ISBN 978-1-330-95337-2
PIBN 10125773

Similar Books Are Available from
www.forgottenbooks.com

MEMOIRS

OF THE

DUKE OF ROVIGO,

(M. SAVARY,)

WRITTEN BY HIMSELF:

ILLUSTRATIVE OF THE

HISTORY OF THE EMPEROR NAPOLEON.

VOL. I.

PARTS I. AND II.

LONDON:

HENRY COLBURN, NEW BURLINGTON STREET.

1828.

LONDON ·

PRINTED BY   J. VALPY, RED LION COURT, FLEET STREET.

PREFACE.

I HAVE been accused of having been the satellite * of the Emperor, and of being so still.

If by this charge is understood my having discovered that the convulsions which shook the world were only the struggles of the principles of the revolution against those of the aristocracy of Europe; if by this charge is meant, that I have set no limits to the sense of my duties, I confess myself to have been the satellite of Napoleon.

If the recollection of former benefits in the time of calamity; if the refusal to abandon my sovereign after his fall; if endurance of personal exile for wishing to share his captivity; if fearlessness in having the hatred of his enemies, who had once been his slaves; if honouring his memory now that he is no more is to be a satellite, I am proud of the title of Satellite of Napoleon.

That great man honoured me with his confidence: I was near his person in the field of battle; I was in the secret councils of his cabinet; he has given me the highest proofs of

---

* This word is in the original *séide:* but as there is no equivalent term in English, it has been translated by the word *satellite.* The French term is borrowed from the name of a character in Voltaire's tragedy of Mahomet, in which Seid is the enthusiastic and unhesitating instrument of the plans of hatred and vengeance projected by the prophet of Mecca.—TRANSLATOR.

consideration, I might almost say of affection ; and could I, or ought I, to have acknowledged all this otherwise than by unbounded devotion to him ? Loaded as I was with his benefits, and intrusted with his secrets, was it possible for me to assume the office of censor in the moment of danger, and blame instead of aiding him ? It is convenient and easy, though not very honourable, to act the part of a censor. But this is not the office I have selected ; and my readers need not therefore expect to find in these Memoirs long critiques, or grave political disquisitions ; I have endeavoured to write simply as I have acted.

Some persons have endeavoured to calumniate the fine and noble character of the Emperor; and the reason is plain— he has no longer any gifts to bestow : but if in eulogizing him, they could at the same time court individuals now in power, how many would gladly compile their recollections of him, and recover the memories they seem at present to have lost !

The Emperor has been represented as a man greedy of war ; and this notion, which will soon be found to be false, passes for true, even in the minds of many unprejudiced and think-ing persons : I trust that the perusal of these Memoirs will tend to enlighten them on the subject. Napoleon required peace above all things : he was the chief of a dynasty which had sprung out of conquest, and which peace alone could consolidate.

I have endeavoured to represent the Emperor as he was, and as I knew him to be ; but it has been my more especial aim to make known the motives of his political actions.

I have passed rapidly over the details of battles and other military operations ; not because I thought them destitute of interest, but because several able officers have already accomplished that task with a talent and genius worthy of the Illustrious Name, which sheds its lustre over all the following pages.

I know not whether an author is obliged to state to the public his motives for writing; but I have no objection to declare mine.

While the Emperor was a captive at St. Helena, I was a prisoner at Malta; and on my return to France, I found that many of my generous friends and public functionaries, guided by the best intentions, had found it convenient to justify themselves at my expense. Calumny must surely be a very fine thing in itself; for although people may despise it, they are always obliged to reply. I thought I could not do this better than by the publication of my Memoirs.

As soon as I declared this intention, the greatest uneasiness was manifested; many persons thought themselves compromised; the alarm spread, and not a few consciences were troubled. Doubtless no one is better qualified than I am for writing a scandalous chronicle, for I have forgotten nothing that I have ever known; but the world may be easy on the subject. I hope my *moderation,* at least, will be acknowledged; for if I had made a more extensive use than I have done of the numerous secret documents in my possession, I could not have been blamed.

Some of my friends have endeavoured to persuade me to leave the publication of my Memoirs to my children. Though sensible of their good intentions in giving me this advice, I do not share their opinion; and I therefore publish them during my lifetime, while I am capable of acknowledging my errors, if I have committed any, and of replying to any calumnious attacks which may be made upon me. Besides, it appeared to me that it was more honourable and courageous to choose a time for publication, when so many witnesses survive to refute me, if I have not spoken the truth.

I have occupied high stations; I have received distinguished honours; I have enjoyed an immense fortune. All this one may be content to resign; but it is not easy to submit to attacks upon the points which every honest man holds most dear. I flatter myself that the perusal of these Memoirs will prove, that if I have been honoured with the confidence, and loaded with the favours of the greatest man in modern times, I have merited them by my services, and acknowledged them by an honourable devotion to him.

I shall only add one word more. I have not tried to compose a literary work; and the reader will consequently discover many faults in my style. But for these I shall not be held responsible; I relate facts, not elaborate a composition: and my military friends know that my talents for writing have never been very remarkable. I might have borrowed the assistance of another and a more practised pen, and so far the public would have gained; but its judgment would not in that case have been so rigorously exercised, as if I had presented myself to my readers as I was, and as I am.

CONTENTS

OF THE FIRST PART.

CHAPTER XXXII.

CHAPTER XXXIII.

CONTENTS

OF THE SECOND PART.

CHAPTER VIII.

CHAPTER IX.

CHAPTER X.

CHAPTER XI.

CHAPTER XII.

CHAPTER XIII.

CHAPTER XIV.

CHAPTER XV.

CHAPTER XXII.

CHAPTER XXIII.

CHAPTER XXIV.

CHAPTER XXV.

CHAPTER XXVI.

SUPPLEMENTARY CHAPTER.

MEMOIRS

OF

THE DUKE OF ROVIGO

PART I.

CHAPTER I.

The author's entrance into the service—Arrival of the representatives of the people at the camp—Execution of M. de Tosia—In danger of being arrested as a royalist—First feats of arms—Secret understanding of Pichegru with the Prince of Condé—Perilous mission to the army of the Sambre and Meuse—Pichegru, suspected, is replaced by Moreau—The author is named captain of a company at the passage of the Rhine—Cessation of hostilities after the preliminaries of Leoben—Aide-de-camp to General Desaix—The author accompanies him to Paris.

THE son of an officer who had grown old under his country's standards, and who had only obtained, as the reward of his long services, the rank of major and the cross of St. Louis, I had scarcely completed my studies when the Revolution broke out. My fortune was to be made. I had no other chance of attaining that object than by the career of arms; and I decided upon running the risks of it.

My elder brother was serving in the artillery; my father wished me also to enter it, offering as it did a certainty of promotion without any danger of being passed over; but I preferred the cavalry; and although that service was con-

sidered to be very expensive, and only suitable to wealthy
young noblemen, I persisted in my determination to join it.
I fancied that a firm resolution, courage, and my sword,
would of course make up to me for the want of fortune.

I proceeded to join the royal regiment of Normandy, in
which my father had served, and which was then marching to
join the small army forming under M. de Bouillé in order to
subdue the revolted garrison of Nancy. I arrived at the
decisive moment; so that, from my very entrance into the
service, my first night was passed in a bivouac, and I stood
fire on the first day.

I formed part of the corps that entered the city through
the gate of Stainville, and the first death which I witnessed
was of the brave Chevalier des Isles, killed by his own
soldiers in attempting to prevent their firing upon us. M. de
Bouillé sent back his army to its garrisons. This general
had a marked regard for the regiment I had just entered, and
the whole regiment answered that feeling by an unbounded
attachment; which, however, it never had a further opportunity of proving to him.

At this time, the greater part of the officers of the cuirassiers
professed principles opposed to those which were venting
themselves in all directions; they accordingly became objects
of animadversion to revolutionary innovators. Provocations
and threats created resistance; proscriptions soon followed.
The officers of the royal Polish regiment murdered at Lyons,
those of the royal regiments of Berry guillotined at Paris,
of Burgundy discharged in a body, of Navarre persecuted at
Besançon, and compelled to quit the town, all became their
victims. We had cause, in our turn, for apprehension; but
fortunately for us the declaration of war created a diversion
to the public mind.

We were ordered to Strasburg. Then it was that I
became acquainted with Desaix, and had the good fortune to
form the closest intimacy with him. He was a captain, and

aide-de-camp to Prince Victor de Broglie, chief of the staff of the army which was forming at that place. Shortly afterwards happened the event of the 10th of August, which served as a pretext for fresh acts of violence. Prince de Broglie was discharged, and Desaix attached to the corps of General Biron. Nearly all the officers of my regiment were obliged to quit the service: a few emigrated; the greater number withdrew to their estates. I now found myself under General Custine's orders.

The invasion of Champagne occurred in the mean time. Verdun and Longwy had been given up. The army collected between Landau and Weissemburg marched through Lorraine to rejoin the army which had fought at Valmy, and had arrested the progress of the Prussians. We had, at the same time, taken Mentz, crossed the Rhine, and pushed on to Frankfort. These successes produced transports of joy, which, however, were but of short duration. Reverses came after them. Defeated almost everywhere, we were driven back to the walls of Landau, leaving a garrison in Mentz on our retreat.

It was attempted to explain away these defeats by the most ridiculous assertions, and suspicions the most absurd; and representatives of the people arrived at the camps. Sent for the purpose of discovering pretended conspiracies, all were conspirators in their eyes; and I must acknowledge they found but too many wretches who, in the hope of reward, degraded themselves into the character of accusers. It has been said that, in a moment of anarchy and disorder, French honour had taken refuge in the armies. It might also have been said that, with this new species of proconsuls, mistrust came to dwell amongst us. Each one avoided his neighbour, and dreaded the vicinity of him who, until then, had been his devoted companion in arms; but, above all, a representative of the people was shunned with the feeling that prompts one to fly from a savage beast. Strange as it may appear, whilst their measures of terrorism created terror around them, their decisions, which they pronounced with all the vain ostentation of ignorance, were such as to cover them with ridicule! A laugh of contempt and a shudder of abhorrence were simultaneous emotions.

At the lines of Weissemburg we were ordered, one morning, to mount our horses at eight o'clock, for the purpose of proclaiming, as general of brigade, a chief of a squadron of dragoons, whose name was Carlin. At eleven o'clock, we were again ordered to mount, and receive him as general of division! The next day he appeared in the general orders as commander-in-chief! The loss of the lines of Weissemburg occurred some days afterwards, before the new general had found time to go over them! He brought the army back to Strasburg, found there his discharge, and if he escaped being condemned at Paris, he owed it to his incapacity, which was admitted by all parties. It was then imagined that the best mode of justifying one's self for public misfortunes or reverses in war, was to cut down with the *sword of the law* those brave men whom the enemy's sword had not reached. On fields of battle death flies at random; but, in the other case, it was discriminating in the choice of its victims. Who could hope to escape its blows? Messrs. de Custine, de Biron, de Beauharnois, perished on the scaffold. Dumourier only saved his head by a precipitate flight.

I was present at the arrest of M. de Tosia, colonel of the cavalry regiment of the Dauphin, upon the denunciation of a quarter-master of his regiment, who had the audacity to address the representative of the people in an open review. Tosia was that instant brought before a military commission, which held permanent sittings, and he was shot two hours after he had been denounced.

I do not recollect if this quarter-master, whose name was Padoue, was rewarded; but I remember well that he became an object of abhorrence to the whole army.

' At this period of time I again fell in with General Desaix: subsequently to some brilliant actions, he had been named adjutant-general, and commanded the advanced guard on the road from Strasburg to Fort Louis. He informed me that my colonel and some officers, as well as myself, had been denounced as greatly suspected, and that I ought to act with prudence. My position was a dangerous one, as will shortly be seen, and the event proved that Desaix was well informed.

Some days afterwards, as I was doing duty in front of the village of Hofeld, on the road from Saverne to Haguenau, my servant came up, and apprised me that the colonel had just been arrested; that I was sought for, and that I had not a moment to lose in effecting my escape. The honest fellow was so sure I was going to fly that he brought me my luggage. Pressing, however, as was the danger, I felt I could not quit the post that had been confided to my charge: I might, besides, make my arrangements so as to ascertain in proper time whether inquiries had been made for me at the advanced posts. I therefore preferred awaiting the event.

. The guard was soon relieved; and the officer who came to take my place removed my anxiety by apprising me that, satisfied no doubt with carrying away the colonel and another officer, the gendarmes had gone off with their prisoners without troubling themselves further about me. I took the hint, however, and instead of returning to the regiment, proceeded to join the adjutant-general, Desaix, at his advanced guard, on the road from Strasburg to Fort Louis; but as I might have compromised him by remaining near his person, I obtained the lieutenant-colonel's permission for my being attached to the head-quarters of the army, in the capacity of a staff-officer.

Meanwhile General Pichegru came to assume the command-in-chief of the army. From the moment of his arrival he openly pronounced himself against the measures of terror displayed by the representatives of the people; from that moment also he made his arrangements for warmly resuming the offensive. On the very day when the army began to move, the general-in-chief entrusted me with a mission for the army of the Moselle, which was encamped on our left. I hastened to fulfil it, and on my return found that there was some fighting going on between Belheim and Haguenau. I soon discovered that it was my regiment and the 11th cavalry which had come into contact with the emigrant corps commanded by the Duke of Bourbon. This was a fine opportunity which fortune opened to me. I hastened to take my share of the danger; placed myself at the head of my troop, and was fortunate enough to attract notice. When the action was over, I went to give the general-in-chief an account of it; and my good fortune would so have it that he was, at the moment, with the representative of the people. I took advantage of the occasion to speak in my own behalf, and Pichegru having taken my part, set my mind at rest by the expression of a single word.

Though very young at this time, I was already known at the advanced guard of the army. Steeled against fatigue, abstemious by habit, having already made some display of temerity, and being gifted by nature with a good memory, I had become an object of preference to my chiefs, when there was some hazardous enterprise to execute, and was soon attached to General Ferino as his aide-de-camp. This general, who had been for some time in the service of Austria, was unfortunately unrelenting in respect to the smallest breach of discipline: the unbounded freedom of the new recruits made him quite furious: he could not dissemble his displeasure; he was, therefore, shortly removed from his command.

I should have found myself unemployed, had not Desaix, who was now a general of division, called me near his person. I was with him at the blockade of Mentz, during that severe winter which was illustrated by the conquest of Holland. Desaïx's friendship for me was unabated : he employed me actively in all affairs of advanced posts, a species of war to which he was partial, because it afforded him an opportunity of forming the young officers upon whom he had set his views.

Previously to the termination of the blockade of Mentz, Pichegru returned from Holland, and resumed the command of the army of the Rhine. He found it in a most destitute condition. The Directory enjoined him to cross the Rhine between Brissac and Bâle ; and he could not find in the arsenals any one of the objects which are indispensable for such an operation. He did not disguise his disappointment —a feeling which was communicated to his dispatches. I have always been of opinion that his mind received then, for the first time, those impressions of hatred, which led him, at a later period, to the commission of a criminal act.

General Desaix's division had left the blockade of Mentz, in order to take up a position between Brissac and Bâle. His advanced guard was commanded by Bellavene; and I was attached to the staff, the head-quarters of which were at Ottmarsheim. The army of Condé was encamped at Neuburg, on the right bank, in front of us. I began to remark that General Pichegru went very often to Bâle, although his head-quarters were at Illkirck, in the vicinity of Strasburg.

As he was returning one day from Bâle to his headquarters, he sent for me, and entrusted me with a letter, to carry to M. Bacher, our chargé-d'affaires at Bâle, who was to hand to me an answer for Illkirck; and as at this period there was not a single crown-piece in the military chest, I noticed that the general had established relays at fixed distances, to render the communication less difficult. I was constantly upon this road for the space of a fortnight; and assuredly had no idea that I was the bearer of letters intended for the Prince of Condé.

We expected to cross the Rhine in this quarter, when we

received orders to proceed to Manheim, which had just
opened its gates, owing to an influence within which was
entirely devoted to France. General Pichegru had directed
General Desaix to assume the offensive on the right bank,
and had obtained the recall of General Ferino. The latter
officer was pleased to express the desire of retaining me near
his person. General Desaix having prevailed upon me not
to refuse the offer, I followed his advice, and joined General
Ferino at Manheim.

The army soon began to move: it advanced along the two
banks of the Necker, when the Austrians were discovered
debouching, and moving to meet it. The action commenced:
we gave way, and were closely pursued. The troops which
occupied the lines of Mentz had an engagement, which was
equally unsuccessful. They suffered an enormous loss in
their artillery, and were forced back in the direction of
Kaiserlautern.

General Pichegru, whose position was rendered more complicated by this double reverse, was compelled to recross the
Rhine in all haste, and established himself upon the small
river Pfrim, in order to rally the fugitives. The situation
was one of difficulty; nothing but a prompt co-operation of
the army of the Sambre and Meuse could protect Lorraine
and Alsace from an invasion: it became therefore of the
utmost importance to prevent it without delay.

The mission was a delicate one. Pichegru, upon General
Desaix's recommendation, confided it to me. I took with
me, in this perilous undertaking, Sorbier, one of my comrades,
in order that, if I should happen to be killed, he might take
charge of the important dispatches under my care.

We placed ourselves at the head of fifty chosen troopers,
all bold and daring men, and at nightfall we quitted the
army. By the help of these precautions—which no officers
of advanced guard should neglect—we crossed the whole of
the country occupied by the Austrian light troops, and had the

good fortune to reach Kaisemark on the Nahe, where we joined Marceau's division, belonging to the army of the Sambre and Meuse. We gave him our dispatches; and as it was of importance that General Pichegru should be informed, as soon as possible, of the position occupied by General Jourdan, we hastened to return. We hardly knew, however, what direction to take, because the army was to have continued its movement. We redoubled our measures of precaution; proceeded only by night, and avoiding the villages; and we arrived at last upon the height of Allzee.

The day was just dawning: some peasants were beginning to scatter themselves over the country. We came up with a young girl, who informed us that we were within a few paces of the Austrians. They were marching towards us; a few steps more, and we should have been discovered. We spurred our horses a second time across the fields, and soon reached the road from Gremstadt to Mentz, at the distance of a long league from General Desaix's advanced posts. We had scarcely arrived there, when we descried a squadron of Austrian light horse hastening towards us. Retreat was out of the question; we made our plans; they were perfectly simple. I desired Sorbier to place himself at the head of the detachment, and make it proceed four abreast, keeping the left side of the road, so that by wheeling round in this order to the right, we must necessarily have the enemy under the edge of our swords: we were soon hotly pursued. We put ourselves into a gallop, in order to break the enemy, with whom we could not come up in a body; and turning sharply round, we bore down those of the enemy whose ardour led them too imprudently forward. We repeated this manœuvre two or three times; and on each occasion we took some men and horses prisoners. We were not, however, out of danger; but, very fortunately for us, the fire of the carbines was heard at the advanced posts, whence a detachment was sent to our relief.

' This expedition procured us the congratulations of the whole army. General Pichegru added his own to the rest; and General Desaix redoubled his kindness for me

Pichegru, on the same day, being pressed by the Austrian army, began to move in the direction of Landau. He took up a position behind the Queich, with his advanced-guard before Landau; where, in case of a blockade, General Ferino was ordered to shut himself up. He had been there some days, when an Austrian flag of truce came to propose an armistice, which was to extend to the two armies of the Rhine, and of the Sambre and Meuse. This was the first armistice that had yet been entered into during the war.

Pichegru availed himself of this moment of relaxation to repair to Paris. He complained warmly of the state of destitution in which the army was left. The Directory, who were averse to encounter difficulties of this kind, declared to him that if he found the load too burthensome, he might lay it down. It has since been said that the Directory already began to suspect his measures: I cannot affirm it; but this is certain, that the army, who were ignorant of the treachery of their general, fancied that he had been sacrificed for no other reason than his having too warmly espoused their interests.

Moreau, who had replaced Pichegru at the army of the north, came again, on this occasion, to replace him at the army of the Rhine. The armistice was almost immediately declared at an end. The Archduke Charles had succeeded Field-marshal Clairfait: it was the first time that this Prince appeared at the head of the Austrian armies: he was impatient to come to an engagement. Moreau, on his side, contemplated marching upon him; but it was necessary to cross the river. With this project in his mind, he endeavoured to deceive him as to the object which engaged his attention.

He concentrated his troops under the walls of Landau; feigned to have objects in view which were furthest from his thoughts; and when every thing was ready, when all arrangements were made, he reached the fortress of Strasburg in two days' march. I was only a captain at this time, but was already known in the army; and although of inferior rank, was directed to effect the passage with a company which was placed under my immediate orders. My instructions were, that I should quit the left bank at midnight, forthwith effect a landing on the right bank, and attract the enemy's attention as much as possible, so as to favour the main passage which was to take place at Kehl. The night was unfortunately dark, and the stream very rapid: part of my boats yielded to the current; another part ran aground. I could only effect a landing with a few boats. I marched, however, upon the Austrians; but weakness compelled me to return to the left bank, and I deemed myself fortunate in reaching it without any accident. I then repaired to the right division, commanded by General Ferino. We quitted Kehl almost immediately afterwards, moved upon the Brisgau, and crossed the Black Forest by the Höllenthal, whilst the rest of the army was moving forward by the road of Wirtemburg. We traversed the whole of Swabia, and had as yet met no obstacle on our march, when we fell in with the corps of Condé in the environs of Memmingen. It occupied the small village of Ober-Kamlach. We charged it: the attack was warm and destructive: the Infantry of Nobles was almost entirely destroyed; and I must say it to the praise of our troops, although political animosities were then at their height, this was a silent and a gloomy victory: our soldiers, when contemplating the horrid field of battle, could not withhold the expression of their regret that the blows they had dealt had not fallen upon foreigners.

We continued our movement, and marched upon Augsburg, which was still occupied by the Austrian rear-guard. It was withdrawn: we pursued; reached the borders of the Lech, and made our arrangements for crossing it. I was directed to reconnoitre a ford above Friedberg, where Ferino's division was to cross, and to conduct the column to the opposite bank. This operation completely answered my expectation. I was so fortunate as only to lose a few awkward fellows, who were drowned in consequence of having wandered from the ford.

The battle immediately began: we gained it, and pursued the enemy as far as Munich. I received, on this occasion, a letter from the Directory, congratulating me on the courage I had displayed.

Whilst we were advancing along the Lech, the army of the Sambrè and Meuse, which had crossed the Rhine at Dusseldorf, had moved upon Bohemia; but, whether from spite or from want of instructions, Moreau neglected the numerous opportunities afforded for crossing the Danube from Donawerth to Ratisbon. This fault proved fatal to us. The Archduke Charles concealed his march from the general who was opposed to him, crossed the Danube at Ingoldstadt and at Neuburg, and effected a junction with the Austrian troops which were retiring before the army of Sambre and Meuse. He lost no time in resuming the offensive; advanced upon Jourdan with all his forces united; defeated this general, and pursued him to the very banks of the Rhine, without its having even occurred to General Moreau to repeat on his part what his adversary had just done. Instead of recrossing to the left bank of the Danube, to endeavour to rally the army of Sambre and Meuse and force the Archduke to desist from the pursuit, he commenced a retreat with his splendid army, amounting to upwards of eighty thousand men. Whilst he was falling back by easy marches, the Archduke kept Jourdan in close pursuit, and crossed the Maine at Frankfort. When the passage was effected, he rapidly reascended the valley of the Rhine, and intercepted the road to Wirtemburg. Forestalled by this march, which he ought, however, to have expected, Moreau was compelled to retreat by the Höllenthal, and recrossed the Rhine at Huningen and Brisach. Thus ended a campaign, which appeared to promise wonders, and terminated like the efforts of the mountain in labour.

Whilst we were performing this military promenade, General Bonaparte was following up his career of victories in Italy. The Austrian armies engaged on the Rhine were constantly compelled to send troops to the assistance of those that were perishing on the Adige. They had been weakened in consequence of those detachments. This was a favourable circumstance for resuming the offensive. The Directory determined to put the armies of the Sambre and Meuse and of the Rhine in motion; but, whether dissatisfied at the want of proper understanding between them or from any other cause, it assigned the command of the first to General Hoche, and ordered that both the one and the other should recross the Rhine.

I was, at this time, General Desaix's aide-de-camp, and was directed to assume the command of General Vandamme's advanced-guard, which was to open the passage. We had to effect a landing in broad daylight, and under the fire of the Austrian batteries. The attempt was full of danger; but all went on well : we landed under protection of the company of light artillery commanded by Foy, who was afterwards a general officer and a deputy. We were both named captains of companies on this occasion.

General Desaix was wounded the next day. I continued to fight at the head of the troops with which I had crossed the river. The enemy was compelled to give way; and we were in close pursuit, when a French officer rode up to us: this was General Leclerc, who had just arrived from Italy, through Germany, and brought us intelligence of the preliminaries of peace agreed upon at Leoben. The firing immediately

ceased ; the army took up a position ; and the contending generals met for the purpose of fixing the lines of demarcation.

I was again employed in these conferences, which were
held at Heidelberg, where I accompanied General Regnier,
who was deputed from the army of the Rhine. All was
soon arranged ; and I was enabled to rejoin General Desaix,
who was at Strasburg for the recovery of his health.

It was during his convalescence that he conceived the idea
of going to Italy, for the purpose of seeing General Bonaparte. At this time he only knew him from his reputation,.
but was in great admiration of his glory. Feeling hurt,
besides, at the state of inferiority in which the Directory held
military men, Desaix longed in secret for the appearance of
a man of character and genius, who might remedy the evil.
The conqueror of Arcole could be no other than such a man ;
he alone had acquired sufficient ascendancy to avow himself.
the protector of those who had covered themselves with,
glory in the field of battle.

He was anxious to hold a conference with him ; and I
went to reside with my family during his absence on this
journey. I rejoined him on his return ; and peace having
been signed in the mean time, I soon after accompanied him
to Paris.

CHAPTER II.

General Bonaparte's return to Paris—Reception given to him by the Directory—
His nomination to the Institute—False project of a landing in England—Secret
mission of General Desaix to Italy—Preparations for the expedition to Egypt—
Bernadotte at Vienna—Harbour of Civita Vecchia—Galley-slaves—Departure
for Egypt.

THE frenzy of the Revolution had already cooled in France:
the mere utterance of rational ideas was no longer a ground
for apprehension; but nothing that revolutionary commotions
had thrown out of its orbit could yet resume its place: the
destruction was complete; and although there was now felt a
desire for reconstructing, there existed no secure centre of
gravitation. No hand was found sufficiently strong to collect
the fragments which the storm had scattered in all directions.
We had before us a heap of ruins: we beheld with terror their
extent and the ravages occasioned by popular ferment; but
no one foresaw an end to so much misery—no one dared
to contemplate the future.

The leaders of the different parties in the civil war, whom
the Directory had succeeded in disuniting, in order to disarm
them, more stunned by the glory which our arms had
acquired and the peace which followed it, than confiding in
the repose held out to them, were well aware that a jealous
government would, sooner or later, call them to a severe
account for the celebrity they had obtained. Volcanic heads
appeared, indeed, to have grown calm; but it was apprehended that they were not at ease; and a spirit of rivalry
was everywhere to be seen, especially amongst men whom the
war had brought forward.

The armies of the north and of the Sambre and Meuse,
possessing a great many meritorious officers, beheld with

regret the finer share of glory which had been reaped by the army of Italy : they were jealous of the preference evinced by the Executive Directory for whatever belonged to that army ; and they thus offered elements of disturbance to those agitators, who are so easily found amongst people of limited understanding, especially after such calamities as those out of which we had so recently emerged. Ambitious projects of every kind were on foot, and could only be productive of some new 18th Fructidor, or of other events of a similar nature.

General Bonaparte had just quitted Italy to repair, through Switzerland, to Rastadt: his journey might almost be said to have been a continued triumphal march. Whole populations came out to meet him : he was hailed as the hero of liberal ideas—as the defender of the revolutionary interests.

Conformably to the treaty of peace, a congress was to be held at Rastadt, for the purpose of regulating the affairs of princes dispossessed of their territories, whether in Germany, in Italy, or on the left bank of the Rhine. As this work required, from its nature, very long preliminaries of etiquette, and circumstantial details, which it was impossible to hurry through, General Bonaparte only gave his attention, at Rastadt, to the object of regulating, in a summary way, the basis of those operations which were to engage the attention of that congress.

He returned to Paris, where public impatience expected to be gratified by his receiving from the government those testimonies of gratitude and admiration which had long since filled the breast of every Frenchman towards him.

The autumn was at its close : winter and its pleasures had brought the population back to the capital : soldiers and citizens went out in numbers to meet him.

The Directory, who had entertained a doubt whether or not they should ratify the preliminaries of Leoben, were compelled, by this manifestation of the national sentiments, to give a solemn reception to the pacificator whom they had been on the very point of disowning.

A magnificent platform had been raised at the end of the court of the palace of the Luxembourg. The Directory took their places under a canopy, and General Bonaparte was presented to them by M. de Talleyrand, then minister for foreign affairs. The acclamations of the multitude formed a contrast with the cold eulogiums of the Directory.

At this period, the army of Sambre and Meuse was united with the army of the Rhine, under the orders of Augereau, who had held the command at Paris on the occasion of the 18th Fructidor.

Moreau had just been discharged from his command, after having denounced Pichegru, who was transported to Cayenne.

The reception of General Bonaparte by the Directory was followed by balls and grand dinners, amongst which should be noticed the dinner given to him by the National Convention: it took place in the long gallery of the Museum: the table was laid along the full length of that extensive place; and the feast would have exhibited a perfect scene of confusion, had it not been for the grenadiers of the Directorial guard, who lined, in arms, the whole extent of the gallery, and presented an imposing appearance.

A few days afterwards, the Institute voted a crown to General Bonaparte, and its council elected him one of its members. He was received by M. Chénier, and his reception took place at night, in the hall of the Louvre, where the Institute then held its sittings. That hall is on the ground-floor: there is before it a balcony or large wooden tribune, worked in the old style. The body of Henry IV. had been deposited here after his assassination. I attended, with General Desaix, at the reception of General Bonaparte. He was in costume, and sitting between Monge and Berthollet: it was, I think, the only occasion on which I saw him in the dress of that learned body. His nomination had all

the effect which he expected from it : it placed the newspapers, the literary characters, all the enlightened part of the
nation, at his disposal.   All felt beholden to him for having
added the academic laurels to the palms of victory.   As for
himself, of plain and retired habits, almost a stranger to the
noise which his name made in Paris, he avoided taking any
part in business ;   seldom   appeared   in   public ;   and   only
admitted a few generals, learned men, and diplomatic characters, into his intimacy.

M. de Talleyrand was of the number : he was a man of
amiable intercourse ; had great facility for business ; a mind
possessed of resources such as I have not discovered in any
other man.   Clever at frustrating or at winding up an intrigue,
he had all the art and ability which the times required : he
was incessant in his attentions to General Bonaparte, and
acted for him the character of mediator, orator, and master of
ceremonies.   Yielding to so much zeal, the general accepted
his attentions.   This mode of proceeding brought on balls
and evening parties, where the minister had taken care to
bring together the remains of the old nobility.

It was at one of these parties that General Bonaparte saw
Madame de Stael for the first time.   The hero had always
excited a lively interest in that celebrated woman.   She
attached herself to him, entered into conversation with him,
and in the course of that colloquial intercourse, in which she
attempted to soar above her height, she suffered a question to
escape her which betrayed the ambition nourished in her
breast.   " Who is the first woman, in your eyes ?" she asked
him.—" Madam," he replied, " the woman who brings the
most   children   into   the   world."   Madame   de   Stael   was
stunned : she expected a totally different answer.

The eagerness, however, with which General Bonaparte
was every where greeted, soon gave umbrage to the members
of the Directory.   Weak depositaries of authority, they felt
that they were losing their hold on public opinion : the nation

compared their personal nullity with the glory that encircled the hero. They were apprehensive that public enthusiasm would create a commotion, and an attempt against their power; and they thenceforward bent their minds upon removing the man who was the object of general attention.

General Bonaparte, having a more correct foresight of the consequences that might result from his longer residence in Paris, where he had, however, avoided taking any part in internal affairs, prepared to withdraw himself from a place which still presented the gloomy prospect of too many elements of disorder, especially as we drew nearer to the moment best calculated for giving effect to the project he had entertained when concluding peace, and for which he had collected the first materials previously to his departure from Italy.

The Directory had no sooner made peace than they decreed the formation of an army of England, of which General Bonaparte was to assume the chief command, but which he had himself been the means of placing under the orders of General Desaix, until he should have completed the object of his journey from Italy to Rastadt.

General Bonaparte sent General Desaix to visit the ports and naval arsenals from the mouth of the Loire to Havre, in order to ascertain their condition, and the resources they might offer for a descent on England. I accompanied General Desaix in that journey, and we returned to Paris at the same time with General Berthier, whom General Bonaparte had sent upon a similar mission to the ports in the Channel.

Both officers agreed in opinion that no reliance could be placed on the resources of those ports for effecting a descent on England, and that other means were, therefore, to be resorted to for waging war against her. A contrary language, however, was held: the conviction was suffered to prevail that the idea of a descent alone was contemplated by government; so that public opinion was bent upon it.

All the generals who were employed in the army of England were ordered to quit Paris : they were sent to their respective posts. Government succeeded in fully impressing the belief that their whole attention was directed towards England, and that all the preparations in the Mediterranean had been made with no other object than to divert the enemy's attention ; whilst the very contrary was the case.

When all this was done, General Bonaparte had no difficulty in proving to conviction the inadequacy of the means possessed by the republic for attacking England on its own soil, and in determining the Directory to undertake the plan of sending an army to Egypt, as the nearest and the most vulnerable point of the commercial power of England, the difficulties of which were not out of proportion with our means of attack. He enumerated to them the resources he had collected in the ports of Italy, previously to leaving that country, and asked for the command of the fleet and army, offering to provide for every thing else.

It was demonstrated to the Directory, that France could never be brought to a state of tranquillity, so long as the multitude of generals and enterprising officers should remain unemployed ; that it was necessary to turn so many ardent imaginations to the public advantage ; that Spain, Holland, Portugal, and England, after their respective revolutions, had been compelled in this manner to undertake expeditions beyond seas, in order to give occupation to restless minds which they could no longer controul ; that to this course was owing the discovery of America and the Cape of Good Hope, and the flourishing rise of commercial powers in distant countries.

It did not, assuredly, require all this reasoning to induce the Directory to avail themselves of an opportunity of removing to a great distance a chief whose popularity they dreaded ; and the proposal was suitable to both.

The order of Malta was still in existence at this time ; and its ships of war were destined to protect all Christian flags against the Barbary states, and against the Turks, who respected no other flag than that of France.

The trading vessels of Sweden and Denmark that frequented the Mediterranean, were protected by ships of war of their own nations which cruised in that sea.

Those of America were few in number; and England had there a fleet of men of war, only while France had kept up a fleet to cover in the Adriatic the operations of the army of Italy; but since the peace, the latter had returned to Toulon, bringing with it the Venetian squadron; and the English fleet had returned to the ports of Sicily.

Its object was to watch Toulon as well as the Spanish squadron at Cadiz; and in furtherance of this object, it cruised at the southernmost point of the island of Sardinia. The trade of Marseilles was not yet wholly destroyed. This city, owing to the protection of its flag, had almost the exclusive command of all the trade carried on by the Turks in the Levant: it kept up a considerable number of vessels known under the denomination of caravan ships, which sailed, throughout the year, to the ports in the Levant to obtain freights, and returned to winter at Marseilles, bringing with them all their profits. Marseilles reckoned as many as eight hundred of those ships employed in that navigation. Those of northern nations wintered in the ports of Italy, where they solicited freights against the spring.

Previously to quitting Italy, and under pretext of an expedition against England, General Bonaparte had caused an embargo to be laid upon all trading vessels then in the ports of the Mediterranean occupied by French troops. He ordered them to be freighted and regularly paid, so that other merchant vessels in the ports of Naples and to the eastward of the Adriatic hurried to the ports we occupied for the purpose of being engaged.

The Roman states had just been seized by the French

troops: the Directory, who sought to establish the republic every where, had not wanted pretexts for raising a
quarrel with the pope, who beheld the metropolis of Chris-
tianity invaded, and himself transported to Valence in the
province of Dauphiné.

From the moment of his return to Paris, General Bonaparte had issued the requisite orders (always under pretence
of a descent upon England) for the squadron at Toulon, to
the number of fifteen sail, one of them a three-decker, to
be immediately placed in a condition to put to sea with troops
on board.

He also gave orders for the equipment and freighting of
all the merchant vessels that could be collected at Marseilles
and at Toulon.

. He had just dispatched General Regnier, whom General
Desaix had recommended to him,* for the purpose of organising the ships collected at Genoa by means of the embargo
to which I have just alluded, and also of taking the command
of the troops placed on board.

There were likewise a great number of similar vessels
detained in all the ports from Venice to Leghorn. He sent
off from Paris, in the most secret manner, General Desaix,
who had the appearance of going to Rome on a voyage of
mere curiosity, because he was a great admirer of the fine
arts. Being his first aide-de-camp, I accompanied him in
his own carriage, as well as the Adjutant-general Donzelot,†
the chief of his staff; and I actually reached Rome without a single word having escaped General Desaix that might
give me an idea of the object of our journey.

He crossed France with the rapidity of an arrow, and

---

* General Regnier was chief of the staff of the army of the Rhine : he was not
known to General Bonaparte, who had never heard of him until after Augereau
obtained the command of the army of the Rhine, and who had requested of the
Directory to remove General Regnier from that army.

† The same who afterwards commanded at Corfu and at Martinique.

entered upon his scientific inquiries, always maintaining his incognito, as soon as he had penetrated beyond the Alps.

He stopped at Turin, Parma, Placentia, Bologna, and Florence, visiting every object worthy of notice in these cities, and reached Rome.

He appeared as if he had come there only as a virtuoso · he was incessantly going about the celebrated environs of that far-famed city; whilst Donzelot carried into effect the orders he had given to him, to assemble in the port of Civita Vecchia all the vessels that had been collected at every other port, from Leghorn to Venice.

We stayed six weeks in Rome, leading a life as active as if we had been in an open campaign. At last, all the *materiel* having been prepared, the circumstance was communicated to General Bonaparte, who was still in Paris; whence he sent his final orders, pointing out the troops that were to compose each convoy. They were not directed to make any special arrangements; whatever they could stand in need of, as well for the sea voyage as for a campaign, having been put on board ship previously to the time fixed upon for their embarkation.

We embarked at Civita Vecchia nine battalions of infantry, taken from the troops which occupied the Roman states;

A regiment of dragoons, with horses for one squadron only;

A regiment of hussars;

A company of light artillery, with its cannon and all its horses;

Two regiments of artillery on foot, with their cannon and their horses;

A park of artillery;

And lastly, a staff, a military hospital, and an establishment complete in all its branches.*

The celebrated Monge, who was then in Rome, had been

---

* The other convoys were similarly composed and organised.

instructed by General Bonaparte to procure, at whatever price, Arabic printing types, correctors of the press, and interpreters, and to embark with them on board of our convoy.

He found interpreters in the Roman college of physicians, to which young men are sent from the Levant, for the purpose of studying medicine. He succeeded in carrying into execution every part of General Bonaparte's orders; whilst the General was forming in Paris that assemblage of learned men, of every class, whose labours have immortalised this renowned expedition.

They had been pointed out to him by General Caffarelli, by Dufalgua,* and by Berthollet.

The multitude of objects that were provided for this splendid operation almost baffles description; nothing was wanting which the most minute or the most comprehensive foresight could imagine.

There were learned men of all classes, and artisans of all professions; materials, in short, for creating, perfecting, civilising, and even giving refinement, at one and the same time, to the populations amongst whom we were going to form an establishment, however barbarous might be their condition.

All these preparations were completed towards the end of March 1797. General Bonaparte had sent off from Paris whatever was to be embarked with him at the ports of Toulon and Marseilles; the troops that were likewise to embark were sent thither from the army which had returned to France after the peace.

General Kleber, whom General Desaix had also pointed out to the notice of General Bonaparte, was entrusted

* An officer of artillery, who had lost a leg whilst with the army of the Sambre and Meuse: he lost an arm at the siege of Acre in Syria, and died regretted by the army and by General Bonaparte, who always mentioned him when he wished to compare the zeal of a person to any thing extraordinary.

with the command of the troops which embarked at Toulon.

There had just arrived at Civita Vecchia from that port a frigate sent by General Bonaparte to General Desaix, to serve as an escort to his convoy. It was not till the arrival of this frigate that he left Rome for Civita Vecchia, in which direction he ordered the troops which were to be embarked at that port.

At the beginning of April, when all the *materiel* was already on board ship, an accident occurred, which nearly put a stop to the expedition.

After the peace of Campo Formio, the Directory had sent General Bernadotte to Vienna, in the capacity of ambassador. At this period he openly professed republican ideas, which were then, for every species of ambition, a sure road to fortune.

He had hoisted over his hotel, in Vienna, a tricoloured flag, which the inhabitants of that city would, right or wrong, consider as an act of provocation. I never could ascertain whether there existed any previous excitement; but after a ferment of some days, a tumult broke out; the mob having repaired to the ambassador's hotel, caused the flag to be removed, and gave itself up to excesses, that compelled the commander of the garrison to order out troops for the protection of the ambassador and of his official suite, which had been formed in Paris with a view to the object contemplated by the Directory at Vienna, under cover of the treaty of peace which had but just been signed.

The first dispatches in which General Bernadotte gave an account of this event were of so alarming a character, that General Bonaparte, to whom they had been communicated by the Directory, sent counter-orders to all the ports, not only for preventing the embarkation, but also for re-landing whatever was already on board, and for the troops to be in readiness to march.

Eight days afterwards, the tone of the correspondence from Vienna had become of a less hostile nature: fresh orders were received to continue the embarkation, which had only been retarded for the space of eight days; a drawback, however, from the time with which fortune seemed to have favoured us.

During this short interval, General Desaix, who thirsted after knowledge, went to visit the Roman mines of alum, situated at a few hours' distance from Civita Vecchia: they are extremely abundant; and the alum extracted from them was considered to be of a quality superior to any other. Monge was in our company, and explained whatever was new to us.

We also went to see the mouth of the Tiber, as well as all the environs of Civita Vecchia. This port was built by Trajan: it is held to be of small extent, considering the magnitude of the ships built at the present day, in comparison with those for which it was intended.

It was with difficulty that the frigate sent to us from Toulon could enter the port; and when it had once got in, there was so little space for its working, that when the moment arrived for setting sail, its manœuvring became an object for deliberate consideration.

The basin of the port has been constructed with all the beauty and solidity which characterise the period of Roman grandeur: its regular quays are formed of layers of enormous blocks of marble; the last is of white marble. The entire circuit of the port is lined with lions' heads in bronze, holding bronze rings in their mouths; not one of them is missing. They are the very same that were placed in Trajan's time for the purpose of securing vessels, and are still used for the same purpose; those of our convoy were moored fast to them.

The port is closed by a jetty raised at the same period. It is formed of layers of lava, which have, up to this moment, resisted the attacks of the sea and of time

The noble recollections which those works bring to mind are, unfortunately, checked by the presence of the debased population bustling in the midst of the remains of Roman grandeur.

The majority of the galley-slaves at Civita Vecchia were, at this time, foreign artisans, who had come to seek their fortune in the Roman territory, and ended by committing crimes. As the pope's marine department was not engaged in any public works, these wretches had been allowed to seek their livelihood in the town, and were readily employed by the inhabitants.

It even appeared to us that this measure had been resorted to by the administration with the view of preventing the malefactors from giving way to despair, and perhaps likewise of some advantage accruing from them to the state. The result was, however, that by degrees the disgrace of fetters had been weakened, and that a galley-slave had become no longer ashamed of his condition. We bitterly regretted the state of degradation we were beholding, and deplored that such a government should possess any influence over the destinies of a nation.

General Desaix had observed two handsome newly built small galleys; he ordered them to be armed and added to the convoy. The galley-slaves were eager in offering themselves, foreseeing that their liberty would be the result of any services they might render us.

The convoys of troops that left Marseilles, Toulon, and Genoa, under protection of the Toulon fleet of men of war, sailed about the same time, and met in the bay of St. Florente, in the island of Corsica. On leaving Toulon, General Bonaparte had received intelligence from sea, through some Spanish frigates which were entering the harbour: they came from Mahon, and informed us that the English squadron was not in that quarter; and that only two vessels of the squadron were at the island of St. Peter, near Sardinia, where they were undergoing repair.*

The convoy of Civita Vecchia was at so great a distance as to render it necessary to leave the entire management of it to General Desaix, under whose orders it was placed: he had been instructed to set sail on a certain day, and to make direct for Malta, taking care on his way to reconnoitre the Maretimo at the extreme point of Sicily ; and when he arrived before Malta, he was there to await fresh instructions.

CHAPTER III.

Arrival before Malta—Junction of the fleet—Attack of the town—Capitulation of the Order—We meet the English fleet in the night-time—Arrival at Alexandria —Landing—The command of the advanced-guard is confided to the author— Contrivance for landing the horses—Attack and capture of Alexandria— Our first march through the desert—Meeting with an Arabian woman.

WE arrived before Malta at the beginning of May: neither the main squadron nor the other convoys had yet made their appearance; and in obedience to the instructions given by General Bonaparte to General Desaix, our convoy kept cruising before the harbour.

We next had to encounter calms, in consequence of which, the currents which prevailed in that quarter dispersed the ships of the convoy to a considerable distance from one another.

Our arrival was on a morning: in the evening of the same day, the grand-master of the Order of Malta, seeing a large fleet, consisting of vessels of all nations, under the protection of a frigate, which not only avoided entering the harbour, but did not even allow the smallest sail to approach it,

---

* They left as soon as our fleet had set sail, and went to join Admiral Nelson at Syracuse.

began to entertain some uneasiness, or felt his curiosity awakened.

He sent a sloop, commanded by one of the grand bailifs of the Order, as a flag of truce, to learn our destination.

This sloop proceeded towards the frigate on board of which was General Desaix; and under pretence of the quarantine laws, the bailif would not come on board, though repeatedly urged to do so: he hailed us from his sloop, which sailed past the frigate's stern.

His mission was one of pure curiosity; and as he saw on board the vessels a great number of soldiers, who had climbed upon each others' shoulders to obtain a sight of him, he was hastening back with an account of what he had seen. He was about to take leave, after a broken conversation carried on in monosyllables, when, with the view of reviving it, General Desaix asked to be allowed to enter the harbour for the purpose of watering. The bailif drew off with the promise of sending an answer.

He returned accordingly the same night, to say that the grand-master could only allow the entrance of the harbour to four vessels at a time. A very ingenious mode of evasion, truly! It did not require any great effort of calculation on his part to discover that we had upwards of eighty sail, and that twenty days would have been consumed in watering the convoy. Assuredly we could not lose so much time before this nest of gentlemen. Nevertheless we pretended to view the matter in a serious light, and in politely refusing the bailif's offer, briefly hinted at the dangers we should be incurring if the English were to make their appearance. This consideration did not appear to create much impression upon him, and he sailed off, informing us that the Order could make no further concession.

Night approached, and the flag of truce was gone, when our signal-man descried two sail to the eastward, bearing down upon us.

They soon neared us sufficiently to enable us to ascertain
that they were a ship of the line and a frigate: we became
rather uneasy; and still more so, when within two gun-shots
of us they omitted to hoist their colours, until at the moment
of passing us they both hoisted the Maltese flag: they proved
to be the line-of-battle ship and frigate belonging to the Order,
and were returning into port from a cruise. The sailors were
taken out the same night, for the purpose of manning the
galleys that were preparing to fight us the following day.

The next morning at daybreak our signal-man descried
several sail to the north-west, and soon afterwards apprised
us that they were in considerable numbers: they proved to
be our squadron and its convoys, just arriving from the Bay
of St. Florente.

General Desaix and M. Monge proceeded from the ship
to one of the pope's small galleys which we had brought with
us, and sailed to meet the squadron, and pay their respects to
General Bonaparte.

In the course of the morning, the entire squadron and the
army were reunited before the mouth of the harbour. Every
thing then assumed a new appearance. Preparations were
every where made for a landing.

General Bonaparte ordered the troops of General Bon's
division to land on the right; and the division of General
Desaix to land at the same time on the left: we disembarked
in the Bay of Maira-Sirocco.

I was entrusted with the command of the troops which
took the lead on this occasion; marched straight up to the
redoubts that protected the landing-place, and thence to
the fort. We encountered very little resistance; every thing
seemed left to itself. The grand-master had scarcely been
able to collect a few detachments for the purpose of defending
the advanced works. There was no emulation amongst the
knights. The population, accustomed to the idea that it was
never to be called upon to man the batteries except in the

event of an invasion from the Turks, refused to carry arms against us. All those splendid fortifications, that indicated the power of the Order and the strength of the place, became useless. We pushed our advances, on this day, to the very foot of the ramparts on the land side. We were amazed at the weakness of the defence, and at a loss to account for the circumstance of a place, which appeared perfectly unassailable, presenting so easy a conquest to our arms ; the mystery, however, was soon unravelled.

General Bonaparte had remained on board L'Orient during the whole day : he had ordered the Maltese galleys to be attacked, and compelled them to return to port. There was an end of the Maltese cross. The general landed the same night ; and we could then discover, from the acts of indiscretion committed around us, that the members of the Order were not all strangers to the success which had just crowned our efforts.

' Ever since the commencement of the French Revolution, and especially since the breaking up of the corps of emigrants, the rock of Malta had become the place of refuge for a multitude of young noblemen, who enlisted under the banners of the Order. These knights of recent creation had not all the ardour of the old Knights of St. John of Jerusalem. Their worldly education made them averse to a monastic life ; and the malady peculiar to the country increased their anxiety to quit the rock upon which they had found an asylum.

The appearance of our fleet before Malta afforded them an opportunity of breaking engagements, which they began to consider in the light of fetters, and of commencing a new existence. Should they be considered as objects of pity or censure ?

Be this as it may, a communication was soon opened between our head-quarters and the government of Malta. The grand-master of the Order, too late, indeed, persuaded of the impossibility of preserving the place, and of the futility of a resistance which had no longer any object, consented to capitulate.

The principal conditions were, the surrender of the forts to our troops; the personal liberty of himself and his followers; and leave for all the knights to withdraw to any place they thought proper.

We accordingly took possession of the place.

M. de Hompesch, the grand-master, embarked on board a neutral vessel, which was placed at his disposal, and was escorted by one of our frigates as far as Trieste. Nearly all the French knights entered the ranks of our army.

The organization of the island immediately engaged General Bonaparte's attention. The national guard; the administration; the means of attack and defence; every thing was planned and completed in less than eight days. The Maltese garrison was incorporated with the semi-brigades, and was replaced by a part of Vaubois' division; and the fleet was ordered to set sail.

General Desaix remained some days longer at Malta, because his frigate was to take on board the Intendant of finances, who had yet some matters to arrange. We employed this short delay in visiting a rock so celebrated in history. I felt a lively curiosity in going over the island, which had always been represented to us as unassailable, and yet, had so quickly fallen into our power.

Civita Vecchia, situated on an eminence in the centre of the island, and the only point which the knights had fortified upon their first arrival, was the first object of our visit: we then proceeded to examine the works in the order in which they had been constructed. It is well known that, upon the fall of the Island of Rhodes, the knights bestowed all their attention on the fortifying of Malta.

Every grand-master of the Order, since that period, seemed to have had no other ambition than that of adding some new work to the harbour or the town. This was the only object of the government. Ostentation, at last, came in for its share; and fortifications were constructed at Malta just in the same manner as palaces were built at Rome, since the throne of the Cæsars had made way for the Holy See. Malta has thus grown into a prodigious heap of fortifications; and we were at a loss what to admire most, the perseverance required in their construction, or the genius that called them into existence. What mostly raised our astonishment was the work of nature—the harbour itself: it is of such extent, that the naval army, and the six hundred vessels of the convoy, only covered a very small part of it. It affords so easy and so safe an anchorage, that the largest ships of war may be moored close to the quay.

. In the midst of so many wonders, we felt again the distress of beholding a sight such as that which had excited our indignation at Civita Vecchia. The galleys of the Order were manned by galley-slaves, composed of prisoners taken on board Turkish vessels. We could hardly credit the assertion that, often, when there was a dearth of these slaves, free men consented to engage themselves, for money, on board the galleys, in the above capacity. We were, however, compelled to yield to the evidence of facts, and believe what we were eye-witnesses of. We saw some of those wretches, who go by the name of *bonovollio*, serving on the same benches with the slaves, in chains like the latter, and taking a part in their painful labours, as they shared in their disgrace.

When we beheld this state of degradation, we no longer felt such surprise at the little resistance opposed to us. It is quite natural that a call to arms should be listened to with indifference by men disposed to obey the voice which summoued them to their own dishonour.

M. Monge had parted from us at Malta, and embarked on board L'Orient, because General Bonapárte was desirous of having him near his person.

General Desaix, with whom I was, could not sail until eight days after the army. On leaving the harbour, we met a fine French frigate arriving from Italy: her boat brought us M. Julien, an aide-de-camp of General Bonaparte's.

Subsequently to falling in with the Spanish frigates, General Bonaparte had ordered this French frigate to be dispatched to General Desaix, and to apprise him of there being two English ships of war at St. Peter's, near the island of Sardinia, from which place they had sailed immediately upon the receipt of intelligence that the Toulon squadron had put to sea.

This frigate (La Diane) proceeded as far as Civita Vecchia, without entering the port; M. Julien had landed in order to ascertain the day of our departure; and whilst he was on shore, the English squadron passed at a great distance in the offing. As La Diane was close in shore, she was not perceived, or at least was not recognised by the English squadron, which was sailing in the clearest part of the horizon; in consequence of which she escaped, and continued her course to overtake the army.

A few days afterwards we met the frigate which was returning from conveying the grand-master of the Order of Malta to Trieste; she was also endeavouring to overtake the army; and such was our good fortune, that this frigate, both upon entering the Adriatic Sea, and quitting it, had repeatedly crossed the track of the English squadron, which was not aware of her proximity.

What were the objects that engaged the attention of the English squadron whilst we were taking every advantage of fortune's favours?—A part of it was at Naples, and the remainder at Syracuse or Palermo, where its admiral, the celebrated Nelson, had found the delights of Capua at the feet of Lady Hamilton.

The two ships that had left St. Peter's on our approach had hastened to give the alarm, and he immediately

set sail for Toulon, steering his way along the coast of
Italy.

From Toulon he proceeded to St. Florente, afterwards
directing his course to the Levant, without stopping at, or
reconnoitring Malta on his way.

We had but just overtaken the army when General Bonaparte gave the signal for the whole fleet to alter its course,
and to make for the island of Candia, which was not yet descried, though at a short distance on our larboard.

The order was punctually attended to. At nightfall the
entire fleet had collected under the coast of Candia, with the
squadron of men of war ranged in two lines on its right.

We repeatedly heard that night the reports of guns on
our starboard side ; and as they were not fired by our fleet,
the circumstance created great alarm. After the loss of our
squadron at the battle of Aboukir, the English compared the
logbooks of our squadron with their own, and it was discovered that the two fleets had sailed several hours that night
at the distance of four or five leagues from each other. The
reports of firing which had reached our ears arose from signals made by the admiral to his fleet ; and had not General
Bonaparte ordered his own to steer for Candia on the preceding day, we must inevitably have found ourselves at day-
break in presence of the British fleet.

We made the land of Egypt a few days after. Alexandria
was in front of us, though, near as we were, we could only
discover its minarets, owing to the extreme lowness of the
coast.

General Bonaparte had sent forward a frigate to bring
off the French consul residing in that city. The consul
had just arrived on board L'Orient, when a signal was made
for the whole army to prepare for landing.

He had informed General Bonaparte that the English
squadron, consisting of thirteen sail, had appeared off
Alexandria forty-eight hours before, and had made inquiries

about the French fleet, which it was chasing, under the impression of its being ahead; but that, on failing to come up with it, the squadron had continued its course for the coast of Syria, conceiving it, no doubt, impossible that the French should be behind them.

General Bonaparte, upon hearing the account given by the French consul, exclaimed, " Fortune! fortune! I ask but three days more !" and he ordered the whole of the troops to land with the least possible delay. The operation began the very night of our arrival : the men of war and the ships under their convoy were at anchor close to the town : the ships' boats all put off, quite full of soldiers, in a few moments, and stood in for the shore, leaving the town on their left. The sea on a sudden became so stormy, as to prevent their landing ; and the boats were compelled to return, and make fast to the ships nearest to the coast. In this manner they passed the night, being loaded with soldiers, and entirely at the mercy of the waves : no sooner, therefore, did calm weather return than they hastened to unmoor, and to reach the shore, which was, in a few hours, completely lined with soldiers. I had the command of the first detachment of General Desaix's corps, and had been forced to return, and make fast to a small galley ; in which situation I passed a very stormy night, and ran the risk of sinking. It was impossible to return on board the ships ; which were, besides, encumbered with soldiers.

In Egypt, the dawn of day is short, and calm weather generally returns with the sun, so that our hardships were soon over. After the landing of the troops, which was completed in the course of the evening, the next object was to bring the horses ashore. I was also charged with the duty of landing those that formed part of our convoy.

This operation could not fail to take up much time : it was perfectly new to me. I resorted to a plan that succeeded : I began by landing six horses ; placing the horsemen in a boat, and letting the horses down into the sea, each dragoon holding his horse by a halter. The first horse thus removed from the ship was obliged to support itself by swimming until the last had been let down into the sea; after which I ordered the boat to steer for the shore, towing after it the six horses that were swimming, and to place them on land, as near as possible to the water's edge, in order that they might be seen by all the horses that were about to follow in the same manner.

I afterwards placed in the boats all the dragoons, hussars, artillery-men, and soldiers of the train, with their saddles and harness, that they might go ashore, and there wait for their horses; and whilst they were on their way, I had the horses of each vessel hoisted out on both sides at once, and let down into the sea, without taking any other precaution than placing the halter round their necks.

A boat was in readiness to pick up the first that were thus sent off, and lead them gently to overtake the others on shore. Those that were taken out of the ships went, by a natural instinct, to join those already in the water; and I thus had a long file of horses swimming, and keeping up with the boat ahead of them. They all arrived safe; and upon arrival were led out by their riders, who had waited for them upon the beach, close to the borders of the desert, and who saddled and mounted them forthwith.

My operation was completely successful; and General Desaix, who was on the seaside, expressed his satisfaction to me, when he beheld the landing of this file of horses.

It was scarcely the hour of sunset when the landing of the *personnel* of the army was effected, and nearly the whole army united close to Pompey's pillar, at the distance of a few hundred yards from Alexandria. This was the first monument presented to our view; but our minds were so engaged in reflecting upon the objects we were about to behold, in a country which did not exhibit the slightest trace

of vegetation, that this column, which stood quite isolated
in the desert, did not attract our admiration.

Kleber's division, the first that was formed, marched at
once upon Alexandria.

The fortifications which enclose the town are the same
that were erected by the Arabs. Towards the angle in the
direction of which we were approaching, there was discovered
a large regular opening, which appears to have been formerly
intended for some particular purpose, but presented now to
the eye nothing more than a large hole, at an elevation of
twelve feet from the lower part of the wall.

Here the Turks had mounted a wretched gun upon a pile
of stones : they loaded it without cartridges or shot, but with
loose powder and stones, and fired it with a lighted brand.
We very soon discovered how perfectly ignorant they were
of the science of artillery.

It will hardly be credited that an army like ours, which
reckoned in its numbers several officers of undoubted talent,
should persist in assaulting this wretched hole, which cost us
many men, and where Kleber, amongst others, was wounded ;
whilst we had, at the distance of a few hundred yards on our
right, the great gate of Alexandria, on the road to Damanhour, which had not even been closed.

As some of our soldiers were wandering along the wall,
which is not protected by a ditch, they discovered that gate :
they entered, and were already near the houses of the town ;*
whilst we still persisted in our attempts against the opening,
which we were bent upon forcing. It occurred to us, at last,
to follow the road taken by our stragglers, and Alexandria
fell into our power.

The whole army was soon united in the midst of these
venerable ruins ; but, with all their admiration for the remains
of so many testimonials of antiquity, the troops began to

* The distance between the enclosure of the town and the inhabited houses is
considerable, and quite choked with ruins and rubbish.

show signs of discóntent, and to murmur at beholding nothing but heaps of dust in the midst of a desert, instead of what they had expected to find in the country to which they had been transplanted.

It need only be observed, in illustration of this feeling, that our army was composed of troops which had left Rome, Florence, Milan, Venice, Genoa, and Marseilles; and that nearly the whole staff came from Paris. The disappointment was generally felt; and the discontent gained ground during the march we had to make from Alexandria across the desert, in order to reach the Nile.

Previously to quitting Alexandria, General Bonaparte caused all the vessels of the convoy to enter the port. He ordered that the squadron should disembark every thing belonging to the army; and, upon leaving it, gave instructions that it should enter Alexandria, if the opening of the harbour did not throw any obstacle in the way; and in the contrary case, that it should proceed to Corfu, at the entrance of the Adriatic Sea.

Admiral Brueys delayed obeying this order, no doubt from a feeling which did him honour, and came to anchor at the point of Aboukir, between Alexandria and Rosetta, conceiving that the choice of this position might enable him to afford assistance to the army, in case of a reverse of fortune, of which he, perhaps, entertained some apprehension.

He remained, however, too long a time at this anchorage, where he was about to be destroyed, with the whole squadron.

The army left Alexandria on the night of the very day of the capture of that city: it consisted of five divisions, commanded by Generals Desaix, Bon, Regnier, Dugua, and Vial, who had replaced General Kleber.

The three last-named divisions took the road from Alexandria to Rosetta, by way of Aboukir; the other two proceeded from Alexandria to Damanhour, marching along the borders of the canal that crosses the desert, and leads from Alexandria to the Nile in the seasons of inundation.

General Bonaparte remained some days longer at Alexandria for the purpose of forming a military administration. He gave the command of the town to General Kleber, who stood in need of repose to recover from his wound; and he organised a flotilla of ships of war and transports, composed of the lightest and smallest vessels, out of the ships of war taken up as escorts at Civita Vecchia; such as the Pope's two small galleys, a few brigs and gun-boats, which had, by his orders, been brought up to the town for this purpose.

After embarking on board this little squadron the ammunition and provisions of which the army might stand in need on commencing its operations, he ordered all the *personnel* of the army and the dismounted cavalry to be put on board.

He next directed the squadron to set sail in his presence, and proceed to the mouth of the Nile, which it was instructed to ascend, keeping always abreast of the army.

He left at Alexandria the commission of learned men, who were not to follow until he should have arrived at Cairo.

After completing these arrangements, he quitted Alexandria, and proceeded on the road taken by Desaix's and Bon's divisions, which he came up with at Damanhour.

I have said that these divisions left Alexandria overnight. We were marching in columns, and at a slow pace, to enable those who lagged behind to keep up with us. We had proceeded but a short distance when a very dark night overtook us: our march was across a white surface of country, which cracked like snow under our feet: on tasting, it proved to be salt, formed by the evaporation of the waters that stagnate in the plain at the time of inundations. The march was painful: we chiefly suffered from the want of water, the canal along which we proceeded being, as is well known, constructed in many places of artificial mounds of earth, and dug out in others, for the purpose of bringing the waters of the Nile to Alexandria ; but it was so obstructed with mud, owing to its never having been repaired since the time of its construction, that it no longer received any water except at the period of the highest rise of the Nile : we therefore had only the water of the preceding year to quench our thirst with ; and this water had settled in the mud at the bottom of the canal, and had, here and there, formed into sinks covered with moss and the most disgusting insects : it was, nevertheless, drunk with avidity.

In Egypt, it is the practice to travel on without any concern about a resting-place for the night, each one who can afford it having with him his baggage and his tent : to those who cannot afford this luxury, the canopy of heaven is the only covering.

Water is the only thing anxiously sought for ; the pains bestowed by the wretched public administration of this country being solely directed to the object of procuring water, by means of wells, for travellers or beasts of burthen.

Beda is the first station on the road leading from Alexandria to Damanhour: this was also to be our first halting-place, and we had been provided with a guide for the journey. We halted from time to time, in order to enable the soldiers to overtake the main body; for they could not find out the road when they had once wandered from it.

I was riding in advance with fifteen mounted dragoons; but kept within call of the column. We had started at a late hour, and marched the whole night to avoid the heat; at daybreak we arrived at Beda, which is not a village, but a well, three feet in diameter, without either cord or bucket, it being indispensable to come provided with them. This wretched spot has not a single tree to afford shelter from the sun, which in Egypt breaks out a few moments after daylight and shines until nightfall.

On arriving at Beda, I found the well filled up with sand to its very mouth : it is impossible to describe our feelings of disappointment at the failure of this resource. My fifteen dragoons gave way to a state of silent despair, which the solitude of the desert carried to its height, and could only be compared to the stillness of the grave.

The absence of any human being, and the non-arrival of our column, which had unexpectedly halted, were circumstances which filled me with apprehension.

I feared I had lost my way, when sharp and plaintive cries reached my ears : some dragoons ran to the spot whence they issued ; perceiving that they stopped close to a human being, I rode up to them.

I beheld a tall blind woman, whose eyes appeared to have been recently put out ; she held a child at the breast, who vainly endeavoured to suck its milk.

I ordered a dragoon to dismount and bring her to the well. She perceived, by a natural instinct, that she had reached the spot she was in quest of ; she felt the edge of the well with her hands and feet, and upon discovering that it was filled with sand, she renewed her lamentations in spite of all our efforts to calm her.

I discovered she was thirsty, and had wine offered to her, of which we had a small quantity left out of the provision we had brought from the vessels. She drank it with avidity, and ate of some biscuit which the dragoons put into her hands. We found it impossible to understand each other. I waited the arrival of General Desaix's column, which had made a short halt, and did not arrive until a quarter of an hour afterwards.

This wretched woman, on recovering a little from her fright, placed her hands upon us, felt our clothes, and the helmets and arms of our dragoons, and must have soon found that we were not the same men whom her eyes had last beheld. The column arrived. She was questioned by General Desaix's interpreter; and before replying to him, she asked if we were not angels sent from heaven to her relief.

She told us that her husband, deceived by another of his wives, had entertained suspicions concerning the birth of his child, and reduced her to that state, after leading her into the desert, where he had abandoned her at a distance from the cistern, which she was in search of when we fell in with her.

She begged we would put her to death, if we could not take her away with us. She was twenty-four years of age, and but for her tawny colour, to which we were not accustomed, we should have considered her a beauty.

Though engaged with this woman's adventures, we had not neglected the object of clearing out the cistern: it had been attended to since our first arrival: the work took four hours, before we could discover any water; the first that was drawn out was distributed in glasses to the men who suffered most from thirst. It had been found necessary to station a guard of officers round the well. We succeeded, at last, in overcoming this first means of defence resorted to by those who were to impede our invasion of Egypt.

Preparations were made for resuming our march, after leaving with the unfortunate woman some bottles of water, and a provision of biscuit; and as it was impossible to bring her away, her adventure was written on a piece of paper, which was tied to her dress; and she was told that other men of our country would come up to her; and that if she remained at the same spot, and showed the paper, they would take care of her.

We continued our march, always starting at nightfall, and learned from the troops that passed the same place after we had left it, that the woman had been found dead, near the cistern, as well as her child, both being covered with wounds.

We inferred that the deed had been committed by the husband, who had witnessed, from a place of concealment in

thé desert, the assistance we had afforded her, and who had
perpetrated the murder after our departure.

CHAPTER IV.

El-Kaffer—Our first meeting with the Arabs—A new species of coin invented by
the soldiers—Damanhour—Danger to which the head-quarters are exposed—
Arrival at the Nile—Order of march in the desert—Galley-slaves in Egypt—
Mamelukes—Engagement on the Nile—Battle of the Pyramids—Capture of
Cairo.

WE had passed the whole day at Beda, where the small
stock of provisions brought by each of us from the vessels
had been nearly consumed; and whatever we beheld was
calculated to create a feeling of despondency.

Nevertheless, we resumed our march at sunset, in the
direction of Damanhour : the place at which we were to find
water was called El-Kaffer, half way from Beda to Damanhour. We were annoyed during our march by Arabs, the
boldness and rapidity of whose excursions, carried to within a
hundred paces of the column, made a forcible impression upon
our soldiers.

We had received orders not to fire; first, because we had
no other ammunition than what each soldier carried in his
cartouch-box and knapsack, and which was to suffice for the
conquest of Egypt, unless a fresh supply could be provided ;
and, in the next place, because, if we had once engaged
the Arabs, the firing would have been incessant, and would
have consumed time, which we could not spare from the
march.

The night was extremely dark when we arrived at El-
Kaffer : and although we could not see the place, we took up
our position as well as we could in its vicinity : each column
formed into a square, and remained in that situation until the

approach of day. A slight but unavoidable disorder was the
result of this position, which could not, however, be altered
until daylight.

The soldiers, in searching for water to allay their thirst,
discovered, outside of the village, a cistern used for the
purpose of watering some cultivated land. The report of
this discovery was no sooner spread than every one rushed
towards the cistern; and the crowd became so great, that
those who were drawing up the water were in danger of
being thrown in.

Those who could not approach the cistern hit upon the
idea of crying out that the water had been poisoned. The
stratagem succeeded; even the most thirsty drew back, and
its contrivers obtained free access to the cistern.

During the stillness of the night a sentinel fancied he saw
an Arab, and fired: the alarm spread in all directions; every
one sprang up; and without reflecting that it had been found
impossible to alter the position of the troops, owing to the
darkness of the night, each soldier fired. This sudden terror
might have occasioned some serious accidents; but it was not
attended with any more fatal consequences than the dispersion of the greater part of our horses.

As the country was wholly unprovided with wood, it had
been impossible to tie them; they were, besides, so completely knocked up, that the precaution was considered
almost superfluous. Being loose, therefore, when the firing
commenced, they took fright, and ran away, without its
being possible to pursue them. The artillery preserved only
such as were attached to the gun-carriages; but the leaders,
which had been untied, for the purpose of enabling them to
turn round and feed with the wheel-horses, were lost, together with the greater part of the horses belonging to the
cavalry and staff; and even the charger usually rode by
General Desaix.

Such of them as were not taken by the Arabs, who were

hovering round us, proceeded, from a natural instinct, in the direction of the Nile (towards Rosetta), where General Dugua's division, which had already arrived there, collected them, and restored them to us a few days afterwards. That division was greatly alarmed at seeing so many horses flying in disorder, with their saddles and harness, and concluded that we must have met with some severe check.

On the morning after this adventure we found ourselves in a very awkward predicament: the loss of the cavalry horses could easily be put up with; not so, however, with respect to the draught horses belonging to the artillery; the order was accordingly given for taking all those that had not fled; and General Desaix, desirous to set the first example, gave up the only one he had saved. The artillery was fortunately provided with a cart-load of harness, which proved of invaluable service to us on this occasion; and we were, eventually, enabled to resume our march.

Previously to quitting our position we entered the small village of El-Kaffer, which the inhabitants had surrounded with a wall built of sun-baked bricks: this wall was about ten feet high, surmounted with battlements, and flanked with towers, as a protection against the Arabs, whose whole life is a scene of plundering warfare.

A real Arab possesses nothing beyond his horse, generally a beautiful one, and his lance. It is a principle with him, that if a robbery can procure him the cost price of his horse, and twenty paras (fifteen sous) besides, he should not hesitate to attempt it. Arab children are reared up in the midst of privations; to abstain as long as possible from drink is a qualification instilled into them as paramount to every other: accordingly, when Arabs praise their children, they lay stress on the number of days they can resist thirst.

General Desaix sent me with his interpreter to El-Kaffer, to endeavour to purchase horses. He was naturally averse to plunder and disorder, and he carried the virtues of disin-

terestedness and probity to so great an extreme, that his soldiers were occasionally the sufferers from them ; but the
respect they bore their general never failed to secure him
their admiration and attachment.

I succeeded in purchasing for him a serviceable horse, the
only one he rode the whole time he was in Egypt, and another
for myself. When about to pay for the horses, which had
been sold to me for fifty Spanish dollars each (the only coin
known to the people), I found I had not any dollars, and
endeavoured, though in vain, to satisfy them respecting the
value of French gold, of which I had plenty about me ; in
vain, also, I offered to double the price of their horses ; I
could not induce them to accept in payment a gold coin with
which they were unacquainted ; and was compelled to return
to the division, change my gold for dollars amongst the officers, and go back to pay for my horses.

A soldier of my escort having noticed the ignorance of these
people, purchased dates and tobacco from them, and gave in
payment a large white button, which he took out of his
pocket; the Turkish tradesman returned him some change,
in a small coin named paras, which the soldier counted before
him, as if to ascertain whether the change was correct, and
went away satisfied ; but he took care to relate the story to
his comrades : it was not thrown away upon them, for they all
availed themselves of the same means to procure the small
articles they stood in need of, and which they could otherwise
have obtained only by means of plunder, which was strictly
forbidden.

This little species of fraud was carried on until the period
of paying the taxes, when these good people must have discovered the deception practised upon them, by the refusal of
the collector to take the buttons in payment.

We had recruited our strength at this little village of El-
Kaffer, where we had purchased an abundance and variety
of provisions, with the exception of bread, which was not to-

be had.   We proceeded on our march this day at an earlier
hour, preferring a slight inconvenience from heat to running
the risk of a renewal of the misfortune of the preceding night.

On leaving El-Kaffer, we followed the road to Damanhour,
where we expected to arrive the same night.   We had heard
so many brilliant descriptions of this town, that we all
marched towards it with the sensations we had formerly felt
on approaching one of the splendid Italian cities.

Great was our disappointment on beholding a heap of
decayed houses, denominated a town, merely because this is
the largest place between Alexandria and the Nile. It stands
in a plain, of an extent which the eye could not reach ; it is
supplied with water from wells only ; and except a few stones,
scattered here and there, amidst the ruins of ancient monuments, the smallest pebble could hardly be met with ; generally speaking, there are no stones to be found in Egypt.

General Desaix caused his division to bivouac in an enclosure of very fine orange and pomegranate trees, having a
cistern worked by a wheel, for the purpose of watering them:
the men found themselves well quartered ; and Damanhour
supplied us with some provisions.

We were overtaken at this place by General Bonaparte
and the whole staff ; Messrs. Monge and Berthollet were with
him.   He showed himself greatly displeased at the manifestations of discontent prevailing among the soldiery, owing to
the privations they had already suffered, and which they were
apprehensive of again encountering.

He could afford them no relief, and promised that, by
perseverance, the army would shortly be in the midst of
abundance.

We remained two days at Damanhour, and then marched
to Rahmanié, another small town at the junction of the canal
of Alexandria with the Nile.

General Bonaparte took the lead with an escort of mounted
guides, his aides-de-camp, and the officers of his staff, leaving

the equipages of the head-quarters in the rear of General Desaix's division, which had resumed its march along the borders of the canal. He knew that Dugua's division had reached Rosetta, and had sent orders for it to march upon Rahmanié, where it was expected to have arrived.

Nothing had yet been discovered in the plain when he left us, and moved forward with his escort.

We had been marching for a few moments, when a firing of musketry was heard behind us.

We made a short halt, and saw a cloud of dust every moment drawing nearer to us. It proceeded from the head-quarters, which had started in a body for Rahmanié with all its baggage, and had been attacked by a cloud of Arabs, who came upon them like a swarm of bees. The escort accompanying that convoy consisted of foot guides, who were too weak to form into a square, so as to protect the baggage, round which they kept constantly turning, in order to drive off the Arabs, who annoyed them and prevented their advance.

This escort was, fortunately, provided with two eight-pounders, attached to the regiment of guides; otherwise it never could have joined us, and must have been destroyed. We waited its arrival half an hour; and indeed it was high time it should come up with us.

We had no sooner resumed our march than we saw before us, on the road to Rahmanié; a considerable body of mamelukes, the first we had yet met with. Their appearance gave us great uneasiness about the fate of General Bonaparte, whom we had seen at the same spot within the last hour, with an escort not one-fourth of the number of the mamelukes who were within sight of us.

This was not the moment for clearing up conjectures, and we instantly halted.

General Desaix formed his division into two strong close columns, at a certain distance from each other; placed his artillery in front, all his camels and baggage in the centre, and in the space intervening between both columns; the guides on foot with their two eight-pounders closing the march.

As soon as these movements were completed, and instructions given that, in the event of a charge, the army should merely move in platoons either to the right or left, and commence firing, we began our march : the mamelukes made a feint upon us, at the head and tail of the column ; but a few cannon-shot soon ridded us of their presence. We continued in this order of march as far as the Nile, where we arrived parched with thirst, and oppressed by the heat of a still powerful sun.

We no sooner saw the river than officers, soldiers, and all, rushed into it ; each, regardless whether it was sufficiently shallow to afford security from danger, only sought to quench the ardency of his thirst, and stooped to drink from the stream ; the whole army thus presenting the appearance of a flock of sheep; no soldier had stopped to take off his knapsack, or lay down his musket.

We found ourselves, on quitting the river, in the midst of fields covered with a great variety of melons and other fruit, which soon made us forget the sufferings of the desert.

The country assumes, indeed, a very different aspect on approaching the Nile: the aridity of the desert is there relieved by a cheerful verdure ; the most luxuriant vegetation presents itself to the eye. Trees, of which we had not had the slightest glimpse since we left Italy, offered us their shade, the value of which can be duly appreciated by those only who have been marching through a desert ; the Nile also was at our feet, the object so eagerly sought for by travellers exposed in the same desert to the rays of a burning sun.

We were much gratified to learn that General Bonaparte had arrived in safety : he had not even met the corps of mamelukes which had made the attack upon us.

The whole army was united at Rahmanié, on the banks of the Nile, and the small squadron which had quitted Alexandria for the purpose of entering the Nile, had actually ascended it, and was at anchor abreast of the army.

We remained in this position nearly a day, previously to resuming our march upon Cairo, which we did without quitting the borders of the river, the flotilla ascending as we advanced.

We no longer suffered from the want of water; we had melons, lentils, and rice in abundance, and heaps of wheat, ready thrashed :* what we felt most difficulty in obtaining was bread ; and, for the greater part, we reached Cairo without having tasted any.

At each step of our advance General Bonaparte quickly foresaw every thing that was to be done ; first, to render available the resources of the most fertile country in the world, and give them a suitable application ; and also to secure to himself a glory of a different character from that which he had so abundantly acquired previously to his arrival.

It requires but the genius of one man to regenerate Egypt and all the East ; and that man should rather be a legislator than a conqueror. This country has so often been the prey of conquerors, in becoming their prize, that it holds them in as much abhorrence as the plague. The monarch, however, who would put an end to the evils attendant upon the yoke which oppresses them, would be hailed as the greatest of human beings by this wretched people, who are strangers to the rights of property, and incapable of acquiring or disposing of any. The harbinger of the benefits of civilization, unat-

* In Egypt, the harvest of each village is piled up, in common, round the village ; each one takes the corn he wants : they have no idea of corn-lofts or granaries ; poultry and birds are hardly excluded from sharing in this common stock, since the children set as a watch to drive them off are generally at play or asleep.

tended by the corruption too often following in its train, might for ever secure their attachment.

There can be no question but that the Directory, in sending General Bonaparte to Egypt, had no other object in view than to get rid of a chief, who had acquired popularity by his victories, and whose services they considered to be no longer necessary to them : on his own part, he had eagerly accepted the mission ; first, in order to be beyond the reach of a jealous government; and, in the next place, to gratify the praiseworthy ambition of restoring to that people their former renown and prosperity. He would, perhaps, have proclaimed himself their chief, no matter under what title ; I have no doubt of this, from what he afterwards told me ; but this was of little consequence as affecting the affairs of the rest of the world.

Continuing his march towards Cairo, General Bonaparte had, on his way, a serious encounter with the mamelukes at the village of Chebreissa.

According to the instructions he had laid down, each division of the army marched forward in squares, six men deep on each side ; the artillery was at the angles ; and in the centre, the ammunition, the baggage, and the few mounted cavalry we had left.

This order of march protected us against all accidents, but retarded our already slow movements, because our cavalry, being already too inferior in its *materiel* and *personnel* to that of the mamelukes, we could not, unfortunately, employ it in scouring the country before us. We therefore commenced our marching movement by forming into squares ; the second square not advancing until the first had begun to form again, for fear of danger ; or else, when the first was in full march, if the great distance of the mamelukes left us no ground for apprehension.

We must, occasionally, have marched four or five leagues

a day in this order, compelled to break our squares, and form again, each time we had to enter a defile; a necessity which repeatedly occurred in the course of the day. These defiles were owing to the road being intersected by canals of irrigation, which the water had not yet reached; they were all very broad, and of considerable depth: it was requisite, therefore, first, to slope down the elevation on both sides, which was a work of time. One can hardly form an idea of the sufferings which the heat occasioned to the soldiers who were in the centre of the square, from which all circulation of air was excluded, besides the difficulty they had to breathe, in consequence of the cloud of fine dust which hovered above their heads.

We all suffered from a parching thirst; several men died of it on the spot: the feeling of self-preservation was sufficient to convince the soldiers that they would have been exposed to be cut in pieces, had they been allowed to return to quench their thirst in the Nile; but when a cistern, or a well worked by a wheel, was met with, we so contrived as to have it in the centre of the square; we then halted, each one drank at his leisure, and our forward movement was then resumed.

General Bonaparte had his tent pitched, every night, on the banks of the river, in the midst of his army, and close to his small squadron, whenever it was able to keep up with us. The two small galleys which General Desaix had brought from Civita Vecchia led the van, because vessels of small dimensions were in less danger of running aground in a river with which we were unacquainted, and which we were navigating without a pilot.

These vessels are well known to work their way in calm weather, and against currents, by means of their enormous oars, which are plied by the galley-slaves put on board for that purpose.

These wretched people are always in a sitting attitude, and

fixed by chains and padlocks to their benches of hard labour, from the first manning of the vessel until they are landed; so that, if by any accident it should sink, they must inevitably perish.

General Bonaparte, seeing from the banks the flotilla passing on its way, noticed the condition of these wretches : this was two days before the encounter at Chebreissa: he immediately ordered the chains to be broken, and the men to be set at liberty.

It was on the next day but one, when the army was moving simultaneously forward, that we descried the army of the mamelukes, whose very want of order, together with their party-coloured dresses, and the splendid trappings of their horses, presented an imposing appearance.

A flotilla, likewise, consisting of all kinds of vessels, manned by Turks and Greeks, was descending the Nile, to attack our small squadron.

They were already close to us, when General Bonaparte ordered his army to halt, for the purpose of forming it into five large squares, checker-wise; the left square resting upon the Nile, and protecting the flotilla, the right square placed in the direction of the desert; and all five reciprocally flanking each other.

The mamelukes came and paraded their horses in our front; but fearing to attack us, wheeled round our right, in hopes of finding in the rear some vulnerable point: we fired a few guns, which were sufficient to rid us of them, especially when they found as little chance of success at that side as at the first they had explored. They made no further attempt on this day.

On the river the case was very different; the enemy's flotilla courageously bore down upon our's, attacked, and instantly boarded it in a position where a turn of the stream, and the elevation of the bank on our side, prevented our affording it any assistance. They at first carried our two small galleys, and cut off the heads of all their prisoners. The galley-slaves, who had scarcely been twenty-four hours at liberty, had thrown themselves into the water, with the remainder of the crews, in order to reach the opposite bank. The other vessels were also endeavouring to escape, though still continuing to fight; and a very warm firing was kept up.

General Bonaparte ordered the left division to move close up to the bank. A fire of musketry and grape-shot soon compelled the assailants to give way, and to abandon the two small galleys, which fell again into our possession.

Our squadron continued to ascend the river, and pressed closely upon the flotilla of the mamelukes. This engagement, however trifling, had been kept up with great spirit. The enemy's flotilla retreated to Cairo on the following night, and must have been burned by order of the Beys; for it never more made its appearance.

The army continued its march the same day, following the course of the river; and two or three days afterwards we fought, exactly in front of Cairo, the celebrated battle of the Pyramids.

The army arrived in five grand squares, each composed of a division. Ours was quite close to the Nile; and our right was in the direction of the Pyramids.

The mamelukes were stationed at the village of Embabé, where the Nile must be crossed in order to reach Boulac, one of the suburbs of Cairo.

They had fortified this village, towards the Nile, by digging a ditch, behind which they were seen ready mounted on their horses.* Behind this ditch they had indiscriminately placed twenty pieces of cannon, which kept playing upon our left square, which was the first that ap-

---

* The mamelukes were strangers to the use of infantry, and considered it disgraceful to fight otherwise than mounted. They were excellent horsemen, but totally ignorant of whatever relates to the art of war, or the composition of armies.

proached them. The other four squares marched abreast of the left, in the direction assigned to each. Desaix's division was on the extreme right, and had Regnier's division on its left.

General Bonaparte was with Bon's division, in the centre. He caused the village of Embabé to be attacked by the left division, which was nearest to it: the village was immediately carried, the artillery taken, and the mamelukes routed. Whilst this attack was going on, the more numerous body of the Beys, followed by their mamelukes, suddenly made their appearance in front of the squares composing Desaix's and Regnier's divisions, the soldiers of which were only attending to the movements on the left. The *mirage*, so prevalent in Egypt, the effect of which was yet novel to us, led us to imagine, when we first saw them, that they were at some distance; and no sooner had we descried them, than, in consequence of the *mirage*, they were almost upon us.[*]

We had scarcely time to give the alarm and open our fire, when we found that this formidable cavalry had already surrounded us. So great had been the rapidity of its charge, that we were unable to alter the position of our two divisions, which masked one another to nearly the extent of half a battalion in front.

The danger was pressing: we commenced firing, never supposing that the two divisions, which were only a hundred paces asunder, would be under the necessity of keeping up a fire towards those parts of their flank fronts which masked one another for a few yards. The contrary, however, came to pass. The charge of the mamelukes was extremely impetuous in our front, where a fire of grape-shot and musketry

---

[*] The *mirage* is produced by the heat of the sun, which condenses the vapourous exhalations from the earth, and prevents their rising in the atmosphere: they form a cloud, extending, in the daytime, over the surface of the ground, and, at a distance, resembling a calm sea. Towards night they fall in copious dews, so that, after sunset, the eye embraces a greater extent of country than it does in the daytime.

brought the men and horses down in heaps round our squares; but what exceeded every thing else in extravagance and daring was, that all who escaped this destructive fire still rushed on with so much rapidity, as to penetrate into the space between Desaix's and Regnier's divisions, under the incessant fire of both faces of the divisions, which played upon them at the distance of fifty paces. Not a single mameluke retreated ; and it is remarkable that a smaller number fell in their charge through this opening than on their first charge upon our fronts.

About twenty of our men fell from each other's fire, an accident occasioned by the too great proximity of the divisions.

Although the troops that were in Egypt had been long inured to danger, and familiarised with all the chances of an encounter, every one present at the battle of the Pyramids must acknowledge, if he be sincere, that the charge of those ten thousand mamelukes was most awful, and that there was reason, at one moment, to apprehend their breaking through our formidable squares, rushing as they did upon them with a confidence which enforced a sullen silence in our ranks, interrupted only by the word of command of the chiefs.

It seemed as if we must inevitably be trampled, in an instant, under the feet of this cavalry of mamelukes, who were all mounted upon splendid chargers richly caparisoned with gold and silver trappings, covered with draperies of all colours, and waving scarfs, and who were bearing down upon us at full gallop, rending the air with their cries.

The whole character of this imposing sight had filled the breasts of our soldiers with a sentiment to which they had hitherto been strangers, and made them attentive to the word of command. Accordingly, the order was no sooner given to fire, than it was executed with a quickness and precision far exceeding what is exhibited in an exercise or upon parade.

No field of battle had ever displayed a similar spectacle to the eyes of two contending parties, who then met for the first time. This action decided the fate of Egypt, and it was the last effort of the Beys, as a united body, to dispute our conquest of the country.

They dispersed the same night: the two most powerful amongst them, Mourad and Ibrahim, whose former misunderstandings had rendered them mistrustful, and exceedingly wary in what related to their personal interests, still continued rivals of each other.

Ibrahim recrossed the Nile with the lesser Beys, his feudatory dependents, and without stopping at Cairo, took the road to Syria: he only waited a few days at Salahié, at the entrance of the desert of Asia, for those of his mamelukes who had not joined him since the battle, and to enable his harem and baggage to reach Syria.

Mourad, on the contrary, took with his vassals the road to Upper Egypt, and ascended the left bank of the river, being followed in his retreat by the flotilla at his command.

General Bonaparte, on the very night of the battle, established himself in the town of Gizeh,* at Mourad Bey's residence; the army followed him, and on the next day he took possession of Cairo.

CHAPTER V.

Murmuring amongst the troops—Citadel of Cairo—The Pyramids—Naval engagement at Aboukir—Formation of establishments of every kind.

OUR flotilla had come up, and was moored before Gizeh. The ammunition consumed was replaced by a fresh \supply'

---

* Gizeh is a large town on the left bank of the Nile, facing the island of Roda, which lies between Cairo and the left bank. The town is surrounded by a strong wall, the two extremities of which are washed by the river.

and we were ready to commence fresh operations when called upon.

The authorities of Cairo, the heads of the law, and magistrates, came to Gizeh to offer their submission to General Bonaparte, who gained their confidence, and drew such information from them as fixed his determination with respect to ulterior operations.

His first object was to secure military occupation of Egypt. He immediately ordered Regnier's division to pursue Ibrahim in his flight.

Vial's division was sent to Damietta, and Dugua's to Rosetta; Bon's division protected Cairo; that of Desaix, which was destined to proceed to Upper Egypt, waited at Gizeh until the others had reached their respective destinations.

This dispersion of the army was the signal for an explosion of that discontent and murmuring, which, in consequence of the severe privations endured by the soldiers, had been fomenting ever since we left Alexandria. They no longer hesitated to give vent to their complaints : the most moderate were sending in their resignations from all quarters ; and had it not been for the firm resolution proclaimed by General Bonaparte, of making an example of the very first who should presume to ask him to take the army back to France, an intention actually entertained by some of the malecontents, no doubt the army would have mutinied and refused obedience. The firmness of their chief kept them within bounds, and preserved these misguided men from the disgrace that awaited them.

So great was General Bonaparte's self-confidence, that, in this state of affairs, he departed from Cairo, followed by what little cavalry he had brought from Europe, and took the road upon which Regnier's division was marching, in order to drive Ibrahim back into Syria, and close the entrance to Egypt in that direction.

He gave the command of Cairo to General Desaix, whilst

he was personally engaged on this expedition; but previously to his departure he had dispatched his aide-de-camp Julien to Admiral Brueys with orders to set sail for Corfu or Toulon; and the aide-de-camp was not to return until he had seen the fleet under weigh.

He had also sent to Mourad Bey, as a negotiator for peace, M. Rosetti, the Venetian consul, who was settled at Cairo; but such was the ignorance of these oriental chiefs, that Mourad rejected General Bonaparte's proposals, because he had just learned the destruction of our squadron, and had persuaded himself that this event would compel us to quit Egypt.

During the time that General Desaix held the command, we went to visit the citadel of Cairo, situated between the town and the chain of Monguatam which separates the Nile from the Red Sea.

This fort is extremely steep in the direction of the desert; and is, generally speaking, in good condition, but has no exterior works connected with it.

We were here shown a breach, at an elevation of upwards of fifty feet towards Monguatam, and were told that, after the battle of the Pyramids, some mamelukes who had retired into the citadel, seeing Cairo occupied by our troops, and not daring to venture out into the town, formed the resolution of escaping through that breach. In order to effect this object, they began by throwing from the rampart all the mattresses and cushions of the divan, and every bale of cotton they could procure: they afterwards made one of their number jump down in order to arrange these as a platform below the breach, and then followed, one after another, with their horses, which they actually rode on the occasion, and, wonderful to say, escaped unhurt! I was shown the materials of the platform at the foot of the breach.

We were also shown the collection, preserved in the citadel, of cuirasses and helmets formerly taken from the crusaders. - They were displayed as trophies above the entrance gate, in the interior of the citadel: the major part were in excellent condition, although they had been exposed to the open air for ages; but the climate, in those countries, possesses the property of preserving objects. The well of the citadel of Cairo also attracted our curiosity: its water is level with the Nile; and although it is of a brackish taste, no means have been neglected to procure an abundant supply.

There had been constructed in the interior of the well a spiral staircase of gentle descent to the water's edge: the well is, therefore, of prodigious dimensions. These noble works attested the progress of arts in Egypt in former times, and they were still in good condition.

We also went to visit the Pyramids; no troops had ever been there before. Every one wished to accompany General Desaix ; so that our party exceeded a hundred persons, independently of a company of infantry which we had taken with us as an escort.

Starting from Gizeh, we crossed the plain where the celebrated Memphis is said to have formerly stood. Of all the ancient Egyptian cities, it is almost the only one of which no vestige remains to point out where it had existed ; and if we had not met now and then, in the plain below the Pyramids, with some broken clay at our feet, nothing would have led us to suppose that even a wall, still less a town, had stood on this spot.

Our conjectures were guided, in the first place, by the canâl that borders the desert at the foot of the pyramids, and which is, at the present day, without water, except at the time of the highest swellings of the Nile; and secondly, by a bridge of masonry-work, which could only have belonged to Memphis, as otherwise it would be without an object ; it must have been constructed as a means of communication of the inhabitants of Memphis with their cemetery or city of the dead, still to be seen by the side of the pyramids, which were nothing more than tombs. The City of the Dead, near Memphis, consists of a countless number of small pyramids, of sizes proportioned to the fortunes of families, many of which pyramids are still standing upon their bases.

I had heard it stated, that the large pyramids were temples; an opinion founded upon the facts of the existence of similar ones in India, where they were consecrated to religious worship, and of the Egyptians having derived their knowledge from the East: I cannot, however, join in this opinion; for the Pyramids of Egypt were, unquestionably, tombs.

I was one of the first to ascend the largest: we were to the number of sixteen on the top, and yet found plenty of space. The view which is embraced from this elevation in the air, is truly delightful.

General Bonaparte was absent about twelve days. We witnessed at Cairo, during this time, the spectacle of the feast of the Ramadan, which is very rigidly observed in the East. It is their Lent. The fasting consists in neither eating nor drinking any thing whatever from sunrise till sunset; the people must work, notwithstanding the excessive heat, and without attempting to quench their thirst; but the sun has no sooner disappeared from the horizon, than they partake of a plentiful repast, served up beforehand.

Every thing was new to us; but what mostly astonished our soldiers, was the dancing of the *almées*, a troop of young girls, remarkable for their elegance and graceful turn of figure, but of a lascivious freedom of action, which must be seen to be credited, and which decency forbids me to describe. All this, however, was going on in the public square, in presence of a crowd of all ages and of both sexes.

We received, one night, intelligence of General Bonaparte's movements: he had overtaken Ibrahim in the vicinity of Salahié, at the entrance of the desert, to which he was endeavouring to retire, and ordered him to be charged by the cavalry, which, being too weak in numbers, incurred a very great danger; and the action would have terminated fatally, had not the infantry promptly come up to relieve it: nevertheless the object contemplated was attained. Ibrahim entered Syria, and ceased to molest us.

General Bonaparte was returning to Cairo, when he met on the road the officer sent from Rosetta to General Desaix; by whom he had been ordered to proceed to Salahié, with the intelligence of the sad catastrophe that had befallen our squadrons, and of which he had been an eye-witness.

I have already said that General Bonaparte, before leaving the squadron, had ordered the Admiral to enter Alexandria, or proceed to Corfu; but whether owing to the entrances into the harbour not having yet been sounded, or not containing a sufficiency of water,* our admiral had gone to take up his moorings at the point of Aboukir, where he remained nearly a whole month.

So great was General Bonaparte's uneasiness, that during his march from Alexandria to Cairo, he had not only twice written to Admiral Brueys, to enter Alexandria, or set sail for Corfu; but also, before quitting Cairo to overtake and engage Ibrahim Bey, he had sent Julien, his aide-de-camp, to repeat the order to the Admiral; but this aide-de-camp, who had embarked in a boat on the Nile, with an escort of infantry, never reached his destination; nor would it have been possible for him to have done so before the squadron was engaged.

He disappeared, with the whole of his escort, at a village on the banks of the Nile, where he had landed to purchase

---

* Two years afterwards, when the English became masters of Alexandria, they took soundings of the entrances into the harbour, and found the middle one to be five fathoms deep in the shallowest part. Had not our squadron lost a month without attempting to try soundings, it would have escaped, and been of essential importance to our future destinies.

some provisions he stood in need of; and it was not till a long time afterwards that we learned the details of his tragical end.

Our admiral had brought his squadron to anchor in a single line, his headmost ship being close to a small island, forming the neck of land upon which the fort of Aboukir is built.

The English, after reconnoitring it, caused two of their ships to pass between the small island and the headmost ship of our line. The first English ship that attempted this passage came too near the island, and ran aground: the next passed between her consort, which had grounded, and the head of our line. The English admiral, finding that the first ship[*] had grounded, and the second had succeeded in forcing a passage, sent a third ship to replace the disabled one. These two ships having joined, sailed up our line, with the land on their right, and attacked each of our ships in succession, whilst the remainder of the English squadron engaged them by sailing up our line on the other tack; a manœuvre that compelled our vessels to fight on the larboard and starboard side at one and the same time.

Ship after ship of our squadron was destroyed, excepting the two last, which, together with a frigate, being at anchor at the tail of the ships at their moorings, weighed and stood out to sea, without waiting to take their turn in the conflict; these were the Genereux and Guillaume Tell, with the frigate Diane, or La Justice. They proceeded to the Archipelago, where they again separated; the Genereux went to Corfu, and the other two succeeded in entering Malta; a proof that the order previously given by General Bonaparte might have been carried into effect.

---

* It is worthy of remark that this English ship was the identical *Bellerophon*, which, being constantly at sea since that period, seemed destined to pursue the remains of the Egyptian expedition in the person of its author. This is the ship which received the emperor sixteen years afterwards. It had yet some sailors of that early period on board, not having been laid up during the peace of Amiens.

The admiral's ship (L'Orient) caught fire, and blew up during the engagement; so that, out of fifteen sail of the line, only the two above-mentioned succeeded in effecting their escape.

The projects of General Bonaparte were necessarily affected by the defeat of this squadron, since it was to have returned to Europe for a further supply of troops, which he could now no longer reckon upon.

The extent of our misfortune was not, however, so great as we had at first apprehended. Egypt was little known at this time, and the English were under the impression that we must all inevitably perish from want in that country. They were the more confirmed in their opinion by the capture of a small vessel, on its way from Rosetta to Alexandria, with a mail containing the first letters written to France by the army subsequently to its landing, and replete, therefore, with complaints of all the privations it had undergone on the march through the desert, until its arrival at Cairo, during which march hardly any bread had been procured.

These details served to confirm the English in their first opinion, and it occurred to them, that they would greatly augment our embarrassment, to increase the number of mouths we should have to feed. They accordingly landed at Alexandria all the sailors, ship-boys, and soldiers of the ships they had captured, furnishing us, by this means, with a supply of seven or eight thousand men, upon which we never could have calculated. They served to complete the different corps; but, above all, we derived invaluable assistance from the many artificers of all trades that were on board our ships. They were added to those brought over with the army, and attached to the various scientific bodies; so that, in this respect, and with regard to the artillery, we more than doubled our means of resources.

It will now be seen with what admirable wisdom every thing was rendered available.

The loss of the fleet had, in some measure, calmed the murmurs of those who desired to be taken back to France. General Bonaparte ordered passports to be delivered to all who had persisted in claiming them ; but, with the exception of a few individuals, who shall be nameless, all determined to remain and cease making complaints.

Works of a gigantic nature and establishments of every kind illustrated the first months of our residence in Egypt.

The commission of scientific men had been removed from Alexandria to Cairo, and each of its members was named chief of some establishment, of which he was entrusted with the formation or the management.

Flour, as fine as could be obtained in Paris, was ground in mills constructed at Alexandria, Rosetta, Damietta, and Cairo.   By the erection of ovens, bread became as abundant as we had hitherto found it scarce.

Hospitals were formed, which admitted of a bed for each patient.   These benevolent establishments were powerfully promoted by the exertions of Messrs. Larrey and Desgenettes, men possessing many claims to celebrity, and who acquired the esteem of the commander-in-chief and the gratitude of the army.

Saltpetre-works and powder-mills were erected.

A foundry was constructed, with reverberating furnaces, by means of which projectiles of large dimensions were recast; and many others were provided, in order to cast smaller ones for the use of our artillery.

Large shops were built for locksmiths, armourers, joiners, cartwrights, carpenters, and ropemakers.

The sailors who were too far advanced in years to change their profession, were employed in the formation of a large flotilla upon the Nile, consisting of all the kinds of vessels on the river, which had been properly rigged and armed. They were commanded by officers of the navy, and were of the greatest assistance in transporting the supplies of the army.

All the troops were dressed in blue cotton clothes, and black morocco caps: to these were added substantial cloaks of the flannel stuff of the country, to serve as a night-covering. At no period had they been so comfortably equipped.

The fare consisted of excellent bread, meat, rice, pease, and a little coffee and sugar, as a substitute for spirits, which were unknown in Egypt until our arrival.

The success of these several improvements was already manifest to all. We provided ourselves with tables, chairs, morocco-leather boots, and linen: the bread we ate was as fine as any in Paris.

We had no sooner procured the objects of primary neces- sity than luxury followed. Plate was manufactured of a light and portable kind. The plate, called hunting-plate, which the Emperor had afterwards in use at Paris, was made from the model of what he brought back from Egypt.

Silver goblets, and services of plate, were now in general use.

Establishments of confectioners and distillers were opened, and proved very successful.

Embroiderers and lace-makers gradually followed: the Turks themselves, who are very quick at imitating, sur- passed us in this line of business; they even succeeded in casting silver buttons stamped with the republican arms, and finishing gold ones in the greatest perfection.

Playing-cards, billiard and card-tables, were seen in Cairo a few months after we had settled in that city. A French and Arabic printing-press was at work: every thing requisite to constitute a regular European establishment was either completed or in progress. The cavalry was recruiting itself: all went on to our satisfaction, and with inconceivable activity.

CHAPTER VI.

Desaix's expedition to Upper Egypt—Action of Sediman—Province of Faïoum—
Faoué—Lake Mœris—City of the Dead—Attempt of Mourad Bey after the
insurrection at Cairo.

THE waters of the Nile had reached their greatest height
when General Bonaparte arrived at Cairo on his return
from the pursuit of Ibrahim Bey. He then ordered the departure of Desaix's division for the twofold purpose of occupying Upper Egypt and fighting Mourad Bey, who had fled
thither. This division consisted of eight battalions only, one
of them, since its arrival at Cairo, having been sent to garrison Alexandria. The whole division was embarked at Boulac
on board of djermes, vessels which navigate the Nile. It
was provided with only two pieces of artillery, and ascended
the Nile, without stopping, as far as Siout, the capital of
Upper Egypt. The whole country was inundated by the overflowing of the river, and the towns and villages, which are
built upon artificial elevations of ground, had become so
many small islands.

General Desaix learned at Siout that Mourad Bey had
again penetrated into the country along the borders of the
desert on the left bank, leaving the inundation on his right,
and contemplating to approach Cairo. He had been informed
of the preparations making for an insurrection against the
French, and was anxious to take advantage of it.

As the inundation compelled him to pass through Faïoum,
so as to secure at any time his retreat into the desert, and as
his march was retarded by the camels loaded with provisions
which followed in his train, General Desaix formed the plan
of overtaking him.

The decrease of the Nile had commenced when he caused

his fleet of djermes to descend as far as the entrance of Joseph's Canal, which is four or five leagues below Siout, between Minieh and Melaoui. He made all his vessels enter, one after the other, into the canal, which is every where ten or twelve toises broad, and in its whole length runs parallel to the Nile, along the borders of the desert.

The current of water in the canal brought the whole fleet close to Sediman, a small village standing on the edge of the desert and on one of the banks of the canal. We descried the mamelukes, who fled into the desert on our approach. General Desaix, however, proceeded no farther on the canal, but landed the troops as well as the two pieces of artillery, and we advanced towards the desert in a compact square, offering battle to the mamelukes, who, however, refused it.

The sufferings from thirst and the approach of night made us retire to the banks of the inundated land, where we had left our boats and all our provisions: the mamelukes followed, and bivouacked at the distance of two hundred paces from us; so that we were obliged to take rest without breaking our square, each soldier holding his musket between his knees.

The merit of French troops in circumstances of difficulty can be appreciated by those only who have lived amongst them. On the present occasion, each soldier was so impressed with the reality of the danger, that he had not to be put upon his guard; the exercise of discipline was wholly uncalled for, so satisfied was he of the necessity of obedience. The troops would, of their own accord, have punished any one amongst them guilty of a neglect calculated to compromise the safety of all.

At daybreak, that is to say, at two or three o'clock the next morning, all the troops were under arms, without being called to it by beat of drum: the boats were immediately set afloat, to spare us the trouble of protecting them: we formed into three squares, a large one flanked by two smaller ones, and advanced towards the desert.

Our two pieces of artillery were stationed at the two angles of our front, and could be removed to the angles in the rear by penetrating through the interior of the square.

We were ascending, in this order, one of the hills of the desert, to take possession of its summit, and command a greater extent of country, when, without receiving any other notice of the approach of the mamelukes than the noise of their tam-tam, and the cloud of dust which they raised in their advance, our squares were suddenly charged by a swarm of this impetuous cavalry, and with such desperate fury, that the right was broken, and lost fifteen or twenty men by the fault of its commander. This officer, who was a man of undoubted courage, had formed the plan of reserving his fire until a sure aim could be taken : he tried the experiment ; it happened, however, that the horses of the mamelukes, though pierced with shot, forced their way through the square, and dropped at a hundred paces beyond it, so that they made openings in the ranks, into which the mamelukes who were behind did not fail to penetrate. General Desaix severely reprimanded this officer, who, with the best intentions, committed an error which was likely, for a few moments, to be attended with serious consequences.

We had but just time to halt, point our artillery, and commence a firing in double files, which, for the space of half an hour, prevented our distinguishing any object, owing to the smoke, dust, and confusion. The action, very opportunely for us, ceased with the firing, as we had only nine cannon-shot left, and our cartridges were nearly exhausted.

The conflict had been very disastrous to the mamelukes, who fled in all directions. The ground was cleared before us in a very few minutes, and we continued to ascend the hill, from the summit of which the beautiful and richly cultivated province of Faïoum presented itself to our view.

We retraced our steps down the hill in order to be in communication with our boats, which had witnessed the late encounter from the midst of the inundated lands: they followed our movement, and came up with us at the small village of Sediman, where we passed the night.

Our departure the next morning was rather accelerated by the decrease of the waters, as it hardly allowed our boats sufficient time to reach the lower entrance of the canal through which they were to return to the Nile.

We therefore quitted Sediman at daybreak, and took up a position at the entrance of the province of Faïoum, a distance of only one league from the village.

Joseph's Canal runs in front of the neck of land that unites this province to the valley of the Nile.

During the heaviest inundations the canal discharges its superabundant waters into another canal which branches off from the first at the village of Illaon, and carries them to the town of Faouë, and thence to Lake Mœris.

The bed of this canal is lower than that of Joseph's Canal. At their point of junction there is a dike of separation, in work of solid masonry, surmounted with a stone-bridge of very great antiquity: we crossed it for the purpose of fixing ourselves at the entrance of the province towards which we were marching.

General Desaix, having landed every thing belonging to his division, sent the boats back to the Nile, and bivouacked his troops in a wood of date trees, quite impenetrable to the sun's rays, and on the borders of the canal of Illaon.

We remained some days in this position, where we had every thing in abundance. The canal was deep enough to admit of our bathing in it. Exhausted as we were by oppressive heat, after marching through the desert for seven or eight successive days, we indulged without restraint in the delightful enjoyment of these baths. The abuse of them was productive of pernicious consequences to us; forty-eight hours afterwards, eight hundred of our men were attacked with ophthalmia, in so severe a manner as to become entirely

blind.   General Desaix himself was of the number, and experienced the most acute sufferings.

Our situation alarmed us to such a degree, that we immediately made arrangements for proceeding to Faouë, where
we expected to find some relief for our numerous sick.

We placed General Desaix, with some soldiers, in a small
boat, which descended the canal, whilst the column followed
the road leading to Faouë along its bank.

The soldiers suffering from blindness exceeded in numbers
those in health : each soldier having the use of his sight, or
only attacked in one eye, led several of his blind comrades,
who, nevertheless, carried their own arms and baggage.   We
bore a much greater resemblance to men discharged from an
hospital than to a warlike body.

After penetrating for several hours through fields in an
admirable state of cultivation, and covered with rose-trees in
full bloom, * we arrived at Faouë in the wretched condition I
have described.   The town is of considerable size, the
capital of Faïoum, and situated in the heart of that province,
which presents to the eye an uniform sheet of verdure.
Its only communication with Egypt is by a neck of land,
of which Illaon is the extreme point.   The canal of Illaon
runs through the province and the capital, whence it branches
out into a multitude of irrigating streams, that fertilise
the surrounding country in their course towards Lake Mœris,
into which they discharge their superfluous waters.

This province enjoys a greater degree of tranquillity than
any part of Egypt, with which country it has very little
intercourse.

Over the canal running through the town is a bridge of
great antiquity, and resembling those I had seen in Egypt;
they appeared to be of kindred origin.   I do not think they
exceeded five in number; one of them, thrown over the canal

---

* The best Egyptian oil of rose is prepared at Faouë.

running at the bases of the Pyramids, and, no doubt, connected with Memphis in former days; another at Illaon; a third at Faouë; and the remaining two at Siout.

We stayed at Faonë until the disappearance of the waters ; an occurrence soon followed by the drying up of the country, or rather by that adherence of the ground which is necessary for sowing; an operation simply consisting in throwing the seed over the mud, and imbedding it by means of men, who tread over the field in every direction. The ground is never ploughed, except when it has become too hard to admit of being sown in the manner I have just described.

At no period since our arrival in Egypt had we enjoyed so much comfort as during our stay in Faïoum : we remained there upwards of a month, at the end of which all our sufferers from ophthalmia had recovered.

Ovens were erected, and the military administration of the province was organised.

We were soon prepared to resume our march, and proceeded across the beautiful and verdant fields of a country which was about to display to our sight its wonderful and unexpected fecundity.

General Bonaparte had signified to General Desaix his satisfaction at the conduct of his division, and instructed him to levy money and horses in the province of Faïoum. This order was punctually carried into effect, and afforded us the opportunity of visiting the famous Lake Mœris, which receives the waters of the canal that forms a junction with Joseph's Canal at the village of Illaon.

Those travellers must have been greatly mistaken who have pretended that this lake was formed as a reservoir for the overflowing waters of the Nile, which it afterwards discharged over the country during the drought. This opinion is probably maintained by people who have not had the advantage of personal knowledge.

We certainly discovered near Illaon, on the right bank of

the canal and of the road leading to Faouë, a very spacious basin, constructed of masonry, which was then full of water; it may be two hundred feet long, and of equal breadth. It is also more elevated than the surrounding land, and can only be filled by the waters of the Nile, when at its greatest rise; or by means of small flood-gates, which were opened for the double purpose of admitting the water, or of letting it out: they still answer the same purpose. This basin, however, cannot be the one alluded to by travellers. There is hardly a single mill in Europe the pond of which does not hold a greater volume of water; and the whole contents of the basin would hardly be sufficient to irrigate a few acres of land: it cannot therefore be the celebrated Lake Mœris, or the exaggeration of historians must have exceeded all bounds.

I had the command of the first detachment of light infantry sent from Faouë to overrun the province. My attention was particularly attracted to the remains which it exhibited of its ancient state of civilization, and to the system of irrigation, which prevailed in as great perfection as in Italy.

A multitude of little canals branch out in all directions from the town of Faouë, and carry their waters into every village of the province: each village has its canal, and keeps it in proper repair.

When a village has excited displeasure, the flood-gate of its canal is closed, and it is deprived of water until the orders signified to it have been complied with. No other means of coercion could be productive of so prompt and effectual a result.

The government of the province requires only the aid of one man to open or close the flood-gates.

I believe I was the first person in the army who visited Lake Mœris; and this imposing sight convinced me that the canal of Faioum formerly ran through the mounds of sand which the winds had collected in heaps at the extremity of the lake, and that its waters discharged themselves into the

Mediterranean through Lake Mareotis, in the vicinity of Alexandria. The winds constantly prevailing in that quarter have by degrees driven these sand-hills into the canal, and completely choked up the part beyond them, which is called at the present day *the Waterless River*, in which the inhabitants assured me that fragments of petrified boats were still to be seen.

As the waters carried every year to this spot, by the rising of the Nile, found no longer any outlet, they must necessarily have overflowed and formed an immense sewer, which has gone on constantly increasing, but which, being in the lowest ground in the province, could never lose its waters by other means than evaporation, under the burning sun of this climate.

I do not think that the existence of Lake Moeris can be accounted for in any other manner.

There is a small island, about the centre of the lake, upon which the inhabitants of the town of Faouë (the Arsinoë of antiquity) constructed their City of the Dead, and erected a temple, which is still in existence. Every opulent family had its tomb in it, with a sepulchral recess for each of its members. In those days, as at the present time, it was an object of constant occupation with the Egyptians to provide for their last home. The City of the Dead had, accordingly, become as extensive as that of the living, and the dwellings were more or less alike in both. This City of the Dead could only be approached in a boat; and in all likelihood the boatman, who was at the same time the guardian of the tombs, went by the name of Charon, since the inhabitants of the province still give to Lake Moeris the appellation of Birket-el-Caron (the Lake of Charon).

The funeral of the higher classes was attended with great pomp: the inferior ranks were buried with less display, and the family of the deceased, after embalming the body, carried it to a spot destined for the purpose on the border of the lake, near the place of embarkation, whence Charon removed it to his boat, and transported it across to the tomb appropriated for its reception. The boatman waited until several bodies had been brought down by the respective families, who never failed to place on each corpse the name of the deceased, and the piece of coin which accrued to Charon as his perquisite. Each family afterwards proceeded to the respective tombs on an appointed day, and rendered the last duties to their deceased relatives.

The poor, who neither possessed a tomb, nor the means of being embalmed, were no doubt carried to the border of the lake by their relatives, who placed on their tongues the piece of coin claimed by Charon as his due previously to burying them. Nearly the same practice is still prevalent in Egypt, in all towns of sufficient extent to possess a city of tombs.

The Egyptians have still the habit of hiding their money under the tongue: it appeared very extraordinary to us, on our first arrival, that a Turk, before he handed us any change, would spit out all the medins * which he kept concealed in his mouth, sometimes to the number of a hundred and fifty or two hundred, without either his voice or his powers of eating and drinking being at all affected by it.

An event occurred during our stay at Faouë which compelled us to resume our march with the soldiers who had but just recovered from the ophthalmia.

Mourad Bey, who had been informed of the plan of an insurrection contemplated at Cairo, had approached that city, which had in reality been the scene of a seditious movement. The populace, urged on by the influential inhabitants and the cheiks, † had repaired to the different residences of the Beys,

---

* A medin or para is a small piece of silver considerably alloyed with copper, and of the value of two *liards*; it is round, of the size of a small wafer, and so extremely thin, that great care is taken in counting them, for fear the wind should blow them away.

† Cheik, a magistrate.

where we had placed some of our establishments. A few assassinations took place in the streets ; but the insurrection was so ill-directed as to afford the garrison time to run to arms, and proceed to the several points threatened with an attack. A prompt and severe example was made of the first who were taken in the act, and the agitation was soon appeased. The leaders sued for pardon ; and it was granted them under the condition of a heavy contribution, which we were not sorry to have an opportunity of imposing upon them.

On being informed of this result, Mourad Bey had again retreated into Upper Egypt, along the border of the desert, and reached the extremity of the province of Faïoum, where he endeavoured to raise an insurrection against us. We quitted Faouë with the intention of encountering him, or driving him back, leaving our sick and the rest of our blind soldiers in the house which the government had deserted on our arrival, and of which we barricadoed the entrance. This house had terraces commanding the approaches to it, and contained our stores of ammunition and provisions. We had scarcely reached the distance of a few leagues from the town, when the mamelukes we were in pursuit of escaped our vigilance, and rushed into the town, hoping to excite the inhabitants to an attack upon the house in which our soldiers were quartered ; having failed, however, in this object, they made the attempt themselves, and prepared to scale the walls.

The sick instantly rushed out of their beds ; those affected with ophthalmia threw the bandages from their eyes : all flew to arms, and ascended the terraces of the house, and by the fire of their musketry succeeded in driving away the assailants, and compelling them to relinquish the attempt.

Mourad Bey retreated through the town, into the desert, in a direction opposite to the one in which he had first made his appearance, and withdrew a second time to Upper Egypt.

The intelligence of this event was communicated to General Desaix by an inhabitant of Faouë, who had been dispatched to him by the commander of the soldiers he had left in the town.

He retraced his steps, and was well pleased to find that an attack, which might have been attended with fatal consequences, had not cost a single life.

In our last excursion we met with a large quagmire of considerable dimensions, since it extended the whole length of the province, from its opening towards Egypt, as far as Lake Mœris, and was as broad as one of the first rivers in Europe. This quagmire seems to have been one of the receptacles for the waters of the Nile; a circumstance tending to confirm the opinion I have expressed respecting the formation of Lake Mœris and the Waterless River.

It is far too deep and spacious to be a work of human construction. The bottom of it still presents a stream bordered by very high rushes; and we were told by the inhabitants that this muddy stream was supplied with water all the year round. We remarked, along the road from Illaon to Faouë, a very ancient bridge, such as the one we had seen in the village itself, and constructed, in like manner, over a projecting dike, made of solid masonry, consisting of enormous stones, and in excellent condition. We endeavoured to ascertain the direction taken by the waters, which, during the heavy swellings of the Nile, exceed the elevation of this dike, the surface of which was an inclined plane of perfect smoothness; and we found that they discharged themselves into this quagmire. In very remote ages, therefore, it must have had a destination, respecting which we did not exert our powers of conjecture.

CHAPTER VII.

Desaix's visit to Cairo—Fresh expedition to Upper Egypt in pursuit of Mourad Bey—M. Denon—The King of Darfour's son—History of Mourad Bey and of Hassan Bey.

THE season was advancing : the whole country presented a verdant scenery, and afforded relief to our eyes, which had become much affected by the aridity of the desert. We had, for the first time in our lives, passed a winter of intolerable and continued heat. The month of January in Egypt had appeared to us like the month of June in Europe. Our spirits had returned ; and the moral character of the soldier was completely restored.

General Bonaparte had ordered General Desaix to withdraw from Faïoum, and to move his division to Benisouef, on the left bank of the Nile, and twenty-five leagues from Cairo. After accomplishing this movement, General Desaix proceeded to Cairo, on a visit to General Bonaparte. I accompanied him in the excursion, which lasted only a few days, and was performed on the Nile.

General Bonaparte had not yet received any intelligence from France : his mind was wholly engaged in the formation of every kind of establishment. His constitution was not in the least affected by the climate ; and he never fell into a state of drowsiness towards evening, as was the case with every one else. He was always dressed the same as in Paris, with his coat close buttoned, and yet he seldom perspired ; whilst we were all in such high perspiration, that the dye ran from our clothes. None but those who have experienced it can imagine the effect produced by such excessive heat.

General Bonaparte, after retaining General Desaix with him for a few days, and showing that officer every mark of friendship, sent him back to Benisouef in a handsome djerme,* which he had caused to be prepared for his own usé : it was called *L'Italie,* and had a very splendid appearance.

He sent off from Cairo, to join General Desaix's division, the whole of the mounted cavalry, to the number of eight hundred horsemen, together with the artillery of the division, which had been left behind on its departure for Upper Egypt.

The campaign by land was about to be resumed, for the purpose of completing the destruction of the mamelukes. We ascended, from Benisouef, along the left bank of the river. On this occasion, however, we no longer marched in a square body, as we had done on the road from Alexandria to Cairo : we were no longer in dread of our enemies, who were terror-struck on our approach. Our march, however painful on account of the heat, was in other respects a military promenade.

Several members of the Institute of Cairo had overtaken our division, in order to visit Upper Egypt.

M. Denon, amongst others, had formed the closest intimacy with General Desaix, and never left him during the campaign. He pleased every one by his gentle and obliging disposition; and his instructive and witty conversation proved a great relaxation to us.

The zeal he displayed in examining monuments, and in searching after medals and other articles of antiquity, was a constant subject of astonishment to our soldiers ; especially when they beheld him braving fatigue, the heat of the sun, and occasionally dangers, in order to sketch hieroglyphics or remains of architecture ; for I do not believe that a single stone escaped his vigilant eye. I often accompanied him in his excursions. He carried across his shoulders a portfolio full of papers and pencils ; and had a bag suspended to his neck, containing an inkstand and some provisions.

* A vessel peculiar to the Nile.

He kept us all at work, measuring the distances and dimensions of monuments, whilst he was sketching them off. In drawings of every kind, he had wherewith to load a camel, at the time of his return to Cairo, whence he accompanied General Bonaparte back to France.

Finding us so eager after things to which they paid no attention, the inhabitants brought us some medals, picked up by them here and there, whilst tilling their grounds, or building their habitations amidst the ruins of ancient cities. They brought them in greater quantities on perceiving that we set some value upon them. M. Denou returned loaded with these medals, from each of his excursions to examine the relics of antiquity. They were nothing more than Roman copper coins, which had remained in immense quantities in a country unexplored by any one until our arrival.

The gold medals had disappeared; the copper ones alone had been preserved, and were found in some places to such an extent, that they might almost have been put again into circulation.

We ascended, at first, as far as Siout, a distance of seventy-five leagues above Cairo, afterwards to Girgeh, which is twenty-five leagues still higher up. We had marched a hundred leagues without meeting any of Mourad Bey's parties, who resigned to us every night the place they occupied in the morning

We stopped some time at Girgeh, in order to recruit our strength, and take some rest, after the fatigues of so long and so painful a march.

A caravan had just arrived in this small town from Darfour; it was commanded by one of the king's sons, who came to solicit General Desaix's protection. He was about thirty years of age, of a mild disposition, and had very strange notions upon the most trivial matters.

Thunder was heard, for the first time perhaps for a century, on the very day of our arrival; and on seeing a few drops of rain, the inhabitants considered the event as a favourable omen.

We asked the king of Darfour to explain to us what thunder was, and if it was ever heard in his country. He replied in the affirmative, and that God appointed a little angel to direct the clouds; that He grew angry when the latter would not obey His orders, and that the late drops of rain were disobedient subjects whom He had hurled from heaven.

We asked him of what country were the slaves composing his caravan, and the merchandise which it conveyed.

He replied that his country was very poor, and was not sufficiently cultivated to subsist its population; added to which, the people of Sennaar, a neighbouring country, often came to plunder their harvests for their own support: this occasioned wars between them; and the prisoners made on either side were brought by them to Egypt for sale. He further told us, that the merchants took advantage of the departure of these caravans, to bring their own merchandise, consisting of gums, ostrich feathers, tigers' skins, some elephants' teeth, and gold dust, which latter he exhibited to us. It resembled the sand in use for writing paper, and appeared to contain many earthy particles. He said that the people of his country gathered it, after the rains, out of the streams that came down from the mountains into the plains.

In this caravan were many children, also destined for sale. He informed us that their parents, being unable to support them, kept the strongest for their work, and sent the rest to Egypt, whence they expected the value to be brought back in grain, rice, and other kinds of provisions; and that the returns of the caravans were generally confined to articles of provisions and clothing, money being of very little use in his country.

Our conversation with this prince of Darfour suggested reflections to us in regard to the slave-trade, and left us

almost unanimous in opinion, that there was greater philan-
thropy in permitting than in forbidding it, or at least that
governments should take the trade into their own hands, by
purchasing the negroes, and transporting them to the colonies
of the torrid zone, where they might be collected under the
protection of a magistracy appointed for the purpose, instead
of being sold as private property.

These caravans leave Darfour in the rainy seasons, in order
to procure water in the desert: they have to march through
it for the space of a hundred days before they can reach the
Oases, which are islands of cultivated ground in the middle
of the desert; the journey thence to Egypt occupies three
days.

They lose many people on the road, when they have the
misfortune to be without rain; and at all times they arrive in
a wretched state of emaciation

General Desaix gave this prince of Darfour a friendly
reception, and made him presents of grain, rice, sugar, and
coffee, which he appeared to receive with much eagerness;
but what seemed to delight him most was a pelisse, which,
with an air of self-importance, he hastened to throw over his
shoulders.

We found at Girgeh a Capuchin friar, who had been sent
thither as a missionary from Rome. He could hardly read
Italian, and had only made one proselyte: this was a little
orphan boy, twelve or fourteen years old, who acted as
his servant. They both seemed pleased at our arrival, and
would no longer leave us.*

Previously to undertaking the present campaign by land,
General Desaix had provided himself with a surgeon-in-chief,
whose society and conversation were a source of satisfaction
to him, and for whom he felt great friendship. This was Dr.

* The little boy entered into the squadron of mamelukes after the evacuation
of Egypt, and was killed on the 2d of May, 1808, the day of the revolt at
Madrid. The Capuchin friar joined one of our military administrations.

Renoult, whose general knowledge and spirit of investigation on all subjects rendered his society highly agreeable and instructive to all.

General Desaix was very partial to the Turks, and often requested Dr. Renoult to give his professional attendance to such of them whose influence and consideration were useful to him.

We were recruiting our strength when we were overtaken by a fleet of armed boats, conveying the ammunition we expected, in order to enable us to resume our march.

We moved forward, still proceeding up the Nile, for the purpose of fighting Mourad Bey, of whom we had just obtained some intelligence. He had at first retreated as far as Esné, and solicited the hospitality of his rival, the celebrated Hassan Bey.

Hassan had, at one time, been a mameluke of Ali Bey, who held sway over the country previously to Ibrahim and Mourad, and who was put to death by the latter, after having been dangerously wounded in one of the affrays so common amongst those petty tyrants.

Ali Bey was, in reality, a man possessed of humane feelings, and of natural talents; he is the only Bey whose memory appeared to be cherished by the Egyptians. Mourad Bey seized upon the sovereignty vacated by his death. Hassan, who had been created a Bey by Ali his master, was a formidable warrior: true to his benefactor, he swore to avenge him.

Having been defeated by Mourad in an engagement near Cairo, he was so hotly pursued that he was driven to the necessity of seeking refuge in Mourad's seraglio, and soliciting an asylum from his favourite sultana. In eastern countries, the laws of hospitality are held sacred: the sultana received the fugitive, wrote to apprise Mourad of what she had done, and to forbid his approaching the seraglio until he had promised to spare Hassan's life. Mourad Bey instantly replied

that he could only allow Hassan a delay of two days to provide for his safety, after which he would infallibly attack the
seraglio.

Hassan was wholly unmoved upon receiving this notice,
though well aware that his death was inevitable. Already,
through the blinds of the seraglio, he could distinguish Mourad's mamelukes on the watch. One of them was stationed at
a wicket gate looking upon a narrow by-street ; over this
gate was a small wooden balcony, surrounded with blinds in
the oriental style, and below the balcony was seen the head of
the mameluke who was on guard at this gate. Hassan removed the blinds of the balcony, and, armed from head to
foot, he gently crept into it, and watched his opportunity so
well, that by a single effort he forced his way through this
slight balcony, and fell, dagger in hand, upon the mameluke, whom he instantly dispatched, whose horse he then
mounted, and fled in full speed to the desert by the road
leading to Suez, taking some Arabs on his way as his
guides, who escorted him to that port. He was no sooner
arrived than he went on board a caravel belonging to Mourad Bey, wrote from thence to inform him of his being at
Suez, and requested to be allowed this caravel to convey
him to Mecca, to which place he alleged his intention of
retiring.

Mourad in reply consented to his having the use of the
caravel, though for that occasion only, and wished him success ; but he gave, at the same time, secret orders to the master
of the caravel, a native of Greece, to strangle Hassan at a
certain distance from the land, and throw the body overboard.

Hassan, though suspecting the treachery, assumed a calm
countenance. On the morning after his departure from Suez
he summoned the master of the caravel to his cabin, and
desired him to produce the secret order which had been received by him. Thus taken by surprise, the latter fancied
himself betrayed, confessed every thing, and, on his knees,

begged hard for his life. " I would have pardoned thee," replied Hassan unmoved, " if thou hadst immediately confessed Mourad's perfidy; but thou hast kept the secret for two days, and it was thy intention to have obeyed the order ;" so saying, he dispatched him as well as his mate. The pilot, seeing what kind of man he had to deal with, hastened to convey him to the sacred city.

The intrepid Hassan levied a heavy contribution upon the scherif and merchants of Mecca, by means of which he secured to himself a few followers, embarked on board the same caravel, and landed at Cosseir. From this place he sent word to such of his mamelukes as had effected their escape to come and join him : he also desired the merchants with whom he was in correspondence to send him a fresh supply of mamelukes ready armed and equipped. He repaired in person to Esné on the banks of the Nile, for the purpose of meeting them, and was shortly at the head of two hundred mamelukes : he then wrote to Mourad, reproaching him with his perfidy, challenging him to fight, and demanding at the same time the restitution of the patrimony which had been wrested from him.

Mourad, taken by surprise, was glad to enter into a compromise with him ; and as, in reality, Hassan was not over-anxious to approach Cairo, he accepted Mourad Bey's proposal to acknowledge him as the rightful owner of all Upper Egypt, from the cataracts of the Nile to a little above Esné, where he resided at the period of our coming to Egypt.

Such was the rival whose protection Mourad Bey unhesitatingly hastened to solicit; and from the impulse of a generous feeling, of which the history of European monarchs affords perhaps no example, Hassan welcomed his guest to his dominions, and forbearing to raise the voice of reproach, condoled with him on his misfortunes, and cheered him with the promise of taking part in his affliction.

It was in his power to have gratified his revenge, and

claimed credit with the French for so doing; but the thought never dwelt, for a moment, on the mind of that extraordinary man: he immediately united his mamelukes to the few still remaining under Mourad's orders, and they advanced toge-ther to meet us. The encounter took place near the small town of Samanhout, on the day after our departure from Girgeh.

Hassan Bey brought also to Samanhout ten or twelve hun-dred men which the scherif of Mecca had sent to him from a motive of religious zeal.

CHAPTER VIII.

Battle of Samanhout—Tentira—Ruins of the city of Thebes—Sienna—Cataracts —Project of the Pacha of Egypt—Rafts of earthenware—Tax of the miri ; mode of levying it.

THE approach of the mamelukes was now made known to us by a few flying corps which General Desaix kept in ad-vance of the main body, so that we had sufficient leisure to form into two large squares of infantry, and place the cavalry in three lines between them; the second line being turned with its back to the first.

In this battle, as in the preceding, the firing of cannon did not exceed twenty-five or thirty rounds: the fire of mus-ketry from our squares decided the day, and completely dis-persed the mamelukes, upon whom we poured the whole of our cavalry, commanded by General Davout ; but the cavalry was unable to come up with one of them, although the pursuit was continued to a great distance in the desert. In return for this disappointment they cut in pieces the wretched infantry sent to Hassan from the city of Mecca.

As the battle was terminating, a mameluke of Osman Bey

Ottambourgi's deserted to us. He was a native of Hungary, and formerly a cornet in the regiment of Wentschal, belonging to the Austrian hussars, and had been taken prisoner in 1783 or 1784, during the war between that power and the Porte. There also came over to us some old dragoon officers of the regiment of La Tour, and even some officers belonging to the Hungarian and Croatian free corps, who had been taken prisoners in the same war, carried to Constantinople, and afterwards sent over to Egypt, where they served as private mamelukes: they were not averse to their condition, and had made no attempt to return to their country although represented in Egypt by a consul. True it is that had they been suspected by their Beys of entertaining such a design, their heads would have instantly paid the forfeit.

As soon as the battle was over we continued our march, and took up our night quarters at Farchout, on the bank of the Nile.

The mamelukes retreated up the river, and we followed them the next day. The valley of the Nile becomes considerably narrowed at this elevated point of land, and continues to contract itself as far as the Cataracts, where it terminates in the shape of a funnel.

On our march from Farchout we saw the ruins of Tentira, and arrived, some hours afterwards, amidst those of the city of Thebes, so celebrated for its hundred gates. On this spot we halted for the night.

Excessive fatigue prevented our bestowing any attention on these ancient monuments, which have exhibited the same ruins ever since the days of Moses. M. Denon, however, who was indefatigable whenever we discovered any thing worth seeing, led us to the place which is strewed over with the fragments, thirteen in number, of the statue of Memnon. I measured one of its arms, above the elbow, and found it to be thirteen feet and a half in circumference.

We went to see the famous avenue of the Sphynx, which appeared very undeserving of attention. What most astonished us was to see capitals of columns painted green and red, the colours of which were as fresh as if the paint had been laid on within the year. This proved to us how little injured by the climate were those monuments, which, it must be owned, would scarcely have excited any curiosity had they been placed at the gates of Paris.

Ever since leaving Girgeh we had traversed a level country, planted with sugar-canes, and covered with all the medicinal herbs peculiar to Egypt; so that the atmosphere was impregnated with a balsamic fragrance, which grew more intense as we approached the villages.

The banks of the Nile began to be unsafe, particularly at night, owing to the enormous crocodiles that come out of the river for the purpose of eating the grain which is sown upon the mud along its borders. Though we often met them, no accident ever occurred. These animals, notwithstanding that they are of prodigious size, are extremely timid : they retreat on hearing the least noise ; especially when they are out of the water, which they never leave except in the night time.

Thebes appeared to us to have been a very large city : and we were enabled to judge of it from the two gates, which are still standing, in a direction opposite to each other : nevertheless, historians have greatly exaggerated on this subject ; for it must have been of less dimensions than one of our largest French cities.

We only stayed there a night, and continued our march up the Nile on the following morning, in order to reach Esné, the place of residence of that Hassan Bey who had bound his fortunes to those of Mourad his rival.

We halted for a night, and no longer, at each station which we took up. From Esné we proceeded to the Chain Passage, which is called by that name, because the valley is here so contracted by the surrounding mountains as to be scarcely of the breadth requisite to admit of the flowing of the Nile ; and although this was the season of its lowest waters, there was barely sufficient space for a gun-carriage to pass between its margin and the foot of the mountain, which, from this point forward, exclusively consists of enormous blocks of red granite. We now beheld this marble for the first time since our arrival in Egypt; and from this spot was, no doubt, obtained the marble which adorned the monuments of Rome, and went by the name of eastern granite. We saw the quarries worked by the ancients, and still found entire obelisks of them, loosened from the rock for the purpose of being roughly hewn, but never completed.

It is probable, that when the river overflowed, these enormous masses were embarked on rafts constructed for the purpose of transporting them to the different towns in Egypt. Some of them are still met with amongst the ruins, which have not been applied to any use.

Beyond the Chain Passage* the valley widens a little, as far as the Cataracts, where we arrived the next morning. This narrow basin, however, is of a soil very different from that of Egypt: it is all sand, which, though fertilised by the inundations, scarcely produces any thing. Our sufferings accordingly returned ; and if, on reaching Sienna, we had not met, at the foot of the Cataracts, with the fleet of boats conveying provisions for the mamelukes, which we seized, we should have been still more distressed ; but they supplied us with biscuit, abundance of dates, and barley for our horses.

We had now reached the foot of the cataracts fronting Sienna, which is on the right bank. We passed the night on the border of the river, where we had collected all the boats to which I have just alluded, and were under the necessity of keeping up a loud noise, in order to frighten away the cro-

---

* It was no doubt thus called from the river being so narrow in this place that the navigation of it was formerly stopped by means of a chain thrown across. The Nile is here of considerable depth ; and the people of the country told us, with great simplicity, that it had been found impossible to sound its bottom.

codiles that came round them in quest of food, with which they instinctively discovered them to be laden.

We crossed the river in the day-time, on our way to Sienna, and stopped at an island rising from the bed of it, which presented a few monuments to our view. This was the Philoë of the ancients, said to contain a well, at the bottom of which the sun was to be seen exactly at mid-day on the 21st June ; for Sienna is well known to be situated immediately under the tropic ; but we tried in vain to discover this well.

Sienna, like every other place, has furnished matter for the exaggeration of historians; that town is at present nothing more than a heap of very low houses, built of sun-baked bricks, and even in the most remote times could never have been a town of any note. It is wholly surrounded with sand, which will not admit of being cultivated beyond a few toises on both banks of the Nile. It could not have possessed any importance, except, perhaps, as a resting-point for the caravans coming into Egypt by the Nile, or as a military station which the Romans appeared to have kept up during the whole period of their occupying the province.

We remained a few days at Sienna for the purpose of watching the movements of the mamelukes, and employed this time in visiting the town and its vicinity.

Sienna is the first place where vaults were shown to us · the inhabitants are under the necessity of having recourse to them in constructing their houses, in the absence of timber of sufficient firmness to support a story above the ground-floor. These vaults have the effect of rendering their dwelling-houses a little cooler than they would otherwise be, which is an invaluable object in a town screened from every wind, surrounded by rocks of granite, and situated under a tropical sun: it would otherwise be impossible to dwell in it. In other respects, neither quicklime nor plaster are made use of in the construction of even the interior of their apartments, which are simply covered over with the black lime of the Nile.

One of the inconveniences of this country is its swarming with vermin, which the greatest cleanliness is not always sufficient to guard one against. We had been told that they died under the oppressive heat of the tropic : this was an imposition upon us ; for, on the contrary, they multiply to an insufferable extent : but the army was obliged to put up with this fresh annoyance.

We discovered in the environs of Sienna some well preserved remains of the Roman way, which ran from that town to the port of Berenice, in the Indian Sea.

We were greatly surprised, on reaching the cataracts a little above Sienna, not to observe any waterfall : the river has forced itself a passage through a heap of granite rocks which obstructed its bed, and compelled it to run in a variety of small torrents ; these rocks extend the length of a league, and form what are called the Cataracts. The river has no sooner broken through this obstacle than it resumes its previons compact body, and forms a beautiful basin, in the centre of which rises the island of Elephantina, abounding in monuments of antiquity. We were struck with surprise at beholding in such excellent state of preservation all the Greek and Roman inscriptions which travellers, on coming to visit the same spot some centuries before us, had engraved in every direction. The greater part of them are more legible than those upon the wall of the gallery which is resorted to for the purpose of beholding the splendid view from the Villa d'Este, near Rome, or those that cover the rock standing at the foot of the cascade of the Rhine, near Schaffhausen.

We passed a night in a situation above the Cataracts which we had left five leagues behind us, and we returned the next day to Sienna.* It is hardly possible to conceive what we had to suffer from the heat during these marches.

* The pacha who at present governs Egypt has been engaged with a plan

We had noticed some rafts descending the Nile, the singular construction of which had greatly excited our curiosity. They were formed of earthenware. We had reached the highest elevation of land in all Egypt without discovering any manufactory of that kind : on inquiring from what place the article was brought, we were told that it came from a much greater distance than Sienna, where we saw one of these rafts : we examined it, and found it as large as those that are met with on our rivers in France, and solely composed of earthen pots, of uniform size, ingeniously ranged close to one another, and bound together, with the opening downwards ; in this manner were placed as many rows, one above another, as the depth of the water would admit of. This mass was kept afloat by means of the air in the bottom of the pots, from which it could not make its escape. The pilots fixed a helm to these rafts, strewed a few mats, and took their stations upon them. In this manner they descended the river from the most elevated point in its course down to

which would be creditable to the most civilised European government. He has procured young engineers from Italy, who had gone through their course of study in the school founded by Napoleon at Modena, and has sent them to survey the cataract dividing Egypt from Ethiopia, and another, a hundred and fifty leagues higher up, which divides Ethiopia from the kingdom of Sennaar. His object was to ascertain whether the obstruction caused by those cataracts could be removed, and the river rendered navigable. The engineers' report has been of a very favourable nature. Nothing but the enormous expense attendant upon such an undertaking has compelled the pacha to postpone the execution of his views, being at that time engaged in redigging the canal that conveys water from the Nile to Alexandria, and the greater part of his finances being absorbed by other expenses. Should he be able, at a future day, to resume his plan, and should it be carried into effect by him or by his successors, the kingdom of Sennaar will be put into communication with the Mediterranean by a good navigable channel. This country, which, like Egypt, is a valley of the Nile, consisting of alluvial soil, produces cotton and medicinal plants ; it also supplies gold-dust and most beautiful timber, which grows in abundance upon the mountains : this is easily accounted for from the circumstance of the heavy rains in Sennaar, and the absence of any rain in Egypt. The power of the pacha and of Egypt will increase in a twofold degree should such a project be ever carried into execution.

Cairo, even passing over the cataracts when covered by the inundation which recurs every year.

There is no other risk with these rafts than that of running aground; but this is attended with little danger in the Nile, owing to the muddy nature of its banks.

Whilst staying at Sienna, General Desaix had occasion to write to Siout; the letter was given to a fellah, who took no other means to execute his commission than to bind two bundles of rushes together, upon which he sat down in the Turkish fashion, with his pipe, a few dates, a lance, to defend himself against crocodiles, and a small oar to assist him in steering his course. Thus stationed upon so weak a craft, he yielded himself to the current of the river, and arrived without any accident.

Our campaign appeared at an end: we imagined that Mourad and Hassan Beys had fled to the Ethiopians; but we were soon undeceived: they were familiar with all the passes of the desert; and, led by faithful guides, had re-entered Egypt, after a toilsome march from the Cataracts.

They reached Esné before us, and there separated, each party to follow his own fortunes. Mourad continued to descend along the left bank of the river, and Hassan crossed over to the right bank.

We were soon apprised of this movement by a large detachment of infantry, which we had left as a corps of observation at the Chain Passage, and we prepared to follow them.

General Desaix left at Sienna a detachment of two hundred infantry, and commenced marching with the rest of his troops along the right bank of the Nile, which he crossed at Esné, and halted for a few days at this place.

Previously to bestowing our exclusive attention on the mamelukes, it was necessary to organise the province, the resources of which were to be applied to our wants: the tax was already a twelvemonth in arrear; the approaching rise of the waters of the Nile would increase the difficulty of collecting it; because, in Egypt, although the tax, or miri, is very exactly paid, it is never brought by the towns and villages; one must take the trouble of going for it; and were it not for the military display made by those who come to demand it, the villages would omit the payment altogether ; and, strange as it may appear, they consider that display as a mark of attention shown to them, and are accordingly grateful for it.

Disgrace attaches to whomsoever pays the miri on the first summons, and great consideration is shown to those who resist; and this sentiment will even rise in proportion to the number of strokes of the bastinado which the people may be able to submit to before they loosen their purse-strings.

This strange custom having existed for ages, we took care not to deviate from it: we were, therefore, compelled to divide our troops, for the purpose of occupying the whole of Upper Egypt, to organise an administration that should provide for the wants of the soldiers, and at last to commence raising the tax, the quota of which was not yet determined on.

General Desaix quitted Esné, and established himself at Kené, a small town situated along the border of the desert, on the right bank, where the road leading to the port of Cosseir, on the Red Sea, terminates. He organised there the expedition which was to proceed to the occupation of Cosseir, which it was of the utmost importance for us to secure as soon as possible, as it was the mart for all the Mocha coffee, and merchandise of Arabia, which is taken in exchange there for corn, rice, and other articles of Egyptian produce. Several hundred camels were collected for the purpose of transporting the troops that were to occupy Cosseir: arrangements were made with some Arabs of the desert for the transport of all kinds of ammunition and provisions. The expedition then moved forward, and reached Cosseir after a march of six days. A few days after its arrival two English frigates from India hove in sight of the harbour, and landed two hundred Indian soldiers, with one piece of artillery. The object of these troops was, no doubt, to take possession of the fort commanding the harbour, an old square building, constructed of very ancient and very solid masonry; finding, however, that it was already in the possession of our troops, they re-embarked, leaving the field-piece behind. The frigates stood out to sea, and never made their appearance again.

CHAPTER IX.

Organization of Upper Egypt — News from France—General Bonaparte at the Isthmus of Suez—Danger he incurs—Jaffa—Massacre of the prisoners—The Druses and Mutuali—Their deputation to General Bonaparte.

THE whole of Upper Egypt was thus occupied by our troops. General Desaix had succeeded in establishing order in the administration of the country; and the advantages of such a system of government over that of the Beys were too evident not to make a suitable impression upon the people, and promote the political revolution which was insensibly developing itself.

No means were neglected for furthering it; and with this view General Desaix, after having organised Upper Egypt, came down to Siout, in order to establish the same mode of organization at that place; and such was the scrupulous rectitude of his decisions and his inflexible impartiality, that the Arabs had surnamed him the *just sultan.*

Egypt was quiet, but nevertheless kept a watchful eye upon us. Mourad and Hassan still continued their inroads, not only without making any impression, but, on the contrary, losing every day some of those intrepid mamelukes, of whom they had so few to spare.

Hope had entirely deserted them; whereas we retained all our moral strength.

Whilst General Desaix was wholly engaged in those important occupations, he learned that General Bonaparte had just taken his departure for Syria, in order to accomplish the second part of the plan he had contemplated in his expedition to the East.

Reports had just been propagated of a fresh rupture between France and Austria, and of the appearance in the Mediterranean of a French squadron of twenty-five sail of the line, under the orders of Admiral Bruix, whom we knew to have been appointed minister of marine since our departure. Such indeed was the fact: Bruix had armed the Brest fleet, and had himself assumed the command: he at first brought it to the Mediterranean, where the Directory informed him that he was to embark troops on the coast of Italy: when, however, he arrived there, he found that the troops were refused, because the army of Italy was short of its numbers. Bruix determined, therefore, to return to Brest, but first touched at Cadiz, whence he was accompanied to Brest, at his own desire, by the Spanish fleet, which the Directory retained as hostages; so little did they rely upon the adherence of Spain to their politics.

In Egypt these rumours were not wholly relied on; but the conjectures they suggested could not be unfavourable to the objects contemplated by General Bonaparte. The occupation of Egypt was secured. The army, in creating for itself a new country, had taken up at the same time a position from which it could deal the most fearful blows to the eastern powers, rush upon Constantinople, or penetrate into India, and strike at the prosperity of England in its most vital point.

The moment seemed to have arrived for giving effect to this second part of his plan; the Egyptians and the French had become familiar with each other.

There did not appear to exist, either from within or from without, any causes for apprehension. Alexandria was well fortified, and provided with a garrison commanded by General Marmont, a skilful officer : the same may be said of Aboukir, Rosetta, Rahmanié, Damietta, and Cairo ; so that, properly speaking, we held all the keys of Egypt in our power. The chance of exciting insurrections was lost to our enemies ; the failure of the first revolts had created a distaste for further experiments ; and we were, besides, superior in strength to the mamelukes. General Bonaparte, previously to proceeding to Syria, determined to visit the remains of the Venetian establishments at Suez, and to have the environs of the town explored for the purpose of discovering traces of the canal which is said to have existed in former days, to carry the waters of the Mediterranean to the Red Sea across the Isthmus of Suez.

The distance from Cairo to Suez is only twenty-five leagues, but the road runs through a desert quite destitute of bushes and water.

He was accompanied by his aides-de-camp, the general of engineers, Caffarelli-Dufalgua, and Messrs. Monge and Berthollet; his only guard consisted of a squadron of guides.

He rapidly crossed the desert, and reached the Kalioumeth. The sun had not yet performed a third part of its course : curiosity induced him to push on to Mount Sinaï, to see in what condition were the reservoirs for fresh water formerly constructed by the Venetians. He crossed the sea at the same point where Moses had crossed it with his Hebrew followers, and, like Moses, he did so at a moment when the lowness of the tide left it almost dry. On their arrival in Asia, the horsemen remained on the seashore with the guides brought from Suez, and took it into their heads to give the latter brandy to drink : these poor people had never before tasted any : they lost their senses, and were still quite drunk when the general returned from his excursion. The tide, however, was about to rise; night was coming on, and there was not a moment to be lost.

The position of Suez having been surveyed, the party proceeded in the direction of that town; but after marching some time in the sea, they lost their way: night had set in, and they knew not whether they were advancing towards Africa, Asia, or the open sea. The waves were gradually rising, when the horsemen ahead cried out that their horses were swimming.

Had they persisted in their course, or lost time in considering, they must have inevitably perished. General Bonaparte rescued the whole party by one of those simple expedients which a calm mind always finds at command.

He made himself the centre of a circle, ranging round him in several rows all those who shared this common danger, giving numbers to the men who composed the first outward circle. He then ordered them to march forward, each man advancing in a straight line from the point at which he was placed, and being successively followed in the same line by other horsemen at the distance of ten paces from the first circle. When the horse of the headmost man of one of these columns lost its footing, or, in other words, when it began to swim, General Bonaparte made the rider draw back towards the centre, as well as those who followed him, and move on in the direction of another column, the extreme point of which had not yet lost its ground.

The radii thus sent out in directions where they had lost their hold had all been successively withdrawn, and placed behind others that still had a firm footing. The right road was thus recovered, and they reached Suez at midnight, the horses being already more than breast-high in the water; for the tide rises to the height of twenty-two feet on this part of the coast.

The non-arrival of General Bonaparte before the setting in of the tide had created great alarm; and the general congratulated himself upon his narrow escape.   He returned to Cairo, in order to complete his final arrangements, preparatory to his departure for Syria with six thousand men.

He left strong garrisons in all the towns of Egypt which I have already named, a moveable corps of fifteen hundred men round Cairo, and General Desaix's division in Upper Egypt.

At the head of his small army he crossed the desert that separates Africa from Asia, captured on his way the fort of El-Arish, the garrison of which capitulated, and was set free, on condition of its proceeding to Bagdad, and not serving against the French for a twelvemonth : he marched from thence upon Gaza (the ancient Cesarea), and arrived before Jaffa (the ancient Joppa), where he found a Turkish garrison, which showed indications of an intention to resist.

Jaffa is situated on the seashore, and defended by a strong wall.   It was found necessary to make an assault before the troops could obtain possession of it ; on which occasion three thousand prisoners were taken, who turned out to be, for the most part, those very soldiers whose lives and liberty had been spared upon conditions which they had immediately violated.

It was ascertained, in the mean time, that the Porte had thrown all the French agents into prison, declared war against France, and was forming, in the Island of Rhodes, an army intended to be conveyed to Egypt.   To restore these prisoners a second time to liberty was, in fact, to send fresh recruits to the Turks ; to forward them to Egypt, under an escort, was to lessen the strength of an army already too weak.   The law of necessity decided their fate ; they were treated, in consequence of such an act of perjury, in the same manner as they treated our wounded after a battle, whose heads they cut off on the spot.

After the capture of Jaffa, the army continued its march, and arrived before St. John d'Acre, the Ptolemais of the ancients.   The conquest of this place was to be followed by that of all Palestine, as had already been the case in the days of the Crusades, and was to open the road for us to Constantinople, by means of the numerous legions which General Bonaparte intended to form out of the fine and swarming population of the country he was now traversing.

The East would, in such a position, have assumed a new aspect, and once more have basked in the rays of that light which it had formerly shed over the world. Its martial people would have infallibly hailed, with delight, the approach of a warrior, who desired nothing more than that they should throw off the ignominious yoke under which they were groaning.

These nations possess extraordinary physical powers; and it is easy to estimate what they might have become after the regeneration of their moral faculties. The East must, sooner or later, fall to the lot of him who shall find the fulcrum for the lever that is to rouse it from its apathy.

We had in our favour the recollection of the old crusaders, though these countries had proved their grave.

The Druses and the Mutuali, two Christian colonies, inhabiting the mountains to the east, are reported, in the country, to be the descendants, in a direct line, from the last crusaders; who, deprived of the means of returning home, were driven by distress to remain on the spot. In their anxiety to avoid the Turks, they retired to the mountains, where their descendants are still living; and it cannot be remembered that any Turk ever succeeded in penetrating into the places they have selected for their abode.

These colonies live in tribes: they have lost all trace of the language of their ancestors, but still retain the same kind of arms, viz. lances of the same form; long swords with hilts in the form of a cross; and small round shields, made of very hard leather.

On the first report of the entrance of the French into Syria, these people descended from their mountains, impelled by the honest feeling that they must be our natural allies, and came to the camp, before St. John d'Acre, to pay homage to General Bonaparte, whose fame had reached their ears: they were treated with great attention; and General Bonaparte, who delighted in recalling the events of this period to his mind, even in the season of his highest prosperity, sometimes did me the honour to tell me that, at the moment when the Druses warriors entered his tent, he was unable to resist a sensation of interest, combined with admiration, for them; and that their visit had afforded him unfeigned pleasure. He could not bring himself, he said, to consider them as Turks · their physiognomies bore an impress of the stock from which they sprung: their eyes, and the contour of their faces, rather presented the character of Europeans than of eastern people: it was plain, in short, to perceive between ourselves and them something of a common origin.

These warlike people had been taught by the tradition of ages that they descended from other warriors belonging to our own country. They lived, however, in complete ignorance of what was going forward in the world, and were only Christians in all the simplicity of the primitive doctrines. They are greatly respected by the whole population of Syria, who occasionally solicit their protection, for the purpose of checking the ferocity of the troops of the Pachas, who are sent by the Porte to govern those unhappy countries.

Out of so many different populations might have been raised a splendid army, which would have cleared the way before our legions, leaving the latter at liberty to husband their resources for occasions of importance, when their exertions would have been called into play; but the first object was to obtain possession of St. John d'Acre.

CHAPTER X.

The English capture a fleet dispatched to St. John d'Acre—Siege of St. John d'Acre—Retreat—General Bonaparte's visit to the hospital of men infected with the plague at Jaffa—Landing of the Turkish army—Battle of Aboukir.

GENERAL BÒNAPARTE, whose foresight anticipated every difficulty, had ordered a fleet to be sent off from Alexandria, with the heavy artillery and engineering utensils on board ; it was escorted by two old frigates, which had sailed from Toulon as transport ships, and had refitted at Alexandria, after the defeat of our squadron. This fleet had on board every thing requisite for the siege of St. John d'Acre, besides a great number of muskets. Thus laden with stores of incalculable value, the fleet proceeded along the coasts of Egypt and Syria. It had been informed of the presence of two English ships in those quarters; but as none of the vessels composing it drew much water, it could sail very close in-shore, and so protect itself from attack, in the improbable event of its not finding the French troops in possession of one of the small ports along the coast, and which it was directed to enter.

It was the fate of the fleet to be commanded by an officer of extremely limited capacity, who, on making the point of Mount Carmel, dared not reconnoitre the port of Caipha, which was only three leagues off, or at least neglected to do so, fearing to find it occupied by the Turks ; whereas we were already in possession of it. He hesitated, and in this state of perplexity stood out· to sea, preferring the risk of being captured by the English to the danger of· falling into the hands of the Turks; a fear which his imagination constantly presented to his view. He fell, accordingly, into the power of the English, with the whole of his fleet : this fault, which it is difficult to qualify, had a prodigious influence over our future operations.

It was impossible to retreat; and there was no resource left but to besiege the place with such means as the artillery of the army would afford.

A line of circumvallation was drawn round it; the trenches were opened, and, by dint of zeal, a breach was effected: no less than ten assaults were given to this paltry fort, into which the soldiers repeatedly penetrated, but were as often repulsed, with heavy loss. The Turks, at all times formidable when protected by walls, were the more eager in defending themselves, as they saw that our means of attack were out of proportion to their means of defence, which were, besides, directed by a French officer of artillery, whom the English had expressly landed at St. John d'Acre.

This unexpected resistance, and the time lost in the operations carried on against the town, had affected, to a certain degree, the high opinion which the neighbouring people had formed of the events of which they had too soon anticipated the results.

Their communications with us began to slacken; by degrees, provisions grew scarce, and disorders followed, as the consequence of want.

The Druses and Mutuali had returned to their homes; and at last the audacious insolence of the wandering Arabs increased to such a degree, that it became necessary to detach whole bodies of troops for the purpose of covering a larger surface of country, and of scouring it to procure provisions for the army. These corps were violently attacked and harassed by swarms of population; and General Bonaparte was obliged to march in person, for the purpose of releasing Kleber at Mount Tabor, and General Junot at Nazareth; but as the detachments did not succeed in the object which they had been sent to accomplish, they returned to the main body.

Scarcity was soon felt ; and, in addition to its distress, the army was attacked with the plague.

In a situation of so much difficulty, General Bonaparte was left without any hope of bringing his operations to a successful issue ; he ran the risk, on the contrary, of losing his army, unless he hastened to take it back to Egypt.

He was induced, by another consideration, to relinquish his original plan : we were approaching the season during which a landing is easily effected in Egypt, where the coast is so low, as to compel ships to anchor at a great distance ; and as they cannot, in such a position, resist the violence of the autumnal winds, they can only ride at that anchorage in summer. General Bonaparte had learned, during his stay in Syria, that an expedition was fitting out in the ports of the Archipelago ; it was of importance, therefore, that he should be in Egypt at the moment of its arrival.

The troops marched back, having embarked all the sick, as well as the wounded, who reached Damietta in safety.

The hospital, however, still contained many soldiers who were in a state bordering upon madness, much more owing to the terror which the malady inspired, than to the intensity of the pain. General Bonaparte determined to restore them to their wonted energy. He paid them a visit, reproached them for giving way to dejection, and yielding to chimerical fears ; and in order to convince them, by the most obvious proof, that their apprehensions were groundless, he desired that the bleeding tumour of one of the soldiers should be uncovered before him, and pressed it with his own hand. This act of heroism restored confidence to the sick, who no longer thought their case desperate. Each one recruited his remaining strength, and prepared to quit a place which, but a moment before, he had expected never to leave. A grenadier, upon whom the plague had made greater ravages, could hardly raise himself from his bed. The general perceiving this, addressed to him a few encouraging words : " You are right,

General," replied the warrior; "your grenadiers are not made
to die in an hospital." Affected at the courage displayed by
these unfortunate men, who were exhausted by uneasiness
of mind no less than by the complaint, General Bonaparte
would not quit them until he saw them all placed upon
camels and the other means of transport at the disposal of
the army. These, however, being found inadequate, he made
a requisition for the officers' horses, delivered up his own,
and, finding one of them missing, he sent for the groom, who
was keeping it for his master, and hesitated to give it up.
The general growing impatient at this excess of zeal, darted
a threatening look; the whole stud was placed at the disposal
of the sick; and yet it is this very act of magnanimity which the
perverseness of human nature has delighted in distorting. I
feel ashamed to advert to so atrocious a calumny; but the man,
whose simple assertion was found sufficient to give it currency,
has not been able to stifle it by his subsequent disavowal. I
must, therefore, descend to the task of proving the absurdity
of the charge. I do not wish to urge, as an argument, the
absolute want of medicines to which the army was reduced
by the rapacity of an apothecary; nor the indignation felt by
General Bonaparte, when he learned that this wretch, instead
of employing his camels to transport pharmaceutic preparations, had loaded them with provisions, upon which he expected to derive a profit. The necessity to which we were
driven of using roots as a substitute for opium, is a fact
known to the whole army. Supposing, however, that opium
had been as plentiful as it was scarce, and that General Bonaparte could have contemplated the expedient attributed to
him, where could there be found a man sufficiently determined in mind, or so lost to the feelings of human nature, as
to force open the jaws of fifty wretched men on the point of
death, and thrust a deadly preparation down their throats?
The most intrepid soldier turned pale at the sight of an
infected person; the warmest heart dared not relieve a friend

afflicted with the plague; and is it to be credited, that brutal ferocity could execute what the noblest feelings recoiled at? or that there should have been a creature savage or mad enough to sacrifice his own life, in order to enjoy the satisfaction of hastening the death of fifty dying men, wholly unknown to him, and against whom he had no complaint to make? The supposition is truly absurd, and only worthyof those who bring it forward in spite of the disavowal of its author.

I return to the infected men. They followed the steps of the army, held the same road, and always encamped at a short distance from its bivouacks. General Bonaparte had his tent pitched near the sick every night, and never passed a day without visiting them, or seeing them file off at the moment of departure. These generous cares were crowned with the happiest results. The march, the perspiration, and above all, the hope to which the general had restored them, completely eradicated the complaint. They all arrived at Cairo perfectly re-established in health.

The army was exhausted; the march and the fatigues of the campaign had been too much for its strength: it returned to Egypt in a state of absolute want; but every thing had been foreseen, and abundance of provisions, rest, and comfortable clothing, soon made them forget all the sufferings they had undergone.

General Bonaparte, on his return to Cairo, endeavoured to ascertain the state of France. At the very moment of proceeding on his expedition to Syria, he had received melancholy accounts of its military and political situation. Messrs. Hamelin and Livron, who came from the coast of Italy with a cargo of wine and vinegar, had crossed the Archipelago, and seen the Russian fleet pressing the siege of Corfu; they had even put into Ragusa, where they were compelled to change vessels. The master with whom they had at first

been in treaty, refused to go as far as Egypt, being apprehensive that his vessel might be confiscated, as he was a Dalma-
tian, and as Austria was again at war with France. They
had informed the general of Suwarrow's march, and acquainted
him that Bruix had in fact penetrated into the Mediterranean ;
but that the army of Italy had been unable to furnish him
with the troops he wished to take on board previously to his
sailing for Egypt; that he had repaired to Cadiz, taken the
Spanish fleet along with him, and carried it to Brest, where
the Directory, not being quite satisfied respecting the protestations of Charles IV., had retained it as a guarantee for
his sincerity.

The general-in-chief was greatly affected at learning this
gloomy state of things, which was confirmed to him by the
newspapers scattered by the English along the coast. Italy
was lost to us; Corfu had surrendered ; we had been defeated
upon the Rhine as well as upon the Adige; fortune had betrayed us in every quarter. To crown all these evils, discord
had followed in the train of our reverses. The Councils
attacked the Directory; the Directory retorted upon the
Councils ; and France, torn by factions, was on the point of
becoming the prey of foreigners.

Such appeared to him to be the confused aspect of the political horizon on his first return to Cairo. His mind was a prey
to every kind of conjecture, when, twenty-two days after his
return from Syria, a Turkish fleet was descried from Alexandria, escorting a numerous fleet of transports, with the very
two English ships in company that had assisted in the defence
of St. John d'Acre under the orders of Sir Sidney Smith.

This news did not take general Bonaparte by surprise;
he had foreseen the event, and had only detained the troops
at Cairo the time requisite for recovering from the fatigue
of their march from Syria; he had afterwards drawn them
nearer to the coast. He had even carried the precaution so

far as to inform General Desaix of what he deemed an un-avoidable occurrence, and ordered him to hold his division in readiness to march.

He no sooner heard of the appearance of the Turkish fleet before Alexandria, than he sent a second order to General Desaix, directing him immediately to bring his division down the country into a position between Cairo and Alexandria, which he pointed out to him. He also left Cairo in the utmost haste, to place himself at the head of the troops which he had ordered to quit their cantonments and march down to the coast.

Whilst General Bonaparte was making these arrangements and coming in person from Cairo, the troops on board the Turkish fleet had effected a landing, and taken possession of the fort of Aboukir, and of a redoubt placed behind the village of that name, which ought to have been put into a state of defence six months before, but had been so completely neglected, that nothing was easier than to ride through the breaches, and through the spaces left by the falling in of the earth, in every direction.

The Turks had nearly destroyed the weak garrisons that occupied those two military points, when General Marmont, who commanded at Alexandria, came to their relief. This general, seeing the two posts in the power of the Turks, returned to shut himself up in Alexandria, where he would probably have been blockaded by the Turkish army, had it not been for the arrival of General Bonaparte with his forces, who was very angry when he saw that the fort and redoubt had been taken; but, in reality, he did not blame Marmont for retreating to Alexandria: what, indeed, would have been his feelings, on the other hand, had he found this important city exposed to any danger by its garrison's being engaged in disputing a barren desert with the Turkish army?

General Bonaparte arrived at midnight, with his guides and the remaining part of his army, and ordered the Turks

to be attacked the next morning. In this battle, as in the
preceding ones, the attack, the encounter, and the route,
were occurrences of a moment, and the result of a single
movement on the part of our troops. The whole Turkish
army plunged into the sea, to regain its ships, leaving behind
them every thing they had brought on shore.

The English sailors had the inhumanity to fire upon these
unfortunate groups of soldiers, who, clothed in their wide
vestments, attempted to swim across the two leagues of sea
that separated them from their ships, which scarcely one of
them reached in safety.

Whilst this event was occurring on the seashore, a Pacha
had left the field of battle, with a corps of about three thousand
men, in order to throw himself into the fort of Aboukir. They
soon felt the extremities of thirst, which compelled them,
after the lapse of a few days, to surrender unconditionally
to General Menou, who was left on the ground, to close the
operations connected with the Turkish army recently defeated.

These three thousand prisoners, who were very fine men,
were employed upon the works of Alexandria and Damietta
(that is to say, of Lesbe), situated higher up on the right
bank of the Nile, between Damietta and the sea, in front of
the space where formerly stood the town of Damietta, which
was taken by the crusaders; but of which we could not discover any traces.

General Desaix was still above Cairo with his division
when he received the letter by which General Bonaparte
informed him of the successful issue of the battle; and as
General Desaix had pointed out to him, each night, the
place where he intended to take up his quarters, General
Bonaparte was enabled to judge that, had he wanted that
division, it could not have been within reach : in his letter,
therefore, he gently blamed General Desaix's conduct.

An Arab courier, dispatched from the field of battle the

very evening of the action, came up with us during the night, at our bivouac, near Benezeh, twenty-five leagues at least above Cairo. This circumstance added greater weight to General Bonaparte's reproaches.

General Desaix, however, was not without an excuse. He had received the instructions to return with his division at a moment when it was broken into several movable columns, which were overrunning the country to collect the tax. He must either have delayed his march until he could bring together all those detachments, or have exposed himself to the necessity of bringing only a part of his troops, if the concentration of those detachments was to have been left to the discretion of their respective commanders. General Bonaparte would not be satisfied with all these excuses, and only scolded the louder; without, however, suffering this circumstance to affect, in any manner, the esteem and friendship he always bore to General Desaix.

CHAPTER XI.

Loss of many distinguished officers—Overtures of Sir Sidney Smith—Disastrous intelligence from France—General Bonaparte prepares to quit Egypt—His departure.

AFTER the battle of Aboukir, the army naturally indulged in the hope of a few months' rest: it was not disappointed in its expectations; for it was soon afterwards sent back to its former cantonments, whilst General Bonaparte, before returning to Cairo, went to visit Alexandria, which place he had not seen since his first arrival there on landing in Egypt.

He had suffered some severe losses in officers of distinguished merit: General Caffarelli-Dufalgua, who commanded the corps of engineers, had died at the siege of St.

John d'Acre, in consequence of having his arm amputated ; he had already lost a leg, when with the army of the Sambre and Meuse: General Dommartin, who was at the head of the artillery of the army, had recently been killed as he was descending the Nile from Cairo to Rosetta; and lastly, he had just lost, at Aboukir, the colonel of engineers, Crétin, who had fortified Alexandria, and whom he had destined to succeed General Caffarelli.   Nevertheless, the officers composing the army of Egypt had been so carefully selected, that these losses could easily be repaired.

The Turkish fleet had weighed anchor, to return to Constantinople; and there only remained before Alexandria the two English ships, the Tiger and the Theseus, under the command of Sir Sidney Smith.

The second of these ships had on board eighty shells, the residue of those made use of against us at St. John d'Acre ; and owing to some unknown accident, they caught fire, and burst all at once, whilst the ship was under sail: twenty of the crew were killed, and the deck was so much injured, that it was found necessary to send the vessel to the Island of Cyprus, to undergo repairs; there consequently remained only the Tiger before Alexandria, with Sir Sidney Smith on board.   This officer, seeing the unsuccessful result of the Turkish expedition, was endeavouring by some stratagem to induce the French army to quit Egypt.   He opened communications with the general in command at Alexandria, by sending him some French prisoners whom he had saved from the swords of the Turks.   He was, no doubt, pleased that what he had done should be known : he received the thanks to which his generosity of conduct entitled him.   As a feeling of ill-will had existed against him during the whole campaign of Syria, the opportunity of being on better terms with him was not neglected.   It must be acknowledged, however, that he was the first to set the example of a return to moderation.

This communication was followed by a second : he sent his

private secretary to Alexandria, under pretence of delivering to General Bonaparte some letters directed to him, which had been found on board a vessel recently captured. These letters were accompanied by a file of newspapers, of a rather recent date, which gave an account of the disasters experienced by our armies in Italy under General Scherer's orders.

In bringing these details to the knowledge of General Bonaparte, Sir Sidney Smith, no doubt, expected to excite in him the desire of transporting his army across to the relief of Italy; and he was, perhaps, anxious to have his name inscribed in the page of history, by opening a negotiation resting upon such a basis; but he had to deal with a man who could not fail to penetrate the snare laid for him, under whatever colour it might be attempted to disguise it.

That the idea was unreasonable, was not, however, a motive with him for its rejection, as at any time a pretext could easily be found for abandoning it. Matters were so well contrived, that the commodore's secretary remained satisfied that he might renew the proposal, and fell into a snare, whilst he had come to lay one. He frequently returned to Alexandria during General Bonaparte's residence there; and when every detail had been obtained from him which it was important to know, with respect to the recent warlike attitude assumed by Europe, General Bonaparte dismissed him, under pretext of his own presence being required at Cairo upon urgent business, and of his being under the necessity of visiting Upper Egypt, thereby putting off the commodore's proposals until his return. He went back to Cairo, spreading, at the same time, the report of his intended journey to Upper Egypt, whither he dispatched some persons whom he had previously stated it to be his intention to send on before him.

Previously to leaving Alexandria, where he had obtained every circumstantial detail respecting the state of Europe, he had been struck with their perfect coincidence with the accounts brought over by Messrs. Livron and Hamelin. He could no longer entertain any doubt of what must occur, whether in France or in Egypt, unless timely assistance were afforded to either country.

After the obstacles that had resisted his progress in Syria, he was no longer under a delusion as to what he could effect with the small army at his command, and he had consequently postponed, until the arrival of fresh reinforcements, the execution of the second part of his plan, which consisted in extending his power in Palestine, marching upon Constantinople, and giving the signal for a revolution in the East.

The details he had just learned respecting the state of Europe removed from his mind all hope of assistance.

Italy was entirely lost : reinforcements could only be sent to him from Toulon, supposing that the Directory were inclined to afford him any, which was at best extremely doubtful.   At all events, the English had now much greater facilities for intercepting them.

He saw by the public papers that France was torn by civil discord, and in danger of sinking under it.   The papers were teeming with revolutionary projects, such as the law upon hostages, the forced loan, &c. &c. ; every thing, in short, was threatened with disorganization.

This intelligence was already six weeks old ; and as a revolution never stops in its course, he calculated the progress which the evil had made, up to the moment when it became known to him. His heart was oppressed at the details which he read of the unaccountable disasters of the army of Italy, of the Russians having crossed the Alps, to enter France, into which they would have penetrated, had it not been for the battle of Zurich, fought at a later period.

In the dissolution of the Cisalpine Republic he beheld the destruction of his own work. The French troops, which were spread, on a former occasion over the whole surface of Italy, were now confined within the Genoese territory.   The people of La Vendée, animated with greater fury than ever, had carried their inroads to the very gates of Paris, and drawn down sanguinary reprisals; and terror was again assuming its former sway over France.

Public credit was threatened with destruction, owing to the disastrous measures recommended and carried into effect by that nest of vampires, who, under cloak of the national interest, are foremost in fomenting disorders, that they may feed at leisure both upon private fortunes and the public revenue. The Directory breathed the atmosphere of these men, the true plagues of a state having the misfortune to be cursed with their presence.

On beholding this gloomy picture, his mind recoiled upon itself; and in his breast he discovered that patriotic feeling, which leads a man of superior stamp to devote himself to the common cause. He wondered that, out of so many celebrated generals whom he had left in France, there was not one whose name was not coupled with some public misfortune.

He felt that, inasmuch as the members of the Directory might have desired his removal, when his presence only reminded them of the glorious services they deemed it painful to recollect, so they ought now to wish for his return, since the disasters that had assailed them during his absence must have forced their reluctant acknowledgment of his being, perhaps, the only man calculated to avert the impending ruin of France, by rallying round his military renown the different parties that divided the republic, at this moment on the verge of dissolution.

The situation of Egypt allowed, besides, of his absenting himself: he had placed it in a formidable attitude of defence; and he availed himself of every means at his disposal to fill up the vacancies which sickness and war had created in our ranks. He not only formed corps out of the mamelukes, and the Copts, as well as the Greeks who were then in Egypt, and who all readily enlisted in our service, and strictly performed their duty; but he caused negroes of Darfour to be brought into Egypt, and had them trained to European discipline.

These several troops were supplied with the arms and equipments of the soldiers who had died in hospital, or on the field of battle.

The system of military administration and of finances was, moreover, so organised as to provide for all the wants of the army. France alone could grant what the colony was still in need of ; and General Bonaparte could alone obtain that object from the government.

Feeling persuaded that his departure was equally for the good of France and of Egypt; that a longer delay, on his part, might compromise the safety of both ; and that in France only could he effectually promote the interests of Egypt, he determined to take his departure, relying upon future events for his justification. Such were the explanations he gave to a person who possessed his intimate confidence at the period in question.

Every thing went on well. A man of even ordinary capacity would have been competent to keep in motion that species of mechanism, which only required not to be put out of order.

The battle of Aboukir had just secured the repose of Egypt until, at least, the ensuing season; as, in Egypt, no landing can be effected except in the fine season of the year.

Contemplating, unmoved, the numberless dangers which would assail him at his very departure from Alexandria, and which would go on increasing at every step of the work he was about to undertake, he resigned himself to his fortune, which he trusted would bring him through all difficulties, unless a fatal destiny had decreed the ruin of France.

Sir Sidney Smith was persuaded that, if General Bonaparte did not quit Egypt by means of a capitulation, which would include his army, and which he hoped to impose upon him, he would at least take his departure alone; and he therefore formed the plan to intercept him ou his way. Unfortunately for him, the prisoners he recently restored had informed us that he was short of water, not having had time to take in any before his departure from St. John d'Acre to escort the Turkish army just destroyed at Aboukir.

He considered, no doubt, that he would find time to proceed to the island of Cyprus, take in his stock of water, and reappear before Alexandria ere General Bonaparte could have returned from Upper Egypt. He accordingly sailed for Cyprus, thus withdrawing the only cruiser that stood in the way.

He was hardly out of sight when a courier was dispatched to General Bonaparte, who was all in readiness. He had communicated the secret of his departure to Admiral Gantheaume, and requested him to have prepared the only two frigates remaining of the squadron, which were not present at the naval engagement of Aboukir, having escorted the transport-ships, and entered with them into the port of Alexandria.

On apprising Gantheaume of his departure from Cairo, General Bonaparte ordered him, at the same time, to leave the port of Alexandria with his two frigates, and fixed the day and hour when he was to send his ships' boats to the small creek of the Marabou, where he intended to embark.

As soon as Sir Sidney Smith left the station of Alexandria Gantheaume set sail, under pretext of going out on a cruise, and came to place himself in front of the small creek of the Marabou, a league to the westward of Alexandria. No right conjecture could be formed from the sailing of those two frigates, since it was imagined, in Alexandria, that General Bonaparte was at Cairo, or in Upper Egypt.

General Bonaparte, who had, as above-mentioned, fixed the day and hour at which Gantheaume was to send off his boats, arrived in the beach about the appointed time, and there found General Menou, whom he had ordered to meet him. He conversed a long time with this general respecting the motives which induced him to brave the British cruisers. He handed to him the dispatches that conferred the command on General Kleber, and hastened to the boat that waited for him, followed by his suite and escort. The boats pushed off from the beach, and General Bonaparte was soon on board the vessel about to convey Cesar and his fortune to the shores of France.

The horses of the escort had been left to run loose on the beach, and all was perfect stillness in Alexandria, when the advanced posts of the town were alarmed by the wild galloping of horses, which, from a natural instinct, were returning to Alexandria through the desert. The picket ran to arms on seeing horses ready saddled and bridled, which were soon discovered to belong to the regiment of guides. They at first thought that a misfortune had happened to some detachment in its pursuit of the Arabs. With these horses came also those of the generals who had embarked with General Bonaparte; so that Alexandria was, for a time, in considerable alarm. The cavalry was ordered to proceed in all haste in the direction whence the horses came; and every one was giving himself up to the most gloomy conjectures, when the cavalry returned to the city with the Turkish groom, who was bringing back General Bonaparte's horse to Alexandria.

Amongst the papers which General Bonaparte had confided to Menou was a letter for General Kleber, to whom he communicated his plan, and transferred the command of the army; and another for General Desaix, who was at Siout, in Upper Egypt, and to whom he made the same communications, with the addition, that he did not assign to him the command of the army, because he hoped to see him in Italy or in France in the month of September following. We were then in June or July.

This packet was accompanied by a proclamation, in which he made known to the army the causes which had determined him to leave it, and fly to the relief of their common country. He recommended the army to persevere in its course; and said that he should always consider every day of his life as ill employed in which he should not do something to promote its welfare.

The stupor that spread in all quarters on the first intelligence of this departure, would almost baffle description. Public opinion did not speak out for some days; but it afterwards vented itself in abusive terms. The determination of General Bonaparte was condemned by the majority: only a few correct minds were able to comprehend its motives: men of limited understanding raved about it for a week; and all parties settled gradually into a right feeling upon the subject.

CHAPTER XII.

State of the public mind after General Bonaparte's departure—Kleber—Negotiations with the Vizier—Noble conduct of General Verdicr—The author accompanies General Desaix on board the Tiger—Armistice.

ALL eyes were soon directed to the new general-in-chief: every one sought to gain his favour.

Since the arrival of the French troops in Egypt, no means had been left untried by the enemies of France to rouse the Porte from its apathy; and this power had just marched a numerous army into Syria under the command of the Grand Vizier.

The approach of that army through Caramania had been mainly instrumental in compelling General Bonaparte to raise the siege of St. John d'Acre and to return to Egypt.

It had already reached Syria before the Turkish fleet had made its appearance at Aboukir ; and General Bonaparte, desirous of gaining time in order to bear upon the army landed from this fleet, had opened a negotiation with the Vizier who commanded the forces in Syria, being well aware that an overture from him to the Turks would have the effect of making them suspend their march ; the more so, as they were not over-anxious to come to close quarters with him ; he also knew them to be discontented at the endeavours made in every possible way to drive them on to the field of battle. The natural good sense of these people pointed out to them that France and the Porte, in coming to blows, were only serving their mutual enemies.

The Vizier returned an answer to General Bonaparte, and there were several interchanges of couriers between them ; but the secret of that negotiation had never transpired. It was known to be still carrying on ; and this circumstance raised a hope in the public mind which was fondly cherished by every one. General Bonaparte held the result in his hands, and husbanded the means of turning it to the account of his ulterior views.

The footing upon which he had placed that negotiation formed part of the instructions which he gave to General Kleber on leaving him the further management of it,* as well as all the documents connected with it. Kleber was soon dis-

---

* *Letter addressed to General Kleber by General Bonaparte, on leaving Egypt to return to France.*

" General, you will find enclosed an order directing you to assume the chief command of the army. I accelerate my departure by two or three days, under the apprehension that from one moment to another the English cruiser may make its appearance. I take home with me Generals Berthier, Andreossi, Murat, Lannes, and Marmont, together with Citizens Monge and Berthollet.

" Herewith you will find the English and Frankfort papers up to the 10th June. They will tell you that we have lost Italy, and that Mantua, Turin, and Tortona are blockaded. I have reason to hope that the first-mentioned city will hold out until the end of November. I hope to reach Europe before the beginning of October, should fortune be favourable to me.

posed to consider this negotiation as the means of quitting a

" Annexed are two ciphers, the one to correspond with the government, the other with myself.

" I request you will send Junot home in the course of October, together with my servants, and all the effects which I have left at Cairo. I should have no objection, however, to your detaining in your own service such of my servants as it might suit you to keep.

" It is the intention of government that General Desaix should return to Europe in the course of November, unless any event of importance should require his further presence in this country.

" The commission of arts will return to France in a flag of truce, which you are to demand for that purpose, agreeably to the cartel of exchange, in the month of November, immediately after having completed the object of its mission. It is at present engaged in visiting Upper Egypt; you need not hesitate, however, in retaining such of its members as you may deem useful to you.

" The effendi made prisoner at Aboukir is now on his way to Damietta. I have written you word to send him to Cyprus : he is the bearer of a letter for the Grand Vizier, of which a copy is annexed.

" The arrival of our Brest squadron at Toulon, and of the Spanish squadron at Carthagena, removes every doubt as to the possibility of conveying to Egypt the muskets, swords, pistols, and cast-iron you may stand in need of, and of which I have a very exact statement, together with a sufficient number of recruits to repair the losses of both campaigns.

" The government itself will then acquaint you with its intentions ; and I shall, both in my public and private character, take every means to enable you to receive frequent intelligence from home.

" Should unforeseen events render all attempts fruitless, and you remain up to the month of May without receiving either news or assistance from France ; and should the plague, notwithstanding every precaution, extend its ravages over Egypt this, year and carry off upwards of fifteen hundred soldiers, which would be a very serious loss, as being over and above what the chances of the war will occasion, I think that, in such a case, you ought not to attempt to take the field ; and that you would be justified in concluding a peace with the Ottoman Porte, even if the evacuation of Egypt should be its principal condition. You would then have only to put off carrying such a condition into effect until a general peace.

" You are as well enabled as I am to appreciate how important is to France the position of Egypt: the Turkish empire is threatened with ruin, and is actually crumbling to pieces; and the evacuation of Egypt would be a misfortune so much the greater, as we should in our own time see that beautiful province fall into European hands.

" Your calculations must be greatly influenced by the news you may receive of the future successes or reverses of the republic.

country against which every one was railing, more especially as
the departure of General Bonaparte had removed the only re-

" If the Porte should reply to the overtures of peace which I made to it previously to your receiving my letters from France, you are to declare that you hold all the powers I possessed, and are to open negotiations, always persisting in the assertion which I have put forward, that France never had the intention of wresting Egypt from the Porte: you will demand that the Porte shall renounce taking part in the coalition, and grant us the trade of the Black Sea; that it shall set all French prisoners free; and lastly, consent to a six months' suspension of hostilities, so as to give time for exchanging the ratifications of peace.

" Supposing that circumstances should make you deem it advisable to conclude a treaty with the Porte, you will point out that you cannot execute such treaty until it shall be ratified; and according to the usage amongst all nations, the interval between the signing of a treaty and its ratification must always be considered as a period of suspension of hostilities.

" You are acquainted, Citizen General, with my sentiments respecting the internal politics of Egypt. Happen what may, the Christians will always be our friends. They must not be allowed to be overbearing, in order that the Turks may not be actuated by the same spirit of fanaticism against us as they are against them, which would have the effect of rendering them irreconcilable enemies. We must lull their fanaticism to sleep, in order to root it out. The good opinion of the whole of Egypt will be secured by obtaining that of the great cheiks of Cairo; and of all the chiefs to whom this people may show deference, none are less dangerous than the cheiks, who are cowardly, unable to fight, and, like all priests, inspire fanaticism, without being fanatics themselves.

" With respect to the fortifications, Alexandria and El-Arish are the keys of Egypt. I had it in contemplation to raise redoubts with palm-trees this winter, two from Salahié to Catiëh, and two from Catiëh to El-Arish; one of these to be on the spot where General Menou found water fit for drinking.

" General Samson, commander of the engineers, and General Songis, commander of the artillery, will each inform you of what concerns their respective branches.

" Citizen Poussielgue has been exclusively charged with the finances. I have found him a hard-working and meritorious man. He has already begun to acquire some insight into the chaos of the administration of Egypt.

" I had intended, should no fresh event interfere, to have established, this winter, a new mode of taxation, which would have enabled us to dispense almost entirely with the Copts; before undertaking this, however, I recommend it to your mature consideration; it is better to embark rather too late than too soon in such an operation.

" French ships of war will undoubtedly make their appearance this winter at Alexandria, Bourlos, or Damietta. Cause a strong tower to be built at Bourlos: try to collect five or six hundred mamelukes, whom, upon the arrival of the French

straint that had kept the freedom of language within bounds.

The new general-in-chief soon showed how little inclined he was to follow up the system of his predecessor : this was manifested by the indecorous conversations held in his house, where censure was busy with General Bonaparte's military operations and private habits: not only did he suffer these conversations to go on, but it was easy to perceive that he listened to them with pleasure.

There arose very soon between the officers who had served in the armies of the north, and of the Sambre and Meuse,

ships, you will have arrested on the same day at Cairo and in the other provinces, and embark them for France. In default of mamelukes, some Arab hostages, or cheïk belets, who might happen to be our prisoners, whatever may be the ground of their detention, might supply their place. These people, when arrived in France, will be detained there a year or two, and by witnessing the greatness of the French nation, and forming some idea of our manners and our language, will, on their return to Egypt, be so many partisans to our cause.

" I had often asked for a company of players : I will take especial care to send you some. This object is of great consequence to the army, and will tend to change the manners of the country.

" The important station you are going to hold, as chief in command, will now enable you to display the talents with which nature has endowed you. There is a very lively interest excited as to what passes here, and the results to commerce and civilization will be immense: from this epoch mighty revolutions will take their date.

" Accustomed to view in the opinion of posterity the recompense of the toils and troubles of life, I quit Egypt with the deepest regret. The interest of our country, its glory, obedience, the extraordinary events that have lately taken place, have alone determined me to force my way to France through the enemy's squadrons. Your successes will be as dear to me as those in which I may have a personal share ; and I shall consider those days of my life ill employed on which I shall not do something for the army I leave under your command, and for the consolidation of the splendid establishment, the foundations of which have just been laid.

" I confide to you an army wholly composed of my children ; at all times, and in the midst of the severest trials, they have ever shown me proofs of their attachment: nourish this sentiment in their breasts ; you owe it to the very great regard I entertain for you, and to the sincere affection I bear towards them.

" BONAPARTE."

and those who had served in the army of Italy, the same jealousy that had already displayed itself between General Jourdan's officers and those of General Kleber at the army of the
Sambre and Meuse.

Those who had served in the last-named army, and whose
discontent had broken out on their first arrival at Cairo, were
the first whom General Kleber took into his intimacy. He
soon became the idol of all who wished for the evacuation of
Egypt, a wish which they were constantly intimating to him.
This feeling pervaded the army to such an extent that Kleber,
so surrounded, was debarred of the means of receiving any
impressions or advice that might be at variance with his own
opinions.

All minds were henceforward bent on finding out the impossibility of executing whatever was calculated to give stability to the residence of the army in Egypt; which object
was no longer one of constant anxiety, as it had been when
General Bonaparte held the command. In a short time, all
thoughts were exclusively directed to France, and each one
made his private arrangements in anticipation of the return
home; in a word, Egypt had no longer any hold on the imagination of the army.

Kleber was a worthy man, and unquestionably a brave and
talented general; but his mild disposition and weakness of
character formed a striking contrast with his athletic and
commanding figure. It appears that he was brought up to
the profession of an architect, which, owing to a relish for the
military life, he relinquished, and entered one of the Austrian
regiments in the Low Countries.

He was living in Alsace when the revolution broke out,
and quitted the service of Austria to embark in it, although
he was diametrically adverse to the system of equality.

He had just been named adjutant to one of the battalions
of volunteers of the Upper Rhine, when that corps was called
to Mentz, where it remained shut up with the garrison which

defended it at its first siege. He distinguished himself on that occasion, proceeded to La Vendée as a general officer subsequently to the capitulation of Mentz, and afterwards returned to serve with the army of the Sambre and Meuse, whence the Directory removed him, in consequence of his perpetual opposition to General Jourdan, its commander-in-chief. Thus matters stood when General Bonaparte obtained an employment for him in his own army.

It was his disposition to be always dissatisfied; and he acknowledged his dislike of *subordination, except in the inferior ranks*. Though an agreeable man, he had not a comprehensive turn of mind; and the least unfavourable opinion formed of him, from his conduct in Egypt, was, that he had not been struck by the conviction of the infallible results with which, sooner or later, the occupation of that country would be attended.

All these disadvantages were increased by a perfect ignorance of the management of political affairs, so as necessarily to place him at the mercy of every one, and of those in particular who were desirous of returning to France through his instrumentality.

There was no difficulty, therefore, in persuading him to follow up the negotiations already opened with the Vizier, and in presenting them to his mind merely as the means of taking back to France an army whose services she stood in need of, in the opinion of men little aware, from experience, of what our country could achieve through the mere impulse given by a clever and active government.

A character of greater importance was given to the communications opened with the Grand Vizier by substituting an officer in the army * for the Tartars hitherto employed, and it

---

* The first officer sent was the chief of battalion, Morand, of the eighty-eighth regiment: he had already attracted the notice of the army at this period, and promised to be one day, what he eventually became, one of the most distinguished lieutenant-generals in the Emperor's army.

seemed as if an anxiety was felt to hurry on the negotiation by connecting the English with it.

The pretence given out for this change was, that whatever stipulations might be concluded with the Turks, nothing would have been done, unless the English, as masters of the sea, were a contracting party to them. The chief of battalion, Morand, was, accordingly, sent to Sir Sidney Smith, instead of the Vizier. That officer only succeeded in finding him by going to the Vizier's camp, near Nazareth, in Syria.

Sir Sidney Smith was flattered by the message, which, being addressed to him, presented him to the Turkish army in a higher character than what properly belonged to the captain of a ship and commodore on a cruise, which were the only commissions he held from his government. He did not hesitate, therefore, in accepting the part of mediator, which was offered to him by the Turks, and not resisted by Kleber. When he saw the contrast between General Kleber's unsuspecting confidence and General Bonaparte's cautious avoidance of such a feeling, his penetration told him at once the turn he might give to the negotiation. Accordingly, from this very first overture, in which the question of the evacuation of Egypt was entertained, General Kleber found himself, perhaps, more deeply committed than he could have wished, because Sir Sidney Smith gave him a reply of so positive a nature, that little more was left to discuss than the basis of the evacuation, the principle itself appearing to have been agreed upon.

The chief of battalion, Morand, returned with this answer to General Kleber at Cairo. He seemed to have been at last awakened to the danger of that influence which had controlled his actions; and whether he felt desirous of averting its consequences by means of a counterpoise, or of linking the highest authorities in the army to his plans, he had already recalled General Desaix to Cairo from Upper Egypt, for the sake of the weight which his name could not fail to stamp upon any measure that might be adopted. He was scarcely arrived when news was brought of the appearance of a fresh Turkish fleet at the mouth of that branch of the Nile which discharges itself into the sea at Damietta.

General Kleber at once saw that this fleet was intended to form a combined system of operations with the Vizier's army, and that the latter would now advance towards Egypt. He hastened therefore to dispatch General Desaix to Damietta, for the purpose of resisting any attempt of the Turkish fleet; but when he arrived, he found that fortune had already favoured us with the most brilliant and complete success.

General Verdier was in command at Damietta, and had a few battalions encamped on the right bank of the Nile, between Lesbe and that town.

Assisted by Sir Sidney Smith's two ships, the Turks landed a few thousand men on the beach leading to Lesbe. They were covered by two pieces of cannon, which the English had brought on shore, intending to mount them upon the ruins of an old tower, seemingly part of the ancient town of Damietta, whence they completely commanded the only road by which alone our troops could advance.

General Verdier, however, did not allow the boats time to go back and bring a second supply of troops ashore. Although his soldiers were at the distance of half a league from the Turkish landing-place, it took him no more than two hours to collect them, bring them down to the beach, and drive the Turks into the sea, at the very moment when the Turkish boats had pushed off from the shore. Those who hesitated to plunge into the water were taken prisoners; and out of all the soldiers who had been landed from the ships, not one effected his escape.

General Verdier had so conducted his attack as to force the Turks back upon the town, against which the English cannon were pointed, and thereby protected us from their fire. Never was success more complete or more decisive.

Nothing was therefore left to General Desaix but to congratulate General Verdier, and he only remained at Damietta the time requisite to enable him to visit Lake Menzale. The Turkish fleet having set sail in the mean time, he came back to Cairo, where he arrived some days after the return of the chief of battalion, Morand, from Syria.

The first proceedings of Sir Sidney Smith had so far advanced the pending negotiations, that, after the reply brought back by Morand, nothing more was left than to discuss the terms of the evacuation, as if the event had come to pass which could alone justify that measure of extremity.

The moment had now arrived when Kleber should have assembled the chiefs of the army : he acted otherwise, however, and determined at once to open negotiations with the Vizier. He again sent a message to that chief, who was attended by Sir Sidney Smith. The reply was still more prompt and decisive than on the former occasion ; and Sir Sidney Smith, who was anxious to become the mediator in the negotiation, veiled his offer of services under a cloak of liberality, which the occasion served him as an excuse for assuming.

He urged as a pretext for his offer the possibility of bad faith or treachery on the part of the Turks ; evils which he, perhaps, in reality apprehended : he also proposed his own ship as the seat of a negotiation which he was most anxious to have at once entered upon, and apprised General Kleber of his intention to proceed forthwith to Damietta, where he would await his answer.

Kleber immediately replied that he accepted the offer, and dispatched General Desaix and M. Poussielgue, the intendant of military finances, to Damietta, with full powers.

I accompanied General Desaix, and was the person whom he sent, with M. Peyruse, on board the Tiger (which lay in the bay of Damietta), to agree upon the day and hour at which General Desaix and M. Poussielgue were to embark.

Having gone off to the ship at a late hour in the day, I was unable to return until the following morning, and had therefore to pass the night on board Sir Sidney Smith's ship, where every mark of attention was shown to me. I was at that time scarcely twenty-four years of age; but was of a reflecting turn of mind, and saw that Sir Sidney Smith had many advantages over us, and would be the winner in the game he was about to play.

It was beyond my power of comprehension to understand how we could submit to lend ourselves to our own ruin ; for we had commenced by acting a secondary part, and were clearing away the difficulties, instead of raising fresh ones. There must undoubtedly have existed a conviction that General Bonaparte would never reach France, or that the Directory would act with severity towards him ; it would otherwise be impossible to account for the conduct pursued since his departure from Egypt.

I returned to General Desaix, and informed him of what I had seen, and what had been agreed upon between Sir Sidney Smith and myself. The embarkation took place the next day, at Damietta, where the English boats came to take up General Desaix and M. Poussielgue, together with the secretary of the latter, who had accompanied me on board Sir Sidney Smith's ship. I again attended General Desaix on this occasion, and we soon got on board the Tiger.

Whilst Sir Sidney Smith was pressing General Kleber to enter into a negotiation, he was urging the Turkish army to commence operations ; and it had, accordingly, broken up from the camp at Nazareth, and taken the road through Gaza, for the purpose of cutting off the small fort of El-Arish, which stands in the midst of the desert that separates Africa from Asia, and is the key of Egypt in that quarter.

General Kleber had just received this intelligence, and,

apprehensive of some misfortune for El-Arish and for himself,
he sent one of his aides-de-camp to General Desaix, who
brought these details to him on board the Tiger, with an order
to demand, as a preliminary condition, a suspension of hostilities—a condition which had not before occurred to the commander-in-chief; although his object was to save his army
when he proposed the evacuation of Egypt.

The suspension of arms was demanded; but Sir Sidney
Smith replied, that he could only interpose his good offices
with the Vizier, to whom he would immediately address a
letter on the subject: he did so; and it was but a few days
afterwards that we heard of the fort of El-Arish having been
carried by surprise, and of the misfortune that befell its garrison, lulled into security by the parleys kept up with it, and
by the hope of being sent back to France.

The commandant was taken off his guard, and yielded to
the courteous requests made to him to allow his fort to be
visited; but the gate was no sooner opened than the Turkish
soldiery rushed in, and fell upon the garrison, who, relying on
the vigilance of its officers, had been equally inattentive to the
snare laid against their confiding candour.

The fort was carried, and the unfortunate soldiers of the
garrison were beheaded, almost to a man, in the presence of a
wretched traitor to his country,* who, bearing the uniform of
England, became their agent in the execution of this sanguinary deed; for we afterwards learned that the very courier
dispatched by Sir Sidney Smith to request the suspension of
arms, conveyed to two French emigrants placed by him with
the Turkish army an order to accelerate, at any price, the
capture of El-Arish; so that the accomplishment of the
latter object might precede the grant of the suspension of
arms, which accordingly followed this event: the entrance

---

* This emigrant came at a later period to solicit employment in the Emperor's
service, and is now an officer in the army of the King of France.

into Egypt was, therefore, no longer interrupted in that quarter.

The intelligence of the capture of the fort, and of the agreement to an armistice, reached General Kleber at one and the same moment.

This gave reason, for the first time, to suspect the sincerity of which Sir Sidney Smith had made so much display, and of which Kleber appeared to have been the dupe.

We could not help remarking that, had we sailed from Damietta, we might have arrived the same night in front of Gaza, where the Vizier was still encamped, and within as short a time as the small vessel which Sir Sidney Smith sent with his dispatches; and that, by negotiating in person for the suspension of arms, we might have saved El-Arish from falling into the enemy's hands.

Sir Sidney Smith, however, under the pretext that military men cannot cope with sailors on their element, carried us first to Cyprus, next to Tyre, and afterwards to St. John d'Acre; and lastly, at the expiration of thirty days, he conducted us to the house of the British consul at the port of Jaffa, and then quitted us, to rejoin the Vizier, who had just removed his camp from Gaza to El-Arish. Previously to his departure he had ordered his ship to proceed to the coast of Caramania for a supply of water; so that we were left wholly at the mercy of the Turks.

CHAPTER XIII.

Arrival of General Desaix and M. Poussielgue at the camp of the Vizier—General
Desaix sends the author to General Kleber—General Kleber's adhesion to the
treaty—Opposition of General Davout—Treaty of El-Arish—Intelligence is
received of the events of the 18th Brumaire—Arrival of M. Victor de Latour-
Maubourg—General Desaix's departure for France with the author—They are
captured and carried to Leghorn—Their arrival in France.

DURING the month we had passed on board the Tiger
General Desaix and M. Poussielgue held several conferences
with Sir Sidney Smith, which left upon their minds an impression of ill omen.

General Desaix might be deemed excusable for erring
in negotiations of a diplomatic nature, never having been
employed on such missions: this excuse, however, could not
be pleaded in favour of his colleague, who had been the diplomatic agent of the republic at Genoa; and yet so blind was
the confidence which had involved them in the situation in
which they found themselves, that Sir Sidney Smith was not
even requested to exhibit the powers he ought to have had
from his government, and from the Turks, on behalf of whom
he pretended to stipulate a treaty.

He acted with so much dexterity, that he was not asked
the question. This neglect on the part of the French
plenipotentiaries was more than Sir Sidney Smith could
have anticipated. It is, moreover, probable, that he had
expected a more cautious conduct; and that, from the very
first communications between General Kleber and the Vizier,
he had applied to his government for instructions and powers,
in anticipation of the event which he foresaw was at hand;
and was yet without an answer, in consequence of that event
having occurred sooner than he expected.

Two days after Sir Sidney Smith's departure from Jaffa,

where he had left General Desaix and M. Poussielgue, his secretary arrived there on a mission from him, with several Turkish officers, and a pass, in order to conduct the plenipotentiaries to the Vizier's camp. They accordingly immediately left for Gaza ; slept the next night at Ramla, on the borders of the desert ; and reached El-Arish at an early hour the next morning. The Vizier had caused some very handsome tents to be pitched at a spot separated from the camp; and a guard had been placed there, for the special purpose of protecting the plenipotentiaries, for whose accommodation those tents were intended.

He sent to compliment them on their arrival ; and to present to them, as a mark of his high esteem, a pitcher of water from Gaza, and about a dozen choice white apples. Our being in a desert could alone account for such objects being deemed worthy of acceptance.

Sir Sidney Smith's tent was placed near ours ; and he had with him some English marines, brought from on board his ship. After a few days' rest, the first conference was opened with the Vizier's plenipotentiaries, and it had well nigh been the last ; for General Desaix was in a perfect rage when he left it.

It had been found impossible to make them comprehend the meaning of a suspension of arms, a capitulation, or a treaty. The Turks could only see two results arising from war ; these were, death or slavery ; nor would they admit of any other stipulations.

M. Poussielgue, though more composed, was not less astonished than General Desaix at what he had just heard : they both upbraided Sir Sidney Smith in bitter terms for his not having communicated to them these dispositions on the part of the Turks, instead of assuring them, as he had done, that it was their intention to accede to a plain and simple evacuation of Egypt. General Desaix broke out in severe reproaches ; and intimating to Sir Sidney Smith his refusal to negotiate any further, he summoned that officer to take him instantly on board, according to what had been agreed upon between them.

Sir Sidney Smith was not at all alarmed at this clamour : he was better acquainted with the Turks of Europe than our plenipotentiaries were. He would not, most assuredly, have allowed the least injury to be done to them ; but he could not be sorry to find his assistance indispensable towards extricating them from the difficulty they were in. He calmed the plenipotentiaries by taking all upon himself: so great, in fact, were his exertions, during the following night, that on the next day he again brought the two parties together, and had the conferences renewed, at which he ever afterwards assisted. By his unheard-of activity, he caused the conditions of that famous treaty of El-Arish to be discussed, settled, and drawn up in the forms prescribed by General Kleber ; thereby destroying General Bonaparte's work. Sir Sidney Smith was urging its signature, because he had already learned the arrival of General Bonaparte in France, as the sequel will show.

General Desaix, however, previously to signing it, recoiled with horror at the idea, and had the signature put off for a few days. He sent for me, at night, to his tent, and said : " What General Kleber desired has been done : go and tell him from me, that before I can sanction the act with my signature, I wish him to read what he has made us agree to ; but that in no case shall I sign without an order from him, of which I request you to be the bearer."

I returned accordingly to Egypt, with an escort of Tartars, who made me cross through the Vizier's army, and joined General Kleber at Salahié, where he had united the army, upon hearing of the capture of El-Arish and the arrival of the Turkish army at that point. I entered just after the holding of a council of war, in which the discussion had turned upon the impossibility of preserving Egypt ; and

General Kleber had not disdained to provide himself with a guarantee, as a relief to his responsibility, by making all the generals sign a declaration, wherein, after the statement laid before them, they acknowledged the impossibility of defending Egypt with the means which the army had at command. Opinions had not been unanimous in this council; as, however, the object of returning to France was flattering to all, they signed in a body; because, in this case, no one could be singled out for censure.

I announced to General Kleber that, at the moment of my departure, intelligence was brought to the camp at El-Arish of General Bonaparte's arrival in France; and I handed to him a file of newspapers which already noticed the event.

I twice repeated the message which General Desaix had specially directed me to convey to him.

General Kleber again assembled the council of war in order to communicate to it the contents of the dispatches I had brought, and made me return the same night in a cartel, with an answer for General Desaix, and the order to sign the treaty, which he had desired me to bring back to him. General Kleber also charged me to claim the wife of a sergeant of the garrison of El-Arish, whom he knew to have fallen to the share of a pacha, being desirous, as he said, not to leave behind him a single individual belonging to the army.

Before my departure, General Davout, one of those who opposed the decision of the council, drew me aside, and desired me to tell General Desaix what had taken place, that the members of the council had only signed out of complaisance to General Kleber, who had succeeded in deceiving them; but that, if General Desaix would refuse signing the treaty, all the generals in the army would side with him.

I had been too many years acquainted with General Davout to doubt the truth of what he said to me; but I observed that the communication was of too serious a nature for me

to make otherwise than by being the bearer of a letter from
him ; adding, that if he felt sufficient dependence upon me to
transmit a verbal message, he could safely entrust me with a
written. one ; that in any case I would execute his commission; but was prepared for the observation General Desaix,
would not fail to make to me, as he would be very justly
disappointed at not seeing the above hints committed to writing, and that from all that had happened he could not run
any risk.

I instantly departed for El-Arish. On arriving at the
Turkish advanced posts, I received an escort which conducted me to the Vizier's tent, round which were strewed
the bodies of wretches who had been put to death during the
day

I found Sir Sidney Smith with the Vizier, and seized that
opportunity to claim the woman I have mentioned. I then
learned from the Vizier that he had given her to the pacha of
Jerusalem ; but he said he would ask for her back, and immediately send her on to us. I went thence with Sir Sidney
Smith to General Desaix's tent, where the treaty was signed
on the night of my arrival.

Upon my executing General Davout's commission, General
Desaix replied to me in these words · " What ! is it possible
Davout could have directed you to give me this message,
when I see his name at the foot of the deliberation which all
have signed, and which you have brought to me ? It were
blameable in me to rely upon such men. Happen what may,
the..dye is cast : this business has caused me uneasiness
enough ; but there has been no fault of mine."

On the next day, or the day following, both parties took
leave of each other. Just as General Desaix was about to
start on his return to Egypt, a letter was brought to him from
Jerusalem ; it was from the poor woman, who thanked him
for .the ˙interest he had shown in her fate, but declared that·
it was not her intention to take advantage of it, as she found

herself well off, and was resolved to remain where she was · she wished us success and a happy journey.

Well satisfied with what had taken place, Sir Sidney Smith left us in order to search the Archipelago for the vessels which the Turks stood in need of for the transport of the army. He was to bring them to Alexandria, where very few were remaining of those that had brought us over to Egypt, they having been successively broken up to meet the wants of the army. Sir Sidney Smith, who, although without any powers, had so well served his country by taking advantage of our credulity, had reason to expect that his government would approve of his proceedings. The contrary, however, was the case.

Conformably to the conditions of the treaty, the Turkish army advanced to occupy Catiëh, between El-Arish and Salahié, as also Salahié and Damietta; and these towns were delivered up to them before the arrival of any one of the transports which ought already to have reached Alexandria; so that we were resigning our advantages without receiving any equivalent.

This circumstance was so mortifying to General Desaix, that, on his rejoining the army, he expressed a desire to avail himself of the permission given him to return to France. General Kleber did not feel himself warranted in refusing him, and at his request allowed him to embark on board the vessel that had brought over Messrs. de Livron and Hamelin, as those gentlemen had freighted her with return goods, and she would be the first to put to sea.

General Desaix also asked for another small vessel, which was likewise ready, and permission to take home General Davout, who would no longer remain in Egypt with General

---

* At a later period, this female sutler became the protectress of the Christian establishments in Syria, to which she rendered important services.

She was of use to us in the time of the consulate, and was provided with the means for supporting the ascendancy she had acquired.

Kleber.   The latter, though he had reason to be displeased
with Davout's conduct, had just appointed him general of
division ; but whether it was owing to bitterness of feeling,
or to a manly pride, Davout had refused the appointment,
unwilling, as he said, to date his promotion from so disgraceful an epoch.   General Kleber, who could not feel otherwise
than vexed at such a refusal, took no other revenge than that
of allowing him to depart.   He returned from Salahié to
Cairo with General Desaix, who remained but a few days at
the latter place, on his way to Alexandria.

Kleber was bringing back the army, and he arrived at Cairo
at the moment when a summary of the events of the 18th
Brumaire had reached that city.   A brig of war from Toulon
had just anchored in the bay of Damietta, and had sent her
boat ashore with General Galbau and his son, whom General
Bonaparte had dispatched to Egypt.

Finding that our troops had evacuated Damietta in the
morning, the boat proceeded up the river, in order to land
General Galban close to our nearest military station, and
returned to overtake its ship, which it could no longer
find.   The fact is, that owing to the protracted absence
of the boat, the sloop of war had sent another boat on shore
to ascertain what had become of the first ; and that boat finding the Turks in possession of Damietta, which they came to
occupy, since the first boat had passed it, no longer doubted
either that it was lost, or had ascended the Nile until it could
come up with our troops.

When the commander of the brig heard the account
brought by the second boat, he took fright, weighed anchor,
sailed back to France, and succeeded in entering Toulon ; so
that the missing boat, not finding its ship in the bay, had
been under the necessity of making the best of its way to
Alexandria, where it had recently arrived.

General Galbau brought the first intelligence of the event
which had transferred the power to General Bonaparte's

hands: this news was not calculated to allay the fears of those who had thought they would only have to account to the Directory for their conduct.

General Galbau had not reached Cairo when General Desaix went to take leave of General Kleber, previously to his departure for Alexandria.

They appeared to meet on terms of cordiality; and General Kleber felt persuaded that General Desaix, on his arrival in France, would not prejudice General Bonaparte against him; he even flattered himself that he might rely upon him in a circumstance so deeply affecting his future prospects.*

I took my departure with General Desaix, who proceeded by the Nile as far as Rosetta, where he went to see General Menou, who was furious at the evacuation of Egypt. Our boats proceeded from the Nile, by sea, to Alexandria, and we cut across the country, because General Desaix was desirous of visiting the fort of Aboukir and all that part of the coast.

We passed the night in a trading caravansary, annoyed beyond description by swarms of vermin, which are brought thither by caravans on their way through; and we were beginning to load our camels, the next morning, in order to repair to Alexandria, when, from a sandy hillock, we descried in the offing a vessel with lateen sails, apparently of a most diminutive size; she was endeavouring to reach the shore on which we stood; and from the whiteness of her sails, and the position in which she appeared, we guessed that she was not an Egyptian vessel. Curiosity got the better of us, and we determined to wait for her, whatever inconvenience we might afterwards suffer from the heat on continuing our journey. We were able to hail her at the expiration of two hours, and

---

* He had cause for uneasiness, since he must have recollected what he wrote to the Directory after General Bonaparte's departure. I have, moreover, been assured that, after Kleber's death, General Menou found amongst his papers a letter from General Moreau, which left no doubt of the secret understanding carried on between Kleber and that general, for the purpose of subverting the power of the First Consul; but I feel a difficulty in believing it, because General Kleber's death occurred at too early a period to entitle the assertion to credit.

learned that she was on her way from Toulon, with a colonel
on board, who was going to join the army, with dispatches
for the commander-in-chief.

The vessel accordingly landed M. Victor de Latour-Mau-
bourg, who gave us the details of the 18th Brumaire, and
immediately proceeded to join General Kleber at Cairo,
taking the road we had just travelled over : we proceeded on
our way to Alexandria.

When we left General Kleber he was very far from entertaining the slightest suspicion of the deplorable issue which
would, in a few days, terminate the negotiations he had so
hastily ventured upon ; but a bitter disappointment was
shortly to come upon him. The first circumstance mentioned
to us by General Lanusse, who commanded at Alexandria,
and which he had communicated to General Kleber on the
preceding day, unfolded to our view what was likely to occur.
The explanation of this circumstance must be prefaced by an
account of previous occurrences.

The Theseus, after proceeding to Cyprus, for the purpose
of undergoing repairs, had come back to resume its cruising
station off Alexandria, where the passing events had rendered
the communications with that ship more frequent than the
ordinary course of the service occasionally required to be kept
up. The captain of the ship had apprised General Lanusse
that Sir Sidney Smith had sent him Turkish passes, ready
signed, to be delivered to the vessels that might sail from
Egypt in consequence of the treaty of El-Arish, and that he
would give up as many as might be demanded of him.

The officer sent by General Lanusse to return thanks to the
captain of the Theseus, happened to be on board that ship at
the very moment of the arrival before Alexandria of a cutter dispatched from England to Sir Sidney Smith. This
cutter, called the Bull dog, had orders to proceed in all
haste ; and the captain brought instructions and powers to
enable Sir Sidney Smith to treat respecting the evacuation of
Egypt ; but whether the English government was under a

false impression in regard to the position of our army, or a delusion had been created by the successes of the allied armies over our troops in Italy, that government would not grant any other terms to the French army than to be made prisouers of war

Previously to sailing in quest of Sir Sidney Smith in the Archipelago, the commander of the cutter communicated his instructions to the captain of the Theseus, who, by the return of the French officer, sent a corresponding message to General Lanusse. No time was, therefore, left for taking advantage of the treaty of El-Arish, except the interval that would elapse before Sir Sidney Smith could be overtaken by the Bull-dog, and could revoke the first orders he had given to the Theseus, and issue counter orders, the course which it was reasonably apprehended he would adopt.

General Desaix, who was furious at the bare contemplation of the misfortunes which he saw thickening around us, felt the utmost impatience to turn to account the short respite we had left; the rather so, as he felt some apprehension, from all he had witnessed, that Kleber, after having placed himself at the mercy of the English, would submit to all their terms without drawing his sword; whereas no consideration in the world would make him stipulate for the surrender of the army.

. He sent me the next morning on board the Theseus, with directions to do all in my power to remove the difficulties that might be thrown in the way of his departure, owing, perhaps, to the merchandise (belonging to M. Hamelin) shipped on board the vessel in which he intended to return to France: in the contrary case, he would engage another vessel.

I found the captain of the Theseus a very worthy, accommodating man, disposed to follow up the first orders given to him by Sir Sidney Smith, regardless of the non-official communication made to him by the commander of the Bull-dog: he accordingly delivered to me a license for General Desaix, and all those who were to return with him. He even carried his attention so far as to send with me one of the officers of his ship, whom he gave us as a safeguard, and directed to embark in our vessel, and see us safe to France.

I have since had a suspicion that his conduct was not altogether disinterested, and that he would have gone much farther to effect the removal of General Desaix.

I returned to Alexandria, where General Desaix anxiously awaited my return : he seemed much pleased to find that the sea was left open to him, and that he might safely undertake the voyage.

He did not trifle with this piece of good fortune, for he sailed the next day. I break off, for the present, from the account of what relates to General Desaix, and return to General Kleber.

The Bull-dog cutter overtook Sir Sidney Smith, who came back to his station before Alexandria, and wrote to General Kleber, assuring him of the sincere distress he felt at having to communicate to him the conditions upon which his government would alone ratify the treaty of El-Arish.

He admitted, what could no longer be doubted, that he had certainly acted without powers, though under the conviction that his government would approve his conduct; and he had now the mortification to acknowledge that he was mistaken. He entreated General Kleber not to permit what now occurred to prejudice him in his opinion, protesting, as he did, that he was no party to it: this was very credible. The upshot of all this was, that we were under the necessity of giving battle to the Turks as soon as possible, and so crown our past operations by the step which ought to have preceded them.

The battle was fought on the ruins of Heliopolis, in the vicinity of Cairo : the Turks were defeated and dispersed ; but having succeeded in reaching the borders of the desert, they contrived to extend their line of march beyond the right of our army, and threw themselves, in numbers, into Cairo.

Kleber now resumed that character which, for the sake of

his army and of his own glory, he never should have laid aside. In a few days he drove back beyond the deserts of Asia those hordes, which were tenfold more numerous than his own forces, recovered all the places he had imprudently evacuated, and returned to besiege Cairo, where a pacha had taken up his quarters with some thirty thousand men.

It became necessary to carry on a destructive war from house to house, and, in the end, to allow the pacha to retire unmolested, before the latter could be prevailed upon to quit the town, and retreat into Asia with his troops.

No price, however, was too great, that would put an end to a destruction of lives, which, considering the position of the army, was daily proving more fatal in its consequences.

General Kleber was thus compelled, as if against his own will, to remain in Egypt, owing to the folly of his enemies. He candidly admitted his error, and saw that his plan of evacuating Egypt had cost him more men than General Bonaparte had lost in establishing himself in that country, or than he himself would have lost if he had adopted a different course.

His conduct altered from that moment: he no longer deceived himself either as to the opinion he might succeed in impressing upon the government, or the judgment that might be passed respecting what he might have done, what he actually had done, and what he ought not to have done; his endeavours, thenceforward, were directed to the object of repairing the errors he had fallen into; trusting to time and to the magnanimity of General Bonaparte for obliterating every trace of that painful period in his career.

Whilst General Kleber was recovering possession of Egypt General Desaix was crossing the Mediterranean, and was on the point of entering Toulon, when he was taken by an English frigate, which carried him to Leghorn, where Admiral Keith's ship was at anchor. The latter, whose instructions were conformable to those sent to Sir Sidney Smith by the

Bull-dog, declared General Desaix a prisoner, and confiscated the vessel.

General Desaix, who had embarked on the faith of a treaty, with a license, and escorted by an English commissioner, claimed to be taken back to Egypt, if he was not permitted to land in France. Notwithstanding the justice of this demand, a month was suffered to elapse before he was informed that he was at liberty to return to France on board the same vessel, the cargo of which had been previously removed.

CHAPTER XIV.

General Bonaparte's voyage to France—Arrival at Ajaccio—The frigates come in sight of English cruisers—Landing at Fiejus—Sensation created at Lyons by General Bonaparte's arrival—He reaches Paris—State of public affairs.

WE had returned on board this vessel, when another brought us M. Poussielgue, who had also sailed for France. We had left him at Cairo, where he was foremost amongst those who wished for the return of the army to France. We were at a loss to account for the motives which had induced him to hasten his departure from Egypt. He sailed in our company. We steered our course towards Provence, and were almost immediately hailed by an enemy's brig; but being provided with a pass from Admiral Keith, the brig sailed off, and we got into Toulon.

Those who have never left their country cannot know the feeling which is experienced on returning to it after a long absence. We were in a kind of mental aberration for three days, running in every direction, and perfectly restless. General Desaix found it a matter of some difficulty to retain us near his person, for the purpose of copying the dispatches he was writing to General Bonaparte on the subject of past events. We felt no other inclination than to walk in the park of the lazaretto.

General Desaix received by return of courier a reply from General Bonaparte. M. Poussielgue, on the contrary, was left without any; this continued to be the case for the whole duration of the quarantine we had to perform.

I return to General Bonaparte. Having already related how his departure was effected, I come to the details of his voyage.

I have already mentioned that there was no cruiser before Alexandria at the time of his setting sail. He reached Corsica in safety. Being ignorant of the existing state of parties in France, he felt it necessary to obtain intelligence; and yet was at a loss how to elude the quarantine laws: his perplexity was relieved by the impatience of his fellow-countrymen to see him. The report having spread that General Bonaparte was on board, the peasantry and towns-people were desirous of conveying to him the expression of their homage. Yielding to the general enthusiasm, the municipal administration gave way, entered a boat, and proceeded in the direction of the Muiron, thus infringing those laws which it was its special duty to enforce. The quarantine regulations were laid aside. General Bonaparte landed at Ajaccio; but only remained there the time requisite for collecting all necessary information, and resumed his voyage. The ship was in full sail, when Gantheaume came to inform him that enemies' ships were descried from the top-masts, and to receive his orders. General Bonaparte, after reflecting for a moment, desired him to trust wholly to chance until the hour of midnight.

The admiral continued his course towards Toulon. The cruisers were lost sight of in the night, and no vessel appeared in the offing the following morning. The English, who had only to watch Toulon, which no longer contained any

ships of war, and Marseilles, whence supplies were forwarded to the army of Italy, kept within the gulf of Lyons:
their whole squadron had assembled at that station, because those ports were "the only two landing points for
vessels attempting to penetrate into France. The cruisers
off Corsica were on the look-out for vessels endeavouring to
reach that island, but neglected to watch those sailing from
it for the coast of Provence, relying upon the difficulty they
would find in eluding the vigilance of the fleet: this was the
cause of their not giving chase to the two frigates.

General Bonaparte arrived at last within sight of the
French coast, and, fortunately, at the approach of night: the
sun had just set, leaving behind a train of light which was
reflected back by the starry heavens. The frigates, beyond
the reach of this refraction, were in a mixed atmosphere of
light and darkness, growing more intense in proportion as it
receded. From the midst of this light the English squadron
was visible to the naked eye; it consisted of fifteen sail stationed before Toulon, and appeared in the centre of the refraction I have just mentioned.

The sea was calm, indeed, but the frigates were bearing down
upon that squadron:* had it not been for these rays of light,
they would have been in total darkness, and persisted in their
course, and would have most undoubtedly got into the very
midst of the squadron on the springing up of the night
breeze.

The frigates no sooner discovered their danger than they
tacked about; escaped under favour of the night; steered
towards Nice, and reached Frejus the next morning. They
were, at first, mistaken for enemies' ships, and fired upon;

---

* I have since met with officers of the English navy who assured me that the two
frigates had been seen, but were considered by the admiral to belong to his squadron, as they steered their course towards him, and as he knew we had only one
frigate in the Mediterranean, and that one in Toulon harbour. He was far from
supposing that the frigates which he had descried could have General Bonaparte
on board.

but no sooner was it known that General Bonaparte was on board than prolonged acclamations were heard in every direction : had he dropped from the skies, his appearance could not have created more surprise or enthusiasm. The people became frantic with joy, and revolted at the bare mention of quarantine regulations. The board of health, the land and naval officers, all hurried pellmell into the boats : hardly any sea-room was left for the frigates, which were hailed from every quarter : the scene in Corsica was again renewed : public impatience broke through the quarantine laws. It was no longer optional with General Bonaparte to resist the acclamations of a people who welcomed him as their liberator.

The population continued flocking to the shore. He thanked them for the expression of their good wishes, and for their offers of service, and prepared to remove himself from a coast where, under pretence of sanitary precautions, his enemies might detain him, or throw serious obstacles in his way ; he therefore availed himself of the first carriage out of the numbers that were brought to him from all quarters, and took the road to Grenoble.

He travelled night and day. Lyons was intoxicated with joy at his arrival : he alighted at the Hotel of the Celestins. The quays were soon encumbered by crowds rending the air with their acclamations, unable to resist their anxiety to behold him. He repeatedly presented himself before them.

The report of his arrival had spread with the rapidity of lightning. The road from Lyons to Paris was covered with people who were eager to obtain a glimpse of him : he evaded these marks of attention, hastened his journey, and actually arrived at Paris, and reached his residence in the Rue de la Victoire, before the government had been aware of his landing at Frejus.

He proceeded to the Luxembourg the same day. He wore

a grey frock, and a mameluke sabre suspended by a silk-twist in the oriental style. He was recognised as he passed along ; and the report of his arrival spread in an instant from one end of the metropolis to the other. The population flocked in crowds round his hotel : it was a continued scene of hurry and congratulation : all rejoiced at possessing at last the man who was to stop the course of our disasters.

Matters had, in fact, assumed a most deplorable aspect. Massena had undoubtedly arrested the progress of the Russians at Zurich. The English, who had landed in Frieze-land, had been defeated at Castricum, and were preparing to evacuate the continent, a retreat they effected a few days after General Bonaparte's arrival. The external position of the republic had improved ; not so, however, its internal condition. The army of Italy, which had been driven back to the territory of Genoa after repeated defeats, was no longer adequate to protect Provence, now threatened by the Austrians ; the civil war, more animated than at any former period, was spreading its ravages over the western and southern departments ; the power of the law had fallen into abeyance, and the administration was without energy : parties the most opposed in political sentiments had united to overthrow a government so totally lost in public opinion.

Every species of credit was destroyed by this distressing state of affairs. The public funds had fallen to seventeen francs, and yet the only resource of government was in bonds and notes of hand to meet the demands with which it was assailed. From this picture some idea may be formed of the expenses of the war and the public administration : we were arrested by precipices in every direction.

Agents were employed by foreign countries to create disturbances in France, and did so with impunity from the heart of the capital, where they fearlessly carried on their intrigues. There was an end to all secrecy : public measures were no sooner planned than they became the talk of every one. The state was falling to ruins : pillage and corruption seemed the order of the day.

To govern had become impossible; to obey almost un-availing :, there appeared no remedy for the evil; none dared to probe the depth of it. General Bonaparte was the object of every hope and every wish ; all France called loudly for him : he heard the voice ; but it required the genius of such a man not to feel intimidated at the magnitude of the en-terprise.

- The state of dejection was such as to revive the pretensions of the party known by the name of the *faction of Orleans,* which had again conceived the design of raising 'the son of that prince to supreme power : an emissary had, even been sent after him to England, where he resided. His answer was unsatisfactory; he refused to promote his own elevation unless the elder branch of his family were to disclaim all opposition to it; which, under existing circumstances, it was not possible to expect. The faction was far from antici-pating such a scruple. It was not, however, disconcerted by it, and determined to call a prince of the Spanish branch to the throne.

Meanwhile General Bonaparte made his appearance, and that project was abandoned.* The state of uneasiness and uncertainty had disappeared : all wishes and all hopes were settled upon the victor of the Pyramids ; but he could only save France by possessing himself of the supreme authority ; otherwise, it were better that he had never quitted Egypt.

After maturely weighing the internal state of France and its exterior condition, he determined upon the line of conduct to be pursued. The Directory were divided in opinion as to the means to be adopted for averting the storm which threatened to overwhelm them ; a still greater want of

* I obtained these details during my public administration.

unanimity prevailed in the Councils; but the nation retained all its energy. It called for a deliverer who might rescue it from its present condition. A party was easily formed, and a solid basis was found whereupon to rest its efforts. All those who had acted a conspicuous part in the revolution, who had acquired national property, and had to apprehend the wrath of some nobleman, or emigrant of note, naturally found a rallying point in General Bonaparte. I only except from the number a few republicans of extravagant ideas; some popular leaders, men more ambitious in their views than even conquerors; but these ardent minds, besides being considerably reduced in numerical strength, were wholly estranged from public opinion: they had long ceased to be objects of apprehension.

All were agreed as to the necessity of a change in the form of government, and on the importance of effecting that change without delay. Convinced that a temporising conduct could only be attended with danger, General Bonaparte put his hand immediately to the work, and the Directory disappeared. The military men who had been principally distinguished by their career of victories, placed themselves at General Bonaparte's disposal.* The Director Sieyes brought

---

* General Sebastiani is one of the officers of the army of whom I have heard General Bonaparte most lavish of his praise on the occasion of the 18th Brumaire; he was at that time colonel of the 9th dragoons, and had under his orders a thousand men, all of whom had served in Italy. General Bonaparte communicated his project to him previously to sounding the other colonels of the garrison. Sebastiani undertook to bring over a great number of officers who were left by the Directory in a state of want.

On a given signal, Sebastiani was the first to throw away the scabbard, by distributing amongst his dragoons ten thousand ball-cartridges, which were deposited in his house, and could only be delivered upon an order from the commandant of Paris. He directed his regiment to mount, and led it to the Rue de la Victoire, as an escort for General Bonaparte, who was about to proceed to St. Cloud. The general passed through their ranks, and was about to address a few words to the men. " We want no explanation," said these gallant fellows, interrupting him, " we know that you only desire the good of France. You may rely upon us." Other regiments soon followed the example thus set them.

over, to his side the most influential men of both Councils; those, in short, who, wearied of the excesses of the revolution, felt the necessity of placing at the head of affairs a man of sufficient moderation to conciliate all parties, and of sufficient firmness to keep them within proper bounds.

Bournonville, Macdonald, Lefebvre, and Moreau himself, all of whom had embarked in the conspiracy, reckoned as their accomplices not only the generals and administrators of the army of Italy who were then in Paris, but also Chénier, Cabanis, Röderer, Talleyrand, and others. It was a coalition between the flower of the army and the most select members of the philosophic party to accomplish the national wish.

With the exception of Bernadotte, who, at that time, could only see the safety of the state in a republic, and the type of a true republic in jacobinism, all the commanders of the army of Italy rallied round their general. Berthier, Eugene Beauharnais, Duroc, Bessieres, Marmont, Lannes, Lavalette, Murat, Lefebvre, Caffarelli (brother of the general who died in Syria), Merlin (son of the director), Bourrienne, Regnault de Saint-Jean d'Angely, Arnault (of the Institute), the commissary Collot; all gave proofs of zeal and devotedness to the cause: all ranks, down to the twenty-two guides lately arrived from Egypt, were eager to promote it: each one served General Bonaparte in his own way.

Augereau himself, who inwardly detested him, after a short hesitation, decided upon joining his ranks. He perhaps came to offer his services because it was not thought worth while to solicit them. "Do you no longer rely upon your little Augereau?" said he to General Bonaparte. When he saw in the Council of Five Hundred, of which he was a member,

---

Calumny was at work, at a later period, against General Sebastiani, and attempts were made to blacken him in the opinion of his sovereign; but the latter constantly replied: " I shall never forget the 18th Brumaire ; he made me acquainted with my true friends."

that the assembly proposed to outlaw General Bonaparte, he could not help saying, " We are in an awkward position." " We shall get out of it," replied the general. " Dost thou forget Arcole ?" If Augereau's words indicated his fears, I will not allow myself to believe that those which escaped Bernadotte were the echo of his wishes. Meeting General Bonaparte at the moment when he was going to review his troops assembled in the Champs Elysées, "Thou art on the road to the guillotine," said he to him, with his Gascon accent. " We shall see," drily replied General Bonaparte.

I shall rapidly run over the events of the 18th and 19th Brumaire, and lay a stress upon those only of which I can speak with certainty; and merely advert to others when I can present details hitherto unknown, which my official situation enabled me to obtain at a later period.

The Council of Ancients gave the first signal, as agreed upon. M. Lebrun, afterwards third consul, arch-treasurer and Duke of Placentia, made a report upon the deplorable condition of the republic, and the necessity of preventing its ruin by the application of immediate remedies.

The Council adopted his suggestions. It issued a decree, which transferred the Legislative Body to St. Cloud, in order that it might deliberate in a place beyond the influence of the capital. At the same time, it charged General Bonaparte with the execution of this measure, and conferred upon him the command of all the troops in Paris and within its constitutional limits. This decree, sanctioned by the Council of Five Hundred, of which Lucien Bonaparte was the president, was immediately transmitted to General Bonaparte, with an invitation to come and take the oath required by his new functions. The general was not slow in making his appearance : he mounted his horse, passed through Paris in the midst of a group of general officers, who had assembled at his house in expectation of this event, and, surrounded by this warlike escort, he presented himself at the bar of the Council. Having taken the oath, he appointed General Lefebvre, who commanded the Directorial guard, to be his lieutenant, and distributed the other appointments amongst the several generals who accompanied him. Lannes received the command of the guard of the Legislative Body ; Murat was named to that of Saint Cloud; and Moreau to the Luxembourg. Three members of the Directory gave in their resignation. The magisterial body to which they belonged was dissolved by this act, the other two directors not forming the number requisite for deliberating upon state affairs.

The events of the 18th Brumaire had prepared the revolution: it was ended by the event of the 19th; not, however, without some difficulty.

The young heads of the Council of Five Hundred, and the old revolutionary ones of the Council of Ancients, had had leisure to reflect upon what was going forward. The new order of things could not be favourable to the principles professed by either: they concerted the means of resisting it. The course that naturally presented itself was, to rally round the constitution of the year III. It was proposed by Duhesme, one of their most spirited demagogues, that they should each be called upon, by name, to renew the oath to defend it.

This motion was intended to cement the union of the conspirators by fresh bonds, and afford time for the affiliated brethren of the suburbs of Paris to come to the assistance of their party at Saint Cloud.

The proposal was unanimously carried. General Bonaparte must necessarily lose the time which it was Duhesme's object to gain. All that the former had done on the preceding day would be turned against him, unless he came at once to the point: he presented himself before the Council of Ancients, invited it, in a speech full of energy, to take into consideration the turn of the public mind, and the danger with which the country was threatened, and no longer to delay adopting some resolution.

A member of the Council, however, now called upon him to explain himself, to calm the prevailing spirit of uneasiness, and to deny his entertaining the projects ascribed to him, and swear to the constitution. " Does the constitution still exist?" rejoined Bonaparte. Enumerating then all the instances in which it had been violated by the Councils, when they pro-scribed the Directory, and by the Directory, when they pro-scribed the Councils, he added, that twenty conspiracies were at work to substitute a new order of things to that consti-tution, the inadequacy of which was proved by the facts which had occurred; that twenty different parties had urged him to place himself at their head, some with the view of recommencing the revolution, others of giving it a retrograde movement; that he had refused to serve any of them, feeling as he did but one interest, that of preserving the good pro-duced by the revolution: he was aware, he said, that some friends of foreign powers spoke of having him proscribed, but that the person who proposed his outlawry was, perhaps, not far from being placed in that dilemma; that, relying on the justice of his cause and the purity of his motives, he trusted to the Councils, to his friends, and to his good fortune.

He repaired to the Council of Five Hundred, there to make the same communications; but he no sooner appeared in the hall, at the door of which he had left the small mili-tary escort that accompanied him, when the cry was raised of *Down with the tyrant! Let the dictator be outlawed!* He had advanced towards the estrade, where the president, his brother Lucien, was seated. He was surrounded and assailed with threats. One deputy, more impetuous than his colleagues, went so far as to attempt to stab him.* A grenadier of the

* It has been pretended that this assertion was not founded in fact. I have even

guard of the Legislative Body, named Thomé, parried 'the blow with his arm. The soldiers left at the door came to his rescue, and forced the general away from the grasp of those madmen.

. He soon afterwards returned to release Lucien Bonaparte, whom these ungovernable men were endeavouring to compel to put to the vote a decree of proscription against his brother.

General Bonaparte had left the hall to join the troops quartered in the court-yard of the castle, where many deputies had insinuated themselves for the purpose of detaching them from the cause of their chief.

. He arrived in the midst of the troops at the most critical moment : a few minutes later, and all would have been lost. He resolved to accelerate the conclusion of the business ; and addressing an officer of infantry (Captain Ponsard, of the grenadiers of the Legislative Body), who was placed with his soldiers at the entrance gate of the castle-hall : " Captain," said he, "go immediately with your company and disperse that assembly of factious men. They are no longer the representatives of the nation, but wretches who have caused all its misfortunes; go in all haste, and save my brother." Ponsard prepared to move, and had scarcely put his soldiers in motion before he retraced his steps. General Bonaparte thought he hesitated; this was not the fact. Ponsard only wanted to know how he was to proceed in case of resistance. " Employ compulsory means," replied Bonaparte, " even your bayonets." " That is enough, General," rejoined the captain,

heard some countrymen of the deputy's, at whose door the guilt was laid, declare that he was incapable of attempting so rash an act.

The contrary opinion was, however, so prevalent, that he was obliged to retire to Leghorn, whence he made an appeal to the justice of the First Consul. " You know better than any one else," said he, in his letter to him, " how unfounded is the accusation I complain of."

The First Consul gave him no reply ; but I never heard him say that he had noticed the attitude attributed to that deputy. I saw the grenadier honoured for his devoted conduct, and rewarded with a pension, which he only lost in 1815. .

giving him the sword-salute. He ordered his drummers to beat the charge, ascended the principal staircase of the castle in double-quick time, and entered the hall with fixed bayonets. The scene changed in a moment: the tumult subsided, and the tribune was left empty. Those who, some minutes before, appeared the most resolute, gave way to fear. They scaled the windows, leaped down into the garden, and dispersed in all directions.

· General Bonaparte felt averse to employ force; but circumstances required it: had he not adopted that course, he would have been lost, and Bernadotte would have prophesied rightly. Fouché had had an explanation on the subject with Regnault de Saint-Jean d'Angely, from whom, I think, I heard the particulars of the conversation. "Let not your general hesitate," said the minister. "It is better he should bring matters to a point, than allow the jacobins time to rally. He is a lost man if a decree of accusation is carried against him. I answer to him for Paris: let him make sure of Saint Cloud."

These sensible observations were in accordance with the language which this old stager of the revolution had held during the preceding six weeks. Judging, from the complexion of affairs, that the Directory could not stand their ground, he took care not to oppose General Bonaparte's conspiracy. Ready to join it if it succeeded, he was likewise ready to denounce it in case of its failure. He was waiting the result to come to a decision, as was afterwards acknowledged to me by Thurot, then chief secretary of police. "The result," said he, "fixed our determination as to the part we were to take. Had General Bonaparte failed, he and his party would have been brought to the scaffold."

Measures were, in fact, so well taken, and Fouché was so well informed of what was going on at Saint Cloud, that when an order was brought from the general to the different gates, not to allow the fugitives to enter, every direction had already been given: the agents of police had already been twenty minutes on the watch. The minister had shown himself anxious to give to the prevailing party that proof of his attachment.

CHAPTER XV.

Formation of the Consulate—Bonaparte named First Consul—Cambaceres—Lebrun—Alterations effected in the conduct of affairs—Composition of the Ministry—The Vendean Chiefs in Paris—Pacification of La Vendée—George Cadoual.

THIS bold measure having dispersed the opposition, the deputies who were favourable to the growing revolution came to rally round the Council of Ancients. A decree immediately passed for the abolition of the Directory, the adjournment of both Councils, the formation of a Legislative Commission, composed of fifty members, to be drawn in equal numbers from each Council. The next object of attention was to organise the government. Three magistrates were created, who, under the name of consuls, were to exercise supreme power until a new constitution could be formed. General Bonaparte, and the Directors Sieyes and Roger Ducos were elected consuls, all of whom took up their residence at the palace of the Luxembourg, where the public impatience, hitherto restrained whilst the issue of the enterprise was yet doubtful, now broke out in loud acclamations.

A new era now opens for General Bonaparte : his reign dates from this time. *We have a master*, said Sieyes, to whom the man he had deemed his superior only in military matters appeared for the first time in his real character, after he had heard him discuss in council the most intricate questions of government and of general administration.

The new constitution was framed in the course of six weeks : the creation of the three consuls was confirmed ; but a change took place in the individuals appointed to fill those elevated stations.

General Bonaparte was named First Consul, and Messrs. Cambaceres and Lebrun second and third consuls, in the room of Sieyes and Roger Ducos, who became the principal members of the Conservative Senate, where they eventually sank into oblivion.

A great part of all the good that was effected at this important epoch of our political regeneration must be ascribed to the two colleagues of General Bonaparte, the one chosen from amongst the wisest and most enlightened magistrates, the other from the civil administrators who were the most esteemed for their probity and experience. To them belongs the merit of a proper selection of prefects, judges, and administrators, and of all those functionaries, in short, who so effectually seconded the efforts of the First Consul to restore integrity to public affairs and equity to judicial decisions.

The first six months of this new administration were productive of an improvement which an age of endeavours, at another period, would not have brought about. All parties were wearied of anarchy and disorder; and a state of things which promised quiet and security could not fail to receive the utmost support that every one could bestow towards its consolidation.

The internal administration began to run in a proper course; but, on the other hand, the war department was in the most deplorable condition. The First Consul bestowed his special attention to restoring the former pride of our standards. The confusion was such, that the war-minister was unable to furnish an exact statement of the army: he neither knew its strength, the number of corps composing it, nor the stations they respectively occupied. It was found necessary to dispatch officers in search of regiments and depôts. They were directed to ascertain their numerical strength, and immediately transmit that information to the war-minister.

The artillery was likewise in a most inefficient state, and the navy completely disorganised, though still possessing great and available resources.

The finances were in so wretched a condition, that, on the night of the 18th Brumaire, the public chests did not contain wherewith to defray the charge of sending couriers to the armies and principal cities that were to be made acquainted with the event. The first expenses incurred were paid out of funds lent to the public treasury, under conditions which the urgency of the crisis rendered it compulsory to accede to.

The diplomatic body consisted of an envoy from Charles IV., who only resided at Paris on account of the detention of the Spanish fleet in Brest, and of a chargé d'affaires of the Prince of Deux-Ponts, lately become Elector of Bavaria. It should be added, that the latter remained rather on the footing of a private individual, than as an envoy vested with a diplomatic character.

It required a man of the genius of the First Consul not to shrink at so fearful an aspect of public affairs. This complication of difficulties, so far from discouraging him, only tended to inflame his resolution; he placed his glory upon conquering so many obstacles, and he succeeded in the attempt.

The appointments which he made to the ministry were received with general approbation. In his first choice, he had the rare good fortune to fix upon men of mature experience, whose age and habits of business made them readier to the task, and could not fail to command obedience. All were convinced of the necessity of extricating the nation from the embarrassment into which anarchy and corruption had plunged it. All placed their glory in seconding the intentions of the First Consul, who soon discovered that he might rely upon them for bestowing the necessary attention to their respective departments.

His military position became the subject of his meditations.

He wanted men, clothing, and horses; every thing was supplied to him with a generous profusion. An alteration was soon effected in the condition of the armies. When he took the helm of the state large forces were employed to suppress the civil war, a fact which the Directory took care to conceal. He immediately sought the means of taking back to the frontiers an army which had become indispensable to make head against foreign enemies. A pacification did not appear to him impossible. The cruelties of which La Vendée had been the theatre dated from the period of the committees. His administration had not yet dealt in acts of reprisal. The chiefs of the insurgents must necessarily be tired of a war without an object : he resolved to make overtures to them, which, if unsuccessful, could not in any way compromise him. He therefore ordered the commander-in-chief of the western army to open a communication with those chiefs, to propose their coming to Paris, and judge for themselves of the sincerity of the motives which actuated him when he invited them to the capital; and he guaranteed their safe return home, whatever might be their determination at the close of the conference he was desirous of holding with them.

They all complied with the invitation. The First Consul made them no reproaches : he told them that if they had only taken up arms for their personal defence and that of the population of those provinces, they had no longer any motive for continuing the war ; government did not wish to molest any of them ; they had henceforward the same claim to the protection of the laws as those against whom they had fought. If, on the contrary, they had taken up arms to revive the feudal yoke, they should consider that they formed the weakest part of the nation ; that it was not probable they could succeed ; and that it was unjust in them to pretend to dictate laws to the majority.

He added that the successes they had hitherto obtained were greatly owing to the external war in which the country was engaged : they would soon find what little advantage could be derived by them from their allies: as he was on the point of proceeding to place himself at the head of the troops, he pledged his word to afford them a proof of what he said.

These considerations could not fail to make a due impression upon men who, for the most part, had taken arms merely to secure themselves from the vexatious proceedings of a jealous government. They asked one day to consider of the subject ; and all, with the exception of George Cadoual, declared they would submit to a government under which their peace and quiet would not be disturbed. They even offered him the use of those means which they had hitherto employed to resist the anarchical system that was prevalent previously to his coming to power.

They went freely through the streets of Paris, called to see their friends, and returned home to their provinces, where they faithfully kept their word.

George Cadoual presented himself with his colleagues at the audience of the First Consul. The latter spoke to him of the glory he had acquired, the rank he had obtained amongst the notables of his province, and added that he should combine with the high feelings that had contributed to his elevation the feelings of a patriot, who would no doubt be averse to prolonging the misfortunes of the soil on which he was born. He stopped. George, instead of replying, muttered a few words that had more meaning than wit, constantly stood with downcast looks, and concluded by asking for his passport. The First Consul not only had it delivered to him, but ordered him immediately out of Paris; an order which he complied with.*

George Cadoual was born at Aurai, near L'Orient. He was a priest before the revolution, but was held in little repute by the clergy. A dangerous hypocrite, incapable of obedience, ambitious beyond bounds, he detested the nobles just as much as the republicans. Napoleon said with truth that he was a wild beast.

The principal chiefs of La Vendée having made their submission, there remained nothing more than a plundering system of warfare, which was, however, carried to such an extent
as to render the communications hazardous, and at times to
interrupt them altogether.   Men to whom the civil war had
given a martial turn were averse to go back to their labour :
they refused to yield to the invitations of their chiefs, and
continued their roving life.   The excesses they were guilty
of soon made them lose the little consideration they had obtained.   They became a burden to provinces which only
desired repose ; and were accordingly pursued, and delivered
up to the tribunals, who made a severe example of such as
fell into their power.

CHAPTER XVI.

Formation of a camp of reserve at Dijon—M. Necker—Passage of Mont St.
    Bernard—Fort de Bard—Arrival of the First Consul at Milan—Action of
    Montebello—General Desaix joins the First Consul.

THE First Consul had succeeded in restoring peace in the
interior ; he had re-established order in the administration,
and subjected to the fiscal laws whole provinces, which, ever
since the commencement of our civil dissensions, had ceased
to pay taxes.   A still more important result of his measures,
considering the circumstances of the time, was his being able
to dispose at once of eighty thousand veteran soldiers, whom
the Directory had kept stationary in La Vendée, to whose
absence from active service was principally to be attributed
the ill success of our arms.

He was, however, gifted with great moral and physical courage, and was not altogether deficient in abilities. Upon the whole, he was deserving of a better fate.

According to the most correct estimates, that cruel intestine war was attended with the loss of upwards of half a million of human beings: all were Frenchmen; and whilst some were put to death in the name of a God of peace, and at the foot of His very altars, others were offered up in sacrifice to liberty. Who can tell where these sanguinary executions would have stopped had not the 18th Brumaire arrested their progress?

Rejoiced at having put an end to a war of extermination, of which it was impossible to foretell what might have been the consequence, the First Consul marched his troops towards Dijon, where he had just ordered a camp to be formed.

He had made an appeal to all military men who had been driven from their standards by the blunders of the Directory. Wonderful to relate! his name operated as a spell to bring them back : not one remained behind, except such as were, from unavoidable causes, prevented from obeying the call.

The cavalry was in a most inefficient state; the greater part of the regiments were reduced to skeletons, and dismounted. A requisition was made for horses, at the rate of one in every twenty, which was afterwards reduced to one in every thirty. They were collected from all parts of France, furnished without murmur, and delivered into the depôts on a stated day. The army was seen, as if by magic, to spring up into a new existence, and present as fine an appearance as in the glorious days of our history. Such were the first results of the confidence reposed in General Bonaparte: he was indispensable to France; and France proved to him that she felt him to be so.

These gigantic measures, accomplished in so short a time, excited the more surprise, as their course had almost been unperceived : every thing had been planned and meditated in secret; the execution of the design followed with the rapidity of thought.

No one in France could imagine out of what elements the

army that was assembling at Dijon was composed : it was
believed to exist upon paper only, because the materials were
nowhere to be seen. The Austrians, being masters of all
Italy, had, doubtless, neglected no means by which they might
be informed of what was going forward beyond the Alps,
which they hoped to force, as soon as they should have taken
Genoa, to which city they were laying siege ; but what was
going on at Dijon was as little known to them as it was in
Paris. The spies they kept up in that capital can have
transmitted none but satisfactory reports, since they continued
their operations before Genoa.

They were not aware that La Vendée was pacified, nor
that it could offer so many resources to the First Consul ;
because the Directory had been on their guard never to
acknowledge that they found it necessary to employ such a
numerous army for the purpose of repressing the disturbances.

The First Consul did not allow the enemy time to become
acquainted with the progress which he had made, or the plans
which he meditated. As he directed every thing in person,
he knew the day on which the troops set in motion were to
arrive at Dijon. He repaired unexpectedly to the spot ;
only stayed the time requisite to see that his orders had been
carried into effect ; to ascertain the numbers of his soldiers ;
to examine into every thing, with a minuteness of detail
hitherto unknown ; and send the army forward, whilst he
completed, during the march, the organization that was still
wanting to it.

He advanced towards the Great Saint Bernard, by way of
Geneva, where he received a visit from M. Necker, who
immediately proceeded to communicate to him his own ideas
of administration, of a constitution, &c. ; but the First Consul
had already his hands full ; added to which, he did not relish
the conversation of the financier. I have heard him say, at
a late period, that it seemed to him like the dissertations of a

man desirous of linking himself to his fortune; but that his opinion had long been fixed respecting that minister, whose talents did not appear to him to accord with the celebrity which he had obtained. The fame, however, which he acquired has nothing surprising in it, he added, so limited was the practical knowledge, in matters of finance and administration, in the days of his power.

The First Consul crossed the Saint Bernard on a handsome mule, belonging to a rich landed proprietor in the valley; he had for a guide a young athletic peasant, whose communicative disposition he felt pleasure in encouraging. "What wouldst thou require to be made happy?" he asked him, as they were reaching the top of the mountain. "My fortune would be made," replied the unpretending countryman, "if I were owner of the mule you are riding." The First Consul smiled, and when the campaign was over, and he had returned to Paris, he ordered the purchase of the finest mule that could be found, added to it a house and a few acres of land, and desired that his guide might be put in possession of that little fortune. The worthy peasant, who had already forgotten his adventure, learned then, for the first time, the name of the person he had guided over the Saint Bernard.

The First Consul had taken the most minute precautions to maintain order amongst the several corps, during a march of so painful a nature as that which they were performing across the Alps, and to prevent the men of weak constitution from quitting the columns to which they belonged. Independently of what the soldier carried about his person, he had caused a large supply of provisions to be collected at the monastery, on the summit of the Great Saint Bernard. Each soldier, on passing it, received from the religious community a large piece of bread, some cheese, and a tumbler of wine. The bread and cheese were ready cut; the wine was poured out according as the troops filed past the monastery. Never did greater regularity preside at a distribution. Each one appreciated the foresight of which he had been the object. Not a soldier left the ranks; not a straggler was to be seen.

The First Consul expressed his gratitude to the community, and ordered 100,000 francs to be delivered to the monastery, in remembrance of the service it had rendered him.

It would require an abler pen than mine to record the courageous efforts made to transport over the Alps the artillery and ammunition that followed the army. It seemed as if the conquest of Italy was an object of personal interest to each soldier. All were ambitious of acting a conspicuous part in so noble an undertaking. So great was the ardour displayed, that the First Consul found, on the following morning, fifty pieces of cannon fixed to their carriages, at the foot of the mountain, together with their caissons, and the requisite ammunition, which had been brought over on the backs of mules. The horses were put to the gun-carriages, all in readiness to proceed.

He stopped to signify his satisfaction to the gunners, and thank them for the zeal they had shown, and then granted them a reward of 1,200 francs; but the sacred fire of glory had inspired these gallant fellows; they declined the grant. "We have not worked for money, said they; do not force us to take any. We will afford you many opportunities of rewarding us for what we have done."

The army having descended from the Saint Bernard, entered the valley of Ivrée, and arrived before the Fort de Bard. The road runs under the glacis. This defile is full of danger for an army, and quite impracticable for artillery.

The time was too valuable, on the other hand, to be lost before a wretched fort, which had only a weak garrison, although it was commanded by an officer fully determined to do his duty. He felt all the importance of the post confided to him, and would listen to no proposal. It became necessary to make the cavalry and infantry file off through by-paths hardly accessible to goats.

The gunners, on their side, found no other means of eluding the vigilance of the Austrians than placing straw round the wheels of their gun-carriages and caissons, and thus rolling them along during the night, until they reached the spot to which the horses had been led.

Every thing was managed in such perfect silence, that the garrison heard no noise, though the passage was effected at pistol-shot distance from the covered way. All who were employed in this dangerous transport were fully sensible that silence and promptitude were equally necessary : every thing accordingly went on as well as could be desired.

The Austrians were far from suspecting an invasion of Italy from this quarter, and had not, therefore, made any defensive preparations. Ivrée was without a garrison; and that town, which might have arrested our progress for some days, opened its gates as soon as our advanced-guard appeared before it. We made it our first strong-hold.

The First Consul, who was in all the ardour of his opening career, anxiously urged the army forward. His mind embraced, at one and the same time, the various objects of securing advantageous positions, recovering at once the ascendancy he formerly held, and presenting himself in the commanding attitude which public opinion confers, upon a theatre where the fate of Italy was about to be decided. He accelerated his movements, and entered Milan, whilst that city was yet in ignorance of his having left Dijon. The Italians, struck with amazement, could not believe that he was amongst them : this doubt was soon dispelled, and they were not long in declaring for us.

The Austrian line of operations was intercepted : no time was lost in stopping the post, containing amongst the correspondence a variety of information of the highest importance.

Having seized the letters coming from Vienna to the Austrian army, and those on their way from the army to Vienna, the First Consul ascertained, the very night of his arrival, the extent of the reinforcements on their way to Italy, and the exact state of the army besieging Genoa, and of its park of artillery and hospitals. The war-minister of the Emperor of Austria could not have furnished a statement more complete than what the First Consul became possessed of.

He had, in a few hours, acquired a knowledge of every thing he was desirous of learning respecting the actual position of the Austrians in Italy. Other secrets were revealed to him by a correspondence which came from Genoa. He saw that the town still held out, but that it was in the utmost distress. A fresh occurrence completed the information he stood in need of previously to embarking upon ulterior undertakings. A courier was stopped on his way with dispatches from Vienna to the Baron de Melas, who held the chief command of the Austrian army in Italy. What was still obscure in the political horizon was cleared up by these dispatches. Strange, indeed, was the position of General Bonaparte, perusing at Milan the dispatches written by the Austrian government to the commander of its army, and the reports of the latter to his government. The First Consul was considering what part he should act, when another courier, sent by M. de Melas to Vienna, was brought to him. He ascertained from his dispatches that Genoa was on the point of falling; that it still resisted, indeed, but was expected very shortly to surrender.

The courier was also the bearer of an account of the state of the army; and had orders for the depôts, the field-equipages, and the parks of artillery in the rear. Information so opportunely afforded was not thrown away, and troops were sent to take possession of all the *materiel* which was now discovered to be so near at hand.

The First Consul had just ordered the castle of Milan to be invested: he had detached two bodies of troops, the one upon Brescia, the other upon the citadel of Turin. He marched upon Pavia, to which he removed his head-quarters. The pontoon train was seized in this place, and, joined to the trading boats, it afforded the means of crossing the Po. He detached troops towards Parma and Placentia, and advanced in person with those that were to cross at Pavia.

The passage was effected by General Lannes at the head of the 6th light infantry, who concealed themselves amongst the bushes on the opposite bank; and the bridge was soon formed with all the activity displayed by Frenchmen in carrying forward any measure calculated to promote their success. The bridge was soon completed. The First Consul made the army instantly cross over to the other side, and took the road from Stradella to Montebello, along which his troops were advancing.

Fortune again supplied him, on this march, with fresh information respecting the enemy's position. An Austrian officer, bearer of a flag of truce, was brought to him at his advanced posts: he was escorted by an officer of Massena's staff, charged to transmit to him the terms of the capitulation of Genoa. This officer informed him how great was the delusion still entertained by the Austrians respecting his march and the forces under his orders.

They had taken possession of Genoa with great pomp, and according to the forms of the most rigid etiquette. General Melas was, indeed, aware that the French had entered Italy by Ivrée; but he refused to believe the reports of their numbers, and had merely sent a strong detachment to watch the banks of the river.

Having left Genoa after that corps of troops, the officer had overtaken it, and succeeded in estimating its strength, which he stated to General Bonaparte, as well as the distance at which he had parted from it. He also informed the First Consul that the Austrian army had pushed no detachment upon Parma and Placentia: those which we had sent in that direction became accordingly useless, and were recalled ; but, without waiting their return, the army marched to meet the Austrians.   The action took place at Montebello : it was ex- tremely brilliant; and, at a later period, General Lannes, who became a Marshal of France, received his title from it as Duke of Montebello.

The Austrians being defeated, were compelled to retrace their steps, and give the alarm to M. de Melas, who had but just taken possession of Genoa.   This corps was closely fol- lowed ; and after the action of Montebello the contending armies kept in sight of each other.

The First Consul was returning from the field of battle when he met General Desaix.   Previously to proceeding to Dijon, he had written to desire he would join him in Italy, unless he preferred waiting for him in Paris, after he should have performed quarantine.   General Desaix, however, was no sooner released from it than he took the road to Italy. He reached the Isére, passed through Chamberry, the Taren- taise, the Little Saint Bernard, and descended into the valley along the track of the army.   He at last arrived in sight of Stradella, where he overtook General Bonaparte.   The First Consul received him with marked distinction, made him mount his horse, and took him to his quarters, where they remained together that night.   General Bonaparte was most eager to obtain details of all that had taken place in Egypt since his departure. They did not separate until daybreak. I was, for my part, extremely anxious for General Desaix's return. His absence was so long delayed, that excessive fatigue at last closed my eyes, and I was sound asleep when he came back. He awoke me, and said, amongst other things, that General Bonaparte had already taken up his residence at the Luxem- bourg when the letters written by General Kleber and M. Poussielgue to the Directory arrived : they were put into his own hands, and, upon reading them, he was no longer sur- prised at the blunders committed after his departure. His safe 'arrival in France, added he, and especially the successes that attended him, had been unexpected ; but he was not at a loss to discover the feeling which dictated those letters, or the object they were intended to effect.

We could then account for the silence he had observed towards M. Poussielgue : he was still feelingly alive to the recollection of the correspondence of that administrator with the Directory.

He did not, however, persist in his rancour ; for, at a later period, on the proposal of the minister of finance to employ him in forming a scale of the distribution of the land-tax, the First Consul, having become Emperor, gave him the place of inspector in that administration; thus affording a fresh proof that no one was more disposed to forget personal injuries than General Bonaparte.

The First Consul determined to avail himself immediately of General Desaix's services : he formed a corps, composed of the two divisions of Generals Boudet and Monnier, and placed it under his orders.

CHAPTER XVII.

Arrival of Melas at Alexandria—The First Consul is fearful of his escaping him by the road of Novi—Battle of Marengo—It is lost until four o'clock—Ma-nœuvres by means of which we recover from our first defeat--Death of Desaix —The Austrian army retreats towards the Adige.

M. DE MELAS had at last gone through all the formalities incidental to the occupation of Genoa, and brought his army back under the citadel of Alexandria : he had descended the country by the Boquetta, and was informed, on his arrival, of the defeat of the corps which he had ordered to oppose our crossing the Po.

His position was rendered complicated from another circumstance. The army that surrounded Genoa was on the eve of returning into line, the period fixed by the capitulation for the resumption of hostilities having now arrived. He was incurring the danger of a double attack in his front and rear at the same time.

He might have moved by way of Turin. The First Consul was even apprehensive, for a moment, that he would march upon that capital, and hastened to advance towards Alexandria, in order to draw nearer to the theatre of war. We met at Voghera some Austrian flags of truce, whose particular mission appeared to be that of ascertaining if our army was really marching upon them. The First Consul had them detained whilst the army was filing before them. He appeared desirous of their seeing General Desaix, who was personally known to one of the party, and he afterwards dismissed them.

We continued our march. Tortona was still occupied by the Austrians. We left this town on our left, and proceeded to cross the Scrivia, at Castel-Seriolo. Boudet's division, followed by General Desaix, was the only one which, bearing to the right, filed along the hill, and crossed the river above Tortona, in order to take up a position at Rivalta. The First Consul so little expected that M. de Melas would march boldly to meet him, that he was apprehensive lest that general should manœuvre to avoid an action which could only turn to his disadvantage. This idea was so strongly impressed upon his mind, that he ordered General Desaix, during the night, to send a detachment towards Novi, for the purpose of ascertaining whether the enemy was not filing along that road to reach the banks of the Po.

This reconnoitring movement was committed to my charge. I pushed on as far as Novi: no detachment had made its appearance; and I returned to Rivalta in the night preceding the 15th June.

The First Consul had employed the 14th in reconnoitring

the banks of the Bormida. He had satisfied himself that, independently of the bridge which the enemy possessed upon that river, and in advance of Alexandria, they had another much lower down, upon our right flank.

He had given orders that all the enemy's troops which had crossed the river should be driven back to the other side, and that a bridge so likely to be fatal to us should be destroyed at whatever cost, expressing at the same time his intention of repairing in person to the spot, if circumstances required his presence. Colonel Lauriston, one of his aides-de-camp, was directed to watch the operation, and not to return until it had been accomplished.

The action began ; a cannonading was kept up the whole day ; but the enemy stood his ground ; it was found impossible to make him break up the bridge. The First Consul, who was exhausted with fatigue, either did not hear or misunderstood the intelligence brought back by his aide-de-camp ; for Lauriston, whom he often reproached afterwards with giving him a false ground of security, as often replied, that so far from having to charge himself with so serious a fault, he had, on the contrary, hastened to inform him that it was found impossible to execute his orders. Lauriston was too well aware of the importance of that bridge to inform him of its having been destroyed without having personally ascertained the fact.

The First Consul had remained until a late hour visiting his lines. He was just returning when the report was brought to him of the reconnoitring I had effected as far as Novi. He did me the honour to tell me, at a later period, that he had found it difficult to persuade himself that the Austrians had not attempted to escape him by a road which was not watched, and which offered them a more secure retreat, since it removed them to a greater distance from Massena, who had resumed hostilities.

This omission appeared the more improbable to him from

the circumstance that, having remained on horseback, with his vedettes, a great part of the night, he had seen but very few fires in the enemy's lines. He had no longer doubted that the Austrians had made a movement; and he had ordered General Desaix to advance to Novi with Boudet's division before daylight.*

We immediately got under arms, quitted the position of Rivalta, and marched upon Novi; but the day had scarcely begun to dawn when we heard a repeated firing of cannon at a distance in the rear of our right. We were in a flat country, and could only perceive a little smoke. General Desaix was astonished at these reports, stopped the march of his division, and ordered me to proceed in all haste and reconnoitre Novi. I took with me fifty horsemen, put them at full speed upon the road, and soon reached the spot to which I was sent. Every thing was quiet and just as I had left it on the preceding day; no troops had yet made their appearance. I galloped back with my detachment, and rejoined General Desaix.

I had been only two hours absent on the commission entrusted to me. It might have an influence over the combinations of the day. I hastened to announce to the First Consul that all was quiet at Novi, that General Desaix had suspended his movement, and was waiting for fresh orders. The firing of cannon increased every movement. I felt anxious to reach the First Consul, and rode across the fields in the direction of the fire and smoke. I was spurring my horse on at full speed, when I fortunately met an aide-de-camp of the commander-in-chief, named Bruyère, who became afterwards one of our most gallant generals of cavalry, and was killed in the Saxon campaign of 1813. He was the bearer of an order to General Desaix to hasten to the

---

* The second division of General Desaix, commanded by General Monnier, had been directed on the preceding day towards Castel-Seriolo, on the right of the army.

field of battle, where the necessity for his return was so urgent, that the aide-de-camp had, like myself, quitted the road and cut across the country in order to come up the sooner with us. I pointed out where he would find General Desaix, and ascertained from him where I could meet the First Consul. The following is a statement of what had taken place.

General Bonaparte, fancying that the lower bridge on the Bormida had been destroyed, had not altered the position of his army, which passed the night from the 13th to the 14th on the causeway leading from Tortona to Alexandria, the right in advance of Castel-Seriolo, and the left in the plain of Marengo. General Desaix was in reserve at Rivalta, and the head-quarters were at Gorrofolo.

We had left in our rear the town of Tortona, which was occupied by an Austrian garrison, and we had therefore been compelled to make our line of operations pass through Castel-Seriolo.

The First Consul was waiting for the corps he had recalled from Parma and Placentia, as well as the one lately engaged in the siege of the Fort de Bard, of which we had just obtained possession. The latter corps was advancing by Pavia, the others by Stradella and Montebello; but neither of those corps had yet joined us.

The position of the army was far from encouraging: it had an enemy in front, who had been reduced to the necessity of making every sacrifice to force his way; it was, moreover, weak, and spread over a large surface of ground: it required all the genius of the First Consul to turn such untoward circumstances to good account. Any other general, even one of no ordinary talents, would undoubtedly have lost the battle we were compelled to accept the next morning.

Our right had been assailed, at daybreak of the 14th of June, by a numerous cavalry, which had debouched across the bridge we ought to have destroyed on the preceding day:

the charge was made with so much fury and rapidity, that in a few moments we suffered an enormous loss in men, horses, and *materiel*.   This part of the army was in complete disorder, though the battle could hardly be said to have commenced. The corps rallied again, but felt during the whole day the effect of that untoward onset.   The disorder was not confined to the defeated troops; those which supported them had caught the alarm at seeing the charge of this numerous body of cavalry, and communicated the panic in all directions.   The First Consul was soon apprised of the check : it was the first report he had received that day.   He concealed the mortification he felt at a misfortune which was owing to the lower bridge on the Bormida not having been destroyed, according to the repeated orders he had given on the preceding day. He had mounted his horse to see what was going forward, when the whole line was attacked on the road of Alexandria. M. de Melas, resolved to force his way through our battalions, had led his army during the night into a position beyond the Bormida : it had formed in front of us, but had not lighted any fires : we did not perceive that those lines had greatly increased.

Their opening attack was a most brilliant one : the Austrians had made it on all points at the same time, and were every where successful : our centre was penetrated, and put to the rout : the left was still more roughly handled.

The shock was most destructive.   The wounded formed, in their retreat, a thick, lengthened column, whose retrograde movement favoured the flight of some pusillanimous soldiers, frightened at an attack as desperate as it was unexpected. The rout had begun ; a desperate charge of cavalry would have completed it.   Had this charge been made, the battle would have been infallibly lost.

The danger grew more pressing at every moment.   The First Consul ordered the troops to give way; and, on rallying, to draw nearer to the reserves he had been collecting between Gorrofolo and Marengo. He stationed his guard behind this small village, dismounted, and placed himself at its head, on the right of the high road. His maps were spread open: he was studying them when I came up with him: he had just ordered the general who commanded his left to send him the few troops that remained uninjured. He was already planning the movement that was to decide the action which he had not foreseen, and which was terminating in so unsuccessful a manner. His left had suffered too much to be of any use to him, since he could not reinforce it. He drew off the few sound troops that still remained of it, and moved them to the centre.

In this state of things, no intelligence could be more acceptable than that of which I was the bearer. He no longer attached any importance to Novi; for it was clear the Austrians had not marched in that direction. Instead of wasting time in a useless march, General Desaix had made a halt: he might reasonably consider that his troops were amongst those that would have to decide the fate of the battle.

" At what hour did you leave him?" said the First Consul, pulling out his watch; at such an hour, I replied. " Well, he cannot be far off; go and tell him to form in that direction (pointing with his hand to a particular spot): let him quit the main road, and make way for all those wounded men who would only embarrass him, and perhaps draw his own soldiers after them."

I hastened to overtake General Desaix, who, informed by Bruyère of the danger in which the army was placed, had cut across the country, and was at the distance of only some hundred paces from the field of battle. I communicated to him my orders, which he carried into effect, and rode up to the First Consul, who explained to him how matters had come to their present pass, and what he contemplated to do as soon as his division should have formed into line.

Our right had been quickly rallied ; the centre, reinforced

VOL. I. *Part* I. M

by the troops withdrawn from the left, had recovered its strength; General Desaix's division formed the extreme left of that centre, and marched in advance of the troops that were about to enter into action. As to our left, it no longer existed.

After dispatching his orders, the First Consul directed the whole army to wheel its front upon the left wing of its centre, moving its right wing forward at the same time. By this movement he effected the double object of turning all the enemy's troops who had continued the pursuit of our broken left wing, and of removing his right to a distance from the bridge which had proved so fatal to it in the morning. There is no accounting for the motive which the general commanding the left of the Austrian army may have had for neglecting to prevent so decisive a movement; but whether he did not anticipate it, or waited for orders, he merely sent some bodies of cavalry to intercept our retreat, not deeming it possible that we could have any other object in view than to secure it. Though placed in such a position as to enable him to dispute, with doubtful success at least, the First Consul's manœuvre, he did not even attempt to obstruct it.

Whilst General Desaix was engaged in conversation with the First Consul the Austrians had not been inactive. Their march had been so rapid, that, when he rejoined his corps, he found them already firing upon his rear: he sent skirmishers against them, and hastened to make his arrangements. His troops, to the number of nine battalions, were ranged upon three lines, a little to the rear of the small village of Marengo, close to the high road from Tortona to Alexandria. The First Consul had deprived General Desaix of his artillery in order to unite it to the artillery of the guard, and thus form an overwhelming battery in the centre.

It was now three o'clock: very few musket-shots were heard: the two armies were manœuvring, and preparing for a last effort.

General Desaix's division occupied the point which came nearest in contact with the enemy, who were advancing in close, deep columns along the road from Alexandria to Tortona, leaving the latter town on their left. They had nearly come up to us, and we were only separated by a vineyard lined by the ninth light infantry, and a small corn-field, which the Austrians were entering. We were not more than a hundred paces apart, and could distinguish each other's features. The Austrian column halted on perceiving Desaix's division, the position of which became so unexpectedly known to them. The direction of its march would infallibly bring it upon the centre of our first line. It was no doubt endeavouring to ascertain our strength previously to opening its fire. The position was becoming every moment more critical. " You see how matters stand," said Desaix to me; " I can no longer put off the attack without danger of being myself attacked under disadvantageous circumstances: if I delay. I shall be beaten, and I have no relish for that. Go then in all haste and apprise the First Consul of the embarrassment I experience; tell him I cannot wait any longer; that I am without any cavalry,* and that he must direct a bold charge to be made upon the flank of that column, whilst I shall charge it in front "

. I set off at full gallop, and overtook the First Consul, who was causing the troops placed to the right of the village of Marengo to execute the change of front which he had directed along the whole line. I delivered my message to him, and after listening to it with attention, he reflected a moment, and addressed me in these words: " Have you well examined the column?" "Yes, General (he went by this title at the time I speak of)." "Is it very numerous?" "Extremely so, General." "Is Desaix uneasy about it?" " He only appeared uneasy as to the consequences that might

* He had no more than two hundred hussars of the first regiment.

result from hesitation.   I must add his having particularly
desired I should tell you that it was useless to send any
other orders than that he should attack or retreat—one or the
other; and the latter movement would be at least as hazardous as the first."

   " If this be the case," said the First Consul, "let him attack :
I shall go in person to give him the order.   You will repair
yonder (pointing to a black spot in the plain), and there find
General Kellermann, who is in command of that cavalry you
now see ; tell him what you have just communicated to me,
and desire him to charge the enemy without hesitation as soon
as Desaix shall commence his attack.   You will also remain
with him, and point out the spot through which Desaix is to
debouch ; for Kellermann does not even know that he is with
the army."

   I obeyed, and found Kellermann at the head of about six
hundred troopers, the residue of the cavalry which had been
constantly engaged the whole day.   I gave him the orders
from the First Consul.   I had scarcely delivered my message
when a fire of musketry was heard to proceed from the left
of the village of Marengo; it was the opening attack of
General Desaix.   He rapidly bore down with the 9th light
regiment upon the head of the Austrian column : the latter
feebly sustained the charge ; but its defeat was dearly purchased, our general having fallen at the very first firing.   He
was riding in the rear of the 9th regiment, when a shot
pierced his heart : he fell at the very moment when he was
deciding the victory in our favour.

   Kellermann had put himself in motion as soon as he heard
the firing.   He rushed upon that formidable column, penetrated it from left to right, and broke it into several bodies.
Being assailed in front, and its flanks forced in,* it dispersed,
and was closely pursued as far as the Bormida.

---

* General Berthier had a picture painted of this battle.   The painter, who is a

The large masses of troops that were in pursuit of our left no sooner perceived this defeat than they retreated, and attempted to reach the bridge in front of Alexandria; but the corps of Generals Lannes and Gardanne had accomplished their movement: those masses had no longer any communication with each other, and were compelled to lay down their arms.

The battle, which until mid-day had turned against us, was completely won at six o'clock.

As soon as the Austrian column was dispersed I quitted General Kellermann's cavalry, and was returning to meet General Desaix, whose troops were debouching in my view, when the colonel of the 9th light regiment informed me that he had been killed. I was at the distance of only a hundred paces from the spot where I had left him: I hastened to it, and found the general stretched upon the ground completely stripped of his clothes, and surrounded by other naked bodies. I recognised him, notwithstanding the darkness, owing to the thickness of his hair, which still retained its tie.

I had been too long attached to his person to suffer his body to remain on this spot, where it would have been indiscriminately buried with the rest.

I removed a cloak from under the saddle of a horse lying dead at a short distance, and wrapped General Desaix's body in it, with the assistance of an hussar, who had strayed on the field of battle, and joined me in the performance of this mournful duty. He consented to lay it across his horse, and to lead the animal by the bridle as far as Gorrofolo, whilst I should go to communicate the misfortune to the First Consul, who desired me to follow him to Gorrofolo, where I gave him

military officer, is unquestionably a man of talent; but, following up the rules of his art, he has removed the charge to the right flank of the column, whereas it took place on its left. This does not affect the merit of the painting; and I only make the observation in adherence to historical truth.

an account of what had taken place. He approved what
I had done, and ordered the body to be carried to Milan for
the purpose of being embalmed.

· Being only an aide-de-camp to General Desaix at the
battle of Marengo, my personal observations were limited to
what the duties of that situation enabled me to see ; whatever
else I have mentioned was related to me by the First Consul,
who felt a pleasure in recurring to the events of this action,
and often did me the honour to tell me what deep uneasiness
it had given him until the moment when Kellermann executed the charge, which wholly altered its aspect.

After the fall of the Imperial government some pretended
friends of General Kellermann have presumed to claim for
him the merit of originating the charge of cavalry. That
general, whose share of glory is sufficiently brilliant to
gratify his most sanguine wishes, can have no knowledge of
so presumptuous a pretension. I the more readily acquit
him, from the circumstance that, as we were conversing one
day respecting that battle, I called to his mind my having
brought to him the First Consul's orders, and he appeared
not to have forgotten that fact. I am far from suspecting
his friends of the design of lessening the glory of either
General Bonaparte or General Desaix : they know, as well
as myself, that there are names so respected that they can
never be affected by such detractions ; and that it would be as
vain to dispute the praise due to the chief who planned the
battle, as to attempt to depreciate the brilliant share which
General Kellermann had in its successful result. I will add
to the above a few reflections.

From the position which he occupied General Desaix
could not see General Kellermann : he had even desired me
to request the First Consul to afford him the support of some
cavalry. Neither could General Kellermann, from the point
where he was stationed, perceive General Desaix's division :
it is even probable that he was not aware of the arrival

of that general, who had only joined the army two days before. Both were ignorant of each other's position, which the First Consul was alone acquainted with ; he alone could introduce harmony into their movements ; he alone could make their efforts respectively conduce to the same object.

The fate of the battle was decided by Kellermann's bold charge : had it, however, been made previously to General Desaix's attack, in all probability it would have had a quite different result. Kellermann appears to have been convinced of it, since he allowed the Austrian column to cross our field of battle, and extend its front beyond that of the troops we had still in line, without making the least attempt to impede its progress. The reason of Kellermann's not charging it sooner was, that it was too serious a movement, and the consequences of failure would have been irretrievable ; that charge, therefore, could only enter into a general combination of plans to which he was necessarily a stranger.

The check recently suffered by the Austrian army was too severe not to be attended with disastrous consequences. General Melas had consumed that time in fighting which he ought to have employed in regaining the Po by way of Turin and Placentia. The favourable opportunity was lost, and that object was no longer attainable.

Massena, having been reinforced by the small corps commanded by General Suchet,* had re-entered Piedmont, and might look forward to obtain successes over a defeated army like that of M. de Melas. Ours, on the contrary, was intoxicated with its victory, and ardently desired to give the Austrians a finishing blow. Had M. de Melas hesitated in coming to some resolution, he would have been irretrievably destroyed.

He was in a disagreeable position, more particularly after his triumphant entry into Genoa. He was compelled, how-

* Suchet had the command of some battalions on the Var, with which he had covered Provence during the siege of Genoa.

ever, to submit to necessity, and have recourse to negotiations. He sent a flag of truce to the head-quarters at Gorrofolo. General Zach, the chief of his staff, was still there.
Having been taken prisoner on the preceding day, he had held
a long conversation with the First Consul; and was acquainted with the desire felt by the latter for peace, and with
his intention not to make a bad use of his victory, by imposing
conditions upon the Austrian army which their honour would
compel them to reject.

General Bonaparte proposed that he should go and acquaint M. de Melas with his intentions. M. Zach accepted
the proposal: he departed with the flag of truce, joined his
commander-in-chief, and hastened back to report that the
latter accepted the bases transmitted to him. General Berthier immediately repaired to Alexandria, and concluded
with M. de Melas a convention, in virtue of which the latter
engaged to retire behind the Adige by filing off through our
ranks: he was also to evacuate the fortified towns of Piedmont, and restore to our possession those of Italy as far as
the Mincio. This convention having been ratified, the First
Consul took his departure for Milan, and left to General
Berthier the care of seeing it carried into effect. Some
difficulties arose with respect to the article relating to Genoa.
Massena had received orders to occupy that city, which had
been only a few days out of his possession. He demanded it
back of the Prince of Hohenzollern, who had been left as its
governor by General Melas with a large body of troops. The
prince, feeling wounded at such an act of humiliation,
refused to comply. Massena made his report of this untoward event; but the Austrian army had already quitted
Alexandria to repair to the Adige. The question was a delicate one. Nevertheless, as the stipulations were quite positive, as the Prince of Hohenzollern's corps formed part of the
army which was to evacuate Italy, and as Genoa was one of
the cities the restoration of which was agreed upon, it became

the duty of M. de Melas to put an end to the opposition lately raised : he acted on the occasion with a frankness which did him honour; he summoned the prince to obey, and declared, that if he persisted in his refusal, he should abandon him and his troops to the consequences that must be the result of his obstinacy. Being summoned in so peremptory a manner, Hohenzollern dared not persist in disowning the capitulation ; he delivered up the city, and followed the road taken by the Austrian army.

CHAPTER XVIII.

The author is appointed aide-de-camp to the First Consul—Return of the First Consul to France—Joy displayed by the women of Dijon—The postmaster of Montereau—Rejoicings in the capital—Carnot—Causes of his dismissal—Formation of various establishments.

THE First Consul had desired General Duroc to tell me, at Gorrofolo, that I was to follow him to Milan, and that he would take care of me. This accorded with my wishes, and I took my departure in his suite.

We met on our road the divisions of Generals Chahran, Duhesme, and Loison, which were arriving from Bard, Parma, and Placentia: they were only a day's march in the rear. The Consul stopped, reviewed them, and continued his journey.

I had ridden in one day from Gorrofolo to Milan upon an Austrian horse I had captured at the battle of the preceding day, though it had a broad-sword cut on the forehead. The First Consul saw me, and several times requested I would follow at a slower pace, and not fatigue myself: I persisted, however, in keeping up with him, and followed him into the court-yard of the castle of Milan.

It was near sunset. The First Consul had travelled so

rapidly, that the courier who was sent to announce him had only arrived an hour before. Nevertheless, the whole population was on the alert: draperies were displayed from the houses; the road, the streets, and windows,. were lined by women of the first rank ; they held in their hands small baskets of flowers, which they threw into the First Consul's carriage as he passed along.

He had not been long in Milan before he brought together the dispersed members of the Cisalpine government. The victory of Marengo had revived the hopes of the Italian people : each resumed his post ; each returned to his functions ; and the machinery of government was in full operation in the course of a few days.

In the midst of this general satisfaction I was overtaken by the equipages of my late general : they had arrived under the care of Rapp, my companion in arms, who had been detained from us by a serious illness. We were both giving way to the bitterness of our regret, and to uneasiness respecting our future fate, when the First Consul caused us to be informed that he retained us as his aides-de-camp. I experienced a transition from anxiety to a species of delirium ; was so happy and so affected, that I found it impossible to vent my gratitude in adequate terms.

The Austrian armies had reached the boundaries assigned to it by the capitulation of Marengo ; but the court of Vienna had not yet ratified the armistice which the First Consul was desirous of extending to the army of the Rhine, in order to bring about a peace : he sent for General Massena, whom he destined to the command of the army at his departure. They had not met since his setting sail for Egypt: he gave him a most flattering reception, and repeatedly congratulated him on his noble defence of Genoa.

The ratification having arrived from Vienna, the First Consul took his departure for Paris, by way of Piedmont and Mount Cenis, and desired me to accompany him.

He soon reached Turin, remained one or two hours to visit the citadel, which had just been given up to the army, returned to his carriage, and did not stop on his way until he reached Lyons.

The road was lined with men of all ranks and of all classes, no less attracted by gratitude than by curiosity. There is no exaggeration in saying that he travelled from Milan to Lyons between two rows of people, who had flocked from the towns as well as from the country to see him, and in the midst of unceasing acclamations. The population of Lyons, in the same kind of intoxicating joy which it had displayed on the return from Egypt, proceeded in a body to the Hotel of the Celestins, where we had alighted to breakfast, forced the gates, and evinced such eagerness and impatience to behold the First Consul, that he was compelled to yield to its wishes, and show himself on the balcony. He then came down for the purpose of laying the first stone of the Place de Bellecour, which he had ordered to be restored to its former state, and proceeded on his way to Dijon, where he intended to review a corps of reserve which was organising in that city, whence it was to go and join the army.

The manifestations of joy were still greater at Dijon than at Lyons : the apartments intended for the First Consul were lined by the most fascinating women of that delightful city ; the crowd of men was immense ; all wished to see and approach him ; the house was full of people ; he could nowhere find retirement in it. The women were remarkable for the vivacity of an unaffected joy, which threw animation into their eyes, and gave their faces as deep a colour as though they had trespassed the bounds of decorum. One of the handsomest amongst them became afterwards one of the ornaments of the court, by the title of Duchess of Bassano.

The First Consul went out to review the troops ; but he could only reach the ground in the midst of this concourse of

young women, loaded with flowers, and myrtle and laurel
branches, which they strewed at his horse's feet. They felt no
dread or apprehension of any kind : their minds were so full
of the hero who was before them, that danger did not alarm
them, provided they could give vent to their admiration. So
careless were they of their own safety, that the First Consul
would not return into the town for fear of some accident
resulting from their impatience. The carriages which followed us came to receive him on the ground where the troops
were stationed: he bowed in the kindest manner to this
swarm of youthful graces, and took his departure; but he
always retained a lively recollection of the reception he had
met with at Dijon : he always felt pleasure in speaking of
that city, and in adverting to the flattering welcome which
it had given him on his return from Marengo.

His train consisted of two carriages: Messrs. Duroc and
Bourrienne travelled in the same carriage with him; I
followed with General Bessières in the other. As we were
about to enter Sens, on the morning following the day of our
quitting Dijon, a mainspring of one of the carriages broke in
going down the hill. This accident detained us six hours.
We arrived at last, and saw the painters, who, doubtless,
not expecting us so soon, were tracing on the front of a triumphal arch the famous words *Veni, vidi, vici*. We alighted
at the residence of Madame Bourrienne, and had the carriage
repaired whilst we were at breakfast.

Sens had a depôt of Russian prisoners of war, who were in
a most wretched condition. The First Consul ordered money
to be distributed amongst those prisoners, and announced to
them that their condition would soon be improved : this actually came to pass.

We left Sens at mid-day, and soon reached Montereau.
The postmaster, who was a warm admirer of the First
Consul, insisted upon personally driving his carriage. His
cleverness did not, unfortunately, keep pace with his zeal;

for, as he came up to the turn which is in front of the bridge, he upset the carriage so suddenly, that we all thought it would have rolled into the river. Neither the First Consul, however, nor any of his suite were hurt: no injury was even done to the carriage. The postmaster, more dead than alive with fright at this accident, was afraid to make his appearance. The First Consul was himself obliged to calm his fears, and to prevail upon him to remount his horse. These different accidences detained us longer than we expected. The First Consul did not arrive until midnight of the 6th July at the palace of the Tuileries, when he was no longer expected.

The population, in fact, repaired at an early hour the next morning to the Fauxbourg Saint Antoine, as it had done on the preceding day; but it was informed of the First Consul's having arrived during the night, and immediately hastened to the Tuileries, the garden of which continued to be thronged during the whole day.

. France had but just emerged from a state of uneasiness and constraint, which made the nation doubly appreciate a victory they had not ventured to anticipate; a victory the more signal, as it repaired every preceding defeat.

Eight months only had elapsed since the First Consul's return from Egypt, and every thing had already assumed another aspect. The revolutionary government was for ever dissolved. The wounds it had inflicted were healed, the torch of civil war extinguished. Belgium, where the approach of an English army had excited some commotions, was now pacified, and Italy reconquered as far as the Mincio by a single battle. Nothing was left unaccomplished to restore France to the state in which General Bonaparte had left it when he took his departure for Egypt except the capture of Mantua, and the extending our operations as far as the banks of the Adige.

Such services were duly appreciated. The first days that

followed his return from Marengo were consecrated to rejoicings, which attested the nation's gratitude. Festivities
and pleasures seemed the order of the day. Each public
body, each individual, felt anxious to take a part in the
general rejoicing. The First Consul was partaking also of the
prevailing gladness when he learned that a courier from Italy
had brought an account of the loss of the battle of Marengo.
The courier had been dispatched at the moment when every
thing seemed desperate ; so that the report of a defeat was
general in Paris before the First Consul's return. Many
projects were disturbed by his arrival. On the mere an-
nouncement of his defeat his enemies had returned to their
work, and talked of nothing less than overthrowing the government, and avenging the crime of the 18th Brumaire.

Carnot, although minister of war, had been remarked
amongst the most prominent, and had not disdained to
welcome, and even circulate this unpleasant intelligence.
The First Consul concealed the impression which these details created upon his mind ; but he did not forget them.
From that moment he determined to separate himself from a
man who, although he consented to be a member of his
government, yet considered him as a public enemy. He had
long destined the seals of that office for Berthier ; but the
services of the latter being still needed at the army, he delayed replacing Carnot for a few months longer.

The 14th July, the anniversary of the Confederacy of 1789,
arrived. It was celebrated in the Champ-de-Mars, in the
midst of a prodigious concourse of people. The population lined all the terraces ; the crowd extended to a great
distance ; the intoxicating joy of that early period of the
revolution seemed to have returned. The First Consul
repaired on horseback to the splendid ceremony : he appeared
just at the moment when the horse and foot guards were
arriving with the numerous standards taken at Marengo.
The appearance of these warriors—the presence of the illus-

trious chief who had led them to victory, could not fail to excite the liveliest acclamations. This detachment had left the field of battle on the 16th June, the day after the action, and performed the distance to Paris in twenty-nine days. Its state of exhaustion, and the wretched condition of its equipments, greatly added to the interest felt for the harvest of glory it had reaped: it was greeted in all directions by acclamations and marks of the general esteem which its presence had inspired.

Amidst all these rejoicings the First Consul was not unmindful of the measures necessary for re-equipping the army for a campaign, and throwing supplies into the fortresses of Italy. The truce was to expire at the end of July. He made all his arrangements in the event of the non-conclusion of peace. Independently of the attention which he bestowed upon the army and its appendages, during the whole time of his stay in Paris, his mind was engaged upon a work of prodigious magnitude. He caused a variety of materials to be collected, which he submitted to the Council of State, and endeavoured to substitute a thorough system of finances to the disastrous want of system pursued by the Directory. He was ably seconded in this object by the minister of that department, M. Gaudin, since Duke of Gaeta, one of the most upright and active men of business that the administration of any period can boast of.

The Directory had often urged him, though in vain, to assume the management of the finances: the First Consul was more fortunate: M. Gaudin accepted the seals of office, because he was certain that in carrying forward any measure he should decide upon, he would receive every support. The First Consul had a particular regard for him: he was the only minister who retained his office from 1799 to 1814.

The First Consul created the sinking fund, the registry office, and the bank: he restored order to all the branches of the administration, and probity in the dealings of private individuals with the government. On this occasion it was that he caused a strict examination to be made of the accounts of all persons presenting themselves as creditors of the state, and took a detailed cognizance of all the frauds and peculations to which the public purse had been a prey during the administration of the Directory. He had had some misgivings on the subject previously to his coming to power; but what he saw soon convinced him that he had not suspected one half of the disorder which actually existed. Accordingly, from that moment, he never could feel either esteem for or confidence in certain individuals, notwithstanding their great wealth. He felt a natural antipathy for those who sought to amass money by disgraceful means. He often said that he thought better of a highwayman, who at least exposes his life, than he did of those leeches who carry off every thing without running any risk. Some of these men of business have imagined that he was their personal enemy, and envied their fortune: this was by no means the case; he had no personal aversion for them; he only condemned the manner in which they had acquired wealth.

He displayed, in combining his resources, that aptitude which characterised him on all occasions; he had a facility in calculating, a quickness of perception which surprised those who transacted business with him for the first time. They were far, however, from anticipating all the wonderful improvements he has since effected.

Such were his occupations during the summer of 1800, conducting the internal affairs of government and those which might pave the way to peace without the necessity of recurring to new efforts. He long indulged the hope of attaining this result; but suspected that the delays of the Austrian cabinet were a cloak to some secret views; and he determined to prepare himself for any event.

CHAPTER XIX.

The author's mission to Italy—Passage of Mount Cenis—The Savoyard peasantry
Brune succeeds Massena—Austria refuses passports to General Duroc—
That power resigns the three fortified places of Philipsburg, Ingolstadt, and
Ulm—Negotiations—Preliminaries of peace.

I WAS directed by the First Consul to repair secretly to Italy, and inform myself of the state of defence and the resources of the several towns which had been surrendered to us, and also of the state of our parks of artillery, depôts, and cavalry.

He handed me a letter for the minister of the treasury, who delivered into my charge a million of francs in gold for the treasurer of the army. This circumstance rendered my journey a perilous one. I was carrying with me a considerable sum of money, and was obliged to cross a country where, for the sake of a few pieces of gold, the people would have taken away my life.* The passage of Mount Cenis, where the carriages had to be taken to pieces, placed me under the necessity of exhibiting my ten little barrels well sealed up, and containing each a hundred thousand francs. From that moment I became indifferent to every thing, so convinced was I that I could never reach my destination in safety. I avoided quitting my carriage either for the purpose of eating or drinking ; and when compelled to leave it, I took care only to do so at night. I must, however, own it to the credit of the Savoyard peasantry, that they loaded my barrels, the value of which they well knew, without manifesting the smallest intention or desire to seize them. They could have found a thousand opportunities for robbing me as we ascended or

* I met on the way the Austrian general Saint Julien, who was proceeding from Italy to Paris, under the escort of one of Massena's aides-de-camp,

descended the mountain ; but the thought of so heinous an act
never once occurred to them.   They had even the attention
to take over my carriage first, that I might find it prepared
to receive me on the other side, and have only to replace my
barrels and continue my journey.   These worthy people were
unconscious of having rendered me more than an ordinary
service.   The frankness of their deportment ought to have
set my mind at ease.   I acknowledge, however, that I felt
greatly relieved on depositing the million of francs in the
chest of the paymaster at Turin.

I examined in detail the places which the First Consul had
instructed me to visit.   None of his orders had yet been
complied with.   I was quite lost in astonishment at finding
that not only they had not been provisioned, but that there
had been a misapplication of part of the resources which
they possessed when evacuated by the Austrians.   The
public voice had even singled out some chiefs as having sold
the objects entrusted to their charge.   These disorders had
created amongst the troops a strong feeling of discontent; they
still retained that bitterness of language which had grown
upon them since the days of their reverses of fortune; and
loudly asked what use to them was the conquest of Italy, if
they were to be as miserable as when cooped up within the
rocks of Genoa, and if plunderers alone were to benefit by
their victories.

I received many reports, during my stay at Milan, respecting depredations committed to a great extent by persons employed in the service of the army, and was requested to
transmit them to the First Consul.   Several related to peculations practised in Genoa since its re-occupation by our
troops.   I then discovered that there were sources of information in Italy of which the First Consul could avail himself
in regard to matters with which it was necessary for him to
become acquainted, and that as he was known to be inexorable respecting misapplications of public money, each was

anxious to point out the particular case which he felt most interest in seeing removed.

I was reluctant to communicate these reports to General Massena, though I had no doubt that they had been exaggerated by the recollection of the sufferings endured whilst he was in command. On the other hand, I wished for certain explanations which the First Consul would not fail to demand of me. Feeling at a loss how to direct my inquiries in a country where I was a perfect stranger, I determined to open my mind to M. Petiet, the intendant of the army, a man who possessed all the confidence of the chief of the state; he readily yielded to my request, and had all the reports verified, a great number of which were unfortunately found to detail circumstances that had really occurred.

I was preparing to return to Paris after having accomplished the object of my mission, when I received a letter from the First Consul, directing me to return by way of Dijon, and examine into the condition of the troops that were stationed there under the orders of General Brune.

I quitted Italy with feelings of disappointment at what I had seen, and recrossed the mountains. Upon my arrival in Paris I delivered to the First Consul the reports which had been confided to me, together with M. Petiet's opinion in corroboration of the facts alleged in them. After perusing these reports he overpowered me with questions, and was greatly indignant at the recital of the disorders pointed out to his notice. Several persons were recalled from the army ; Massena himself had to resign his command to General Brune a few months afterwards.

The enemies of the defender of Genoa appeared for a moment to have carried their point; but the First Consul was under the necessity of keeping on terms with every one : he was more especially desirous of conciliating the good opinion of the Italians, for whom he entertained a natural predilection, and whose wounded feelings might be productive of unpleasant consequences in the event of the war again breaking out. He very justly observed that it was the duty of General Massena to foresee such consequences and to repress the disorders that gave rise to them. He was more particularly displeased at the collecting of an unlawful impost upon every sack of corn that entered Genoa. It was an outrage to humanity, calculated to drive the people to despair, to have imposed a tax upon agricultural produce, after all the sufferings which the unhappy population had endured, after the famine and horrors occasioned by a long siege. This infamous traffic was, no doubt, carried on unknown to the commander-in-chief; but this did not alter its political consequences. The city would have been reduced to all the extremities of want if the chance of war had again brought the Austrians under its walls.

The truce concluded with Austria had not yet expired. This power pleaded the treaty which bound her to England as a pretext for not negotiating without her intervention. She had the loss of Italy at heart, and could not submit to it with a good grace. England, on the other hand, to whom the war was more profitable than burdensome, was in no hurry to bring it to a close. She resorted, on the contrary, to every means in her power for inducing the allies to persevere, so great was the influence which she derived from the coalition. The fine season was drawing to a close, and matters remained in the same state as in the month of July. Disappointed in his expectations, the First Consul regretted having given way to a feeling of generosity, and having allowed M. de Melas' army to retire behind the Mincio, when he might have compelled it to surrender. The mischief was done: his determination was soon taken, and he prepared once more to place himself at the head of the army.

He ordered his guard to proceed to Italy; sent off his horses and those of his staff, and instructed General Brune to announce his arrival, and prepare to cross the Mincio. In

Germany, the army of the Rhine, which had acted upon the armistice ever since the battle of Marengo, prepared at the same time to resume its forward movements; but the unsatisfactory account which Moreau had given of the operations of the troops under his command had considerably lessened the opinion which the First Consul had formed of the talents of that general from the reports which had been made to him. He even repeatedly told us that if Moreau had well understood the plan of operations which he had traced for him; and if, instead of adhering to his antiquated method, he had crossed the Rhine with his whole force towards the extreme left of the enemy, he would, by such a step, have come much nearer than the Austrian army into contact with the hereditary states; that the Emperor, on being defeated at Marengo, would have been informed of the loss of Italy at the same time that he would have heard of the arrival of the French upon the Inn. In this dilemma, he added, Francis would have infallibly concluded peace, whereas we now had fresh risks to encounter before we could secure it.

Preliminaries of peace had been signed at Paris between the. Austrian general Saint Julien and the French government. Duroc was made the bearer of them to the Emperor for his ratification. He repaired to the head-quarters of the army of the Rhine, where he applied for a pass to enable him to proceed on his journey. This having been refused him, he reported the circumstance to the First Consul, who, by return of courier, ordered him to come back to Paris. General Moreau was, at the same time, instructed to break the truce, and renew hostilities, unless the Austrians delivered into his hands the fortress of Philipsburg, which they occupied upon the Rhine, as well as the two fortresses of Ingolstadt and Ulm, where bridges were thrown across the Danube, which might endanger the safety of the army in the event of its making any forward movement; and in case of compliance with these terms, General Moreau was authorised to agree to a fresh armistice, which would include the army of Italy. The Austrians consented to the surrender of those three fortresses, and offered, at the same time, to treat upon new bases.

This proposal was accepted by the First Consul. M. de Cobentzel repaired to Luneville, where the conferences were soon opened: Joseph Bonaparte represented France on the occasion. The negotiation was in progress; but England had succeeded in obtaining a disavowal of M. de Saint Julien's conduct, and flattered herself with the hope of again obstructing the contemplated pacification. Lord Minto, who was her representative at the Court of Vienna, demanded to take a part in the discussion of the interests which were agitated at Luneville. The First Consul was not at a loss to comprehend the motive of this tardy proceeding: he did not, however, oppose it; but, in order to baffle the views meditated by England, who only sought to make him lose time, he required, as a preliminary step, that she should agree upon a cessation of hostilities with France, as the latter had done with respect to Austria: this was affording an unquestionable proof of the desire he felt for an immediate pacification. The British cabinet, which had other objects to promote, refused the armistice, and yet persisted in its demand of sending a plenipotentiary to the congress, a demand wholly inadmissible. M. Otto, who was residing in England as a commissioner for the exchange of prisoners, and was vested with the necessary powers of negotiating a suspension of arms, detailed the grounds of his proposal in a note of the following tenor:—

" The undersigned having communicated to his government the note which His Excellency Lord Grenville caused to be delivered to him, under date 29th August, is desired to submit to him the following observations:—

" Preliminaries of peace had been concluded and signed between his Imperial Majesty and the French Republic. The ratification of His Imperial Majesty was prevented by the intervention of Lord Minto, who has demanded that his court should be admitted as a party to the negotiations.

"The suspension of arms, which had only taken place on the continent in the hope of a speedy peace being concluded between the Emperor and the Republic, must accordingly cease, and will cease in effect, on the 24th Fructidor, since it was only to this hope of an immediate peace that the Republic sacrificed the immense advantages which victory had secured to it.

"The question of a peace with Austria becomes so complicated by the intervention of England, that it is impossible for the French government to prolong the duration of the armistice on the continent, unless His Britannic Majesty will extend its operation to the three powers.

"If therefore the British cabinet should persist in making common cause with Austria, and if its desire of being a party in the negotiation be entertained with a sincere object in view, His Britannic Majesty will not hesitate to adopt the proposed armistice.

"But, in the event of the said armistice not being concluded before the 24th Fructidor, hostilities with Austria will have then been resumed, and the First Consul will thenceforward no longer consent to any other peace than a complete and separate peace with that power.

"Whilst awaiting the explanations demanded relative to the armistice, the undersigned is directed to make known to His Excellency that the places which it is attempted to assimilate to those of Germany are Malta and the maritime towns of Egypt.

"If it be true that a long suspension of hostilities between France and England might appear detrimental to the interests of His Britannic Majesty, it is no less true that a prolonged armistice on the continent is essentially injurious to the French Republic; so that, whilst the maritime armistice would be a guarantee to France of the zeal with which

England is disposed to concur in the re-establishment of peace, the continental armistice would also be a pledge to the British government of the sincerity of the pacific intentions of France ; and as the position of Austria would no longer afford her an excuse for delaying to bring matters to a conclusion, the three powers would find, in their respective interests, weighty reasons for consenting, without delay, to make the sacrifices that are reciprocally called for, with the view of soon coming to terms, and of concluding a general and permanent peace—such a peace as the wishes and the hopes of the world so loudly demand.

"London, 17th Fructidor, year VIII."

These arguments were of a peremptory nature, and the decision upon them demanded serious reflection. If England would not consent to a special armistice with France, the armistice which the latter had concluded with Austria would not be renewed. The Aulic Council, having no means of carrying on the war, would be compelled to yield, and the peace would thus be agreed upon without the intervention of England.

The British government perceived the danger ; but whether they were not sufficiently alive to the extent of it, or deemed it enough to have saved appearances towards the court of Vienna, they did no more than present, in an extremely diffuse and laboured note, a counter-project of an armistice, which would have left to France none of the advantages she had a right to expect as a compensation for those which Austria derived from the suspension of hostilities that had been granted to her. This was a sufficient indication of the spirit by which their councils were actuated. Nevertheless, the First Consul was determined to exhaust every means of conciliation. He presented to England two modes according to which a treaty might be framed. If she desired to become a party in the negotiation with Austria, he required that she should accede to the armistice, there being no other means of establishing a point of resemblance in the respective relations of the contracting powers, and of imposing upon each the desire as well as the necessity of coming to a conclusion.

If, on the other hand, England wished to enter into a separate negotiation with France, the First Consul accepted the project of armistice presented by the British ministry.

He went still farther: he put off, for eight days, the resumption of hostilities, as a fresh proof of his pacific intentions: but this considerate conduct on his part only gave rise to fresh doubts, to unjust allegations. He spurned them through his plenipotentiary, and trusted to the chance of war the settlement of a question which the trammels of diplomacy were endeavouring to elude. The official document ran as follows :—

" It has been a source of regret to the undersigned during the whole course of the negotiation entrusted to him, that the absence of more direct communications with his Britannic Majesty's ministers should have made it impossible for him to give the requisite developements to his official overtures. This inconvenience is greatly enhanced by the result of his last communications, which are answered by the note he has had the honour to receive under date the 20th instant.

" The first part of that note appearing to doubt the sincerity of intention of the French government, in its endeavours to open negotiations for a general peace, the undersigned must, on this subject, enter into some details which will fully justify the conduct of the First Consul.

" The alternative proposed of a *separate* peace, in case His Britannic Majesty should not agree to the conditions of a general armistice, is so far from exhibiting a want of sincerity, that it furnishes, on the contrary, the strongest proof of the conciliatory dispositions of the First Consul: it is a necessary consequence of the declaration made by the undersigned on the 4th instant. He, in fact, did himself the honour

to intimate to the British ministry, that if that armistice were
not concluded before the 11th September, hostilities would
have then recommenced with Austria ; and that, in the latter
case, the First Consul could no longer admit, in respect to
the latter power, of any other than a separate and a complete
peace.   That armistice was not concluded at the above-mentioned date : it was therefore natural to expect eventually *a
separate peace with Austria,* and, in such an hypothesis, *a
separate peace with Great Britain* likewise, unless it be
taken for granted that the calamities which have afflicted a
great part of Europe for the last eight years are to be perpetuated, and are never to terminate, except in the moral
destruction of one of the contending powers.

" It is not therefore a proposal of the French government that His Britannic Majesty should separate his interests from those of his allies ; but having in vain attempted
to unite them to one common centre, and finding them
separated *de facto* by the refusal of England to lay down at
the shrine of peace some private advantages, which France on
her part had already sacrificed, the First Consul has given a
fresh proof of his pacific intentions by pointing out another
means of conciliation ; which proof the course of events will
sooner or later bring to light.

" In conformity with the intimation given by the undersigned on the 4th of this month, the continental armistice has
been in reality notified as terminating at the stipulated
period ; but the counter-project of the British ministry,
transmitted by the undersigned on the 8th instant, having
reached Paris on the 10th, and His Britannic Majesty having
appeared convinced that his ally would not reject an armistice
founded upon admissible terms, the First Consul has determined to postpone, for eight days, the resumption of hostilities.   Orders have been accordingly dispatched to the
armies of Germany and Italy ; and in case those orders
should have arrived too late in the latter country, and the

French generals should have obtained some success consequent upon any military operations, they have been instructed to resume the position which they occupied on the precise day on which hostilities were renewed.

"This plain statement of facts will no doubt suffice to demonstrate that the French government never could have contemplated cloaking, by feigned negotiations, a fresh attack upon Austria; and that, on the contrary, the whole negotiation has been met on its part by that frankness and candour which are alone calculated to secure the restoration of general tranquillity, an object which His Majesty and his administration have so much at heart.

"Vain would be the attempt to discover proofs of any other intention in certain terms of the official communications of the French government with His Majesty's allies, the less so if allusion be intended to one of the last letters written by the Baron de Thugut, which the undersigned himself would have felt no difficulty in communicating had the opportunity offered for his so doing. That letter would furnish a proof that the French government, always friendly to peace, only appeared to complain of the intentions of Great Britain because it had every reason for viewing them as being opposed to a solid system of pacification.

"The undersigned has had no other reason for entering into these details than that, on the eve of the negotiations likely to be set on foot, it was of importance for the councils of both powers to be reciprocally satisfied of the sincerity of each other's intentions, and because the confidence they may entertain of such sincerity is the surest guarantee of the success of the negotiations.

"With regard to the second point adverted to in the note which the undersigned has had the honour to receive, he must refer to his letter of the 16th, wherein he has intimated to His Excellency Lord Grenville that he was instructed to give *satisfactory explanations* respecting the principal objections of the British government to the proposed armistice, and to urge upon his attention the necessity of affording facilities to verbal communications with the ministry. How therefore could the impression be entertained that the French government would admit of *no modification* to its first overtures, since in such a case it would have been quite superfluous to solicit an interview for the purpose of affording *satisfactory explanations* ?

"In adverting to the compensations required previously to allowing a naval armistice corresponding in principle with the continental one, His Britannic Majesty's ministers find that the balance set up by the French government is open to the charge of exaggeration. A formal discussion on this subject would no doubt be out of place after the varied successes of a war which has produced so many extraordinary events. . It is difficult to discredit the moral influence of those events upon armies ; upon whole nations; upon governments themselves ; and the inferences that may be deduced from them, at the present moment, appear to justify the opinion which the undersigned deemed himself warranted in expressing upon the subject. If that opinion be exaggerated, it is shared by the very enemies of the republic, who have done every thing in their power to prolong the truce, and have even made no scruple of resorting to feigned negotiations for the purpose of gaining time.,

"A memorable instance of this is to be found in the preliminaries signed by the Count de Saint Julien and disavowed by his court : and the continuation of the continental armistice must be considered as a *sacrifice* on the part of the republic, since such efforts have been made to obtain it from France.

"His Majesty's ministers, however, in admitting the reality of this sacrifice, formally declare that a corresponding sacrifice ought not to be required of them. It certainly does not behove France to determine how far His Majesty's engagements towards his allies may restrain his intentions on this point ; but France has an incontestible right to demand the price of the sacrifice she has made, and is still ready to submit to.

" The First Consul has afforded to Europe repeated pledges of his pacific intentions: he has never ceased manifesting them to the cabinets interested in this struggle ; and even if his moderation should have no other effect than to raise the hopes of the enemies of the , French government, he will always persist in it as his only rule of conduct.

" Notwithstanding the existing difference of opinion as to the mode of considering several accessory questions which are preliminary to the contemplated pacification, the under-signed cannot but rejoice to find in all the communications he has hitherto had the honour of receiving, the same assurances of His Majesty's desire to second, by every means in his power, the re-establishment of the tranquillity of Europe ; and he will neglect no opportunity of laying a proper stress on those intentions in his intercourse with his own government.'

"Hereford Street, 23d September, 1800 (1st Vendémiaire, year IX)."

CHAPTER XX.

Transfer of the remains of Turenne—Ceremony at the Invalids—The armistice is declared at an end—Battle of Hohenlinden—Joseph Bonaparte sent to Lune-ville—General Clarke—Canal of St. Quentin—Peace is concluded—The Russian prisoners sent home.

THE intelligence of the occupation of the three fortresses had reached Paris on the 1st of Vendémiaire. The deputies from the departments were assembled in the capital for the first time as a political body since the 18th Brumaire : a hope

had no doubt been indulged that the actual conclusion of
peace might be communicated to them. Be this, however,
as it may, there happened to be a public ceremony on that
day, partly in consequence of the inauguration of the opening
century, partly owing to the transfer of the remains of Marshal de Turenne, which the First Consul had directed to be
deposited near those of Vauban at the Hospital of the Invalids.

After the violation of the tombs in the abbey of Saint Denis,
where the remains of the marshal were reposing amongst
kings, his coffin had been carried away, and deposited in the
upper part of the surgical amphitheatre at the Jardin des
Plantes, where it was still remaining on General Bonaparte's
departure for Egypt. I recollect seeing it there at that time,
when General Desaix was visiting the establishment; it was
shown with great veneration, though having no mark to distinguish it from the other skeletons in the room. At a later
period, a respectable citizen, having obtained leave to collect
in the convent of the Grands Augustins, which he had transformed into a museum of French monuments, the mausoleums
that had escaped the outrages committed at Saint Denis,
had caused the body of Marshal de Turenne to be transported to this spot. The government removed it thence for
the purpose of transferring it to the Invalids. The church
had been decorated for the ceremony. The deputies from
the departments, who had been invited, were already in their
places when the body of the marshal was brought in. The
clergy had not yet reappeared in France at this time: there
was no celebration of the divine office nor any other religious
duty performed: the ceremony was purely one of oratorical
speeches and pageantry.

Lucien Bonaparte, who was minister of the interior,
ascended the pulpit, and gave a bold sketch of the misfortunes
that had oppressed the republic during the period of the revolutionary storm; he made an affecting allusion to the scenes
of mourning which the closing days of the century just ex-

pired had witnessed, and offered as a contrast a brief statement of the improvements effected in the commencing century. He then turned to the hopes we were justified in entertaining; but as the word peace was not uttered, the gloom of uneasiness was not dispelled. He at last came to the topic of the external position of the republic : a profound silence reigned throughout the church. He was listened to with the most anxious attention whilst relating the anecdote of Duroc's journey; the refusal to allow him passports to proceed to Vienna; the order given in consequence to General Moreau, that he should declare the armistice at an end, and immediately resume hostilities unless Ulm, Ingolstadt and Philipsburg were delivered up to him.

The minister concluded by announcing to the assembly that at the moment when he was leaving the palace for the purpose of attending the ceremony which brought them together, government had received intelligence that the three fortresses demanded had been occupied by our troops, and that the armistice was prolonged. A movement of satisfaction was immediately manifested throughout the assembly : peace was eagerly wished for: it was clearly perceived that the First Consul also desired it, and it was anticipated at no distant period. All left the church well pleased with the communication.

The refusal made by Austria to grant passports to General Duroc, at the same time that it compelled that power to purchase the prolongation of the armistice at so high a price, denoted a spirit of irresolution the cause of which was not to be mistaken. It was clear that Austria was under the influence of England, and that the latter swayed her decisions; but as it was unlikely that Germany would sacrifice herself for the gratification of her ally, it is clear that she expected support, or had agreed upon an *ultimatum* beyond which she was at liberty to enter upon a separate treaty. Whatever that *ultimatum* may have been, the First Consul, who was quite prepared, could only lose by prolonging the armistice.

He determined upon breaking it, as I have already related, and ordered the armies of the Rhine and of Italy to announce the resumption of hostilities. Brune crossed the Mincio, and Moreau the Iser. The battle of Hohenlinden took place ; Moreau occupied Lintz, and pushed on some advanced posts as far as Saint Polten, at the distance of eight or ten leagues from Vienna.

On being informed of this victory, the First Consul felt persuaded that it would compel the Austrians to come to an explanation ; and in order not to lose time, as soon as he heard by a telegraphic dispatch that Count de Cobentzel,` who was coming in all haste to resume the negotiations, had arrived at Strasburg, he sent off his brother Joseph to Luneville, there to discuss the interests of France.

Joseph had not yet passed Ligny when he met Count Lewis de Cobentzel, who was on his way to Paris in all haste with the necessary powers to conclude the so long wished for. peace.

Joseph retraced his steps, and brought M. de Cobentzel back with him. They alighted at the Tuileries, where the First Consul received them both in their travelling dresses. He, held a conference with the Austrian plenipotentiary during. part of the night, and made him take his departure the next day, with Joseph, for Luneville, which place had been fixed upon for holding the conferences.

General Clarke, * who was already doing all in his power to '

* General Clarke was descended from an Irish family which had emigrated to France with the Stuarts. He entered at an early period into the Duke of Orleans' household, in the capacity of secretary, which was the means of his obtaining the rank of supernumerary captain in the regiment of hussars, of which the Duke was the colonel-general.

During the revolution he made himself subservient to the political principles of that prince. Having, in his turn, become lieutenant-colonel of the second cavalry regiment, he was employed with the army of the Rhine, under M. de Custine, and was present, in that capacity, at the first retreat from Mentz to Weissenburg. After the departure of this general, who had been called to the command of the

force himself into importance, was sent to Luneville as
governor of the town. His mission was simply to give

north, the representatives of the people appointed Clarke to the functions of chief of
the staff; but these proconsuls, who every day adopted the most whimsical determinations, almost immediately dismissed him from that duty, and sent him to the
distance of twenty leagues from the frontiers. He was again reinstated by the
revolution which established the power of the Directory. Clarke was placed at
the head of the topographical department of the war ministry. He directed its
labours, and knew every thing that related to the military plans of the republic.

The Directory having become jealous of General Bonaparte, sent Clarke to
Italy, under the pretext of his endeavouring to open communications with Vienna.
It was not their object to accredit him, but merely to have a safe agent at head-
quarters, who would report the political views of the commander-in-chief.

Clarke accordingly crossed the mountains, and was replaced for the time in the
topographical department by General Dupont, with whom he corresponded. (I
shall hereafter dwell upon this correspondence, which I once had in my possession.)
General Bonaparte was not at a loss to guess the object of this officer's mission.
He set his secretary to work, and soon obtained proofs of what he had merely suspected. He sent for the agent of the Directory, and ordered him to explain himself. Clarke did not attempt any disguise; he confessed every thing, and pledged
to the general of the army of Italy that faith which was already promised to the
Directory. Nevertheless, he did not consider himself obliged to give up reporting
to Paris. He continued to correspond with Dupont, to whom he took care not to
confide the secret of the reception he had met with, and transmitted regular notes
to him respecting the views and projects of the commander-in-chief. The Directory, however, was not long the dupe of this artifice. The 18th Fructidor took
place, and Clarke was dismissed from his functions. Impelled by a feeling of
generosity towards the now disgraced observer of other men's actions, General
Bonaparte threw the influence of his power round him, and kept him in Italy
until the moment when he recrossed the mountains. He had saved him from the
rigorous treatment which the Directory had in store for him, after the negotiations
of Campo Formio; and he saved him from misery after the events of Saint Cloud.
When the 18th Brumaire was over, he drew him away from a small estate upon
which he was residing near Strasburg, and, by a telegraphic dispatch, called him
near his person. He restored to him his topographical department, gave him
apartments at the Tuileries, and employed him in every circumstance that could
flatter his ambition. At a later period he appointed him ambassador, named him
governor of Vienna, then of Berlin, minister of war, a duke; in short, on the
occasion of his marriage, he made a settlement upon him out of his private purse.
This is what, to my knowledge, Clarke had obtained from the munificence of
Napoleon. We shall see by the sequel of these Memoirs what he did for his
benefactor in the hour of danger.

dinners and to listen.   At the same time that the First Consul
was opening conferences he was infusing a new life into all
kinds of public and private works.   Confidence was returning;
manufactories and new speculations were springing up in all
directions.

Winter had just set in.   The First Consul repaired to
Saint Quentin, for the purpose of visiting the works of the
subterranean canal which was intended to unite the river
Oise with the Scheldt, and of which he was contemplating
the completion.   The director-general of high-ways, as well
as Messrs. Monge, Berthollet and Chaptal attended him on
the occasion.

Great damage had been occasioned by the abandonment of
the works : fresh expenses were called for to an enormous
amount ; and the statements made by competent judges
created some hesitation as to the course to be adopted : there
were doubts whether it would be proper to prosecute the
excavations already made, or whether a lower tunnel should
be cut in a different direction.

The First Consul was determined to see every thing with
his own eyes, and discovered, in fact, that an undertaking
commenced on so bad a plan could never be successful.   He
abandoned the defective excavations, and ordered that the
canal should receive the new direction which it now has.   The
vault under which it runs is much shorter than the one
which was at first contemplated.   France is therefore indebted
to the First Consul for this canal, which is the source of
so great profit to the northern departments.

On his return from Saint Quentin he found at the Tuileries General Bellavene, who brought him the treaty of peace
which Joseph had just signed with M. de Cobentzel.   The
stipulations were the same as at Campo Formio, and the renewal of such terms proves that no rancorous feeling lurked in
the breast of the First Consul.   The beaten generally pay the
forfeit : not so, however, in this case ; the Austrians resumed
their limits as marked out at Campo Formio.

The First Consul hastened to ratify his brother's work; and the news of the conclusion of peace was forwarded in every direction with the utmost dispatch.

Some months afterwards, Austria named as its accredited ambassador to Paris Count Philip de Cobentzel, the plenipotentiary's brother; and France sent to Vienna, with the same title, M. de Champagny, who was at this time a councillor of state, and was created Duke of Cadore at a later period.

Peace was hailed throughout France with transports of joy: it eased the public mind, revived its long-banished hopes, and confirmed the restoration of tranquillity in the western provinces. The suspicion was never entertained for a moment that evil counsellors would soon persuade foreign courts of their having more to apprehend from the power of the moral lever of which the First Consul had acquired possession, than they had at the time when the only object of those vested with authority before him was to destroy; or when the Directory, in its vague and restless uneasiness, could discover no means of security except in the ruin of ancient governments.

It was an opinion generally prevalent in France that the war out of which she had just emerged had been undertaken by foreign powers only with a view to prevent the diffusion of republican principles, which the Directory had not relaxed in its endeavours to propagate ever since the peace of Campo Formio.

The more prudent course pursued by the First Consul, the moderation he had just displayed in victory, ought to have calmed the fears of the allies. Having no longer any reason to dread the fomenting of agitations amongst their subjects, it behoved them to show a similar spirit of moderation.

The First Consul himself was under a delusion on this subject. His confidence was heightened by knowing as he did how deeply he might have injured Austria after the battle of Marengo; still, if his moderation were not duly appreciated, he was justified in concluding that this power would take care not to incur the risk of again placing itself at his mercy.

So great was the First Consul's anxiety to reconcile the republic with its enemies, that he sought a renewal of negotiations wherever the door was not absolutely closed against them. Russia had brought no army into the field since the battle of Zurich, and yet she was in a state of war with France. The Emperor Paul wielded the Russian sceptre. It occurred to the First Consul to collect all the soldiers of that monarch whom the fate of arms had thrown into our power: he had their national uniform restored to them; caused them to be armed and equipped anew, and sent them home. The Russian general who was directed to lead them back to their country, merely received from him a letter to the Autocrat, wherein he told him that, as he felt no desire to wage war against his people, the gallant men who were thrown by chance into his power had no longer any prospect of being exchanged: in this state of things he had determined to put an end to their captivity. Entertaining full confidence in the Russian government, he had restored to them their arms, which, on the score of bravery, they had proved their claim to bear, and left them at liberty to wield those arms as their sovereign might think fit to direct. This noble and hitherto unexampled conduct had its desired effect. The Emperor Paul, who had declared war against an anarchical power, had no longer any motive for waging it against a government which proclaimed every where its respect for order, and only rendered its victories instrumental to securing peace: he accordingly dispatched M. de Sprengporten to Paris without delay, in order to return thanks to the First Consul for his generous action, and to treat for a peace, which was almost immediately concluded. This was the first of our friendly communications with foreign powers that was attended with complete success. The two countries had waged war against each other; but there existed no national animosity between them that could obstruct the way to a perfect reconciliation.

The French Consul adopted a peace establishment, and brought the troops back to their garrisons, which they had not seen since 1792. All those gallant volunteers who had flown to arms when the country was in danger were now disbanded and sent home. Leave of absence was granted to such an extent, that many corps were reduced to their skeletons; and even these were incomplete. The army having thus been placed upon a peace establishment, the First Consul withdrew the seals of the war department from M. Carnot, and confided them to General Berthier.

CHAPTER XXI.

Peace of Luneville—State of Europe—Negotiations with England.

THE peace of Luneville had been in the highest degree detrimental to the views of Mr. Pitt, then prime minister of England. He had openly declared that a war of extinction ought to be waged against France, and his last remaining ally had just withdrawn herself from his influence; he accordingly foresaw, that unless he could again set a general coalition on foot, England would also be under the necessity of concluding a peace with the French Republic.

Russia was governed by the Emperor Paul, who had manifested the intention of coming to terms with France; and the First Consul was not behindhand in this happy disposition, which soon led to a treaty of peace.

Prussia was immovably bent upon the system of neutrality to which she had adhered ever since the peace of Basle.

Austria, after an unsuccessful struggle, had just laid down her arms.

Spain was still wrapped up in her ancient habits, and was quite devoted to France.

The whole of Italy was in the power of the First Consul.

Holland was bound to France by the ties of a policy and of a revolution that were common to both.

The other petty powers of Germany were not then possessed of the military importance they have since acquired.

In such a state of things, Mr. Pitt would be compelled to carry on the struggle single-handed : he accordingly retired from the ministry as soon as he found that it became a matter of necessity for England to conclude a peace.

On quitting the helm, however, he caused Mr. Addington to be appointed his successor, the political sentiments of this minister being in accordance with his own. The names were changed, but their views and maxims were the same. Necessity was submitted to ; a truce was concluded with the firm intention of suffering it to last no longer than the time requisite for renewing a general coalition against France, which inspired so much dread, and was represented as the more dangerous to the common security of all, from her having confided to the First Consul the task of protecting the interests that had grown out of the revolution. The department of foreign affairs in France was held at this time by M. de Talleyrand, a very intelligent man, no doubt ; but who, on the present occasion, was entirely the dupe of his opponents, and did not sustain the reputation of talent he had acquired. I have often heard the First Consul express his astonishment at never learning any thing from his minister at the period of the rupture of the peace of Amiens, and of the coalition which soon followed it ; especially when he found that the coalition had not been formed without the previous interference of a variety of private proceedings, of which his minister ought to have acquired a thorough knowledge.

I now return to the overtures made by the new British ministry. Orders had been given by the preceding one to chase and capture fishing boats. This measure, which was only calculated to increase unnecessarily the evils of war, was contrary to all usage.

M. Otto intimated to the British cabinet that his presence could be no longer useful; that it behoved him to quit a country which abjured every sincere disposition to peace, and disregarded, and even violated the laws and usages of war. The measure he complained of was instantly revoked. Lord Hawkesbury informed him, at the same time, that the King was ready to renew the interrupted negotiations, and willing to send a plenipotentiary minister to Paris.

The First Consul, whose intentions had not undergone any change, warmly hailed this overture; convinced, however, that a mere display of negotiations was not the most expeditious mode of settling a dispute, which had only been rendered more complicated by a war of eight years' duration, he proposed either to suspend hostilities at once, or to decide immediately · upon the preliminary articles of pacification. The British ministry agreed to the latter course, but endeavoured to put forward all the pretensions to which they had publicly laid claim. They had acquired confidence from late occurrences in the north of Europe, the passage of the English fleet through the Sound, and the unexpected death of Paul I. ·They proposed inadmissible conditions. The First Consul rejected them, · and intimated to the British cabinet, that although he desired peace, he would affix his signature to an honourable one only, resting upon an equitable balance in the several quarters of the globe ; that he could not leave in the power of England those countries and possessions to which she laid claim, and which were of so much weight in the balance of Europe. He acknowledged, at the same time, that the extraordinary events which had occurred in Europe, and the changes which had taken place in the boundaries of the continental states, might justify, to a certain extent, the pretensions advanced by the British government; but he was at a loss to understand upon what principle it could demand as its *ultimatum* to be allowed to retain Malta, Ceylon, all the countries wrested from Tippoo Saib, Trinidad, Martinico, and other possessions.

The French and Spanish armies had invaded Portugal : its court, driven to extremity, offered to make the most painful sacrifices. The First Consul, who, in the advantages which he had obtained over that kingdom, only sought means of compensation calculated to balance the restitutions to be made by England to the allies of France, proposed to the British cabinet, in consenting to its arrangements respecting the East Indies, the adoption of the *status ante bellum* for Portugal on the one side, and for the Mediterranean and America on the other. Lord Hawkesbury rejected the proposal : he consented to give up Trinidad, but insisted upon retaining Malta, Martinico, Ceylon, Tobago, Demerara, Berbice, and Essequibo.

These pretensions were at variance with the pacific professions so constantly put forth by the English ministers : the contradiction was pointed out to them. They replied : a feeling of acrimony crept into the discussion; and it was feared that such recriminations would dispel the hopes to which France still fondly clung.

The First Consul was determined if possible to avert so painful a result of his efforts : he resolved to fix anew the basis upon which the question was to rest, and specified the conditions he was prepared to agree to. M. Otto's note was conceived in these terms :—

"The undersigned has communicated to his government Lord Hawkesbury's note of the 20th July, and is directed to return the following answer :—

"The French government has at heart not to neglect any means calculated to bring about a general peace, which is equally called for by humanity and by the interests of the allied powers.

" It remains for the King of England to consider whether that peace is also consonant with his political, commercial, and national interests : in such a case, an island more or less remote, cannot be a sufficient ground for prolonging the misfortunes of the world.

"The undersigned has made known, by his last note, how deeply the First Consul regretted the retrograde course which the negotiation had taken; but as Lord Hawkesbury disputes the fact in his note of the 20th July, the undersigned will now recapitulate the state of the question with that frankness and precision which ought always to attend the discussion of matters of so much importance.

"The question is divided into three points :

"The Mediterranean ;

"The East Indies ;

" America.

" Egypt shall be restored to the Porte ; the republic of the Seven Islands is recognised; all the ports of the Adriatic and the Mediterranean that are occupied by French troops shall be given up to the Pope and the King of Naples.

" Mahon shall be returned to Spain.

" Malta shall be restored to the Order ; and if the King of England should deem it consistent with his interests, as a preponderating naval sovereign, to rase its fortifications, that clause will not be objected to

" In India, England shall retain the island of Ceylon, and thus become the unassailable sovereign of those rich and extensive countries.

" The other possessions, including the Cape of Good Hope, shall be restored to the allies.

" In America, every thing shall return to its former possessors. The King of England is already so powerful in that part of the globe, that, being absolute master of India, if he pretends to more, he must be aiming at the sovereignty of America.

" Portugal shall be maintained in all its integrity.

" Such are the conditions to which the French government is prepared to subscribe.

"They offer immense advantages to the British government; to aim at still greater, would be to reject the tender of a just and mutually honourable peace.

" As Martinico was not conquered by British arms, but merely surrendered in trust by its inhabitants, until France should have a settled government, it cannot be considered as an English possession : France will never renounce her right to it

" It now rests with the British cabinet to make known its determination : if these conditions do not meet its wishes, it will at least be proved to the whole world that the French Consul has left no means untried, has shown a readiness to submit to every kind of sacrifice, for the purpose of restoring peace, and sparing humanity the tears and effusion of blood which must be the unavoidable results of another campaign.

"4th Thermidor, year IX."

Lord Hawkesbury's reply did not bear the stamp of that frankness that might have been expected. The minister, however, announced his sovereign's determination to retain only such portions of his conquests as were indispensable for guaranteeing his ancient possessions. With respect to Malta, the King of England was ready to enter into arrangements for the eventual disposal of that island, and was seriously desirous of concerting the means by which Malta might be rendered wholly independent of Great Britain and France.

The only difficulty that embarrassed the first part of the negotiation was thus removed. The second difficulty next came under consideration. It was pointed out to Lord Hawkesbury that the security of the ancient British possessions in America did not stand in need of the extension which it was thought necessary to give to them, since they had the island of Jamaica for their central point. This vast and opulent colony, strong by its natural position, had been fortified in a manner that secured it from any attack. An attempt to preserve the recent acquisitions which England had made in America was tantamount to an endeavour to secure in the West Indies that absolute dominion which she already exercised in oriental India.

Lord Hawkesbury appeared to admit the truth of this reasoning, and offered to restore Martinico, with the alternative, however, of retaining in the West Indies the islands of Trinidad and Tobago; and, in such case, of declaring Demerara, Essequibo and Berbice free ports, or of keeping possession of Saint Lucia, Tobago, Demerara, Berbice, and Essequibo.

This was a perplexing alternative.

By giving up Trinidad, the First Consul subjected Spain to a serious loss: by ceding Berbice, Essequibo, and Demerara, he made Holland bear all the weight of the sacrifices which a peace rendered necessary: on the other hand, he resigned to England the whole commerce of the American continent, and inflicted upon Spain a much deeper wound than she could suffer by the abandonment of the island of Trinidad. The First Consul would have willingly yielded Tobago, in order to consult the interests of his allies: he even offered to add Curaçoa to it. England persisted in her demands, whilst he was, according to his own expression, unwilling to hazard the peace of the world by throwing it in the scale against the possession of an island which was divested of its former political importance; and he submitted to the sacrifice.

Nothing more remained than to come to a definitive understanding with regard to Malta. Lord Hawkesbury evaded the question: he cavilled about terms: it was at last agreed upon, however, that the island should be given up to the

Order of St. John of Jerusalem,* and that the evacuation should take place within the time agreed upon in Europe for a measure of that description. The preliminaries of peace were ratified by both governments.

CHAPTER XXII.

M. Clement de Ris forcibly carried off—The author is sent by the First Consul to Tours, to inquire into this event—Various kinds of evidence obtained—M. Clement de Ris is restored to his family—News from Egypt—Preparations for a fresh expedition—The author is sent off to Brest by the First Consul, for the purpose of accelerating its departure—General Sabuguet—Infernal machine.

THE administration was beginning to breathe. It was no longer necessary to impose sacrifices upon the nations, or to draw upon the finances to meet extraordinary expenses. Nothing but reform and economy was talked of: a happy futurity opened every where to our view. A strange adventure suddenly occurred to throw a gloom over the picture. We were in the month of September, when a deputy of the senate, M. Clement de Ris, was carried away from an estate

---

* " His Majesty has only consented to resign the island of Malta under the express condition of its remaining quite independent of France, as well as of Great Britain. The only means of attaining this object will be to place it under the guarantee or protection of some power able to assert the right. His Majesty will no longer persist in retaining a British garrison in that island until such time as the government of the Order of St. John shall have been established. The King is even anxious to direct the evacuation within the delay usually prescribed in Europe for a measure of that description, provided that the Emperor of Russia, in the character of protector of the Order, or any other power that may be so acknowledged by the contracting parties, will undertake the defence and security of Malta in the most effectual manner.

" HAWKESBURY."

where he resided in the vicinity of Tours. A crowd of men had come to his house in disguise, compelled him to mount a horse, and forcibly conveyed him into the heart of the neighbouring forest.

Madame Clement de Ris had hurried off to Tours, and, bathed in tears, had implored the prefect's assistance : the latter had made a report of the event; and as the peace of the country was threatened by this abduction, which might be the forerunner of some insurrection, the First Consul ordered me to repair to the spot.

I was not long in reaching Tours, where stupor was still marked on every countenance: no search had yet been made to discover M. Clement de Ris. At the end of a few days his wife received a communication, stating, that if she would deposit 50,000 francs in Blois or Amboise, at a certain tavern which was named to her, she would recover her husband. This respectable lady did not hesitate a moment ; she applied secretly to her friends, borrowed money from each, and succeeded in collecting the required sum. I had it intimated to her that she should provide the sum in silver money only. She proceeded on the journey with her treasure, and repaired to the tavern pointed out; but on the first display made of the quantity of silver taken out of the carriage, a man came up and sharply told her: " Nothing can be done to-day ; go back; a letter will be written to you:" so saying, he disappeared.

She returned to Tours in the utmost despair, and with the impression that her husband had been murdered. I thought otherwise ; I had ascertained that a country doctor, on going the round of his patients, had met the group by whom M. Clement de Ris had been carried off. Being also seized by the abductors, who feared his giving the alarm, he had travelled with the prisoner, was led to a spot where he was detained the whole night, and then dismissed with the necessary precautions to prevent his finding out the track they had pursued.

On my sending for him he particularly described the spot where he had fallen in with M. Clement de Ris; but as the abductors had immediately bandaged his eyes, he could give no clue to the road he had taken. All he could tell was that he had heard the clock of the village of Montresor on his left striking the hour of eight. They soon afterwards reached the station at which they dismounted. He had been conducted to a house, which was entered by ascending three steps; the bandage was then removed from his eyes, and he was led to a chamber situated on the left of the entrance, where a pie, ham, and artichokes were set before him. After supper a letter was handed to him for Madame Clement de Ris: he was again blindfolded, replaced on horseback, and led through a thousand winding turns, to the neighbourhood of Montresor, where he was set at liberty. The letter to which the doctor alluded was the identical one which Madame Clement de Ris had received.

I had no other guide in my inquiries than the evidence of this lady, whose head was quite bewildered by the apprehension of the danger to which her husband was exposed, and the information afforded by the doctor, who displayed great shrewdness.

His deposition tallied with a fact I have not yet mentioned. A hat was picked up in the neighbourhood of Montresor which was found to belong to M. Clement de Ris. I questioned the doctor on this subject, and he replied that M. Clement had in fact dropped his hat a short time before his arrival at the station where they dismounted. The field of our inquiries thus became much circumscribed. We had only to search the vicinity of Montresor, without proceeding beyond the distance within which the clock could be heard. I had assembled the brigade of gendarmerie stationed at

Loches and Chinon ; I now caused copies of the doctor's deposition to be distributed amongst them, and directed them to search every one of the isolated houses of which there was abundance in this part of the country, and to extend their inquiries over a surface of two leagues.

A quartermaster soon came to tell me that he was upon the right scent. He had found out a house which exactly tallied with all the circumstances mentioned in the doctor's deposition ; he had entered it by ascending three steps, and turned to the left into a room where he had noticed near the steps of the staircase some old artichoke leaves, which even appeared to have been there some time, as they were faded and half covered with dirt ; lastly, the remains of some ham had been served up to him, when not more than ten days had elapsed after the disappearance of M. Clement de Ris. This quartermaster had hastened back in all speed to relate these particulars.

The minister of police, however, M. Fouché, had already sent agents to the prefect. These men, who were formerly of the Vendean party, had immediately opened a communication with the abductors of M. Clement de Ris, and reproached them with compromising those of their party whose only desire was to live in peace. They dwelt upon the deposition just made by the quartermaster of the gendarmerie, and pointed out that their prey was about to escape from their grasp, and that consequently they were lost men.

The abductors took the alarm, ran to the house in which M. Clement de Ris was guarded, brought him out of the vault, led him, blindfolded, to a certain distance in a forest, and under pretence of a skirmish with some of their party just arrived from Paris, they fired a few pistol shots close to the ears of M. Clement de Ris, and disappeared amongst the trees. Those who next presented themselves appeared as the avengers of M. Clement, and hastened to inform him that he was free : the prisoner, quite beside himself with joy, tore the bandage from his eyes, embraced his deliverers, and re-entered Tours at the moment when every one despaired of seeing him again.

The public safety was compromised by this abduction; the First Consul was inexorable towards the guilty; he insisted upon justice taking its course.* The information obtained established the fact of the identity of the house pointed out by the quartermaster with that in which M. Clement had been detained. In consequence of the account given of it by the prisoner, I sent to have it examined. The hole in which he had been detained was concealed under a heap of faggots, in a shed close to the barn: had it been of larger dimensions, it would probably have also become the little doctor's habitation.

M. Clement de Ris had remained concealed for ten days in this hole, which only required to be stopped up in order to bury him alive; an event which would probably have come to pass had Madame Clement de Ris paid the sum which was demanded of her.

Whilst the First Consul's attention was directed to restoring the influence of the laws, he was not unmindful of Egypt. He had sent back, in the month of September, the aide-de-camp who had brought him the convention of El-Arish; and as he was informed of the consequences that had resulted from the non-execution of the treaty, he had apprised General Kleber, by that officer, of the period at which he would dispatch the relief which it was intended to afford him.† He could only send it from Brest, the only harbour in which we had any ships of war.

The directorial administration had carried their neglect so far, as to permit the dismantling of the greater part of the

---

* On this occasion several young men, who had been ruined by dissipation and bad company, were brought to the scaffold.

† The aide-de-camp reached Alexandria in safety, though after Kleber's death.

squadron which had been armed by Admiral Bruix ; only ten ships of the line were in a fit condition for sea.

The Spanish fleet was still in Brest, and would not have shared a better fate than our own, had not the government of Charles IV. taken upon itself to provide every thing that was necessary for keeping it in proper repair: it therefore still presented a respectable appearance, whilst our fleet was reduced to a state of nullity.

Ever since the month of September the First Consul had been considering of the means of relieving Egypt ; he had given orders to get ready for sea six of the best line-of-battle ships belonging to the Brest fleet, to which were to be added four of the best frigates that could be found ; he had caused them to be very carefully selected and fitted out, without communicating to any one the destination for which he intended them ; and only waited for the long winter nights to order them to get under sail.

In the mean time 2000 infantry, 200 cavalry, and 200 artillerymen had been assembling at Brest ; the naval arsenal was preparing a considerable supply of arms, powder, melted lead, balls, shot, iron, copper, and other materials connected with an armament. The report had been spread of an expedition to St. Domingo, and all believed that these preparations were intended for the colony to which the convoy had been directed to proceed.

I was desired by the First Consul to proceed to Brest, to superintend the execution of the orders he had given, and to deliver up his youngest brother, Jerome Bonaparte, to Admiral Gantheaume, who commanded the squadron : it was at this period that Jerome first entered the navy.

I was not to quit Brest until the admiral should have set sail. This did not happen for a long time ; he was detained two months in port by contrary winds and by the presence of the English who were cruising off Ushant, and in daily communication with the land. Those islanders still held the strings of that vast system of espionage which they had spread over those provinces at the period of the civil war; it was impossible to keep from their knowledge the sailing of the smallest vessel without resorting to the most mysterious conduct.

Gantheaume's departure at last took place one evening during the prevalence of a high wind, which almost threatened to blow the houses of Brest into the sea, and had forced away the British cruisers. No better moment could offer for sailing with a certainty of being neither seen nor pursued, because the English would not fail to return when the weather moderated; advantage was therefore taken of it: the wind was very favourable; but our ships sailed in a tremendous storm, and all suffered very severe damage, which they had to repair in the open sea.

Admiral Gantheaume had foreseen the dispersion of his fleet, and had given to each captain secret written instructions, which he was only to open at sea, and in which he named Cape Finisterre as the first point of rendezvous, afterwards Cape St. Vincent, then the southern part of the island of Sardinia, and lastly, Alexandria on the coast of Egypt.

General Sahuguet was still on shore when Gantheaume's ships were weighing anchor to set sail. M. Caffarelli, the maritime prefect of Brest, and brother of the officer who died in Syria, was urging him to embark, observing to him that the squadron would not wait his arrival on board. General Sahuguet resisted, and demanded for the use of his troops a considerable sum of money, which the maritime prefect had not the power of giving to him, and which he, moreover, knew to be uncalled for, since he was in the secret of the destination of the squadron, which was not known to General Sahuguet. The discussion was growing warm; and General Sahuguet was urging, with great vehemence of language, the interests of his expedition to St. Domingo, to which he thought he was proceeding.

M. Caffarelli had in vain used every means in his power to persuade him to depart: the general was immovable, and declared he would not embark without his money. I was compelled to interfere in the discussion; and M. Caffarelli and I both agreed upon the propriety of telling the truth to General Sahuguet, who showed a momentary ill-humour at what we unfolded, and went off without uttering a word.

Gantheaume had already been forty hours at sea: no unpleasant event had occurred, nor did the English fleet make its appearance. I returned to Paris by way of L'Orient and Nantes. I was at Brest when the crime of the 3d Nivose was attempted. On my arrival in Paris, I found it still greatly agitated, in consequence of the explosion of the infernal machine, and was enabled to collect the most minute details of that criminal attempt. There was to be that night at the opera a first representation of Haydn's oratorio: the First Consul was to attend: the conspirators concerted their measures accordingly.

At this period several of the houses in the Carrousel had already been demolished: nevertheless, the angle of the Rue Saint Nicaise still fronted the principal gate of the Hotel de Longueville, so that in going from the Tuileries to the theatre it was necessary to turn first to the left, and afterwards to the right, to pass through the Rue Saint Nicaise at once into the Rue de Malte; the consequence was, that coachmen were obliged to slacken the paces of their horses to enable them to turn in opposite directions. The conspirators had built their hopes of success upon the delays which these windings would necessarily occasion.

The First Consul left the Tuileries at the usual hour of representation. He was accompanied by General Lannes, and, I believe, by his aide-de-camp, Lebrun, with an escort, consisting of a picket of grenadiers. In one moment he reached the angle where stood the cart upon which the infernal machine was laid: his coachman, a bold man, and a very

dexterous driver, who had been with him in Egypt, fortunately took it into his head to turn at once into the Rue de
Malte, instead of following the direct line of the Rue Saint
Nicaise. The carriage of the First Consul was thus placed
beyond danger. At that moment the explosion took place,
killed or wounded about forty people, sacrificed many victims,
but missed the very one against whose life it was levelled :
the glasses of his carriage only were broken, and the horse
of the last trooper of the escort was wounded. The First
Consul arrived safe at the opera, where the report of the
event had almost immediately become known.

The police, taken by surprise, set every inquiry on foot ;
but whilst the researches were going on the different parties
in the state indulged in conjectures which displayed the
intention of laying hold of any occurrence that might afford
them an opportunity of injuring each other.

The nobility insisted that the jacobins were alone capable
of such an attempt; that they alone had a design upon the
life of the First Consul; and that if the minister of police did
not discover any trace of so infamous a conspiracy, it was for
no other reason than its having been got up by his old accomplices. They urged, in their own behalf, the gratitude
they owed to the protector of the state, who had put an end
to their exile, and reinstated them in their property : so far
from making any attempt on his life, they were ready to shed
their blood in its defence : in short, they pleaded their zeal
and attachment with so much earnestness, and so beset Madame Bonaparte, who was of very easy access to them, that
the First Consul began to attach some credit to their accusations. This opinion was greatly strengthened by the representations of many of those who were about his person. They
felt an abhorrence of the jacobins, and did not fail to euve-
nom the reports made against them. Many others bore a
personal hatred to Fouché, and neglected no opportunity of
injuring him. Clarke, in particular, gave a loose to his ani-

mosity with a violence quite unaccountable to those who were ignorant of his old enmity to him. The First Consul, on the other hand, was not over-satisfied with his minister another plot had been hatched against his life some time before, and not only the police had not given him any notice of it, but it was clearly proved to him that he would have been assassinated at the opera, had it not been for the timely information of a noble-hearted man.

The assassins were, on that occasion, seized in the lobby, where they had stationed themselves until he should quit his box, which, at that time, was in the first tier in front, between the two columns towards the left when facing the theatre. His access to it was by the public entrance. In this attempt originated the idea of a private entrance, which ever after existed until the theatre was pulled down.

These were not the only two grounds of complaint which the First Consul had against the administration of police : he complained of the disturbances in the western provinces, and was highly incensed at the depredations committing all over Brittany. Audacity had never gone to greater lengths: not only were the diligences plundered of the taxes that had been collected, but those taxes were even forcibly seized in the chests of the collectors by bands of armed men. The public conveyances and couriers could not pass from one place to another without being attacked and plundered. Matters had come to such extremities, that it had been found necessary to place detachments of infantry on the tops of diligences—a precaution which did not always prove effectual. The lawless men who met together in this disgraceful pursuit were the terror of the country they overran. Paris, which delights in ridicule, only looked at the measures which had been adopted for repressing those excesses in a humorous point of view, and gave the name of *armées impériales* to the detachments with which the public conveyances were loaded.

Envy, which works upon the slightest materials, laid hold

,of the most insignificant trifles for the purpose of injuring
M. Fouché. All the old stories of the police, whether true,
or false, that were current under the peaceable administration
of M. Lenoir, were raked up and repeated, and the minister's
character was tortured by comparisons of the most unfavourable nature. He was in a delicate situation: his dismissal
was daily expected. The First Consul was attentive to every
report, but he was not coming to a decision. He pretended
to have adopted the conviction that the attempt upon his life
was, in reality, the work of the jacobin party against whom
the general accusation was directed. On the other hand,
many respectable people, who were bound from principle to
the revolution, and who adhered to the consular government,
proposed that this opportunity should be laid hold of to act
with severity against those restless minds which never grow
weary of promoting disorders. This measure suggested, in
their opinion, a double advantage; it had the effect of
relieving society from certain elements of interminable discord, and of eliciting whatever the party might have to reveal,
supposing that the guilty were to be found in its ranks. It was
M. Fouché's impression that they lurked elsewhere; but he
had not courage to oppose the plan suggested, and he assisted
in drawing up the list of those individuals who had taken a
conspicuous part in the revolutionary excesses. They were
arrested, conducted to Rochefort, and shipped off to Cayenne,
without the least appeal being made in their favour by any of
those of the minister's companions in the revolutionary career
who had become reconciled to the First Consul.

The whole odium of the affair of the 3d Nivose had been
cast upon these unhappy men: public indignation vented
itself throughout their journey. I witnessed their arrival in
Nantes. This city had not yet laid aside the feelings of
exasperation created by those revolutionary scenes which had
deluged it with blood. They would have been torn to pieces
had not the military been called to arms. The assistance

thus afforded was hardly sufficient to protect them from being thrown into the river.

The party of the nobles had gained the ascendancy. They had repelled the bare suspicion of being concerned in the attempt, and gravely asserted that men of rank were incapable of entertaining so iniquitous a design.

Nevertheless the researches continued. The First Consul kept urging on the prefect of police, whose zeal acquired new ardour from the sluggishness imputed to the head of that department.

The horse which was harnessed to the infernal machine had been killed on the spot, but not in the least disfigured. Some fragments of the vehicle were strewed about the carcase. The prefect ordered they should be collected, and sent for all the horse-dealers of Paris. One of them recognised the horse that had been killed as having been sold by him, and delivered at a house of which be indicated the street and the number. This intelligence was followed up, and the whole mystery unravelled. The portress gave the names of its inmates. By degrees it was ascertained that an old Vendean chief, named Saint Regent, had worked for six weeks, with several of his party, at the construction of the infernal machine, which they had placed in a water-carrier's barrel, and in which it actually exploded.

Every plan of a complicated nature, however well combined, will always miscarry when put to the proof. The driver was too late in lighting the train that was to set fire to the inflammable machine. The carriage of the First Consul had already turned the corner of the Rue de Malte before the explosion took place.

This discovery, although made at too late a period to reach the guilty, had at least the advantage of pointing out to which party they belonged.

CHAPTER XXIII.

THE First Consul was at Malmaison when I returned to
Paris, and I immediately waited upon him. He expressed
great satisfaction at the sailing of Admiral Gantheaume, the
accomplishment of which object was the most difficult part of
my mission. He fancied that the squadron had achieved every
thing, since it had triumphed over the obstacle that prevented
its departure. His confidence, however, was soon shaken.

The squadron, having been dispersed by the storm on its
quitting Brest, had rallied at Cape Finisterre: it had afterwards doubled the Straits of Gibraltar, passed on to Cape
Bon without encountering any obstacle, and was almost within
reach of its destination, when on a sudden it tacked about,
and entered Toulon at the moment when it was expected to
be in the roads of Alexandria.

Disappointed beyond measure at this extraordinary and
unaccountable return, the First Consul dispatched Lacuée,
his aide-de-camp, to Toulon, with orders that the squadron
should again set sail, and that he should bring him an account
of the motives which had induced the admiral to return to
France.

My curiosity was awakened on the subject, and I learned,
upon inquiry, that the admiral's conduct was influenced by the
false notions entertained of the state of our army in the East,
and of the efficiency of the British naval force on the coast
of Africa. The officers of the fleet had taken it into their
heads that, once arrived at Alexandria, they should never be

able to quit it: they were apprehensive of being made prisoners; and under pretence of the damage experienced by some of the ships running foul of each other, they brought the squadron back to Toulon. They made, by these means, a voyage three times longer than what they had yet to perform in order to gain their destination, and ran infinitely greater risks of coming into contact with the English squadrons, to avoid incurring the mere chance of meeting them along a coast all the commanding points of which were in our power. The feeling of disappointment was heightened when it was afterwards learned that they might, without the least difficulty, have entered the passes, which were perfectly free from cruisers. The whole of the English ships had repaired to the Archipelago, in order to stimulate the Turks to fresh efforts.   Admiral Gantheaume could not have been ignorant of this, since he had met on his return and captured an English ship of war, which had made him acquainted with those facts. Nothing could be more pitiful than the motives alleged by Gantheaume. Nevertheless, he obstinately refused to put to sea again. It was found impossible to overcome this determination; and the First Consul, notwithstanding his displeasure, was under the necessity of giving way, and of combining some other mode of sending assistance to Egypt.

As the late expedition had succeeded in getting under weigh in spite of the weather and of the English, a fresh one might be equally successful. The First Consul directed preparations to be made for a second expedition in the same harbour from which the first had sailed. He ordered six line-of-battle ships to be equipped, and entrusted the command of them to Vice-Admiral Latouche-Tréville, who had the charge of accomplishing what Gantheaume had left undone. He sent me, at the same time, to Rochefort, for the purpose of collecting and organising every thing that was to be embarked in another expedition which was preparing at that place. I first repaired to L'Orient,* where I was to send out to sea two new ships and a frigate that were lying in that port. I communicated my instructions to the maritime prefect, Vice-Admiral Decrès, who afterwards became minister of marine and a duke. He caused the ships to set sail immediately, and come to anchor at L'Ile d'Aix, close to the mouth of the Charente, whence they were ordered to join the squadron then fitting out at Rochefort.

I revisited Nantes, and penetrated through La Vendée on my way to Rochefort. Over this unhappy country were still scattered the embers of the conflagration by which it had been desolated. Not a man, not a house was to be seen: in a space of fifteen leagues through the richest part of those so lately flourishing provinces, I discovered only women, children, and ruins. Every dwelling-house had been destroyed.

" Paris, 11th Ventose, year IX. of the French Republic.

' * " The chief of brigade Savary will proceed in all haste to L'Orient : he will deliver to the maritime prefect the letter from the minister of marine. He will remain in that port until the Argonaute, the Union, and one of the three frigates shall have sailed for Rochefort. With the view to expedite their departure, he is to confer every day with the maritime prefect and with Rear-Admiral Ledoux: he will then repair to Rochefort, where he will stop until the squadron shall have got under weigh. He will report to me every night, from each place, the progress made in provisioning and fitting out the ships, the state of the wind, and the strength of the enemy's cruisers.

" When he shall have any doubt on the latter point, he will himself go out to sea, or ascend any cape whence he can personally ascertain the strength and number of the cruisers.

" On the occurrence of any extraordinary event, he may send off a courier to me.

" In his second dispatch from L'Orient, he will let me know the actual condition of all ships on the stocks, and what may be required to expedite their construction.

" On his arrival at a port, he will never fail to wait upon the maritime prefect, the commandant of the town, the sub-prefect, and the mayor.

" In every place where he may be detained, he will note down his remarks on the principal public functionaries, and on the state of the public mind.

" He will wait upon the minister of marine before his departure.

" (Signed) BONAPARTE."

The lands were untilled, the villages buried as it were under the briers and grass which were growing out of their ruins : the roads were entirely broken up. In whichever direction I turned my eyes, I beheld a vast picture of desolation, which harrowed the soul. It was the close of day; and hesitating to venture during the night upon such wretched roads, I took shelter in a cabin which had been made a post-house station. I found there some priests who were returning from Louisiana, whither they had fled for shelter when driven by persecution from their native land. I was struck with the attentions paid to them by the peasantry. My carriage, my money, my military dress, every thing yielded to the reverence which their cassocks inspired ; the supper and apartments were kept in reserve for them. They had the complaisance to divide their meal with me; but I was compelled to sit by the fireside until the return of day.

I at last got to Rochefort, after encountering many difficulties : Admiral Bruix had already reached that post with the two ships from L'Orient; those, however, that were fitting out in Rochefort were very far from being ready for sea.

Several extraordinary couriers were sent to me every week by the First Consul, to whom I was to return, on the day of their arrival, an answer to each of his questions, which originated in his having just learned that an English army was on the eve of embarkation for the purpose of attacking Egypt : he kept urging me on, as well as the admiral, not to neglect any means of accelerating the expedition. His letters, some of which were of great length, were indicative of the extreme anxiety he felt for the colony. He noticed every object which it stood in need of; the artillery and small arms, medicines and projectiles; he pointed out and ordered every thing ; carts, harness, spare stores, instruments for every trade, cases of mathematical instruments, pencils, surgery cases, chemical instruments ; all the most minute articles used by the

engineer, the chemist, and the mechanic had shared his
attention. Many of these objects were not to be had at
Rochefort or La Rochelle, and I went in person to Bordeaux
in search of them. Admiral Bruix, on his part, had succeeded by dint of perseverance in fitting out three sail of the
line and as many frigates. He made them get under weigh
for L'Ile d'Aix, where they formed a junction with the ships
lately arrived from L'Orient.

This squadron had thus on board not only a considerable re-
inforcement, but also whatever the colony could stand in need
of for its several establishments. The First Consul had given
me the superintendence of the detachments of each service
about to be sent on board, and directed me to distribute the
men and the objects of various descriptions to be embarked,
in such a manner that no one ship should have a greater
proportion than another. Having therefore eight ships to
supply, I had to divide the men, powder, ammunition, projectiles, &c. and send on board each ship an eighth of the
aggregate amount. In this manner each ship had its proportion of every thing ; and if one vessel should be lost, this was
only attended with the loss of a portion of each object,
instead of the whole of one description, and which might have
been the one most needed by the colony or the army.

This was an unusual mode of distribution, and was warmly
resisted by the marine department. I reported this oppo-
sitiou to the First Consul, who imperatively settled the question, by replying that I should see to the punctual execution
of his orders, and desiring me to point out to the admiral the
advantage of the distribution he had enjoined, which afforded
us a security that a part of the various objects of which the
armament was composed would reach Egypt, and protected
us from the consequences which might have resulted to the
colony from the loss of a vessel exclusively loaded with the
supply it stood in need of.

I had to send a detailed statement of the number of men of

each corps, and of the quantity of each kind of articles embarked on board each ship. It was approved by the First Consul, and returned without any alteration. Every thing was in readiness, and the fleet about to sail, when he sent me an order to load a fast-sailing corvette with timber for the use of the artillery; with wheels, wheelwrights' timber, and gun-carriages ready mounted, which I was authorised to take from the arsenal of La Rochelle. I proceeded immediately in search of a corvette of the swiftness required, loaded it to its full admeasurement, united it to the squadron, and reported progress to the First Consul. His reply was soon received : it was an order for Bruix to proceed immediately to the Mediterranean, where he was to rally under his command the squadron of Admiral Gantheaume, and continue his voyage in all haste for Alexandria.

It was unquestionably a work of some magnitude, with the weak resources possessed by the marine department when the First Consul assumed the supreme authority, to have succeeded in fitting out eleven sail of the line and seven or eight frigates, of which force the two squadrons were composed. Had these ships reached Egypt, which it has since been ascertained they might have done, the colony would have been saved. They were conveying to it upwards of 8000 fighting men, and 50,000 stand of arms, besides a variety of other objects that would have contributed to its defence. Unfortunately the favourable season for setting sail had elapsed amidst the difficulties which attended their fitting out. That season was succeeded by calms and contrary winds; and it was found necessary to put off the expedition to the autumnal equinox; but it was then too late; we had already lost every thing in Egypt, as will presently be seen.

Whilst the First Consul was urging the departure of the succours he was sending to the army in the East, he neglected no means of annoying the English. Portugal might be considered a colony of England, and he determined to expel them from it. This enterprise had the twofold object in view, of taking possession of a country with which we were still at war, and of compelling the English to send to the relief of their ally the troops which they destined for an attack upon Egypt.

Spain entered into his views, formed an army in Estremadura, and granted a passage through Biscay and Castile to the corps of French troops that were intended to join and assist her in her operations.

The junction took place at Badajoz. The King of Spain came in person to assume the command of the combined forces. The celebrated Godoy, who will be spoken of in the sequel of these Memoirs, was second in command.

Our troops were under the orders of General Leclerc, brother-in-law of the First Consul, and did not exceed ten or twelve thousand men, of all arms.

Lucien Bonaparte, who had recently quitted the ministry of the interior, had just been named ambassador to Spain, and followed the King to the army.

The Portuguese government, conscious of being too weak to resist the forces about to invade their territory, only exerted themselves to avert the storm. Their ally having left them to their own resources, they submitted to the conditions of peace imposed by us, and sent an ambassador to the First Consul. This was the first diplomatic appointment from Portugal to France since the breaking out of the revolution.

Don Manuel Godoy, who had already been created Prince of the Peace on account of the treaty of Basle, obtained as a reward for the late insignificant expedition an extension of favours and patronage of which no example had yet been found in history. He brought his sovereign back to Madrid, was considered the only man calculated to manage the internal and external affairs of Spain, and very shortly drew down upon himself the animadversion of all Spaniards.

As a consequence of this peace, and in execution of the treaty of Luneville, the First Consul raised to the throne of Tuscany the son of the Infant of Parma, who had espoused the daughter of the King of Spain. That prince was acknowledged by the title of King of Etruria, and came to thank the First Consul for his elevation. He was received by General Bessieres, who had gone as far as Bayonne to meet him, and traversed France under the name of Count of Leghorn, which he retained during his sojourn at Paris.

This unexpected visit was looked upon by the old republicans with an eye of suspicion: it was, on the other hand, strenuously applauded by the nobility ; and they took care to point out the difference between the First Consul, who had just created a king, and the Directory, who dreamed of nothing but republics.

This unfortunate prince was, however, very ill-calculated to recommend, by his personal character, the institutions to which the nobility clung with so much fondness. Nature had endowed him with an excellent heart, but with very limited talents; and his mind had imbibed the false impress consequent upon his monastic education. He resided at Malmaison nearly the whole time of his visit to Paris. Madame Bonaparte used to lead the queen to her own apartments ; and as the First Consul never left his closet except to sit down to meals, the aides-de-camp were under the necessity of keeping the king company, and of endeavouring to entertain him, so wholly was he devoid of intellectual resources. It required, indeed, a great share of patience to listen to the frivolities which engrossed his attention. His turn of mind being thus laid open to view, care was taken to supply him with the playthings usually placed in the hands of children ; he was therefore never at a loss for occupation. His nonentity was a source of regret to us: we lamented to see a tall, handsome youth, destined to rule over his fellow-men, trembling at the bare sight of a horse, and wasting his time in the game of hide and seek, or at leapfrog with us, and whose whole information consisted in knowing his prayers, and in saying grace before and after meals. Such, nevertheless, was the man to whom the destinies of a nation were about to be committed.

When he left France to repair to his kingdom, " Rome need not be uneasy," said the First Consul to us, after the audience of leave, " there is no danger of *his* crossing the Rubicon."

The departure of the King of Etruria gave rise to a highly unbecoming act, which was likely to be attended with serious consequences for the individual who had been guilty of it. Madame de Montesson, who had contracted a left-handed marriage with the Duke of Orleans, the grandfather of the present one, without, however, at any time assuming his name, conceived the idea, no doubt, that the revolution, in destroying all titles, had sanctioned her intercourse with a prince of the blood ; she suddenly took it into her head that she was the only relative of the Count of Leghorn in Paris, and that, as such, it devolved upon her to pay him the honours he had a right to claim from the remains of the old court society. She was, undoubtedly, adopting the revolution with all its consequences, when she conceived the thought of bringing together all the returned emigrants who were to be found in the capital, in the same company with those who had risen by their deeds, and inviting them to the house of an old mistress of the Duke of Orleans to pay their respects to the Infant of Parma, the son-in-law of the King of Spain. Madame de Montesson dared to go farther : she invited the family of the First Consul, as well as the persons of his suite. We went thither, without giving the First Consul any previous intimation, and were severely reprimanded the next morning for so doing : he dwelt with warmth upon the great impropriety of such an invitation ; and if he abstained from any severity towards the individual with whom it originated, his indulgence is, I believe, to be ascribed to Madame Bonaparte, who undertook Madame de Montesson's defence, as well as to the necessity he still felt of keeping on terms with every one.

CHAPTER XXIV.

Assassination of General Kleber—Regret of the First Consul—General Menou assumes the chief command—Arrival of the British army commanded by Abercromby—Battle of Alexandria—Capitulation of General Belliard at Cairo—Capitulation of Menou—Return of the army of Egypt.

WHEN I broke off the thread of my narrative of the affairs of Egypt I left General Kleber in that country, just after he had repaired his error, the cause to him of a heavy loss of men, and after he had become acquainted with the revolution of the 18th Brumaire, which had made him renounce all idea of returning to France without a previous sanction of that measure by the First Consul.

After driving the Grand Vizier back into Syria, and recovering possession of Cairo, where the head-quarters were again established, Kleber's whole attention was directed to the object of restoring whatever had been destroyed during the momentary occupation of that city by the Turks. He was walking one morning upon the terrace of his garden, and in conversation with an architect respecting certain plans of improvements which he contemplated for his residence, when his attention was drawn to a wretched fellah (a peasant), who had just issued from a group of fig-trees almost in a state of nudity, and who handed, on his knees, a folded paper to the general : the architect had turned his head to the other side of the terrace whilst Kleber was unfolding the paper. The

VOL. I. *Part* I. Q

wretch availed himself of this moment to stab Kleber to the heart with a dagger which he had kept concealed under his cloak, and repeated the blows until Kleber fell to the ground.

The architect, Protain, ran up with the measure he held in his hand; but having also received a wound, was unable to lay hold of the assassin: his cries, however, drew people to the spot; but it was too late; Kleber was expiring. The fellah was found concealed in the garden, and arrested: he was interrogated, brought to trial, and condemned to death · he met the punishment of having his right hand cut off, and of being impaled, with the same indifference which he had displayed in the perpetration of the crime.

This fellah was, at most, eighteen or twenty years of age · he was a native of Damascus, and declared that he had quitted his native city by command of the Grand Vizier, who had intrusted him with the commission of repairing to Egypt, and killing the grand sultan of the French; that for this purpose alone he had left his family, and performed the whole journey on foot, and had received from the Grand Vizier no other money than what was absolutely requisite for the exigencies of the journey.

On arriving at Cairo, he had gone forthwith to perform his devotions in the great mosque, and it was only on the eve of executing his project that he confided it to one of the scherifs of the mosque.

The death of General Kleber was made known to the First Consul in the winter of 1799—1800. I was on duty about his person when a courier coming from Toulon, with large fumigated packets, brought them to me at the Tuileries at ten o'clock at night. All was then quiet; and I was unwilling to awake the First Consul for the mere purpose of his reading, a few hours sooner, the contents of dispatches from Egypt: I accordingly delayed presenting them until the hour of Bourrienne's repairing to his presence. He made me remain to open the packets, which contained an account of all that had taken place in Egypt since the departure of the Turkish army.

The loss of General Kleber had a powerful influence over the fate of the colony. The First Consul had already forgotten his causes of complaint against him, and evinced sincere regret at losing that officer by so melancholy a catastrophe.

He considered the event as injurious and fatal to his future views, and openly spoke his sentiments of Kleber on this subject : had he found any one capable of succeeding him, he would have sent him off without delay ; but there were few men calculated for so important a command ; and this gave him a fresh occasion for deploring the loss of General Desaix. He reflected a long time upon the choice he was to make : he even did me the honour of mentioning the matter to me one day, when he appeared to have set his views upon General Richepanse ;* but he did not appoint him, because his chief reliance was upon the effect he contemplated from the arrival of his squadrons, the departure of which he still hoped to be enabled to effect.

The remains of Kleber were interred with the utmost pomp, and a monument was raised to his memory. The command of the army unfortunately devolved, by seniority, upon General Menou, a very respectable man, but utterly ignorant of his profession ; and, indeed, so free from any pretension to a knowledge of military matters, that he candidly owned they had never engaged his attention : he had, moreover, exposed himself to ridicule by marrying a Turkish woman, notwithstanding his advanced age ; and had, in consequence, become a butt for the jests of the officers of the army, which were not restrained even by the presence of the Turks, naturally a grave people, who consider raillery as a very serious offence when directed against the officer in

* He had served in the army of Sambre and Meuse, and has since died at Guadaloupe.

command.   Independently of his services not being illustrated by any act of renown, General Menou had to command
an army very fastidious on that subject, and quite unma-
nageable in respect to many other requisites.   Such was the
state of military discredit in which the British forces found him
at the head of those with whom they came to contend in Egypt.
The British army, under the orders of Abercromby, after the
lapse of several months consumed in forming and organising it
in the Gulf of Satalia, at the extremity of the Mediterranean,
came at last in sight of Alexandria, the access to which
would have been perfectly free to our squadrons during two
entire months, without being interrupted by a single cruiser.
The English cast anchor in the road of Aboukir, between
Alexandria and the mouth of the Nile, and effected a landing
on the same part of the coast where the Turks had landed
fifteen or eighteen months before.   From this moment began
a series of blunders which, for the sake of history, I deem it
proper to detail.

    Although, upon quitting Egypt, the First Consul had left
directions for keeping the army close to the seashore during
the favourable season for effecting a landing, those orders had
not been attended to: the army was still divided, and scattered over the country, for the greater comfort of the troops
and of the general officers, without any preparation being
made for their forming again.   The consequence was, that
the British army found no other obstacle to its landing than
a weak corps from the garrison of Alexandria, commanded
by General Friant, who was governor of that city.   The remarks passed upon one of his predecessors similarly situated
on the occasion of the landing of the Turks, were fresh in
Friant's recollection : whether owing to this or to some other
cause, he attacked the British army, but was very roughly
handled, and compelled to retreat, after suffering, without
any corresponding advantage, a loss which, considering the
position of our army, was extremely serious to it.

General Menou, who had received information of the sudden appearance of the English army, had at last quitted Cairo, after hesitating for many days upon the plan of operations to be adopted. He had sent forward General Lanusse with part of the division formerly commanded by General Desaix. This division arrived after the check sustained by Friant, and attacked in its turn the English army, but with as little success, being defeated in like manner, and driven back with still greater loss.

These disastrous results of partial attacks made by troops whose position imperatively prescribed to them not to act otherwise than in concert, were the necessary consequence of the injudicious plans of General Menou, who had conceived the notion of sending forward a part of his forces along the borders of the desert, and retaining the other part at Cairo, instead of sending them off in a body to the coast.

He at last arrived in person with the rest of the army, made his arrangements for attacking, and, on the 30th Ventose, gave, under the walls of Alexandria, the battle of that name, the loss of which decided the fate of Egypt.

Our numerical strength would have been greater than that of the English army had it not been for all the losses which Kleber on the one side, and those two unconnected attacks on the other, had occasioned it. We had an unquestionable superiority in cavalry and artillery : our infantry was less numerous; but an insuperable obstacle to success was to be found in the jealousy or mistrust felt by General Menou towards most of the distinguished officers of that army. He could hardly muster courage to call in aid of his inexperience the practical knowledge of men whom he had long injured. He was, however, compelled at last to adopt this course. He asked General Lanusse for a plan of attack, which the latter concerted with General Regnier. The dispositions agreed upon were immediately inserted in the orders of the day, and every thing was prepared for action; but Lanusse was shot at the first onset. The attempt which was to be the principal feature in the action failed of success, and it was found impossible to remedy the failure.

Many were the deeds of bravery performed, as usual, by the several corps; but they were rendered unavailing. The commander-in-chief of the English army was killed: our army, notwithstanding, retreated the same night to the lines of Alexandria, leaving the English in possession of the field of battle. They soon approached the city, which was, indeed, quite unassailable with the means of attack they had brought up; but they carried on the rest of the campaign in the most skilful manner.

General Menou had shut up the army in Alexandria. He could no longer communicate with Egypt except by way of the canal of Rahmanié; so that the English were masters of the sea as well as of the peninsula of Aboukir.

Their engineers reconnoitred the banks of the canal dug by Alexander the Great. They soon discovered that it had been effected by means of stupendous constructions across Lake Mareotis, which is to the right of the canal, on the road from Alexandria to the Nile, and is only separated from the Lake of Aboukir, and therefore from the sea by that same canal, the banks of which served as dikes to both lakes. They also discovered that the Lake of Aboukir was more elevated than Lake Mareotis, the waters of which were absorbed by the sun's heat, and left the ground covered with saline crystallizations.

After ascertaining the lowest point of Lake Mareotis, the English engineers cut open, at that point, the two dikes forming the banks of the canal, and existing ever since its original construction; and after making all the troops pass beyond the cut, they introduced the waters of the Lake of Aboukir into the old Lake Mareotis, which, in a few days, was filled with water as far as the Arabs' Tower, a distance of eight leagues westward of Alexandria.

The effect of this operation was to encircle Alexandria by the sea on the one side, and by this new Lake Mareotis on the other; and by means of a small body of troops stationed in such a manner as to obstruct the filling up of the cut made to the canal, the English kept the army of General Menou blockaded in Alexandria, where it was fortunately provided with resources in abundance.

Lake Mareotis had been so completely filled with water, that if General Menou had attempted to return to Cairo, he could only have succeeded by making the round of that inundated land, and passing close to the Arabs' Tower. But the army would have to perform a march of twenty-six leagues through the desert before it could obtain any supply of water fit for drinking, and was not provided with camels for transporting the requisite supply for those twenty-six leagues of country; whereas, before the inundation of the lake by the waters from the sea, they had only a distance of five or six leagues to perform in order to obtain fresh water.

Such being the situation of the army, it could have been no otherwise employed than in consuming its provisions. After the English had taken all the requisite measures, they had caused their stores of all kinds to be transported to the mouth of that branch of the Nile which runs into the sea at Rosetta; they then marched upon Cairo, by ascending along the banks of the Nile, and arrived without encountering the smallest interruption: they found there General Belliard, whom General Menou had left in that city with a small body of troops to protect it, as well as the hospitals, stores, and the various establishments of the army; or, to speak more correctly, General Belliard was surrounded by difficulties on all sides, and had not the shadow of an army. Our affairs were in a condition the very reverse of what they should have been.

Menou was blockaded in Alexandria with his whole army

by a small body of British troops who protected the cut of the canal, and Belliard was in an open town with all the *materiel* of the army, and but a very small body of men to oppose to the whole British army. Placed in this dilemma, he had no resource but in a capitulation; and he entered into one.

It has been much insisted upon that he should have ascended the country and retired into Upper Egypt. There was no impossibility of his so doing; but what purpose could it have answered? what provisions or resources could he have derived from that country? what means had he of carrying on the war? were they to be found in a handful of men under his orders, to make head at one and the same time against the sepoys on their way from India, and the troops which Europe and Asia had already poured upon him? what useful purpose, besides, could he have found in incurring fresh risks of a much more formidable nature than the former ones? could it have been with the view to afford time for sending assistance to him? But how could the mother-country have furnished him with those succours in the deserts of the Saïd, which it had been unable to supply when he was in the heart of the Delta? was it easier to penetrate to the Red Sea than to effect a landing on the shores of the Mediterranean; to disembark at Cosseir, than to reach Alexandria, Bourlos or Damietta? Fate had decided the question; it would have been a useless effusion of blood to prolong the contest. Criticism often wields its too ready weapons, and becomes an easy task for those who deal in it at a distance from all danger.

Belliard capitulated upon condition of being taken back to France with his body of troops.

The English army brought back to the sea-coast all those extensive establishments, and arrived just in time to receive the surrender of General Menou, who had nearly exhausted all his provisions, and was unwilling to wait until he should be absolutely reduced to extremities, lest he should not then obtain such favourable terms.

The English, on the other hand, whose fleet was moored in Aboukir roads, were extremely desirous of bringing it up to Alexandria, so great was their anxiety to close the war without delay.

Thus ended that brilliant enterprise, which had emanated from the mind of a mighty genius, bent upon giving a new existence to the East, and who had attended with greater care to its smallest details than his successors had bestowed upon its main interests, and which proved the grave of their glory. Every thing that was done in Egypt since his departure bore the stamp of mediocrity, and prepared the First Consul for the catastrophe that necessarily ensued. The return of the army of the East dispelled the hopes which the occupation of the colony had nourished.

Malta had been taken possession of by capitulation in the preceding season. There existed no longer any means of restoring an expedition to its former state of efficiency, which at one time bade fair to change the aspect of the universe.

The First Consul had received the official news of those events in the summer of 1801. It therefore became useless to dispatch the squadrons from Toulon and Rochefort. Whatever had been embarked was, on the contrary, relanded, and the necessary arrangements were made in the first-named port for receiving the army of Egypt, which the English were bringing back on board the same ships that had conveyed their own to that country.

However great was the displeasure of the First Consul at what had taken place, and in particular at the conduct pursued by several general officers of that army, not an expression of ill-humour escaped him against any one; nor did he make inquiry into the conduct of a single individual. He showed at all times a marked preference for those who formed a part of that army, whether in the distribution of favours, or in the

nomination to lucrative employments; with the exception, however, of a few officers who had belonged to the army of Italy,
but had made themselves conspicuous by their bad spirit and
ingratitude; and the only revenge he took on these was
to forget them altogether.

CHAPTER XXV.

Internal improvements—Macdonald's Letter—Preliminaiies of Peace.

I HAVE anticipated the course of events, in order not to
interrupt the narrative of the affairs of Egypt. I now return
to what was taking place in France whilst the fate of this
colony was being decided at the point of the sword. The
whole attention of the First Consul was devoted to the indispensable duty of repairing the evils occasioned by civil discord and revolutionary anarchy. He instituted commissions,
caused a revision of the accounts of all persons who had had
any dealings with the different branches of the administration;
and the public treasury had now, for the first time, counter-
claims to set up, instead of being, as heretofore, declared
indebted for incomplete or imaginary supplies alleged to have
been furnished. This exercise of severity had an influence
upon the national credit. The Council of State reckoned, at
this period, a great number of men of talent and of untainted
patriotism : the greater part were competent to undertake the
management of the principal branches of the administration,
and to give them a proper direction. Never had the machinery of any government yielded more readily to the impulse
given to it: it appeared as if every one had measured the
depth of the precipice into which the state was well nigh
plunged by the blunders of the late government, and was on

his guard against a return of them. Regularity had taken the
place of disorder; the system of public accounts was clear;
the administration prompt in all its acts; nothing was suffered
to fall into arrears; our present condition was a promising
augury for the future.

The state of the public mind at that time will be better
appreciated by the following document:—

" ARMY OF THE GRISONS.

" French Republic.

" Liberty.   Equality.

" Head-quarters at Trent, the 3d Pluviose,
" Year IX. of the Republic.

" Macdonald, general-in-chief of the army of the Grisons,
to General Regnier.

" As I was crossing the snow-capt and icy mountains of
the highest Alps, I received, with inexpressible delight, my
dear Regnier, the letter you had the kindness to write to me,
under date of 12th Brumaire. I have never failed inquiring
after you whenever a vessel arrived from Egypt; but I experience a much livelier pleasure in hearing from you direct.

" You are now, then, become a living mummy, separated
from your family and friends. It must be a source of consolation to them and to yourself to reflect upon the courage
and the grandeur of the French name, which you have carried to those barbarous people, and caused to be respected by
them: accordingly, the national rewards that await you have
been anticipated by the admiration of the world.

" Soon after your embarkation war was again kindled,
and we have marched to Naples, and driven an imbecile and
weak monarch from a throne which he has not dared to
resume, any more than to return to his capital, in spite of the
opportunities offered him by the inconstancy of fortune: we
have since had to bewail the capriciousness of this dame, and
have been defeated every where, owing to the pusillanimity
of the old, tyrannical, and too arrogant Directory.

"Bonàparte at last made his appearancè, upset that presumptuous government, seized the reins, and now directs, with a steady hand, the car of the Revolution to that goal which all honest men were desirous of its reaching. This extraordinary man is not alarmed at the pressure of the burden: he reforms the armies, calls back the proscribed citizens, throws open the prisons in which innocence was left to groan, abolishes the revolutionary laws, restores public confidence, extends his protection to industry, gives life to commerce; and the Republic, triumphant by his arms, dreaded by her enemies, and respected by Europe, assumes, at the present day, that first rank in the scale which Providence has eternally assigned to her.

"I am, my dear Regnier, as great a stranger to adulation as to flattery: such is my austerity of principles, that I blame and condemn what is wrong with no less candour than I praise what is right. I am not the trumpeter of Bonaparte, but merely pay homage to truth. Our military and warlike affairs are as prosperous as we could wish; and it is to be hoped at last, that the Emperor, better enlightened upon his real interests, will shake off the odious influence of the freebooters of England, and conclude a peace no less durable than wished for.

"Whilst we are invading the hereditary states M. de Cobentzel is proceeding slowly with the treaty at Luneville, and giving the formal assurance of an early peace. May this event come to pass, my dear Regnier, and restore you to your family! your friends long for your return, and I request you to consider me in the foremost ranks of them.

"Your general-in-chief has been confirmed in his appointment: if we are to judge of men by their outward acts, General Menon's nomination will be universally approved of; those who, like you, are upon the spot, can better appreciate his real worth.

" Lacroix and —— are still with me : the former intends writing direct, and giving you a detailed account of events. I have but few people of your acquaintance about me.

" Farewell, my dear Regnier : I have deeply regretted the loss of our poor Kleber : he was, like yourself, a great enthusiast for your expedition.

" It is affirmed that 12 or 15,000 English are gone to pay you a visit: you will probably give them such a reception as they met with from us in 1794.

" I embrace you and Millet cordially.

" Signed   MACDONALD."

The preliminaries of peace having been ratified at Paris, the First Consul dispatched one of his aides-de-camp, General Lauriston, as the bearer of them to London, where they were duly exchanged. That event was soon announced by the firing of guns from the Invalids. The intoxication of joy exceeded all bounds. The contracting powers, France, Spain, and Holland, on the one part, and England on the other, had pledged themselves to send plenipotentiaries to Amiens: we were on the eve of a general peace: the proceedings of France in her foreign relations were earnestly directed to that object.

CHAPTER XXVI.

Congress of Ratisbon—Lord Cornwallis—Negotiations at Amiens—Communications in respect to the affairs of Italy.

M. DE TALLEYRAND had accelerated the execution of the clauses of the treaty of Luneville which were to determine the indemnities to be allowed to the princes of the Empire who had suffered losses owing to the concessions made to France, as well as to the new arrangements that had taken place in Germany. He had hastened as much as possible the proceedings of that congress, in order to verify the new order of things. It appeared to him that no time was to be lost in doing away with difficulties which were only calculated to keep up a spirit of acrimony, and to prevent France from giving stability to her new condition.

Those negotiations had lasted a twelvemonth, without reconciling the various pretensions and intrigues that had been set up. France and Russia interposed to bring them to a termination. The First Consul gave a proof of his satisfaction to M. de la Forêt by naming him his minister plenipotentiary at Ratisbon, where he appeared as the equal of M. de Buller, thither sent by Russia for the same object, and in the same character.

These two ministers succeeded in bringing the labours of the congress of Ratisbon to a close; which, in consequence of the many new territorial arrangements placed under the protection of France, afforded to the First Consul a powerful influence in Germany.

Reports began to circulate at this period of extortions levied upon those princes who had claims to bring forward: many were the interests crushed on this occasion. Some would not submit to any loss; others strove to obtain every thing. The general discontent shortly vented itself in open language. The first had only failed because they would not submit to the tribute; the others found that part of their claims were admitted, but denied the right of any one to impose such high terms as were demanded of them. Such is the world; neither rank nor distinctions will alter its nature. The language of complaint was so often repeated, that at last it reached the ears of the First Consul, who afterwards loudly complained in my hearing on the subject. It is even affirmed that, in 1810, and 1811, he received proofs of those extortions, together with a list of the sums illegally levied on the occasion.

Be this as it may, the negotiation of Ratisbon was managed with very great dexterity, and affairs had taken a favourable turn.

The English had long hesitated to evacuate Egypt; they had even openly supported the insurrection of the mamelukes; but they had yielded at last to the just representations of the Sultan, and set sail for Europe. A great number of officers had passed through France on their way home. They had met in Paris with the most marked attention; some of them had been even admitted into the company of the First Consul. All had had an opportunity of satisfying themselves of the baseness of the stories by means of which public opinion in their country was misled with respect to the state of France and its government. The curiosity to visit the banks of the Seine was not confined to military men. The same desire was felt by a great number of persons no less distinguished by the rank which they held in their native country than by their personal character and talents

The notions imbibed by men of such high repute, and expressed by them on their return to London, proved useful auxiliaries to the First Consul's policy; for an apprehension was beginning to be felt that the English, who had exhausted every diplomatic subtlety in order to evade the restoration of Malta, would no longer agree to a peace. The plenipotentiaries entrusted with the mission of concluding it were to assemble at Amiens; but the British minister was slow in making his appearance: some uneasiness was felt for the motives of such an unexpected delay. The First Consul kept urging Lord Hawkesbury, and signified to him his anxiety to convert the preliminaries of peace into a definitive treaty, which was alone calculated to consolidate the repose of the world. His importunities, and no doubt also the language held by the English who had visited France, succeeded in overcoming the repugnance of the British cabinet. Lord Cornwallis at last arrived in Paris. He was presented to the

First Consul, who received him with marked distinction, and on the occasion of the preliminaries complimented him by the grandest fête that had yet been given to any public character. We had inherited this custom from the Directory, who gave orders for fêtes on the most trifling occasions, and laid out in concerts and illuminations that money which was drawn from an already exhausted treasury.   '

The conferences, however, kept pace with the fêtes. The negotiation was opened at first under an unfavourable aspect. Lord Cornwallis, in a conference which he held with Joseph Bonaparte, who had the charge of negotiating on the part of France, gave some insight into the difficulties which would spring out of the possession of Malta. Nevertheless, as the preliminaries had decided the question, and nothing remained but to name the power to whom the charge should be assigned of guaranteeing the independence of the island, very little distrust was occasioned by the transfer of the negotiation to Amiens. The parties, however, had scarcely met in that town, when the British minister raised the most unexpected pretensions. He demanded, that since there was a *French language* at Malta, there should also be a language there of his own nation. The difficulty was met at once by an effort to stipulate that both powers should renounce such a claim.

He next expressed some anxiety as to the eventual fate of that island. He demanded, that not only some guarantee on this subject should be pointed out, but that its protection should be expressly stipulated for by the establishment of a foreign garrison in Malta. A simple course was proposed to him as calculated to obviate every inconvenience ; this was to restore the Order to its primitive institution, and render it a mere order for exercising hospitality as in its early days, instead of an order of nobility, into which it had grown in the course of time ; to rase the fortifications that covered the whole island, and convert it into an extensive lazaretto, open alike to all nations frequenting the Mediterranean. This course did not meet the views of his government, and he rejected it. Joseph Bonaparte, whose natural bias, as well as his instructions, led him to soften down every difficulty, presented a new project, in which he offered to place the island under the protection of the great powers of Europe. This proposal did not meet with a better reception than the preceding ones. England demanded that Malta should be confided to the custody of the King of Naples. The plenipotentiary replied by claiming the literal execution of the preliminary articles. " Those stipulations," he added, " are become a primitive law which none of the contracting powers can retract. A refusal to carry them into effect is tantamount to a refusal of peace. To the strict observance of this principle I have sacrificed many articles which prejudiced in no way the interests of Great Britain. I have felt myself bound to relinquish them, so soon as it was proved to me that they were not strictly comprised in the preliminaries. How can an article be now set up which is in all respects opposed to them ? What do the preliminaries say? that Malta shall be restored to the Order of St. John of Jerusalem. Is the Order of St. John of Jerusalem centred in the King of Naples ?

" Is it pretended that the Order is too weak in itself? the project secures to it the guarantee and protection of the principal powers of Europe.

" The preliminaries only mention one power. It has occurred to the French government that the object of the preliminaries would be more effectually accomplished by the simultaneous guarantee of the great powers, as being a more imposing and a more suitable one. Nevertheless, as it claims above all, the absolute, and even, if that should be insisted upon, the literal execution of the preliminaries, it is ready to sacrifice to them this article, which a kind of political decorum had suggested to it."

Lord Cornwallis replied by a counter-note, wherein, taking advantage of the word *protection*, which was expressed in the preliminaries, and of the hatred of the natives for the knights of St. John, he insisted upon the necessity, as well as the propriety of delivering Malta to the custody of Ferdinand IV. The distressed state of the Order, which was unable to pay the troops required for the defence of the forts, and certain words that had escaped the French plenipotentiary in the previous conferences they had held together in Paris, appeared to him to be sufficient grounds for persisting in this demand. Joseph Bonaparte thought otherwise; he commented in warm terms upon the pretensions of the English ministry, and required the insertion, in the protocol, of the following note :—

"The undersigned has read, with the greatest care, every document connected with the negotiation, without discovering any trace of the proposal alleged to have been made by France for the delivering up of Malta to His Sicilian Majesty's troops

"The 4th article of the preliminaries cannot bear that interpretation.

"When the undersigned had the honour of meeting Lord Cornwallis for the first time, at Paris, on the 24th Brumaire, he was far from supposing that their mutual congratulations on the facility of terminating the mission confided to him could be considered in the light of proposals, or of groundworks for treaties. He had not then even received his powers, which were not delivered to him until the 30th Brumaire, and were communicated to the British minister on the 14th Frimaire only. The case was otherwise with the latter, who came to Paris ready provided with instructions from his government on his very first visit: he spoke of Malta as a perplexing article, although it was agreed that the garrison of that island should consist of troops belonging to a third power, until the Order should be able to organise its means of defence. Lord Cornwallis considered Spain to be wholly *inadmissible* as a guaranteeing power, owing to its alliance with France; Russia appeared too far removed, and Naples too weak.

' " The British government, always adverting to a guarantee
to be furnished by the guaranteeing power, as being a basis
agreed upon, observed that Naples was inadequate to the
expense. The undersigned may possibly have added that two
such powers as France and England should not be arrested by
a consideration of that nature. The actual discussion of all
these matters was, however, adjourned to the period of the
opening of the negotiation.

" In the conferences that have taken place at Amiens, in the
protocols, in the plan of a treaty of the 14th Nivose (4th January), the undersigned has never uttered a single expression
which could convey the idea that his government would consent to the island of Malta being delivered over to the protection of the Neapolitan troops for a period of three years.
He proposed, on the contrary, in the protocol of the 23d
Nivose (13th January), that Malta should be placed under the
protection and guarantee of the principal powers of Europe,
each of which was to have furnished two hundred men for its
garrison. That island would thus have been guarded by
twelve hundred experienced soldiers, to be paid by the Order,
Lord Cornwallis having himself made the observation that
the revenues of the vacant commanderships would afford
them sufficient means for so doing.

" The anonymous writing which has been handed to the
undersigned by desire of Lord Cornwallis bears no authentic
character ; it appears to have been drawn up by discontented
people. It does not speak the language of the inhabitants of
Malta ; an island possessed of no importance except through the
Order: when they shall be made acquainted with the articles of
the treaty that concern them, they will be delighted at the re-
establishment in Malta of an Order of which they will become
an integral part. Admitting that circumstances might require
a temporary and intermediate garrison to occupy Malta, from
the moment of its evacuation by the British forces until the
moment when the Order shall have formed a corps composed

of Maltese and foreigners, it is still demonstratively proved that
there should be as little departure as possible from the 4th
article of the preliminaries, which stipulates that *the island
should be restored to the Order* ; that article anticipates the
necessity of a guaranteeing and protecting power; the means
of carrying it into effect are left to the wisdom and good
faith of both governments.　All their endeavours must aim at
this sole object—that Malta should belong to the Order : they
must avoid any thing that might fetter its prerogative; or
that, instead of affording a protector to the knights, would
have the semblance of giving them a master, or diminish the
influence they should exclusively exercise over Malta.　The
French government proposes, by its project, England, Austria, Spain, Prussia, and Russia, as protectors of the Order:
it would be difficult to attach greater splendour to it, or to
afford it a more effectual protection.　Why retain a Neapolitan garrison during a period of three years?　Can it be from
apprehension of foreign enemies?　The above six named
powers would no doubt be sufficient protection to the island.
Is it from a fear of the Maltese themselves?　The Order
will secure to itself the affections of the people if the
stipulations are faithfully observed; these will be their best
internal defence.

"Admitting, however, the necessity of a garrison, were it
only for the purposes of security and internal police, does it
require three years to form a corps of a thousand men, who,
with the addition of four hundred knights, and six hundred
Maltese, would be more than sufficient to meet every exigency?
Since the plan of delegating the protection and guarantee of
the Order to the great powers is now agreed upon, would it be
either necessary or proper that the King of Naples should
hold a garrison in Malta for the space of three years?　Will
the protectors, the protected, the grand-master, in short, to
whatever country he may belong, view with any feeling of
satisfaction the Order placed under the guardianship of the

troops of the only prince who has any pretensions to set up
to Malta? Would it not be more becoming, and more in
accordance with the preliminaries, if there be an admitted
necessity for a foreign force at Malta, that a body of a
thousand Swiss should be raised, whose officers should be
named by the existing landamman, and selected amongst those
who had not borne arms in the present war? They would in
the end settle at Malta, at a distance from all foreign influence ; being dependent on the grand-master only, they would,
in reality, be the soldiers of the Order, and Malta would become their adopted country. The Order, therefore, would
have every thing to gain on the score of consideration and
independence, with a garrison composed of knights, of Maltese, and of a corps of Swiss soldiers, such as other powers
keep in their pay.

"The result of the foregoing observations is, that France
has never consented to the introduction of Neapolitan troops
into Malta ; and still less *that the island should be given up
to His Sicilian Majesty, who would furnish, in conjunction
with the Maltese forces, the troops requisite for garrisoning
the principal forts during the space of three years.* This
proposal proceeded from Lord Cornwallis in the conference
of the 23d Nivose (13th January).

"From the perseverance of the British government in
insisting upon prolonging for three years the stay of a foreign
garrison in Malta, and upon delivering up that island, in the
most formal manner, not to the Order itself, but to His Sicilian
Majesty, the French government was led to think, and was
justified in asserting, that a departure was made from the preliminaries laid down; which preliminaries, it is well known,
are the basis of a peace. If that language was not thought of
so conciliatory a nature as heretofore, the cause is not to be
ascribed to any change in the sentiments of France ; but
when, in a discussion, all arguments have been exhausted,
and have failed to carry conviction, the natural inference to

be drawn by one of the parties is, that the other rejects every kind of arrangement.

"If it be the intention of the British government to maintain the Order of St. John and the island of Malta in a state of perfect independence (a hope in which the undersigned wishes to indulge), he trusts that the foregoing project, drawn up with the object of removing all foreign influence, will meet with the approbation of Lord Cornwallis. This project is unquestionably preferable, in all respects, to every other hitherto presented. The undersigned cannot find words too strong to urge its adoption.

"Should, however, the British government have irrevocably adopted the plan of establishing a Neapolitan garrison in Malta, the undersigned, with the view of hastening the moment of peace, would consent to admit it in the manner in which it is drawn up in the sequel of this note.

"Lord Cornwallis will discern in the two versions of the plan relating to Malta the application of the principle just developed by the undersigned.

"He is further directed to insist upon the insertion into the treaty of the article concerning the Barbary states, such as it is drawn up in his project, and upon the concurrence of the contracting powers to put an end to the hostilities carried on by those states in the Mediterranean, to the utter disgrace of Europe and of modern times.

"The mere notification that would be made to the Barbary states of the determination of the contracting powers on that subject, would restore security to the commerce of the United States, of Portugal, of the King of Naples, and of all the other states of Italy; and if the competition in the Mediterranean trade, which such a measure would considerably augment, could be a ground of apprehension to any nation, it would unquestionably be so to France and Spain, which, from their natural positions, and their separate intercourse with the Barbary states, carry on that trade at all times with greater security and advantages than other powers. To them therefore the sacrifice would be greatest; but in a question which involves the political morality as well as the dignity of European nations, motives of mere personal interest should be discarded.

" Strength is given to political bodies as it is to individuals, for the protection of the weak : how glorious and consoling would be the reflection, that a war, productive of such great calamities, had terminated at least by an act indicative of the deep interest taken in the prosperity of all commercial nations!

" This question, besides, is bound up with that of Malta, from which it cannot be separated ; for if the contracting parties do not take upon themselves to put an end to the hostilities carried on by the Barbary states, it may be said, with great truth, that the Order of St. John cannot cease to wage personal war against those states, without failing in their primitive engagement, and incurring the loss of all their property.

" The generous founders of the commanderships had no other object in view than to afford protection to Christians against the piracies of the Barbary states ; and every civilian in Europe would agree in opinion, that the Order of Malta, if they renounced the fulfilment of that duty, and thus overlooked the object of their primitive foundation, would lose their title to the possession of the property conceded to them for that specific purpose."

A new occurrence started up to render the negotiation more complicated, and brought on a declaration of which England should have taken advantage. The question of the new states formed in Italy had been agitated. The British ministry had replied, by the formal declaration, that they could not, amongst others, acknowledge the King of Etruria. The First Consul endeavoured to make them understand the imprudence of such a resolution, and addressed to them the following observations through the channel of his accredited minister :—

" In reply to the declaration of the British minister respecting the King of Etruria, which is contained in the same protocol, and to his preceding verbal declarations concerning the Italian republics, Citizen Joseph Bonaparte has intimated that he would make known to his government the repugnance felt by His Britannic Majesty to recognise the King of Etruria, the Italian republic, and the republic of Genoa.

" As the recognition of those states by His Britannic Majesty can be of no advantage to the French republic, the French plenipotentiary will no longer insist upon it. He is desirous, however, that the observations he is about to offer may be taken by the British cabinet into its serious consideration.

" The political system of Europe is founded upon the existence and recognition of all the powers that divide its immense and beautiful territory between them. If His Britannic Majesty refuses to recognise three powers standing in so distinguished a rank, it necessarily renounces taking any interest in the people composing those three states. Can it be possible to admit the hypothesis that British commerce is indifferent to the trade of Genoa, Leghorn, the mouths of the Po, and the Italian republic; and if her commerce should suffer from any shackles imposed by those three states, to whom could His Britannic Majesty apply for redress, as he cannot hold out any reciprocity, since the states of Genoa, of Tuscany, and of the Italian republic, carry on no sort of trade with England, though they are found to be useful and even necessary channels for British commerce? And if these three powers, offended at not finding themselves acknowledged by the great powers, should introduce any change in their internal organization, and seek protection by incorporating themselves with a great continental power, His Britannic Majesty likewise shuts himself out from any right of appeal, though he could not be indifferent to those changes. Complaints are sometimes raised against the continental extension of the French republic; but is not that a necessary consequence of the small Italian states being driven by the greater powers to the necessity of looking for refuge and protection to France alone?

"The Cisalpine republic, though acknowledged by the Emperor in the treaty of Campo Formio, could never obtain the admission of her minister at the court of Vienna; that republic was still considered by the Emperor as if the treaty of Campo Formio had never had any existence. As the general peace was not then concluded, the court of Vienna, no doubt, viewed its treaty in the light of a truce; now, however, that there exists a general peace, if those states are still kept in uncertainty as to the recognition of their independence, they will become apprehensive of a renewal of the slights which they have already experienced, and feel the necessity of drawing closer the ties that unite them to the French nation. The same principle that induced France to relinquish three-fourths of its conquests, has dictated to the First Consul the course of not interfering in the affairs of those small states any farther than was deemed indispensable towards restoring order, and establishing in them a firm organization. Frankness will naturally suggest the question, whether his moderation is destined to contend against any false and ill-judged measures of other powers, or whether the peace is considered in no other light than as a truce? This would be a prospect equally painful and discouraging to a man of upright principles, and would infallibly be attended with results which no human foresight can calculate."

CHAPTER XXVII.

Mr. Fox in Paris—Meeting of the Italian assembly (la consulte) at Lyons—They decree the presidency to General Bonaparte—M. de Melzi named vice-president —Marriage of Louis Bonaparte—Peace of Amiens—Expedition to St. Domingo —Defeat and submission of Toussaint Louverture—He is forcibly carried off —Particulars respecting that leader—Death of General Leclerc—General Rochambeau assumes the command—Fresh insurrection of the blacks—Cruelties exercised against them.

WHILST the only remaining unconcluded peace engaged the attention of government, the English of note continued to flock to Paris.

One of the most eager to visit us was the celebrated Fox, an opposition member of the British parliament. The curiosity to see General Bonaparte had induced him to anticipate the period of peace. The First Consul was not behindhand in his desire to hold a colloquial intercourse with him. He was much pleased with his society, and I have often seen them pass long nights in close conversation together.

Mr. Fox appeared to have formed a correct notion of the First Consul's character, and to have felt an affection for him. Having, on his return to England, heard of a conspiracy against his life, he communicated the information to him, which afterwards proved of service.

The First Consul's attention was turned towards Italy. That country was still in the same state in which the battle of Marengo had replaced it. It had an executive directory, councils, and, as a necessary consequence, renewed elections, which opened a field for intrigues, and consequently for disorders. A national vote had just decided in France that the dignity of First Consul should be held for life: all admitted the necessity of such a measure to prevent the discords that might be occasioned by rival ambitions, of which some glim-

merings were already breaking out. The First Consul sought
to place Italy in harmony with France, and caused it to be
suggested to the former country that it should adopt the modifications adopted by the latter; in other words, that it should
substitute a president, a senate, and a legislative body, for its
then existing form of government. He was desirous that
this change should be insensibly effected, and he would readily
have gone in person to bring it about. But his presence in
France could not be dispensed with; he could not cross the
mountains, and was unwilling to delegate the task to other
hands. He adopted a middle course; convoked at Lyons the
deputies of the departments and cities of Italy, who were to
give utterance to the wishes of their country. All hastened
to the appointed place with a zeal against which the rigour
of the season, and the snows that almost blocked up the
roads on the mountains, proved inefficient barriers.

The First Consul, on his part, was not long in making his
appearance. The welfare of the Italians was the object of his
journey; his attention was exclusively engaged with their
affairs. The remains of the army of Egypt, which he had
brought together at Lyons, where he was desirous of meeting
them, afforded him but a momentary diversion from this
task.

He received the whole Italian deputation in a solemn audience, but only by sections of forty deputies each at a time;
because he felt desirous of impressing them all with the sincerity of the interest which their country had excited in his
breast. He addressed to each section a long speech on the
dangers resulting from revolutions. He depictured the fatal
consequences ever attending political agitations, civil war,
proscriptions, and all the evils incident to them. He dwelt
upon the necessity of forgetting animosities and injuries, of
assuming an attitude which would be in harmony with neighbouring nations, in order to inspire them with confidence.

This was not, assuredly, the language of a ferocious conqueror. It would have done honour to the greatest phi-

losophers of antiquity, and was hailed with general approbation.

The Italians had sent to Lyons the most distinguished characters amongst the clergy, nobility, and gentry of their country. They seemed to have placed a sort of national pride in the choice of their deputies. They were vain of displaying to the view of the second city of France the treasures of their civilization.

The First Consul was much pleased with this assembly, whose principles and composition were in accordance with his wishes. He has often dwelt at a later period upon the proper sentiments which animated them.

The Italians, on the other hand, were no less pleased at the speech he addressed to them. They were more particularly grateful for his forbidding the French to interfere in their discussions.

They opened their sittings after several deliberations, in which many of the members displayed considerable talents. They accepted the mode of government proposed to them, that is to say, a president, a senate, a legislative body, and a council of state. The First Consul was appointed to the presidency; which, at first, he neither accepted nor refused.

When all proceedings had been gone through, and the modifications adopted, nothing remained but to dissolve the assembly. He decided upon closing the session in person; repaired to the hall of deliberations, and said to them, in Italian, that he should always feel an interest in the prosperity and welfare of the people they represented; but that being unable to devote to Italy, their native country, all that attention which she had a right to claim from him, he was under the necessity of naming a substitute who should reside on the spot, and that he therefore appointed M. de Melzi as their vice-president. In this election he had been guided by the desire of proving his solicitude for the Cisalpine republic, where he knew that M. de Melzi, upon whom he set a great value, was held in the highest esteem.

' This appointment was hailed with the loudest acclamations. The assembly broke up; the deputies retired to their homes, and the First Consul returned to Paris.

A few days before his journey to Lyons he had united his brother Louis to Mademoiselle Hortense Beauharnois, and shown, on that occasion, a fresh proof of the austerity of his religious principles. He had himself been married during the reign of terror. His sister Caroline had been united to General Murat in the interval between the 18th Brumaire and the battle of Marengo. The exercise of religion was forbidden at both periods, nor was it yet tolerated at the moment of which I am speaking, the churches still exhibiting the same state of profanation as before. Accordingly, the marriage of Louis was celebrated in conformity with the custom at this time, at the private residence of the First Consul in the Rue de la Victoire, at the Chaussée d'Antin. A priest came to give the nuptial blessing to the youthful couple. The First Consul availed himself of the opportunity to have a like blessing bestowed on the union of his sister Caroline, who had not been married in the church; conceiving, no doubt, that this important act of our life should be sanctioned by religion after having been sanctioned by the presence of the civil authority. In his own case, however, he dispensed with the religious ceremony, a circumstance which gave rise to some conjectures amongst us.

He was therefore only bound to Josephine by the civil act, a bond susceptible of being broken asunder, agreeably to the legal clauses concerning marriage. The ecclesiastical discipline had therefore nothing to do with his divorce, whatever may have been its pretensions in the year 1810.

Winter was drawing to a close: the plenipotentiaries had at last overcome the feelings of repugnance manifested by the British ministry. They had closed their discussions, and repaired to Paris. , The peace with Russia and the Porte, respectively, the preliminaries of London, and the peace of

Badajoz with Portugal, were published in Paris between the 11th and 19th Vendemiaire. On the 18th Brumaire following general peace was restored, and celebrated with great splendour. Of all the works of the First Consul, none afforded such uniform satisfaction, or gave rise to such flattering hopes. The public rejoicings attested the delight felt every where at the event.*

England named Lord Whitworth as her accredited minister in Paris, and the First Consul selected General Andreossi for his representative in London. For the first time since the breaking out of our troubles we were at peace with the whole world ; the French republic was universally acknowledged. Such were the fruits of moderation combined with talent ; and accordingly, no head of a government ever excited at any time an admiration so general, or so deeply felt as that which the First Consul commanded at this period.

Peace restored to us the possession of the small factories we formerly had in the East Indies, and of all our American colonies.

---

* This event brought on, as I have already stated, a change of ministry in England. It was found impossible to conquer Mr. Pitt's repugnance to any terms with, what he persisted in calling, the French revolution : he therefore retired from the cabinet, but caused his place to be filled up by Mr. Addington, a mere dependant upon him, who was only to act by his directions. Mr. Pitt did not renounce the hope of renewing a coalition ; and in the shades of retirement he was able to set his springs in motion. He particularly stood in need of a repose of some months, in order to open an intercourse with the ministers of those powers which had been successively driven to the necessity of making peace with France. He built his principal hopes upon Russia; and it was only in consequence of the peace concluded between France and that power that he consented to a peace between England and France : he therefore used his utmost endeavours to obtain a copy of the treaty concluded between the Emperor Paul and the First Consul: he first obtained it at Paris through some breach of trust, and afterwards at St. Petersburgh by the like means. When the comparison of these documents one with the other no longer allowed him to doubt their existence, a fact of which he had been informed, from that moment he set about forming new 'projects for the future.

The Dutch lost Ceylon. A few other stipulations of minor importance took place.

No difficulty was felt in the resumption of those colonies, in which all labour had not been destroyed by the liberty granted to the blacks. The case, however, was otherwise with St. Domingo, the richest of our colonies previously to its revolution; but it had now become the most fatal present that France could have received. It was, nevertheless, necessary to make arrangements for sending troops thither; the interest of the mother-country required it, as well as that of a multitude of families utterly ruined by the disorders to which the colony had-been a prey. They flattered themselves that they should recover possession of the property they had lost, just in the same manner as one might return to an estate which had been quitted for a time; and in their anxiety for the sailing of the expedition, they complained that the distress to which they had been reduced was unnecessarily protracted. The First Consul was not to be overawed by such clamours. He attempted nothing in haste. He wished to make himself acquainted with St. Domingo before the expedition should set sail, just as he had taken the precaution to study Egypt previously to effecting a landing at the Marabout.

He was upwards of a month engaged in collecting information respecting that island from all those who had resided in the Antilles, whether as administrators, military men, or planters. The profession of the party was of little consequence to him; he desired that all those who could throw some light on the subject should be sent to him to Malmaison. I have known him to be closeted for hours with inferior clerks in the marine department, who had been pointed out to him as possessed of positive information respecting St. Domingo. This was the occasion on which he became more particularly acquainted with M. Barbé Marbois, who had been intendant general of that colony, and was then a councillor of state. He was pleased with him, and, on the demise of M. Dufresne, he named him director, and some months afterwards minister of the public treasury. This alteration, however, in the title of office only took place, I believe, in order that he might intro- duce M. Marbois into the council, and work with him without exciting the envy of the other councillors of state who were placed at the head of the various branches of administration.

I have already said that the First Consul neglected no means of acquiring the information he stood in need of re- specting St. Domingo; he was engaged whole days in col- lecting it, and employed part of the night in issuing orders on the subject of the expedition : he had asked of Charles IV. the loan of his squadron, which was still in Brest, for the performance of a voyage to St. Domingo previous to its returning to the ports of Spain, and the king had placed it at his disposal.

The squadrons which were to have sailed for Egypt from the ports of Rochefort and Toulon were again put in a con- dition for sea, as well as every ship that had been brought into Brest and L'Orient: a great number of transports were also collected; and on board these several ships not a mere corps of occupation, but a formidable army was embarked.

This army contained a great many persons who had ex- pressed a desire of forming part of the expedition; it also numbered a multitude of those restless and uneasy minds for whom a state of peace is insufferable, and who require a per- petual change of scene. Such elements are more available for promoting a conquest than for preserving or forming a permanent establishment in a country which only stood in need of hope and consolation. St. Domingo was, accord- ingly, treated as a hostile country.

The First Consul had sent back to Toussaint Louverture his two sons, who were completing their education in Paris. He had written a letter to him at the same time, congratu- lating him on the prosperous state in which he had maintained the colony ; announcing, that he could no longer return to the level of his fellow-citizens; that the government would seize with eagerness the opportunity of proving to him the high sense it entertained of his services; and that it sent back his children as a first indication of its esteem.

The squadron having arrived off Cape Français, detached a division towards Port-au-Prince. Toussaint was absent, and Christophe commanded in his stead. He hesitated at first, and endeavoured to gain time; but he soon returned to his natural ferocity, and set fire to Port-au-Prince. A landing was effected, and the town occupied ; but the blacks, in their retreat, spread the conflagration, and extended their ravages in all directions.

They were closely pursued, and shut up in their mountains: some of them surrendered to us, the remainder persisted in following the fate of Toussaint, under whose orders they sustained a defeat at the Crête à Pierrot. Feeling himself unable to continue the war, the governor began to treat for terms.* General Leclerc granted him peace and personal security: the black troops enlisted in our ranks, and the country submitted to the laws of the mother-country.

This transaction, which so happily terminated the struggle, afforded a hope of seeing the colony resume its former flourishing attitude. Unfortunately, General Leclerc, who was really a clever man, had not illustrated his name by any success calculated to command respect. He was unable to effect

---

* Agreeably to this convention the colony was delivered up to the troops sent by the mother-country to occupy it, and Toussaint and his people were to return to their respective homes, and live there in peace, under the orders of the generals about to be named to the command of the districts in which they resided.

By the same convention it was stipulated that the black troops should be kept up for the service of the colony, and should retain their arms, which consisted of muskets taken by their leaders in the arsenals of the Cape and of Port-au-Prince at the time when the Europeans were compelled to evacuate those towns.

It was also agreed that they should mount garrison with the whites, and be treated in all respects like the latter troops.

a prompt and absolute obedience, and the expedition failed. His general officers chose rather to attend to their own interests than to the glory of their chief. All restraint or discipline was at an end. To crown all other evils, Leclerc was attacked with the yellow fever, which carried him off before he had an opportunity of justifying the First Consul's choice.

The disease which had spread amongst a part of the troops continued its ravages : the reinforcements daily arriving from the ports of France and Italy were inadequate to fill up the vacancies which it occasioned in our ranks : whole regiments fell victims to it in the space of one week after their landing.

The First Consul was deeply afflicted at this misfortune. He sent for those whom he knew to have long resided in St. Domingo, but obtained no information that could enable him to avert the results of which he now had a foreboding. He could not understand why the colonial administration and that of the army had neglected taking measures for preserving the troops from a contagion, the effects of which were well known ; still less could he account for the circumstance of the troops which he had sent out having been instantly landed, and brought into contact with those attacked by the epidemical disease. The island of Tortuga and the mountains offered numberless means of preserving them uninjured until the arrival of the ordinary period at which the malady disappears.

The simplest sanitary precautions were omitted. The army was left in places where the fever was carrying off a tenth of its numbers. Its destruction bore witness to the guilty indifference of those who were but too much accustomed to consider soldiers as mere instruments of their own advancement.

The hopes of the blacks began to revive when they beheld this dreadful consumption of human beings. Their troops had escaped the rage of so cruel a scourge : they were more numerous than the whites, and resolved to raise anew the standard of revolt. General Leclerc was still alive at this time, and at the head of the army: he obtained intelligence of their plots, and determined to do what he ought to have done in the early part of the peace. Whilst guaranteeing to the negro army the ranks and honours they had acquired, the First Consul had summoned their principal leaders to France, well aware that he who has once sipped the cup of power will not easily submit to act a secondary part: he had therefore instructed his brother-in-law to send the black generals to Europe. Leclerc, deceived by their protestations of fidelity, omitted to do so, and had soon cause to repent his neglect. The mountains were becoming the depositories for arms and provisions: the troops evinced a restless spirit: every thing portended an explosion. Had not Toussaint's correspondence fallen into the power of Leclerc, those preparations, that state of anxiety would have been sufficient to raise his suspicions against him. Toussaint, who had formerly belonged to M. Galifet's plantation, independently of that acuteness which is a characteristic feature of the blacks, had been gifted by nature with a sound judgment and a strength of mind which are seldom found combined in one person. He had listened to the imprudent dissertations of the planters, and read with avidity all writings that adverted to slavery or liberty : his imagination was kindled at the perusal of Raynal : he had indelibly impressed on his memory the chapter in which this philosopher, after picturing the degradation of the blacks, announces that a noble-minded negro will one day appear, who will break the fetters that enchain his race, and take signal revenge for the outrages inflicted upon it by the whites : he fancied the part to be cut out for himself; bestowed all his attention on conciliating the affections of his fellow-countrymen, and shortly acquired an unbounded ascendancy over them.

This formidable man held in his hands every thread of the

general movement which was in preparation. Leclerc determined to anticipate him, and caused him to be arrested. It
has been contended that more wisdom would have been
shown in taking advantage of his experience; that the
difference between a negro and a white, between men who,
in different hemispheres, had raised themselves to the pin-
nacle of power by means of revolutions, was a question in
which vanity alone was concerned; that the colour of the
chief was a matter of little consequence, so long as he had
the talent of making the colony flourish.

These are specious considerations. If Toussaint, however,
had been a man likely to be satisfied with the second rank,
he would not have placed General Laveaux under the
necessity of receiving a deputation which had not originated
in any suggestion from him ; he would not have insult-
ingly dismissed General Hedouville, raised the standard of
revolt, and risked every thing to conquer what was not
contested to him. He was aware of the consequences of
rushing to arms ; and after having insulted a fresh and powerful army, he was not likely now to remain passive when it
was sinking under the malady of the climate. Toussaint was
playing his game whilst preparing to take advantage of our
misfortunes : Leclerc acted his part in forestalling him. The
proofs against him were, besides, incontrovertible ; but had
they not been so, who could believe that a man of the character of Toussaint Louverture would see an opportunity of proclaiming the liberty of the blacks, and neglect taking advantage
of it ? He was sent to France, and confined in the castle of
Joux. Anxiety, age, a climate too severe for his constitution,
soon put an end to his days : he died some months after his
arrival. The most absurd reports were sedulously propagated
respecting that event; and whilst young and vigorous Frenchmen were perishing by thousands in St. Domingo, it appeared
unlikely that an old man, driven from the summit of power,
and removed to a distance of two thousand leagues from the

climate in which he had lived, should end his days according
to the course of nature, in the fort in which he had been
confined.

It was hoped that the repose of the colony had been secured
by Toussaint's removal; quite the contrary; his abduction
spread the alarm among the black chiefs. The white troops
were not in a condition to keep the field; the blacks were
fresh, and in all their strength. Fortune was declaring for
them; they threw off the mask, and retreated one after the
other to the mountains. The yellow fever continued to
spread its ravages in our ranks; nearly the whole army had
perished; desertion became general; we had only a few negro
soldiers left us. The blacks were on the point of bearing
down upon us, and hostilities were about to begin again, when
Leclerc died. He was succeeded by General Rochambeau,
who was next in seniority; a man of tried courage, but the
least qualified for the command in the then state of the
colony. There was wanted a man of a mild and conciliatory
disposition; whereas Rochambeau was only known by his
harshness of conduct.

Leclerc, when at the head of a powerful army, had preferred the course of negotiations to that of hostilities: his
successor adopted a contrary system: although possessed of
a mere skeleton of an army, he pretended to put down the
insurrection by force of arms, and displayed a severity which
bordered on madness. Since veracity is the bounden duty of
a writer, I will state all that I afterwards learned of those
events, and of the indignation felt by the First Consul when
he heard of the deep stains that had tarnished the glory of
his arms.

The new general-in-chief, whose name was enrolled amongst
those who had contributed to the independence of America,
established himself at the Cape, where he was soon surrounded by that crowd of proprietors who were exasperated
at the Revolution, and were not disposed to stop at any thing,

when the object was to recover what they had lost: no means
were indifferent to them. The violence of the general-in-
chief rather favoured their views: they applauded him, flattered his passions, and neglected no opportunity of exaspe-
rating his ardent mind. General Rochambeau soon lost
all self-command: he became a blind instrument of the
atrocious schemes of his flatterers, who had conceived
the thought of exterminating the whole black population.
This horrible idea was followed up: all hands were set to
work: a degree of barbarity was displayed which is a
disgrace to our age, and will inspire horror in succeeding
ages. The wretches who had been proscribed were indiscriminately carried off in all directions: they were embarked
under pretext of being transported from the island, and were
drowned at night in the open sea. Worse remains to be told:
when the terror inspired by this wholesale condemnation had
driven a wretched population to seek its safety in flight, dogs
of a peculiar species were procured from the island of Cuba
for the purpose of hunting them more effectually in their retreats: these animals were let loose in the underwood. The
blacks were followed to the deepest recesses of the mountains.
This new mode of dislodging an enemy, who laid himself flat
on the ground under the fallen leaves, was revolting to the
feelings of the troops: they refused to shoot some of these
wretches who were forced out by the hounds, and to assist in
hunting them out of the woods. The soldiers went farther;
when they learned that the poor creatures who fell into their
hands, instead of being transported to some other land, were
actually drowned at sea, they mutinied, and declared,
" that they had come to St. Domingo, not for the purpose of
promoting savage executions, but of fighting; that they were
not disposed to accept as auxiliaries the packs of hounds
which led them on; that if the same scenes were revived, they
would inflict summary punishment upon the hounds and their
savage guides." It was found necessary to yield: that bar-

barous hunt, against which those gallant men had raised their voices, was relinquished.

Such were the occurrences in St. Domingo, whilst France was indulging in the pleasing illusion of shortly seeing that rich colony supply the mother-country with its wealth. Many private letters, which contained the details of those savage executions, had reached France from various parts of America, and had been communicated to the First Consul. Nevertheless, although they all agreed in their accounts, he refused to give credit to such savage acts, so revolting was the picture they exhibited. He wondered at not receiving reports from those whose duty it was to make them, and often repeated, in the deepest distress of mind, that if those atrocious executions were true, he discarded the colony for ever; that he never would have directed its occupation could he have foreseen the guilty excesses which had arisen out of the expedition.

CHAPTER XXVIII.

Details of internal affairs—M. de Bourrienne—Means resorted to for the purpose of defaming him—Visit of the First Consul to some of the departments—M. de Menneval—Ecclesiastical discussions—The Concordat.

EVER since the First Consul was invested with the supreme power his life had been a continued scene of personal exertion. He had for private secretary M. de Bourrienne, a friend and companion of his youth, whom he now made the sharer of all his labours. He frequently sent for him in the dead of the night, and particularly insisted upon his attending him every morning at seven. Bourrienne was punctual in his attendance with the public papers, which he had previously glanced over. The First Consul almost invariably read their contents himself; he then dispatched some business, and sat down to

table just as the clock struck nine. His breakfast, which
lasted six minutes, was no sooner over than he returned to
his closet, only left it for dinner, and resumed his close' occupation immediately after, until ten at night, which was his
usual hour for retiring to rest.

Bourrienne was gifted with a most wonderful memory;
he could speak and write many languages, and would make
his pen follow as fast as the words were uttered. He could
lay claim to many other advantages; he was well acquainted
with the administrative departments, was versed in the law
of nations, and possessed a zeal and activity which rendered his
services quite indispensable to the First Consul. I have known
the several grounds upon which the unlimited confidence
placed in him by his chief rested; but am unable to speak
with equal assurance of the errors which occasioned his losing
that confidence.

Bourrienne had many enemies; some were owing to his
personal character; a greater number to the situation which he
held. Others were jealous of the credit he enjoyed with the
head of the government; others, again, discontented at his
not making that credit subservient to their personal advantage. Some even imputed to him the want of success that had
attended their claims. It was impossible to bring any charge
against him on the score of deficiency of talent or of indiscreet
conduct: his personal habits were watched; it was ascertained that he engaged in financial speculations. An imputation could easily be founded on this circumstance. Pecu-
lation was accordingly laid to his charge.

This was touching the most tender ground; for the First
Consul held nothing in greater abhorrence than unlawful
gains. A solitary voice, however, would have failed in an
attempt to defame the character of a man for whom he had
so long felt esteem and affection; other voices, therefore,
were brought to bear against him. Whether the accusations
were well founded or otherwise, it is beyond a doubt that

all means were resorted to for bringing them to the knowledge of the First Consul.

The most effectual course that suggested itself was the
opening a correspondence either with the accused party direct,
or with those with whom it was felt indispensable to bring
him into contact; this correspondence was carried on in a
mysterious manner, and related to the financial operations
that had formed the grounds of a charge against him. Thus it
is that, on more than one occasion, the very channels intended
for conveying truth to the knowledge of a sovereign have
been made available to the purpose of communicating false
intelligence to him. I must illustrate this observation.

Under the reign of Louis XV., and even under the regency, the postoffice was organised into a system of minute
inspection, which did not indeed extend to every letter, but
was exercised over all such as afforded grounds for suspicion.
They were opened; and when it was not deemed safe to
suppress them, copies were taken, and they were returned
to their proper channel without the least delay. Any individual denouncing another may, by the help of such an
establishment, give great weight to his denunciation. It is
sufficient for his purpose that he should throw into the post-
office any letter so worded as to confirm the impression which
it is his object to convey. The worthiest man may thus be
compromised by a letter which he has never read, or the pur-
port of which is wholly unintelligible to him.

I am speaking from personal experience: it once happened
that a letter addressed to myself relating to an alleged fact,
which had never occurred, was opened. A copy of the letter
so opened was also forwarded to me, as concerning the duties
which I had to perform at that time; but I was already
in possession of the original, transmitted through the ordinary
channel. Summoned to reply to the questions to which such
productions had given rise, I took that opportunity of pointing
out the danger that would accrue from placing a blind reliance

upon intelligence derived from so hazardous a source. Accordingly, little importance was afterwards attached to this means of information ; but the system was in full operation at the period when M. de Bourrienne was disgraced : his enemies took care to avail themselves of it ; they blackened his character with M. Barbé Marbois, who added to their accusations all the weight of his unblemished character. The opinion entertained by this rigid public functionary, and many other circumstances, induced the First Consul to part with his secretary, and the duties of the latter were for the most part united to those of M. Maret, who had hitherto acted only as chief secretary to the consulate.

M. de Bourrienne's place in the cabinet was filled up by M. de Menneval, a man of honour and talents, who won the First Consul's esteem, and justified the favour he acquired by a zeal for his service which has stood the test of time.

We were now in the season of autumn, when the First Consul made a tour through the departments bordering the river Seine. He started from St. Cloud, crossed the department of the Eure, went over the field of battle of Ivry, and proceeded to Evreux, Louviers, and Rouen, which latter place he entered by the Pont de L'Arche. He visited the manufactories of that city and of Elbeuf, and pushed on as far as Havre, whence he repaired to Dieppe. He was on the road between these two ports when he received the dispatch announcing the death of General Leclerc. It also apprised him of the approaching arrival of his sister Pauline,* who had sailed with her only son on board the ship of war which conveyed home the remains of her husband. This intelligence made a painful impression upon his mind. He returned to Paris sooner than he had intended, taking the road of Neufchatel, Beauvais, and Gisors, and was greeted every where with the loudest acclamations. The

* Afterwards Princess Borghese, since dead.

constituted authorities of Beauvais, in particular, went a great distance to receive him, and were preceded by a group of very elegant young ladies, the handsomest of them carrying the flag which the celebrated Jeanne Hachette wrested, in a sortie, from the troops of the Duke of Burgundy, who had laid siege to the town. Delighted at this instance of bravery, Louis XI. resolved to perpetuate the remembrance of it, and granted the right of precedence to the ladies of Beauvais, by decreeing that they should take the lead of the other sex in all public ceremonies.

The First Consul had been some days in the capital when he learned that the ship in which Madame Leclerc had embarked had just entered Toulon, having been prevented by contrary winds from reaching the western ports. He immediately dispatched General Lauriston to the south, who brought Madame Pauline back to Paris.

Our internal tranquillity was uninterrupted, and peace was restored with foreign powers. A question extremely important and difficult to settle now engaged his attention, and rivetted it for the remainder of the autumn and part of the succeeding winter.

A habit had grown up during the revolution of saying mass in private houses: it was celebrated by nonjuring priests. Devotees pretended that their masses were of more avail, and more agreeable to God, than those celebrated by priests who had taken the oaths. They were attended by many through a spirit of opposition: an affected zeal for hearing them was even put forth by atheists, in order to thwart the government.

Almost every old family had its private chapel: mass was alternately said at one or other of them. The affiliated brotherhood received a previous intimation, and met together under various pretences, sometimes even as if merely to return a visit. In a very short time other ceremonies were also performed in those chapels ; such as baptisms, confessions, nuptial blessings, and burials ; in short, a real schism had sprung up.　This state of things dated from the early days of the revolution.　The First Consul had felt unwilling to resort to measures of severity for putting a stop to it ; he viewed it as the result of the alarms felt by some persons of a timorous conscience, and not as the invention of malevolence.　He resolved, however, that this should cease, by the application of an effectual remedy.　He probed the evil to the root, and determined that whatever was connected with the interests of religion, or with ecclesiastical discipline, should be established upon a solid foundation.　The chargé d'affaires of France at the court of Rome was instructed to broach the subject; and as it was the wish of the First Consul, in this discussion, not only to terminate the quarrels which disturbed the harmony of the clergy, but to guard against an influence which was already on the increase, he reserved to himself the management of the negotiation.　Accordingly he complained to the Pope of the breaking out of a schism, which threatened the repose of the faithful, and perhaps of religion itself.　He manifested the desire he felt of averting such an evil, and begged His Holiness would send a legate with whom he might confer upon the subject.

This proposal was eagerly accepted by the Pope, who sent to Paris Cardinal Gonsalvi, Spina, Archbishop of Genoa, and Caselli, to discuss the question of a concordat.　The First Consul named, on his part, his brother Joseph, M. Crettet, and Abbé Bernier, *curé* of Saint Lô d'Angers, to consider its articles, conjointly with the prelates.　The concordat was signed on the 18th July, 1801.

The clergy became in France, in consequence of that act, a branch of the administration, which was governed by M. Portalis the elder, who was appointed by the First Consul to the place of minister of public worship.　The Pope sent to

Paris as his legate, in the course of the following year, the venerable Cardinal Caprara, who completed the work begun by his predecessors.

The reconciliation of France with the church was another triumph for the First Consul, who thereby secured the favour of all devotees. It was productive of the further advantage to him of causing the suppression of all that parade of the celebration of the divine offices in private houses. The faithful returned to the churches, which he had ordered to be thrown open ; and the priests of different opinions in orthodox matters felt no objection to officiate in them. The Pope enjoined the same discipline to nonjuring clergymen as to those who had taken the oaths. He summoned the absent bishops to return immediately to their dioceses, or to send in their resignations. A few obeyed the mandate; those who resisted were replaced.

The First Consul determined to celebrate the reconciliation of France with the church ; and a splendid ceremony accordingly took place at Notre Dame. At the time of the First Consul's accession that metropolitan church was in a most deplorable condition: it had been stripped of its marble and ornaments; every thing had been plundered or sold. This was not all; the edifice had been divided into sections, forming a series of storehouses, which had been let to the highest bidder. The First Consul put a stop to such odious profanation ; he repaired the cathedral; had fresh altars and tables substituted for those which jacobinical rage had broken down; and, accompanied by all the members of the government, he assisted at the ceremony of its inauguration.

This conduct, which was praiseworthy in itself, and promoted the interests of his policy as well as of religion, increased his popularity on the one hand, but created an explosion of discontent on the other.

The First Consul had, on several occasions, urged M. de Talleyrand to return to holy orders. He pointed out to him that such a course would be more becoming his age and high birth, and promised that he should be made a cardinal ; thus raising him to a par with Richelieu, and giving additional lustre to his administration.

However little was the vocation of M. de Talleyrand for the church, he nevertheless took the proposal into serious consideration ; but such was his weakness of character, that a woman, who had acquired an ascendancy over his mind by doing the honours of his house, completely paralysed the direct influence exercised over him by the chief of the state. She set so many springs in motion to protect herself from a dismissal, which must have been the immediate consequence of M. de Talleyrand's return to the prelacy, that she eventually prevailed upon him to marry her, and bore a conspicuous character afterwards, not at the Tuileries, but in the midst of the representatives of all the courts of Europe, under the title of Princess of Benevento. On this occasion the First Consul carried his condescension so far as to solicit from the Pope a brief to secularise M. de Talleyrand, and permission for him to marry. He particularly yielded in this to Madame Bonaparte's entreaties.

CHAPTER XXIX.

Discontent of some general officers—Bernadotte—A singular scene at General Davout's residence.

I HAVE stated that the ceremony at Notre Dame had created an explosion of discontent; it remains for me to relate what effects it produced.

Envious, mischief-making, and for the most part narrow-minded men, who claimed, however, the right to decide upon matters they did not understand, were busy in stirring up the people. They narrowly watched the proceedings of government, criticised its acts in the most bitter language, imputed views to it which were the offspring of their own imaginations, and protested their readiness to encounter death at the shrine of liberty in danger. Unable, or unwilling as they were, to penetrate the real intentions of the head of the state, they attributed such to him as squared with the objects they had in view. The First Consul, they said, was resolved to restore the clergy to the condition in which the revolution had found them; it was never too soon to oppose such a nefarious attempt. All arms, all means were indifferent; any course of proceeding was justifiable which would avert the storm. Such conduct was not confined to mere talking: the mode of resistance to be adopted was taken into consideration; their proceedings were altogether treasonable. These senseless meetings, which became alarming from the very madness of those who composed them, were headed by General Bernadotte, who at this period held the command of the western army. Though nearly allied to the Bonaparte family,* he had often attended the meetings in which the mode of getting rid of the First Consul had come under discussion. It is fair to acknowledge that he always opposed any attempt being made upon his life; but he advised his being forcibly carried off; a course which must necessarily have been attended with such a result. Every other member was for putting him to death.

The First Consul, whose preservation was indispensable to France at this time, was soon apprised of those meetings, and of the bad spirit which animated them; but he was so much steeled against fear, that he merely sent to a distance from Paris the madmen who attended them. With respect to Bernadotte, he was ordered to return to his army.

One general in particular, who was at that time lost in the

---

* Madame Bernadotte was sister to Madame Joseph Bonaparte.

crowd of commanding officers, was on terms of close intimacy with one of the most violent amongst those who felt the effects of this measure of the First Consul. He was originally a soldier in the service of Spain, clandestinely forsook it to return to France, where the revolution had just broken out. He attached himself to the representatives who went to stir up the spirit of the armies and purify them, and hunted down the aristocrats with a zeal which proved very serviceable to him. He now found a fresh opportunity of serving the state; he took advantage of it, and pointed out to the First Consul the views and resources of those meetings which he had so often excited with his republican ideas. He named, amongst others, Colonel F . . . . and General D . . . ., with whom he was united by the closest terms of intimacy. He represented them to be so ardent in the cause as not wholly to reject the idea of an attempt upon the First Consul's life ; a consideration which could alone, he said, have determined him to give the information he had just communicated., Being provided with a document of so detailed a nature, the head of the state ordered the arrest of the two officers who were named to him. The minister of police had allowed him to remain ignorant of the existence of such odious conspiracies. He knew not whether they had escaped its vigilance, or whether Fouché had any interest in deceiving him. In the uncertainty what to do, he would not have recourse to ordinary channels, but directed the select corps of gendarmerie, of which I was the colonel, to secure the parties denounced. F . . . was arrested ; but D. escaped by the officious attentions of his informer.

The latter had no sooner transmitted his report to the First Consul, than he ran to inform his friend that all was discovered, and that he should take care of himself, hoping, doubtless, to relieve his conscience by such gratuitous advice. D., greatly affected at this semblance of anxiety for his fate, and fully relying upon an old intimacy, contracted amidst the chances of political fortune which they had run together, asked him for an asylum. . . . He dared not refuse the fugitive, and afforded him shelter: but he gave information at the same time that he was unable to resist the importunities of friendship, and that D. had sought an asylum from him.

I was at Malmaison when this piece of intelligence was brought. - The First Consul, who was vexed at such intrigues, sent me immediately to Paris, with an order to dispatch a detachment of gendarmerie to the country-house of that general. The detachment proceeded to the village, but found no one there. D. was on his way to his own home, and the First Consul desired that he should be left undisturbed. ;

The sudden appearance of the gendarmes at the house of the general whose conduct appeared to be guided on the occasion by his zeal for the service of the First Consul, was the cause of a misunderstanding between him who had provoked the measure and myself, who had received orders to carry it into effect. He complained of the insult offered to him, appealed to his brother officers, wrote to the First Consul, and insisted upon obtaining satisfaction at my expense. So much clamour for a mere visit of gendarmerie created suspicion. I could not give credit to the sincerity of that inflexible anger which appeared to possess . . . ., and originated, after all, in an unpleasantness to which every one is exposed. I demanded satisfaction in my turn. "I endure," said I to the First Consul, " the language I am subjected to by the command with which you have vested me, because the good of the service requires it; but if this is always to be the case, if I am always to be persecuted by the clamours of those against whom I may receive any orders to execute, deign to relieve me of the duty, and give me a regiment of cuirassiers in exchange for my own." " Why should you mind those clamours?" replied the First Consul; "do you not see from whence they spring? . . raises his voice so loud, merely because he informed me himself of the views entertained by D. . ., and of the place of shelter he had chosen. You may be quite at ease, however; I take upon myself to quiet him." I learned, in fact, his having hinted to him that his conduct was not calculated to do him any good; that he should take part one way or the other; and had only to make his selection.

My surmises were verified; there remained but one more point to clear up. I was determined to set my mind at ease on the subject, and I therefore afterwards asked D ...,* who had retired to his own home, who it was that advised him to quit the house in which he had sought shelter; it turned out again, as I suspected, to be his officious friend who had apprised him that the gendarmerie was in quest of him. He might have said more ; he might have apprised him how they happened to go there at all.

I retain a vivid recollection of those unhappy circumstances, which only afforded me a fresh proof of the weakness of man. If the individual to whom they apply should read these Memoirs, let him not imagine that the new character in which he is clothed has prevented my naming him. I owed the omission to the welfare of my children.

My eyes were opened by what the First Consul had confided to me, and I turned a deaf ear to every harsh remark. That loud clamour, which was echoed through the saloons of Paris, had no other object in view than to throw a veil over the secret intercourse kept up with the cabinet. It was wholly undeserving of notice.

Amongst the very indifferent characters who composed the meetings was a superior officer, who was pointed out by the disclosures of . . . . as capable of the most nefarious attempts. He had been dismissed from his regiment for motives of which I am quite ignorant, was without any fortune or employment, and naturally became one of the fire-

---

* He remained ten years in disgrace before he received any employment, and was killed at the battle of Leipsic.

brands in the contemplated explosion. The death of the First Consul was again to throw open the career of fortune to him. He loudly avowed his intention of compassing it. His sentiments became so publicly known, that he was arrested and thrown into the Temple. His confinement led him to turn his conduct over in his mind : it was only calculated to alarm him, and he determined to solicit the First Consul's pardon. He was the rather disposed to do so, as he doubted not that the loss of his liberty was owing to the secret information given by some false associate, who had become reconciled to government at his expense : this was really the case.

He offered to make some disclosures. General Davout was instructed to receive them, and repaired to the Temple, where that cavalry officer made certain communications to him of the highest importance. The First Consul desired he would see the prisoner again, and make him an offer of five hundred louis if he would undertake a mission to London, where, by spreading the report of his having effected his escape from the Temple, he might acquire a knowledge of the plans projected by the English and the emigrants for an invasion of the western department, as well as of the correspondence they still kept up with the coast.

General Davout sent for the prisoner, and had him brought to the house where he then resided at the Tuileries, on the spot now occupied by the terrace, in front of the Rue St. Florentin.

Meanwhile General . . . ., who has been already adverted to, happened by chance to call upon Davout, and was as clamorous as ever. The object of the First Consul, he said, was to restore the ancient order of things: he had begun by opening the door to emigrants : he was now bringing the clergy back, and would soon dispossess the holders of national property. To sum up the whole, added he, that poor cavalry officer, who was carried prisoner to the Temple, has just been strangled by his orders.

General Davout, who was still at a loss to understand the aim of his interlocutor, fancied at one moment that all he desired was to be asked such questions as might afford him a colouring for relieving his conscience from some heavy weight; at another moment he imagined that he was endeavouring to detach him from the service of the First Consul. Nevertheless, General Davout allowed his language its free range, listened to all the nonsense he uttered, and at last suffered an emotion of pity to escape him, which put an end to the tirade. He gave him no other reply than to see him out of the house by the common entrance, leading him through an apartment where D.... was in waiting at that very moment.

General .... suddenly saw before him the cavalry officer whom he had just reported to have been strangled: he was quite beside himself at the occurrence; but recovering his composure, and well aware of the motives which brought that officer to the residence of the commandant of Paris, he returned to Davout's closet with a hurried step, and said to him, " I perceive that every thing is known, since D.... is here. I have been deceived. I beseech thee to accompany me at once to the First Consul." Davout complied with the request. General .... threw himself at the feet of the head of the government, confessed every thing, gave by this mode of proceeding a fixedness to his then vacillating conduct, and opened the way to the position which he was afterwards to assume. He devoted himself from that moment to the First Consul, for whom he affected to feel an exclusive attachment. With respect to the cavalry officer, he had little to add to the disclosures already known. He accepted Davout's proposal, repaired to London, made some stay in that capital, and did not leave it until he had succeeded in obtaining detailed and positive information concerning a project in agitation for the purpose of overthrowing the First Consul. He rejoined the marshal at the camp of Ostend, and disclosed to him the conspiracy, which was attempted a few months afterwards to be carried into effect. He remained quiet for some time ; but nature broke out again: he returned to his former habits, in consequence of which he was strictly watched. The severest orders had even been issued, in the event of his being seen to loiter about the First Consul's. Several endeavours were afterwards made to procure him employment ; but age had not ripened his judgment; his usual unsteadiness followed him every where. He claimed, in 1814 and 1815, the merit of having been the victim of the late government. The pages of history will unfold the remainder.

At the period of the occurrences I have just related the First Consul had just taken up his residence at the palace of St. Cloud, which he had caused to be repaired, in order that he might have the advantage of stepping from his closet into a walk which was on the same level with it, and also of being nearer to Paris than the residence of Malmaison ; a very important object for those who had to hold daily communications with him.

CHAPTER XXX.

Discussions respecting the Civil Code—The Tribunate—Exhibition of the produce of industry—Canal de L'Ourcq.

TOWARDS the end of March 1802 a commission of the Council of State, consisting of Messrs. Tronchet, Portalis the elder, Merlin of Douay, and others, under the presidency of Cambaceres, the second consul, was appointed to draw up and present the plan of the civil code. The First Consul directed that the Council of State should enter upon the discussions of so important a subject. This body generally held its sittings three times a week : they opened at two o'clock, and closed at four or five : during the present winter, however, the Council never separated before eight o'clock at night, and the First Consul never failed to attend every one of its sittings.

At no time had there been held so important a course on the law of nations. The Council of State contained, at this period, several men of mature experience, and in the prime of life : the discussion was, accordingly, no less profound than enlightened ; it bore the stamp of deep meditation.

The First Consul took so lively an interest in the debate, that he generally detained a few state councillors to dinner, in order to resume the discussion afterwards. When he returned alone, he remained only ten minutes at table, and then withdrew to his closet, where he shut himself up for the evening.

If he had not to go to the Council of State, he proceeded to the Institute, to which place I have sometimes attended him. The meetings were held at the Louvre. He repaired to the sitting by the gallery of the Museum ; and when it was over, he would sometimes keep back one or two of the members, seat himself on a table like a schoolboy, and enter into a conversation, which was often extended to a late hour of the night. If he met any one whose intercourse was pleasing to him, the time would run on imperceptibly.

The labours of drawing up the civil code were no sooner completed, than this splendid work was submitted, with the usual formalities, to the discussion of the Tribunate. This body had already shown, on many occasions, a spirit which foreboded that it would eventually prove an obstacle to the proceedings of the administrative branch of government. Though mostly composed of men of acknowledged talent, it had assumed an attitude of hostility towards the Council of State, and displayed at times a resistance, which was, perhaps, more owing to party feeling, and to a rivalry of talents than to intrigue, or a tendency to exaggerated ideas.

This spirit was made known to the First Consul, who refused to credit its existence, so unreasonable did it appear to him. He was not long in discovering that he had formed a better opinion of that body than it deserved. A minute and angry discussion took place : it now became hopeless to pass the code without considerable mutilations. The necessity of carrying that great measure through was deeply felt ; but as it was to be apprehended that a similar opposition would be manifested by the Legislative Body, and thus a character of discredit be stamped upon the first work of the consular legislation, the project was given up. The elections were the means of introducing men of more enlightened wisdom into the Legislative Body. The Tribunate, which was reduced to half its numbers, from the effects of a measure dictated by a prudent foresight, returned of its own accord to a less hostile system. The code was again produced before that body and adopted.

The First Consul abolished the Tribunate at a later period ; and as his objection was not to the members, but to the institution itself, which was only calculated to impede his measures, he gave appointments to all its members, the greater part of whom distinguished themselves as members of the administrative branches of government, and all as men of considerable merit.

I have often heard him say, with reference to some one of those with whom he had cause to be most satisfied, "You see, now, how it is: in the Tribunate, he would have opposed what he performs at present with greater alacrity than any one else : such is the effect of party spirit. How true it is," he added, on the same occasion, "that men are generally no more than grown children !"

Since the First Consul had taken the helm of government the labours in every branch of the public administration had grown to a prodigious extent; and yet fresh work was in progress. A water-and-forest department was formed, which effectually stopped the plunder of wood, and substituted a wise and rational system of felling trees. Lyceums were established ; the means of gratuitous instruction increased in a twofold ratio, and were completed at a later period by the formation of a body of teachers ; stockbrokers became authorised agents ; the lottery was remodelled, and had the effect of: destroying a multitude of small lotteries, and private banks, quite as ruinous to the public, and wholly unproductive to the state ; and lastly, the excise laws were instituted.

M. Chaptal, the minister of the interior, protected and encouraged all manufactures and objects of industry with a zeal which obtained general approbation. With him originated the idea of establishing museums in each department, and afterwards in Paris, for the purpose of exhibiting, at stated periods, the produce of national industry. This happy idea was immediately carried into effect. The exhibitions were opened, and proved what unexpected strides the arts had made during an epoch which was deemed productive of nothing but a series of calamities. M. Chaptal conferred on this occasion a signal service upon France: he opened the eyes of a vast number of sceptics, who had hitherto insisted upon the superiority of foreign manufacturers over our own. The comparison now instituted had the effect of removing their doubts: they were forced to admit that some of the articles which they purchased as being of English manufacture came from our own workshops, and were made by the artisans whose capacity to the task they had disbelieved. It was by such simple means that he put a stop to the petty frauds of some manufacturers, who were not ashamed to fix upon their goods a foreign mark, in order to procure their readier sale. The agricultural interest was not less indebted to him: he was the founder of the prizes, which are still decreed at the present day in the several departments for the best agricultural produce. By the aid of time and of similar institutions a country cannot fail to undergo considerable improvements, and to attain the height of prosperity. It may be said of **M. Chaptal,** that all the acts of his administration were not less marked by an enlightened patriotism, than those of his private life by uprightness of character.

The First Consul seldom passed a week without visiting some establishments. Administrative order, general embellishments and improvements, were objects upon which his mind was constantly bent: his attention was also directed to tracing canals, opening new roads, or repairing the old ones, which had been wholly neglected during the revolution. The head of the state had given the impulse, and animated the whole of the republic to follow his example. Repairs, labours, and reconstructions were going on in every direction, not unlike the attempts made after a storm to set afloat a ship, which an unskilful pilot had suffered to run aground.

At Lyons, the place Bellecour was about to be restored: in Paris, the works of clearing the Louvre, of removing the obstructions from the Carrousel, and of repairing the public monuments, were rapidly proceeding: the churches which had escaped destruction were restored to religion; those which a senseless fury had levelled with the ground were on the point of being rebuilt.

The works in harbours or on the canals; in short, constructions of every kind were simultaneously going forward. It was unaccountable to all how the First Consul could meet the expenses which such undertakings entailed: all were astonished, and cried wonder! It was, however, no such extraordinary wonder; order and probity were the corner-stone of all this superstructure. I will explain my meaning.

Previously to the 18th. Brumaire the receivers-general kept back the public revenue, under pretext that the sums they had to collect came in very slowly. Being thus deprived of any certain returns, and unable to ascertain the exact state, of his different public chests, the finance minister was obliged to carry on the service by means of checks drawn at a more or less remote date upon the receivers-general. These

checks were in public circulation ; but as no greater dependence was placed on the solvency than on the good faith
of the government, the confidence which it was attempted to
infuse into public opinion was daily affected by the checks in
circulation. The receivers-general took advantage of this
deplorable state of things ; they acted the part of bankers,
bought up the checks which they were bound to discharge,
and thus realised enormous profits. This scandalous traffic
ceased with the extinction of the government which tolerated
its existence. M. Gaudin put an immediate stop to it when
he assumed the management of the finances. Every one
saw a spell in the rise of the public funds : the only spell was
honesty and the return of order. The taxes were collected
with rigid economy ; no funds were any longer misapplied ;
no government securities fell in value ; public credit and
public confidence had completely revived.

This year was rendered remarkable by another undertaking
which exclusively contemplated the interests of the metropolis and of trade. It had long been intended to dig a canal
for the purpose of receiving the waters of the river L'Ourcq,
and introducing them into Paris ; but the labour requisite
for this object was immense, and the difficulty in the way
of accomplishing the work had discouraged the attempt.
Some trials had, however, been made from the plans of
M. Girard, of which the First Consul had had occasion, in
Egypt, to estimate the value ; but so great was the obstacle
raised that every idea of it was abandoned, until the moment
when the head of the government happened by chance to go
out hunting in the forest of Bondi.*

The hounds led him amidst the works of the canal, which
partly encroached upon the forest ; he immediately left the
chase, and ordered us to follow him. He examined in person

* The doctors had recommended that exercise for the First Consul's health. He
had at the time a *small* pack of hounds, wholly unlike what we see at the present
day.

the works that were already completed, and as he had, long
before this time, visited the work which extends along the
river L'Ourcq, and that of the projected canal, as far as it
extended, the obstacles which had caused their being suspended now recurred to his mind : he gave up all thoughts
of resuming the chase, returned at once to Paris, and issued
orders for assembling at the Tuileries that very night all the
superintendents of highways who were for and against the
plan. He brought them together, closely attended the discussion, found the objections untenable, the replies to them
most satisfactory, and immediately ordered the resumption of
the works, which were continued with great activity, but of
which it was not reserved for him to witness the completion
he so anxiously looked for.

CHAPTER XXXI.

Suppression of the ministry of police—General Rapp—Helvetic mediation—
Interior of the Tuileries—Anecdote.

THE state of peace we enjoyed had gradually removed the
public mistrust. The First Consul had erased from the list
of emigrants the names of all those who solicited that favour :
he had even restored to them such part of their property as
had not been sold, and was still under national sequestration.
His ready compliance tended to increase the applications, and
he was obliged to adopt a general course, in order to put a
stop to the claims which constantly poured in upon him.
His first intention was to cause the repeal of the law respecting emigration ; but it was represented to him that such
a measure would be attended with worse consequences than
the evil to which he was desirous of applying a remedy. - An

early decree of the Council of State excepted from the list of emigrants the clergy who had been transported beyond seas, children under sixteen years of age, labourers, artisans, &c. A senatus-consultum of 1802 granted them a full amnesty. The First Consul afterwards caused a list to be drawn up of the persons whose actions or birth had brought them into a state of hostility against the new system of laws, and expunged in the mass all other names.

The suppression of the ministry of police became a necessary consequence of this measure. There was no longer any occasion for exercising a rigid watchfulness when nothing was left to be guarded against. This opportunity was taken for pointing out to the First Consul that such an authority could not now be kept up without seriously endangering the popularity and consideration with which he was endeavouring to invest his power. By continuing to tolerate that authority he was affording pretexts for calumny, and raising suspicions as to the intentions of government. The First Consul pretended to be convinced by these arguments, and did not perhaps regret attempting what no one had ventured before him, the maintenance of order by means of the gendarmerie and of the public tribunals. M. Fouché was furious against M. de Talleyrand, whom he looked upon as the author of a measure which removed him from the council, and at the same time deprived him of an office which he considered as an irremovable appanage. He accordingly resorted to reprisals; threw out doubts of the sincerity and political intentions of the minister for foreign affairs, and endeavoured, by every possible channel, to convey those suspicions to the knowledge of the First Consul, who, unfortunately for himself and for M. de Talleyrand, attached more importance to them than they deserved. Nevertheless the ministry of police was suppressed, and M. Fouché was appointed a member of the Conservative Senate.

M. Abrial, who held the seals of the ministry of justice,

received a similar appointment. The First Consul united both ministries into one, under the name of ministry of the chief judge, which he confided to M. Reignier, then a councillor of state: he gave him for assistant M. Réal, to whom he entrusted the management of every thing that was connected with the public safety, or that required proceedings which would have been inadequately carried on by a solicitor-general. Matters went on tolerably well at first: all were tired of war and discord: all were anxious for repose, and desirous of repairing the losses they had sustained. No one dreamed of disturbing a state of prosperity which was solely to be ascribed to the late concentration of power.

The Swiss were still ruled by the government which the French Directory had imposed upon them; but the exasperated feelings excited against a power exclusively resting upon a foreign invasion, had reached the highest pitch. They ran to arms in every quarter: a general scene of confusion ensued; and the storm, which had settled with us into a calm, was raging with violence over Switzerland. The contending parties were not long in coming to blows.

The party opposed to the Directory was so numerous that it overpowered the other in the very onset of the contest. The defeated party immediately availed itself of a treaty concluded with France, and claimed the First Consul's assistance. He was placed in a position of great difficulty: he would neither allow a civil war to be kindled, nor the Helvetic independence to be crushed. He had, however, instructed General Ney to enter Switzerland with a corps of troops, and caused Reding, the instigator of the disturbances, to be arrested; and he dispatched Rapp, his aide-de-camp, in all haste, who providentially arrived at the moment when the parties were coming to blows. Rapp, with a rare presence of mind, alighted from his carriage, placed himself between the two armies, loudly declaring, in the German language, that he was authorised to denounce as an enemy of the French nation whichever of the two parties should commence firing, and that he was ordered to introduce a fresh body of French troops into the Swiss territory. His firmness produced the greater effect, as both parties had the same consequences to apprehend from a second invasion. They became reconciled, agreed to assemble the cantons, and to leave to the First Consul the mediation of their misunderstandings.

The latter accepted the part of mediator, received in a friendly manner the deputation sent to lay before him the wishes and wants of a nation which had been driven to arms by the worthlessness of the Directory, and appointed a commission of senators, M. Fouché amongst the rest, to discuss with the deputies the groundwork of the constitution most suitable to the mountain people of whom they were the chosen representatives.

The constitutional act was soon agreed upon : the deputies, pleased with the result of their mission, requested the First Consul to retain the title of mediator, which had been conferred upon him. The country was restored to its wonted tranquillity, without the least effusion of blood ; and the celebrated M. de la Harpe,* who had governed it under the title of director, came to fix his residence in Paris.

The winter which followed the conclusion of peace was rendered remarkable by the great influx of distinguished foreigners : they came to France from all quarters. Our civil discords had, however, been represented to them in such a light, that they had pictured to their minds the capital as half destroyed. They were greatly surprised at not discovering any trace of such devastation, and at hearing it said in every direction that the city exhibited a finer appearance than it did before the troubles which had been represented to them in such gloomy colours.

The formalities of etiquette had not yet been established. Madame Bonaparte did not give any public receptions : she feared to involve herself in unpleasant scenes, by the preten-

---

* Formerly tutor to the Emperor Alexander.

sions that might be started by some foreign ladies, in a palace into which etiquette had not as yet found its way, or to offend their pride, by the claims which she felt conscious were due to her rank: accordingly, nothing could be more dull at that time than the palace of the Tuileries. The First Consul never left his closet. Madame Bonaparte, in order to while away the time, was under the necessity of going every night to the theatre with her daughter, who never left her sight. When the representation was over, of which, however, she seldom waited to see the conclusion, she returned to finish the evening by a game of whist; or if the party was not sufficiently numerous, by a game of piquet, which she played with the second consul, or some other state personage.

The ladies of the First Consul's aides-de-camp, who were of the same age as Madame Louis Bonaparte, came to keep her company: every day brought with it the same round of visitors and the same amusements: the week ran on at Malmaison in the same way as it did in Paris. The second consul gave public receptions to the functionaries of government and the members of the magistracy: his residence was the only one in which any thing of the parade of state was to be seen. Foreigners, on the other hand, filled the state apartments, of which M. de Talleyrand did all the honours.

It was in the course of this winter that the First Consul caused M. T—— to be arrested, and confined in the Temple, on his return from England by way of Holland. This arrest was represented as an act of tyranny. The following, however, were the real grounds for it:—

M. T . . ., who had formerly been a member of the parliament of Paris, had been leading a very restless life ever since he had quitted France. He had successively resided in England and in Germany, and at last taken shelter in America. His unquiet spirit had crossed the seas with him; but he was a slave to his opinions: he preferred enduring

every privation to the sacrifice of them.   Such was his
distressing condition when he learned the events that followed
close upon General Bonaparte's return.   Tired of roaming
about the world, and anxious to see his children, he determined upon returning to Europe.   He met some Dutchmen
of Surinam on board the ship in which he had taken his passage, formed an acquaintance with them, and ascertained that
the colony, unwilling to continue to belong to a government
which could not afford it protection, was sending to treat with
the British ministry ; or, in other words, to invite them to
take possession of the settlement.   They were perfect strangers in London, and, nevertheless, felt desirous that their
mission should not be known in Holland, from which they
were now at so short a distance, and with which they kept
up an intercourse.   M. T . . . . removed all their difficulties : he had still retained some old connexions in England : he opened a correspondence with the government, and
succeeded in quietly procuring for the Dutch the protection
which they had come to solicit.

The ministry, who obtained possession of Surinam by this
intrigue, acted generously towards the manager of it ; so that
M. T . . . . saw before him the double prospect of returning
to France, and of repairing his fallen fortunes.   The negotiation which he had carried on opened a kind of intercourse
between him and the British ministry.   Mr. Pitt consulted
him as to the degree of confidence which was due to a French
ambassador, who had just addressed a paper to him respecting the means best calculated for curtailing the power of the
First Consul.

M. T . . . ., who had known that personage previously to
his emigration, imagined from such an overture that he had
remained true to his original principles, and gave the minister
a flattering account of him.   Pitt entrusted him with the
paper ; and T . . . ., on running it over, discovered in it his
own opinions, and felt persuaded that he might rely on his old

friend. He hastened to his place of residence, paid him a visit, related his good and bad fortune, and solicited his assistance. The other made him very fine promises; but threw out some expressions, in the course of conversation, which indicated political principles of a complexion widely foreign from those which his friend had anticipated. "How canst thou tell all this to me?" was T .'s exclamation: "I know thy real thoughts, having read thy memorial. Pitt himself confided it to me."

The diplomatist denied the fact, and yet redoubled his caresses and offers of service. The emigrant trusted to those protestations, and took his departure for Paris; but he had been pointed out to the police as an English spy sent with large sums of money. His obliging friend had taken care to make known the part he had acted in the Surinam intrigue.

The First Consul could not avoid ordering his arrest. Anxiety of mind, and that state of irritation which treachery never fails to create, soon brought T... to the grave. He died in the bitterness of heart of a man perishing the victim of the designs of a false friend.

CHAPTER XXXII.

First reception given by the Consular Court—Warm remonstrance of the First Consul to the British ambassador—Calculations and hopes of England.

TOWARDS the end of March, 1802, some formality of etiquette was established, and the wife of the head of the state was thenceforward attended by ladies, and by officers of the household, who had the charge of superintending all matters of ceremony. The ladies did not at first exceed the number of four: these were Mesdames de Rémusat, de Thalouete,

de Luçay, and Madame de Lauriston, for whom the First
Consul entertained a particular regard. The four officers of
the consular household were Messrs. de Cramayal, de Luçay,
Didelot, and de Rémusat.

This court had only been installed a few months when foreigners were introduced for the first time. The reception
took place in Madame Bonaparte's apartments, on the ground-
floor looking upon the garden. It was numerously attended,
and consisted of the most elegant women from the neighbouring country, who exhibited a rich display of jewels, of
which our rising court had not yet any idea. The whole
diplomatic body were also in attendance. So great, in short,
was the concourse of visitors at these ceremonious receptions,
that the two saloons on the ground-floor were hardly sufficient
to contain them. When every thing was ready, and the
places were all taken, Madame Bonaparte entered, preceded
by the minister of foreign affairs, who introduced the foreign
ambassadors. She then went round the first saloon, the
minister still preceding her, and naming each of the per-
sonages that lined the way. Just as she had completed the
round of the second saloon, the door suddenly flew open, and
in walked the First Consul, who appeared for the first time in
the midst of this brilliant assembly. The ambassadors were
already known to him ; but the ladies beheld him for the first
time. They all rose spontaneously, and exhibited the most
marked indications of curiosity. He made the round of the
apartment, followed by the ambassadors of the several powers,
who named to him, in succession, the ladies of their respective
countries.

One of these receptions was the occasion on which he
afterwards vented his displeasure at the conduct of England.
He had just been reading the dispatches of his ambassador
at the court of London, who sent him a copy of the King's
message to Parliament respecting alleged armaments in the
ports of France.

His mind being wholly biassed by the reflections to which the perusal of the dispatches had given rise, he omitted going that day into the second saloon, but went straight up to the ambassadors. I was only at the distance of a few paces from him, when, stopping short before the English ambassador, he put the following hurried questions to him in a tone of anger : " What does your cabinet mean ? What is the motive for raising those rumours of armaments in our harbours ? How is it possible to impose in this manner upon the credulity of nations, or to be so ignorant of our real intentions ? If the actual state of things be known, it must be evident to all that there are only two transports fitting out for St. Domingo ; that this island engrosses all our attention, all our disposable means. Why then those complaints ? Can peace be already considered as a burden to be shaken off ? Is Europe to be again deluged with blood ? Preparations making for war ! To pretend to overawe us ! France may be conquered, perhaps even crushed, but never intimidated !"

The ambassador made a respectful bow, and gave no reply. The First Consul left that part of the saloon ; but whether he had been a little heated by this explosion of ill-humour, or from some other cause, he ceased his round, and withdrew to his own apartments. Madame Bonaparte followed. In an instant the saloon was cleared of company. The ambassadors of Russia and England had retired to the embrasure of a window, and were still found conversing together after the apartments had been cleared of visitors. " Indeed," said one to the other, " you could hardly expect such an attack ; how then could you be prepared to reply to it ? All you have to do is to give an account of it to your government : in the mean time, let what has taken place suggest to you the conduct you ought to pursue."

He took the advice. The communications became cold and reserved. England had already formed her determination. A spirit of acrimony soon sprung up between the two governments.

An interchange of notes took place; categorical explanations were demanded; the demand for passports soon followed. The latter were immediately granted by the First Consul. I was in his closet at Saint Cloud when M. Maret was introduced, who brought with him the corrected draft of the reply which was to accompany the passports. He had it read out to him, and expressed himself in the kindest terms respecting the personal character of Lord Whitworth, for whom he felt great regard. He was quite satisfied that on this occasion the ambassador had not at all influenced the conduct of his government.

Some points had remained in dispute ever since the treaty of Amiens: Malta, according to its stipulations, was to have been restored to the Order of St. John of Jerusalem. England refused her consent, because the possession of that island secured her dominion over the Mediterranean. France likewise expected that England would, in conformity with her engagements, evacuate Egypt and the Cape of Good Hope. France, on her part, had faithfully fulfilled her own engagements.

It was absurd to urge our naval armaments as a reason for declaring war against us, since those were notoriously inadequate to afford to the colony of St. Domingo the assistance it stood in need of. The genius of the First Consul, and the state of prosperity to which he had raised France, were the real ground of England's alarm. That country had formed a correct estimate of his importance, and had therefore vowed a war of extermination against him. The fixed determination to renew it at the first favourable moment was evident from the circumstance of these armaments affording the only pretence for doing so.

It would, I think, have been much more consonant with truth

to have avowed that the real ground of the war was, on the contrary, the absolutely disarmed condition of France; a condition, therefore, which presented some prospect of success against her; and that the favourable moment which was looked for, when the peace was submitted to, had now arrived.

I became more and more confirmed in this opinion when, at a later period, I acted a part in public affairs, and when my official situation enabled me on a variety of occasions to attend to preceding occurrences.

Since the battle of Zurich, won by Massena over the Russians, this nation seemed no longer to take any active part in the events of the war in Germany and Italy; and the relations established between the Emperor Paul and the First Consul having brought on a peace between their respective countries, the Russians disappeared from the fields of battle. Prussia, ever since the treaty of Basle, had maintained the strictest neutrality.

Austria stood alone in the struggle. England had indeed promised her the assistance of a civil war in France; but the First Consul had triumphed over the efforts she made to foment it. He had led into Italy all the republican troops which the pacification of the western departments rendered available to him. The Emperor was no longer in a condition to continue the contest; and if the army of the Rhine, after its victory at Hohenlinden, had been commanded by a more skilful general, Vienna would have fallen into our hands. Austria had, accordingly, hastened to avert the storm, and had consented to a peace, because it could not prolong the war without putting its existence to hazard. Of all the enemies of France, England therefore alone possessed all her physical and moral strength unimpaired. This condition was to be ascribed to circumstances which it may not be superfluous to dwell upon.

All the continental states mainly rely upon their agri-

cultural condition for their resources, and can only flourish
when that condition is prosperous. England rests upon a quite
different basis; she depends upon her commercial power;
and the resources with which commerce supplies her can
alone support her power as a state. An extension and de-
velopment of the one power must, therefore, necessarily give
greater range and augmentation to the other. Whatever
tends to desolate the rest of Europe, whatever crushes industry and throws impediments in the way of trade, such as a
state of war, or a system of prohibitions, are the grounds of
England's prosperity. She disowns the rights of neutral
flags, seizes and carries off the vessels that put out to
sea, and by dint of violence compels the continental nations
to draw their supplies from herself. Having thus acquired
the monopoly of purchasing, manufacturing, and selling, she
commands any price, and is in possession of every market.
A state of war, which is the ruin of other nations, is a state
of prosperity to her: she has, accordingly, never missed an
opportunity of forcing Europe into the field of battle.

A rational peace would be a calamity for England, and a
deadly blow; but how can she be compelled to accept such
a peace so long as the European cabinets are swayed by
cupidity or ambitious views? England holds the sinews of
corruption in her power: these will for a long time prove her
bulwark.

At the period of the peace of Luneville, the agents of
England, who, with a tariff of duties in their hands, sought to
raise enemies against France in every direction, were astonished at finding the continental nations tired of a war which
was only productive of disastrous consequences to them.
They held out the promise of more abundant subsidies than
the preceding ones; but the offers proved ineffectual. The
continent was exhausted: it became necessary to renounce the
hope of perpetuating the war, and to assent to a peace which
could no longer be averted. This measure, besides, was no

more than a truce intended to render the First Consul's situation more complicated. The British government had formed an erroneous idea of the internal state of France. From the reports made to them by a crowd of spies they kept up amongst us, they had been led to believe that peace would bring about what a war had proved inadequate to accomplish.

They had laid down to themselves the principle that the First Consul's power could never acquire consistency; that it had not a moral character, and merely rested on the strength of his bayonets. By subscribing to a peace, they would place their adversary under the necessity of disarming, from his inability to pay such an extensive war establishment, and of proportionably weakening his resources. Private ambition would thus be revived, a civil war rekindled, and the consular power, standing between the ruins of the revolution and the resisting force prepared to oppose that power, could never recover from its financial difficulties. It would be compelled to weigh the people down with taxes, and thereby create discontent, or to press heavily upon foreign countries, and resort to a spoliating system, which would again draw it into a war.

Another consideration suggests itself: the French nation had grown indifferent to all contests that related solely to the possession of power; it had become quite impossible to bring about any internal commotion.

Every thing held out a hope of the downfall of the consular authority; the only difficulty was how to direct the attack with a prospect of success. What period could be more favourable than the moment when he had disbanded his army?

Matters had, however, gone on since the peace in an inverse ratio to the expectations of the British ministry. La Vendée had remained quiet: the First Consul, whose popularity had greatly increased, had continued to carry on the public works he had in view. He had raised into new existence what the political storms had destroyed, and given birth to branches of industry hitherto unknown to us. His system of administration was equally rapid and uniform; all hailed the happy chance that had restored him to us. The public funds were on the rise : no rival ambition had started up to resist him : all the hopes of England had been baffled except in regard to the disbanding of the army ; a measure which had, indeed, been fully accomplished.

CHAPTER XXXIII.

Situation of the army—General Marmont—Patriotic donations—Conscriptions— Occupation of Hanover—Napoleon's journey to Belgium—The invasion of England is determined upon.

THE First Consul had indulged a hope of the duration of peace. He believed in it the more as the rumour had been industriously spread, that of all countries France was the only one calculated to excite apprehension. He had, indeed, acted with so much candour and good faith, that he had caused an unlimited leave of absence to be granted to every soldier who had applied for it ; and this permission had been taken advantage of to so great an extent that the major part of the infantry regiments were nearly reduced to skeletons. They would even have been wholly broken up but out of consideration for the officers, who, having lost all habits of working for their support, could not exist without the aid of their pay.

The cavalry was, comparatively speaking, in a still more deplorable condition ; it had almost dwindled away to nothing. Some regiments of cuirassiers, the 6th regiment, amongst others, were unable to furnish three squadrons of sixty four men each. The park of artillery, and of course the field equipages, were broken up. Every other consideration had made way for economy.

The *materiel* of the artillery was also in a very bad condition. General Marmont, who had been appointed chief inspector of that branch of service, had recently introduced new plans, which would have required the recasting of all field-pieces, and a complete remodelling of the caissons and gun-carriages. Every thing had been taken to the large foundries, where they had already begun to break up the cannon for the purpose of throwing them into the furnaces. None of the elements requisite for the composition of an army were either ready or in a state of forwardness.

I therefore ask whether such a condition was calculated to excite the apprehensions of our neighbours; or rather, if it did not tend to revive the hopes of our enemies, and make them take up those arms which they had reluctantly laid aside? Is it not clear that they had long combined to attack France when off her guard, and give stability to the old aristocratic government, threatened by the consolidation of the new social order established amongst us, as well as by the power which it had had the effect of concentrating in the hands of one man? The interruption of the peace of Amiens was not to be ascribed to any other cause; and the First Consul was for a long time displeased with his minister of foreign affairs for having lulled him into a mistaken security, or at least for not having seen through the plots that were preparing in every direction around him. At no time had he stood in greater need of correct information; and the minister did not on this occasion establish his claim to the reputation he had acquired.

In France, where every one could bear testimony to the zeal which the First Consul evinced for promoting works that were only suitable to a state of peace, the imputations of foreigners, who charged him with entertaining views of aggression, were indignantly repelled. It was too manifest indeed to all that the whole activity of his genius was exclusively devoted to objects connected with the internal administration, with manufactures, and with the advancement of the national industry. But all such exclusive cares bestowed in a manner that justified him in the eyes of the nation, had well nigh compromised its welfare. As he only sought repose, and the promoting of internal improvements, he had signed, without reading it, the decree presented to him by the war minister (General Berthier), just as it had been unsuspectingly received by the latter from General Marmont, in whose well-known zeal and talents he had confided; so that the breaking up of the whole field of artillery was going on without the First Consul's knowledge, when the cry of war suddenly sounded in his ears.

He was greatly vexed, as he could not fail to be, at so untoward a circumstance. He sent for the minister of war, and for Marmont, with a hastiness of manner which I never saw him display on any other occasion. On their appearance shortly afterwards, I announced their arrival; but neither would venture to go in first. He was obliged to call them both into his presence. " Really," he said, " if you were not my friends, I should suspect that you were betraying me. Send immediately to the arsenals and foundries: let your fatal projects be suspended, and get as much artillery in readiness as you can immediately collect."

He had reason to complain of the two oldest participators in his glory; but their evident embarrassment completely disarmed him.

The navy was not in a more promising condition. All the sailors had been sent to take possession of the colonies restored to us, where a great part of our ships of war were still in commission. The marine department had just dispatched the flotilla intended to occupy the small factory in the East Indies, into which we had been reinstated. Thus, by a strange fatality, it had sent out ships at the moment when it became dangerous to put to sea. Under whatever aspect our military position might be considered at this period, it afforded no pretext for an aggression. The prevailing opinion therefore was, that England had again taken up arms because she felt as much alarmed at the progress of our internal industry as enraged at our political principles.

This interruption of peace was a source of excessive dis- appointment to the First Consul, who was accordingly com- pelled to postpone all his plans of internal improvements, and bestow all the energies of his mind on matters of war: they called for immense pecuniary means. It became necessary to suspend useful works for the purpose of meeting the exigen- cies required by the attitude of defence imposed upon him.

He had to contend with unheard-of difficulties, such as any other mind than his must have recoiled at; but the more insurmountable they appeared, the greater was his pride in surmounting them. If at times he felt at a loss, he never showed any signs of embarrassment. Antwerp was still in the same condition in which it had been restored to him: the works were not yet begun which it was in contemplation to erect with the view of making it a warlike arsenal: no naval construction was yet commenced; the requisite materials had not even been procured.

It was the admirable practice of the First Consul, at this time, to make France acquainted with her real position. The accounts of his administration, which he transmitted to the Legislative Body, had given general satisfaction, and been hailed as a favourable omen for the future. He repeated a course that had already proved so successful to him: he laid before the constituted bodies the several communications which had taken place previously to the rupture; and as they proved beyond a doubt that he could not avoid a war, more unjust on the part of his enemies than any other of which history affords an example, the nation warmly took up his cause, pressed round her chief, and cheerfully bestowed all the means he required for coming victorious out of a contest in which he was not the aggressor.

The larger towns voted the sums requisite for obtaining

ships of war, which were built and armed, and named after the places which had respectively provided the means applicable to each.

This was the period at which the system for recruiting, better known by the name of the conscription, was adopted. The First Consul had caused the plan to be discussed in the Council of State a short time before; but as we were at peace, he had not established it into a law. Circumstances were now altered, and the exigencies were of the most pressing nature. The decree was issued, and the army soon numbered in its ranks a multitude of hardy young men, accustomed to the labours of the field, and capable of enduring the hardships of a soldier's life.

The provocations to war had imposed the necessity of resorting to this measure. The conscription, besides, has not had the effect of diminishing the population; it has given the nation a right sense of its own dignity. The orders of knighthood, and the promotions and appointments distributed amongst the soldiery, tended to give the nation a new character. Great, however, as may have been to the nation itself the advantage resulting from that system, I must acknowledge that it has sometimes been found necessary to abuse it; and that if it had been acted upon with less severity, France would have escaped an invasion.

The cavalry and artillery were remounted: every thing was put upon a war footing. The soldiers were drilled; the superior officers submitted plans of operation to the government. The First Consul was constantly receiving projects of attack against England. He gave his attention to all, but adopted none, conceiving them to be premature. When every thing was prepared, he determined to strike the first blow. He put in motion a part of the troops that were stationed upon the Lower Rhine, and sent them forward towards Hanover, one of the possessions of the King of England. The management of this expedition was confided to General Mortier, who was then in command of the first military division (Paris). The Hanoverian army withdrew on our approach, and successively occupied the different positions which the nature of the country presented; but it was wholly unable to resist us: it accepted the terms proposed by General Mortier, laid down its arms, and was immediately dispersed.

Tranquillity was thenceforward restored to that country, which supplied us with horses in great abundance, and was the means of remounting our cavalry. The regiments in France were sent to Hanover to be remounted, as they used to be sent to Normandy for the same purpose. We found there a quantity of artillery sufficient for the wants of a powerful state. This country was, in short, of invaluable assistance to us by furnishing every thing requisite for the restoration of the *materiel* of the army.

Ever since the First Consul was at the head of the government he had been prevented from carrying into effect his intention of visiting Belgium: he determined to make that excursion during the summer following the rupture with England, and availed himself of the same opportunity to inspect the coast and harbours.

I was one of those selected to accompany him. He left St. Cloud with Madame Bonaparte, who was desirous of making the journey, and dined at Compiegne, which he had never yet seen. He visited the palace, where the school of arts and trades was established. The apartments of that splendid edifice had been turned into workshops for artisans of all trades; containing anvils, bellows, forges, joiners' tables, tailors' and coblers' boards, and showed no trace of the purposes for which they were originally intended. The mirrors, marbles, floors, and wainscots had been taken away; nothing but the bare walls and ceilings remained: the only part that did not exhibit any sign of devastation was the landing-place at the top of the great staircase; nor could any fitter place be found for serving the dinner.

The First Consul could not repress a feeling of displeasure at beholding the degraded condition of so noble a building. He wrote on the same day to the minister of the interior, desiring he would present him a plan for the removal of the school to some other place; and Chalons was, afterwards, selected to receive it.   He ordered the immediate repair of those parts of the palace which stood most in need of it; and, by degrees, that immense pile of ruins rose into the majestic palace of the present day.   Continuing his journey from Compiegne, he slept at Amiens, where the population welcomed him with an enthusiasm bordering upon frenzy.   He remained some days in that town, visiting all its establishments and manufactories, to which Messrs. Monge, Chaptal, and Berthollet invariably accompanied him.

Proceeding on his journey, he passed through Montreuil, Etaples, Boulogne, Ambleteuse, Vimereux, Calais, and Gravelines, and arrived at Dunkirk, where he rejoined Madame Bonaparte, who had travelled from Amiens by way of Arras and St. Omer.

He had sent saddle-horses beforehand to the different places through which he intended to pass, and ordered the most skilful civil and naval engineers at those several stations to fall in with his suite.   With this retinue he proceeded along the coast, and overwhelmed with questions every scientific person he met with on the way.   He had soon made up his mind upon the principal part of the plans they had submitted to his inspection, and directed them to follow him to Dunkirk, where he discussed the several points, and came to a resolution respecting them.   From Dunkirk he went to Lisle, from Lisle to Bruges, and thence to Ostend, to which place the engineers had gone to wait his arrival. From Ostend he repaired to Blankenberg, returned thence to Bruges, and proceeded to Ghent, on his way to Antwerp.

He caused the latter city to be thoroughly examined in all its parts.   A beginning was at once made of those gigantic works of which no idea can be formed by those who had not seen the then condition of Antwerp. The First Consul attentively observed every thing on his way, made remarks upon what he saw, and brought together the several persons of his suite to discuss each case with them. He then noted down his ideas, wrote to the several ministers, and seldom retired to rest until he had sent off his observations to them upon the matters connected with their respective departments.

He assembled a naval council for the purpose of discussing the means he had to contend with the English, and was soon convinced that the resources at his disposal were wholly inadequate to the object which he had in contemplation. The council was unanimously of opinion that the fleet of men of war afforded no chance of success. It required to be created anew and exercised, and in its present condition it might be destroyed before it could be in a condition to fight. The only means, therefore, of contending with England on an equal footing was to attempt a descent; because, if once we could accomplish it, we should be enabled to fight with means more powerful than those which the English would bring against us. We stood, however, in need of a flotilla to effect a descent. It was certainly not yet in existence; but we had all the necessary materials for raising such an armament, although not in sufficient abundance for the building of ships of war. M. Decres, the minister of marine, who attended the council, was not in favour of the plan; he observed that, if we constructed a flotilla, the English would also raise one, and come to meet us. Admiral Bruix replied to this observation that much would be achieved if we compelled them to do so, as they would then be under the necessity of disarming their fleet for the purpose of fitting out their flotilla. Their means of recruiting for the navy were not, in fact, at that period, so extensive as they have since become: the sailors of the maritime countries of which we had successively obtained posses-

sion were not yet compelled to volunteer to man their fleets
for the purpose of earning their livelihood. The opinion of
Bruix prevailed, and the descent was determined upon.

The First Consul's attention was immediately devoted to
the construction of a flotilla. He gave orders to the civil
engineers to draw up the plans and estimates of the works
which related to their branch of the service, desired the
naval engineers to present models of the vessels which they
deemed best adapted for the undertaking, and fixed for both
a period within which they were to bring him the result of
their deliberations. He then proceeded to Brussels, which
he was visiting for the first time, and entered that city on
horseback, with his retinue and guards. His presence
created an intoxicating joy in all classes of the population.
The poor and the rich, the soldier and the citizen, the friend
of legal authority, the advocate of rational liberty, all were
desirous to see him, and to testify their gratitude by their
acclamations of welcome.

The First Consul staid some days in that city, where
every kind of fête was given to him. He then went on to
Maestricht, and returned to Paris bv way of Liege, Givet,
Mezieres, Sedan, Reims, and Soissons.

During the whole of this journey he did not pass through
a single town that was famed for any particular branch of
industry without visiting its workshops and manufactories.
M. Chaptal did not allow a single one to escape him : he
seemed, besides, to take a pleasure in this occupation, and
expressed the deepest regret at being compelled to withdraw
his attention from that source of national prosperity to objects
of a very different nature.

Having, shortly after his return, received the plans
and estimates which he had demanded of the engineer departments, he caused them to be discussed ; and he definitively decided upon ordering the construction of an immense
quantity of gun-boats, flat-bottomed boats, and other small

craft. Each considerable city had voted money for the building of a man of war: those which were less wealthy and less populous offered gun-boats, the others flat-bottomed boats. These offers were accepted; and in order to prevent any' delay in their building, or any obstacles in the way of the men of war which were on the stocks, the keels were laid along the banks of navigable rivers, where the carpenters and other workmen of the adjacent places were brought together under the superintendence of the ship-builders whom the naval department had sent for the purpose of carrying on their work.

In this manner the banks of the rivers, which discharge their waters into the ocean, were lined with regular docks. The materials and workmen of the several districts being thus made use of and employed, the money remained in the places by which it had been voted, whilst it would otherwise have been withdrawn to defray the same expenses at other places. Holland likewise furnished her own flotilla, which was first assembled at Flushing: it was formed on the exact plan of the French flotilla, and commanded by Vice-Admiral Verheul, a resolute and able seaman; who, in spite of every obstacle, brought it from Flushing to Ostend, and from the latter place to Dunkirk, Calais, and Ambleteuse.

END OF PART I.

PART II.

MEMOIRS

OF

THE DUKE OF ROVIGO.

PART II.

CHAPTER I.

Camp of Boulogne—Discipline—Works of the troops—M. de la Bouillerie.

WHILE the navy was displaying this activity, the army finished completing itself. The regiments, two-thirds of which were composed of conscripts, quitted their garrisons, and proceeded to form camps of instruction, which extended from Utrecht to the mouth of the Somme. The camp of Utrecht was commanded by General Marmont, who had been succeeded in the general inspection of the artillery by General Songis. It extended to Flushing, and was numbered 2, because the corps of Hanover, then commanded by General Bernadotte, had taken number 1.

The 3rd, under the orders of General Davout, had its centre at Ostend, and extended to Dunkirk inclusively.

General Soult commanded the 4th, which was formed at Boulogne, and extended from Gravelines to the left of Boulogne.

The 5th, commanded by General Ney, comprised Montreuil and Etaples. It was subsequently known as No. 6, because a new corps was formed at Boulogne, and called No. 5. It was placed under the command of General Lannes, who returned from Portugal, where he was ambassador.

A reserve, composed of twelve united battalions of grenadiers, assembled at Arras, under the orders of General Junot, who relinquished the government of Paris to take the command of this division.

All the regiments of dragoons that were in France, were formed into divisions of four regiments each. They were cantoned from the mouth of the Scheld to the banks of the Oise and of the Aisne.

The chasseurs and the hussars were collected at St. Omer and Ardres.

The troops thus distributed, were employed and disciplined in the manner of the Romans. Each hour had its employment: the soldier but laid down the musket to take up the mattock, and the mattock to resume the musket.

The engineers had to undertake immense works, which were all executed by the troops. They excavated the harbour of Boulogne; they constructed a pier, built a bridge, erected a sluice; and finally, they dug a basin to receive the vessels of the flotilla. They did still more: the port of Vimereux was to be entirely created; the site which it was to occupy was fifteen feet above the surface of the water in the highest tides. They fell to work, and in less than a year they had excavated and lined with masonry a basin capable of containing two hundred vessels of the flotilla. It had a sluice for the purpose of cleansing it, and its piers and channel for outlet.

At Ambleteuse it was necessary to begin afresh the works which had been commenced during the reign of Louis XVI. The bed of the river was so obstructed, that the water could not run off, and had covered several thousand acres in high cultivation. This inundation had not only reduced numbers of families to poverty, but generated dangerous effluvia, which obliged the inhabitants of the neighbouring villages to come away every year during the dog-days.

In the first place, the fall which the water had lost was restored ; the works previously commenced were resumed and completed, and a sluice was constructed. The river, returning within its bed, gave back to agriculture the land which it had overflowed, and to the adjacent country the salubrity which it had banished from it.

This done, they set about the harbour of Ambleteuse. They excavated it, constructed its pier, and deepened its channel: every thing was speedily completed. The soldiers who executed these various works laboured at them with assiduity. They were paid : work put money into their pockets ; they relinquished it only when compelled by the tide, and then resumed their arms and went to exercise.

It was the same at Boulogne : the troops went from work to exercise, from exercise to work. The mattock and the musket were never out of their hands. Hence all the naval establishments of a great port sprung up as it were by magic. Magazines were formed, ammunition was collected, stores of all sorts were brought together. Never did the head of man embrace so vast a conception; and above all, never did it cause the different parts to move simultaneously with such activity, such unity, and such precision.

Ports were dug, ships built, cannon founded, cordage and sails made, biscuit baked, and the army trained at the same time. The superintendence of these different operations seemed to surpass human powers; and yet the First Consul found time to attend to the affairs of France and Italy besides. The activity which he displayed cannot be conceived by those who were not witnesses of it. He hired near Boulogne the small mansion called Pont de Brique, which is on the road to Paris. He arrived there in general at the moment when the corps least expected him, immediately mounted his horse, rode through the camps, and was back again at St. Cloud, when he was supposed to be still in the midst of the troops.

I made several of these trips in his carriages. He usually set off in the evening, breakfasted at the post-house at Chantilly, supped at Abbeville, and reached Pont de Brique very early the next morning. He was presently afterwards on horseback, and most commonly did not alight again till dark. He returned not till he had seen every soldier and every workshop. He went down into the basins, and ascertained with his own eyes to what depth the men had dug since his last visit.

He usually brought back to dine with him, at seven or eight in the evening, Admiral Bruix, General Soult, Sganzin, superintendent of the works in the engineer department, General Faultrier, who commanded the *materiel* of the artillery, and the commissary charged with the supply of provisions ; so that before he retired to bed, he was better acquainted with the state of his affairs than if he had read whole volumes of reports.

Works were carried on with no less activity in the interior than on the coast. Boats were built, and being consigned to the currents of the rivers, they thronged to Bayonne, Bordeaux, Rochefort, Nantes, and all the ports of Bretagne. They were equipped, armed, and even manned, by the detachments with which they gained the mouths of the rivers that run between Honfleur and Flushing. When they had arrived there, they were rendered fit to put to sea, formed into small squadrons, and sent forth successively from their retreats, as soon as it was judged that they could leave them with safety. For this purpose such breezes were chosen as allowed them to keep close along shore ; and for their better security, the light artillery of the army was placed on the capes or promontories, at the base of which there was sufficient depth of water to permit the English cruisers to intercept them. This was by no means an unnecessary precaution on various parts of the coast of Bretagne.

Good luck and skill carried this great enterprise to a high pitch : our squadrons reached their destination without sustaining any other losses than those occasioned by the ordinary accidents of navigation. Every thing had succeeded to the wishes of the First Consul. All then vied with one another in zeal and devotedness.

The army began to be expert in military exercises, and enjoyed excellent health. It was divided into twelve corps, including the troops which were on the coast and those which had been stationed on other points of the frontiers. It was the first time that trial was made of this organization. The First Consul had adopted it, because he was fond of celerity, and, besides the military advantages with which it was attended, it possessed that of simplifying the accounts. In consequence, he ordered the then minister of the treasury, M. de Barbé-Marbois, to organize a treasury-office for each corps.

The minister submitted to him his ideas; but the First Consul would have been obliged to transact business with the paymaster of each *corps-d'armée*, and he rejected the plan. He directed M. Petiet, intendant-general of the army, to inform M. Marbois, that he would have to do with but a single individual, to whom all the paymasters should be subordinate. He therefore required the minister to give him for this service the most capable of the persons in the department of the treasury.

M. Petiet proposed M. de la Bouillerie, who had been paymaster-general of the army of the Rhine under General Moreau, whose intimate friend he was. The First Consul was unacquainted with him, but he recollected that an officer of that name had formerly been at the head of the finances in Corsica,* where he had left behind him an excellent character. On the strength of this recollection, he accepted

* This was the father of M. de la Bouillerie.

him, and desired the intendant-general to communicate to the minister the choice which he had made.

M. de la Bouillerie, who already possessed an independent fortune, and who was moreover connected with General Moreau, with whose secret sentiments he was more intimately acquainted than any other man, excused himself upon various pretexts. Petiet had recourse to the intervention of the general, and M. de la Bouillerie accepted the office.

The minister of the treasury, who viewed this nomination with an evil eye, apologized for not having proposed it. He had not done so because M. de la Bouillerie, after giving in his accounts, owed to the treasury a sum of four hundred thousand francs, for which he tendered a bill of General Moreau's "Out of what fund was this sum paid?" asked the First Consul.—"Out of the fund placed at the disposal of the general-in-chief," replied the minister. "In this case," rejoined the First Consul, "M. de la Bouillerie is quite right, and you must accept the bill."—"*Parbleu*," added he, "you might as well require me to account too for all the sums which I ordered to be given when with the army of Italy, to the officers with whom I was pleased. That is neither just nor reasonable."

M. de la Bouillerie, in accepting the office of paymaster-general, stipulated that no security should be demanded of him. On the other hand, he never once inquired what salary he was to receive, and he was even three years without drawing any. The First Consul, who had meanwhile become emperor, was apprized of it; and made such liberal amends for this forgetfulness, that M. de la Bouillerie was more than satisfied.

The First Consul placed the utmost confidence in him, and was not backward to testify it. He subsequently appointed him to the management of all his personal finances, and also of those of the extraordinary domains; and, in 1815, I saw him bitterly deplore having occasion to reproach him with misconduct.

CHAPTER II.

Sensation produced in England by the project of invasion—General Moreau—
His opposition to the government of the First Consul—Sinister rumours—Important warning of a Vendean chief—The First Consul sends the author on a
secret mission to La Vendée.

WHILE these preliminary arrangements of the grand operation of the First Consul were proceeding with a success for
which he had not himself dared to hope, censure began to fix
itself upon his enterprise; and it even made progress in a city
like Paris, where no opportunity for it is lost. Accordingly,
the projected invasion of England was there generally considered as a scheme that could not be carried into effect. It
was regarded as wild and extravagant, on a comparison of the
gun-boats which were on the stocks, from the Gros Caillou to
the Corps Legislatif, with men of war: people vied with each
other in condemnation of the measure, and even talked a
great deal of nonsense, as they almost always do when they
pretend to pass judgment on what they know nothing about.
It was much easier to find fault with the First Consul than to
comprehend him. When, however, they saw that in spite of
all imaginable difficulties, he persisted in the execution of his
design, and that the union of all the different flotillas from
Bayonne to Flushing had been effected, notwithstanding all
that could be done by the English cruisers to prevent it, they
began to reflect and to admit very generally that the final
success depended solely on a turn of fortune ; and it is impossible to conjecture what might have been the result had not
events occurred to divert the army from that operation, after
they had brought about a change in the form of the government.

While the project of the First Consul was censured in

France, in England, where people are cooler, they took the threat seriously, because they had measured the whole extent of the danger, instead of amusing themselves with making puns.

The English ministers could no longer help confessing to themselves that the commotions, which ever since the peace of Amiens they had predicted as inevitable in France, had not only not happened, but, on the other hand, things had taken such a contrary turn, that the man, whose ruin they had considered as certain, had succeeded in forming such a bundle, * as already threatened the existence of England. The ministers judiciously abandoned the illusions into which they had at first been led, when they were induced to make peace, and afterwards to break it. They had doubtless observed that the wonderful restoration of things in France, and that in so short a time, was purely the work of a mighty genius, which conceived, arranged, and executed, with the rapidity of thought; that the First Consul was the legislator, the magistrate, and the absolute master, of a country and of an army, of which he was at the same time the general and the first soldier; that it was consequently at him that the blow which was to preserve England from ruin ought to be aimed; and that the success of this single blow would suffice to plunge France back into the abyss of calamities from which he had drawn her, and to sink her to that depth to which the powers of the continent that had made war upon her could not reduce her.

The success of such a scheme would have produced cousequences too positive to admit of any hesitation respecting the choice of the means calculated for ensuring it : they were accordingly sought in human passions.

I have now to treat of the conspiracy of George Cadoual, and the singular part which the friends of General Moreau wished him to take in it. For his own person, far from being

---

* In allusion to the bundle of sticks in the fable.—TRANSLATOR.

desirous to promote the plan, he was so averse to it as to be in some measure the cause of its failure.

Ever since the peace of Luneville, General Moreau had lived almost unknown, and kept aloof from the government. A love of retirement, an indifference, perhaps affected, to honours which could not exalt him above the second rank, and a real aversion to every kind of employment, had led him to adopt this mode of life.

Those who knew him can admit, without the least prejudice to his good qualities, that General Moreau was most unfit for business requiring assiduous attention; that he possessed but very limited information, which rendered him incapable of governing; and that, nevertheless, the contempt which he affected for honours was but a kind of distinction which he had assumed, and by which a courtier could scarcely have been deceived. One might have said to Moreau as to Diogenes: " I see thy pride through the holes in thy cloak." With great firmness in danger he united a weakness of character in private life, which rendered him the most accessible and the most easily persuaded of men

As he occupied himself but little with business, his judgment was slow, his foresight short, and he had need of assistance in his determinations: hence his kindness to persons who at length acquired control over him, and who under the veil of friendship ruined him, by endeavouring to make him subservient to their own ambition. Soon after his return from the army to Paris, General Moreau, at the instigation of his pretended friends, attempted to lecture the First Consul on politics, organization, and administration: the trial which he made of his influence failed, and perceiving what sort of character he had to deal with, he never recurred to those subjects. In consequence, with the exception of a few wrongheads, all the generals and officers of his army pursued the right line of the respectful obedience due to the head of the government.

Moreau had at length retired to his estate, to enjoy the wealth which he had acquired in the service of his country. Other generals of that army, who had amassed money, lived in like manner in mansions which they had purchased, and strove to habituate themselves to a country life.

Some of them were early disgusted with it, and not having been able to obtain appointments on the first formation of the army of the coast, they had turned grumblers ; others lived in repose, because they had expressed a wish to be left in the enjoyment of it ; but both put on the look of ill-used persons; which gave them a position that cost but little, and was favourable to their plan of keeping aloof. At a distance, the eye of the observer confounded all these people with General Moreau, and made out of them an opposition party, which had even acquired a sort of lustre from all the frothy declamations that were put forth on the impossibility of the success of the enterprise of Boulogne.

There had been persons silly enough to advise Moreau not to *compromise his glory by mixing himself up in such a mess,* and he had been weak enough to listen to this advice.

Ever since the rupture of the treaty of Amiens, that is to say, upwards of a year, we had remarked that he had not appeared at the Tuileries, even on occasions when not only decency, but the duty of a citizen as well as a soldier, would have dictated the propriety of his attending there and offering his services.

General Moreau could not be considered as a private individual, which he affected to appear ; and when cities and whole provinces, filled with generous indignation, imposed on themselves the sacrifices required by the most unparalleled aggression that had ever been witnessed, and those provinces sent deputies from all quarters to convey their offerings and their good wishes to the head of the government, was it the duty of General Moreau to remain an indifferent spectator of the new dangers of his country? Was he another Achilles, whom Agamemnon ought to have solicited to resume his arms? And if even he had been disposed to obey the orders which there might have been occasion to give him, ought he not, after the line of conduct which he had held, to have transmitted an assurance to that effect, if he had not thought it his duty to offer it in person? It was such advice as this that his friends ought to have given him.

But be wrapped himself up in silence; and we shall soon see why he could not break it.

He had lent an ear to counsels which flattered his indolence; and it was doubtless the perverse temper into which it was but too well known that this general had fallen, which gave to the agents of England, vulgarly called Vendeans, the idea of attempting to bring about a union that antecedent circumstances appeared to have rendered impossible between General Moreau and General Pichegru.

Fouché, who was no longer minister, caused Moreau to be haunted by men of his province, and at the same time of his party: he closely watched to discover his sentiments, for the purpose of influencing and taking advantage of them upon occasion; but I believe he was a stranger to the plan of an accommodation between the Vendeans and Moreau, because the character of the latter did not offer a sufficient guarantee for him in case of the success of that party: but I believe too that he would have urged it himself, had be seen a possibility of reviving the republic by the overthrow of the First Consul, which at that period would not have been impracticable. Perhaps, too, M. Fouché had no other intention than to induce serious circumstances, in order to provoke the necessity of re-establishing a ministry which had been suppressed, and which he considered as his appanage.

The aversion of Moreau to the Vendeans was the consequence of his opinions: perhaps, too, fear of the revision of his conduct in 1797 towards his comrade, Pichegru,* prevented his compliance with the solicitations of the latter. A stanch republican, he turned a deaf ear to every proposal incompatible with the existence and the restoration of the republic : having known him intimately, I am convinced that he did not communicate to the government the proposals that were made to him, because he was persuaded that Pichegru's plan was so extravagant, that he should have had nothing to do but to fight him the very next day after that general should have overthrown the First Consul. It did not appear possible to Moreau that any other but himself could be invested with the consular power : he therefore suffered Pichegru to proceed, under the conviction that it was for him (Moreau) he was labouring ; and this it was that caused Pichegru, when speaking of Moreau, to observe : " It seems that fellow has ambition too !" †

After I was invested with the ministerial authority, I had the means of ascertaining that the First Consul owed his life at that period solely to the diversity of plans of the two intrigues, both which aimed alike to destroy him, but with wholly different objects. It was during their disunion that a knowledge of them was obtained, and all their plots discovered. For some time dark rumours had been afloat; and without affording the certainty of a completely-organized conspiracy, they still gave warning that something was going forward which it was daily more and more important to sift to the bottom.

A thousand sinister reports were circulated, as if to pre-

---

* It will be recollected that he transmitted to the Directory the correspondence found among the baggage of the Austrian general, Klinglin, which proved that Pichegru was in criminal communication with .the Prince of Condé, and that he was preparing the disasters of his own army.

† An expression reported by George's companions, when questioned respecting what they had done, seen, and heard.

pare the public mind for some event; the possibility of arresting the political career of the First Consul was talked of: letters from London even stated that he would be assassinated, and that the information was derived from an authentic source. The certainty of this intelligence, though it was not incontestable, was nevertheless sufficient to excite the alarm and consequently to deserve the attention of the government.

There was not at this time, as I have observed, any minister of police : it was a counsellor of state who directed the investigation of every thing relative to the general *surveillance*, and whose operations were carried on in concert with ·the grand-judge.

At this period I received a letter from one who had formerly been a Vendean chief, whom I had laid under obligation, and who had now no other wish than to live in quiet on his estates. He informed me that he had just been visited by a band of from thirty to forty armed men, who had come to talk to him about the *follies* which he had heartily renounced ever since the 18th Brumaire; and that, as well to keep the promise which he had then given, as to secure himself against the consequences which might result from this event, he lost no time in apprizing me of it; adding that, in order to keep out of danger, he should repair to Paris as soon as the vintage was over.

I laid this letter before the First Consul, who judged, from the stamp of truth which it bore, that I should probably obtain some particulars concerning this matter, which began to engage his attention ; and that at any rate it would be well to ascertain the political sentiments of La Vendée, in circumstances which might become aggravated, in consequence of the events that were preparing.

I set out therefore *incognito*, and went to my Vendean chief, who furnished me with further details; and at my reiterated proposal we both set out, after I had disguised myself, in quest of the band which he had mentioned in his letter.

On the third day we saw some men belonging to it, and who had parted from it the day before; and from them we obtained all the details requisite to enable me to form a judgment of its designs.

This band was headed by two men, who had recently landed on the coast : it scoured the country, announcing a speedy change in affairs, and giving notice to people to hold themselves in readiness for this moment. I actually saw the peasants numbering themselves by small districts, as if preparing for an insurrection : some of them even said to me in their jargon: *Comment est-ce que je ferons? je n'avons plus de fusils, les bleus les ont pris*—"What am I to do? I have no guns; the blues have taken them away." It is well known that this was the name by which the Vendeans denominated the republicans.

In this journey I had occasion to ascertain that this unhappy country was still capable of suffering itself to be again set on fire; and I also convinced myself that many Vendean chiefs, whom we supposed to possess a great moral power in those parts, had entirely lost all consideration with the people on account of their connexion with the government. I was told repeatedly, that none of them would be able to excite insurrection in the country, but that it was probable that this time it would be George himself who would come; and some even went so far as to say, that it was not believed he would run the risk of coming through Bretagne, where every body was sold (meaning that they would betray him), but that he would probably come by Normandy. I saw evidently, from the hopes which they entertained on the subject, that he was the only man who could yet inspire them with any confidence, and excite them to insurrection.

I returned with this gentleman to his mansion, whence I set out the following day for Paris.

CHAPTER III.

Trial of several Vendean chiefs—Querel—Young Troche—Mission to the beach of Biville.

THESE particulars greatly surprised the First Consul, who began to be uneasy at not having heard from me since I left Paris ; he said some flattering things to me about my courage and resolution in running such dangerous risks, and he certainly set them down to my credit.

He then determined to employ severe measures, to elicit truth from darkness. He had an inconceivable tact for judging when he was upon a volcano, and for laying his finger on the precise spot where any thing was to be discovered.

Since he had been at the head of the government, trials by council of war had been extremely rare ; he had even entertained the intention of suppressing them, excepting in cases of military discipline.

There were nevertheless in the prisons several persons detained by the police as spies, or charged with political machinations ; and they were not ordered for trial, because the First Consul said that the time would come when no further importance could be attached to those intrigues, and they might then be set at liberty.

On this occasion he desired to be shown the list of all those persons, with the date of their apprehension, and notes of their different anterior circumstances.

Among them was a man named Picot, and another named Le Bourgeois, who had been apprehended a year before at Pont Audemer in Normandy, as coming from England: on their departure from London, a description of their persons had been given by an agent whom the police kept there,* and who had learned from themselves the atrocious design with which they were going to France, and which was nothing less than to assassinate the First Consul. The government had hitherto contented itself with keeping them in prison. The First Consul directed that they and three others should be tried: they were brought before a commission. The first-mentioned two manifested an obstinacy that was not expected; they refused to answer, and were condemned, and shot, without making the slightest confession. They seemed even determined to defy authority; and perished, declaring that it would not survive the war. This bravado diminished the painful impression which an execution always produces. Not a single step had been gained. The First Consul nevertheless directed the trial for which he had given orders to be deferred.

The government being obliged to have recourse to inquiries concerning a design, the existence of which it guessed, had excited the zeal of all the functionaries. These set on foot inquiries; and Mr. Shee, uncle of the Duke of Feltre and prefect of the Lower Rhine, gave notice of an intrigue which wore an alarming appearance. He had ascertained that the English resident at the court of Wurtemberg kept up an extensive correspondence on the right bank of the Rhine; that he was continually travelling, and frequently visited a party of emigrants who had recently thrown themselves into the territory of Baden, and into the vicinity of Offenburg. He encouraged them, succoured them, and assured them that there would be a speedy change in France. He had, moreover, for an auxiliary a Baroness von Reich, who lived at Offenburg, and who had long figured in all the counter-revolutionary plots. It was well known what the resident was capable of. It was determined to penetrate his intentions, and the plans which he had formed; and a cunning, insi-

---

* It was only in London that a *surveillance* was kept up among the refugees from the war in the West.

nuating emissary was dispatched, who intoxicated him with hopes, wormed from him the secret of the connexions which he kept up with the interior, and fascinated him to such a degree, that the diplomatist proposed to associate him in his designs. The emissary assented. He weighed and discussed the chances which the enterprise presented; pleaded falsehood to come at truth; obtained all the information that he wanted; and set out for Paris, furnished with large sums of money which he had had the address to draw from the credulous envoy. The designs which he reported were too paltry to deserve notice. Nothing was learned from his mission. We were obliged to seek other sources of information.

The First Consul reverted to the prosecutions which he had suspended. He ordered the list to be laid before him. It began with a person named Querel:—"Who is this man?" he inquired. He was told that he was a native of Bas Bretagne, who had served under George in La Vendée. Having arrived at Paris about two months before, he had been apprehended upon the denunciation of a creditor whom he was unable to pay, and who in revenge gave information to the government concerning him. "This man knows something, or I am much mistaken," rejoined the First Consul. It was impossible that Querel, under all the circumstances of his case, could escape condemnation. He was actually condemned; but the sentence awakened reflections: for, next day, when preparations were making to conduct him to execution, he declared that he had disclosures to make to the First Consul which concerned his life. The execution was deferred. The officer commanding the picket came to acquaint the aid-de-camp on duty with the disposition in which Querel was. The aid-de-camp in his turn reported it to the First Consul, who sent him to receive the declaration. It was circumstantial, precise, and dispelled the cloud which still enveloped the meditated assassination. Querel, in fact, declared that he had been at Paris for six months past, and that he had come from England with George Cadoual, and six other persons whom he named. They had since been joined by fourteen more, who had likewise come from England, and been put on shore by a cutter of the English royal navy. They had all been landed at the foot of the cliff of Biville, near Dieppe : they had been met by a man from Eu, or Treport, who had conducted them to some distance from the coast to a farm-house, the name of which was unknown to him. They had afterwards proceeded from farm to farm to Paris, which they entered singly, and where they never showed themselves, but when they were summoned by George. Thus George had been at Paris six months ; and what had hitherto appeared but an empty rumour acquired peculiar importance by this disclosure.

Since the restoration of internal tranquillity, the police had kept lists of all the persons who had borne a part in civil commotions, or had excited notice in districts where diligences had been robbed, or any other acts of that nature committed. These lists were divided into several classes : first, the instigators ; secondly, the actors ; thirdly, the accomplices ; fourthly, and lastly, such as had favoured the escape of any of these persons.

The table for Eu and Treport noted a watchmaker, named Troche, as having formerly been an emissary of the party. He was now, to be sure, grown old, but his son was capable of supplying his place. The gendarmerie were ordered to apprehend and bring him to Paris. The suspicion proved well-founded. This young man, of eighteen or nineteen years, was recognised by Querel ; and being equally acute and ingenuous, he easily guessed, on seeing the latter, the subject on which he was to be examined. He sought not to deny a fact which was too palpable to be disputed ; besides, his part had been so simple, that he would not run the risk of making himself more culpable by a denial, which, in any case, could not have been of the least personal benefit to him.

He related all that he had done, all that he had seen or heard; that he had conducted Messrs. de Polignac to Biville, where they had passed the day in the house of a sailor; that he had gone to them again at night to take them to the farm-house, which formed the first stage on their route to Paris. The details fixed the opinion that was to be entertained of this enterprise.

Troche had declared that three disembarkations had already taken place, and that there was to be a fourth in the evening of the very next day. This circumstance was immediately communicated to the First Consul. He sent for me into his cabinet, where I found him measuring with a pair of compasses the distances of the different points of the coast of Normandy from Paris.

He explained to me the business in hand, and made me set off without delay to secure the persons concerned in this new landing; and he directed me to return by the route followed by these little parties, and to explore myself these different focuses of disturbance.

I set out at seven in the evening, followed by a waggon from the stables of the First Consul, which was full of *gendarmes d'élite*.

I took young Troche along with me, because the party would not have landed unless it had perceived him on the shore. On the road he related his adventures to me with the utmost frankness. He had but just discovered that he had been employed in intrigues which might have brought him to the scaffold; and he showed as much zeal in laying a snare for those who were coming, as he could have done to serve those who had already passed.

I had the powers of the minister of war for any case that might occur; I had no apprehension of any impediment. I arrived at Dieppe the next evening after dark, that is to say, twenty-four hours after my departure from Paris.

I instantly demanded the signals of the coast. The only

information they furnished was, that an enemy's cutter continued to hover off Treport : this I communicated to Troche, who told me that it was the same from which the landing was to be effected, and which had already brought three other parties. She kept in this position that she might be able with a single tack to reach the foot of the cliff, where she was accustomed to put the people ashore. He promised when he should have seen her by daylight to give me more positive information. The sea was very rough, and by no means favourable for the coming ashore of a boat upon a coast studded with reefs : nevertheless, I would not stay at Dieppe. I disguised myself and set out on horseback for Biville, taking with me young Troche, as well as my gendarmes, who were also disguised. They were all men of tried courage. With such men one might run all risks without uneasiness. I made them alight at some distance from Biville. I sent the horses to the inn ; and before I pushed on further, I waited till my little party, which had orders not to show itself, had rejoined me. It soon came back : we set out under the guidance of Troche, who led us to a house which was the habitual resort of the emissaries thrown on the coast by the English packets. There they warmed and refreshed themselves, and made arrangements for proceeding to the first stage, which, being several leagues inland, was beyond the circle of the habitual *surveillance* of the authorities. Situated at the extremity of the village which faces the sea, the house offered to those who frequented it the advantage of being able to enter and leave it unseen by any one.

In the garden of this cottage I posted myself, with my people : I listened for any sound indicative of the steps of men, when I perceived through a small window a large table, on which were placed wine, pies, ready cut, and a large lump of butter. I called Troche, and pointed out to him these preparations. " It is the collation," said he, " which is usually given to those who arrive from the coast : if they are not come, they will be here presently, for the tide is about to ebb. If they miss the moment for disembarking, they will not be able to get ashore to-day, because the reefs prevent boats from landing." Time pressed : I determined to enter the house, without exactly knowing what was in the second room, the door of which I saw.

I had with me a gendarme, whose courage was proof against every danger. I ordered him to follow me, to post himself at that door, and not suffer it to be opened till all his comrades should have entered. I had decided on instantly closing the first; fully persuaded that, let the cottage contain what it would, with men so determined I should carry my point. My arrangements being made, I desired Troche to go in, keeping my eyes fixed on him, to watch lest any look, any sign, might betray us. The precaution was superfluous ; the sailor's wife, not doubting for a moment that we had just landed, asked Troche how many he had brought. Troche replied that he had not come from the coast, but was going thither. " Well," said she, " you will there find little Pageot de Pauly, who has been gone this hour, after waiting for you a long time." I was curious to know who this little Pageot could be : he was a comrade of Troche's, who sometimes came to the beach, but had in general no other duty to perform than to guide the persons who landed to the second station, and to carry their luggage.

The good woman was alike ignorant of what had befallen Troche, and who I was. I hastened out of the house to proceed to the coast, where the landing was at the very moment supposed to be taking place. From Biville to the shore it is but a few minutes' walk. The ground was covered with snow, and we had the wind in our faces : we were walking cautiously along when we heard some one speaking a few paces ahead of us. Troche fancied that he recognised the voice of Pageot ; but, as the night was dark, and the conversation was held in a hollow, it was impossible to judge of the number of the interlocutors. I placed my gendarmes in ambush, behind the avenue by which they were coming, and took post myself at the spot by which they were obliged to debouch, in order to reach the house of the sailor. There were but two of them : nevertheless, I gave the signal. My men sallied from their ambush, and seized them. Their sudden appearance frightened the villagers : they gave themselves up for dead men ; but Pageot, perceiving Troche, took courage, and informed us that he was returning from the coast, that the boat had not been able to land because the surf ran so high, and that the crew had told them they should come ashore the next day. Every evening, for two or three days past, they had been trying to land, but the sea had always been too rough. The foot of the cliff was covered with reefs : a boat could not approach but during flood-tide, and when the water was calm.

I passed the rest of the night in the house of the sailor, and went at daylight with Troche to reconnoitre the enemy's cutter, which he knew to be the one for which I was looking out. The vessel bore away from the shore as soon as day began to dawn, but stood in tacking at dusk, and took her station opposite to a signal-tower on the coast, washed by a wide and deep ravine, at the extremity of which was fixed a rope, known in the neighbourhood by the appellation of " The Smugglers' Rope."

This rope, of the thickness of a merchantman's cable, was fixed perpendicularly against the cliff, which at this place rises abruptly to the height of two hundred and fifty feet : it was fastened to stout stakes driven into the ground at intervals of six feet. The person who ascended last coiled it up, and hung it on a post destined for that purpose, lest it should be seen by the patroles who might be watching along the coast. This method of smuggling must be very ancient ; for this rope seemed to me to be a regularly-organized establishment. It had its superintendents, whose duty it was to keep it in order; and the smugglers punctually paid the charge imposed upon them for the use of it.

Never did danger appear to me so imminent as that incurred by a man thus scaling the cliff with a load on his shoulders. Had but one of the stakes given way, it had been all over with the smuggler, and with the smuggled goods too. It was this way that George and his companions had come to France; and certainly no one would have dreamt of a passage effected within less than one hundred paces of a signal-tower, inhabited by watchmen, who, it is true, retired at night. I made some painful reflections on witnessing the thousand dangers which men were not afraid to encounter, in order to sell a few prohibited commodities; and above all, to commit a crime which, in its result, could not change the situation of any of those who undertook it. This excited my curiosity to learn how far these people knew what it was they had been induced to do; and I was soon convinced that they suspected that they were doing wrong, but none of them ever thought of making the least inquiry on the subject. This rope was an income to the most needy: as it produced them a good deal, they kept it up with care; but not one of them strove to penetrate what had not been told him. They respected all the secrets of others—that the secret which afforded them a livelihood might be respected; and they were more affected at the suppression of that rope than at having been instrumental in introducing George into France:—for the rest, they all firmly believed that it was only smugglers they had been aiding. No attempt was therefore made to punish them as accomplices in an offence of which they had no suspicion.

I returned in the evening to the coast, and posted myself at the outlet of the defile; but the sea continued to be rough. I passed six or seven nights waiting for a landing, which could not be effected.

I had been twenty-eight days in this position, when I received orders to return to Paris.

CHAPTER IV.

Activity of the police — Various measures — Moreau — Mysterious personage — Conjectures on this subject—Royal family—Attention is directed to the Duke d'Enghien—An emissary is dispatched to the banks of the Rhine.

WHILE I was at Dieppe, the police had continued the inquiries which it was making in Paris. It had not only gained a knowledge of each of the emissaries who had followed George, but had found means to secure them all, from the leader to the meanest individual of the expedition.

These apprehensions had broken the silence in which the first of them were wrapped. The newspapers, in which they were mentioned, had reached England: whence a warning was instantly sent to the cutter cruising off Dieppe, where, fortunately for her passengers, the unfavourable weather had prevented their being landed.

The cutter proceeded to the coast off Morbihan, where we shall presently meet with her again. I remained some days in the environs of Dieppe, and returned to Paris. I was surprised, at my arrival, to find what activity had been exerted to secure George and his followers. The cavalry of the guard and that of the garrison furnished guard-posts on the outer boulevards, and had vedettes round the wall, inclosing the capital. Continually moving from one towards the other, the latter formed permanent patroles, who had orders to apprehend every one who should seek to scale the walls for the purpose of gaining the country.

A corresponding measure had been taken at the barriers. Every one going out at them was most rigidly examined.

But this was not all: a law had been enacted, enjoining every citizen to declare what persons were lodging in his house, and pronouncing the penalty of death against any one who should harbour George's accomplices. Such measures might be expected to produce disclosures, and this expectation was not disappointed.

All the individuals who had belonged to this association were soon known. A list of their names, with a description of their persons, was printed and posted up in Paris, and all over France; where no one could now travel, even with passports, without being examined from head to foot. From the disclosures of some of the persons apprehended, it was discovered that General Moreau was no stranger to the enterprise.

The presence of George, and of several persons whose high birth might have been expected to keep them aloof from such a man, left no doubt of the existence of a conspiracy, or of the end at which it aimed. It seemed too serious to forbid the idea that the conspirators had neglected nothing in order to associate General Moreau in their schemes. This conjecture appeared the less improbable, as the line of conduct which that general affected to hold, strengthened the suspicions which already arose respecting his fidelity to his old political principles.

George's servant declared, that one evening he went out in a hackney-coach with his master, who was accompanied by a little lame general, whose name he knew not, and by another person, who was also a stranger to him. He added, that, on their arrival at the Boulevard de la Madelaine, the little general alighted, and went to fetch General Moreau from his house, Rue d'Anjou; that his master and the other person then alighted, and both walked about with General Moreau, while he and the little lame general waited in the coach. When they returned to the coach, he heard the person who accompanied his master, in speaking of General Moreau, observe—" It seems that fellow has ambition too."

The grand-judge made an official report in council on this circumstance, and orders were issued for the apprehension of General Moreau. He was taken on the bridge of Charenton, as he was returning from his country-seat, Gros Bois, and conducted to the Temple. His secretary also was secured; but Fouché, who probably had his reasons for not investigating too closely the conduct of Freniere—this was the name of the secretary—set every engine to work to procure his liberation. He feigned zeal, affected a regard for forms, and told the First Consul that when one had a good job in hand, it was a pity to spoil it by arbitrary measures and injustice; that Freniere had been apprehended, though he was not accused, nor was any thing laid to his charge. " You must," said he, " show yourself equitable, and release that man."

The First Consul fell into the snare : notwithstanding the remonstrances of the police, who wished to detain Freniere for a week, he was set at liberty. No sooner was he released, than he was deeply compromised by the depositions of all those whom George had brought into contact with the persons about General Moreau. Search was made for him again, but too late; he was already in safety. This circumstance excited suspicions of M. Fouché; but as he was already known to be a man of very light character, they led to nothing further.

Fouché followed with particular anxiety the inquiries made under the direction of M. Real; and when he had caught up some new incident, he ran to retail it at the Tuileries. The First Consul, who was sometimes amused by his wit, said, " You will stick to the police, then ?"—" I have retained some friends there," replied Fouché, " who furnish me with any thing new." The conversation turned in this manner to the enterprise of George; the ramifications of which incessantly engaged the thoughts of the First Consul, who liked to talk of them in confidence. Fouché seized every thing that dropped from him, and made it the groundwork of fresh inquiries.

Placing himself in this manner between the head of the state and the person who directed the investigation, it is scarcely possible but that he should find opportunities of promoting his private interest; and he cared not at whose expense he did that. But, while flattering power, he was not unmindful of his brethren and friends of the good times, and used such language as this—that "the First Consul wanted no more patriots;" that "he permitted the emigrants to return for the purpose of making use of them;" and other expressions of the like kind, which are sure to find acceptance in a city where nothing is lost.

This plot against the life of the First Consul produced a profound impression upon the public opinion. The mind revolted at the bare idea of a project, the least important consequences of which would have been to plunge France back into the abyss of calamities from which she had scarcely escaped. The people were indignant at the means of execution which had been adopted, because in France they dislike assassination. Every department, every town of any cousequence, nay, even La Vendée itself, sent a particular deputatiou to the First Consul to congratulate him on the discovery of so odious a plot. These deputations could not find terms sufficiently strong to express the indignation which animated them, and the attachment they felt for a man in whose preservation all France was interested. They invoked the vengeance of the law; they besought the First Consul, for the sake of the future, to turn a deaf ear to clemency. This was the unanimous cry of the whole republic. Every functionary, whether present or at a distance; every officer, of every rank whatsoever, and particularly all who aspired to favour, thought of nothing but how to avail himself of this circumstance to prove his devotedness to the person of the First Consul.

I have often seen him weary of all that was said to him on this subject: he was nevertheless deeply affected by the demonstrations of attachment poured in upon him from all parts of France, as had previously been the case in regard to

the infernal machine.   This was just the time of his greatest
power over the nation.   The army, assembled in the camps,
shuddered with rage at the mere idea of a design to take the
life of him whom it considered as its guardian angel.   Had
General Moreau been sent before a council of war the day
after the presentation of the report of the grand-judge, it
had been all over with him.

It was proposed that he should be tried in that manner;
but the First Consul rejected that mode of proceeding, be
cause he judged coolly of the state of things.   He was right:
for in fact there was no military offence to take cognizance
of; and besides, the presence of Moreau would be necessary
in the prosecution of the examinations.   These proceedings
took place at the Temple itself, and almost publicly, for it
was easy to obtain admittance.   The *juge-instructeur* took
up his residence there, so numerous were the confrontations.
Independently of this, the police continued its researches.
George was considered as merely a principal instrument: the
question was, for whom, in whose name, he would have acted
the day following that on which he should have dispatched
the First Consul.   It was very naturally concluded, that a
more important personage was somewhere concealed, and
waiting for the blow to be struck before he made himself
known.   Search was made every where; George's people
and those of the house where he had lodged were examined,
but nothing was discovered.   At length two of his servants,
being separately interrogated, declared that every ten or
twelve days there came to their master a gentleman, whose
name they did not know, about thirty-four or thirty-five years
of age, who had light hair, was bald on the forehead, of mid-
dling height and ordinary corpulence.   They related that he
was always extremely well-dressed, both as to his linen and
other clothes; that he must be a person of consequence, for
their master always went to the door to receive him: when
he was in the apartment, every body, Messrs. de Polignac

and de Rivière, as well as the others, rose, and did not sit
down again till he had retired ; and that whenever he came
to see George, they went together into a cabinet, where they
remained alone till he went away, and then George attended
him to the door

This declaration, which the parties were made to repeat
and to circumstantiate with care, augmented the anxiety that
was felt.   Inquiry was made who could be the person whom
George and his accomplices treated with such respect : the
deponents could not tell.   They had never seen him till he
came to visit their master.   All were puzzled what to conjecture : the search was prosecuted with increased ardour, and
inquiries set on foot whether scouring and cleaning was
going forward in any of the apartments with gilt ceilings in
the hotels of the Marais, or the Faubourg Saint-Germain,
almost all of which had long been uninhabited ; but nothing
was discovered.   From the different depositions of the persons
first apprehended, it appeared that they had all been embarked in England in a cutter belonging to the royal navy,
which had landed them on our coast : besides, the considerable
sums of money found upon them at the time of their apprehension, and on George in particular, proved that this was the
enterprise of a government which had neglected no means to
ensure its success.   Notwithstanding the disclosure made by
certain subordinate agents of George's, relative to daggers
which they carried about them at the moment of their apprehension, every one felt convinced that this enterprise was no
other than the work of the English ministry, which was bent
on getting rid at any rate of the First Consul.   It was thought
that, alarmed at the wisdom with which he had repaired
every thing, and tranquillized the country, it had determined
on his destruction ; but, to avoid the odium of such an attempt,
it had contrived to engage the wretched relics of a party,
which it had never ceased to feed with false hopes, in the
execution of its design.   It abused their unfortunate condition

by deceiving them with the assistance of the reports furnished by the agents whom it kept in France : it violated hospitality by causing an attempt to be made, in their name, to
commit a crime which could not fail to extinguish the interest
excited by their misfortunes.

Luckily for them, this conception required means which
they no longer possessed : for rarely does misfortune meet
with any thing but abandonment and perfidy.*

CHAPTER V.

The question of the seizure of the Duke d'Enghien discussed in council—Opposition of the Consul Cambaceres—Orders issued for his apprehension—The.
Duke d'Enghien is brought to Paris—The author is appointed to the command
of the troops sent to Vincennes—Sitting of the military commission.

PEOPLE began generally to agree respecting the real
source of this enterprise, and great impatience was felt to

---

* M. de Rivière, whom I had occasion to see in the Temple, confirmed me in
the opinion which I here express. I declared to him my astonishment to see
himself and M. de Polignac associated with such company : I spoke to him of
what he must have suffered on hearing in the pleadings the details of the atro-
cities committed by these wretches. He admitted that his situation had indeed
been very painful, and informed me what had induced him to come to Paris.

Count d'Artois had long received none but the most improbable reports : according to those by whom they were addressed to him, it would appear that he
had only to show himself, and all would be ready to obey him. It was difficult,
considering the source whence these reports proceeded, to ward off the impression which it was natural they should produce. " Still," said M. de Rivière to
me, " I took not the least share whatever in the hopes that were held out to us.
I told the prince what I thought ; I asked his permission to come and judge for
myself, telling him that he might make up his mind from my report, because I
should not give way to any illusion. His royal highness assented to this proposal. I came to Paris, was soon convinced that we were imposed upon, and was
about to return when I was apprehended."

come at the discovery of the mysterious personage who was as yet but a subject of conjecture, and the knowledge of whom could not fail to fix all opinions. Every one puzzled his brains without being able to arrive at any conclusion : every one, great and small, manifested his attachment. The First Consul was perhaps the person who gave himself up least to his imagination. He was incessantly repeating that it was not his business to unravel the plot which threatened him. Hence, I conceive, originated the combinations of certain persons, who determined to make the most of this circumstance for their own advantage. Of all the conjectures submitted to him, he seemed to be most struck by the following, which was at once plausible and perfidious. He was told that the party of the revolution might benefit, as well as the house of Bourbon, by the blow which George meditated. The latter had certainly not failed to take measures for repressing the Jacobins : it had infallibly sent to the spot some one of its members to serve as a rallying point, as soon as the stroke should have been struck ; and might not this member, it was added, be the mysterious personage who had visited George, and not Moreau, who was then rather intractable the moment republicanism was attacked ?

This reasoning was plausible enough. A review was taken of all the princes of the house of Bourbon.

The description given by George's people corresponded neither with the age of the Count d'Artois, nor with the person of the Duke of Berri. Besides, George's men, who personally knew the latter, declared that it was not he.

The Duke d'Angoulême was at Mittau with the King. The Duke of Bourbon was known to be in London. Next came the Duke d'Enghien, who resided at Ettenheim on the right bank of the Rhine. The proximity of his residence, and the resolution of his character, had not escaped those who directed attention to him. He was named to George's people, but they knew him not. Their declaration only served to provoke curiosity. All trace of the Duke d'Enghien had been lost since the treaty of Luneville; there was indeed no motive for thinking of him : it was not even known whether he continued to reside at Ettenheim.

The minister for foreign affairs, through whom at this period all information from abroad was received, had not himself any more positive intelligence concerning this prince than what had been furnished by Mehée. The First Consul could not conceal his astonishment which such ignorance excited, and ordered some one to be sent to the spot to learn what the Duke d'Enghien had been doing for six months past.

M. Real, who was charged with this business, went himself, for the purpose of preventing any mistake, to explain the intentions of the First Consul to the chief inspector of gendarmerie. The inspector selected a person in his office, to whom he gave instructions conformable with those which he had just received. The unlucky officer took it into his head that the Duke d'Enghien was the person of whom the government was in search, and imagined that he was charged to confirm what he was only appointed to investigate. He had put a wrong construction on his mission ; his judgment was equally wrong.

It is nevertheless but just to admit, that this officer learned at Ettenheim, or elsewhere, that the Duke d'Enghien went almost every week to the theatre at Strasburg : a fact which was attested to me by a person who was in the service of that prince at the time of his seizure.* Hence it was concluded

---

* An officer of the Duke of Bourbon's, who was at that time about the Duke d'Enghien, has disputed this assertion. I am not inquiring the motives which influenced his actions; for my part, I had no other interest in noting it but that of historical truth, which was far from questioning the courage of the Duke d'Enghien. For the rest, this prince may very possibly have kept secret from his officers certain proceedings which he concealed not from his domestics. I persist, therefore, because the person who related the circumstance to me is worthy of credit, and certainly known to my refutator. A Strasburger has even assured me, that it was notorious at the time at Strasburg, that facilities were

that he was attracted to Strasburg by something more important than a play; and that, besides, if he exposed himself to such danger for a gratification of that kind, he would not be deterred by perils when a higher interest was at stake. It has even been asserted, that in the time of the Directory he ventured as far as Paris; and that it was Bernadotte, then minister at war, who warned him to make his escape. The minister for foreign affairs ought to know what credit is due to all this: as for the First Consul, he was then in Egypt.

The officer from Paris, on his arrival at Ettenheim, observed, questioned, learned that the Duke d'Enghien lived more than modestly. Since a number of emigrants had come back to his neighbourhood, the prince received several of them; he invited them to dinner, and probably he even gave them some money : there was nothing in this that could give umbrage. He was fond of hunting, kept up a tender connexion with a French lady, who shared his exile, and was frequently absent for several days at a time. To those who know what a passion for hunting is, and are acquainted with the mountains of the Black Forest, this will appear nothing extraordinary.

The emissary viewed the matter in a different light: he disbelieved both the hunting and the love-affair of the prince; and hurried back to Paris with a report, in which he declared that the Duke d'Enghien led a mysterious life; that he was frequently visited by emigrants; that he supported them; and that he was frequently absent eight, ten, or twelve days, without any one knowing whither he went.

The report to which I have just adverted could not fail to produce its effect. When the chief inspector of gendarmerie received it, he carried it himself to the First Consul, instead of transmitting it to M. Real, whom this peculiarly concerned.

---

afforded for suffering the Duke d'Enghien to repass at night by the citadel, and to regain the bridge of the Rhine.

Surprise was even manifested to the latter, because he knew
not a syllable of the Duke d'Enghien's mode of life. The
First Consul, who expressed this surprise, had doubtless forgotten the order which he had given to M. Real for the chief
inspector of the gendarmerie; and did not consider that the
report which the latter had just laid before him was the consequence of the order transmitted to him by M. Real.

The following calculation, among others, was submitted to
the First Consul. It requires sixty hours to travel from
Ettenheim to Paris, crossing the Rhine at the ferry of Rhinan,
and sixty to return—this makes five days; and at least five
days to stay in Paris to observe and direct every thing : just
the time occupied by the absences of the Duke d'Enghien and
the interval between the mysterious visits paid to George,
which are thus accounted for. This coincidence proved fatal
to the Duke d'Enghien.

M. Real had answered the expression of surprise at the
ignorance of the police, by saying that it was waiting for the
report of the gendarmerie " Why," rejoined the First Consul, " it is precisely from the gendarmerie, as well as the
prefect of Strasburg, that I derive this information. For
the rest, I have given orders for the seizure of the Duke
d'Enghien with all his papers : this is beyond a joke. To come
from Ettenheim to Paris to plot an assassination, and to fancy
one's self safe because one is behind the Rhine ! I should be
too simple to suffer it !"

The First Consul, however, had not decided alone upon the
seizure of the Duke d'Enghien : he had assembled a council,
composed of the three consuls, the minister for foreign affairs,
the grand-judge, and M. Fouché, who was then but a senator,
but who was taking great pains to regain a place in the
ministry.`

At this council, the grand-judge gave an account of the
state of the conspiracy with regard to the interior: the minister
for foreign affairs then read a long report concerning the rami-

fications of the conspirators abroad, in which were detailed all the follies of Drake, extracted from the report of Mehée, and supported by certain officious correspondence concerning the emigrants residing in the electorate of Baden. This report concluded with proposing the seizure of the Duke d'Enghien by force, and thus putting an end to the matter.

The Duke Cambaceres, from whom I received these particulars, and whom I durst not name in his lifetime, added, that he had made a strong objection to the proposal of the forcible seizure; observing that since the Duke d'Enghien came sometimes into the French territory, as it was alleged, it would be more simple to lay a snare for him, and to carry the law relative to emigrants into effect against him: on which he had been thus answered—"*Parbleu!* what pretty fools you would make of us! After the newspapers have been filled with the particulars of this affair, do you suppose he will let himself be entrapped?" And he persisted in the conclusions of his report.*

A long conversation on the subject succeeded this discussion: the First Consul demanded the voices which had supported the opinion of the minister for foreign affairs, and leaving the council went to his cabinet, where he dictated to his secretary the necessary orders for the seizure of the Duke d'Enghien. The minister at war, in consequence, ordered the colonel of horse-grenadiers to go to Neuf Brisac; and on his arrival there with the gendarmerie placed at his disposal, to take a detachment of cavalry belonging to the garrison, to cross the Rhine at the ferry of Rhinan, to proceed expeditiously to the residence of the Duke d'Enghien at Ettenheim, to make him prisoner, and to send him to Paris with all his

---

* I know that since the death of the Duke Cambaceres great pains have been taken to suppress this circumstance, which is stated in his manuscript memoirs; but it is not the less true, that it stands there just as I have given it above; and assuredly had he lived, he would not have made any sacrifice to the person who is most interested in wiping away the record of it.

papers, in hopes of finding among them some useful information concerning the connexion which he must have had with
this conspiracy.*

This order was punctually executed; and to prevent the
remonstrances which the Elector of Baden would not' have
failed to make, it was intimated to him that he must immediately remove that band of emigrants which had made its
appearance again on the banks of the Rhine.†

The Duke d'Enghien was seized on the 15th of March, and
carried the same day to the citadel of Strasburg, where he
remained till the 18th, when he set out for Paris under the
escort of the gendarmerie. There he arrived on the 20th of
March, about eleven in the forenoon: his carriage, after
having been detained at the barrier till four in the afternoon,
was driven by the outer boulevards to Vincennes, where the
prince was kept prisoner.‡

I had been two or three days in Paris, after returning from
my mission to Dieppe which had lasted two months, and was
on duty at Malmaison, when the Duke d'Enghien arrived at
Paris. I had noticed that the minister for foreign affairs had,
contrary to his usual custom, come that day about noon to the
First Consul: this I remarked, because his visits in general
took place very late in the evening. About five in the afternoon of the same day, I was summoned into the cabinet of
the First Consul, who delivered to me a sealed letter, with
orders to carry it to the governor of Paris, then General
Murat. On reaching his residence, I met at the door the
minister for foreign affairs, who was just leaving the house.

---

* See the *Documents*, No. 1. This letter from the First Consul to the Minister
at War, is dated the 10th of March, 1804. See No. 2, *Letter from the Minister
at War to General Ordener.*

† See No. 3, *Letter from M. Talleyrand to the Elector of Baden,* dated the 10th
of March, 1804.

‡ I was ignorant of the circumstance of the stoppage of the prince's carriage
from eleven till four o'clock at the barrier, when I published in 1823 what I knew
concerning that event.

General Murat, who was so indisposed as to be unable to walk, told me that this was sufficient, and that he would presently send me the orders that concerned me.

I knew not what could be the drift of these orders; and I was far from being aware of what was going forward with the Duke d'Enghien, whose name had scarcely been uttered on the arrival of a telegraphic dispatch at the moment of his departure from Strasburg. I supposed that I was to return to Malmaison, when I received orders to take under my command a brigade of infantry, which was to be assembled the same evening at the Barrière St. Antoine, and to proceed with it at night to Vincennes.

The gendarmerie d'élite, of which I was colonel, and which did not then form part of the guard, but belonged to the garrison of Paris, had received orders from government to send its infantry and a strong detachment of its cavalry to keep garrison at Vincennes. This castle was then a neglected building, and in the last stage of decay. The duplicate of this order had been sent to me; and that my legion might be prepared to comply with it, I hastened myself to its barracks, to cause proper orders to be given to every body: for it was just the hour at which both officers and privates were accustomed to go out to amuse themselves, and not to return till the hour of beating the tattoo.

I then repaired to Vincennes, which I entered for the first time: it was dark; I saw no place where I could station the gendarmerie which was just arriving, as well as the brigade that was to follow: nevertheless, I made the former march in at the castle-gate, and posted it in the court, forbidding it to suffer any communication with the exterior on any pretext whatever. I then placed the infantry of the garrison on the esplanade, on the side next to the park.

The barracks of Paris are situated in quarters remote from each other: some of the corps which received orders to march on this occasion had to traverse the city from points opposite

to, and very far distant from the Barrière du Trone.   Owing
to this distance they did not arrive at Vincennes till past three
in the morning, because it was already late when the order for
their departure reached their barracks.

While I was engaged in placing all these troops, the president of the military commission and the judges who were to
compose it arrived.   I had been informed, since I was at Vincennes, that the Duke d'Enghien had arrived there at five
o'clock in the afternoon, escorted by the gendarmerie of Strasburg, whom I still saw at the castle.   But for this I should
have firmly believed that he had been found in some hiding-
place in Paris, as well as George's companions; and I was
very curious to hear what he would say for himself.

The Duke d'Enghien was interrogated by the captain-
reporter, before the commission met for his trial.   This interrogatory must have been grounded on the materials which
had been transmitted to the commission, that is, on the report
of the officer who had been to watch the prince at Ettenheim.
I imagined that I had been the bearer of it in the letter which
the First Consul had given to me for Murat ; but I was mistaken, as will be seen at the conclusion of this volume, from
what General Hullin himself has said.

The military commission, which had not been selected for
this duty on account of any exaggeration of principles, was
composed only of colonels of regiments of the garrison of
Paris, and its president was their natural chief, the commandant of the place.

This commission knew not a syllable of the disclosure of
George's people, which had led to the present proceeding.   Its
members shared the general indignation against the plan of
assassinating the First Consul, and against all those who had
taken part in it : they were not ignorant of the opinion which
was most generally adopted, that George's operations were
carried on under the direction of a prince who was to make
himself known after the blow should be struck.   The situa-

tion of the residence of the Duke d'Enghien, the journeys which he was said to have made to Paris, where it was even asserted that he had very lately been, led to the notion that he must be the director of George, and consequently the dispositiou of men's minds was far from being favourable to him.

The commission assembled in one of the large rooms of the inhabited part of the castle, that is, the building over the gate of entrance on the side next to the park.

It was not mysterious, as those who have written on this point of history have asserted : it was public for all who could come at that hour ; and there must have been people there, since, having been detained out of doors by the duty of posting my troops, which gave me a good deal of anxiety, perceiving the serious circumstances in which I was placed, I was one of the last to enter the room where the commission was sitting. I had even great difficulty to get so far as behind the president, where I at first wished to station myself that I might see the better ; and afterwards, being chilled with the cold of the night which I had passed amidst the troops, I went to warm myself at a large fire, before which was placed the chair of General Hullin. Thus I happened, for a few moments only, to be seated behind him during the sitting of the commission.

When I entered, the reading of the examination was finished, the discussion had already begun, and was very warm. The Duke d'Enghien had even already answered so sharply, that it was obvious he had no notion of the danger of his situation.

" Sir," said the president to him, "you seem not to be aware of your situation, or you are determined not to answer the questions which I ask you. You shut yourself up in your high birth, of which you take good care to remind us ; you had better adopt a different system of defence. I will not take an undue advantage of your situation, but observe that I ask you positive questions, and that, instead of answering, you talk to me about something else. Take care, this might become serious. How could you hope to persuade us that you were so completely ignorant as you pretend to be of what was passing in France, when not only the country in which you resided, but the whole world is informed of it? And how could you persuade me that with your birth you were indifferent to events, all the consequences of which were to be in your favour? There is too much improbability in this for me to pass it over without observation: I beg you to reflect upon it, that you may have recourse to other means of defence."

I wrote down these words of the president's the very next day; and it was out of delicacy that I omitted to notice them in the work which I published at the end of October, 1823.

The Duke d'Enghien, after a moment's silence, replied in a grave tone: " Sir, I perfectly comprehend you ; it was not my intention to remain indifferent to them: I had applied to England for an appointment in her armies; and she had returned for answer that she had none to give me, but that I was to remain upon the Rhine, where I should soon have a part to act, and for that I was waiting. I have nothing more to tell you, Sir."*

Such was the answer of the Duke d'Enghien; I committed it to paper at the very moment: this I wrote from memory long afterwards, but I do not think that I have forgotten a single syllable. If it is not in his trial, it must certainly have been abstracted from it, or have been omitted to be recorded.

I have had occasion to satisfy myself that the criminal

---

* On quitting the Bellerophon in Plymouth-road, in 1815, I was carried on board the Eurotas frigate, to be conveyed as a prisoner to Malta. The captain of this frigate was a Mr. Lilycrap: during the voyage he frequently related to me, that he was at this period employed about Drake on the banks of the Rhine ; that he was sent by him in all directions, to all the petty courts of Germany, to the emigrants at Offenburg, and to Ettenheim to the Duke d'Enghien.

He still launched out furiously against Mebée, who, he said, had so completely bamboozled them.

papers, as they were called, on which the condemnation of the Queen of France was pronounced, have been taken away from the archives of the Palace of Justice, so that the bundle of this trial is reduced to a few paltry scraps of paper; and I know that, immediately after the restoration in 1814, the imperial archives were rummaged for several days by trusty agents of those who were deeply interested in the removal of documents, which no doubt might have compromised the safety of their new position.

So carefully was this search conducted, that neither the archives of the foreign office nor those of the government afford any trace of that event, which nevertheless was the subject of a correspondence with the foreign courts.

Previously to his last avowal, the Duke d'Enghien had declared that he received an allowance from England; but he had expressed himself in such a manner, that it might be supposed that instead of sums destined to defray his household expenses, it was money paid for corrupt purposes that he received. As none of the judges could know any thing of the financial situation of the prince, this declaration aggravated the prepossessions already entertained against him. This money was assimilated with that which had been found upon George; and a fatality decreed that all the doors to escape should thus be closed against the prince.

After the last answer of the Duke d'Enghien's, the president of the commission declared the discussion closed, and ordered all those who had been present during the debates to leave the room. The commission resolved itself into a council to deliberate.

I retired like the rest, and went, as did several of the officers who had attended the sitting, to rejoin the troops that were on the esplanade of the castle.

I cannot tell exactly how long the commission continued in deliberation; but it was no more than two hours after the room was cleared, that the commandant of the infantry of my legion, who was posted in the court of the castle, came to inform me that the commission had passed sentence, and that a picket was required for its execution. I recommended to him, as usual in such cases, to place it so as to prevent accident. The spot which seemed to him best suited for this purpose was a spacious ditch of the castle.

While this officer was making his arrangements, I ordered the troops under arms, and acquainted them with the sentence which the commission had passed, and that they were to attend its execution.

Meanwhile, the Duke d'Enghien was brought down the staircase of the entrance tower on the side next to the park. His sentence was read to him, and the execution immediately followed. It was then about six in the morning.

I thereupon took the orders of the president of the military commission to send back the troops to their barracks.

CHAPTER VI.

The author makes his report of the execution to the First Consul—His astonishment—Sensation in Paris—Absurd rumours—Reflections—Discovery of the mysterious personage—General Lajolais—Apprehension of General Pichegru.

I REPAIRED to Malmaison, to report to the First Consul what had passed at Vincennes.

He immediately admitted me, and appeared to listen with the greatest surprise. He could not conceive why the trial had been hurried on before the arrival of M. Real, whom he had ordered to proceed to Vincennes to examine the prisoner. Looking stedfastly at me with lynx's eyes, he said, " There is something in this that I cannot comprehend. That the commission should have pronounced sentence upon the confession of the Duke d'Enghien, I am not surprised at .

But then they had not this confession till they were proceeding to judgment, which ought not to have taken place till M. Real had interrogated him on a point which it is of importance to us to clear up." He then repeated: " There is something in this that I cannot fathom . . . . Here is a crime, and which leads to nothing."

M. Real afterwards had an interview with the First Consul, at which I was not present.

The news of this sentence produced a great sensation in Paris. Some approved it, and roundly asserted that the Duke d'Enghien had made himself the chief of the corps of emigrants, and that all the conspiracies against the life of the First Consul had been hatched for his sole benefit; others disapproved, and asked in what respect this execution consolidated the consular power: these termed it murder and useless crime—those an act of sanguinary tyranny. Each reasoned and talked nonsense at pleasure: amidst this manifestation of all opinions, the government alone kept silence; either because this line of conduct appeared most suitable to its dignity, or because, at the moment of engaging in a new war, it was afraid to make it known that the germs of civil discord were not yet destroyed in France, and that they still offered chances to discontented and audacious spirits.

So long as I believed that it was these motives which decided the plan of conduct adopted by the government, I confess that I considered it as bad, because malignity took advantage of it, and did more mischief by its interpretations than the consequences of the greatest publicity could have done. It was not till long afterwards that I learned that the First Consul had given the strictest orders to preserve silence. His instructions had been transgressed: he was displeased with what had been done, but he would not be severe towards men whose fault originated in excess of zeal, and who had no doubt conceived that they were rendering him a service.

Malevolence had fair scope for its efforts. It circulated a thousand absurd stories relative to the circumstances attending the death of the Duke d'Enghien. It even went so far as to invent a tale about a lantern said to have been fastened to his breast, without considering that on the 21st of March the sun rises at six o'clock, and that it is light at five. People said also that the commission refused the application of the prince to send for a priest, without reflecting that the ministers of religion were then very rare, and that it is more than probable that the parish of Vincennes was then without a pastor. Party animosity has invented a multitude of particulars as well circumstantiated and quite as plausible as those which I have just mentioned, but with which it would be useless to load these pages, because time and sound reason have done them complete justice.

It has been related that Madame Bonaparte threw herself at the feet of the First Consul, imploring the pardon of the Duke d'Enghien, but that it was refused her. Not only is this assertion false, but wholly destitute of probability. Till my return to Malmaison, Madame Bonaparte was not only ignorant, like every one else, of the result of the commission, but she could not even form any conjecture before M. Real should have identified the Duke d'Enghien with the person described in the disclosures of George's subordinates. Not that I mean to say that Madame Bonaparte would not have interceded in behalf of an unfortunate person : the known goodness of her heart would assuredly have induced her to make this application; and she was too well acquainted with the humanity of the First Consul, not to hope that he would suffer himself to be persuaded to show a clemency, which moreover was consistent with the interests of his policy.

A handle was sought to be made of this affair to excite the public indignation against the First Consul. People vied with each other in these efforts, because they thought to promote thereby the interest of a party which was hostile to the revolution, and strove to obscure its glory. It is quite natural: those who lose the game, always find a consolation in saying that they have been cheated.

Few months, nevertheless, had elapsed, before it was to be remarked that those who had shown the strongest animosity thronged to the ante-chambers of the Emperor; and in truth they were crowded by them so long as his prosperity lasted. This conduct, on their part, at least authorizes a belief that they were subsequently satisfied that the orders of the First Consul had been transgressed, and that his conduct had not been so reprehensible as they had at first conceived: perhaps, too, they hoped that the Emperor would not bear in mind the injuries done to the First Consul.

If a person coolly examines the share which the head of the government had in this tragic event, he cannot refuse to admit the following remarks :

The object of George's enterprise was not more doubtful than the point from which he set out. It was the third attempt against the life of the First Consul in less than two years. On this occasion, the conspirators were not to confine themselves to the commission of that single crime : their object was nothing less than to overturn the revolution completely, and to rekindle the flames of civil war at the very moment when France was about to have a foreign war to support.

Men whetted their daggers against the head of the government; they came from foreign countries to strike him in the midst of a nation, the independence of which he protected, and against which they conspired as much as against him : on what ground then could he be required to respect a right which was violated in regard to him ? And when means were employed for the purpose of dispatching him, which were without the pale of the rights of nations and of morality, could he alone be expected to con-

fine himself within limits which others had not hesitated to
pass?

And besides, was not the First Consul responsible for all
the political interests placed in some measure on his head?
What would have been thought of the solidity of a government, the chief of which should have been deficient in firmness in such a circumstance?

Such were probably the thoughts of the First Consul; but
very different were those attributed to him. Some have said
that in putting to death the Duke d'Enghien, it was his object
to strike terror into the princes of the house of Bourbon, and
to break up with a single blow all the corps of emigrants
which threatened the frontiers. Others have asserted that
his only aim was to give guarantees to the Jacobin party. To
the former I shall reply, that the conqueror of Marengo relied
upon his sword to disperse his enemies; and I will ask the
latter, if the Jacobins were to be feared after the 18th Brumaire; and if that day, which was the first of the power of the
First Consul, was not the last of theirs. They were already
imploring his all-powerful protection; what guarantee then
did he need to give them?

It has also been asserted, that the First Consul had a direct
personal interest in ridding himself of a prince, whom he
knew to be of a firm and enterprising character. To reason
in this manner, is to admit that the First Consul had not
rejected the proposal of a crime. But then, instead of making
such a stir at Paris, the same end might have been attained
with greater certainty and less noise at a hunting-party on the
other side of the Rhine, or even at Ettenheim. There would
have been no want of assassins had they been sought after;
and he would only have appeared to be using reprisals.
Would not this have been merely fighting with the same
weapons, as others had not been ashamed to employ several
times against him?

He was ignorant of the existence of the Duke d'Enghien;

he was much better acquainted with the names of the generals whom he had fought, than with those of the members of
the family which had reigned in France. The Duke was
described to him as the head of George's party: he consented
to his seizure. History will judge the rest.

At this period, the moral power of the First Consul over
the nation was in all its force and all its purity. This event,
it cannot be denied, gave a serious shock to it.

Was it wantonly that the First Consul thus weakened the
public affection which he possessed; and if this can be supposed, why should he have taken so many precautions? Why
direct M. Real to go and interrogate the prince, when he
knew that he had been put to death by his own orders?—for
people have even gone so far as to risk this assertion.

In 1810, when I was elevated to the ministry, I requested
M. Real to explain to me how it happened that the Duke
d'Enghien was fixed upon, since there had been no allusion to
him in the proceedings against George. He then informed
me that it was the disclosure of George's two attendants
which had determined the seizure of the Duke d'Enghien for
the purpose of confronting him with them; and that it was
only in case he should have been recognised as the mysterious
personage mentioned in the disclosures that he was to be tried.

On this occasion M. Real reminded me, that during the
time the police was actively engaged in researches, it had
learned that the little lame general, who went to fetch
General Moreau to conduct him to the Boulevard de la Madelaine, was General Lajolais. It cost some trouble to find
him; and it was not till he had been confronted with George's
servant, who knew him, that all his proceedings since his
arrival at Paris were strictly scrutinized. He chanced to let
slip at what house he had alighted on his arrival in that city;
and in consequence of this avowal, it was ascertained from the
very people of the house that he had come with General
Pichegru, whom nobody had yet thought of.

Lajolais afterwards admitted this, and declared that he had travelled with General Pichegru from London to Paris, passing through the environs of Amiens and Gisors; in consequence of which, though he had also been landed at the cliff of Biville, he was not known to the emigrants who had proceeded to Paris by another route.

After some search General Pichegru was apprehended. He was first interrogated alone; and as he adopted the system of an absolute denial, it was found necessary to confront him successively with all those of George's subordinates who had been arrested. It was not till then that he was ascertained to be the mysterious personage who had come every fortnight to George's, and in whose presence every one assumed a respectful attitude. He was also recognised by George's servant as the person who had gone with him in a hackney-coach to the rendezvous of la Madelaine.

The luminous information furnished by this confrontation could not but astonish M. Real in the highest degree. He lost no time in making his report to the First Consul, who became thoughtful, and who expressed by an exclamation of sorrow the regret which he felt at having consented to the seizure of the Duke d'Enghien. It was too late. The First Consul could not but be deeply interested in having this affair elucidated; and yet he enjoined secrecy, either because this appeared most conducive to the interest of his policy, or because he chose rather not to make known the mistake into which he had fallen.

Our history, however, is not destitute of examples of justice itself having been in error: the religion of the parliaments, the composition of which forbade any suspicion of its rigid equity, has sometimes been abused, and condemnations that were afterwards deplored have been the consequences.

I have since frequently heard the Emperor thus express himself before his ministers: "Gentlemen, I am a minor: it is your duty to inform yourselves before you report to me; but when once I have your signature, so much the worse for you if an innocent person suffers ;" and he has often repeated the same words to me, with reference to the reports which I have had occasion to submit to him in the course of my administration.

CHAPTER VII.

Death of General Pichegru — Particulars relative to it—Gendarmes d'élite— Captain Wright—His confrontation with George and his accomplices.

THE presence of Pichegru in George Cadoual's conspiracy seriously compromised Moreau, inasmuch as it afforded room to suppose that there was some connexion between them. The next question to be resolved was, how these two persons could have come together. Means were dexterously contrived to convict General Moreau of having seen Pichegru: as he was unacquainted with the progress of the examinations, he perceived none of the snares that were laid for him; he admitted that Pichegru had come to his house, and that it was General Lajolais who had brought him; but that, for fear of compromising himself, he had not admitted him any more, and yet he had seen him elsewhere. He was asked where; " I do not exactly recollect," replied he, " except once at the Boulevard de la Madelaine, at nine in the evening." Being questioned respecting the manner of this meeting, he answered, that he knew nothing about it; that General Lajolais had come to fetch him, and conducted him to the boulevard, and that after leaving him for a moment, he had rejoined him and taken General Pichegru along with him.

He was not examined further on this point; but Lajolais was taken aside, and after being questioned and cross-questioned, it was ascertained that he had gone from George's lodging in a hackney-coach, with George and Pichegru on the back seat; himself (Lajolais) and Picot, a trusty attendant of George's, on the front : that he had ordered the coachman to drive to the Boulevard de la Madelaine, whence he went to fetch Moreau from his house, Rue d'Anjou, where the latter was waiting for him ; that he had conducted him to the foot of the boulevard ; that he had then gone to the hackney-coach to fetch Pichegru, who had alighted with George, and that he had led them to Moreau, who was walking to and fro till they came up ; that then he, Lajolais, had returned to the coach, in which he remained during the whole time that this interview lasted. Picot confirmed this deposition of Lajolais'; and added, that when his master had returned to the coach with Pichegru, he had heard the latter, speaking of Moreau, say, as I have already related, " It seems that fellow has ambition too." *

Neither George nor Moreau would admit the particulars of this interview. To all the questions that were asked, George replied, " I know not what you mean ;" and Moreau said, " I have never seen George." As Pichegru was just dead, it was impossible to obtain any greater certainty respecting the circumstances of this affair which might implicate General Moreau.

I have said that Pichegru was just dead : his death has given rise to so many reports equally stupid and calumnious,

---

* This expression has a coincidence with the hope entertained by General Moreau of being invested with the consular power, and with the refusal which he gave to enlist under George's principles. I have learned since the restoration that, at another interview, George told him that his plan was quite ripe ; that he should despatch the First Consul on such a day, which he named ; and that he only begged him to set out beforehand with General Pichegru for the environs of Boulogne, to wait there for the news of the event, and to lose no time in using his influence with the army : to which Moreau gave a positive refusal. George was in consequence obliged to defer the blow, from the conviction which he acquired that he should have despatched the First Consul merely for the benefit of General Moreau. It was on this occasion that he said—*Un bleu pour un bleu, j'aime encore mieux celui qui y est que ce j . . .f . . . . . là.*

that it needs some explanation. What I know about it is this.

Pichegru, after his apprehension, had been closely confined in one of the ground-floor rooms in the tower of the Temple. His examination was deferred a few days in order to gain time to collect the materials for his interrogatory; and this delay proved fatal to the Duke d'Enghien.

Pichegru was separated from George merely by a small room, which was the common ante-chamber to their abode.

The keeper of the Temple had the key to their rooms; and to prevent their communicating to each other the questions put to them severally by the *juge-instructeur*, this same judge had directed a sentinel to be placed in this ante-chamber, where, by means of a little noise, any conversation which they might have attempted to keep up could be rendered ineffectual. Both were sent for several times a day to be confronted; that is to say, whenever they were implicated by a fresh deposition of the accused or of witnesses.

George had doubtless made up his mind respecting the issue of the proceedings; but General Pichegru, with different preceding circumstances, probably felt himself in a different predicament. Every time that he was sent for into court, he perceived that his situation grew worse, and that an abyss was opening before him at every step, and he could not help changing countenance.

He had perhaps flattered himself that in the judicial investigation of his affair it might not be possible to obtain sufficient proofs of his participation in a crime, against which the public opinion of all France revolted *en masse;* but he must soon have been convinced that it would be impracticable for him to touch the sensibility of even the most generous hearts; and that moreover his presence before a criminal court, as a co-operator in George's project, would carry back the conviction of his guilt to the circumstance in which Moreau had denounced him to the Directory (in 1796 or 1797), after the latter had caused him to be transported to Cayenne ; and that he would thus lose even the interest which some of his assembled friends had manifested for him at that period of his career.

I presume that this afflicting consideration, continually present to his mind beneath the vault of his prison, powerfully influenced his determination to put an end to his life.

General Pichegru was naturally gay and fond of the pleasures of the table, but the horrors of his situation had altered him. He had sent to request M. Real to come and see him ; and after the conversation which he had with him, he begged that he would send him some books, and among others Seneca.

Some days afterwards, being at the Tuileries, about eight o'clock in the morning, I received a note from the officer of the gendarmerie d'élite, who that day commanded the guard posted at the Temple. He informed me that General Pichegru had just been found dead in his bed ; and that this had occasioned a great bustle in the Temple, where they were expecting some one from the police, to which intelligence of the circumstance had been sent.

This officer communicated the fact to me, as well on account of its singularity, as because I had made it a rule in the corps which I commanded, that all the officers employed in any duty whatever should give me an account of what they had done, seen, or heard, during the twenty-four hours. I forwarded this note to the First Consul: he sent for me supposing that I had further particulars, but as I had none, he sent me to make inquiries, saying, " This is a pretty end for the conqueror of Holland !"

I arrived at the Temple at the same time as M. Real, who came on behalf of the grand-judge to learn the particulars of this event. I went with M. Real, the keeper and the surgeon of the prison, straight to General Pichegru's room; and I knew him again very well, though his face was turned of a crimson colour, from the effect of the apoplexy with which he had been struck.

His room was on the ground-floor, and the head of his bed against the window, so that the seat served to set his light upon for the purpose of reading in bed. On the outside there was a sentinel placed under this window, through which he might easily, upon occasion, see all that was passing in the room.

General Pichegru was lying on his right side; he had put round his neck his own black silk cravat, which he had previously twisted like a small rope: this must have occupied him so long as to afford time for reflection, had he not been resolutely bent on self-destruction. He appeared to have tied his cravat, thus twisted, about his neck, and to have at first drawn it as tight as he could bear it, then to have taken a piece of wood, of the length of a finger, which he had broken from a branch that yet lay in the middle of the room (part of a faggot, the relics of which were still in his fire-place): this he must have slipped between his neck and his cravat, on the right side, and turned round till the moment that reason forsook him. His head had fallen back on the pillow and compressed the little bit of stick, which had prevented the cravat from untwisting. In this situation apoplexy could not fail to supervene. His hand was still under his head, and almost touched this little tourniquet.

On the night-table was a book open and with its back upward, as if laid down for a moment by one who had been interrupted while reading. M. Real found this book to be the Seneca which he had sent to him; and he remarked that it was open at that passage where Seneca says, that *the man who is determined to conspire ought above all things not to fear death.* This was probably the last thing read by General Pichegru, who having placed himself in a situation to lose his life on the scaffold, or under the necessity of having recourse to the clemency of the First Consul, had preferred dying by his own hand.

While I was at the Temple, I questioned the gendarme who had passed the night in the ante-chamber which separated George from Pichegru: he told me that he had heard nothing all night, except that General Pichegru had coughed a good deal from eleven to twelve o'clock; that, not being able to get into his room because the keeper had the key, he was unwilling to rouse the whole tower on account of that cough. The gendarme was himself locked up in this ante-chamber; and had any thing occurred to oblige him to give the alarm, it was by the window that he was to apprize the sentinel who was at the door of the tower; the sentinel was to give notice to the post, and the latter to the keeper.

I questioned also the gendarme who had been on duty under the window of General Pichegru from ten o'clock till twelve, and he had heard nothing.

M. Real then said to me, " Well, though nothing was ever more clearly proved than this suicide, yet in spite of all we can do, it will be said that because he could not be convicted he has been strangled." For this reason, the grand-judge determined from that moment to have a guard without arms placed in the room of each of the persons implicated in George's business, to prevent any attempt on their own lives: of course no such thing was ever thought of as to take them away by secret executions. Party spirit, which always welcomes whatever is likely to be prejudicial to power, publicly circulated a report that Pichegru was strangled by gendarmes. This opinion obtained to such a degree that a high functionary, a friend of mine, mentioned it several years afterwards as a fact of which he had not the least doubt; and notwithstanding all I could say to convince him of the contrary, I am not sure that I succeeded. For the rest, it was not from a carping disposition that he had adopted this opinion: he had heard it repeated so often, that he at length believed it.

It would have argued an absolute want of sound sense to employ for such an office subordinate persons, who would have divulged this crime on the first occasion of discontent, or who would every day have set a fresh price on their silence.

There was no necessity to destroy Pichegru; his presence was even requisite for the *instruction* of the process. Besides, having come to France with George, he was inseparable from him before justice, which would not have failed to condemu him, in spite of the talents of the ablest advocate;* but I cannot think that the First Consul would have suffered him to perish: of this I need no other proof than the pardon which he granted to those who were condemned to death in this affair, and who had nothing to recommend them to the public opinion, as was the case with the conqueror of Holland. Besides, Pichegru, condemned in a criminal court before the face of the world, could no longer prove dangerous, and would have been worthy of pity alone.

If, under these circumstances, there was any one whom it would have been desirable to put out of the way by extraordinary means, that one was Moreau; who was far more formidable to the First Consul than Pichegru, and who had not injured himself in the public estimation by coming from England.

The three persons whom France may interrogate respecting this event are, first, the keeper of the Temple, who is still living;† secondly, M. Manginet, captain of gendarmerie at the residence of Evreux—he was then irremovable commandant of the Temple; thirdly, M. Bellenger, *chef d'escadron* of gendarmerie at the residence of Alençon: he was then lieutenant of the legion d'élite, and was that day on duty at the

---

* The monument erected to General Pichegru, since 1815, is the best answer that can be given to those who at that time (1804) considered him in the light of a victim as well as Moreau.

† This was written in 1815. The facts and disclosures which have come to my knowledge since 1823 have been stated above.

Temple; it was he who wrote me the note of which I have made mention above. It was impossible for any one to enter the tower without his knowledge: had gendarmes gone in, he must not only have seen them, but he would have known them; for the legion d'élite was not so numerous as that the gendarmes composing it could be unknown to each other. They actually did know one another: it was I who had formed this corps, composed of four hundred and eighty horse, and two hundred and forty gendarmes on foot, all picked from the entire corps of gendarmerie: most of them had been subalterns in the army.

I had infused into them all the zeal for the First Consul with which I was myself animated; and I had no greater pleasure than in availing myself of the advantages of my situation to do good for them or their relatives. Their attachment to me assisted me to endure the many vexations brought upon me by a command which was the object of much jealousy; and I feel it to be my duty to declare in the face of the world that I knew not one among them to whom one would have proposed an equivocal mission, while on the contrary most of them were deserving of particular confidence. Out of several instances which I could give, I shall cite the following. Two of them taken without selection, in their regular turn upon the list, were appointed to escort a sum of money from Paris to Naples: the treasurer of the crown delivered it to them ready packed in a carriage prepared for the purpose. They set out from the court of the palace of the Tuileries, and reached Rome without molestation. After quitting that city they were attacked near Terracina. The two postilions having been killed, the robbers came to plunder the carriage; but the two gendarmes plied their weapons with such success that they put the villains to flight, and then mounting the horses themselves, they conveyed the treasure untouched to Naples.

A gendarme d'élite who should have been capable of accepting a mission equivocal for honour, would have been removed from that corps as capable also of betraying the general honour.

The officers of this corps had been selected with the same care: I have never had occasion to do otherwise than commend them in all the delicate circumstances in which they have been employed, and that sometimes by the Emperor himself. This respectable corps fell a victim in 1814 to the basest calumny. It was the first disbanded. It is to be wished, for the sake of the King of France, that he may replace it with servants having hearts as honest and as attached to his person as those were to the government which they served.

The long *instruction* of the process was drawing to a close, when a strange incident occurred to delay the opening of the judgment.

A multitude of depositions had re-echoed the name of the English captain, Wright, and the newspapers had talked of him in all sorts of ways. This captain, who had landed George and his people at the cliff of Biville, had afterwards gone to cruise off the coast of Quiberon. Having had the misfortune to be wrecked on the coast of Morbihan, he was conducted with all his crew to Vannes, where nothing was just then talked of but what was passing at Paris. The administration of that department reported the shipwreck, and was ordered to send Captain Wright and all his crew to Paris. They entered the court of the Temple when George and his people were walking there: the English and French officers did not seem to recognise one another; but the English seamen, not supposing there could be any harm in it, frankly accosted some of their acquaintance among George's subalterns.

Captain Wright was separated from them; and the court proceeded to confront the rest with George's subordinates, which confirmed the rigid truth of the information previously obtained. Wright persisted in declining to answer the questions put to him, and said, " Gentlemen, I am an officer in the British navy; I care not what treatment you reserve for me, I shall give no account of the orders which I have received:* I know none of these gentlemen."

From whom then could Wright, an officer in the royal navy of England, and moreover commanding a ship of war of that navy, have received orders to take on board George and his people, and to land them on our coast? Is there in England any other authority which issues orders to the navy than the government offices?

Captain Wright had been thrown upon the coast by shipwreck: instead of making him a prisoner of war, a criminal prosecution might have been instituted against him by the *procureur-general,* on the ground of his being an accomplice in the conspiracy. Regard was nevertheless had to his devotedness and his character; he and his men were brought forward as witnesses, but no proceedings against him personally were commenced.

This unfortunate man remained in the Temple till 1805, when he died. So many stories have been told concerning his death, that I too was curious to learn the cause of it, when,

---

* The English ministry alleged that it was a stranger to the plans of George. The following is part of a note from Lord Hawkesbury, principal Secretary of State for Foreign Affairs, transmitted on the 30th of April, 1804, in the name of his Britannic Majesty, to the Ministers of Foreign Courts, resident at the Court of London.

"His Majesty has in consequence directed me to declare that he hopes he shall not be reduced to the necessity of repelling, with merited scorn and indignation, 'the atrocious and utterly unfounded calumny, that the government of his Majesty have been a party to plans of assassination.'—an accusation already made with equal falsehood and calumny by the same authority against the members of his Majesty's government during the last war—an accusation incompatible with the honour of his Majesty, and the known character of the British nation; and so completely devoid of any shadow of proof, that it may be reasonably presumed to have been brought forward at the present moment for no other purpose than that of diverting the attention of Europe from the contemplation of the sanguinary deed which has recently been perpetrated, by the direct order of the First Consul in France, in violation of the right of nations, and in contempt of the most simple laws of humanity and honour."

as minister of police, the sources of information were open to me ; and I ascertained that Wright cut his throat in despair, after reading the account of the capitulation of the Austrian general, Mack, at Ulm, that is, while the Emperor was engaged in the campaign of Austerlitz. Can one, in fact, without alike insulting common sense and glory, admit that this sovereign had attached so much importance to the destruction of a scurvy lieutenant of the English navy, as to send from one of his most glorious fields of battle the order for his destruction ? It has been added, that it was I who received from him this commission: now I never quitted him for a single day during the whole campaign, from his departure from Paris till his return. For the rest, the civil administration of France is in possession of all the papers of the ministry of the police, which must furnish all the information that can be desired respecting that event.

CHAPTER VIII.

Trial of George and of General Moreau—Pleadings—Condemnation—Clemency of the First Consul—Departure of General Moreau for the United States.

THE famous trial of George, so eagerly expected, at length commenced : the palace of justice was beset by an innumerable concourse of people, composed of individuals of all classes and all opinions, who thronged thither to make their observations. Persons of the better sort, who were also to be seen there, were not carried thither by curiosity alone. The spirit of opposition was a principal ingredient in the interest which attracted the greater part of the people of all ranks who attended all the sittings; and this opposition was not silent. The stories circulated respecting the death of the Duke d'Enghien and that of Pichegru had produced audacity, and public opinion was loudly expressed.

The pleadings lasted twelve days: they were constantly attended by a crowd which filled all the avenues of the palace. A fault had been committed in persuading the First Consul to agree to the suppression of the jury for this occasion only; in consequence of the alarm, whether well or ill-founded, excited by the language held since the catastrophe of the Duke d'Enghien. This measure, though vigorous, produced a bad effect, and awakened still more distrust in the public mind in general.

The pleadings in the affair of General Moreau were awaited with impatience: at length they were opened. His advocate was eloquent, and found in history an apposite quotation in the work of the President de Thou: he dwelt on the ignominy with which Lombardemont had covered himself; but he passed over the interview at the Boulevard de la Madelaine with all the rapidity allowed by the denial of Moreau, the silence of George, and the death of Pichegru: this, in fact, it was that saved him. I was present at this sitting; the public was all eye and all ear.

Moreau admitted that General Lajolais had come to his house for him, conducted him to the Boulevard de la Madelaine, fetched Pichegru from the hackney-coach, and brought him to the spot where he, Moreau, was walking.

Lajolais acknowledged all this to be true, but added, "George was with Pichegru: you knew that he was to be there; and he alighted from the coach with Pichegru." Picot, a trusty attendant of George's, said, "I was with George when he got out of the coach with Pichegru; and I stayed in the coach with Lajolais, who had got in again, till they came back and rejoined us."

Nothing could be more clearly proved than this truth; but (as it luckily happened no doubt in this case) two and two do not always make four: nevertheless, Moreau was obliged to affirm upon oath that he had not seen George. All eyes were fixed upon him: the spectators suffered on account of what he must have suffered; but at length he swore that he had not seen George, and assuredly he did very right : but ought the conqueror of Hohenlinden to have placed himself in this situation? *

The guilt of the other accused persons was too evident to leave room for hope ; they were all condemned.

It was useless to suppress the jury : for the very same day that Moreau was sworn, I saw a very clever man who said aloud in the court, " Had I been on the jury, I should have declared Moreau guilty on such depositions as that of Lajolais and Picot."

He was nevertheless sentenced jointly with the girl Izai to two years' imprisonment. The audience burst into a laugh on hearing this ridiculous sentence.

The girl Izai was a poor creature, who to the kindness which she had shown for one or two of the least important persons of George's party, had added that of going on all sorts of errands for them. Can any rational man persuade himself that in a conspiracy, all the circumstances of which are proved, and which aims at the overthrow of a state, for the success of which the actors think that they need the concurrence of one of the principal leaders of the army, who gives his consent to it, because he has seen the conspirators and admitted them into his house ; but who, it is true, has fettered his participation with restrictions which have suspended the enterprise, and perhaps caused it to miscarry—can, I say, any rational man believe that this chief had no more share in this conspiracy than could have been taken by a pot-house girl? Such a supposition would revolt the meanest understanding. Either Moreau was not guilty, and then the court ought to have had the courage loudly to declare his innocence and to send him

* His advocate, speaking to me concerning this affair during my administration, told me, that if in his defence he had admitted this interview as proved, he should have had no means left to save General Moreau, whom the slightest contact with George would have irretrievably ruined.

home in triumph; or he was guilty, and in this case he was more guilty than George, for George was at least acting up to his principles—whereas Moreau, after denouncing to the Directory, subsequently to the 18th Fructidor, the correspondence between Pichegru and the Prince of Condé, behaved a thousand times worse than Pichegru: at this period he lent himself to an assassination and to a manifest treason, after he had pledged his faith to his country. But such is blind passion: he had been slighted at the time when he denounced Pichegru, and the latter had been exalted into a hero.

It has been strongly asserted that the members of the criminal court, being thoroughly acquainted with the republican opinions of Moreau, had given him the benefit of them; and that a brother of General Lecourbe's (a partisan of Moreau's), who was a member of the criminal court, assisted by M. Fouché, had gained over many voices in favour of Moreau. I know nothing of the matter: but something of the sort must have taken place.

He was advised to ask permission to go to America: the First Consul granted it the same day. Moreau quitted the Temple at night, after taking leave of his family: he was conducted to Barcelona, and embarked in a Spanish port for America. I have since seen an Englishman who knew Moreau when he commanded the army of the Rhine, and afterwards met with him again in America. He told me that he had heard him congratulate himself on having got off so well as he did; and that he moreover expressed his astonishment that the police had not sooner discovered his intercourse with Pichegru, because he supposed that he was strictly watched; and on this subject he related the following anecdote. It is given in Moreau's own words.

" Pichegru had already been some time in Paris, and we were in the habit of seeing each other every night.

" When he came to my house he was accustomed to ask for one of my servants, who was the only one that knew him, and whom I had ordered to be always in readiness to receive him and to usher him into my cabinet, whither I went to join him if I was not there already.

"It once happened that when my drawing-room was full of company who had dined with me, Pichegru came earlier than usual. Not finding upon the stairs the servant who was in the habit of waiting for him there, he went up to the ante-chamber, and not meeting with any one there either, he opened the drawing-room door, but seeing it full of company, he immediately drew back. Luckily he had not been perceived by any person but my wife, who had turned her head towards the door at the moment of its opening, and recognised him. I instantly retired, and conducted him myself to my cabinet, where we remained part of the evening.

"Next day I had a sharp altercation with my wife, who insisted that I was ruining myself; because General Pichegru could scarcely have come to Paris for any other purpose than to engage in some enterprise in favour of the Bourbons, and whenever he should have no further occasion for me, he would make me repent what I had written against him to the Directory. She talked to me a long time in this strain, and I was in an agony lest she should communicate her grievances to some of her female friends; but it appears that she kept them to herself, for it was not through any indiscretion of hers that the first intelligence of this affair was obtained."

Such was the language of General Moreau during the first year of his residence in America; while in France a party was striving to represent him as the victim of a jealousy which his great talents had excited.

General Moreau possessed property in France, by the sale of which, as it would have been difficult to turn it into money, he must have suffered a considerable loss. The First Consul bought the estate of Gros Bois near Paris, and gave it to General Berthier, minister at war. He also purchased of him his house in the Rue d'Anjou, which he gave to Bernadotte, as if it had been decreed that this house should not cease to be the focus of conspiracy against him.

For these two properties General Moreau was paid the price which he himself asked, and he was moderate in his demand.

It has been generally believed that the First Consul was vexed at the non-condemnation of Moreau. If he was vexed at this result of the trial, on which point I am ignorant, it was no doubt merely because it deprived him of an opportunity to humble Moreau by pardoning him. He was not fond of revenging himself by capital punishments. After the condemnation of George and his people, he pardoned several of them at the first application. If I recollect rightly, there were seven pardoned in all. Would he have suffered the conqueror of Holland and the victor of Hohenlinden to perish? It would be unjust to think so.

Did he leave Moreau to suffer the two years' confinement to which he was sentenced, and during which he might have found occasion to get rid of him had he harboured a thought of so doing? No; for on the night of the very day that Moreau solicited by letter permission to go to America, he granted him leave to depart.

I was the person whom the First Consul sent to him in the Temple to communicate his consent, and to make arrangements with him for his departure. I gave him my own carriage, and the First Consul paid all the expenses of his journey to Barcelona. The general expressed a wish to see Madame Moreau; I went myself to fetch her, and brought her to the Temple. These, I think, were attentions which I was not obliged to pay.

Thus terminated this long affair: it was during the proceedings that the form of government changed once more in France.

CHAPTER IX.

Creation of the empire—Motives for the adoption of that form of government—
Addresses of the army—The First Consul is proclaimed Emperor—New institutions—Distribution of crosses of the Legion of Honour at the camp of Boulogne—The Pope crosses the mountains—Interview at Fontainebleau.

THIS event requires some developement. The so oft repeated enterprises against the life of the First Consul began
to excite alarm: he had hitherto been preserved from them,
but the efforts for this purpose might not always be so fortunate. Up to this time it had been supposed that he was
threatened only by a few violent Jacobins; and people tranquillized themselves with the idea that the political fervour
must cool sooner or later; but they had already been forced
to acknowledge that it was not Jacobins who had prepared
the 3rd Nivose, as attempts had been made to persuade the
public. In George's affair it was not possible to doubt for a
moment the object which had armed the conspirators and
the party to which they belonged.

From all these reflections flowed the natural consequence
that some power or other wished to destroy the First Consul;
that it might possibly succeed: that if this calamity should
happen, France would be without strength or guide amid the
elements of discord and revolution, of which it could not be
denied to be still full; and that thenceforth it would be liable
to be subjected to the yoke.

The returned emigrants, and they were very numerous,
were afraid to see the power wrested from a hand which had
the strength to protect them. The patriots feared the return
of the house of Bourbon, and the reaction which as they conceived must be the inevitable consequence of it: all minds
were weary of commotions, and satisfied with the port in

which the revolution had been laid up in safety from fresh storms. On all sides people were alarmed at the bare idea of seeing the First Consul cut off; and they seriously set about remedying so much in this form of government as tended to make us uneasy and to enccurage our enemies.

The first idea was to appoint a successor to the First Consul; but this measure, besides being unconstitutional, might perhaps have hastened the death of him whom its projectors wished to preserve. Ambition is impatient. After turning over and thoroughly examining the histories of all revolutions, they reverted to the monarchical form of government, which, fixing the order of inheritance, ensured the succession to power without convulsions, and destroyed at least that part of the hopes of our enemies.

It was not without considerable trouble that the majority of opinions were brought over to the adoption of this measure. It was only upon the breach that the old friends of liberty signed this capitulation; but at last monarchical ideas were adopted.

They were propagated, and they struck root with astonishing promptitude. Fouché, who only sought occasion to climb again to power, spread them in the senate and among the men of the revolution with the zeal of a new convert.*

In the army the proposed change went down of itself: this

---

* After George's affair, in which the First Consul had been well served, good care was taken to make this observation to them :—" Only see, he has been six months at Paris without its being suspected. It is clear that if there had been a ministry of police, this risk would not have been incurred : nay, more, George would not have dared to come had Fouché still been minister." The First Consul was easily persuaded to re-establish this ministry; it became necessary, especially on account of the changes which were preparing, and which were likely soon to set intrigues at work. The First Consul inclined to M. Real. I know not what led him to decide in favour of M. Fouché, who returned to the ministry. The latter was persuaded that he had been turned out of it solely by the machinations of M. de Talleyrand; he therefore resumed his post with a resolution to do him all the harm he could, and accordingly he missed no occasion of doing it.

is easily accounted for. The dragoons, who were all collected into divisions of four regiments each, and preparing to approach Boulogne, gave the first impulsion. They sent an address to the First Consul, in which they alleged that their efforts would be of no service if wicked men should succeed in taking away his life; that the best way to thwart their designs and to fix the irresolute was to put the imperial crown on his head, and to fix that dignity in his family. After the dragoons came the cuirassiers; then all the corps of infantry, and then the seamen ; and lastly, those of the civil orders who wished for the change followed the example of the army. This spirit spread in an instant to the smallest parishes : the First Consul received carriages full of such addresses.

Pains were taken, I dare say, to foment this zeal ;* but at any rate the bodies of the state were assembled, these documents were communicated to them, and independently of their deliberations, all these manifestations of a desire for the restoration of the monarchical system were submitted to the sanction of the people. A register for the reception of votes was opened in every parish in France; from Antwerp to Perpignan, and from Brest to Mont Cenis. I am not sure that Piedmont was comprised in it.

It was the summary of all these votes laid before the senate that formed the basis of the *proces-verbal* of inauguration of the Bonaparte family to the imperial dignity.

This *proces-verbal* is in the archives of the senate, which

---

* It is but right to observe, that it was the army which gave the signal, and which set the example. But what was it that had caused the new social order es-tablished in France to be respected, as well as the institutions that were the consequence of it ? Was it not the efforts of the army ? Under what guarantee was all this placed ? Was it not under that of the army ?

To destroy these institutions, where was a beginning to be made unless with their author ? and next to him, who was most threatened if not the army ? (Witness the events of 1815.) The latter having, like all France, passed through the revolution, perceived danger for itself: what wonder then that it should be the first to seek to secure itself from that danger ?

went in a body from Paris to St. Cloud to present it to the
First Consul. M. Cambaceres read a very excellent speech,
which concluded with a statement of the number of votes; and
in consequence proclaimed, with a loud voice, Napoleon Bonaparte, Emperor of the French. The senators, placed in a line
facing him, vied with each other in repeating *Vive l'Empereur!* and returned with all the outward signs of joy to Paris,
where people were already writing epitaphs on the republic.*

Thus, then, the First Consul had become Emperor. It was

* Before the First Consul put the imperial crown on his head, he had been appointed consul for life, in consequence of a popular vote, on the 2nd of August,
1802. His enemies have reproached him for his assent to the *senatus-consulte*,
which thus perpetuated him in authority, as an ambitious act, by which he designed to pave the way to his elevation to the throne.

On an impartial examination of all that they have been able to advance on this
subject, we discover the characters of passion and envy. We need but refer back
to that period to convince ourselves of this.

The consulate was, at first, to be held for ten years only; and it will be recollected how party spirit disturbed internal tranquillity, and to what discords we
should still have been liable, had not a firm hand curbed all the factions. Now,
what would have happened, when the time should have arrived for electing a
successor to the First Consul? The parties would probably have been in commotion; and as the soldiery would have given law, the votes would have been divided between the First Consul and General Moreau.

Supposing that the latter had been elected, what would he have done? None
but inexperienced persons will deny, that he would have undone all that his predecessor had done; and as he would have had every reason to fear that, owing to
the discontent which this would have excited, General Bonaparte would be re-
elected at the ensuing election; he would have been solicitous to throw obstacles
in his way, if even he had not done something still worse, upon pretext that he
was conspiring against the tranquillity of the republic. The history of governments
of this kind is filled with similar events.

After Moreau, another would have been elected, who, in his turn, would have
pursued the same course, and so on, as at Constantinople. General Bonaparte
would have been an idiot to run this risk; and he would have been laughed at for
not knowing how to make use of power when he was invested with it. In such
cases, the first who occupies the place acts wisely not to quit it. Besides, how
was it that the friends of liberty did not establish this government while the Emperor was in Egypt? They were then masters of the ground, and might have
made themselves what they pleased.

believed that he had now attained repose : we shall soon see what labours yet remained for him to perform.

The day after his inauguration, he received all the constituted bodies, the administrative authorities, and the learned corporations. Each speaker had exhausted his rhetoric to fill his censer, and from the very first day there was nothing more to be desired : the most furious Jacobins were all courtesy.

The oath was administered to the troops ; they took it with shouts of enthusiasm which rent the air.

It was in the two or three succeeding days that we witnessed the nomination of dignitaries, marshals, and all the appendages of a throne, as well with reference to the military appointments as to the high offices of the crown.

The Emperor arrogated nothing to himself on account of his situation : in sanctioning this restoration of principles, he secured nothing additional for himself. He had no children, and the families of kings have in general some bad relations

He thought much less, therefore, of all these new honours than of the prosecution of his operations at Boulogne, at which he laboured morning, evening, and night ; but how this inconceivable head found time for every thing remains to be discovered.

On the 14th of July, in the same year, he conferred the crosses of the Legion of Honour, which he had instituted some months before, but without making known the circumstance. On this occasion there was a national ceremony, to which all the military, from boys to invalids, were admitted : it took place at the Hôtel des Invalides.

Napoleon then announced that he was going to distribute these decorations among the army at Boulogne : this was a pretext for collecting and reviewing it, because his expedition was on the point of being carried into effect.

Accordingly he set out for Boulogne, where all the corps

d'armée, stationed between Ostend and Etaples, were assembled in the open country; and thenceforward the decoration of the Legion of Honour was substituted for the weapons of honour, such as muskets, sabres, &c. previously given—an institution which dated from the first war in Italy.

From Boulogne the Emperor went a second time to Belgium,* where he made the Empress join him: it was the first time that they occupied the palace of Lacken, near Brussels, which the Emperor had had repaired and new furnished. He extended his journey to the Rhine; and from Mentz he sent General Caffarelli to Rome, to negotiate the visit of the Pope to Paris, of which I shall speak presently.

It was likewise from Mentz that he sent orders for the departure of the two squadrons equipped at Rochefort and Toulon. The former was commanded by Vice-admiral Missiessy, and had on board General Lagrange, the same who has since been in the gendarmerie: the Emperor had been partial to him ever since the war in Italy and in Egypt. Vice-admiral Villeneuve commanded the latter: he received on board with his troops General Lauriston,† whom the Emperor sent from Belgium to embark there. These two squadrons were to have started at the beginning of autumn; but, owing to many contrary circumstances, it was winter before they sailed: I shall say no more about them till their return. Their departure was a commencement to carry into effect the Boulogne expedition. That of Toulon was joined by a Spanish squadron under the command of Admiral Gravina. The apparent destination of both was to carry out succours to our colonies; but they were stinted to time, and were to return the following year in such a way as to make some noise, as will be seen presently.

The Emperor returned from this tour at the end of October;

* It was on occasion of this journey that he sent for M. de Massias. See the supplementary chapter, at the end of this Part.

† Lauriston, as aide-de-camp to the Emperor, accompanied him in this journey.

and his attention was occupied during the month of November with all that related to the ceremonies of the coronation : the Pope himself had set out from Rome for the purpose of anointing the Emperor.

The court went to Fontainebleau to receive him : it was also the first visit paid by it to that palace, which the Emperor had received in ruins, and which he had caused to be repaired and completely re-furnished.*

He went to meet the Pope on the road to Nemours. To avoid ceremony, the pretext of a hunting-party was assumed : the attendants, with his equipages, were in the forest. The Emperor came on horseback and in a hunting-dress, with his retinue. It was at the half-moon on the top of the hill that the meeting took place. There the Pope's carriage drew up; he got out at the left door in his white costume : the ground was dirty; he did not like to step upon it with his white silk shoes, but was obliged to do so at last.

Napoleon alighted to receive him. They embraced ; and the Emperor's carriage, which had been purposely driven up, was advanced a few paces, as if from the carelessness of the driver; but men were posted to hold the two doors open : at the moment of getting in, the Emperor took the right door, and an officer of the court handed the Pope to the left, so that they entered the carriage by the two doors at the same time. The Emperor naturally seated himself on the right; and this first step decided without negotiation upon the etiquette to be observed during the whole time that the Pope was to remain at Paris.

After resting at Fontainebleau, the Emperor returned to Paris : his Holiness set out first, and was received with sovereign honours on the road. The pickets escorted him to the

---

* After the first survey made by his direction by the architects, whom Duroc and I accompanied, they were so frightened at the quantity of repairs required by this monumental palace, that they unanimously agreed that it would cost more to repair than to rebuild it.

palace of the Tuileries, where the pavilion of Flora was assigned for his residence.

The presence of the Pope in Paris was so extraordinary a circumstance that every one was anxious to see him: he seemed affected by this, and graciously received the religious corporations which were presented to him, and which at that time were but few in number.

All the bishops were at Paris; they had been summoned thither for the coronation: each of them had brought with him several ecclesiastics, so that there were as many of them as could have been met with at Rome.

The officers in waiting on the Emperor were placed about the Pope; he was treated in every respect as if he had been at home.

The government in changing its form had also changed its manners: etiquette was introduced into every thing; it became daily more difficult to obtain admittance to that which formerly was quite easy of access. The oldest servants submitted to this with repugnance; but zeal and necessity stifled their complaints and remonstrances; they were obliged to accustom themselves to the mortification of being forbidden access to the Emperor's apartments by those who shortly before were the objects of their particular vigilance. All the individuals of the ancient nobility most distinguished by their birth, their fortune, and the part which they had acted in the revolution, either against it or in its favour, were then seen successively arriving and being admitted to the intimacy of the sovereign. The aim of the Emperor was to bring about the amalgamation of the different parties; he succeeded, though imperfectly, because jealousy and intrigue entered at the same door as ambition. The old servants were so injudicious as to fall out with one another; they seemed to think that the Emperor was wresting from them their inheritance: the new ones skilfully profited by their estrangement.

CHAPTER X.

Ceremony of the coronation—Distribution of eagles to the army—Creation of the kingdom of Lombardy—Papal pretensions—Mission to Belgium—Napoleon at Milan.

THE day fixed for the ceremony of the coronation arrived. It was the 2nd of December: the weather was as usual at this season of the year, that is, very bad. It was nevertheless a fine sight to see that assemblage of the deputations of all the departments, of all the considerable towns, and of all the regiments of the army, joined to all the public functionaries of France, to all the generals, and to the whole population of the capital.

The interior of the church of Notre Dame had been new-painted; galleries and pews magnificently adorned had been erected, and they were thronged with a prodigious concourse of spectators.

The imperial throne was placed at the end of the nave, between the principal entrance, and on a very elevated platform. The pontifical throne was in the choir, beside the high-altar.

The Pope set out from the Tuileries, * and proceeded along

---

* The departure of the Pope from the Tuileries for the archiepiscopal palace was delayed for a short time by a singular cause. Every body was ignorant in France, and even at the Tuileries, that it was customary at Rome when the Pope went out to officiate in the great churches, such as that of St. John de Lateran, for example, for one of his principal chamberlains to set off a little before him, mounted on an ass, and carrying a large cross, such as is used in processions. It was not till the very moment of departure that this custom was made known. The chamberlain would not, for all the gold in the world, have derogated from the practice, and accepted a nobler animal. All the grooms of the Tuileries were instantly despatched in quest of an ass; and they were fortunate enough to find a tolerably well-looking one, which was hastily caparisoned. The chamberlain rode with a composure which nothing could disturb, through the innumerable multitude who lined the quays, and could not help laughing at this odd spectacle, which they beheld for the first time.

the quay to the archiepiscopal palace, whence he repaired to
the choir by a private entrance.

The Emperor set out with the Empress by the Carrousel.
The procession passed along the Rue St. Honoré to that des
Lombards, then the Pont au Change, the Palace of Justice,
the court of Notre Dame, and entered the Archbishop's
palace. Here rooms were prepared for the whole of the
retinue, each of whom dressed in state for the occasion : some
appeared in the costume of their posts of honour, others in
their uniforms.

On the outside of the church had been erected a long
wooden gallery from the archiepiscopal palace to the principal
entrance of the church. By this gallery came the Emperor's
retinue, which presented a truly magnificent sight. The procession was opened by the already numerous body of courtiers : next came the marshals of the empire wearing their
honours ; then the dignitaries and high officers of the crown ;
and lastly, the Emperor in a dress of state. At the moment of
his entering the cathedral there was a simultaneous shout,
which made but one explosion, of *Vive l'Empereur*. The immense quantity of figures which appeared on the sides of this
vast edifice formed a tapestry of the most extraordinary kind.

The procession passed along the middle of the nave, and
arrived at the choir facing the high-altar. This scene was not
less imposing : the galleries round the choir were filled with
the handsomest women whom the best company could produce, and most of whom rivalled in the lustre of their beauty
that of the precious stones with which they were covered.

His Holiness went to meet the Emperor at a desk which
had been placed in the middle of the choir : there was another
on one side for the Empress. After saying a short prayer
there, they returned, and seated themselves on the throne
at the end of the church facing the choir ; there they heard
mass, which was said by the Pope. They went to make the
offering, and came back ; they then descended from the plat-

form of the throne, and walked in procession to receive the
holy unction. The Emperor and Empress, on reaching the
choir, replaced themselves at their desks, where the Pope performed the ceremony.

He presented the crown to the Emperor, who received it, put
it himself upon his head, took it off, placed it on that of the
Empress, removed it again, and laid it on the cushion where it
was at first. A smaller crown was immediately put upon the
head of the Empress. All the arrangements had been made
beforehand : she was surrounded by her ladies ; every thing
was done in a moment, and nobody perceived the substitution
which had taken place. The procession moved back to the
platform. The Emperor there heard *Te Deum*; the Pope
himself went thither at the conclusion of the service, as if to
say, *Ite, missa est.* The Testament was presented to the Emperor, who took off his glove, and pronounced his oath, with
his hand upon the sacred book.

He went back to the archiepiscopal palace the same way
that he had come, and entered his carriage. The ceremony
was very long ; the procession returned by the Rue St. Martin,
the Boulevard, the Place de la Concorde, and the Pont Tour-
nant: it was getting dusk when he arrived at the Tuileries.

The distribution of the eagles took place a few days afterwards. The weather was extremely unfavourable : the crowd
was nevertheless prodigious. At the moment when the deputations of the regiments approached to receive the eagles, the
enthusiasm was general: the citizens as well as the soldiers
burst into long acclamations.

Thus monarchy was consecrated anew in France—but this
was not all: the form of government of the Cisalpine Republic
had been modified, because it could not accommodate itself
to that of the consular government; it was found necessary
to modify it once more, and this business was set about immediately.

The Emperor had ministers and a number of able men, who

spared him the trouble of expressing the same wish twice:
accordingly every thing proceeded rapidly. Lombardy was
erected into a kingdom, and the Emperor put the iron crown
upon his head.

The Pope had come to do all that was required of him, and
he thought that he might demand the reward of his compliance : he modestly desired that Avignon, in France, and
Bologna and Ferrara, in Italy, should be restored to him.
The Emperor turned a deaf ear: the Pope insisted, and was
flatly refused. His Holiness went away in not the best humour; leaving us to believe, that if he had anticipated the
chance of a refusal, he would have attached this condition to his
journey, and not have granted the spiritual till he had made
sure of the temporal. The Emperor, nevertheless, made him
magnificent presents of furniture and pontifical ornaments:
he also bestowed valuable presents on all who had accompanied him. They took leave of each other: the Emperor
left the Pope at Paris, and set out for Italy. He went by
way of Troyes and Burgundy, which he wished to visit. He
stopped at Lyons, and thence proceeded to the castle of
Stupinitz near Turin.

About a fortnight before his departure from Paris, the
Emperor had sent me to Belgium,* by Lille, Mons, Brussels,

* " Monsieur, the general of division, Savary, my aide-de-camp,

" You will set out in the course of the day with all speed for Brussels. The
annexed papers will acquaint you with the object of your mission. You will call
upon the president of the criminal court, and the imperial *procureur ;* and without
making any fresh noise, or suffering the aim of your journey to be discovered, you
will collect the information requisite to enable me to form a precise idea respecting that affair, as well as respecting the necessity of the measures which are proposed to me.

" You will also go to my palace at Lacken, to see in what state the works are
there.

" You will thence go to Antwerp : you will there most minutely inspect the arsenal, the docks for ship-building, the magazines, the gun-boats, and other vessels
of the flotilla that are equipping. You will return by Bruges, Ostend, Dunkirk,
Calais, Ambleteuse, Vimereux, and Boulogne. You will make a sufficient stay in

and Antwerp. In this last city I had many things to inspect; and never, I dare say, had any one such satisfactory reports to make to him. It was scarcely two years since I had last seen Antwerp, and it seemed as if a miracle had been wrought there: it might have been compared with Thebes, which started up at the sound of Amphion's lyre. I found ships half-built, immense dock-yards, work-shops of all kinds, extensive buildings, where two years before stood ramparts and a great number of houses which it was found necessary to demolish. From Amiens I turned back to take the right of the army, which was already drawn together between Dunkirk and Etaples. I had orders to see all the generals and colonels, and to tell them that in going to Italy the Emperor was mindful of them, and that he would soon be back in the midst of their camps, and put an end to the impatience which they were manifesting ; that they were not to lose their patience, or to consider what they had done as useless. I also inspected the troops : the Emperor had particularly recommended to me to do so.

While I was at Boulogne, I was not a little surprised by the arrival from Turin of long instructions from the Emperor respecting the manner of embarking the army. He had divided his immense flotilla into squadrons, divisions, and subdivisions, with such order, that even at night the troops might have proceeded to embarkation. Each regiment, each company, knew the numbers of the vessels which

each of these towns to examine the state of the land and sea forces, and to enable you to give me an account of every thing that can interest me. You will write to me from Brussels concerning the affair of ——, and from each of the other towns, on every thing connected with your mission. You will talk to General Davout and the other generals, and always give them to understand that I expect the army and the flotilla to be constantly kept on a respectable footing, and in the best discipline. Whereupon, I pray God to have you in his holy keeping.

" NAPOLEON."

' Malmaison, 24 Ventose, year 13."

were to take it on board : the same was the case with regard
to each general and officer of the staff.

The Emperor must have devoted a month at least to this
immense and minute work; which demonstrated that events
which had engaged the attention of all the world besides had
not caused him to lose sight of his plans.

I rejoined him at Stupinitz. He was eager after news
from the coast of Boulogne, and was well pleased with what I
brought him. He prolonged his stay at Turin, and was still
in that city when the Pope arrived there. His Holiness had
lodgings provided for him in the royal palace in the city ; the
Emperor went thither to see him, and set out the next day by
Asti for Alexandria: the Pope took the road to Casal on his
way back to Rome.

On his arrival at Alexandria, the Emperor inspected the
immense works which, by his direction, were carrying on
there. He held a review on the field of battle of Marengo ·
he put on that day the same coat and laced hat which he
wore in the engagement; the coat was quite moth-eaten.
Next day he went by Pavia to Milan.

All heads were turned at his entrance into that city. He
remained there the time required for the ceremony of the
coronation, which took place in the cathedral. A detachment
of the guard of honour of Milan went the day before to fetch
the iron crown of the ancient kings of Lombardy, which was
carefully preserved at Muntza; it became once more that of
the king of Italy.

On this occasion the Emperor instituted the Order of the
Iron Crown.

It was at Milan that the insignia of the different orders of
Prussia, Bavaria, Portugal, and Spain, were received in exchange for the cordons of the Legion of Honour, which had
been sent to those powers.

After the ceremony of the coronation, the Emperor went in

procession to the Italian senate, where he invested Prince Eugene with the viceroyalty of Italy.

During the Emperor's stay at Milan, he directed his attention toward the embellishment of that city with the same zeal as if it had been Paris : all that concerned the interests of Italy and the Italians was one of his favourite occupations. He had always regretted that none of the governments of that country had undertaken the completion of the cathedral of Milan, which is well known to be the largest edifice of the kind after St. Peter's at Rome. He ordered the works to be immediately resumed, forbidding them to be interrupted on any pretext whatever, and created a special fund for defraying the expenses. The Milanese have no doubt not forgotten that to him they are indebted for the completion of that beautiful structure, which would probably have long remained in the unfinished state in which it then was.

On his return to Paris, after the battle of Marengo, he had resolved to perpetuate the memory of the conquest of Italy, by erecting, in the *hospice* of the great St. Bernard, a monument which should attest to future ages that glorious epoch in the history of our arms. He had directed M. Denon to go and survey the spot, and to submit to him various plans. Out of these he had selected one, and the building was just finished while the Emperor was at Milan. He resolved to have it solemnly inaugurated, and the remains of General Desaix, surrounded with the laurels amid which he had fallen, removed thither. A small column was formed of the deputations of different regiments of the army of Italy, and of a civil deputation of Italians, who were to proceed from Milan to the *hospice* of Mount St. Bernard. Every thing was arranged, when M. Denon came to inform the Emperor that the body of General Desaix was not to be found. The Emperor recollected the order which he had given to me on the field of battle of Marengo, and desired me to neglect no means for discovering what had been done

with it. · M. Denon assured me that he had made many inquiries without success.   I begged him to come with me just
for an hour, and conducted him straightway to the convent where I had caused the body of General Desaix to be
deposited.   The monastery had been secularized ; one of the
monks only was left there : at the first question he comprehended what I wanted ; he took me into a little sacristy,
contiguous to a chapel, and there I found the body of General
Desaix, in the same place and in the same state that I had
left it some years before, after having had it embalmed, then
put into a leaden coffin, that into one of copper, and lastly
the whole enclosed in a wooden one.   M. Denon rejoiced at
this discovery, for he was afraid that he should be obliged to
perform the ceremony without the remains of the illustrious
general who was the object of it.

Since that time General Desaix has reposed in the church
of Mount St. Bernard.

CHAPTER XI.

Premature return of Admiral Missiessy's squadron—Review of Monte Chiaro—
Annexation of Genoa to the empire—Preparations for the embarkation.

FROM Milan, Napoleon proceeded to Brescia, where he
stayed two days : there he received intelligence at which he
was equally surprised and mortified.   This was the return to
Rochefort of Admiral Missiessy's squadron, which had gone like
lightning to Guadaloupe, and returned with the same rapidity.
He was two or three months earlier than had been calculated
upon ; and brought back to our coasts the English fleet, which
had been in pursuit of him ever since his departure.   Thus was
the object of this trip frustrated ; for the ships which we had

at Toulon, Cadiz, and Rochefort, had been sent out with no other design than to disperse the English squadrons over the Indian seas, and to keep them aloof from the coasts which we purposed invading.

General Lagrange, who had accompanied this squadron, had likewise returned; he himself arrived at Brescia, where he was very ill received.

The Emperor, however, betrayed not all the vexation which this return occasioned him

From Brescia he went to review the army assembled in the plain of Monte Chiaro : it filed off, the infantry by battalions formed in order of battle, and the cavalry in regiments likewise in order of battle, and night had nevertheless set in before it had finished. The Emperor pursued his journey and repaired to Verona, which was then the frontier of the kingdom of Italy. The Austrian general, Baron Vincent (afterwards ambassador at Paris), begged permission to pay his respects to him, and caused him to be saluted, according to custom, by his artillery. The Emperor received him the next day with his whole corps of officers ; and two days afterwards set out for Mantua, and then crossed the Po opposite to Bologna. He entered that city, proceeded thence to Parma, to Placentia, and then to Genoa, of which he went to take possession.

The doge and senate of that city had come to Milan to beg him to accept them, and to incorporate them with the French empire. I have no doubt that this resolution had been somewhat assisted. Such was the state of this unfortunate republic, that its inhabitants were almost famishing : the English closely blockaded it by sea ; the French *douanes* cooped it up by land : it had no territory, and could not without difficulty procure wherewithal to subsist. Add to this that whenever a quarrel took place in Italy, the first thing was to send it a garrison, which it had not the means of refusing. It had therefore all the inconveniences arising from a union with France, without possessing any of the advantages : it determined therefore to make application to be incorporated with the empire.

To France this was no great acquisition. The country had a passive quality which far surpassed its active; so that its annexation caused an increase in the expenditure of the imperial treasury. Genoa had long possessed nothing but marble palaces, the relics of its ancient splendour.

Hither had come, by the Emperor's direction, M. Lebrun, arch-treasurer, whom he appointed governor, and the minister of the finances, who immediately regulated what belonged to his department. The Emperor then set out on his return to Paris, being impatient to get back to the capital. At Fontainebleau he stayed some days before he entered Paris. It was then the end of June. He could no longer repress his impatience. At length he set out with the minister of the marine for Boulogne, stealing away according to his custom.

He had caused the line of signals along the coast from Bayonne to Calais to be organised in a particular manner. He inspected his army man by man, and his flotilla boat by boat. He had placed guards at the avenues to his head-quarters, who stopped all the couriers coming to the minister of the marine and brought them to him; so that he read the dispatches before the minister, to whom he sent them after he had run them over. This precaution he took that he might not lose a moment, but have the army embarked as soon as he should be assured that the event which he expected had taken place. He thus gained a few hours on the minister of the marine, who was fixed at Boulogne; while he, as the reader knows, was at his little country-house at Pont de Brique, about a league from Boulogne on the road to Paris.

All this being finished, he ordered the parks of artillery to be brought up; they were embarked, and afterwards the cavalry. There was nothing left but the infantry, which was kept in the camps ready to take arms at the first sound of the drum. The order for going on board was expected every moment; it came not, but on the contrary what was already on board was again landed. The reason for it was this.

The squadron which had left Toulon the preceding winter, with that of Spain, was to have been joined by that of Missiessy; but the latter had sailed for Europe before the appointed time. The two squadrons consisted together of fifteen ships: they were to appear off Ferrol, without entering that port. Admiral Gourdon, who was there with six sail, had orders to join them. These twenty-one ships were then to proceed together, take Missiessy in the road of Rochefort, rally his squadron, and all steer for Brest, where lay twenty-one vessels which had orders to push out as soon as the combined squadron should heave in sight. After this junction, they would have formed a force of sixty sail, which might arrive off Boulogne in two or three days. On the departure of the squadrons from Rochefort and Brest, a courier was to be dispatched to the minister of the marine; and at the same time notice was to be given by the coast-signals, that is, from Rochefort to Brest, and from Brest to Boulogne.

On the arrival of this courier, or on the coast-signal, the rest of the army was to be embarked; the flotilla, collected at Etaples, Boulogne, Vimereux, and Ambleteuse, was to begin to move, and it was calculated that it would be in the roads in three tides. This operation was to have been commenced as soon as the fleet of men of war should have been discerned. We had before us only two or three English frigates: who can tell what might have happened had the Emperor's orders been executed?*

How was a combination so far-fetched and so long calculated rendered abortive? By these circumstances:—the

---

* The army which would have crossed the strait was that which afterwards fought the Russians and Austrians. If it had not conquered England, as I think it would have done, at any rate it would have brought about a very different sort of peace from what we are accustomed to make with that country.

French and Spanish squadron, consisting of fifteen sail, fell
in, about a hundred leagues off Ferrol, on its return from
America agreeably to its instructions, with the English squadron under Admiral Calder.   The latter had but nine ships,
and probably would not have been there but for the return of
M. de Missiessy to Rochefort: not only did our squadron of
fifteen ships not beat Admiral Calder, but it suffered two of
its number to be taken.   We had the wind: it is said that
the two ships were dismasted, and that they fell into the
English line; but how happened it that our thirteen others
did not follow them?   They would at least have saved their
two ships.   This is what I never could learn.   In consequence of this action the squadron did not appear off Ferrol,
or give notice to Admiral Gourdon, as had been concerted:
the latter of course did not call for the Rochefort squadron,
or for that at Brest.   Here then was an operation thwarted,
in consequence of particular faults and a slight accident.

The Emperor, who stopped the couriers of the minister of
the marine, read the report of this engagement in a dispatch
coming from Bayonne; he shrugged his shoulders in pity on
learning the conduct of his admiral: it was the already unfortunate Villeneuve, and he was dejected the whole day.

What was to be done?   What punishment, what vengeance,
what example, could make amends for a fault which rendered
abortive the efforts and the enormous expenses which he had
been making for two years past?   It was necessary, however,
to be resigned to it, and to devise a new combination for
rallying our squadrons and removing those of the English
which had followed them.   The Emperor meditated the
means of attaining this result, but events of very different
importance supervened to divert his projects.

CHAPTER XII.

Irruption of Austria into Bavaria—Breaking-up of the camp of Boulogne—Mission of Duroc to Prussia—The Emperor of Russia visits Berlin—The Duke of Wurtemberg.

ABSORBED by his expedition against England, the Emperor was far from expecting an aggression on the part of any continental power, when he learned by dispatches from Munich that the Austrian army was marching upon that capital.

Austria, no one knew why, unless it was for the purpose of making war upon us, had collected a considerable army at Wels, under the command of Field-marshal Mack: the pretext for the assemblage of this force was military manœuvres and exercises, but all at once this army broke up and approached Bavaria. .

The Emperor was puzzled to account for this procedure; he had no point in dispute with Austria. That power, it is true, had not recognised the Emperor, but its ambassador had not left Paris.

I am not sure, however, that it had not acknowledged him; for when the Emperor went to Verona, after the coronation at Milan, the Austrian general, Vincent, who commanded the troops of his nation in the Venetian states, came, as I have already related, to pay a personal visit to the Emperor, with all the officers of the troops under his orders; and the Austrian artillery fired the customary salute. This occurred at the end of June; and, according to all appearance, nobody had the least suspicion of what was to happen in the month of September in the same year. The ambassador of France was at Vienna; the Russian ambassador, indeed, had long before left Paris, but we had yet heard nothing of the march of Russian troops except from the newspapers.

The intelligence, however, was of too serious a nature for the Emperor to neglect it, and he was engaged in too important concerns to give them up lightly. He dispatched his aide-de-camps from Boulogne itself to meet the Austrian army; so difficult was it for him to believe the report of such an incredible aggression. General Bertrand was sent on a similar mission in another direction. I pushed on to the Inn; and, agreeably to my instructions, I reconnoitred a different road for returning from Donauwert to Ludwigsburg and the banks of the Rhine, from the ordinary high-road of Wurtemberg: but before his aide-de-camps had got back, the Emperor received information, not to be doubted, of the departure of Mack's army from Wels, and of the entry of the Austrian territory by the Russians. From this iniquitous aggression date the calamities of France. He hesitated no longer what course to pursue: in fact, he had already lost some time from distrust of the veracity of the intelligence received: he caused, therefore, every thing to be landed, and the army to be re-organised for long marches. It accordingly set out by all the shortest routes for the banks of the Rhine, where it arrived at the same time that the Austrian army reached the Danube. The Elector of Bavaria, with his family and his army, had retired to Wurzburg.

The Emperor, before he left Boulogne, had in haste sent orders to the banks of the Rhine to collect draught-horses, and to provide as large a quantity as possible of *materiel* for artillery. We were taken quite unawares; and it required all the activity of the Emperor to supply that army, on the spur of the occasion, with what it needed for the campaign into which it was so suddenly forced.

General Marmont, who was in Holland, had to traverse such countries only, the sovereigns of which have no right to say to a stronger enemy—Why do you pass through my territory? But Bernadotte, who was in Hanover, had part of the Prussian territory to cross; and at the same time that the Emperor sent him orders to march, he dispatched the grand-marshal, Duroc, to Berlin. We were on good terms with Prussia, and in friendly intercourse with its court ; and scarcely two months had elapsed since honorary distinctions had been exchanged between the two countries.

Thus attacked, without declaration of war, the Emperor communicated to the King of Prussia the critical situation in which he was placed by this unexpected aggression : he assured him that he was extremely sorry to be obliged to march his troops over certain portions of the Prussian terri- tory, without any previous negotiation on the subject. He sent his grand-marshal to give him notice of it, and to ex- press his anxious wish that this step might be considered as the result of absolute necessity alone.

Marshal Duroc was received not quite so well as he had been in former missions on which he had been sent to the court of Berlin. The King said little to him concerning the march of Bernadotte : he seemed to be convinced of the validity of the Emperor's motives ; and expressed great regret at seeing him forced into a war, which, however, he had no doubt would terminate to his advantage.

Baron Hardenberg was less moderate : on the 14th of October he presented a very warm note to the grand-mar- shal. " His master," he said, " knew not whether he ought to be more astonished at the violence committed by the French army, or at the motives employed to justify it. Prussia, though she had declared herself neuter, had ful- filled all the obligations which she had contracted : nay, perhaps, she had made sacrifices to France which her duty condemned. And yet, how had the honour and the perse- verance which she had shown in her relations of friendship with France been repaid ? The wars of 1796 and 1800 were adduced, when the margraviates had been open to the bel- ligerent parties ; but exception is no rule ; and besides, at the periods referred to, every thing had been regulated and stipulated by special conventions. They were left in the dark as to our intentions; but intentions sprang from the very nature of things: the protestations of the royal authorities made them known. Matters of this importance required a positive declaration. But what need has he of a declaration who relies on the inviolability of a generally acknowledged system? Is it for him to act, when he who meditates the overthrow of what he has sanctioned abstains from doing so? Unknown facts were cited; wrongs of which they had never been guilty were attributed to the Austrians: what result were such means likely to produce, unless to show in a still stronger light the difference there was between the conduct of the cabinets of Paris and Vienna? The King, however, would not dwell on the consequences with which they were pregnant: he should merely believe that the Emperor of the French had sufficient motives for annulling the engagements which bound them, and consider himself thenceforward as released from every kind of obligation. Thus re-established in a position which imposed upon him no other duties than those enjoined by his safety and justice, the King of Prussia would adhere to the principles which he had never ceased to profess, and would neglect nothing to procure for Europe, by his mediation, that peace which he desired for his subjects; but he declared at the same time that, obstructed every where in his generous intentions, unfettered by engagements, without guarantee for the future, he would provide for the security of his dominions, and set his army in motion."

This declaration was not supported by any direct measure; the grand-marshal continued his stay in Berlin, where he remained nearly a month, during which he witnessed the arrival of the Emperor of Russia, * who repaired to that

---

* I have since had occasion to ascertain that at the time of the assemblage of the Russian troops on their frontier to operate this movement, Russia demanded a

capital upon pretext of going, before he took the field, to visit his sister, the hereditary Princess of Saxe-Weimar. Nobody could mistake the secret motive of this journey. A person would not quit an army on the eve of important operations, for the purpose of paying a visit more than a hundred leagues distant from the country where it is to act. It was evident that he sought to draw Prussia into the coalition.

I cannot tell what was done and said on this occasion; but so much is certain, that while Marshal Duroc was still in Berlin, the Russian army, under the command of General Buxhövden, crossed the Vistula at Warsaw, and marched through Polish Prussia upon Breslau, whence it was to proceed to Bohemia.

The Emperor Napoleon had already calculated and foreseen every thing. The maps of England had disappeared; those of Germany alone were admitted into his cabinet. He made us follow the march of the troops; and one day addressed to us these remarkable words: " If the enemy comes to meet me, I will destroy him before he has repassed the Danube; if he waits 'for me, I will take him between Augsburg and Ulm." He issued the last orders to the navy and to the army, and set out for Paris. As soon as he had arrived there, he repaired to the senate, explained the motives which had obliged him all

---

passage of Prussia; and that the court of Berlin not only refused it, but set in motion an army to oppose the passage. It was during these transactions that Prussia was apprized of the violation of her territory by the corps of Bernadotte. She expressed the same ill-humour, and allowed a passage to the Russians. The Emperor availed himself of this unfavourable disposition to France, and hastened his journey to Berlin to hurry Prussia into his policy.

Ever since that period things have gone worse and worse with that country. This is not the least inconvenience of its geographical position. It will be obliged to remain for a long time to come in the disk of the power by which it is most threatened. Had the French army, instead of being entirely occupied at Boulogne, been able to afford her the certainty of being succoured in time, never would Prussia have deviated from an alliance which was so natural and so necessary to her.

at once to change the direction of our forces, and started next day for Strasburg. He reached that city while the army was passing the Rhine, at Kehl, Lauterburg, Spire, and Manheim. He inspected the establishments of the fortress, and pointed out the means of turning to useful purpose a great number of little resources, the application of which he regulated.

He passed the Rhine himself, after giving orders for the reconstruction of the fort of Kehl and seeing the works begun. He had sent proposals to the Prince of Baden and to the Landgrave of Hesse-Darmstadt to ally themselves with him : the two princes delayed answering. The latter thought to elude the question by disbanding his troops, and by making an official communication of the circumstance to the Emperor, as a proof of his neutrality; but, after the battle of Austerlitz was won, he was in a great hurry to send protestations of his attachment. The officer who had fulfilled the first mission was charged with the second : two very different parts to act at so short an interval.

The court of Baden acted more frankly; its troops had joined ours before the battle.

While the Emperor was occupied with these matters, the different corps of his army approached the foot of the mountains, situated on the right bank of the river, and entered the country of Wurtemberg. He had sent one of his aide-de-camps to the sovereign of that country, to apprize him that he was obliged to pass through his dominions; that he was sorry for it, but hoped the passage would take place without disorder.

The Duke of Wurtemberg, shocked at seeing our troops debouch, had collected his little army near Ludwigsburg, his summer residence, and was preparing to make resistance, when the aide-de-camp of the Emperor appeared. This mark of respect pacified him : he, nevertheless, insisted that no troops should pass through his residence. The Emperor arrived a few moments afterwards : the court of Wurtemberg gave him a magnificent reception ; he slept two nights at the palace of Ludwigsburg. It was during his stay there that hostilities commenced on the road from Stuttgard to Ulm, which the corps of Marshal Ney had taken. The Austrians, commanded by the Archduke Ferdinand, under the direction of Field-marshal Mack, had their head-quarters in the latter of those places.

The Emperor manœuvred on his left, and remained at Ludwigsburg, making Marshal Ney debouch by the high Stuttgard road: the enemy, fully believing that our whole army was following him, manœuvred accordingly. The Emperor, satisfied with having deceived him, moved with the rapidity of lightning to Nordlingen, where at the same time arrived the corps of Marshal Davout, who had come from Manheim by the valley of the Necker to Bettingen; that of Marshal Soult, who had come from Spire by Heilbron; and lastly, that of Marshal Lannes, who, leaving Ludwigsburg on his left, had reached Donauwert at the very moment when an Austrian battalion appeared on the right bank of the Danube to destroy the bridge. These troops were driven back to a distance ; and the whole of the cavalry, and afterwards the infantry, were made to cross the river.

CHAPTER XIII.

Various combats—Manœuvres of the Emperor—The Archduke Ferdinand escapes from Ulm—Marshal Soult takes Memmingen—Answer of Napoleon to Prince Lichtenstein sent with a flag of truce—Marshal Mack capitulates— Plans of the coalition—The Austrian army lays down its arms—Address of the Emperor to the Austrian officers made prisoners.

THE Emperor caused the country to be scoured as far as the Lech, and placed himself in communication with General

Marmont, who debouched by Neuburg, where he had passed
the Danube, and was marching upon Friedberg.   He also
placed himself in communication with the Bavarian army,
which was leaving Ingolstadt with the intention of advancing.
The cavalry fell in with an Austrian corps at Wertingen,
defeated it, and drove back what had escaped it upon Ulm.
The Emperor moved his head-quarters to Zumnershausen,
between Augsburg and Guntzburg.   He ordered Augsburg
to be occupied ; and sent the corps of Marshal Soult upon
the only line of operations left to the enemy, by Memmingen,
a small town, into which he had thrown six thousand
men, whom Marshal Soult blockaded in it.   Desiring
also to place himself in communication with the corps of
Marshal Ney, who had remained on the left bank of the
Danube, he sent orders to him to force the passage of the
river at Guntzburg.

He then went and fixed his head-quarters at Augsburg,*
to observe what course the Austrian army was about to
pursue, and to organise the means of administration and hospitals in that city, which he had been obliged to make the
centre of his operations.   He was there joined by Marmont's
corps, and received intelligence of the march of Bernadotte.
In this manner he found himself in the midst of all his corps
d'armée.   From Augsburg he moved his head-quarters to
Zumnershausen, and caused Ulm to be hemmed in on all
sides.   Not one of us could conceive why the Austrian army
had not come to the resolution of leaving it or of offering us
battle.   It did neither, and waited till it was impossible for it
to avoid us.   It may easily be imagined how many opportunities of extricating itself from the dilemma it might have

---

* It was on this occasion that he became acquainted with the Bishop of Augsburg, formerly Elector of Treves : he conceived an esteem for him, and this Prince
in return became attached to the Emperor, whom he considered as having caused
the bishopric of Augsburg to be given to him, but for which he would have had
no indemnity for the loss of his electorate.

seized, in the immense movement which we had been forced
to make in order to turn it so completely as we did. The
corps which formed the circle in the rear of it had traversed,
from Donauwert, the one hundred and eighty degrees of the
last circumference, to arrive at its position.

These arrangements being made, the Emperor approached
Ulm by Guntzburg. His army had arrived by the right
bank of the Danube within sight of Ulm, when he learned
that a very strong detachment had escaped from the place, and
was proceeding along the left bank by forced marches toward
Bohemia. At the same time he received intelligence that
one of the divisions of the corps of Marshal Ney, under the
command of General Dupont, which was closing Ulm in by
the left bank, had been forced in the position which it occupied, and had not been strong enough to oppose the sortie of
a very large Austrian corps which had taken the road to
Nordlingen. He conjectured for a moment that the enemy's
whole army was about to take that direction, and immediately
manoeuvred in such a manner as to harass the Austrian corps
with his cavalry. The latter recrossed the Danube, and
marched with such celerity, that every day it overtook and
dispersed some fragments of that corps which was commanded
by the Archduke Ferdinand. Worn out by an incessant
pursuit, the enemy sought to escape us by stratagem. It
made overtures, and affected a wish to treat; but it was
perceived that its only object was to gain time. It was
charged, and driven fighting into the mountains of Bohemia.

At the same time that the Emperor sent his cavalry in
pursuit of the Archduke Ferdinand, he caused Ulm to be
more closely invested. He ordered the passage from the
right to the left bank to be forced at Elchingen. It so happened that the very same day a second column left the place
and took the direction of the village. The bridge, though
very bad, was not destroyed. The part of Marshal Ney's
corps which was on the right bank went to meet it, and over-

threw and drove it back into Ulm. It was this part which a few days before had forced the passage of the Danube, in order to cross from the left bank to Guntzburg on the right.

That division, out of the six which had been sent in pursuit of the Archduke Ferdinand, continued to descend the left bank of the Danube. The corps of Marshal Lannes was ordered to support Marshal Ney, and also crossed the bridge. The same evening the two corps slept on the crest of the heights which overlook Ulm on the left bank, while Marmont approached it on the right. The Emperor on his part took post at Elchingen, and then Bohemia was ours.

Next day we drove back into the place all the troops that the enemy's army had outside it : his very posts were driven in. He remained in this situation four days without making any proposal. During this interval Marshal Soult took Memmingen with its garrison of six thousand men. This intelligence reached the Emperor in a wretched bivouac, which was so wet that it was necessary to seek a plank for him to keep his feet out of the water. He had just received this capitulation, when Prince Maurice Lichtenstein, whom Marshal Mack had sent with a flag of truce, was announced. He was led forward on horseback with his eyes covered. When he had arrived, he was presented to the Emperor. The look which escaped him proved that he did not imagine he was there. He admitted that Marshal Mack had no notion of his presence. He came to treat for the evacuation of Ulm. The army which occupied it demanded permission to return to Austria. To be impartial, without at the same time ceasing to be a patriot, I must confess that, during the course of the war, the enemy's generals have always thought to outwit ours wherever the Emperor happened not to be.

The Emperor could not forbear smiling, and said, " What reason have I to comply with this demand? In a week you will be in my power, without condition. You expect the Russian army, which is scarcely in Bohemia yet ; and besides, if I let you go, what guarantee have I that your troops will not be made to serve when once they are united with the Russians. I have not forgotten Marengo. I suffered M. de Melas to go; and Moreau had to fight his troops at the end of two months, in spite of the most solemn promises to treat for peace. Besides, there are no laws of war to appeal to, after such conduct as that of your government towards me. Most assuredly I have not sought you; and then again I cannot rely on any of the engagements into which your general might enter with me, because it will depend on himself alone to keep his word. It would be a different thing if you had one of your princes in Ulm, and he were to bind himself: I would take his word, because he would be responsible for it, and would not allow it to be dishonoured; but I believe the Archduke is gone."

Prince Maurice replied in the best manner he could, and protested that without the conditions which he demanded the army would not leave the place. " I shall not grant them," rejoined the Emperor · " there is the capitulation of your general who commanded at Memmingen; carry it to Marshal Mack, and whatever may be your resolutions in Ulm, I will never grant him any other terms. Besides, I am in no hurry: the longer he delays, the worse he will render his own situation and that of you all.* For the rest, I shall have the corps which took Memmingen here to-morrow, and we shall then see."

Prince Lichtenstein was conducted back to Ulm. The same evening Marshal Mack wrote a very respectful letter to the Emperor, in which he intimated that the consolation which was left him in his misfortune was that of being obliged to treat with him: assuring him that no other person should

---

* According to the capitulation of Memmingen, the officers returned home. It was hinted to Prince Maurice that in case of delay on the part of General Mack, this favour would not be granted.

ever have made him accept such mortifying conditions; but since fortune would have it so, he awaited his orders.

Next morning the Emperor sent Berthier to Ulm with instructions, and still remained himself at his wretched bivouac, that he might be at hand to answer objections should any be started. Berthier returned in the evening with the capitulation, by which the whole army surrendered itself. It was to march out with the honours of war, file off before the French army, lay down its arms, and set out for France. The generals and officers alone had permission to return home, on condition of not serving till a complete exchange.

For the eight days we had passed before Ulm it had rained incessantly: all at once the rain ceased, and the Austrian army filed off in the finest weather imaginable.

The Emperor went to pass the two days allowed as stipulated, between the signature of the capitulation and its execution, at the abbey of Elchingen, where Marshal Mack paid him a visit; he kept him a long time, and made him talk a great deal. It was in this interview that he learned all the circumstances which had preceded the resolution of the Austrian cabinet to make war upon him. He was made acquainted with all the springs which the Russians had set to work to decide it; and lastly, with the plans of the coalition. Their object was nothing less than to wrest from France all the conquests of the revolution; and, to arrive at that result, they were resolved to employ any means—war, division, internal intrigues; and, in short, so confident were they of success, that they had not hesitated to allot Lyons to the king of Sardinia.

Such disclosures would have appeared the follies of a morbid brain or the ravings of a maniac, had they not issued from the lips of a field-marshal, whose situation had initiated him in the greater part of the measures of his government. The Emperor could not divert his thoughts from the subject: he needed this confidence to soothe his mind, and to account for a multitude of petty intrigues, which he remarked without guessing their aim. He could not conceive how it happened that though he had ministers every where, he should have known nothing of all this. He then comprehended the attempts against his life, the projects of Drake, and other matters of that kind; but he could not conceive how a monarch could be so destitute of understanding as to lend himself to such extravagancies. Such, nevertheless, was the fact: the Emperor was affected by it, as he sometimes testified to us; but these plans seemed so insane that he concerned himself but little about them. They were, nevertheless, but postponed by our victories: the coalesced powers realized them in a great measure, as soon as success furnished them with the means.

The Emperor treated General Mack extremely well, and strove to make him forget his misfortune: he ordered General Mathieu Dumas to accompany him back to Ulm, having directed that general to arrange the enemy's columns which were to march out on the following day. The day of that painful ceremony for the Austrian army arrived. Our army was drawn up in order of battle on the heights; the troops being admirably clean, and their dress and appointments in the best state that their situation permitted.

The drums beat—the bands played; the gates of Ulm opened; the Austrian army advanced in silence, filed off slowly, and went, corps by corps, to lay down its arms on a spot which had been prepared to receive them.

This day, so mortifying to the Austrians, put into our power 36,000 men; 6000 had been taken in Memmingen, and about 2000 at the battle of Wertingen. If to this be added what fell into our hands in the battle of Elchingen, and in the pursuit of the Archduke, we shall find that there is no exaggeration in estimating the total loss of the Austrian army at 50,000 men, 70 pieces of cannon, and about 3500 horses, which served to mount a division of dragoons which had come from

Boulogne on foot. The ceremony occupied the whole day. The Emperor was posted on a little hill in front of the centre of his army : a great fire had been lighted, and by this fire he received the Austrian generals to the number of seventeen ; among whom were Marshal Mack, commander-in-chief, Klenau, Giulay, Jellachich, Maurice Lichtenstein, Godesheim, and Fresnel : the two latter were French officers, and had emigrated with the regiment of the hussars of Saxony. I do not recollect the names of the others. They were all very dull ; it was the Emperor who kept up the conversation. He said to them among other things, " It is a pity that such brave men as you, whose names are honourably mentioned wherever you have fought, should be the victims of the follies of a cabinet which dreams of nothing but insane schemes, and is not ashamed to compromise the dignity of the state and nation by trafficking with the services of those who are destined to defend it. It is of itself an iniquitous proceeding to come, without any declaration of war, to seize me by the throat ; but it is being criminal towards one's own subjects to bring upon them a foreign invasion ; it is betraying Europe to mix up Asiatic hordes in our quarrels. Instead of attacking me without motive, the Aulic council should have allied itself with me to repel the Russian army. What a monstrous thing for history is this alliance of your cabinet ! It cannot be the work of statesmen of your nation : it is, in short, the alliance of the dogs and the shepherds with the wolves against the sheep. Supposing France had succumbed in this struggle, you would very soon have perceived the fault which you had committed."

This conversation was not lost upon all : none of them, however, made any reply.

A circumstance occurred there, in the presence of the Austrian generals, which exceedingly displeased the Emperor.

A general officer, who piques himself on his wit, repeated

aloud an expression which he put into the mouth of one of the soldiers of his *corps d'armée.*

He was passing before their ranks he said, and had addressed them in these words: " Well, soldiers; here's plenty of prisoners."—" Very true, general," replied one of them; we never saw so many *j . . .)f . . . . .* together before."

The Emperor, whose ears caught up every thing, heard this story: he was highly displeased, and sent one of his aide-de-camps to tell that general-officer to retire; saying to us in a low tone, " He must have little respect for himself who insults men so unfortunate."

<hr />

CHAPTER XIV.

March of the Russian army—Entry into Braunau—Return of Duroc from his mission to Berlin—General Giulay sent to Napoleon by the Emperor of Austria—Occupation of Vienna—Action at Krems—Surprise of the bridge of the Tabor — General arrangements — Napoleon examines the ground where he intends to give battle.

THE Emperor returned to Elchingen, slept there, and next day set out for Augsburg, where he lodged at the bishop's. Here he remained during the time requisite for organising a new combination of marches, and then departed.

He had learned, in such a manner as to be nearly certain, that the Russians were approaching. Travellers from Lintz had seen the first troops of that nation enter the town; as fast as they arrived, they placed themselves in carts and waggons collected before-hand, and set out post for Bavaria: this haste was probably the result of the intelligence received by Kutusow, the commander-in-chief, that we had passed the Rhine. It was not long before he was apprized of the events which had taken place at Ulm, and changed his plans.

From Augsburg the Emperor went to Munich: he there received all the Bavarian authorities, and promised not to forget their country in the treaty of peace.

The Elector had not yet returned to his capital; but he had not omitted to give orders that the reception of the Emperor should be suitable and proportionate to the advantages which Bavaria derived from the first success of the campaign. The Bavarians expressed their gratitude by illuminations; and though the city was full of French soldiers, no complaints were heard. It was not possible, however, but that some excesses should be committed.

Our army crossed the Iser over all the bridges, from that of Munich to that at Plading, and approached the Inn.

The Emperor, with a large portion of the army, took the road to Mühldorf: the first Russian troops had advanced as far as that place, and returned, after they were apprized of what had befallen Marshal Mack.

Beyond Mühldorf we found not a single bridge that we had not to rebuild entirely: the Russians burned them in a manner that was till then unknown to us; so that we were obliged to send on with the advanced-guard companies of sappers, together with engineers, who had plenty to do.

From Mühldorf the Emperor proceeded to Burkhausen, and, then to Braunau. It was believed that there was a garrison in that place; but to our great surprise we found the gates open, the fortifications in very good condition, well palisaded, artillery on the ramparts, and the magazines full of provisions. The bridge over the Inn was burned. Two thousand men in this place would have done us a great deal of injury, because they would have obliged us to blockade them, and to derange all the directions of our communications; which would have been a great inconvenience to us, as the season had become very wet.

The Emperor judged that people must have lost their senses to commit such faults, and ordered the rebuilding of the bridge to be set about immediately. He was always on horseback whatever weather it might be, travelling in his carriage only when his army was two or three marches in advance: this was a calculation on his part. The point where he was always entered into his combinations, and to him distances were nothing; he traversed them with the swiftness of the eagle.

He stayed but one night at Braunau, and took the road to Lintz: the army was nearly collected. He marched cautiously, so that he might be able to manœuvre and to be every where himself: he proceeded therefore by short marches to Lintz.

We followed the track of the Russians; but the repair of the bridges took us so much time that they gained upon us.

The bridge of Lintz was burned; the Emperor ordered it to be rebuilt: he made infantry cross to the left bank, and, as he animated every thing by his presence, it was not long before the cavalry also was enabled to cross.

It was pushed forward on the roads to Bohemia; and two divisions of infantry, under the command of Marshal Mortier, were marched to support it. The Emperor made these dispositions, because he was apprehensive lest the Russians should cloak their retreat from him by crossing the Danube unawares; and as he was stopped at every step by the breaking-down of the bridges, he conceived the idea of marching troops along both sides of the river, since the corps which was descending the left bank, not having the same obstacles to encounter, might easily keep close upon the Russians, and consequently oblige them to seek a passage further off.

In this town the Emperor received a visit from the Elector of Bavaria, who, having arrived at Munich after his departure, had hurried away to pay his respects, and brought his eldest son along with him: they both dined with the Emperor, and returned to Munich.

Marshal Duroc, dispatched, as I have already mentioned, to the King of Prussia, before the departure from Boulogne, likewise joined the Emperor in that town. He brought back nothing satisfactory from his mission: but at least he gave the assurance that the conduct of the cabinet of Berlin would be governed by events, or, in other words, that we should have to fight that power if fortune proved unfavourable to us. The Emperor thought that the events at Ulm had caused it to make reflections; but concluded that we had nothing solidly fixed in Berlin.

At Lintz the Emperor received intelligence from the army of Italy, under the command of Marshal Massena; it had crossed the Adige, and attacked the army of the Archduke Charles in the position of Caldiero: the action, though indecisive, was very sanguinary; the Archduke however retired, probably because he knew of the march of the Emperor upon Vienna.

There came to Lintz a flag of truce from the Emperor of Austria: it was General Giulay, who had been included in the capitulation of Ulm. He had seen our army on that occasion, and had given an account of it at Vienna. The monarchy was seriously endangered, notwithstanding the resources which it still possessed: it had need to gain time to bring together the army of the Archduke and the Russian army, and wished to unite them by the bridge of Vienna. Had it been able to effect this junction, it would have found itself in a respectable situation.

General Giulay came, in consequence, to bring assurances of the pacific intentions of his sovereign, and to propose an armistice. The Emperor replied that he desired nothing more than to make peace, but that negotiations might be opened without suspending the course of operations. He observed to General Giulay that he was not furnished with any powers on the part of the Russians, who would therefore have a right to disregard the armistice; he desired him to go and put matters into a regular train, and dismissed him.

He left Lintz, and took the road for Vienna. He arrived at St. Pölten, where he was detained a day or two by an accident which had befallen the corps of Marshal Mortier, on the left bank of the Danube; one of his two divisions had got considerably in advance of the other, and pushed on to Krems: apprized of this circumstance, the Russian army made its dispositions and marched towards us; it attacked the French division, to which it was incomparably superior in number, enveloped it, inflicted on it severe losses, and would infallibly have destroyed it, had not the second division come to its relief. The Russians took from us three eagles: these were the first that we lost.

This little check threw the Emperor into an ill-humour, and caused him to stay twenty-four hours longer at St. Pölten. General Giulay, who had already been to receive his instructions, rejoined him in that town. He was more urgent than on the former occasion, for the evil was becoming worse; but he was not more regular, so that he met with no better reception. Austria was evidently solicitous to save Vienna, and to gain time: there would have been nothing but danger for us to grant what she demanded.

The troops set out from St. Pölten for Vienna: Marshals Lannes and Murat had entered that capital. They effected a surprise, which had so powerful an influence on the rest of the campaign, that it cannot be passed in silence.

General Giulay had not yet returned to the advanced posts of the Austrians, when our troops entered Vienna. The report of an armistice was circulated there by our enemies themselves: it was known that General Giulay was still with the Emperor. For a fortnight past he had been seen continually going and coming. As he had not returned, the rumour of the armistice acquired plausibility. The Austrians, placed on the left bank of the Danube, had made the necessary dispositions for burning the bridge of the Tabor, and had merely covered it by a post of hussars.

Marshals Lannes and Murat, wishing to save this medium of crossing so essential to the army, went themselves, accompanied by a few officers, to the Austrian post, where they repeated all the rumours that were afloat respecting the armistice. The commandant of the post took them for mere officers ; they walked about with him, and led him upon the bridge itself, which is of very great length. Some Austrian officers belonging to the troops on the other side, that is, on the left bank, came and joined in the conversation. Marshal Lannes' column of grenadiers, headed by an intelligent officer. took advantage of the moment when they had their faces turned toward the left bank. It had advanced through the streets of the suburbs of Vienna, which are in the island of the Prater; it prevented the vedettes of the hussars from turning about to give the alarm : the French officer told them that it was a post which he was going to place on the bank of the river ; they believed him, gave no warning to their post, which all at once saw soldiers debouching in its rear, and the head of the column at the entrance of the main bridge. The Austrian hussars of this main-guard not seeing their officer, who was on the bridge with Marshals Lannes and Murat, and besides having their heads full of the ideas of an armistice, stirred not a step. The column of grenadiers moving in double quick time entered upon the bridge, and hastily gained the other bank, after throwing into the water all the fireworks prepared for destroying the bridge.

The Austrian officers perceived the fault which they had committed ; but it was too late : and their gunners, who were at their pieces on the other bank, not aware of what was passing before their faces, durst not fire, because they saw their own officers on the bridge in conversation with ours. They suffered the column to come up to them ; and soon saw their cannon, themselves, and all that was there taken.

Never was surprise better executed, and never had it a more important result. The junction of the Russian army with that which the Archduke was bringing from Italy was thenceforward impracticable.

The army advanced from all points upon Vienna : it crossed the Danube, and marched on by the road to Znaim, to come up with the Russians, who had repassed the Danube at Stein.

This surprise of the bridge of the Tabor gave the Emperor great pleasure. He moved his head-quarters to the palace of Schönbrunn, and made preparations to manœuvre with all his forces, either upon the Russians or upon the Archduke Charles, according as either the one or the other should be within reach.

The army of General Kutusow, which had recrossed the Danube at Stein, was marching by Znaim to rejoin the main Russian army at Olmütz, where the Emperor Alexander was. If that general, instead of repassing the Danube, had come and occupied Vienna, he would have given quite a different aspect to affairs. His reason for not doing so was —at least it is believed to have been—because he was afraid that the corps of Marshal Davout, which marched on our right, would descend from the mountains of Tyrol, after having beaten and dispersed the Austrian corps of General Meerfeld, and contrive to enter Vienna before him, which might have been the case ; but had he adopted this resolution at the time of his departure from Lintz, and marched, nothing would have stopped him.

In the magazines and arsenals of Vienna were · found artillery and ammunition enough for two campaigns : we had no further occasion to draw upon our stores at Strasburg or Metz, but could, on the contrary, dispatch a considerable *materiel* to those two great establishments.

Vienna was now the Emperor's capital, and the source of all his means. The march of all the convoys became more rapid on this account.

The occupation of Vienna, and the surprise of the great bridge of the Tabor, changed the situation of affairs. The Archduke Charles was obliged to throw himself on the right, and to gain Hungary: to lengthen the way for him, troops were immediately marched upon Presburg, which removed to a much greater distance the point at which he could have placed himself in contact with the Russians.

The Emperor stationed in Vienna the corps of Marshal Mortier, and outside, to watch the roads to Italy and Hungary, the corps of General Marmont; which made together four divisions.

Marshal Ney had remained in the country of Salzburg before Kuffstein, which had a strong garrison.

All these troops would have been the first employed, had it been more advantageous or more urgent to act against the Archduke Charles. The Emperor expressed some dissatisfaction that Marshal Massena did not march in such a manner as to be able to join him, at the same time that the Archduke should have it in his power to join the Russians, which he thought he might have done. The Emperor never would imagine that, where he was not, zeal though the same frequently had obstacles to encounter in the hierarchy of subordinates. The fact is, that the arrival of Marshal Massena would have given him extreme pleasure ; but he was obliged to manœuvre in such a manner as to be able to dispense with him.

After making his dispositions on the right bank, he set out for Znaim, taking with him the rest of the army. On the very day of his departure, our advanced-guard, under the command of Marshals Lannes and Murat, overtook the rear-guard of the Russian corps of General Kutusow : it was at Hollabrunn that the action took place. From the time which had elapsed since the Russians recrossed the Danube, they ought to have been at a great distance ; but, in short, there they were found. The affair was warm : they behaved like brave soldiers, and we like men who had long been seeking them. General Oudinot was wounded on this occasion. We afterwards learned that the enemy's force consisted of the division of Prince Bagration alone; it had a great number killed: we, on our part, had three brigades employed.

The Russians continued to retreat upon Znaim, and we to pursue them with all our means.

The Emperor had ordered the corps of Marshal Davout to march upon Vienna by the road of Nicolsburg.

Ever since we had been in the line of retreat of the Russians, we might have tracked them by their stragglers and their sick. Their soldiers, who entered the lists for the first time, had a look of stupidity, which rendered them anything but formidable to ours. It was easy to see how many things were deficient in the mechanism of that army, which has since learned a great deal.

At Znaim the Emperor was informed that the Russian army had marched by the road to Brunn, and he made his army take the same road.

In that city he was joined by Marshal Bernadotte's four regiments of light cavalry, which were commanded by General Kellermann; they arrived by the Budweis road, and had left Bernadotte* and his corps at Iglau in Bohemia. The Bavarian infantry had gone with him; and the cavalry of the same nation was sent to him to replace that of Kellermann.

This Bavarian cavalry, commanded by General Wrede, was worn out with fatigue: it had been marched about in all irections; but, as it approached the theatre of more important operations, the Archduke Ferdinand, whom it was pursuing from Ulm in that direction of Bohemia, was no longer the object which engaged the most attention.

The Emperor set out from Znaim for Brunn. He had given the command of the united grenadiers to Marshal

* It has been stated above that he had been sent from the environs of Ingolstadt against the Archduke Ferdinand, to prevent his junction with the main army by Bohemia.

Duroc, being desirous that he should distinguish himself during the campaign.   General Oudinot had been conveyed wounded to Vienna.

On his arrival at Brunn, the Emperor found the citadel evacuated, the magazines full of stores, and, from a negligence which is beyond conception, ammunition ready prepared so that we might make immediate use of it.   The Austrian functionaries delivered all this to us with such fidelity, that one would have supposed that they had received orders to do so.

The same evening the Emperor pushed all the cavalry on the road to Olmütz, and followed himself.   At the first post on that road we fell in with the enemy's rear-guard.   The Russian cavalry bravely charged all that pursued it, and would have kept up a running fight, had not the horse-grenadiers of the guard, who were there, cut this Russian line in two.   The cuirassiers completed the dispersion of the other part, which was closely followed by our light troops.

It was dark before this warm affair was over.   The Emperor returned to Brunn, and came next day upon the ground where it had occurred to place his army, which was coming up in different directions.   He moved on his cavalry of the advanced-guard to Vichau; he went thither himself, and on his return he walked his horse over all the sinuosities and undulations of the ground situated in front of the position which he had ordered to be taken.   He paused at every height, had the distances measured, and frequently said to us, " Gentlemen, examine the ground well; you will have a part to act upon it."   It was the same on which the battle of Austerlitz was fought, and which was occupied by the Russians, that is, the position which they had before the battle. He passed the whole day on horseback, inspected the position of each of the corps of his army, and remarked, on the left of General Suchet's division, a single hillock, overlooking the whole front of that division.   The Centon was there, as if for the express purpose; here he caused to be placed the same night fourteen Austrian pieces of cannon, part of those found at Brunn. As caissons could not be placed there, two hundred charges of powder were piled up behind each of them: the foot of the Centon was then cut away *en escarpement*, so as to secure it from assault. The Emperor returned to sleep at Brunn.

CHAPTER XV.

Fresh envoys fiom the Emperor of Austria—Defeat off Trafalgar—Mission to the Russian head-quarters—The Emperor Alexandei—Long conference with that sovereign—His views and plans—M. de Novosilzow—Return to the French camp—Fresh mission to the Emperor of Russia—Prince Dolgorouki is sent to the Emperor Napoleon.

AFTER the occupation of Vienna and the affair of Hollabrunn, the Emperor was strongly solicited by all about him to make peace: he was himself disposed to do so; but the Russians were in presence, and it was first requisite to measure his strength with them.

Next day two envoys arrived from the Emperor of Austria: one of them was M. de Stadion; the name of the other I do not recollect, but I believe it was General Giulay again. The Emperor received them, and no doubt spoke to them concerning his intentions; but, as these gentlemen came to treat once more for Austria alone, announcing that the Emperor of Russia would himself send some one immediately for what concerned him, the Emperor Napoleon, who absolutely insisted that this power should be comprehended in the treaty, as he had previously intimated, dismissed them.

M. de Talleyrand had received orders to come to Vienna; of which General Clarke had been appointed governor.

The Emperor referred the Austrian deputies to him, and

gave some particular instructions respecting them to General Clarke, after which he continued his military operations.

He had already been several days at Brunn, when he ordered the corps of Bernadotte to draw nearer. He had a peculiar tact for feeling the approach of any event, which enabled him to turn it as best suited himself.

He sent for me at day-break : he had passed the night over his maps; his candles were burnt down to the sockets : he held a letter in his hand; he was silent for some moments, and then abruptly said to me, " Be off to Olmütz ; deliver this letter to the Emperor of Russia, and tell him that, having heard of his arrival at his army, I have sent you to salute him in my name. If he questions you," added he, " you know what answer ought to be given under such circumstances." *

I left the Emperor, and proceeded to our advanced posts at Vichau, where I took a trumpeter, and repaired to those of

---

* The Emperor had received intelligence of the disastrous sea-fight off Trafalgar.

Admiral Villeneuve, after his action with Admiral Calder, had called for the Ferrol squadron, and sailed with it to Cadiz. The Emperor had no doubt ordered the minister of the marine to take from him the command of his fleets; for the latter sent Admiral Rosilly to supersede him. He apprized Villeneuve of this by a courier : whether he added any reproaches I know not ; but something of the kind must have passed, since Villeneuve quitted Cadiz without occasion, with the French and Spanish fleet, to attack the English squadron commanded by Nelson.

The engagement took place off Cape Trafalgar. We had thirty or thirty-one ships in all. The English had not more than thirty-two or thirty-three, and yet we were not only beaten but destroyed : the result was that we lost eighteen ships ; the rest got back to Cadiz. Admiral Nelson, indeed, fell in the engagement; but that had nothing to do with the honour of arms. Villeneuve was taken prisoner, and carried to England.

The Spanish admiral, Gravina, was wounded, and died in consequence. Admiral Dumanoir, who commanded four ships of reserve, was severely censured for having struck without fighting : it was alleged that if he had attacked he might have retrieved matters : he was tried by a council of war and acquitted, as it was customary.

the Russians, only about a league distant from ours on the road to Olmütz.

I found that we were far advanced at Vichau, and out of our natural line; but the officers who were there could not help being aware of it, and keeping upon their guard. I pursued my route.

I was detained at the first post of Cossacks, till notice could be given to Prince Bagration, who commanded the Russian advanced-guard: he sent Prince Trubetskoi to receive me, and to conduct me to him. From the advanced-guard I was taken to Olmütz to Kutusow, the commander-in-chief: this little journey was performed at night, through the whole Russian army, which I saw assembling and taking arms at day-break.

I arrived at General Kutusow's at eight in the morning; he lodged in the suburbs of Olmütz: every thing was packing at his house; and I saw plainly that he was preparing to follow the movement of his army. He asked me for the dispatch which I had brought for the Emperor Alexander; observing that he slept in the fortress, and that the gates could not be opened to me. I replied that I had orders to deliver it myself; that I was not in a hurry, and would wait till the hour most convenient to the Emperor; that if this could not be permitted, I begged him to let me be conducted back to our advanced posts, and the Emperor Napoleon would afterwards send the letter by a trumpeter. General Kutusow did not insist, and went away, leaving me with an officer of his staff.

I saw there a great number of young Russians, belonging to the different ministerial departments of their country, who talked wildly of the ambition of France;* and all of whom, in their plans for reducing her to a state of harmlessness, made

---

* The French might now talk with much stronger reason of the ambition of Russia.

much the same kind of calculations as the maid with her pail of milk.

From the nature of my situation, I was obliged to listen to all this idle gossip without replying. It was ten in the forenoon when a bustle took place in the street. I inquired the cause of it, and was answered, " It is the Emperor himself." He stopped before the house where I was, alighted, and entered: I had but just time to throw off my cloak, and to take my dispatch out of my pocket-book, before he was in the room where I had been waiting.

He made a motion for all present to retire, and we were left alone. I could not help feeling a certain fear and timidity on finding myself in the presence of that sovereign; he awed me by the majesty and nobleness of his look. Nature had done much for him; and it would have been difficult to find a model so perfect and so graceful: he was then twenty-six years old. I felt regret at seeing him engaged in so bad a business as that of Austria then was; but I was aware too of all the facilities possessed by intrigue to influence a mind, that could not yet have sufficient experience to grasp all the difficulties which existed, for conducting to a successful issue all that was on the political horizon of Europe in the winter of that year, 1805. I delivered to him my letter, saying, that " the Emperor, my master, having been informed of his arrival at the army, had ordered me to carry to him that dispatch, and to salute him in his name." Alexander was already somewhat hard of hearing with the left ear, and he turned the right to hear what was said to him.

He spoke in broken sentences : he laid great stress upon his finals, so that his discourse was never long. For the rest, he spoke the French language in all its purity, without foreign accent, and always used its elegant academic expressions. As there was no affectation in his language, it was easy to judge that this was one of the results of an excellent education.

The Emperor, taking the letter, said to me, " I duly appreciate the proceeding of your master ; it is with regret that I have armed against him, and I shall seize with great pleasure the opportunity of giving him that assurance. He has long been the object of my admiration."

Then, changing the subject, he said to me, " I will go and peruse his letter, and bring you an answer to it."

He went into another room, and left me in that where I was. In half an hour he returned, and holding his answer, with the address turned downward, he thus began :—

" Sir, you will tell your master that the sentiments expressed in his letter have given me great pleasure ; I will do all that lies in my power to return them. I have no wish to be his enemy, or that of France. He must recollect that in the time of the late Emperor Paul, while I was yet but grand-duke, when the affairs of France were thwarted, and had to encounter opposition in most of the cabinets of Europe, I interfered, and greatly contributed, by causing Russia to speak out, to induce by her example all the other powers of Europe to recognise the order of things which had been established in your country. If at this moment I am swayed by other sentiments, it is because France has adopted different principles, which the leading powers of Europe have deemed dangerous to their tranquillity. I am called upon by them to concur in establishing a more suitable order of things, and which shall be satisfactory to all. It is to attain this aim that I have left my own country. You have been admirably served by fortune, it must be confessed ; but, as a faithful ally, I will not desert the King of the Romans (meaning the Emperor of Germany) at a moment when his future existence depends upon me. He is in a bad situation ; but it is not yet irremediable. I command brave men ; and if your master compels me, I shall order them to do their duty."

Answer. Sire, I shall not fail to remember the message

which your Majesty has just done me the honour to deliver to me. I take the liberty to observe, however, that I am not here in any character, nor have I any other mission than to bring a letter; but your Majesty speaks to me of events and circumstances with which I am acquainted. I have passed through the revolution of my country; and if your Majesty would deign to listen to me on the subject concerning which you have done me the honour to speak to me, I could satisfy your Majesty on many points. I think I can answer for it that the Emperor is more than inclined to peace: this very proceeding of his might furnish evidence to that effect, independently of all that I should advance in support of it,

The Emperor. You are right; but the proposals which preceded it ought by right to have been conformable with the sentiments which have dictated this step. It does the greatest honour to his moderation; but does it argue a wish for peace to propose conditions so disastrous to a state as those which are offered to the King of the Romans? I perceive you are not acquainted with them.

Answer. No, Sire; but I have heard of them.

The Emperor. Well, if you know what they are, you must admit that they are not such as can be accepted.

Answer. Sire, respect here imposes upon me a duty which I fulfil; but since your Majesty condescends to listen to me, I have the honour to remark, that the Emperor demands nothing that is beyond the pretensions which he is able to support, and which are the result of a resolution induced by events that he has not provoked. He considered himself as being in profound peace, especially with Austria; he was completely absorbed by the preparations for his expedition against England: he has been suddenly diverted from this occupation, obliged to relinquish the enormous expenses which it has cost him, and to order new ones for the support of a war begun against him without any previous declaration; so that, but for an accident which has befallen one of our fleets, our army might very possibly have been in England by the time that the Austrians appeared' on the Rhine. Fortune crowns the efforts of the Emperor, and puts him in possession of all the resources of the Austrian monarchy. His army has as yet sustained but insignificant losses. In this situation, what has he to fear from the consequences of the war? Should it be protracted, it cannot but augment his power. Admitting that he may lose a battle, it would not be productive of any very calamitous consequence to him. Vienna is at this moment his capital: his army has now nothing to do with the frontier of France. But, Sire, if Austria sustains a defeat, what may be its results? On what basis will she set on foot negotiations? If then, in this situation, the Emperor is ·the first to make overtures of peace, it is impossible to suspect their sincerity. He has thought it right to take the first step, in order to spare the dignity of his adversary; but he wants a durable peace with good guarantees.

The Emperor. It is precisely for the purpose of obtaining a durable peace that reasonable conditions, such as are not offensive, should be proposed: without this, it cannot be durable.

Answer. Yes, Sire; but war must not be made at his expense. Your Majesty will be pleased to consider what the Emperor sacrifices by his departure from Boulogne; what an opportunity he loses for putting an end to the war with England; the time uselessly employed; and lastly, Sire, the fleet which he has just lost, in consequence of all this. What would the nation say, were it not to see some compensations for the inutility of all the sacrifices which have been imposed upon it for an operation, the success of which was bound up with its existence? And then what guarantee for the duration of this peace will be given to him beyond what had been given for the duration of the preceding, which nevertheless has been broken in a manner hitherto without a parallel?

To me it seems that whatever peace the Emperor may make with Austria, the allies alone will be gainers by it; and that, for his part, he will always come off with real losses: the only advantage that he can derive from it is the diminution of the power of his enemy.

The Emperor. It is precisely this disposition to diminish the power of his enemies and to increase his own that alarms every body, and is continually exciting wars against him. You are already a nation so strong of yourselves, by your union under the same laws, by the uniformity of your habits and your language, that you naturally inspire terror. What need have you to be continually aggrandizing yourselves?

Answer. I know not what your Majesty means by our continual aggrandizements; for, with the exception of Genoa, I am not aware that we have acquired an acre of land beyond what has been ceded and recognised by our treaties of peace, which we have been obliged twice to seal with our blood. If it is to this point that the allies would revert, here is an account to be opened afresh, though this first quarrel of the revolution, in which we were not the aggressors, has been settled in so many fields of battle: we shall not be afraid to appear in them again. I see nothing but Genoa that we have acquired since the treaty of Luneville.

The Emperor. Genoa first, and then Italy, to which you have given a form of government that subjects it to your laws.

Answer. To this, Sire, I may reply, that we took Genoa against our will.

The Emperor. What obliged you to do so?

Answer. Its position, and its moral and physical situation. Your Majesty would be mistaken, were you to suppose that this annexation originated in motives of interest or ambition.

Genoa has long possessed nothing but its marble palaces:

that little republic has long subsisted solely on capitals acquired by a commerce formerly considerable, but since nearly annihilated, through the weakness of a government which could no longer protect its navigation even against the states of Barbary : in this respect it was in the same predicament as Venice.

Before we entered Italy, Genoa had nothing left but its name and its ancient reputation : its port had become useless to it from the blockades of the English, whose ships we had excluded from it. Its territory, too, was next to nothing, compared with the wants of its population; and as our custom-houses bordered its frontier, the Genoese were on all sides beset with difficulties.

Add to this, that the excellence of its port and the extent of its fortifications drew to it a foreign garrison, which was sent thither by the principal power the moment a war broke out in Italy.

Placed thus amidst all the inconveniences of its position, and having none of the advantages of the protection of a great power, it could do no other than either consummate its ruin, or throw itself into the arms of a protector. I ask your Majesty, whom could it have chosen to obviate the inconveniences which I have mentioned ?

We have taken Genoa with its active and its passive : this latter was superior to the other. A burden for the public treasury has consequently been the result.

Had the annexation of Genoa been a calculation of ambition, it would not have been so long delayed; because it is easy to perceive what is most advantageous for ourselves. Formerly, in our different transactions with Austria, we were in a position to insist on this stipulation, which she could not have obliged us to renounce.

With respect to Italy, I have a still stronger argument. It is entirely our conquest : we have moistened it with our blood ; it has twice recovered its liberty and its political existence by our efforts. If it set out with a republican form, it was that it might harmonize with the protecting power. The two changes which have since taken place are a consequence of the interest which associated it with our destinies. It has the same laws, the same usages, and the same administrative regulations, as France. We have reciprocally communicated to each other so much of our habits as we conceived ought to be adopted; and if Italy finally resolved to place herself under the protection of a monarchical government, as France had just done, ought she not to choose a powerful monarch, of whose support a new state always stands in need? In this case she had no option but between Austria and France.

We had been fighting ten years to conquer it—to aggrandize it—to wrest it piecemeal from the Austrians—to give it a constitution: should we have suffered a choice which would have destroyed our work? If Austria has not renounced Italy, we will fight again for the latter; if she has sincerely renounced it, to her it must be a matter of indifference how Italy is governed.

As for the latter, could she, needing as she does a protector, help placing her destinies with confidence in the hand of her founder and regenerator, more deeply interested than any one else in the fate of the countries which are the cradle of his glory?

The Emperor, in sending me to your Majesty, was far from surmising that the war originated in these questions; and if these are the motives for it, not only do I perceive no possibility of making peace, but I foresee, on the contrary, a universal war.

The Emperor. That is not my meaning; and if the intention of your master is such that every one can be satisfied of its sincerity, he will add to his immense labours the greatest of all glories, that of having put an end to so many calamities by making a sacrifice of the advantages to which he might lay claim ; and I am persuaded that he will not be insensible to the gratitude which will be felt for him for having won by his moderation what he could not wrest by force.

Answer. I will accurately report to him what your Majesty does me the honour to say to me ; but I beg you to consider, that this is the third time we are treating on that point with Austria; that, in the second transaction, when we had a right to demand much, we imposed no other condition than the ratification of the first. If on the present occasion we still adhere to that point, how do we know but that, under circumstances which may be deemed favourable, we may have again to recur to that question?

The Emperor. On that very account you ought to adopt reasonable ideas, and renounce a domination which raises apprehensions in all your neighbours.

Answer. Then it is a revision of all that has been done for ten years past which is insisted on : if this is required of us in our present situation, we may thence augur what would have been imposed on us had we been vanquished : we, too, have consequently a right to profit by the favours of fortune, and to make demands proportionate to those which would have been made upon us.

It was not we who stirred up or began the war : it has been prosperous for us; we ought not to bear the expense of it, and I am thoroughly persuaded that the Emperor will not consent to that.

The Emperor. So much the worse ; because, notwithstanding the high estimation in which I hold his talents, and the wish I have to be able soon to accommodate matters with him, he will oblige me to order my troops to do their duty.

Answer. That will be a pity ; but we shall not have come so far to avoid an occasion of giving them a fresh proof of our esteem : we flatter ourselves that it will not detract in the least from the good opinion which they have conceived of us. If it must be so, I beg your Majesty to consider that I have not come to you as a spy; and what an injury you would do me, if, exerting your power, you were to detain me, and thus deprive me of an occasion of performing my duty, if the armies are to try each other's strength.

The Emperor. No, no; I give you my word you shall not be detained, and that you shall be conducted back to your troops this very evening.

Here the conversation ended: the Emperor, delivering to me his answer to the letter which I had brought, still holding the address downward, said to me, "Here is my answer; the address does not express the title which he has since assumed. I attach no importance to such trifles; but it is a rule of etiquette, and I shall have great pleasure in changing it as soon as he shall have furnished me occasion to do so."

I read the address, which was—" To the Chief of the French Government."

I replied, " Your Majesty is quite right; that can be nothing but a rule of etiquette, and the Emperor, too, will not think otherwise of it.   As general-in-chief of the army of Italy, he formerly commanded more than one king: content with and happy in the suffrage of the French, it is for their sakes only that he derives satisfaction from being recognised. Nevertheless, I will repeat to him the last words of your Majesty."

He dismissed me: I was conducted afterwards by the road to Brunn to a town, four or five leagues distant, which the Emperor of Russia had just quitted, but where his whole chancery still was.   I was kept there the remainder of the day: during this interval, I saw the Russian guards pass by on their arrival from St. Petersburg to join the army.   It was a magnificent body, composed of men of prodigious stature, who did not appear to be very much fatigued with so long a journey.

Towards evening, M. de Novosilzow, belonging to the foreign relations of Russia, came to inform me that the

Emperor of Russia had set out for the army, and that he had given orders to Prince Adam Czartorinski, his minister for foreign affairs, to cause me to be conducted back to our advanced posts; that, from what I had said to the Emperor, he had thought fit to direct him (M. de Novosilzow) to accompany me, for the purpose of ascertaining the intentions of our Emperor; that, at any rate, he (M. de Novosilzow) must have an interview with M. de Haugwitz, minister of the King of Prussia, who either was at Brunn, or on the point of arriving there; and that the mission of M. de Haugwitz to the Emperor required previously that he (M. de Novosilzow) should have a conference with that Prussian minister.

This strange proposal I could not entertain for a moment. I should have had to lend myself to facilitate the communication between the ministers of Prussia and Russia: I could not help laughing, and told M. de Novosilzow that if his cabinet wished to send a mission to ours, there were forms and usages to be observed with which it was well acquainted; I declared that, for my part, if I was obliged to take him with me, I would drop him at the first post of our troops, where he would remain till I could inform the Emperor of his arrival, and he had received permission to proceed to the head-quarters.

As this would have frustrated the object which M. de Novosilzow had in view, he gave up the idea of accompanying me further than Vichau, where the whole Russian army was posted, after driving out our advanced-guard and taking from it a few hundred prisoners.

I was conducted to Vichau to the quarters of the Emperor of Russia, who was in the same apartments where I had left the general of our advanced-guard two days before: he did not receive me, and ordered me to be conducted to our advanced posts.

I found them at less than a cannon-shot from those of the Russians; and though it was night, I was permitted to pass on to our army. My trumpet sounded: this was contrary to custom, nevertheless a party came, recognised, and received me: I sent back the Russian escort, and desired to be taken to the Emperor. He had been all day on horseback upon the ground where the affair with the advanced-guard had occurred; and he was still at the post-house of Posorzitz, six hundred toises from his last vedettes, when I rejoined him.

He was surprised that I had been allowed to return at that· hour; I delivered to him the letter of the Emperor of Russia, and repeated to him, word for word, what he had said to me.

I added, as my own observation, that all the Russian youth of the highest quality were there, and eager for battle; that I considered an engagement as inevitable, unless means were found to conciliate matters agreeably to the wish that had been expressed (in allusion to the Emperor of Russia).

He appeared thoughtful for some time : he then connected what Marshal Mack had told him at Ulm with what I reported to him.* All this unfolded to him the existence of very extraordinary projects; and he still expressed his astonishment at not having heard any thing concerning them from his minister for foreign affairs.

He took me aside, and said, " Take a trumpeter, and contrive to return to the Emperor of Russia: tell him that I propose to him an interview to-morrow, at any hour that suits him, between the two armies; and that of course there

---

* The Emperor had just received from M. Delaforest, his minister at Berlin, intelligence that the court of Prussia had espoused the cause of the allied powers, and was sending M. de Haugwitz to his head-quarters to signify this to him. The minister actually arrived at Brunn a few days after me ; but, as the Emperor had already enemies enough upon his hands, he would not afford Prussia an opportunity to compromise herself again. He therefore referred M. de Haugwitz to his minister for foreign affairs, who was at Vienna, and to whom he wrote in consequence, persuaded that if he should win the battle for which he was preparing, the business of Prussia would be easily arranged ; and that, on the other hand, if he lost it, his situation would not be worse. This policy was advantageous to Prussia.

shall be meanwhile a suspension of arms for twenty-four hours."

I set out after having given the Emperor some other particulars; in consequence of which, he ordered the retrograde movement which he had prepared to be commenced, for the purpose of taking the position which he had reconnoitred and definitively fixed upon a few days before.

Since my first departure for the head-quarters of the Emperor of Russia, he had given orders for the concentration of the army; and he expected in the course of the next day all the troops he had on the left bank of the Danube, and even the corps of Bernadotte, whom he had recalled from Iglau, where he had left only the Bavarian general, Wrede, with the troops of that nation.

I reached the Russian advanced posts again, about two hours after I had left them; as I was recognised—for the vedettes had not even been relieved—I was conducted to the general commanding the advanced-guard at that point, who deemed it his duty not to suffer me to be taken any where else but to his immediate superior, Prince Bagration. I was therefore led about at night on horseback, from bivouac to bivouac, to Prince Bagration, whom we at length found, and who would not send me to the Emperor of Russia without the permission of the general-in-chief. The night was passing away; there was not too much time for preparing the interview that was proposed for the next day. I determined to write from the place where I was a note to the following effect:

" To Prince Czartorinski.
" Prince,
" Scarcely had I quitted the Russian advanced posts before I returned to them, bearing a verbal communication to his Majesty the Emperor of Russia: it is of such a nature as to be likely to produce explanations, which I do not feel autho-

rized to commit to writing; and I think that your excellency could not take upon yourself to answer it, or to prevent me from proceeding to the Emperor. At any rate, I apprize you of the communication which I have to make, that the events which may result from a refusal to hear me may not, in any case, be imputable to me.

" I am, &c."

This note was carried to Vischau to Prince Czartorinski, by an officer of Prince Bagration's staff, who brought back an order for me to be conducted to the general of cavalry, Wittgenstein, whose head-quarters were on the high-road, very near Posorzitz. I arrived there at day-break, and waited not more than an hour.

The Emperor of Russia came himself. He was advancing; and while I was at General Wittgenstein's, an account was brought to him that we were retreating. All the young people who were there really believed that we were afraid, and endeavouring to escape from them.

The Emperor entered, and asked me what message I had brought.

" Sire," I replied, " I have faithfully reported to the Emperor all that your Majesty did me the honour to say to me yesterday. He has directed me to come again to your Majesty, and to express the desire which he has to see you: in consequence, he proposes an interview to-day between the two armies. The Emperor will conform to your Majesty's wishes in regard to the hour, the place, and the number of persons by whom each of the sovereigns shall be accompanied. He merely attaches one preliminary condition; namely, that an armistice of twenty-four hours shall be tacitly agreed upon for this occasion.

" Your Majesty will yourself judge of the sincerity of the Emperor's intentions; and you will be able to convince yourself that he has no reason to fear an event which perhaps inconsiderate persons would fain hasten, without caring for the consequences that might result from it."

The Emperor. I should with pleasure accept this opportunity of seeing him, were I persuaded that his intentions are such as you intimate; besides, the time is too short for us to see each other to-day. I should wish before I go to this interview to see the King of the Romans, who is at a cousiderable distance; and, in the second place, it is of no use to meet him, if I am not to come back satisfied.

Answer. But in what hands can your Majesty place your interests more safely than in your own? It seems to me that you would settle all that concerns you better than third persons would do; at least there would be no after-thoughts.

The Emperor. I have a particular desire to see him, and to terminate all the differences which separate us.

Then, changing the conversation, he said to me; " I will send with you a person who possesses my entire confidence. I will give him a message for your master; contrive to let him see him: the answer which he shall bring back will decide me, and you will do yourself in particular great honour by arranging all this.

Answer. Since your Majesty commands it, I will take with me whomsoever you please; but the success of what you desire will depend much on the particular character of the person whom you shall send.

The Emperor. It is Prince Dolgorouki, my first aide-decamp. He is the man in whom I place most confidence, and the only one to whom I can give this mission.

He sent for him: I retired while he gave him his orders.

The Emperor dismissed us both, and went away. We set out for the French advanced posts, which were so near that the vedettes could see and speak to one another.

I left Prince Dolgorouki with our main-guard, and hastened to give the Emperor an account of what I had done.

He was walking in the bivouacs of the infantry, amidst which he had slept upon straw.

His desire to make peace was carried to such a pitch, that, without allowing me time to finish, he mounted his horse and hastened himself to the main-guard: his picket had difficulty to keep up with him.   He alighted, ordered every body to retire, and walked alone with Prince Dolgorouki upon the high-road.

The conversation became animated, and presently very warm: it seems that Prince Dolgorouki had been deficient in tact in the manner of delivering the message with which he was charged; for the Emperor drily replied, " If that is what you have to say to me, go, and tell the Emperor Alexander that I had no notion of these dispositions when I asked to see him ; I would only have shown him my army, and referred to his equity for the conditions : if he will have it so, we must fight; I wash my hands of it."

CHAPTER XVI.

The carbineer—Preparations for battle—Dispositions—General attack—Battle of
  Austerlitz—The Russians are overthrown at all points—Solicitude of the Emperor for the wounded.

NAPOLEON dismissed Prince Dolgorouki ; I stayed behind to bid adieu to the latter, and to ask if he needed any thing to regain the Russian advanced posts : I sent the officer of the main-guard to accompany him as far as the communication with the Russian vedettes.

At separating, he said to me, " On your part you are bent on war ; we will meet it like brave men."   I replied, that I feared he would have to reproach himself for having changed dispositions which I knew to be excellent; that this would be unfortunate, because the Russian army would not only be beaten but destroyed, and he ought to bear in mind that it was his master who commanded it in person. He rejoined, " I have said no more than he ordered me to say After that it is of no use to talk."—" Then," said I, " we shall presently have work enough cut out for us—" and left him.

The Emperor sent for me again already to repeat to him to satiety all that I had told him before : he went away, saying, " But those people must be mad to insist on my evacuating Italy, when it is impossible for them to take Vienna from me. What plans had they then, and what would they have done with France, if I had been beaten? Let it end as God pleases; but by my faith before eight-and-forty hours I shall have given them a sound thrashing."

While thus speaking, he returned on foot to the first post of infantry of his army ; it was carbineers of the 17th light. The Emperor was irritated, and he vented his ill-humour in striking with his switch the lumps of earth that were on the road. The sentinel, an old soldier, overheard him; and having placed himself at ease, he had his gun between his legs, and was filling his pipe. Napoleon, as he passed close to him, said, at the same time looking at him, " Those —— fancy they have nothing to do but to swallow us up !" The old soldier immediately joined in the conversation. " Oho !" replied he ; " that won't be such an easy job—we'll stick ourselves right across."

This repartee made the Emperor laugh ; resuming a serene look, he mounted his horse, and returned to his head-quarters.

He now thought of nothing but the preparatory dispositions for the battle, which he resolved to delay no longer. Bernadotte joined him with two divisions of infantry ; Soult had three ; Marshal Lannes two ; the united grena-

diers formed a strong one; the foot-guards one. Marshal
Davout had one within reach: the Emperor had, besides
his light cavalry, three divisions of dragoons, two of cuirassiers, and the two regiments of carbineers, with the horse-
guards.

He caused abundance of provisions and ammunition of all
kinds, taken from the magazines of Brunn, to be brought
upon the ground.

It was the last day of November, 1805; the next day,
the 1st of December, he himself placed all the divisions of
his army: he knew his ground as well as the environs of
Paris.

Marshal Davout* was on the extreme right, *en échelons*,
on the communication from Brunn to Vienna, by Nicolsburg.
His right division was commanded by General Friant: it was
this that acted with us.

Marshal Davout was separated from the corps of Marshal
Soult by ponds, which presented long narrow defiles, and of
difficult communication.

Marshal Soult was also on the right of that part of the
army which was opposed to the Russian army.

His right division was that of General Legrand, who
was close to the ponds which separated him from General
Friant. On the left of General Legrand was the division of
Saint Hilaire, and on the left of the latter that of General
Vandamme.

In the second line, behind Marshal Soult, was first the
division of united grenadiers, and on their left were the two
divisions of Marshal Bernadotte.

On the left of Marshal Soult, upon a configuration of
ground somewhat more advanced, was the corps of Marshal
Lannes, having its first division (that of General Caffarelli)

* It will easily be perceived that the author frequently mentions a marshal to
indicate his *corps d'armée,* and a general of division to denote the division commanded by that general.

on the right of the road from Olmütz to Brunn, and its second division (that of General Suchet) supported on its right upon the same road, and on its left upon the Centon.

The infantry of the guard was the natural reserve of Marshal Lannes. As the ground on our left seemed to offer an extensive space, it was deemed prudent not to place the cavalry at a distance from it: the light cavalry therefore was first put on the right of Marshal Lannes, where it did not at all incommode the corps of Marshal Soult, which was on a vast *plateau*, a little in the rear, and to the right.

Behind the light cavalry were placed the dragoons.

The cuirassiers also remained that day near the corps of Marshal Soult, with the horse-guards.

The Emperor passed the whole day on horseback, inspecting his army himself, regiment by regiment. He spoke to the troops, viewed all the parks, all the light batteries, and gave instructions to all the officers and gunners. He afterwards went to inspect the *ambulances*, and the means of conveyance for the wounded.

He returned to dine at his bivouac, and sent for all his marshals: he enlarged upon all that they ought to do the next day, and all that it was possible for the enemy to attempt.

It would require a volume to detail all that emanated from his mind in those twenty-four hours.

The Russian army was seen arriving the whole afternoon, and taking positions very near to our right.

The Emperor was ready either to receive the attack of the enemy, or to attack himself.

In the evening of the 1st of December there was on our extreme right an irregular firing of small-arms, which was kept up so late as to give the Emperor some uneasiness. He had already sent several times to inquire whence it proceeded; he sent for me, and ordered me to go as far as the communication between the division of General Legrand and that of General Friant, and not to return till I had ascertained what the Russians were about, adding that this firing must be designed to cover some movement.

I had not very far to go; for no sooner had I got to the right of Legrand's division than I saw his advanced-guard, which was repulsed from a village situated at the foot of the position of the Russians, who wished to possess themselves of it for the purpose of thence debouching on our right: the nature of the ground favoured their movement, which was already begun when I arrived.

The moon shone very bright; nevertheless, they did not continue this movement, because the night soon became overcast: they were content with concentrating themselves on that point, so as to deploy rapidly at day-break.

I returned with all possible expedition to relate what I had seen: I found the Emperor lying upon straw, and so fast asleep, in a hut which the soldiers had made for him, that I was obliged to shake in order to waken him. I made my report: he desired me to repeat it; sent for Marshal Soult, and mounted his horse, to go himself and inspect his whole line, and to see the movement of the Russians on his right: he approached as near to it as possible. On his return through the lines of bivouac, he was recognised by the soldiers, who spontaneously lighted torches of straw: this communicated from one end of the army to the other: in a moment there was a general illumination, and the air was rent with shouts of *Vive l'Empereur!*

The Emperor returned very late; and though he continued to take repose, he was not without uneasiness as to what might be the result of the movement of his right on the following day.

He was awake and stirring by day-break, to get the whole army under arms in silence.

There was a very thick fog, which enveloped all our

bivouacs, so that it was impossible to distinguish objects at the distance of ten paces. It was favourable to us, and gave us time to arrange ourselves. This army had been so well trained in the camp of Boulogne, that one could rely on the good condition in which each soldier kept his arms and accoutrements.

As it became light, the fog seemed disposed to clear off. Absolute silence prevailed to the very extremity of the horizon: nobody would ever have thought that there were so many men, and so many noisy engines of destruction, enveloped in so small a space.

The Emperor sent me again to the extreme right to watch the movement of the Russians: they began to debouch on General Legrand, when I had got very near him; but, on account of the fog, I could not well judge of the movement.

I returned to make my report. It was scarcely seven in the morning: the fog had already cleared away so much, that I had no reason to follow the line of the troops, lest I should lose my way. (We were about two hundred toises from the Russians.)

The Emperor saw his whole army, infantry and cavalry, formed into columns by divisions.

All the marshals were near him, and teazed him to begin: he resisted their importunities, till the attack of the Russians on his right became brisker: he had sent word to Marshal Davout to support General Legrand, who was soon afterwards attacked, and had his whole division engaged. When the Emperor judged, by the briskness of the fire, that the attack was serious, he dismissed all the marshals, and ordered them to begin.

This onset of the whole army at once had something imposing: you might hear the words of command of the individual officers. It marched, as if to exercise, to the very foot of the position of the Russians, halting at times to rectify its distances and its directions. General Saint Hilaire attacked

in front the Russian position, which is called in the country
the hill of the Pratzer. He there sustained a tremendous fire
of musketry, which would have staggered any one but himself.
This fire lasted two hours: he had not a battalion that was not
deployed and engaged.

General Vandamme, who had rather more space to traverse
to get within fire of the enemy, came upon the column, overthrew it, and was master of its position and its artillery in an
instant.

The Emperor immediately marched one of the divisions of
Marshal Bernadotte behind Vandamme's division, and a portion
of the united grenadiers behind that of Saint Hilaire. He
sent orders to Marshal Lannes to attack promptly and briskly
the right of the enemy, that it might not come to the assistance of their left, which was wholly engaged by the movement of the Emperor.

The portion of the enemy's army, which had begun its
movement upon General Legrand, would have fallen back
and re-ascended the Pratzer; but General Legrand, supported by Friant's division (belonging to Marshal Davout),
followed it so closely that it was forced to fight where it
stood, without daring either to retire or to advance.

General Vandamme, directed by Marshal Soult, and supported by a division of Bernadotte's, made a change of
direction by the right flank, for the purpose of turning and
attacking all the troops that were before Saint Hilaire's
division.

This movement was completely successful; and the two
divisions, united on the Pratzer itself by this movement, had
no further need of the assistance of Bernadotte's division:
they made a second change of direction by their right flank,
and descended from the Pratzer to attack in the rear all the
troops who were opposed to General Legrand. These troops
quitted, for the purpose of attacking the Russians, the position
from which the latter had descended during the preceding

night to attack General Legrand: they had thus traversed a complete semi circle.

The Emperor made the united grenadiers and the division of the foot-guards support the movement: it had complete success, and decided the battle.

General Vandamme received a check at the commencement of his first change of direction to the right. The fourth regiment of the line lost one of its eagles in a charge of cavalry made upon it by the Russian guard; but the chasseurs of the guard and the grenadiers on duty about the Emperor charged so seasonably, that this accident had no bad cousequences.

It was after the second change of direction to the right of this same division of Vandamme's, then in communication with Saint Hilaire's, that the Emperor ordered the division of Bernadotte's which followed the movement to go right before, and no longer to follow the direction of Vandamme. That division did so: it fought the infantry of the Russian guard, broke it, and drove it fighting a full league; but it returned to its position, nobody could tell why. The Emperor, who had followed the movement of Vandamme's division, was exceedingly astonished, on returning in the evening, to find that division of Bernadotte's on the spot from which he had himself dispatched it in the morning. We shall presently see whether he had reason to be displeased at the retrograde movement of that division.

The left of our army under Marshal Lannes, and where all our cavalry was under the command of Marshal Murat, had broken and put to flight the whole right of the Russian army, which, at night-fall, took the road to Austerlitz, to join the relics of another portion of that army with which Marshal Soult had been engaged. Had Marshal Bernadotte's division continued marching another half hour, instead of returning to its first position, it would have been across the road from Austerlitz to Hollitsch, by which the right of the Russian army was retreating. By checking that movement it completed the destruction of the latter.

The whole day was a series of manœuvres, none of which failed; and which cut the Russian army, surprised in a flank movement, into as many pieces as there were heads of columns brought up to attack it.

All the troops that had descended from the Pratzer to attack Generals Legrand and Friant were taken on the spot, in consequence of the movements of the divisions of Saint Hilaire and Vandamme.*

In short, there were left to us, with the field of battle, 100 pieces of cannon, and 43,000 prisoners of war, exclusively of the wounded and slain who remained upon the ground. There could scarcely be a more victorious and decisive day.

The Emperor came back in the evening along the whole line where the different regiments of the army had fought. It was already dark: he had recommended silence to all who accompanied him, that he might hear the cries of the wounded; he immediately went to the spot where they were, alighted himself, and ordered a glass of brandy to be given them from the canteen which always followed him. I was with him the whole of that night, during which he remained very late on the field of battle: the squadron of his escort passed the whole night upon it in taking the cloaks from the Russian dead, for the purpose of covering the wounded with them. He himself ordered a large fire to be kindled near each of them, sent about for a muster-master, and did not retire till he had arrived; and, having left him a picket of his own escort, he enjoined him not to quit these wounded till they were all in the hospital.

These brave men loaded him with blessings, which found

---

* It was at this moment that the Emperor dispatched his aide-de-camp, Lebrun, from the field of battle, to carry the news of his success to Paris; and that he likewise sent an officer to the Elector of Bavaria and the Elector of Wurtemberg.

the way to his heart much better than all the flatteries of courtiers. It was thus that he won the affection of his soldiers, who knew that when they suffered it was not his fault; and therefore they never spared themselves in his service.

The night was so dark that we had been obliged to pass through Brunn, so that it was late when Marshal Davout received the order; and he could do no more that day than re-unite his corps, and approach near enough to reconnoitre the enemy.

CHAPTER XVII.

The Emperor of Austria proposes an interview—Motives of Napoleon for accepting it—Interview—The author is charged with a mission to the Emperor of Austria —Is sent by that sovereign to the head-quarters of the Emperor of Russia— Convention with the Emperor Alexander—Operation of Marshal Davout after the battle of Austerlitz.

It was the 3rd of December, the day following the battle; and it was already late, when Prince John of Lichtenstein arrived at the castle of Austerlitz, charged with a message from his master for the Emperor. He was a long time with him, and then returned : we knew the same evening that he had come to express a wish for an interview, to which the Emperor had assented.

The Emperors of Austria and Russia were in a ticklish situation, from the direction of the retreat which the events of the 2nd had forced them to cause their army to take. They had no point of passage on their march but the bridge of Göding at Hollitsch. The corps of Marshal Davout was nearer to this bridge than the wrecks of the Russian and Austrian army, which were to retire by it; and the allies believed Marshal Davout to be much stronger than he really was, so that they had no way left to save themselves but the interview which they solicited.

On the other hand, Davout was still ignorant of the results of the battle of the 2nd, and consequently of the real state in which the enemy was; he nevertheless made his dispositions for attack, and even attempted to force the defiles which separated him from Göding.

The Emperor Napoleon, the only one who was acquainted with the state of things, was not without anxiety respecting the result of the attack which he had ordered Davout to make; because he was well aware that he was inferior in force to the enemy. He no longer looked upon the retreat of the latter as impossible; and then he considered that the Prussians were urged to enter the lists, and that they had an army united with a Russian corps at Breslau: he knew, moreover, from the intercepted dispatches of M. de Stadion, that the Archduke Charles had arrived on the Danube, while the army of Italy, under the command of Massena, was still far on the other side of the Julian Alps; it was not therefore impossible that all these united armies might combine a movement which would oblige him to incur fresh risks, that might compromise the success of Austerlitz. In this situation he accepted what fortune offered him. The allies proposed an interview to gain time; in point of fact, the Emperor had the best of the bargain.

It may be added, that there can be no doubt that if the Emperors of Russia and Austria had received M. de Stadion's dispatches, they would not have proposed the interview.

Prince John returned the next morning to take the orders of the Emperor, who left to him all the arrangements. On the 4th, at nine in the morning, we all set out with the Emperor and the horse-guards, and proceeded along the high-road of Hollitsch to a mill in front of the advanced posts of Bernadotte, about three leagues from Austerlitz. We arrived there first: the Emperor caused two fires to be made, and waited. The horse-guards were drawn up in order of battle, two hundred paces in the rear.

It was not long before the Emperor of Austria was announced. He came in a landau, accompanied by Princes John and Maurice Lichtenstein, the Prince of Wurtemberg, Prince Schwartzenberg, Generals Kienmayer, Bubna, and Stutterheim, and two superior officers of Hulans. There was with the Emperor of Austria an escort of Hungarian cavalry, which remained, as ours had done, about two hundred paces from the spot where the interview was held.

The Emperor Napoleon, who was on foot, went to meet the Emperor of Austria from the place where the fire was to the carriage, and embraced as he accosted him. Prince John Lichtenstein alighted from the same carriage, and followed the Emperor of Austria to the Emperor's fire ; there he remained during the whole interview, as did Marshal Berthier by the Emperor. All the other persons of the suite of the two sovereigns were together at one and the same fire, which was separated only by the high-road from that of the Emperors. I was at this fire ; our conversation turned solely on the events of the battle : we studied to say nothing that might be galling to those gentlemen.

I know not what was said at the Emperors' fire ; we were as curious to learn that as the Austrians who were at the same fire with us, but neither they nor we could make it out. At any rate, the parties seemed to be in an excellent humour; they laughed, which seemed to us all to be a good omen: accordingly, in an hour or two the sovereigns parted with a mutual embrace. Each of us ran to his duty ; and, as I approached, I heard the Emperor Napoleon say to the Emperor of Austria, " I agree to it ; but your Majesty must promise not to make war upon me again."—" No, I promise you I will not," replied the Emperor of Austria; " and I will keep my word."

I know not on what occasion this was said, but I heard it;

and I repeat it, because the Emperor has frequently mentioned it to me since.

The day was drawing to a close when the two Emperors
separated, and took the road to their respective armies : we
followed the Emperor, who rode his horse at a foot-pace,
musing on what he had just said, and on what he meant to do.

He called me, and without adverting to what had passed,
said to me, " Run after the Emperor of Austria ; tell him
that I have desired you to go and wait at his head-quarters
for the adhesion of the Emperor of Russia, as far as he is
concerned, to what has just been concluded between us.
When you are in possession of this adhesion, proceed to the
corps d'armée of Marshal Davout, stop his movement, and
tell him what has passed."

This is too important not to be well circumstantiated.

I ran after the Emperor of Austria, and, as soon as I had
acquainted him with my errand, he permitted me to accompany him to his head-quarters, which were at a little distance,
in a domain belonging to him. We soon arrived there ; and
though it was not yet very dark, I perceived scarcely any
troops, which astonished me much.

The Emperor supped, and gave orders that I should not
want for any thing : I heard talk in the house of an action
which had taken place in the morning (it could only have
been with Marshal Davout). Anxiety had been felt for a
moment as to the issue that it might have ; but, it was added,
as soon as the French general (Davout) had received the
letter of the Emperor Alexander, he had desisted from the
attack.

All this was an enigma to me, and the Emperor Napoleon
knew no more about the matter than I did. When he had
come to the interview solicited of him, he certainly presumed
that Marshal Davout would attack ; but as it was necessary
to pass through Brunn again to communicate with him, it was
impossible to receive intelligence from him so soon.

After supper, the Emperor of Austria sent for General Stutterheim, and gave him his orders; then, desiring me to be introduced, he told me to accompany that general, whom he was sending to the Emperor of Russia: that I should know much better the answer he should give to the proposals which he had charged General Stutterheim to communicate to him, and that it would be nearer for me to proceed thence to the *corps d'armée* of Marshal Davout, which was at a very little distance.

I took leave, and set off with General Stutterheim: we went to Göding, where all was bustle and confusion; the Russian troops were packing their baggage. We found Russian sappers already destroying the bridge; their troops were still on the right bank; General Stutterheim was obliged to send them away. From Göding to Hollitsch the distance is not more than half a league at furthest: the Emperor of Russia had arrived there the preceding evening, and though it was but four or five in the morning, he was already up. He lodged at the castle, and had with him Prince Czartorinski.

I recollect having a feeling of mistrust, while waiting at the castle of Hollitsch to see the Emperor Alexander. I could not conceive why the Emperor of Russia had not been at the interview with the Emperor of Austria; I recollected that he had not assented to that which the Emperor had proposed to him before the battle, alleging, among other things, that the Emperor of Austria was too far off to communicate with him before he went to this interview. There they were together, when the Emperor of Austria had come to see the Emperor Napoleon: it was, moreover, of importance to him to know what should be concluded between them: if he had told me the truth, he was ardently desirous to smooth difficulties to settle all our differences; and notwithstanding all this he had not come to the interview. He had suffered the Emperor of Austria to go to it by himself.

I sought the cause of this, and was not long in discovering it; what it was I shall state presently.

General Stutterheim came out of the cabinet of the Emperor Alexander; I was ushered into it: it was scarcely light, and we had candles to converse by.

Alexander spoke first, and said to me, " I am very glad to see you again on an occasion so glorious to you: this day will not disgrace any of those in the military career of your master. It is the first battle that I have been in; and I must confess that the rapidity of his manœuvres never allowed time to succour any of the points which he successively attacked: you were every where twice as numerous as we.

Answer. Your Majesty has been misinformed; for altogether your army had a numerical superiority over ours of at least 25,000 men: besides, we had three divisions of infantry which had no share in the battle, and but six of infantry that were warmly engaged. We manœuvred, indeed, a great deal: the same division fought successively in different directions—this is what multiplied us during the whole day. This is the true art of war: the Emperor, who has fought forty battles, never fails in this point. He could now compose with the troops that were not engaged as strong an army as that which fought the day before yesterday, and march against the Archduke Charles, if all were not over; at least that depends on your Majesty.

Alexander. What is your business?

Answer. To learn, Sire, whether your Majesty accepts the proposals that concern you in what was agreed upon yesterday between the Emperor of Austria and the Emperor Napoleon.

Alexander. Yes, I accept them: it was for the King of the Romans that I came; he releases me: he is content with what is promised him, and I ought to be so too, since I have nothing to ask for myself.

Answer. The Emperor has charged me to add, that he

wishes the army of your Majesty to leave the Austrian states with the least possible delay, and by the shortest military route, proceeding every day the distance usually travelled by troops on march.

Alexander. Why, your master wishes me to be gone in great haste; he is in a prodigious hurry.

Answer. No, Sire; he does not wish you to return more speedily than you came: but what other rule can we take to guide us than to admit the military route, and the distance from magazine to magazine for the march of each day? One would not even stipulate that the unity of measure should be adopted: it is therefore not unreasonable to agree to that at once.

Alexander. Well, I agree to it: but what guarantee does your master require? and what guarantee have I myself, that, while you are here, your troops will not make some movements against me? Am I safe?

Answer. The Emperor has provided against that objection.

Alexander. Well! what guarantee does he desire of me?

Answer. He has directed me to request your Majesty's promise; and ordered me, as soon as I shall have received it, to proceed to the *corps d'armée* of Marshal Davout to suspend his movement.

Alexander. (With a look of great satisfaction) I give it you; and shall instantly prepare to perform what has been agreed upon.

He paid me a compliment, saying, " If more fortunate circumstances should some day bring you to St. Petersburg, I shall be happy to render your abode there agreeable."

I was far from supposing that this would happen so soon. Alexander strictly kept his word to me, as will be seen hereafter.

I left him, returned with M. Stutterheim, and recrossed

the Marche at Göding: we were obliged to wait till the Russian army, which appeared on the opposite side, had passed. I alighted with M. Stutterheim to count it: it did not exceed in number 26,000 men of all arms, without cannon, without baggage-waggons, many without arms, the greater part without knapsacks,* a very great number wounded, but marching courageously in their ranks.

After the Russian army had filed off, I was suffered to pass, and the bridge was destroyed.†

As soon as we were on the other side we met with the Austrian general, Meerfeld, who ordered us to be conducted, though day was scarcely dawning, to the advanced posts of Marshal Davout.

I was not a little surprised to find him so near; and we shall presently see what had passed at the corps of this marshal: these particulars are most strictly true. The Emperor of Austria had reason to tell me that he was not far distant.

In the first place, I communicated to Marshal Davout all that concerned him; and I came very seasonably, for he was about to commence the attack. In fact, the Russians were no longer before him, for I had seen them recrossing the Marche two hours before; that is to say, they crossed it on the 5th of December, between the hours of two and four in the morning. I now come to the operations of Marshal Davout since the battle.

Gudin's and Friant's divisions of infantry being united, as also a division of dragoons and light cavalry, the marshal himself, at the head of the whole, approached Göding on the 3rd, and on the 4th he briskly attacked the Austrian corps, which, being weaker than he, was nearly obliged to abandon·

---

* Till 1806, we saw the Russian infantry lay its knapsacks on the ground before it began to fire, so that when it was repulsed it lost all its baggage.

† This was the 5th of December, at day-break: the battle took place on the 2nd.

to him the bridge over the Marche at Göding, from which
he was only a very short half-league distant, having before
him a defile which constituted the whole strength of the
Austrians, and where they had placed their artillery.*. The
marshal was nevertheless on the point of forcing this passage,
when a flag of truce was sent to him to propose a suspension
of arms: he refused, and continued his attack. A second
flag of truce arrived, with a Russian officer, to make the
same demand: but this time General Meerfeld sent a note,
just written to him by the Emperor Alexander, no doubt
according to an agreement made between that sovereign and
General Meerfeld. This note ran thus:—

" I authorize General Meerfeld to acquaint the French
general, that the two Emperors of Germany and France are
at this moment holding a conference; that there is an armistice on this occasion, and that it is consequently useless to
sacrifice any more brave men.

(Signed) " ALEXANDER."

"The 4th December."

This note, written in pencil, and which I read when in the
hands of Marshal Davout, is deposited in the office of the
secretary of state in France

Marshal Davout, who had not received any intimation
from the major-general, attributed this delay to the great
circuit which it was absolutely necessary to make by Brunn
to come at him: he deemed it his duty to defer to the positive assurance of the Emperor Alexander;† in consequence

---

* It should be observed, that the wrecks of the Russian army had a great way
to march in order to come and oppose Davout.

† Yet the armistice was not to concern the Russians till after the Emperor
Alexander should have accepted the conditions agreed upon at the interview
between the two Emperors; and it was not till the night between the 4th and 5th
that he gave me his promise to subscribe to it.

he suspended his movement, and I found him at the place where he was on the morning of the 5th, whereas on the preceding day Marshal Davout might in half an hour have been master of Göding and of the bridge over the Marche, when the Russian army was still two or three leagues off on the Austerlitz road, facing Bernadotte. It was at the moment when the Emperor of Austria parted from the Emperor of Russia to go to the interview that Marshal Davout threatened most to force Göding, the only retreat of the Russians : the Russian army could not have arrived in time ; and besides, Bernadotte's troops, on seeing it move off, would have pursued it. It was in this position that the Emperor Alexander thought fit to write that note, to which Marshal Davout, out of respect for the character of the monarch, deemed it right on his part to give credit, not entertaining the least idea of a trick.

But, supposing Marshal Davout had doubted the veracity of the note, notwithstanding the presence of the Russian officer, who appeared to have been sent with the flag of truce merely to give it more force, and had kept marching on for another half hour, I ask any military man what would have become of the Russian army and its Emperor ; and what would have been the consequence if, on the 3rd, instead of having engaged unseasonably on the Olmütz road, our cavalry had immediately pushed on to Hollitsch. The Russian army would have been attacked at three in the afternoon ; it would have been driven upon Marshal Davout: there would have been a second representation of the scene at Ulm, because then there would have been no flag of truce, no proposal for an interview ; that would have been rejected as ridiculous.

When I had returned and reported this to the Emperor, I crossed over again to the advanced-guard of the Austrians, who had remained on the left bank of the Marche. Prince Maurice Lichtenstein was there ; M. Stutterheim was still with me: I dropped a word on the subject to those gentlemen:

the colonel of O'Reilly's regiment of light horse was present. They began to smile; I knew what that meant. My eyes were opened; I saw clearly enough why the Emperor of Russia had not come to the interview, and also why the Emperor of Austria had come to it. They had divided between them the two parts which weie to extricate them from their dilemma; and they werё far from suspecting that they were furthering the views of the Emperor Napoleon.

CHAPTER XVIII.

The Emperor fixes himself at Brunn—Gratuities to the wounded—Departure for Schönbrunn—Treaty with M. de Haugwitz—The King of Prussia disavows it—Austria signs—Partition of territories—Entry df the Russians into Naples—Unpleasant news from Paris—Signature of peace—The young damsel of Vienna—The Countess ****—Departure from Vienna—Arrival at Munich—Marriage of the Viceroy to the Princess Augusta of Bavaria—Departure for Paris.

WHEN I came back to the Emperor, Marshal Murat was in his cabinet: he was rating him soundly for having made him lose, in consequence of a false report, four hours of valuable time, which he had been obliged to employ in bringing back the movement commenced on the road to Olmütz: this circumstance was the only one that vexed him; he was pleased with all the rest.

Prince John of Lichtenstein came back in the evening with General Bubna; and the Emperor went and fixed his quarters at Brunn, whither he sent them word to follow him.

He remained there but a few days; during which he distributed his army into cantonments, caused the losses which it had suffered to be ascertained, sent his aide-de-camps to inspect the hospitals, and to deliver in his name a napoleon to each wounded soldier: he sent a gratuity of **3000** francs to each wounded general officer, and successively 2000, 1500, 1000, and 500 francs, to the officers of the different subordinate ranks who were in the same predicament. I need not say whether this bounty was welcome to them, and whether they blessed the hand which sent it.

The Emperor issued several orders relative to the administration; and after having had several interviews with Prince Lichtenstein, he set out for Schönbrunn, to accelerate the conferences for peace which were held at Vienna, and also to see how he stood with Prussia. For several days M. de Haugwitz had been near M. de Talleyrand, but had made no communication to him; he was to have concerted matters with the envoys of the other powers, whose calculations we had just deranged.

The Emperor passed through Vienna at night, and proceeded direct to Schönbrunn: it was the next day that he received M. de Haugwitz. At first he abstained from reproaches, but he let him see clearly that he was not the dupe of the intentions with which he had been sent to him. He conversed with him on the passage of the Russian army to Warsaw, and on its arrival at Breslau, where it still was.* At last he asked him, what was the meaning of that other Russian army which was in Hanover, communicating by Prussia with the main army

The Emperor began to grow warm and to speak loud; we heard him in the next room. " Sir," said he, " is this conduct of your master's towards me frank and sincere? It would have been more honourable to him to have openly made war upon me, though you have no motive for that: you would at least have served your allies, because I should have looked twice before I had given battle. You wish to be the allies of all the world; that is not possible: you must choose

---

* Thirty-six thousand Russians were actually there with Buxhövden; they would have been joined to the Prussians if we had lost the battle.

between them and me. If you are resolved to throw yourselves into the arms of those gentlemen, I shall not oppose
your doing so; but if you remain with me, I wish for sincerity, or I will separate myself from you. I prefer open
enemies to false friends. If your powers are not sufficiently
extensive to treat on all those questions, qualify yourself to
do so: for my part, I shall go and march upon my enemies
wherever they are."

This address was delivered with great warmth: the Emperor looked down upon M. de Hangwitz from the elevated
position on which he had been placed by victory. He had
not the least doubt that Austria would make peace: the
Russians were gone, and the French army might in a few
marches turn the whole Prussian monarchy; it was not therefore to be supposed that the Prussians would choose that
moment for making war: he therefore treated M. de Haugwitz with severity.

The cabinet of Berlin could not have anticipated the
position in which its minister then was: in fact, M. de
Haugwitz had only been commissioned to declare the alliance
of his country with the Russians; but, considering the state
of the affairs of the latter, and the precise terms of the Emperor, he took it upon himself to conclude an arrangement,
which he flattered himself he could induce the King to
sanction on his return to Berlin. The Emperor, on his part,
well knowing all that there was eventual in that arrangement,
had caused every thing that could be adapted to the policy of
the two countries to be inserted in it, hoping, like M. de
Haugwitz, that it would be the more easily ratified, inasmuch
as it was beneficial to Prussia. In consequence, the treaty
which was concluded gave Hanover to Prussia in exchange
for the margraviates.

While M. de Haugwitz was signing this treaty with the
Emperor at Vienna, M. de Hardenberg, who was at Berlin,

ignorant of the events at Austerlitz, and still more so of the mission which M. de Haugwitz had taken upon himself, signed another at Berlin with the ambassador of England.

He dispatched Colonel Pfuhl to Vienna to convey intelligence of .this treaty to M. de Haugwitz. In Silesia, on his way to Vienna, the colonel met M. de Haugwitz returning to Berlin with the treaty concluded at Vienna, which he was carrying for the ratification of the King. He took Colonel Pfuhl back with him, conceiving that if the treaty was not ratified, the King of Prussia would still be in time to send the new stipulations to Napoleon.

On his arrival in Berlin, the hopes of M. de Haugwitz were disappointed ; the King of Prussia loudly expressed his displeasure at what he had done.

He summoned a council : never was situation more delicate. It would have been madness to go to war, in the state in which the victorious armies were, as I have shown above; and he could not abandon his allies with whom he had just contracted. The discussion was warm : it was concluded not to accept Hanover without the ratification of England ; while it was conceived that a middle course had been found in accepting it, by causing it to be occupied as a deposit till the peace. Such were the proceedings at Berlin before the Emperor had left Vienna to return to Paris.

The Russians having departed, and having no relations with us, the Austrians were left alone to take care of their own interests : they made a peace analogous to the disastrous situation of their affairs. They lost the old Venetian states, which were annexed to the kingdom of Italy. They were to cede to Bavaria the Tyrol and the country of Salzburg, with some other possessions in Suabia; among the rest, those of the Teutonic order, Guntzburg, &c.

The house of Austria lost also the Brisgau, which had been assigned to the Grand-duke of Tuscany in preceding transactions; but, as the Emperor Napoleon had a particular affection for that prince, he caused the country of Wurtzburg to be ceded to him by Bavaria.

Compensations of territory likewise took place between Bavaria, Wurtemberg, and Baden; all which acquired an extent of power equal to half what they possessed before.

The Emperor caused, by the same treaty of peace, the Electors of Bavaria and Wurtemberg to be recognised as kings, and the Margrave of Baden as grand-duke.

Notwithstanding the repugnance of Austria, she was obliged to sign this disastrous treaty of peace.

The Emperor had nothing more to do at Vienna; he had hoped to treat with the Russians: in this view he had written, after the battle, from Brunn, to the Emperor of Russia. It was General Junot * whom he sent with his letter; but when Junot reached the Russian army, the Emperor Alexander had set out for St. Petersburg: the general, conceiving that he ought not to run after him, brought back his letter to the Emperor, who was already on his return at Vienna. There is reason to believe that had he ventured to proceed to St. Petersburg, peace would have been made that year. England, too, would perhaps have concluded peace, seeing no means of kindling war against us: there is reason at least to believe so, and then what evils would have been avoided! Fate had decreed otherwise. Before his departure from Vienna, the Emperor received intelligence of the entry of the Russians jointly with some English into Naples.

He immediately made dispositions for marching troops thither. He had an old grudge against the Queen of Naples; he had many a time had occasion to complain of her, and on receiving this news, he said—" Ah! as for her, I am not sur-

---

* General Junot was ambassador to Portugal. The Emperor, wishing to afford him occasion to distinguish himself, had sent him orders to come and join the army: he arrived two days before the battle. Had he measured his ground from Lisbon to Austerlitz, he could not have come more opportunely.

prised at it; but woe betide her if I enter Naples: never shall she set foot there again !"

He sent from the staff of his own army officers to compose that of the army which was about to assemble on the frontiers of Naples; and ordered Prince Joseph, his brother,* whom he had left at Paris, to go and put himself at the head of that army. He received also at Vienna unpleasant intelligence from Paris, which was no doubt exaggerated, but, even if it had not been, still it was bad enough.

The bulletin of the battle of Austerlitz, which had been read with extreme avidity throughout all Germany, might naturally be expected to produce the same effect in France. It did actually excite enthusiasm there: yet at Paris great uneasiness had been felt respecting the fate of the Bank, and in a short time the alarm spread so rapidly that people came in crowds to change notes; it was unable to satisfy all who presented themselves at once. It was believed to be embarrassed for cash, and the run became still greater. The stock-brokers interfered; bank-notes were sold like any other public stock, and at a discount of 70 francs per thousand.

The public funds were somewhat affected by this state of things, which caused the Emperor some anxiety. This was increased by another incident, which I am about to mention.

An officious person at Paris wrote to some one who had facilities for seeing the Emperor frequently, and denounced a fraud of the public treasury, which had already subscribed for 80,000,000 of rescriptions of the receivers-general, in anticipation of the revenues of 1806: now, we were in the month of December, 1805.

It was thence concluded, that the Emperor was expending the revenues of the state by anticipation: this again con-

---

* He had a year or two before caused his brother Joseph to embrace the military profession, and had given him the command of the 4th regiment of the line at the camp of Boulogne. This prince was president of the council of ministers at Paris in the absence of the Emperor.

tributed to lower the public funds. All these circumstances put him into an ill-humour, and made him ardently desirous to finish at Vienna, that he might go to Paris and investigate the cause of this disorder.

He was so urgent for peace, which was retarded only by certain difficulties relative to contributions, that at length it was signed: he ratified it the same evening, and set out the next day.

Before he left Vienna, a circumstance occurred which I ought to relate here.

People have talked a great deal about a decided passion of the Emperor's for women : it was not predominant in him. He loved them, but knew how to respect them ; and I have witnessed the delicacy of his intercourse with them, when his long absences placed him in the same case with all the officers of his army.

During his residence at Vienna, between the battle of Austerlitz and the signature of the peace, he had occasion to remark a young female who pleased him. As chance would have it, she had herself taken a particular fancy to the Emperor, and she accepted the proposal made to her to go one evening to the palace of Schönbrunn. She spoke only German and Italian ; but as the Emperor himself spoke the latter language, they soon became acquainted. He was astonished to learn from this young woman that she was the daughter of respectable parents, and that in coming to see him she had been swayed by an admiration which had excited in her heart a sentiment she had never yet known or felt for any person whatever. This, though a rare circumstance, was ascertained to be a fact : the Emperor respected the innocence of the young lady, sent her home, caused arrangements to be made for her settlement in life, and gave her a portion.

He delighted in the conversation of an intelligent woman, and preferred it to every kind of amusement. A few days after the adventure just related, the following occurrence took place.

A French agent, who resided at Vienna, had had occasion to distinguish there a certain countess, to whom an English ambassador (Lord Paget) was said to have paid particular attentions. There could scarcely be found a more fascinating woman than this countess, who, at the same time, carried the love of her country to enthusiasm. The agent took it into his head to prevail upon her to go and see the Emperor, by causing it to be insinuated that the proposal was made by the order of that sovereign himself, who, however, had never harboured such a thought.

An officer of the horse-police of the city of Vienna, who was acquainted with this countess, was employed to speak to her. She listened to the proposal, which was made to her one morning, with a view to its being carried into effect in the evening; but she could not decide immediately, and required a day for consideration, adding, that she wished to ascertain whether it really was by the Emperor's order that this overture had been made to her.

In the evening, the carriage being in waiting at the appointed place, where the officer was to receive the countess, and to consign her to the care of another person, who was to accompany her to Schönbrunn, he called upon her: she told him that she had been unable to make up her mind that day, but she pledged her word that she would do so without fail the following day, desiring him to come in the afternoon to be informed of her determination.

The carriage was bespoken for the same hour the next day. The officer, apprehensive of another whim, called the following day, according to appointment, on the fair lady. He found her fully resolved: she had arranged her affairs, as if preparatory to a long journey; and she said in a decisive manner, addressing him familiarly in the second person, " Thou mayst come and fetch me this evening; I will go and see him ; thou mayst rely upon it. Yesterday I had business to settle; now I am ready. If thou art a good Austrian, I will see him. Thou knowst what injury he has done to our country ! Well, this evening, I will avenge it ; come and fetch me without fail."

Such a confidence startled the officer, who would not incur the responsibility ; he afterwards went and communicated the matter, and was rewarded. The carriage was not sent to the place of rendezvous, and the countess was spared the opportunity of acquiring a celebrity which would doubtless have blasted her reputation as a lovely woman.

This adventure took place the day preceding that on which the Emperor set out from Schönbrunn for Paris.

The Austrians, for the first instalment of the contributions, were obliged to cede to us the amount of the subsidies which they were to receive from England : they were expecting them just at that moment, and gave orders at Hamburg that when they arrived they should be placed at the disposal of the minister of France. This was then **M.** Bourienne, whom the Emperor had consented to employ again : he received the English subsidies destined for Austria, and remitted them to Paris.

Some days before the Emperor's departure from Vienna, the Archduke Charles solicited an interview. I know not why the Archduke did not come to Schönbrunn ; but the interview took place at a hunting-seat, called La Venerie, on the road from Vienna to Beckersdorf. The Emperor had gone thither as if for the purpose of hunting ; the Archduke came with two officers only : they conversed a long time alone in an apartment of the hunting-seat. We returned rather late to Schönbrunn. The Emperor had a particular esteem for the Archduke Charles, and was attached to him.

The Emperor left Vienna : in his way to Munich, he passed through Scharding and Passau, where he met General Lauriston, who was returning from Cadiz ; he sent him

as governor to Venice.   He arrived at Munich in the night,
a few days before new-year's day, 1806.   The Empress had
come thither by his order a fortnight before: she had previously been at Strasburg. *

The Princess Caroline was there too.   There was, as may
be supposed, great rejoicing at the court of Bavaria: not
only was the country saved, but almost doubled in extent;
and the Bavarian troops had not been engaged, that is, they
had sustained but slight losses.   The greatest delight was
therefore expressed at seeing us, and we were welcomed
with every demonstration of kindness.

It was at Munich that we began to perceive something
which we had as yet only heard vaguely talked of.

A courier was sent by the Tyrol with orders to the Viceroy of Italy to come immediately to Munich: accordingly,
five days afterwards he arrived.   No secret was any longer
made of his marriage with the Princess Augusta of Bavaria,
daughter by his first wife of the King of Bavaria, and born
while he was yet but Prince of Deux-Ponts.   The Viceroy
was much beloved; and the greatest pleasure was expressed
to see him unite his destiny with that of a princess so vir-
tuous and so lovely as the Princess Augusta.

The religious ceremony was performed by the Prince-
primate of Germany, formerly Elector of Mentz.

The nuptials were celebrated at Munich: the customary
festivities took place on this occasion; they lasted a whole
week, after which the Emperor returned to Paris.   The
Viceroy stayed some time longer at Munich, and then returned
to Milan.

---

* It was during his stay at Munich that the republican calendar was given up,
and the old calendar again adopted.

CHAPTER XIX.

A new army assembled at Strasburg—Marriage of the hereditary Prince of Baden with Mademoiselle de Beauharnois—Arrival of the Emperor at Paris—Causes of the depression of the public funds—M. Mollien succeeds M. de Barbé-Marbois—Victualling Company—Dismissal of the officers of the treasury—Sequestration of the property of the members of the Victualling Company—Their imprisonment—M. Ouvrard—Board established for victualling the forces—Deplorable result of that measure.

THE Emperor stopped one day at Augsburg, another at Stuttgard, and spent two or three days at the court of Baden. He then proceeded to Munich in a carriage with the Empress. At Carlsruhe we learned that the marriage of the hereditary Prince of Baden with Mademoiselle de Beauharnois had been determined on : previously to the opening of the campaign, a projected union between the Prince of Baden and Princess Augusta of Bavaria had been spoken of. The Emperor, wishing to ascertain the truth of this report, sent M. Thiars to Baden, during the watering-season, with orders to inquire into the particulars of the intended marriage, and to use his endeavours to thwart it. These orders were executed with punctuality and intelligence.

Every thing being arranged with the court of Baden, the Emperor came to Strasburg, where he found a new army assembled. But this must be explained.

When he found himself unexpectedly attacked, and that Prussia had held equivocal language with him, he became fearful that the war would linger. He called out a conscription, and the troops assembled at Strasburg and Mentz : they were already clothed and armed, and presented a fine appearance. The national guards of the frontier departments had also been assembled ; and these corps, joined to the conscription, formed a fine army.

This was the second conscription that had been raised since the treaty of Amiens; and, like the first, it was composed of remarkably fine men.

The Emperor remained but a few days at Strasburg; and he arrived in Paris one day about the end of January, at five in the afternoon.

Immediately on his arrival he sent for the arch-chancellor and the minister of finance, in whose prudence he reposed great confidence. He wished to know the cause of the depression of the public funds. He gave no credit to the accounts he had received from the police, which informed him that the mischievous reports which had been circulated, and the doubts respecting the success of the army, had originated in the Faubourg St. Germain.

The Emperor had forced the minister to explain the matter, and to point out the guilty parties, whom it was to be presumed he of course knew. M. Fouché, to extricate himself from the difficulty, presented to the Emperor a list of fifteen persons of the Faubourg St. Germain, whom he accused of having inflamed the public mind. The consequence was that they were exiled. These were the first individuals who suffered this punishment; and they had to thank the minister of police for it. The order of banishment was sent from Munich.

There was no doubt that the public securities had fallen into discredit; and the Emperor was now determined to ascertain the cause. He first of all sent for M. de Barbé-Marbois, the minister of the treasury, who had but little to say in his defence. His well-known probity placed him above suspicion; but he had been entrapped into so many imprudent speculations, that the Emperor would not allow him to retain his situation. He was succeeded by M. Mollien, who had been director of the sinking fund.

An issue of 80,000,000 bonds, on the credit of the receivers-general, had actually taken place. This operation

was undertaken with the view of favouring private speculations.

The Victualling Company, which had the contract for bread
to the army and navy, and also for the supply of corn, was
composed of capitalists possessing great wealth and great
commercial experience : they had been born in the trade,
and had pursued it all their lives.

Their transactions were immense ; and they rendered essential services to the government in times of scarcity.

Their accounts had to pass through two, and often three
ministerial offices ; namely, those of the war, the marine, and
the home departments: so that if they succeeded in obtaining
full payment of their claims, it was not without considerable
trouble and delay.

While the Spanish fleet lay at Brest, the government of
Charles IV. contracted with this company for supplying it
with provisions. This rendered it necessary for one of the
company to go to Madrid to obtain the liquidation of the
accounts against the Spanish government. M. Ouvrard was
employed on this mission. At Madrid he necessarily came
in contact with the Prince of the Peace, who then governed
every branch of administration in Spain.

The Prince of the Peace not only settled the accounts due
for the fleet, but proposed to Ouvrard that the company
should undertake in Spain the same service which it performed
for France; that is to say, the supply of corn, as well as the
victualling of the army and navy. The company took the
contract, under the condition that the Spanish government
should obtain from the French government permission to ex-
port grain, without which the supply could not be effected.
Spain negotiated for this permission, and obtained it. As to
the payments, the Prince of the Peace declared that he had
nothing to give but bills on Mexico ; for which value would
there be obtained, but which it would be necessary to negotiate. M. Ouvrard not only took bills for the sums due to

the company on account of the contract, but also engaged to get all the bills due to the Spanish government by Mexico discounted. This was, unquestionably, the greatest service which could at that time have been done for Spain. The government was extremely well pleased with the arrangement, more especially as Ouvrard's transactions raised the value of this kind of paper. - The operation was immense, and entirely unconnected with the business of the Victualling Company.

In carrying his plan into effect, M. Ouvrard freighted American ships for Vera Cruz with cargoes consisting of such articles as the Spanish colonies were in the habit of receiving annually from the mother country. The bills granted in payment were discounted in favour of the royal treasury, and the ships returned to the United States.

The amount of the bills was invested in American produce, or sent in specie to London, whence the value was transmitted to Amsterdam and Paris.

Never was any commercial enterprise of so extensive a nature managed with so much boldness and skill. M. Ouvrard had a chain of correspondence and agents from Madrid, Paris, Amsterdam, and London, to Philadelphia, Vera Cruz, and Mexico. No obstacle remained to impede the success of this great undertaking, when the affair of M. de Barbé-Marbois caused its failure.

While M. Ouvrard was devoting all his attention to this particular enterprise, his partners were exerting themselves to meet the demands to which the Spanish contract gave rise. What they wanted was sufficient funds. Their existing capital was employed in the provision-trade in France, and another capital was necessary to enable them to carry on the same business for the service of Spain.

M. Ouvrard's enterprise was calculated to produce immense returns; but time was requisite for the communications between America and Europe. Allowing for all expenses and risks, his transactions would have yielded a net annual profit of more than 20,000,000 francs. He was in Spain attending to this business, when his partners, in their anxiety to obtain the command of more capital, thought it advisable to give the secretary-general of M. de Barbé-Marbois an interest in their speculations. They explained the state of their affairs to him, and succeeded so well, that he gave them all the support they desired. He induced the minister to assign to them 80,000,000 of bonds on the service of 1806.

Unfortunately, in a country in which the government is always in a state of great activity, the transactions of the treasury and the circulation of its securities are the constant objects of vigilant observation : accordingly, whenever any financial operation is a departure from the ordinary routine, conjectures commence and distrust follows.

Notwithstanding the precautions observed by the secretary-general, the affair soon transpired ; in consequence of part of the 80,000,000 of paper being negotiated to supply the required capital. A panic was the result, and every holder hastened to realize his security. The Bank could not answer the demands made upon it, and the disorder was at its height. The Emperor, who had received his appropriation-sheet, attributed the deficiency, which he soon discovered, in the first instance, to some error which might have occurred in making the accounts. He however ordered an investigation : in consequence of which he ascertained that an issue of treasury-bills had actually taken place ; and then he perceived, with alarm, the dreadful situation in which he would have been placed had fortune proved unfavourable to him. Had he been beaten in Moravia, while he was, by an inconceivable imprudence, deprived of the resources on which he calculated that he could confidently rely, he would have had no means of repairing his loss, and his ruin would have been inevitable.

The error which had been committed was of a very serious nature. The minister, however, persisted in defending the transaction.   At last the Emperor, as I have already stated, superseded him ; he also dismissed all the officers of the treasury who had contributed to mislead the judgment of the head of their department.

The Emperor next ordered all the paper in the possession of the contractors to be returned to the treasury ; and, as a considerable part had been thrown into circulation, he placed their property under sequestration : the payments which they had to receive from different ministerial offices were suspended ; and finally, the company's supplies of provisions were sequestrated.   These measures spread consternation among all the creditors, who proceeded to enforce their claims.   Thus the discredit of the company, which daily augmented, terminated in a declaration of bankruptcy.

The contractors, being unable to meet the demands of the government, were arrested, and sent to prison.   However, much was not gained by this proceeding.   Some loosened their purse-strings, but the greater part chose to stay in jail rather than to pay.

In the midst of this confusion M. Ouvrard arrived from Spain : he was examined respecting the nature of his transactions.   The Emperor sent for him ; and M. Ouvrard, having explained the business, was severely treated.   It is much to be regretted that the company could not command sufficient resources without implicating the treasury in its speculations ; for the enterprise was in itself calculated to be beneficial to the public.   We could not but be gainers by the progress of financial distress being checked in Spain.   France could not only lose nothing, but immense advantages would have accrued to the great French capitalists, independently of the profits which a multitude of men of business would have obtained by their participation in the commercial activity which this singular enterprise must have produced : but coming forward as it did, in the way of a surprise, it was dangerous to the state, which it might have involved in ruin ;

and it cost the government much time, various negotiations, and considerable sums, to correct the disorder which took place. It was even with great difficulty that the government could obtain value for the securities which it had been necessary to take to cover the treasury-paper circulated by the company.

When the Victualling Company was dissolved, it became necessary to resort to another mode of supplying the troops. It was proposed to the Emperor to constitute a board of administration for this service, with all the clerks and establishments of the company attached to it. A question which will long continue to afford matter for difference of opinion was then quickly settled. It was represented to the Emperor, that by placing a counsellor of state, with a certain number of auditors, at the head of the board, every thing would go on smoothly; and that, besides, the gain to the public would be great. A gross error was thus committed. The counsellor of state, placed at the head of the board, was M. Maret, brother of the minister of the same name; a man of probity and zeal for the public service; but the result of his administration remains to be seen.

While the supplies provided by the company lasted, the business went on very well: some economical prunings were even made on the baking, the firewood, and the consumption. It was thought that the board had performed miracles.

But the stock of provisions left by the company melted away. How was it to be replaced? For this money was wanting. M. Maret could not obtain any supply on credit, because, as agent of the government, he was not liable to be sued. Recourse was then had to the Emperor; but he would not consent to an issue of money until he knew into whose hands it was to go. Only auditors, with whom the ministerial offices were well provided, were now employed on this service : accordingly, these auditors took their departure for the principal corn-markets. On their arrival, the merchants were at no loss how to deal with their new customers : they knew that these gentlemen were not born factors, and that they came to purchase for the government : of course they gave them no great bargains.

Some of these gentlemen had devoted themselves to the study of civil and natural law, and knew nothing either of corn or the mills that grind it. Nevertheless, it was singularly enough supposed, that young men of this description would manage better for the board, and be more saving of the public money — though such care and economy was foreign to their private interests—than the members of the Victualling Company managed their own affairs, and saved money which belonged solely to themselves.

The Emperor was not slow to suspect that he had been misled ; especially, when the result of the management of the board was, that at the end of the year it had cost 10,000,000 more than the expense of the company, though it had been necessary to supply the board with funds in advance. During the scarcity of 1811, this board had nearly proved fatal to us; and the government was obliged to have recourse to the experience of some of the old members of the company. Thus the Emperor had to abrogate and re-establish the Victualling Company, at a time when he was obliged to direct his attention elsewhere.

Such are nearly all the most remarkable changes which occurred in this branch of the public service.

CHAPTER XX.

Occupation of the kingdom of Naples—Distribution of favours—Marriage of the Prince of Baden—Joseph, king of Naples—Louis, king of Holland General Sebastiani is sent to Constantinople—Pitt dies, and is succeeded by Fox—Overtures made to England—Lord Lauderdale's arrival in Paris—Movements of the other foreign ministers—Fresh discussions with Prussia—Luchesini—Respective situations of Prussia and France—The Grand-duke of Berg—Prussian armaments—M. de Talleyrand prosecutes the negotiations with England.

LONG before the commencement of the campaign, M. Chaptal * had been succeeded in the post of minister of the interior by M. de Champagny, who was our ambassador at Vienna. M. de Talleyrand arrived at Vienna soon after the peace of Luneville.

Shortly after the Emperor's return, accounts were received of the occupation of Naples by our troops. The remainder of the winter was spent in fêtes and amusements.

Murat was invested with the sovereignty of the grandduchy of Berg, which Bavaria ceded to France in return for other territories. M. de Talleyrand received the principality of Benevento, and Marshal Bernadotte that of Ponte-Corvo, both in the kingdom of Naples. It was a

---

* The retirement of M. Chaptal was justly regarded as a misfortune. Of all men in France, he was most capable of giving an impulse to national industry. He had an opinion of his own, and he had courage to maintain it. He invariably recommended peace. Malignant reports of pretended speculations, in which M. Chaptal was said to be engaged, had reached the ears of the Emperor: being the proprietor of some extensive chemical establishments, it was not to be expected that he should sacrifice them because he was a minister.

The Emperor subsequently discovered that he had been deceived. M. Chaptal was one of the men in whose conversation he took most pleasure, and to whose acquirements he attached most value: consequently, he was always one of the first on the list of those who enjoyed the favour of private entry.

matter of some surprise, that Bernadotte should be among the first to share in the distribution of favours.

The Prince of Baden came to Paris to contract his marriage, which was celebrated in the chapel of the Tuileries. The hereditary Prince of Bavaria had also been in Paris since the 10th of February. On this occasion, magnificent entertainments were given at the Tuileries. The ladies of the court, most of whom were distinguished for youth and beauty, danced in character at the balls; and these fêtes, independently of the peculiar interest attached to them, presented all the elegance and splendour of enchanted spectacles. During this same winter, the Emperor determined to place the crown of Naples on the head of his brother Joseph; and twelve senators were deputed to invest him with the sovereignty. Joseph was at the head of the army which had recently taken possession of Naples. The Emperor also resolved to change the government of Holland, by substituting the monarchical for the elective form; and the choice of the leading men of the country (who, I believe, were wholly favourable to us) fell on Prince Louis, the Emperor's brother, to whom the crown was offered.

It is strictly true, that Louis was perfectly indifferent to this accession of greatness : indeed, it was doing violence to his taste for retirement to force him to ascend a throne.

Thus the battle of Austerlitz created three new kings in Europe, and overthrew the Neapolitan dynasty.

About the spring of 1806, our external political situation was still unsettled. Russia had made no declaration : Austria had but ill-executed the conditions stipulated at Vienna, as will hereafter be seen; and our position with respect to England continued unchanged. The Emperor immediately saw what measures he had to adopt; and he began to think of strengthening his interests at Constantinople. He sent thither, as his ambassador, General Sebastiani, who had just arrived in Paris, scarcely recovered from a serious wound which he had received, when leading a brigade of dragoons, at the glorious battle of Austerlitz.

In addition to his public character of an ambassador, the general was the bearer of private instructions from the Emperor to guide him under circumstances which, it was foreseen, must inevitably arise. Sebastiani speedily justified the Emperor's confidence.

In the month of April following, all the distinguished individuals who had passed a portion of the winter in Paris returned to their homes.

The King of Holland likewise set out to take possession of his states. The Emperor, who was now more solitary than heretofore, lived almost constantly shut up in his closet. He now seriously considered of the means of making peace with England. M. de Talleyrand neglected nothing for the attainment of this object. He was one of those who ardently wished for peace, and a circumstance now occurred which appeared to favour his views.

In consequence of the death of Pitt, Fox had become prime minister of England. The Emperor knew him personally, and had conceived a great regard for him, in the long and frequent conversations they had had together when that distinguished statesman visited the continent.

Lord Yarmouth was in Paris in May, 1806. He was fond of company ; and amidst the gaieties and amusements with which Paris abounded, he became acquainted with an individual whom M. Talleyrand employed to sound his inclination for becoming the bearer of pacific overtures between the two countries. After some explanations, he consented to enter upon the negotiation, and he received a passport for London. His mission was favourably received ; and he was sent back with authority to commence a negotiation which was to pass through several preliminaries before it assumed a regular form. The conferences soon commenced ; and the

Emperor thought proper to make M. de Champagny and General Clarke attend them.*

Lord Lauderdale came to Paris as the English chargé d'affaires in this business; and it was then publicly understood that we were treating with England. It is very certain that no opposition to this negotiation would have proceeded from the Emperor. He was the more sincere in wishing for peace, because it would have irrevocably determined his situation with respect to the continental powers. All who were about the Emperor likewise wished for peace. It was an object which his ministers would have purchased by any sacrifice; and yet it was not attained. When the different foreign ministers who were in Paris learned that France and England were treating directly and exclusively for their own reciprocal interests, they endeavoured by all the means in their power to become acquainted with the particulars of the conferences.

Fortunate as had been to us the results of the campaign of 1805, the natural allies of England did not yet relinquish hope. Thus the ministers of these powers in Paris easily contrived to become acquainted with whatever might interest their respective courts in the conferences above mentioned: some of them pretended to be well informed, with the view of learning more than they knew; thus circulating falsehoods for the sake of getting at truth

Every spring was set in motion: women—intrigues— nothing was neglected.

The ministers of those powers whose colonies had been reduced, were also anxious to ascertain what would be stipulated for them; and by dint of plotting and contriving, every

---

* The Emperor used to treat Clarke as a child, who would whimper if he were neglected. Never was there a man so unfortunately organised as Clarke. He was a courtier by nature; and there was nothing he would not have done to obtain an approving look from the Emperor.

one gradually discovered what they had to hope or to fear from the issue of the negotiations.

Prussia stood in a very peculiar situation. She was ashamed to accept the spoil of a prince with whom she had recently leagued against us, but, being at the same time impatient to gain possession of Hanover, she thought of receiving that country as a deposit, until the acquiescence of England should enable her to add it definitively to her dominions. On all other points she wished to continue on the same footing on which she had stood with respect to France up to the time of the peace. Napoleon rejected stipulations which would have annulled the treaty concluded at Vienna. Fresh negotiations were commenced; and the cabinet of Berlin, after refusing Hanover, with a considerable extent of territory to be ceded by Bavaria, now accepted it without any addition. Prussia became indignant, and exclaimed against breach of faith; but the ratifications were exchanged, and she was obliged to submit to the consequences of the blindness which had made her reject the work of Haugwitz, when a new incident arose to excite further dissatisfaction. Murat, who had just been created grandduke of Berg, indicated his design of taking possession of the three abbeys of Etten, Essen, and Werden, in the county of Marck. The Prussians wished to retain them. Disputes and recriminations ensued; and both parties prepared to occupy them. A few musket-shots were fired, and Blucher then withdrew.

The Grand-duke, on his part, allowed himself to be misled by ambition. He already dreamed of aggrandizing his newly-acquired power; and he was not content with a lot which would have gratified the utmost wishes of a prince of royal birth.

It is difficult to guess what had dazzled him, but he could not endure the thought of peace. He availed himself of every opportunity which his new situation afforded to instigate the Emperor to the continuance of war : he inspired him with distrust of M. Talleyrand, and all who were favourable to peace. He went still farther : he alarmed the Prussian minister respecting the approaching loss of Hanover, while at the same time he spoke to the Emperor of the dissatisfaction of Prussia, which wanted only the assurance of support in order to declare herself against France. Another misfortune was, that the Grand-duchess of Berg, who was endowed with grace and beauty, and all that could render a young princess interesting, was fond of power, and she contrived to fire the ambition of those who had to endure her caprices. But as she could not exercise power under the control of a husband, she looked favourably on all projects which, while they promoted the glory of the Grand-duke, ensured to herself the gratification of reigning with undivided sway, and of seeing all bow to her will : she therefore excited instead of checking the ambition of the Grand-duke ; and there soon appeared on the scene a troop of young admiring courtiers, all eager to march to new fields of battle.

But, in spite of all this, the conferences pursued their ordinary course ; and the Emperor thought that peace was already attained, when, to his great mortification, he found himself forced to renounce it. The Prussian minister at the court of France * quitted Paris on the 16th of February, and returned on the 3rd of May. He was panic-struck by the results of the campaign of Austerlitz ; and he could not fail to perceive that the sudden change in the policy of the Prussian court, and its equivocal conduct at the close of the campaign of 1805, had produced an alteration in the sentiments of France. He was exceedingly anxious to ascertain what would be the result to Prussia of the conferences between Lord Lauderdale and the French ministers. He listened to

---

* M. Luchesini, the same who had been plenipotentiary at the celebrated congress of Sistow, under Frederick the Great.

what was said by all parties, and opened his own mouth only to make inquiries about the fate of Hanover. He kept continual watch upon the Grand-duke; but he saw nothing that could tend to ease his apprehensions. Thus his reports kept the Prussian cabinet in a state of continual alarm.

Another circumstance contributed to increase the uneasiness of M. Haugwitz, who had come to Paris to negotiate the treaty of the 15th of February. He was succeeded as minister extraordinary by M. Knobelsdorf. The Emperor conceived a great regard for this diplomatist, and he treated him with marked attention. This preference offended M. Luchesini, and contributed not a little to his dissatisfaction.

It was scarcely possible but that the King of Prussia should feel uneasy at the accounts which he received from France. On the other hand, however, he received encouragement at home. He was told that he was destined to be the liberator of Germany: the example of Frederick the Great was cited for his imitation, and he was constantly reminded of the battle of Rosbach.

- In this state of mind, he began to adopt precautions; and these precautions gradually assumed the aspect of threatening measures. Alarm increased with the arrival of every courier from Paris; and preparations for war commenced, as soon as it was understood at Berlin, by the communications of the King of England to parliament, that he had received the offer of the restitution of Hanover. Instead of viewing this proposition as a step towards peace, which would be followed by an indemnity to her, Prussia thought herself trifled with: her evil star impelled her to take up arms, and she deceived herself respecting the consequences of this measure.

But to return to the conferences. M. de Talleyrand urged them forward with the utmost activity, and he would have made any sacrifice to attain peace with England. He assured all who would listen to him, that without peace there was no certainty for the Emperor; that nothing but a succession of victories could consolidate him, and that these were reduced to a series of which the first term was *a* and the last *y* or *zero*. He was very indignant when he discovered the little plots of the ambitious intriguers, who stirred up war by their reports of the arming of Prussia, which they had themselves daily provoked by their ostentatious boasting and threats. Letters, either genuine or forged, dated from Berlin, and filled with invective against the French, were artfully circulated. In some of these letters it was affirmed that the Prussian cavalry had sharpened their sabres under the windows of the French ambassador. Some young men in Berlin had indeed thrown stones at the ambassador's windows; and there was no insult or offensive allusion of which he had not been the object.

CHAPTER XXI.

Death of Fox—The conferences are broken off—Lord Lauderdale is recalled—
Ultimatum of the cabinet of Berlin—The Emperor quits Paris—Warlike preparations—Marshal Lannes defeats Prince Louis of Prussia—The Emperor
fixes his head-quarters at Auma—His arrival at Jena.

THE Emperor was ready to make any sacrifice for the sake of a general peace, when an event occurred which obliged him to relinquish all hope of attaining it.

Mr. Fox, the English minister, had been ill for a considerable time. His illness suddenly assumed a serious character, and he was soon pronounced to be in danger.

We relied wholly on him for terminating our eternal differences with England; and at every fresh report of the state of his health, the negotiations were urged forward, because it was hoped that if peace were once concluded, some means would be found of rendering it permanent, even in the event of Mr. Fox's death.

' But fate had decided otherwise. The English minister died, and his successor recalled Lord Lauderdale : the conferences were then broken off. We tacitly accused Lord Lauderdale of not having been as zealous as we were in smoothing away the difficulties which opposed the conclusion of peace; and it was even suspected that when Mr. Fox's recovery was found to be impossible, he had studied only the sentiments of the minister who was destined to succeed him. *

* This opinion was founded on the circumstance of Lord Yarmouth having carried on the negotiation until the month of August, the period at which Lord Lauderdale was sent to Paris. The latter was supposed to be favourable to the Grenville party, and opposed to Mr. Fox, who, being attacked with the disorder of which he died in the middle of the following month, had but little influence in the choice of the negotiator, or on the management of the negotiations.

We suspected that Lord Lauderdale was sent only for the purpose of embarrassing and breaking off the negotiations ; for he had no sooner arrived, than he refused to acknowledge the basis on which Lord Yarmouth had negotiated. From that moment all appeared to be at an end ; though he did not quit Paris until after the Emperor had set out to join the army, doubtless for the purpose of strengthening the opinion that the rupture had originated with France.

Perhaps, from what I have said, the reader may be too much inclined to attribute the cause of the rupture to the boasting of the youth of Paris, and those who surrounded the Grand-duke of Berg, who himself was not the only one to form plans. But the Emperor was not the man to suffer himself to be led away by these little intrigues : he looked upon the war as inevitable, because it was only the consequence of the plans of the coalition, which had never been dissolved, and which had modified, but not changed its plans.

On the prejudiced minds and vain and vindictive heads by which the foreign cabinets were directed, England had too strong a hold to lose the opportunity of renewing the alliance ; and she had just caused the rejection of the treaty made between France and Russia by M. d'Oubril. The two courts of Prussia and Russia were already connected by friendly relations ; the part therefore to be taken by England was easy. It is certain that the Emperor was very far from wishing for war, which could only have the effect of rendering the future problematic ; and it is no less certain that war was not desirable to the King of Prussia. The one was driven to it, and the other led into it. Intriguing women, young men, and ambitious plotters, contributed more to it than the two sovereigns.

Thus then, on the one hand, the war continued with England, and on the other, a rupture was ready to take place with Prussia. It is impossible to refrain from attaching blame to those who started so many obstacles to a reconciliation which might have been so easily effected.

. The dissatisfaction of Prussia had originated in her fear of losing Hanover. The rupture of the conferences of Paris eased her apprehensions; and there now remained only some little private misunderstandings, arising from trifling causes, which could be easily settled by presents of snuff-boxes, &c.

The Emperor was perfectly disposed to make every accommodation. The matter being arranged, it was still possible to bring back his army to Boulogne. His flotilla was unharmed: his fleet had indeed been destroyed; but he could have found means to restore it.

He relied so implicitly on peace, that he began to think seriously of fulfilling the promise he made to the army in his proclamation from Vienna. In this proclamation he said that the whole army should be assembled in Paris, before it proceeded to Boulogne, that the troops might fully enjoy the happiness they would experience from having honourably served their country. He repeated that his greatest pleasure would be to see every man in the army assembled round his palace, and daily to call to mind the courage and attachment of which they had given him so many proofs.

In several of the public offices he reserved a number of trifling places, and successively some of greater importance, for the purpose of satisfying the applications he received from the soldiers, at every review, to provide for some of their relatives. During the whole time I served the Emperor, I never knew him to neglect the petition of a soldier, particularly when he solicited a favour for another. A sure way to forfeit the Emperor's good graces, was to ill-treat or to repulse a soldier or an officer of inferior rank. He had already mentioned to several individuals his plan of re-assembling the army of Austerlitz; but the genius of evil prevented him from accomplishing this design.

The Grand-duke of Berg and several others were over-joyed at the rupture of the conferences with England. The least important consequence which they calculated from the circumstance was, that it would be necessary to attack and overwhelm Prussia while her attention was occupied with the marching and counter-marching of her troops. The ultimatum of the cabinet of Berlin aided the Grand-duke's impatience. This document, from its tone and the terms in which it was couched, was a defiance rather than an exposition of grievances, and it consequently gave offence to the cabinet of the Tuileries.

On the other hand, Marshal Berthier wrote from Munich, where his head-quarters were established, urging expedition : he began to fear that the Prussians would commence hostilities, without making any communication (which was the case in 1805), and consequently it was impossible to proceed too speedily. The Emperor left Paris on the 21st of September, 1806; he had only returned on the 26th of the preceding January. The Empress accompanied him as far as Mentz. The imperial guard had scarcely begun its march : it had returned to Paris after the campaign of Austerlitz. The Emperor stopped at Metz only long enough to visit the arsenal and the school of artillery, and to inspect the garrison. He proceeded rapidly from Metz to Mentz, where he stopped two or three days. Various couriers which he received made him hasten his arrangements. At Metz, orders were given to put the troops in position as soon as they should arrive. Orders were also sent to Strasburg for embarking on the Rhine all that were to depart from that fortress and the towns situated on the banks of the river. An officer was dispatched to the King of Holland, to direct that the Dutch army should without delay enter the territory of Munster, and advance towards the Weser.

After receiving visits from the Princes of Baden, Darmstadt, and Nassau, and finally determining the plan of the *tête-de-pont* across the Rhine, the Emperor proceeded to Aschaffenburg. He dined with the Prince-primate; and then continued his journey by the way of Wurtzburg, where he arrived on the evening of the day on which he left Mentz. The Grand-duke received him in the handsomest way; and he put up at the residence of that prince, for whom he entertained a very high esteem. Here he awaited news of the enemy.

At Wurtzburg he settled the plan of his operations, and he resolved to make the town of Bamberg his first point of departure.*

The different *corps d'armée* occupied the territory of Bayreuth and the banks of the Mayne, and approached the frontiers of the little principalities of Saxony. All had been assembled at their respective positions since the Prussian army had established itself at Erfurt and Weimar.

By a singular error, the Prussian army remained in this position until the union of our forces was accomplished, and our movements determined. The Prussian army having been concentrated before ours, it might easily have attacked one or several of our corps before they were united. An enterprise of this kind would at least have justified the inconceivable presumption of supposing that the Prussian army was in itself sufficient to oppose our columns: or, if the Prussians had prudently thrown a good garrison well commanded into Erfurt, and had then come with all their collected forces to dispute the passages of the Oder and the Elbe,

---

* Marshal Lefebvre, who had commanded the 5th corps, was succeeded by Marshal Lannes, whom the Emperor had brought from Paris; and the command of the foot-guards was given to Marshal Lefebvre.

fortune might have given them some favourable chance in the series of movements and manœuvres which we should have been obliged to make in consequence of theirs. But no, they remained quietly in their position, and suffered us to debouch by Saalfeld, where Marshal Lannes defeated the corps of Prince Louis of Prussia, who was killed in the action.

The Emperor himself marched by the valley of the Maine; having with him the corps of Bernadotte and Ney, and being flanked on his right by the corps of Marshals Soult and Davout, who, leaving Bayreuth, advanced upon Hoff. The Emperor at last debouched from Cronach, passed the Saale at Saalburg, and arrived at Schleitz, where a small Prussian corps was met, and pursued in the direction of Gera.

This movement ought to have brought the Prussian army to a decisive course: it was concentrated, and might easily have made an offensive movement; but prudence suggested the necessity of holding back.

The Emperor halted one day behind the Saale, where he was rejoined by the foot-guards; and meanwhile, the corps on the right, commanded by Soult and Davout, followed by all the cavalry under the command of the Grand-duke of Berg, advanced on the banks of the Elster.

On the day after this halt the Emperor established his head-quarters at Auma, where he received, through Marshal Lannes, notice of the march of the enemy, who had resolved to abandon his position at Erfurt, and to advance towards the Saale.

The Emperor immediately ordered Marshals Bernadotte and Davout to proceed to Naumburg: Marshal Soult was directed to march to Gera, and Marshal Lannes to maintain a communication with him. The Emperor then proceeded to Gera, preceded by all the cavalry, and followed by the foot-guards and Marshal Ney's corps.

At Gera we took a small Saxon convoy, which had been ordered to march to Naumburg, by the way of Zeitz. We profited by the indication which this circumstance afforded, and all the cavalry turned into the corresponding route.

Besides, we captured at Gera the post-office mail, which had just arrived there; and ascertained that the Prussian army was still at Weimar. The Emperor then formed his resolution. He ordered Marshals Lannes and Ney to march on Jena. He moved towards that point himself, and made Marshal Soult take the same direction. The rest of the army continued its march on Naumburg, and was ordered to advance against the enemy, who, we believed, was at Weimar. By this movement the Emperor completely turned the Prussian army; for we arrived by a road which the Prussians should have taken in marching from Prussia to meet us, and they were advancing to force the passage of the Saale by a road which would have been ours had they manœuvred better. In such a position it was difficult to suppose that a conflict could be avoided, or that on its taking place it could fail to be decisive.

On the 13th of October, at sunset, the Emperor arrived at Jena, with Marshal Lannes and the foot-guards. He was in communication with Marshals Soult and Ney, whom he ordered to join him. Bernadotte, Davout, and the Grand-duke of Berg, had on their part also arrived at Naumburg.

CHAPTER XXII.

Situation of the Prussian army—The Emperor's dispositions—Embarrassment of the artillery—Conduct of the Emperor on that occasion—Battle of Jena—Napoleon visits the field of battle—His solicitude for the wounded—He returns to Jena—News of Davout.

THE Emperor had detached me from Gera, with the 1st regiment of hussars, to collect intelligence on the road towards Jena. He proposed that I should take with me M. Eugene Montesquiou, one of his orderly officers, whom he made the bearer of a letter to the King of Prussia; and directed me to accompany him until we met the first Prussians, which took place in the valley of the Saale, about a league above Jena.*

On entering Jena we obtained certain news of the Prussian army. It had left Weimar in two great corps: the largest, under the immediate command of the King of Prussia and the Duke of Brunswick, had taken the road from Weimar to Naumburg; the other, which was under the orders of the Prince of Hohenlohe, had directed its march on Jena.

In fact, the first companies of chasseurs, which debouched on the summit of the mountain which commands Jena, discovered the enemy's line; the left of which had just taken an appui in front of the point by which we debouched. The Emperor reconnoitred it himself, alone and within pistol-shot. The sun had not set; he alighted from his horse, and advanced until some muskets were fired at him. He returned, to hasten the march of his columns: he himself conducted the

---

* Prince Hohenlohe, who commanded this army-corps, detained Montesquiou during the whole battle. It is even said that he did not deliver the letter to the King until after the battle.

generals to the positions which he wished them to occupy during the night, and recommended to them not to take their positions until it was so dark that they could not be seen from the enemy's line.

He slept in the bivouac amidst his troops, having first made all the generals who were there sup with him. Before he lay down he descended the hill of Jena on foot, to be certain that no ammunition-waggon had been left at the bottom. He there found the whole of Marshal Lannes' artillery sticking in a ravine, which in the obscurity of the night had been mistaken for a road, and which was so narrow that the linch-pins of the wheels rubbed against the rocks on both sides. There was thus no getting forward or backward; and there were a hundred waggons one behind the other in the defile. This artillery was intended to be the first in service; the artillery of the other corps being behind it.

The Emperor was excessively angry, but showed his displeasure only by a cold silence. He inquired frequently for the general who had the command of the artillery, and appeared greatly astonished at his absence; but without wasting time in reproaches, he set to work himself to do the duty of an artillery officer. He collected the men, made them get their park-tools, and light the lanterns, one of which he held for the convenience of those whose labours he directed. In this way the ravine was sufficiently widened, and the extremities of the axle-trees cleared of the rocks. I shall never forget the expression in the countenances of the men on seeing the Emperor lighting them with a lantern, nor the heavy blows with which they struck the rocks. They were exhausted with fatigue, but no one uttered a complaint: all felt the importance of the service in which they were engaged; and they did not refrain from expressing surprise at finding that it should be necessary for the Emperor himself to set this example to his officers. The Emperor did not leave the spot until the first waggon had passed through, which was not until late in the night. He afterwards returned to his bivouac, and issued some orders before he reposed himself.

' This happened on the night between the 13th and 14th of October. On that night there was a hoar frost, accompanied by a thick fog, similar to that which we experienced at Austerlitz ; but it was favourable to us, for we were upon a level height of a limited extent, which obliged us to form the troops in large masses, almost touching each other, in order to facilitate their deploying in the morning. This level was not more than two hundred toises from the position occupied by the left of the Prussians. Had it not been for this fog, our fires would have served as a direction for the enemy; and their artillery would have done us considerable mischief, for every shot would have told. However, fortune favoured us wonderfully ; for the fog lasted until eight o'clock next morning.

We were under arms at day-break ; but the fog was still so thick, that we could not see our way in advancing on the enemy's line. Beside the wood on which his left rested, there was a tract of ground by which we could pass, as had been ascertained on the day before, but in seeking it during the fog we came upon the wood which the enemy occupied. A skirmish then began, which afforded the Prussians a point of direction. We now got into the right road by turning a little to the left, and the artillery was conducted in that direction in close columns. ' The Prussian line finding itself attacked, and fearing a grand movement in front, proceeded to manœuvre to gain a position nearer its main body. It was now nine in the morning : we had fired only a few guns, and, with the exception of the 17th light infantry which attacked the wood, none of our troops had been engaged. The atmosphere cleared up, the sun shone bright, and we were in presence of the Prussians. The cannonade commenced in the centre, and was more brisk on the side of the enemy than on ours.

, Marshal Ney, who was on the right of Marshal Lannes, attacked the extreme left of the Prussians. He carried a village which formed its appui, was repulsed, retook the village, and was again driven from it. He would in all probability have lost a great many men, had not one of Marshal Soult's divisions, which arrived by our extreme right, and which, notwithstanding its excessive fatigue, was marched forward, completely out-flanked the point which Marshal Ney was so obstinately set upon holding, though it was quite out of our natural position.

The movement of Marshal Soult's division caused the evacuation of the village; and had only half an hour's patience been exercised before it was attacked, the lives of many brave men would have been spared.

The Emperor was very much displeased at Marshal Ney's obstinacy. He said a few words to him on the subject, but with delicacy. This movement, for occupying the point on which the extreme left of the Prussians rested, was seconded by a vigorous attack operated on their centre by Marshal Lannes, who wished to give them a close discharge of musketry. The boldness of his advance made the Prussian army change front on its right wing, the left wing in the rear. This obliged us to perform the opposite movement; namely, to change front on our left wing, with our right wing in advance. The action recommenced along the whole front, and a fortunate incident gave us the victory. The Emperor had left Marshal Augereau at Mentz, to form a corps with the regiments which after the peace of Austerlitz had been sent to France, and which were ordered to repair to Mentz by forced marches. Augereau made so rapid a march from Mentz, that he arrived at Jena while the action was going on. He did not pause a moment, and appeared in the field of battle at the moment when the Prussian line was attacked in the position I have described. Marshal Augereau's column advanced through a fir-wood, in such a manner that it debouched in the rear of the Prussian right: the 14th regiment of the line was at the head of the column. It commenced an attack of musketry before the Prussians had time to reconnoitre it. This attack being vigorously maintained, caused a retrograde movement on the right of the Prussians, which made their whole line waver.

The Emperor had but few cavalry with him. The parties which were in the direction of Naumburg had not yet arrived, so that we had on the field of battle only one brigade of light cavalry, commanded by General Durosnel, another commanded by General Auguste de Colbert, and the 1st, 9th, and 11th regiments of hussars.

The above corps of cavalry were all assembled in our centre; and the moment the oscillation in the Prussian line was observed, they were sent forward, and ordered to charge with desperation. The charge succeeded; and disorder and rout began to appear among the Prussians. They tried the effect of bringing forward their own cavalry, by which ours, being weaker, were for an instant checked; but this did not enable their army to rally, and it was completely broken. The head of the Grand-duke of Berg's cavalry arrived at this moment on the ground, and uniting with the rest, proceeded on the route to Weimar, along which the Prussians were flying.

The Emperor, at the point where he stood, saw the flight of the Prussians, and our cavalry taking them by thousands. Night was approaching; and here, as at Austerlitz, the Emperor rode round the field of battle. He often alighted from his horse to give a little brandy to the wounded; and several times I observed him putting his hand into the breast of a soldier to ascertain whether his heart beat, because, in consequence of having seen some slight appearance of colour in his cheeks, he supposed he might not be dead. If he found a greater number of dead on one part of the field than another, he looked at the buttons to ascertain the number of the regiment ; and it was his custom at the first review in which he saw that regiment to ask questions as to the manner in which it attacked, or had been attacked, in order to discover the cause of the loss he had observed.

While thus making the tour of the field of battle, I saw him two or three times discover, in the manner I have mentioned, men who were still alive. On these occasions he gave way to a joy which it is impossible to describe, but which was quickly followed by a melancholy expression, occasioned by the reflection that there were many others in the like situation whom he could not hope to find.

This evening he was upon the whole pretty well satisfied with what he saw done. The commissariat had performed its duty. The wounded were collected without delay, and every where attended with the greatest care.

He returned to pass the night at Jena, where he received the professors of the university. He made a present to the vicar of that town, who had distinguished himself by his humane attention to the comfort of the wounded and the prisoners.

He took some repose at Jena, and received, during the night, very satisfactory news from Davout's corps.

CHAPTER XXIII.

The Prussian army takes a position at Auerstädt—Arrival of Davout and Bernadotte—Dangerous position of Davout—Bernadotte refuses to support him—Battle of Auerstädt—Adjutant-general Romeuf's report—The Emperor's address to the Saxons—General Pfuhl—The Emperor releases the Saxon prisoners—He goes to Weimar—The King of Prussia solicits an armistice—Capitulation of Erfurt—The Emperor's observations on the conduct of Bernadotte—The column of Rosbach.

THE grand Prussian army, under the immediate command of the King, which was marching on Naumburg, had halted, and taken position at the village of Auerstädt, in front of Sulz, which formed its head-quarters, when information was received there of the arrival of Davout and Bernadotte with a numerous body of cavalry at Naumburg.

On the same day (the 14th of October) on which the Emperor attacked the Prince of Hohenlohe in front of Jena, Davout and Bernadotte, in pursuance of their instructions, marched from Naumburg by the Weimar road, on which the Prussian army was advancing.

Our cavalry, so spirited in the field of battle, was seldom directed with judgment when the object was to obtain intelligence of the enemy. On this occasion, among others, Marshal Davout was unable to gain any information respecting the march of the Prussian army, except what he learned in consequence of a bold reconnoissance made by one of his aides-de-camp, Colonel Burck, now a general and peer of France. He had, in fact, no fixed opinion as to the force coming against him, except that which he formed on the report of a deserter from the Prussian body-guard, who had formerly served in France in the King's regiment, in which he was a serjeant. This very intelligent man communicated to Marshal Davout most minute details concerning the Prussian army.

Davout's corps was at the head of the column. He communicated the information which he had received to Marshal Bernadotte, whose troops immediately followed his.

Davout had no sooner reached the summit of the hill, which it is necessary to ascend after passing the stone-bridge on the Saale, about a league from Naumburg, than he discovered the Prussian army. He immediately dispatched a messenger to Bernadotte, and requested that he would support him. Bernadotte insisted on passing to the front. Davout replied, that chance having placed him at the head of the column, it was not just that he should retrograde; and besides, that this movement would expose them both to total destruction if they were attacked while executing it, and remarked that there was not a moment to be lost. He further observed, that he gave him this notice in the name of the Emperor's service; and that as to himself he was going to debouch, and would immediately attack the enemy. Bernadotte, from motives which have never been well explained, replied, that he was looking for a passage higher up the river, and that Davout might attack with safety, because he would second him.

Marshal Davout attacked with an inferiority of one to four. Scarcely was his corps formed, when he was assailed by a cannonade and discharges of musketry which were vigorously maintained, as the enemy thought 'they were sure of destroying him; and it is but justice to say, that had it not been for his great courage and firmness under fire, his troops would have been completely disheartened. He had lost one-third of his force by three o'clock in the afternoon. He could only retain his men in the field of battle by showing himself every where. His aides-de-camp hastened in every direction to Marshal Bernadotte to request him to debouch, but all in vain; for he spent the whole day in seeking a passage by roads where none was to be found, and allowed Marshal Davout to be crushed. Marshal Davout also experienced the same obstacles when he sent for cavalry. His aides-de camp carried repeated orders to divisions of cavalry to join him immediately, as the danger was imminent; but Bernadotte detained them, and prevented them from taking part in the action. It happened with this cavalry to which he had no right to give orders, as with the corps which he commanded: it was of no use either at Kösen or at Jena, where it did not arrive in time.

Davout was indebted to his great valour, and the confidence placed in him by his troops, for the glory he won on this day, which was to him one of the most honourable that a general officer could expect in his military career. Notwith-

standing the loss which he sustained, he took from the enemy
seventy pieces of cannon, and forced him to retreat. Had he
been supported by a corps of cavalry, he would have made a
great number of prisoners; but he might consider himself
extremely fortunate that he was able to keep the field. This
day justly obtained for him the admiration of the whole
army.

The loss of the Prussian army which he attacked was
great. The Duke of Brunswick, who was wounded, died at
Altóna. The King, on learning what had happened to 'the
duke, made a movement by his left flank to regain the Oder,
and rally the corps which was retreating from Jena on Weimar and Erfurt.

Marshal Davout could not follow the King of Prussia's
army in consequence of the want of cavalry, so that the
retreat of that monarch was not obstructed.

Adjutant-general Romeuf, who brought the report of this
affair to the Emperor at Jena, said nothing of the inaction of
the cavalry, nor of the refusal of Bernadotte to take part in
the battle. The Emperor allowed him to go on to the end of
his narration, and then asked him what those corps had done
during the conflict. Romeuf was obliged to confess that
none of them were present, and appeared not to know any
thing of the motives which had withheld them. The Emperor saw that something was concealed from him. He did not
insist much upon explanations; but he bit his lips, and became only the more impatient to ascertain the truth.

Prisoners poured into Jena the whole of the night; and
among them was almost the whole of the Saxon infantry, and
several generals. The Emperor assembled these generals,
together with all the Saxon officers, in a hall in the university; and as none of them could speak French, M. Demoustier,
who belonged to our foreign office, acted as interpreter.
The Emperor thus addressed the officers :—

" Saxons! I am not your enemy, nor the enemy of your

Elector. I know that he has been obliged to follow and to aid the designs of Prussia. You have fought, and ill fortune has made you forfeit your liberty. If you have sincerely entered into the interests of Prussia, you must follow her destiny; but if you can assure me that your sovereign has been constrained to take up arms against me, and that he will seize this opportunity of resuming his natural policy, I will overlook the past, and will henceforth live on friendly terms with him."

M. Pfuhl, a Saxon general officer, who was particularly attached to the Elector of Saxony, replied, that he would undertake in two days to go to Dresden as the bearer of this generous proposition to his sovereign, and to bring back his reply. He said he was convinced that the proposal would not only be conformable to the sentiments of the Elector, but that the Emperor's generosity would fill him with gratitude.

" May I rely on you?" said the Emperor: " Yes, Sire," replied M. Pfuhl. " Well," resumed the Emperor, "depart, and tell the Elector that I send back his troops, and that I beg he will command those who are yet in the Prussian army to leave it."

The Saxon prisoners set out immediately; they went by the way of Leipsic.

The Emperor departed instantly, in an open carriage, for Weimar. On reaching the top of the mountain, commonly called the Snail, we saw a Prussian officer coming up to us, conducted by an officer of our advanced-guard. This was an aide-de-camp of the King of Prussia's: he was the bearer of a letter from the King to the Emperor, in which an armistice was proposed. The Emperor desired me to direct the officer to follow him to Weimar, where he would give him an answer.

The Emperor then continued his journey rather more speedily; and on arriving at Weimar, before he received the officer, he made some arrangements, which led me to suppose that either from the date of the King of Prussia's letter, or from some other circumstances, he had ascertained the situation of the principal Prussian army

He dispatched orders to Marshal Bernadotte to march immediately to Halle by the way of Merseburg, and to force the two passages of the Elster, which were defended by the corps of Prince Frederick of Wurtemberg.

The corps commanded by Marshal Lannes had marched upon Erfurt. The rest was directed upon the Elbe, part by Merseburg and part by Leipsic. The Emperor stopped two days at Weimar, in order to ascertain what the enemy would determine upon. During this short interval, the town of Erfurt, where the Prince of Orange commanded, capitulated, and 18,000 prisoners were taken. This event afforded us the opportunity of carrying our line of operations through that place, which was a great advantage, because it considerably shortened the march from Mentz to the army.

After sending back the King of Prussia's aide-de-camp, the Emperor received the Prussian general, Schmettau, who had formerly been aide-de-camp to Frederick the Great, and who was a man celebrated in various ways. He had been wounded in the late battle, and remained at the castle of Weimar, where he died shortly after.

The Emperor did not grant the armistice applied for by the King of Prussia, because our army was advancing; and if it had halted, we should have oppressed our allies with the maintenance of our troops; and besides, it was necessary that we should take up a military position.

In seeking an armistice, the King of Prussia had evidently no other object in view than to preserve his own states from the burden, against which we wished to secure our allies: we therefore continued our march.

The Emperor left Weimar and slept at Naumburg, where Marshal Davout and his corps were stationed. Here he expressed his entire satisfaction with the conduct of Davout; and

he received a true account of the conduct of Marshal Bernadotte and the cavalry on the 14th.* He was silent for a
moment, and he then burst into reproaches. "This is so
shameful;" he added, "that if I were to bring him to a
court-martial, it would be equivalent to ordering him to be
shot. The best way is to overlook it. I think he is not so
devoid of honour as not to feel the full extent of his misconduct, respecting which I shall not fail to let him know my
opinion."

Next day we left Naumburg to proceed to Merseburg and
Halle. In this march we passed over the field of Rosbach.
The Emperor was so perfectly well acquainted with the dispositions of Frederick's army and ours, that, on arriving at
Rosbach, he said to me, "Gallop on in that direction
(pointing the way he meant), and at the distance of half a
league you will see the column which the Prussians erected in
commemoration of the battle of Rosbach."

If the harvest had not been over, I should not have discovered the object of my search: for the column, which stood
in the middle of a vast plain, was not higher than one of
those posts which are fixed up in harbours for the purpose of
attaching vessels by ropes to the quays.

When I found it, I waved my handkerchief as a signal to
the Emperor, who had deviated a little from his road to
inspect the field of battle. He came to see the column. The
inscriptions were so much obliterated that they were almost
illegible.

The Emperor observed General Suchet's division passing
at some distance; and he sent to order it to come up and
remove the column, which he wished to convey to Paris.
General Suchet set his company of sappers to work, and the
column was speedily placed on some carriages.

---

* On his way from Weimar to Naumburg, the Emperor first passed the position
in which the King of Prussia had fought, and next that which Davout had occupied. The two fields were yet covered with the slain.

The whole army was now approaching the Elbe. The Emperor received information that the bridge of Dessau had been burned by the Prince of Wurtemberg, whom Marshal Bernadotte was pursuing. The bridge of Wittenberg had however been saved.

We had commenced our movement on Dessau, and nothing would have been saved by countermanding it and directing it upon Wittenberg: besides, we hoped that our sappers would be enabled to repair the bridge of Dessau, so that we might continue our march in that direction. If the Prince of Wurtemberg had not burnt the bridge, it is impossible to say what would have been the fate of the Prussian army; which, after fighting at Jena and Austerlitz, had no passage across the Elbe but at Magdeburg. We were a vast distance in advance, and another battle must have been fought before the Prussians could have debouched in that direction. The event must have been fatal to them, had not the King adopted other plans.

On arriving at Dessau, the residence of the Prince of Anhalt, the Emperor went himself to inspect the bridge, which was two-thirds burnt. The repairs were actively commenced; but finding that it would be a work of consider-able time, the Emperor preferred crossing at Wittenberg. Next day all the troops marched in the direction of the latter place, which they reached the same evening. By this movement nearly a day was lost.

CHAPTER XXIV.

Duroc's secret mission to the King of Prussia—The Emperor's arrival at Witten-
berg—Singular meeting in a forest—Surrender of Spandau—The Emperor at
Potsdam—He visits Sans-Souci and the apartment of Frederick the Great—
Discovery of a memorial drawn up by Dumouriez—The Emperor enters Berlin
—A flag of truce from Prince Hohenlohe—Capitulation of Prentzlau.

ON the road from Dessau to Wittenberg we met Marshal
Duroc, who was returning, in an open carriage, with intelligence of a mission with which he had been charged. The
Emperor made him mount a horse, and directing every one
else to go forward, he rode by the side of the marshal, at a
sufficient distance behind us to prevent their conversation
being overheard.

It was not until long after that we understood Duroc
had been sent from Weimar to the King of Prussia. He
managed the affair with so much secrecy, that we knew
nothing of his departure until after he was gone. He never
informed us where he had been ; but, as reports of peace
were circulated as soon as we entered Berlin, we concluded
that he had been charged with some pacific negotiations, as
will subsequently be seen.

As soon as the Emperor arrived at Wittenberg, he inspected the fortress, and ordered some new works to be
added to those which were already executed. Here he remained two days, to afford time for the whole of the army to
cross the Elbe. The French effected this operation before
the Prussians, and thus we still had the start of them in the
subsequent movements. The Emperor intrusted Marshal
Ney with the blockade of Magdeburg. The marshal surrounded the fortress in the best manner he could, that is to
say, after the Prussians had recrossed the Elbe.

The Emperor, with the rest of the army, advanced to Berlin by the Potsdam road, in order to dispute with the enemy the passage of the Spree. The whole army was one or two marches in advance, when he set out from Wittenberg. It was about one in the afternoon. The sky was overcast, and a storm was gathering. As we passed through one of the suburbs of Wittenberg, the hail began to fall.

The Emperor alighted to get shelter, and he entered the house of the district inspector of forests to the Elector. The Emperor thought he was not known; and he regarded merely as ordinary civility the respectful manner in which he was received by two young women, who were in the apartment which he entered. They appeared much surprised and embarrassed; and having risen from their seats, they continued standing, as well as some children who were with them; and the prettiest of the two exclaimed, in an under-tone, "Heavens! it is the Emperor."

The Emperor did not notice this; but I observed it, as I happened to understand a little of German. He asked the lady whether she was married. "Sire, I am a widow," she replied. The Emperor appeared surprised, and again addressing her, he said, "Where did your husband die?" The lady replied, "In war, Sire—in your Majesty's service." "You know me then?"—"Yes, Sire, you are not altered; and I recognised you immediately, as well as General Berthier and General Savary." "Where have you seen me before?"—"In Egypt, Sire."

The Emperor was now more astonished than before. "What!" said he, "have you been in Egypt? How happened you to go thither?"—"Sire," said the lady, "I am a native of Switzerland, and I married M. de . . . , a physician in the army. He died of the plague at Alexandria, and I married again. My second husband was colonel of the 2nd regiment of light infantry, and he was killed at Aboukir. He left me with a son, whom I have brought up. On my return to France with the army, I could not obtain my pension ; and tired of the repulses I experienced, I returned to Switzerland, which I again left on being engaged by this lady to educate her children."

" But," said the Emperor, " were you really married to the colonel, or was it merely a connexion which your circumstances induced you to form ?"

" Sire, my marriage-contract is up stairs." (She ran to fetch it.) " Here it is. You see that my son is born in lawful marriage."

, The Emperor was much pleased, and he exclaimed, " *Par Dieu!* this is a curious meeting." He then ordered Bertrand to take down the names of both the mother and the son.

The storm was now over, and the Emperor being about to depart, he said, " Well, Madame, as a memorial of this day, I grant you an annual pension of 1200 francs, with the reversion to your son."

He then mounted his horse, and set off. In the evening, before he retired to rest, he signed the order for the widow's pension.

He passed the night at the distance of a short march from Potsdam. Next morning we met some of the Saxon cavalry, who were quitting the Prussian army to return to Saxony. We now learned that the Prussian army had recrossed the Elbe, and was making every exertion to regain the Oder towards Stettin.

The Emperor ordered Marshals Soult and Bernadotte, who were on the right bank of the Elbe, to press the enemy as closely as possible. He was harassed with fatigue, and experienced great privations.

Marshal Ney remained on the left bank of the Elbe, for the twofold purpose of observing Magdeburg, and guarding the passage of the river against the Prussian army, if, being too closely pressed by the corps of Soult and Bernadotte, it should attempt to recross to the left bank, and throw itself into another part of Germany, by which means the French army would be drawn to a distance from Prussia.

The corps of Marshal Lannes was directed on Spandau, which surrendered at the first summons; so that this corps, being afterwards disposable, was carried behind the Havel on the other side of the Spree.

The Emperor arrived at Potsdam, and was lodged in the castle. It was broad day when he entered the town, and he immediately went to visit the two palaces of Sans-Souci. He admired the beauty of the large palace, and made some remarks on the site chosen for that beautiful residence. The soil is so unfavourable to vegetation, that the trees never attain any considerable growth.

The little palace of Sans-Souci greatly interested him. He examined the apartment of Frederick the Great, which is religiously respected. None of the furniture has been displaced; and certainly splendour constitutes no part of its value: plainer or commoner furniture could not be found in any broker's shop in Paris.

The writing-table appeared to me to be similar to those which are still seen in the offices of our old French notaries: the inkstand and pens were still upon it.

The Emperor opened several of the books which he knew Frederick the Great was fond of reading, and which contained marginal notes written in the king's own hand, upon which the Emperor made some observations. Some of these notes seemed to have been written under the influence of ill-humour. The Emperor ordered the door to be opened by which Frederick the Great used to go down to the terrace beside the garden; and also the door through which he used to pass, when he went to review his troops on the great sandy plain, near the palace, on the side opposite to the garden.

The Emperor returned to Potsdam to pass the night.

He was much pleased with the elegance of the King of Prussia's apartments ; and he forbade that the Queen's private apartments should be occupied by any person whatever.

He gave the same order at Berlin, with reference to some apartments which were prepared for the Queen in a small house which was one of her favourite residences.

On the 20th of October the Emperor's head-quarters were at Charlottenburg. Curiosity having induced some persons to visit the Queen's apartments at this place, they found in a drawer a memorial drawn up by Dumouriez, on the means of destroying the power of France. It was carried to the Emperor, who, on seeing it, could not repress his indignation.

Next day (the 21st), one month after his departure from Paris, and having taken rather a circuitous route, the Emperor entered Berlin. He was on horseback, accompanied by the guard, two divisions of cuirassiers, the foot-guards, and the whole of Marshal Davout's corps, for whom he had reserved the honour of being the first to enter the Prussian capital. The weather was delightful. Almost all the population of the city seemed to be out of doors, and the windows were filled with ladies.

To the honour of the ladies of Berlin, I must observe, that though they evinced considerable curiosity on this occasion, yet the most profound grief was expressed in the countenances of all, and many were bathed in tears. They were generally very exceedingly beautiful : their patriotic feeling powerfully excited our interest and respect.

The Emperor alighted at the King's palace, where he took up his abode. The troops were stationed on the Custrin and Stettin roads, with the exception of the guard which was quartered in Berlin.

The Emperor sent me with a detachment of a hundred

dragoons on a reconnoissance. * He had not received so much intelligence of the enemy as he wished; and he had an admirable tact in anticipating any approaching event.

I directed my course on Nauen; and, at first setting out, I proceeded so expeditiously, that before day-light I had established myself in ambuscade between Nauen and Spandau, where I suspected some stray Prussian detachment would take refuge, the surrender of Spandau being not yet known. Accordingly, at day-break, some baggage and a number of led horses approached. These were accompanied by fugitives from all the Prussian regiments. I allowed them to advance a good way into the defile where I was stationed, and I then went forward to address them. None attempted to escape, except those in the rear, who took to flight, and were pursued in vain.

This was a good capture, and my men made a tolerable booty. I did not however obtain much information; for among the whole party, who had quitted the army long since, there was not a single man who could give me any satisfactory intelligence. I sent the column to Spandau. As I conjectured, they knew nothing of the surrender of the fortress. About two hours after, a man on horseback, followed by baggage of the Prince of Orange, appeared in sight. He was better informed than those who preceded him; he had come from Rattenau, where he left Prince Hohenlohe. All the Prussian troops were in the neighbourhood, and were about to march by Alt-

---

* " General Savary, remain all day in your position. Go wherever your horses can carry you. If you can, go as far as Fehrbellin, where it is possible you may fall in with something. If you capture horses, send them to Spandau, to mount the dragoons. Above all things send me intelligence; and if you have anything of importance to communicate, you may forward it straight to the Grandduke of Berg, who will be at Oranienburg.

" On this, &c.

{" NAPOLEON."

" Potsdam, Oct. 26, 1806, 4 in the morning."

Rupin on Prentzlau. I immediately sent information of this to the Emperor.

The Prince's baggage immediately arrived. The man who had the care of it gave me some satisfactory accounts. I captured none of the baggage except a box of claret, which was a valuable thing in Prussia.

On my march from Nauen to Fehrbellin, I met a Prussian flag of truce, who was sent by Prince Hohenlohe with orders to deliver his dispatch, and then return. I was not to be duped. Prince Hohenlohe's object was to ascertain precisely where we were, that he might either quicken or retard his march accordingly. I blindfolded the flag of truce, and sent him by express to the Emperor at Berlin.

I did right, for we learned from the flag of truce that he had left Prince Hohenlohe at New-Rupin preparing to depart for Prentzlau; and on this information the Emperor directed the dragoons and the corps of Marshal Lannes to proceed up the Havel by forced marches on Prentzlau. They reached the bridge of Prentzlau a few hours before the head of the Prussian column appeared on the other bank of the river.

Both sides were so much fatigued, that a parley readily ensued. The Prussian troop which was most in advance was a regiment belonging to the King's guard, which, supposing all was lost, were very glad to return to Berlin. An arrangement was proposed, and immediately concluded.

Prince Hohenlohe surrendered with all the troops who were there, which was a very considerable number;* and he transferred to General Blucher the command of those troops who were too distant to be included in the capitulation.

The regiment of the King's guards, and all the colours and standards of the troops composing the corps of Prince Hohenlohe, were sent to Berlin.

* These capitulations were, properly speaking, dismissals from service ; for most of the men returned to their homes.

This event was very satisfactory to the Emperor, who urged Marshals Soult and Bernadotte not to leave General Blucher a moment's respite. He again sent me from Berlin with two regiments of light cavalry to pursue all the troops whom Blucher might detach from his army with the view of misleading Bernadotte and Soult.

CHAPTER XXV.

The Emperor sends the author in pursuit of Blucher, who is also pursued by Bernadotte and Soult—The remainder of the Prussian army is separated into two divisions—Capitulation of General Husdom—The author enters Wismar—Capture of twenty-four Swedish vessels—Capitulation of Blucher—The Prince of Hatzfeld.

I ASSEMBLED the two regiments before-mentioned, namely, the 1st hussars and the 7th chasseurs, at Fehrbellin; and advanced immediately, by forced marches, through New-Rupin, Rhinsberg, and Strelitz. In the last town I found Prince Charles of Mecklenburg, a younger brother of the Queen of Prussia's, and a major in the guards. He had left the army to return to his family. I allowed him to proceed, contenting myself with making him sign an indorsement, by which he bound himself not to bear arms against France until after a peace, or his exchange. There would have been no great merit in making a prisoner in this situation; and besides, I could not have carried him with me.

I was well received by the Prince of Mecklenburg, in whose residence I passed the night. Next morning I proceeded in the direction of Surburg, in order to reach Wharen at an early hour.

On the road I heard a cannonade in advance of me; I made all haste, and found Marshal Bernadotte engaged with Blucher before Wharen.

Blucher had rallied the wrecks of the Prince of Hohen-

lobe's corps, and added them to what he had previously collected of the army which fought against Marshal Davout.
His corps formed nearly the only remnant of the Prussian
force.

The King had left the army, as soon as the armistice which
he applied for was refused : he passed through Magdeburg,
on his way to Berlin, where he had orders to give, as he foresaw that he could not prevent that city from falling into our
power.   He then directed his course to the Oder, and thence
to Graudentz, where he ordered the bridge of boats over the
Vistula to be withdrawn.   It was after he had passed that
river that he was informed of the surrender of his army at
Lubeck, in the manner I shall now relate.

General Blucher manœuvred so as to draw Marshals
Soult and Bernadotte from Berlin ; but had he led them even
to Mentz, he would not have escaped the fate which awaited
him.   However, he succeeded in giving our two marshals the
slip from the field of battle at Wharen, where they engaged
him.   He escaped from them so completely, that they only
reached in the evening the positions which he had left in the
morning.   He passed through Schwerin, and gained Lubeck.
He wished to defend the bridge of that place, but it was taken
by our troops.   Driven then to the last extremity, and destitute of ammunition, he capitulated, and surrendered his
troops prisoners of war.

As flanker of the right, I marched in the same direction as
Marshal Bernadotte ; and the day after the battle of Wharen
I had the good fortune to separate the Prussian general, Husdom, and his small corps, from General Blucher. Informed of
the position he occupied by one of his officers, whom he had
dispatched to General Blucher, and whom I made prisoner,
I immediately went in pursuit of him, and was so close
upon him every evening, that it was impossible for him to
escape me ; but he drew me after him to the gates of Wismar.   He had with him the hussar regiment which bore his

name, Kat's regiment of dragoons, and two pieces of light artillery.

With my two regiments united, I had only four good squadrons, when I sent out my flankers ; but fortune befriended me.

On the last day of my march, General Husdom had passed the night in bivouac, about a league from Wismar on the Rostock road. He deliberated during the night whether he should march next day on Rostock, or try to form a junction with Blucher ; of whose disaster he was as ignorant as I. Opinions were divided in his little council of war ; and next day, fortunately for me, Kat's dragoons left him, and directed their route across the country towards the states of Upper Prussia. I halted for the night at a short distance from General Husdom ; and, by a lucky thought, I made my men mount their horses two hours before day-break. I was on the point of reaching the branch of the road which goes from Rostock to Wismar, when my advanced post brought in two Prussian hussars, who had deserted. They told me that they had left their regiment about a quarter of an hour before, at the moment when it was ordered to proceed to Wismar. While I was examining these men, my servants, who were bringing up the led horses for my own use from the rear of the column, arrived in a state of alarm, and told me that the Prussians had turned us. I hastened to the rear, and took with me one of the deserters, who recognised Kat's dragoons, and informed me of the separation of that regiment from the corps to which he had belonged. These troops had no inclination to commence an attack ; on the contrary, they carefully avoided it, and were very happy that I had not arrived half an hour sooner, which would have stopped their march. They found the road, and took advantage of the opportunity to hasten their march, at which I was very well pleased ; for, in fact, I was not strong enough to attack two regiments. Had they come to me, I should have been obliged to submit to the fate which I wished to impose upon them.

I returned, with my mind much eased, to the head of the column. I had with me a man of uncommon courage and presence of mind : he set out with a detachment of forty men ; and with a hardihood akin to Quixotism, he threw himself into Wismar, assembled the Mecklenburg troops which formed the garrison, and made them shut the gates of the town, in which he remained. General Husdom's vanguard presented itself at day-break before the town, and attempted to enter it ; but was repulsed by this small detachment, which very prudently did not venture out in pursuit.

General Husdom's position was becoming delicate. I spared him the first step in a disagreeable business, by sending one of my aides-de-camp to him with a trumpet to propose an arrangement. He had no other course to take: it was his belief that I was stronger than he; and, on the contrary, I was persuaded that he was the stronger party; but as I did not allow him to come near to reconnoitre me, he capitulated, and surrendered his regiment, with two pieces of cannon more than I had, independently of a superiority of about two hundred men.

I was very glad to find that I had made such an acquisition. The number of horses I now had was so great that I could not carry them with me; and I was obliged to order the surplus to be hamstrung under the walls of Wismar. After supplying an escort for the prisoners whom I sent to Spandau, I had still with me three good squadrons.

From Wismar, where I learned the capitulation of Lubeck, I proceeded to Rostock. None of the enemy's troops remained there : I took possession, however, of twenty-four Swedish vessels, which I found in the port; they were all loaded and ready to sail, but were wind-bound. We were at war with Sweden, and these ships were therefore good prize. Having only cavalry with me, and considering that when we left the town the vessels might escape, I called a meeting of the magistrates; and, without explaining to them my plan, I required them to make out an estimate of the value of the Swedish vessels in the port, which they did, ship by ship. I then ordered them to take possession of these merchantmen, and to hold themselves answerable to me for the whole. They objected, that they were not at war with Sweden; and that to do what I desired, would be to commit an act of hostility against that state.

I admitted that what they said was true; but observed, that I was determined not to be duped, and therefore required that they, the magistrates, should pay me down the sum at which they had valued the ships and their cargoes. I added, that on receiving the money I would sign a declaration, acknowledging that I had seized the twenty-four vessels, and compelled the magistrates to purchase them from me for that sum, and would give them an acquittance for the same. This was the only way in which I could turn my capture to account.

The magistrates were not very well pleased with this arrangement, but I was too strong for them. I did not drive a hard bargain with them; but in making the sale of my flotilla, I let them off for one-half of the estimated price, as may be easily conceived, when I say that they paid for the whole only something between 120 and 130,000 francs. On this being settled, all the scruples of the worthy burghers vanished. I gave the two regiments which were with me 60,000 francs; which, added to the little booty they obtained by the capture of General Husdom's corps, satisfied them that they had made a good campaign. The Emperor gave up the whole of the other 60,000 francs to me. He was still at Berlin when I arrived there. It is proper to state what had passed in that city.

We no sooner established ourselves in a place of any importance, than a system of police superintendence and means of acquiring information were organised. It was generally believed that I managed this department; but that supposition was erroneous.   During the sixteen or seventeen years in which I served the Emperor, he had sufficient esteem for me never to propose to employ me in any such business. I have, however, often found placed to my account actions of which I am incapable, of which I even had no knowledge; and which were the work of certain low-minded adventurers or intriguers, who, being naturally the servile adulators of all governments, were always ready to flatter the Emperor, as they had before flattered the Commissioners of the Convention, and as they have since flattered the restored Princes;— men who never hesitate to betray the power from which they have obtained all they can hope for, in order to gratify any other power from which they may still expect more, and who are willing to make themselves useful by any means.   These men, who rendered my situation with the Emperor embarrassing, and some of whose actions I shall make known, used to address to him directly, or transmit through Marshal Duroc, reports which sometimes came into my possession: after denouncing their comrades, they often told them that the accusation came from me; that the Emperor had asked their opinion on the subject, and that they had settled every thing.

The circumstance of my being commandant of the gendarmerie of the Emperor's guard favoured their duplicity, and lent a colour of truth to their base calumnies.

On our arrival at Berlin, possession was immediately taken of the Post-office.   The examination of correspondence was so skilfully managed, that for some time the people in the Prussian service had no suspicion of the fact : until apprehension was excited, it was pretty certain that the letters would have real addresses, dates, and subscriptions; and that thus a knowledge would be obtained, on the one hand, of the places to which important persons, whose employments necessarily determined the positions of troops, had retired ; and, on the other hand, the functions with which persons remaining in the places we occupied might be invested.

The packets addressed to the postmaster, containing letters to be called for, were those in which the most interesting matter was found. In this way, within a few days after our arrival in Berlin, a letter, forwarded from the office of the postmaster of that city, and addressed to the King, was stopped. This letter was written and signed by the Prince of Hatzfeld, who had remained in Berlin. It contained a detailed report of every thing which had occurred in the capital since the King's departure, and a minute description of our force, corps by corps. As the letter was written by a prince, it was laid before the Emperor, who ordered a court-martial to be formed to try the writer on the charge of giving secret information to the Prussian government: an offence likely to be attended by danger to an invading force; as it would be easy in this way to convert every burgomaster into a spy, instructed to make similar reports: in consequence of which an army might be so watched on every point, that scarcely an enterprise could be planned without some information respecting it reaching the enemy.

On the order for the court-martial being given, the Prince of Hatzfeld was arrested. The court-martial met; but as the Emperor had not returned the original letter, which was the only document on which the charge was founded, an application was made for it in the usual way through the major-general.

The Emperor had gone to some distance from Berlin to review one of Marshal Davout's divisions. It was another fortunate circumstance, that on his return he paid a visit to the old Prince Ferdinand, the great Frederick's brother, so that the day was nearly spent before he got home.

These lucky incidents afforded the Princess of Hatzfeld the time necessary to make inquiries, and to see Marshal Duroc, whom she had known during his former visits to Berlin. The marshal knew nothing of the business; and being so occupied that he could not leave the palace, he begged of me to ascertain the nature of the charge against the Prince of Hatzfeld. On our first arrival in Berlin all the military duty of the city was done by the gendarmerie. I therefore soon learned that the captain appointed reporter to the court-martial was waiting for a letter from the Prince of Hatzfeld to the King of Prussia, and that the charge was a capital one. I ran back to inform Marshal Duroc; and I observed to him that not a moment was to be lost, that the life of the Prince was at stake, and that it was necessary to procure for the Princess an immediate audience of the Emperor. I had scarcely said this when the guard was called out under arms. The Emperor had just arrived. Marshal Duroc, giving his arm to the Princess of Hatzfeld, who had never left his apartment, hastened forward, and arrived at the door of the saloon at the moment the Emperor had got to the top of the staircase. The Emperor said to him, " What, has something new occurred, grand-marshal?" *—" Yes, Sire," said Duroc, and followed the Emperor into his cabinet.

I remained at the door to prevent any person from being announced before the Princess of Hatzfeld had seen the Emperor. Duroc soon came out, and immediately introduced the Princess. She knew not why her husband had been arrested; and in the simplicity of her nature demanded justice of the Emperor for the wrong which she supposed was done to him. When she had finished her statement, he handed to her the letter written by her husband. She began to read, and became alarmed as she proceeded. She turned pale, and interrupted her reading with exclamations: " Good God! it is indeed his writing!—Alas! how unfortunate I am!" When she had run over the letter, she seemed motionless, and looked as if she had lost sensation. She stared with haggard eyes at the Emperor; but articulated not a

---

* Duroc was not thus in the habit of waiting on the Emperor, whenever he went out or returned.

word. The Emperor said to her, " Well, Madam, is this a calumny—an unjust charge? I leave you to judge."

The Princess, more dead than alive, was going to answer only with her tears, when the Emperor took the letter from her, and said, " Madam, were it not for this letter, there would be no proof against your husband."—" That is very true," she replied; " but I cannot deny that it is his writing." " Well," said the Emperor, " there is nothing to be done but to burn it ;" and he threw the letter into the fire.

The Princess of Hatzfeld knew not what to do or to say ; but she spoke more by her silence than the most eloquent orator could have done. She retired quite happy. She soon saw her husband, who was set at liberty ; and owed his life solely to the concourse of incidents which I have faithfully related. The Emperor always cherished in his heart similar feelings. He was, on this day, as happy as the Princess of Hatzfeld.

CHAPTER XXVI.

Prince Paul of Wurtemberg taken prisoner—Surrender of Stettin and Custrin— Capitulation of Magdeburg—New mission of Duroc to the King of Prussia— Negotiations between Luchesini and Maret—Arrival of the Prince of Bene- vento—The King of Prussia refuses to sign the peace—Deputation from the senate—Conduct of the police minister on this occasion—Capitulation of Ha- meln—Measures for preventing the dilapidation of the magazines—Capitula- tion of Nieuburg.

AMONG the Prussian prisoners was Prince Paul of Wur- temberg, the second son of the King of Wurtemberg. He had left Stuttgard without his father's permission to serve in the campaign against us. On his arrival, the King of Prus- sia made him a general ; and almost immediately on his ar- rival, he became a prisoner.

The Emperor had reason to be offended at his conduct: nevertheless, he treated him with gentleness; exercising no other vengeance than that of not receiving him. He ordered him to be re-conducted to Stuttgard by a captain of gendarmerie, leaving what was afterwards to be done with him to the King, his father.

While these things were passing at Berlin, our cavalry had approached the Oder; and in consequence of a panic, which it is impossible to explain, the fortified towns of Stettin and Custrin surrendered to some troops of horse, which summoned them from the left side of the river. The cavalry were quite astonished at finding their summons complied with, and at seeing boats come to them, sent by the governors of the towns, to enable them to take possession.

These detachments of cavalry sent notice of what had happened to the corps of infantry in the rear, and they hastened forward to occupy the two towns. * At the same time, Magdeburg, with a garrison of 23,000 men, commanded by General Kleist, formerly the Great Frederick's aide-de-camp, surrendered to Marshal Ney, whose army-corps was not much stronger.

Fortune every where smiled upon us. Prussia was occupied: her troops were prisoners—her fortresses had surrendered; and our army could be assembled in one mass, and undertake new operations.

It was only in Silesia that a Prussian corps kept the field, and opposed Prince Jerome, to whom the Emperor had given the command of an army-corps. It was chiefly composed of allied troops; such as Bavarians, Wurtemberghers, &c.

There remained also in the possession of Prussia two fortresses on the Weser, Hameln and Nienburg; the gar-

---

* These governors must have lost all presence of mind; for only a few days before, some wandering detachments, which appeared before the same fortresses, were refused admission.

risons of which amounted to about 13,000 men. The Emperor ordered me to take these two places. I shall speak of them by and by.

Marshal Duroc was again sent to the King of Prussia, whom he did not find until he reached Osterode, on the other side of the Vistula. He was the bearer of an ultimatum, in reply to the propositions which the King had made through his minister.

The Marquis Luchesini had joined the King before the commencement of hostilities; and it was through him that Prussia negotiated on the overtures of which Marshal Duroc was the bearer, after the battle of Jena. The Emperor was alone. M. de Talleyrand, whom he had left at Mentz with the Empress, had received orders to repair to Berlin, but had not yet arrived.

General Clarke, who was to come from Erfurt, where he had been left governor, to take the government of Prussia, including the city of Berlin, had also not arrived. The Emperor, therefore, made M. Maret conduct the negotiations. In the meantime, the Prince of Benevento arrived, and drew up a note, which was far from being well calculated to bring the negotiations to a favourable issue. He declared to the Prussian plenipotentiaries that the policy of the Emperor was immutable; that he neither wished to aggrandize nor oppress any of his neighbours; but that he was determined not to part with his conquests, except for the sake of obtaining peace. The fortune of arms had placed Prussia in his power; but he was ready to accept a compensation: let then England restore the colonies taken from France and her allies—let Russia desist from assuming the protectorate of Wallachia and Moldavia—let the rights of the Ottoman Porte be re-established in their full plenitude, and he would readily give up all the provinces he had conquered

If even the King of Prussia had wished it, he could not have obliged his allies to subscribe to these conditions. In answer, he observed, that it was not in his power to make the Russian armies, which were covering what territory remained to him, retrograde; that, as to the demand that he should induce the courts of St. James's and Petersburg to join him in negotiating in concert a general peace with Napoleon, he could not flatter himself with any expectations of success in that object; that, however, he did not repress all hope, and that accordingly he would not yet recall his minister from the Emperor's head-quarters. When Duroc presented himself to the King, he refused to ratify the armistice, saying, " It is no longer time; the matter does not now depend upon me: the Emperor of Russia has offered me support, and into his arms I have thrown myself." After this declaration, the Emperor could not carry the negotiations farther; and he had only to consider how he was to put himself in condition to seek peace, wherever he might find the Russians.

The Emperor had established his great magazines of provisions at Berlin and Potsdam. All the horses of the Prussian cavalry were used to remount ours. All the artillery-horses were in like manner collected: so that in less than a month our army was completely refitted.

At Berlin the Emperor received a deputation from the senate. The deputies were sent to compliment him on his astonishing success; and, at the same time, to thank him for the standards and colours which he had transmitted to the senate to decorate the hall in which its sittings were held.

This deputation, which consisted of twelve senators, thought fit to make representations to the Emperor on the danger which he might incur by advancing beyond the Oder, and to express to him a wish to see his conquests brought to a termination. This observation offended the Emperor; and he replied to the deputation, that he would make peace as soon as he could, but in such a way as to make it once for all; that, as they themselves well knew, he had made every endeavour to obtain that object; and that he could not refrain from showing his dissatisfaction at their want of consideration, in exhibiting the shameful spectacle of disunion between the chief of the state and the first constituted body of the nation, at the very time when they knew that the Russians were advancing to join the Prussians. He farther observed, that before they took this step they ought to have ascertained on what side the opposition to peace existed, and to have brought with them the means of causing that opposition to disappear.

In other respects the Emperor treated these deputies well, and they went away satisfied; but he wrote to Paris with the hand of a master on the mission of the twelve senators. Their representation might have been well intended; but how could peace be made, since it no longer depended on the King of Prussia, who had placed himself in the hands of the Russians?

It ought also to have been recollected, that the Emperor's residence at Berlin had been dedicated to negotiations for peace with Prussia, which had only been broken off in consequence of the arrival of the Russians.

The Emperor began to suspect that the minister of the police had acted improperly on this occasion; because he ought either, as a senator, to have explained the state of affairs to the senate, and then that assembly would not have voted such a measure; or, as minister, to have opposed it: but he wished to conciliate the senate, by conniving at the making of the representation. Had it succeeded, he would have asserted that he had influenced the whole proceeding, and would thereby have augmented his popularity and credit. At all events, he took care to secure a cover for his ministerial responsibility, by making a report to the Emperor on what had passed; and stating therein, that, notwithstanding all his endeavours to the contrary, the senators persisted in the course they had adopted. This was the cause of the displeasure expressed by the Emperor towards them; but, nevertheless, he was far from being satisfied with the minister. Had it not been for the continuation of the war, and the protection afforded him by the Grand-duke of Berg and Marshal Lannes, Fouché would probably have been, at this time, dismissed.

The Emperor had sent to Italy for the Polish general, Dombrowski, who joined us at Potsdam. This was an indication of the Emperor's intentions, though as yet he had not allowed a word on the subject to transpire in Poland. It was not until after the final refusal of the King of Prussia to negotiate, that he appealed to the patriotism of the Poles to augment his force.

With a view to this object, the mere presence of General Dombrowski was of great advantage.

The Emperor, who was extremely provident, never moved without being accompanied by all the means which he anticipated he might on some future day have occasion to employ. This obliged a great number of persons to follow his headquarters, where there was always to be found not only a sufficient administration for an army, but for a whole state.

Besides the army which we had in Prussia, the Emperor ordered from France some more regiments, which he draughted from the garrisons of Paris and Brest. These formed the rudiments of a corps of which Marshal Mortier took the command, and with which he marched from Mentz to occupy the Hans towns. This corps was afterwards reinforced by allied troops; and Mortier was master of the shores of the Baltic, by the time that the Emperor was making his preparations for the invasion of Poland.

The Emperor sent me from Berlin to take the command of the Dutch troops before Hameln. The King of Holland, after having summoned that place, experienced an attack of a disease to which he was subject, and was obliged to return to Amsterdam.

The Emperor directed me to take Hameln with the force then before it; and prohibited me from detaining or diverting for my aid any troops which might be on their way to join the grand army *

The Grand-duke of Berg advised me to spare the country which I was about to enter, as he expected that it would belong, to him. On this possession he already calculated.

I found the Dutch corps posted at the distance of two leagues from Hameln. In force it was about equal to half the garrison of the place, and the weather was horrible. On my arrival, I wrote to the governor, proposing an interview on the glacis, and leaving it to him to settle what precautions

---

* My instructions were in these terms:—

Head-quarters, Berlin, November 18.

In pursuance of the Emperor's desire, you will be pleased, general, to depart forthwith, and present yourself before Hameln.

You will take the command of the troops blockading that fortress, and you will take care to entrench all the posts of the blockade with good redoubts

You will take from the fortress of Rinteln the howitzers and guns necessary for bombarding and cannonading the town, and accelerating the surrender. You will mount small field-pieces on the redoubts, to prevent the enemy from raising the blockade; and to supply, by means of these works and a well-executed service, the deficiency of the troops placed under your command.

Immediately on your arrival you will transmit to the Emperor a report on the state of the blockade, and you will correspond with me as often as possible.

You will draw your provisions, and whatever else you may want, from the Hanoverian territory

The 12th regiment of light infantry was to march this day from Cassel for Hameln. Should it not be arrived, you will write to General Lagrange, at Cassel, to send it forward without delay; and if you really do need a greater number of troops, you will also ask General Lagrange to give you some of the detachments of cavalry which he has at Cassel. The intention of his Majesty is, that you shall make up by judicious dispositions, by activity and energy, for the small number of your troops.

His Majesty farther authorizes you to grant a capitulation to the troops in garrison on their surrendering prisoners of war; the officers on their parole, and the soldiers to be sent to France. You will take care that all the regimental chests, and every thing belonging to the King of Prussia, shall be delivered up. Send me also, general, a report on the condition of the fortress of Rinteln.

he might think necessary on the occasion. He replied immediately, and fixed next day for the meeting.

I was first at the appointed place. I brought with me the
capitulations of Magdeburg, Spandau, Custrin, Stettin, Prentzlau, and Lubeck. These were certainly my best means of
attack. The place had somewhat more than six months' provisions; and contained, besides the garrison, a small disposable corps, commanded by General Le Cocq, who, finding it
impossible to form a junction with any Prussian army, had
taken refuge in Hameln. He came to the rendezvous with
the governor, who was General Schell, an old officer, who had
served under Frederick.

I told them that, having come to take the command of the
military operations against the fortress, I thought it right to
make them acquainted with the state of affairs in their country; that what that state was they would learn from the
documents which I should show them; that after their decision I should know how to act; that at present I was authorized to allow them all to return to their homes except the
soldiers, as had been the case at other places; and that if mv
proposal was refused, I should proceed immediately with the
attack; but that the siege once opened, I would listen to no
capitulation.

I had remarked that the Prussian officers set great importance upon their baggage; for, at this period, as in the time of
Frederick, any one of them had more than a colonel in our
army carried with him.

The gentlemen who met me on this occasion requested that
I would allow them to be in private while they examined the
documents I had brought with me, and deliberated on my
proposal. I gave them a chamber in the mill which I occupied. In about half an hour they announced that they had
resolved to treat on the conditions which I had offered them:
they only wished farther to stipulate for payment of a month
or half a month's pay, as travelling expenses.

I had not money enough to pay the instalment of a crown on the sum they demanded ; but the bargain was too good to allow me to hesitate about it. I agreed to their terms, and we signed the capitulation; according to which, the place, with its forts, was to be surrendered to me next day at noon.

We separated : I returned very well satisfied to my head-quarters, to make such dispositions as were necessary.

Next day the garrison mutinied ; and General Schell wrote to me, that he feared he should not be able to deliver up the place unless some new articles were added to the capitulation, to the effect that the soldiers should be allowed to return home ; and, I believe, that some other advantages should be granted to the officers.

I adhered firmly to the capitulation, and would consent to no addition or alteration. I sent an answer by one of my aides-de-camp, and made arrangements to possess myself of the place, at all events, by some means or other. As good fortune would have it, the soldiers of the garrison proceeded to plunder the magazines, and to give themselves up to intoxication. The officers found it quite impossible to maintain order ; and General Schell sent a message to me, begging that I would not delay taking possession, and informing me that the soldiers had forced one of the gates ; a circumstance which the weakness of my blockading force had prevented me from observing ; and were leaving the fortress in a disorderly state. I lost no time in sending forward the Dutch column, which entered the town some hours sooner than the time stipulated by the capitulation. We were obliged to collect the Prussian soldiers in a kind of park near the town; and for that purpose we had to pick them up dead drunk from the streets. The spectacle was altogether hideous. However, we succeeded at last in getting the place evacuated, and the column of prisoners sent off on its route.

I found in the town, besides a prodigious quantity of artillery, fifteen stand of Prussian colours, and, what I was most proud of, the standards of Blucher's regiment of hussars ; the commander of which had deposited them in Hameln as a security against the chances of war. This was a novel method, with which I was not before acquainted. One of these standards, which was lighter than the rest, was adorned with a quantity of ribbons bearing embroidered devices; which proved that many fair ladies felt very warmly for the honour of this regiment. They appeared to have lavished all their tender sentiments in these embellishments; and they surely had not been consulted when such a testimony of their interest and affection was delivered into the keeping of other hands than those for which it was originally intended.

I remained at Hameln only as long as was necessary to draw up an inventory of what I found in the place, and in particular of the magazines. I took care that these magazines should be given up only to the Hanoverian regency, which had furnished the supplies on the requisition of the Prussian government. I made them be delivered in the state in which they were, informing the members of the regency that they were robbed in a thousand ways, but that all their complaints would go for nothing when the account of those munitions should be required of them. The deputies of the regency were quite astonished when they found that I made no demand upon them of any thing for myself. They had been so long accustomed to purchase what belonged to themselves, to see it taken from them the next day in order to be paid for again, that on coming to this place from Hanover they expected to experience similar conduct: they had even brought money to answer the demand which they thought would be made upon them : they were therefore very well pleased, and I performed a useful service; for the first thing the Emperor ordered was to re-provision this fortress for six months. I left at least provisions for four months, so that the regency had only to replace what the Prussian garrison had consumed.

The states of Hanover did not forget my conduct ; for, at the end of the following summer, I received from them a grand order, set with diamonds.

I sent the Emperor the capitulation of Hameln, the standards, and an account of every thing relating to the place; and I prepared to march towards Nieuburg on the Weser, where there was a bridge over the river. The garrison of that place consisted of 4500 men, and the fortifications mounted 80 pieces of cannon.

I prepared in Hameln a small howitzer-train, with the necessary ammunition. I had only that and the field-artillery to begin the siege of Nieuburg. Fortunately, on the eve of my departure, the 12th regiment of light infantry, which had been ordered to join me instead of proceeding to its first destination at Cassel, arrived. I took it with me, and also all the Dutch corps, except one regiment which I left in garrison at Hameln.

My first day's march brought me to Minden, and the second within gun-shot of Nieuburg. It was night, otherwise I might have experienced a warm reception. However, late as it was, I sent a flag of truce to the governor, with copies of the capitulations of the other fortresses, to which I added that of Hameln. The governor was General Stracwitzch, another old officer, and aide-de-camp of Frederick. He postponed the negotiation to next day ; and sent back my flag of truce, whom he treated with great politeness.

In fine, he signed on the morrow the same capitulation which had been signed by his comrades of the seven years' war, and, on the following day, surrendered to me the place and the garrison.

SUPPLEMENTARY CHAPTER

ON THE CATASTROPHE OF

THE DUKE D'ENGHIEN.

SUPPLEMENTARY CHAPTER.

On the catastrophe of the Duke d'Enghien.

THE catastrophe of the Duke d'Enghien was yet unexplained : nothing was certain but the Duke's melancholy death, when, in 1823, I published an abstract of my memoirs, in which I explained the causes of that event. In this publication, I had two objects in view. The first certainly was to repel the base insinuations which were cast upon me, when, during my imprisonment at Malta, I was supposed to be lost beyond redemption : the second was to defend the memory of the Emperor, to whom I had wholly devoted my existence ; for I accept this reproach as an honour conferred on me. My only wish was to unfold the truth ; but that which was merely the elucidation of an historical fact, has suddenly become a personal question. Adversaries, whom I had never even thought of, rose up against me. Of these, General Hullin, who had hitherto been on as friendly a footing with me as I had with him, and whom I had informed of my publication before it appeared, was the first to present himself.

He was soon followed by two others : one wishing, no doubt, to repel in anticipation a portion of the blame which a profound investigation of the affair could not fail to cast upon him, published a letter, which, among many offensive things to which I did not condescend to reply, contained false assertions, which cannot with propriety remain unanswered.

The other only *wrote that he would not write :* he declared that he had transmitted a letter to the King. I certainly was not aware that I was so far honoured as to be the object of his attention, until I received a letter * prohibiting my appearance in a place to which I had always had free access in the days of our glory and danger.

I was doubtless bound to respect the will of the sovereign, and to submit to it; but I regarded it only as a decision wrested from him by surprise from his misled equity. Besides, it was not before him that this cause was to be tried ; and the judgments of a king are not without appeal, when the reputation and honour of a citizen are concerned.

It is public opinion, tested by public discussion, that judges in the last instance. To this I might immediately have had recourse ; and some of my friends have blamed me for not doing so. I considered, however, that delay was more advisable ; and it was not without well-founded motives that I came to this determination.

Like all political publications mine had its inconveniences and advantages. It drew public attention to transactions which some persons had good reason to wish for ever buried in oblivion ; it compromised some personal interests ; it disturbed securities which were believed to be well secured ; and committed the unpardonable offence of alarming certain Parisian saloons. But, on the other hand, it brought to light

---

* " Monsieur le Duc,

" The King has observed with extreme dissatisfaction, that you have directed public attention to fatal recollections, which he had commanded all his subjects to bury in oblivion.

" His Majesty orders me to acquaint you, that it is his desire you should refrain from presenting yourself at the palace.

" I have the honour to be, with respect, Monsieur le Duc, your very humble and obedient servant,

(Signed)   " Count de Villfle,

President of the council of ministers, and minister of the King's
household, in the absence of the Marquis de Lauriston."

important facts; it resuscitáted incontrovertible documents which had escaped the search of those who would willingly have destroyed them; and it excited a polemical discussion 'from which history cannot fail to profit, and by which truth must unavoidably be elicited. It became me then to wait, that I, as well as others, might be benefited by these new lights.

Besides, at the point to which the question had been brought, was it proper to reply by a pamphlet to pamphlets, or to oppose a justificatory memorial to vague or false assertions? I know not whether such a contest would have convinced my adversaries, but it certainly was not in my opinion worthy of me. I owed it to my honour to make a more noble and more complete defence. I owed it also to my children to whom I have to transmit a name, the lustre of which is proved by titles which cannot be disputed. I therefore resolved to publish my Memoirs—that is, to submit my whole life to public examination.

Let my adversaries then descend into the arena with me, and take up this new kind of gauntlet. A fine opportunity is afforded them for doing homage to the memory of him who loaded them with benefits, and for explaining events much more serious and of much higher historical importance than the question which has awakened their inquietudes or disconcerted their views.

A day will come when public opinion will judge, without reserve and without partiality, all who have acted a part in the great drama of the empire. The course of nature puts a period to personal influences; the petty animosities and gossiping traditions of drawing-rooms sink into oblivion. Men then decide on documents—and to that decision I submit mine.

I wish, but I doubt, that my adversaries would follow this example.

Among the works which have appeared since 1823, I must particularly mention :—

1. Examination of the Proceedings of the Court-martial instituted to try the Duke d'Enghien.

2. A justificatory Memorial published by the Duke de Vicenza.

3. Some Letters published by the Duke de Dalberg, minister from the Court of Baden to the French Government in the year XII. (1804.)

4. An important Note from the Baron de Massias then French Minister at the Court of Baden.

5. Minutes made on the Exhumation of the Duke d'Enghien, in 1816.

6. A Deposition of the Sieur Anfort, brigadier of Gendarmerie at Vincennes, preserved and separately published, in 1822, by a writer who styles himself a Bourgeois de Paris.

Such are the documents which ought to be referred to for the solution of a question which it is in vain attempted to render personal, and which belongs wholly to history.

For the sake of that clearness with which it is necessary that this examination should be conducted, I shall successively discuss :—

1. The causes which brought the Duke d'Enghien before the court-martial.

2. The conduct of General Hullin as president of the court.

3. My conduct as commander of the troops.

§ I.

Causes which brought the Duke d'Enghien before the court-martial.

I shall not repeat here what I have stated in the first chapters of this volume, respecting the circumstances which transpired on the trial of George, and which would lead to the conclusion that the mysterious personage whom certain subaltern agents alluded to was the Duke d'Enghien. What I have written gives on this subject every desirable explanation. I have nothing to add.

But what I did not state, and what, for the elucidation of other important circumstances which require investigation, must not now be omitted, is, that at the time of that trial the Duke de Dalberg was the envoy from the Elector of Baden to the French republic: though descended from a princely German family he was then only a baron. He was nephew of the last Elector of Mentz, who had not yet become Primate of Germany. Thus, in 1804, Baron Dalberg was from relationship, and as feudatory of the German empire, connected with the ambassador of the chief of that empire. His transactions must naturally have been intimately combined with those of that ambassador ; unless it be supposed, contrary to all probability, that the court of Baden had instructed the baron to sacrifice the general interests of Germany for the sake of favouring the extension of the French republic.

Be this as it may, Baron Dalberg, in his apologetic letter, declares that " M. de Talleyrand, during his ministry, had constantly endeavoured to moderate the violent passions of Bonaparte."

Had then Baron Dalberg private communications with M. de Talleyrand? It certainly could not be in any intercourse between them, as minister with minister, that he was informed by Talleyrand of the efforts which he might or might not have made to calm the violence of the First Consul's passions.

Baron Dalberg, indeed, dates this confidence only from the war of 1806; but I will soon fix its real date.

In the first place, I would ask how it happened that, according to these premises, Baron Dalberg left a country where his birth ensured him the highest consideration, to come to France and connect himself with a republican system

against which all Europe had risen? How came he to renounce the high honour of being proclaimed at every coronation of the German emperors, when the Emperor himself
used to ask aloud, in the presence of the nobility of Germany
assembled in the church of Frankfort, "Is there a Dalberg
here?"

It may be readily conceived that the First Consul, on becoming emperor, had to reward great services in war; and
there is nothing extraordinary in the political fortunes of men
who astonished the world by their toils and their deeds.

It was the same in the civil administration, where great
talents and efforts, supported by patriotic zeal, substituted a
code of laws for the anarchy which desolated society, a system
of finance for the waste of the republic, and restored order
and economy in every branch of the government.

All these superior men naturally became the objects of particular attention, and the causes of their elevation were perfectly honourable.

But when Baron Dalberg joined our fortunes, he had
neither incurred the danger of our battles, nor shared the
labours of our administration. What then were the *potent*
services which he could have rendered us, and which warranted his sudden entrance into the service of France as
Duke de Dalberg, instead of Baron—the title he had borne
in Germany—and being, in the course of *a few months*, endowed with the sum of four millions, and with the appointments of counsellor of state and senator?—*None.* It must
then be presumed that *officious* services already performed,
but not publicly known, drew upon Baron Dalberg all these
accumulated favours.

The Emperor Napoleon was not ungrateful; but he was
not in the habit of rewarding services before they were performed. Why then has not Baron Dalberg, himself explained his private services? I can supply what his modesty
has omitted. He knows this well; for he admitted me

sufficiently into his confidence.—His zeal to bring about the marriage of the grandson of his elector with Mademoiselle Stéphanie de Beauharnois—the choice which was made of Cardinal Fesch to succeed to the primateship of Germany in preference to a German ecclesiastical prince—the good offices and the particular relations of Baron Dalberg when a member of the diplomatic body at Warsaw in 1806—the eagerness of M. de Talleyrand to summon him to Tilsit, in order that he might mingle with the foreign diplomatists, though the Emperor ordered me to prevent his arrival at Tilsit, when I was governor of old Prussia, at Konigsberg —the *officious* part which he acted at Erfurt, and even the anecdote which forced him to enter the service of France— are all known to me. But this is not the place to break the prudent silence which the Duke de Dalberg thinks proper to maintain with reference to these circumstances. An explanation of all these facts, and others not less characteristic, will perhaps find a place in the course of these Memoirs. What I have now said is sufficient to show that Baron Dalberg never thought that, while engaged in an *official* correspondence arising out of his ostensible functions, he was not also at liberty to maintain *officious* communications.

Let us now examine the conduct of Baron Dalberg, the minister representing that venerable and respected prince, the Elector of Baden, at the period of the catastrophe of the Duke d'Enghien, and we shall see whether he was not at once the *official* agent of his sovereign, and the *officious* agent of a French minister.

The affair of George then occupied the attention of the French government. Our diplomatic agents were making investigations in all directions. Baron Dalberg had, doubtless, given official information of this affair to his sovereign; for in his letter to M. de Talleyrand, dated 13th November, 1823, he acknowledges, " that he had received orders to inquire whether there was any complaint against the emigrants who resided in the electorate, and whether their abode there excited any dissatisfaction."•

Could the *pretended* distance at which Baron Dalberg kept himself from the French ministry have made him the dupe of M. de Talleyrand's assertion? and could he really believe that he might transmit to his court, as sincere, this reply of the minister of foreign affairs for the Republic— " That he did not think the government of Baden should be more severe than the French government; that he was not aware of any complaint on the subject, and that the emigrants must be left unmolested?" Or did Baron Dalberg transmit this reply merely in discharge of his *official* duties, and in opposition to other positive opinions? It is not to be expected that Baron Dalberg will make an honest confession on this point : we must therefore seek the truth in comparisons, which are likely to lead to it.

Baron Dalberg had scarcely transmitted M. de Talleyrand's letter to the court of his sovereign, when the territory of Baden was violated. Previous to this violation, a privy-council had been assembled on the 10th of March, composed of the three consuls, the grand-judge, the minister for foreign affairs, and M. Fouché. In this council, a report was read on the foreign ramifications of George's conspiracy. The evidence of these ramifications rested on the reports of the Sieur Mehée. From these reports it was inferred, that it could be no other than the Duke d'Enghien who was to head the insurrection after the blow should be struck. This opinion was held to coincide with the declarations of the subordinate confederates of George; and the report terminated with the proposition for carrying off the Duke d'Enghien, and *getting rid of him.*

A diplomatist like Baron Dalberg could not be ignorant of the assembling of this council. According to his own confession he knew, on the 12th of March, of the departure of General Caulaincourt, who, he says, it was suspected had orders for the arrest of Dumouriez on the territory of Baden.

I was at Rouen on the 12th of March ; and I learned through the ordinary channels the departure of General Caulaincourt and of General Ordener.

Baron Dalberg was the advanced sentinel of the court of Baden. He had hitherto had no guarantee for the safety of the emigrants, to whom his sovereign granted an asylum, but the law of nations, and the assurances of the minister for foreign aff.irs. If the French government, in the very face of Baron Dalberg, violated that law, and acted in opposition to those assurances, it was the incumbent duty of the minister of Baden, who knew that the Duke d'Enghien and other emigrants resided at Ettenheim, to make immediate communications to his court. The emigrants were especially compromised by the depositions of the agents] of George. Not a single individual in Paris was ignorant of this fact : for the first proceedings on the trial took place publicly in the Temple.

Thus, on learning the fact of the holding of the council on the 10th, and the departure of M. Caulaincourt, which took place on the 11th, Baron Dalberg, if he had not voluntarily allowed himself to be misled by the minister for foreign affairs, ought immediately to have dispatched couriers to his sovereign, to rouse him from the false security into which he had been plunged some days before, by the transmission of the reply of the minister for foreign affairs. From that moment there could exist no doubt that the territory of the electorate would be violated ; and from that moment Baron Dalberg might have appreciated the just value of the assurances he had received from the minister for foreign affairs.

An estafette may go from Paris to Carlsruhe in forty hours : to this I have myself been many times a witness. A courier dispatched by Baron Dalberg even on the 12th, would have reached Carlsruhe, or rather Ettenheim (where he might have been directed to the grand-bailli of the place), in the course of the 14th, and in sufficient time for warning to have been given to the Prince, who was not arrested until the 15th: yet Baron Dalberg remained inactive. Surely there is no injustice in affirming that this inactivity was not in unison with his official duties.

But what are we to think, when we find that it was only on the 20th of March, the day on which the Duke d'Enghien arrived in Paris, that Baron Dalberg wrote to the court of Baden to announce the departure of M. Caulaincourt, and the object of his journey; that it was not until the 21st, when all Paris knew that the Prince had perished at six o'clock on that very morning, that he again wrote to Baden, stating, that the Duke d'Enghien *had arrived, escorted by fifty gendarmes,* and that " every body was inquiring what was intended to be done with him?"

The courier then left Paris at four in the afternoon; and at that hour, on the 21st of March, Baron Dalberg writes, that the above question was asked with reference to the Duke d'Enghien!

Finally, it was not until the 22nd of March, *when the Moniteur published the sentence of death, that, in a postscript to a letter of the same day,* the minister of Baden informed his court that the unfortunate prince was no more.

All these circumstances are now revealed by the correspondence of Baron Dalberg. Nothing but the publication of the Moniteur would have forced him to mention the catastrophe. Thus far his official duties had not been forgotten; they might, according to his combinations, yield to his officious duties . . . . But let us proceed.

The Duke d'Enghien was arrested at Ettenheim at five in the morning of the 15th of March. This news must immediately have been conveyed to Carlsruhe. The letter of the 11th, of which M. de Caulaincourt was the bearer, written by M. de Talleyrand to the Baden minister for foreign affairs, was transmitted on the 15th. This is proved by the decree published by the Elector of Baden on the 16th, in which the arrests of the preceding day are alluded to.

It is impossible that an event of this importance could take place without the court of Carlsruhe writing on the same day, or at latest on the 16th, to its minister at Paris, to remonstrate against this violation of territory, or at least to attest the peaceable and inoffensive conduct of the Duke d'Enghien, and to intercede in his behalf. The spirited M. de Massias, the French minister at the court of Baden, himself wrote to the minister for foreign affairs ; and he could only have done so on the communications made to him the same day by the Baden minister. M. de Massias did not fear to affirm, that, during his residence in the electorate, the conduct of the Duke d'Enghien had been *moderate and innocent.*

The dispatches of M. de Massias to the minister for foreign affairs, and those of the minister of Baden to Baron Dalberg, ought therefore to have been received in Paris at the latest on the 18th or 19th of March ; but certainly before the arrival of the Duke d'Enghien, who did not reach Vincennes till the 20th, at six in the evening

Baron Dalberg himself admits, in his letter of the 20th of March, "that, on Thursday the 15th, he knew positively the order of which M. Caulaincourt was the bearer ;" that is to say, he was informed that M. de Talleyrand had written to his court, stating that General Ordener was directed to arrest the Duke d'Enghien and General Dumouriez.

But on learning the object of this expedition, why did not Baron Dalberg immediately repair to the minister for foreign affairs ? Why did he not instantly assemble the diplomatic body to intercede for the Duke d'Enghien? Had Baron Dalberg taken these measures, they certainly could not have failed in their object; if, as he affirms in his letter of the 13th November, 1823, the minister for foreign affairs was of opinion that the emigrants ought to remain unmolested in the electorate ; or if, according to the letter he addressed to the court of Baden on the 22nd March, 1804, " M. de Talleyrand himself seemed, until the last moment, to be ignorant of the resolution that was adopted."

Nevertheless, the First Consul, who, as every circumstance proves, entertained no private resentment against the Duke d'Enghien, except indeed that which might have been excited by the report on which he ordered the arrest of the prince, might have suspended the sentence. Communications between Baron Dalberg and other members of the diplomatic body and the minister for foreign affairs—had the latter been as favourably disposed as Baron Dalberg pretends he was— might have produced this result ; especially, as such communications would have induced the minister to lay before the First Consul the letter of Baron Massias, which was concealed from him, as I shall soon have occasion to show, and all would have terminated by explanations in favour of the Duke d'Enghien.

Instead of pursuing this course, Baron Dalberg remained passive until after the catastrophe. It was not until the 22nd of March that he wrote to the court of Baden : " I cannot, in the very difficult and delicate situation in which I stand, do anything else than explain to the ministers of the courts with which we are most intimately related, the circumstances such as they are."

This was the language which Baron Dalberg held on the 22nd, when the Prince was no more ; but were these also his sentiments on the 15th ?

But what need was there of express orders, when, on the 20th of March, and consequently before the trial of the Duke d'Enghien, Baron Dalberg wrote that he was informed of arrests having taken place at Ettenheim ? And when he knew that the honour of the respectable Elector of Baden was offended, the territory of his electorate violated, the law of nations disregarded, and a prince of the house of

Bourbon at a critical moment arrested; were there not in these circumstances sufficient motives to give a generous impulse to Baron Dalberg, had he been entirely devoted to his duty as minister of the court of Baden? Besides, how could Baron Dalberg, a man of high monarchical principles, as he would have himself believed to be, allow those principles to yield, on so very important an occasion, to the childish considerations stated in his dispatch of the 20th of March?

The conjectures which must unavoidably be deduced from the conduct of Baron Dalberg, acquire additional force from the consideration that he knew on the 20th of March what degree of reliance he ought to place on a minister who was contemplating the arrests at Ettenheim, at the very moment when he was giving assurances that the emigrants residing in the electorate should not be molested.

It even appears that Baron Dalberg, on writing at this period to his court, pronounced an official judgment on the conduct of this minister which was far from being favourable.

In fact, there appears in a letter written on the 12th Nov. 1823, by Baron Berstett, minister for foreign affairs at Carlsruhe, to Baron Dalberg, permitting him to publish some parts of his diplomatic correspondence, the statement that Baron Dalberg would find in No. 27, dated March 27, 1804, "that, at the fatal epoch, he (Baron Dalberg) had not yet reason to be proud of the confidence of the minister for foreign affairs at Paris."

I need not stop to consider what are the causes which afterwards obtained for Baron Dalberg the confidence of the minister for foreign affairs; but I must remark, that Baron Dalberg has taken care not to publish this letter, No. 27. The reason of this reserve may be easily divined. The *official* judgment, then pronounced by Baron Dalberg on the minister for foreign affairs, would form too revolting a contrast with the *officious* judgment contained in his letter of the 13th of

November, 1823, in which he states, "that it is well known that, during his ministry, M. de Talleyrand never ceased to moderate the violent passions of Bonaparte."

But what Baron Dalberg did not wish to say, doubtless, because since that time he had obtained the confidence of M. de Talleyrand, may be easily conjectured from Baron Berstett's letter.

Be this as it may, it is easy to estimate at its true value Baron Dalberg's recent apology for the conduct of the minister for foreign affairs, respecting the catastrophe of the Duke d'Enghien. It will also readily be conceived, that the most favourable judgment which can be formed of Baron Dalberg's conduct is, that, though he knew every thing which was going on, his scruples had been satisfied by being told that the Duke d'Enghien would only be detained as a hostage; and that this was told him because it was foreseen that Baron Dalberg must transmit some statement on the subject to his court; and that, on finding himself placed between the fear of compromising his government, and of compromising himself in his relations with France, on which he probably had already founded projects for the future, he would quietly allow the affair to take its course; being persuaded that his court would easily exculpate itself as to an event which, in the absence of previous information, it could not prevent.

But if Baron Dalberg was only the dupe of those who contrived this plot—if his diplomatic self-love induced him at that epoch to disguise from his court a part of the mystification which was practised upon him, instead of acknowledging his fatal mistake, the odium of the atrocity does not fall with the less weight on those who planned and effected its accomplishment.

Who were those machinators? I conceive that I have sufficiently indicated them; and that I have supported my assertions by circumstances and comparisons of dates, which carry with them at once the stamp of truth and of authenticity. M. de Talleyrand has referred for his justification to his letter to the King, the contents of which are not known ; to the attestations which Baron Dalberg and himself have reciprocally given for each other in their own cause, and which they affect to regard as the public opinion; and finally, to General Hullin's memorial, which does not say one word about the circumstances personally implicating M. de Talleyrand. I might acknowledge all the part of the catastrophe of the Duke d'Enghien attributed to me in that memorial, or rather that with which General Hullin must himself remain charged, and still the part assigned to M. de Talleyrand would not be changed.

My accusation then remains complete against him. Neither the cautious silence which he observes, nor his secret intrigues affect it.

When I preferred this accusation against him, what were, it may be asked, my antecedent relations with M. de Talleyrand ? On this it is proper to say a few words.

At the period when I was promoted to the ministry, Talleyrand was in a deplorable situation, both as to his pecuniary and political circumstances. Many avoided him, believing thereby to pay their court to superior power. I was not one of the number.

It is to me he was indebted for payment of the rent of his chateau of Valençay, which was occupied by the Spanish princes. This, doubtless, was only an act of justice; but in fact, from motives which I do not pretend to judge, the payment had been withheld from M. de Talleyrand, and he solicited it in vain. Had it not been for my interference, this state of things would have long continued ; but my applications procured him payment of the rent of his chateau, at the rate of 75,000 francs per annum.

It was I also who ventured to speak to the Emperor respecting threats of prosecution by some of M. de Talleyrand's creditors. In consequence of what I said, the Emperor was induced to purchase the Hotel de Valentinois, completely furnished, which belonged to M. de Talleyrand, and for which he gave him the sum of 2,100,000 francs. For this he was indebted to me ; and besides that, he was not obliged to bring back the articles which he had already moved to furnish his present hotel.

Again, it was I who, during four years, suspended the effect of certain disagreeable manœuvres, which could not have failed to reach him ; and I went so far in my services, as to throw an obstacle in the way of the unexpected return of a member of his family from Berne to Paris : an event which, at that moment, would have placed him in a most embarrassing situation.

Such was my perseverance in reconciling the Emperor, whom this affair had greatly displeased, that, in 1812, when he departed for the Russian campaign, he was inclined to take M. de Talleyrand with him.

If, from the conduct of M. de Talleyrand towards his benefactor, I turn to that which he has held with regard to me, it is there proved that, in return for my good offices, I owe to him my being placed on the most fatal of the two lists of proscription.

It is impossible to mistake the secret object of this testimony of his gratitude. My crime was the being able to show what his part had been in the affair of the Duke d'Enghien. This explains M. de Talleyrand's efforts to obtain my removal from Malta in 1815; and why, during the whole period of my imprisonment, I could look to no security until after he left the department of foreign affairs. In 1815, it was intended to bring me before a court-martial at Toulon or Marseilles ; I have evidence of this fact before me. I should, as a matter of course, have been condemned and executed : after which, M. de Talleyrand would have boasted to my family of his efforts to save me. It is a maxim with M. de Talleyrand, that a man who can speak only ceases to be an object of fear when he is no more.

After what has now been said, few will be surprised at the pains I in my turn take to leave to M. de Talleyrand the share which duly belongs to him in a catastrophe in which I took no part, for which I can with justice be reproached.

What farther encourages my efforts in this respect, is my perfect conviction that the Emperor Napoleon did not act on the impulse of his own mind, when he ordered the arrest of the Duke d'Enghien. My opinion is fully confirmed by the works written at St. Helena. The authenticity of these works is unquestionably augmented by the circumstance of the authors, who composed them without communication with each other, being unanimous on this point.

The Emperor Napoleon, whose words and even autograph notes these works record, had no motive for blaming or accusing any one person more than another. He knew that what he was writing was to come under the severe scrutiny of history, and to its judgment he looked forward with respect. He besides expressed himself in a way which proves that he had no wish to rid himself of any part of the transaction which could reasonably be attributed to him.

The Emperor ought then to be believed, when he himself wrote that " the death of the Duke d'Enghien must be ascribed to those who laboured by reports and conjectures to represent him as the chief of a conspiracy ;" and when in familiar intimacy with his faithful followers at St. Helena, he added—" that he had been suddenly urged ; that his opinion had been taken as it were by surprise, his measures precipitated, and their result secured beforehand. I was alone one day, he says ; I was still at the table where I had just dined, and was finishing my coffee : I was hastily told of a new conspiracy. I was vehemently reminded that a period ought to be put to such horrible attempts ; that it was full time to give a lesson to those who were in the daily habit of plotting against my life ; *that there was no way of putting an end to the business but by shedding the blood of one of them;* that the Duke d'Enghien ought to be the victim, since he might be taken in the fact, as forming part of the existing conspiracy. I did not rightly know who the Duke d'Enghien was. The revolution came upon me when I was very young, and I had never been at court. I did not even know where the Duke was. *All these points were explained to me.* If it be so, I said, he must be seized ; and the necessary orders were given in consequence. Every thing had been provided beforehand ; *the papers were prepared, and there was nothing to do but to sign them ;* and the fate of the Prince was already decided."

Mr. O'Meara's veracity cannot be suspected when, agreeing in his work with the other publications from St. Helena, he affirms, that having asked Napoleon whether it was true a letter written to him by the Duke d'Enghien had been received by M. de Talleyrand, and not delivered until two days after, the Emperor replied—" After the Prince's arrival at Strasburg, he wrote me a letter ; that letter was delivered to T. —— who kept it until after the execution."

But who then were those who, by *reports* and *conjectures,* represented the Duke d'Enghien as chief of a conspiracy? Who was at that time in a situation to induce the First Consul to compromise himself by shedding the blood of a Bourbon? Who could it be that had foreseen every thing, who had in anticipation *prepared the papers,* which were *instantaneously presented for the First Consul's signature,* and which decided the fate of the Prince.

The minister for foreign affairs under the Directory shall now himself declare what interest he had in making the First Consul compromise himself. The functions and the personal transactions of that minister under the First Consul will also show, whether it was he who prepared the reports and the papers which determined the fatal measure.

In a pamphlet which was published in the year V. and which was addressed by Citizen Talleyrand to his fellow-citizens, he thus expresses himself:

" I should be unworthy to have served the noble cause of liberty, if I dared regard as a sacrifice what I then did (1789) for its triumph. But I may at least express my surprise, that after having so many just claims on the implacable hatred of the heretofore clergy and nobility, I should draw upon myself the same hatred from those who style themselves the vehement enemies of the nobility and clergy."*

The man whose former conduct authorized such language, could not, without fear, see the French republic ready to expire in the year XII. in the person of the First Consul, without wishing to place that personage in a situation which would render it impossible for him ever to become a Monck ... Citizen Talleyrand, in his foresight, might not repel the idea of one day becoming Prince of Benevento under a new dynasty: but, priding himself in the advantage of having merited the implacable hatred of the clergy from whom he was a renegade, and of the nobility to whom he was a traitor, he must doubtless have shuddered at the very thought of their return under the banner of the Bourbons.

M. de Talleyrand has unfortunately learned in the course of his political life that rule by which certain men make interest the sole motive of their actions. This may explain the motive he had to be one of those who endeavoured "by *reports* and *conjectures* to represent the Duke d'Enghien as the chief of a conspiracy ; to take the judgment of the First Consul by surprise ; and to advise him to finish the business by steeping his hands in the blood of a Bourbon."

His terror at the bare idea of the possible return of the Bourbons was perhaps peculiarly strong at this time, as, when

---

* *Eclaircissemens donnés par le citoyen Talleyrand à ses concitoyens.* (Page 3.)

the conspiracy of George was detected, the First Consul had not disclosed his project of ascending the throne. On the contrary, it is alleged that he formally refused the title of King of France, which was offered to him during the nego-tiations at Amiens, in compensation for sacrifices of conquered territory, which it was wished to prevail on him to make.

The official transactions of the minister for foreign affairs, and his general conduct, add greatly to the evidence by which the truth of the facts stated has been demonstrated. The minister for foreign affairs was the only person who could answer the questions which the First Consul declared he had asked respecting the Duke d'Enghien, of whose name even he was ignorant, when that prince was pointed out to him as the chief of a conspiracy. He alone corresponded with foreign cabinets, and with our ministers at foreign courts. To him only belonged the duty of watching the proceedings of the emigrants. Of this, proof may be found in the diplomatic note which he addressed, on the 11th of March, to Baron Edelsheim, minister of state at Carlsruhe, of which M. de Caulaincourt was the bearer. In this note, which officially announces the order given for the arrest of the Duke d'Enghien, M. de Talleyrand admits that he had previously transmitted another note, which contained a demand for the arrest of the committee of French emigrants at Offenburg.

The nature of M. de Talleyrand's functions sufficiently ex-plain why the arrest of the Duke d'Enghien was decreed and ordered on his report in the privy-council, which preceded the departure of General Ordener.

It could not have taken place on the report of any of the three Consuls; for it was clearly foreign to their functions. M. Fouché, who was admitted to the council, was not then in office, and was only called as an assistant in the deliberations, and because he was considered to be greatly interested in the adoption of the proposed measure. It is, however, but just to state, that it was warmly opposed by the Consul Cambaceres.

He recommended that instead of forcibly seizing the Duke d'Enghien as the report proposed, the measure should at least be postponed until the Prince entered the French territory. It was on this occasion that Cambaceres was asked, How long it was since he had been so sparing of Bourbon blood.

This information was communicated to me by the Duke de Cambaceres; who, besides, assured me that he had recorded the facts in his memoirs.

It, however, may be asked, whether it be true, that when M. de Talleyrand instigated the arrest of the Duke d'Enghien, before that of Pichegru had explained the fatal mistake respecting the real head of the conspiracy, he participated in the common error, or rather whether such error ever existed on his part. His anterior correspondence with the French minister at Baden had given him such positive information on the Duke d'Enghien's mode of living, that it was not possible for him to believe that the Duke d'Enghien could be the mysterious personage spoken of in the examinations preliminary to the trial of George.

If such was M. de Talleyrand's belief, still it must be asked, why did he not put in the balance against it, in the privy-council of the 10th March, the previous reports of M. de Massias? Why so much zeal in accusing the Duke d'Enghien? In a case of doubt, to abstain from proposing a forcible removal was an indispensable duty.

I have been informed that M. de Talleyrand presented to the King an attested declaration of the Princess de Rohan, from which it appears that the Duke d'Enghien was warned to go out of the way some days before he was arrested. He also pretends that he sent this information by a courier; who, according to his statement, broke a leg at Saverne. This, however, is nothing but a fable; for such a fact could at any time be proved, and yet no proof whatever is offered of it. It is not at all probable that he sent a courier; but had he wished to do so, there were many persons in his family who would have gladly undertaken the mission, and the messenger would now be ready to declare himself.

But the degree of credit due to this attested declaration of the Princess de Roban's may be easily appreciated. M. de Talleyrand only obtained it at Paris after the restoration ; and for the possession of it he has to thank the urgent applications made to the Princess de Rohan-Rochefort by Madame Aimée de Coigny, formerly Duchess de Fleury.

The truth is, that M. de Talleyrand never sent. The information which was conveyed to the Duke d'Enghien, and to which Madame Rohan-Rochefort bore witness, without specifying whence it came, proceeded from another source. The King of Sweden, who was then at Carlsruhe, and the Elector himself, warned the Prince of the danger he might incur, and advised him to depart. Baron Dalberg, a witness whom M. de Talleyrand will not certainly refute, admits this in his letter of the 13th of November, 1823. The warning thus conveyed to the Prince was the consequence of the diplomatic note sent by M. de Talleyrand to Carlsruhe, previously to the 10th of March, in which he demanded the arrest of the committee of French emigrants at Offenburg. The Duke d'Enghien did not immediately depart, and his delay proved fatal. The whole of M. de Talleyrand's conduct controverts the idea that he ever wished to save the Duke d'Enghien ; and, certainly, if the Prince had received from Paris any intimation confirming that which was given him by the King of Sweden, it cannot be doubted that he would have quitted Ettenheim without delay.

Let us now hear what M. de Massias says, in a note which he thought it necessary to publish on this subject

" Some days after the catastrophe, I received a letter from the minister for foreign affairs directing me to go to Aix-la-Chapelle, where I should find the Emperor Napoleon, to whom I had to render an account of my conduct. On my

arrival, I called on General Lannes, with whom I had served
in the wars of Spain and Italy, and to whose friendship I was
indebted for the post I held, and for all my future prospects.
He informed me that I was accused of having married the
near relation of a dangerous intriguer, and of having contrived the conspiracy of the Duke d'Enghien.

" On leaving General Lannes, I went to the minister for
foreign affairs, to whom I repeated that which I had mentioned to him in my correspondence; viz. *that the conduct
of the Prince was peaceable and innocent, and that my wife
was no relation of the Baroness de Reich: a fact, of which
he was assured by an authentic certificate which I had sent
him.* He told me that all would be arranged.

" The Emperor began by asking news of the Grand-duke
and his family; and, having heard my reply, without any
further observations, he said, ' How could you, M. de Massias,
whom I have treated with kindness, join in the miserable intrigues of the enemies of France ?'

" I knew his address; and I was aware that if I entered
immediately on my justification, he would seize and draw
inferences from certain circumstances, on which I should not
be able to give categorical explanations: I therefore determined to manifest astonishment, and to appear not to understand what he meant.

" ' Ah!' he exclaimed, with a gesticulation and a start
back ; ' one might almost believe that he does not know what
I am talking about.' (The same astonishment and the same
appearance of ignorance on my part.)

" ' How,' continued he, emphatically, but not angrily;
' have you not married a near relative of that wretched
intriguer, the Baroness de Reich?'—' Sire,' said I, ' this
gentleman (pointing to the minister) has unworthily deceived
your Majesty. He was informed by me that my wife was no
relation of Baroness de Reich. Of this fact I sent him an
authentic certificate.' On hearing this, the Emperor smiled

and stepped back, and then paced up and down his closet, still looking at us. He afterwards stepped up to me, and said in a softened tone, ' You, nevertheless, permitted meetings of emigrants at Offenburgh ?'—I rendered a faithful account of all that had taken place during my mission. 'How could I,' said I, ' think of persecuting a few unfortunate men, while, with your permission, they were crossing the Rhine by hundreds and thousands ? I was merely acting in the spirit of your government.'—' You might, however,' resumed the Emperor, ' have prevented the plots which the Duke d'Enghien was organising at Ettenheim ?'—' Sire, I am too old to learn to utter falsehoods. Your Majesty has also been deceived on this point '—' Do you think, then,' said he, with vehemence, ' that if the conspiracy of George and Pichegru had succeeded, the Prince would not have crossed the Rhine, and posted to Paris?' I hung down my head, and said nothing. Then assuming a careless air, he spoke to me of Carlsruhe, and some other subjects of little interest, after which he dismissed me." *

* On the following day, adds M. de Massias, there was a public and solemn distribution of crosses of the Legion of Honour, which the Emperor had then newly instituted. According to the regulations, I was entitled to one ; both on account of my post of chargé d'affaires, and my rank as a colonel in the army.

The honour was, however, conferred on all my colleagues who were present, and I was the only person who did not receive one. General Lannes, whom I saw in the morning, told me, that the Emperor was perfectly satisfied with my courage and honourable conduct, but that he wished to punish my want of respect to my superior.

I returned to Carlsruhe ; and in about a month or two afterwards, one of his Majesty's chamberlains called on me. This was the Count de Beaumont, who delivered to me a letter from Duroc, the grand-marshal of the place. This letter informed me that the Emperor would shortly send to Carlsruhe his adopted daughter, Princess Stephanie, wife of the Grand-duke of Baden, whom he intended to confide to my care ; and that in every thing concerning her, I was not to correspond with the minister for foreign affairs, but directly with the Emperor himself.

About a year after the arrival of the Princess, the Emperor appointed me resident-consul-general at Dantzick. I had scarcely held this new situation a

M. de Talleyrand then deceived the Emperor, in not rendering him a faithful account of the tenour of the correspondence of M. de Massias;—he deceived M. de Massias himself, whom he misrepresented to the Emperor;—he deceived the Elector of Baden, by assuring him, through Baron Dalberg (whom he was doubtless at the same time deceiving), that the emigrants residing in the electorate would not be molested, while he was preparing his diplomatic note of the 11th of March, which was not to be transmitted to the Baden minister of state until after the arrest of the Duke d'Enghien!

M. de Massias thus continues :—" As soon as I learned that the Prince had been arrested, and removed to the citadel of Strasburg, I wrote without loss of time to the minister for foreign affairs, to inform him that, during his residence in the electorate (*of which my former dispatches had apprized him*), the conduct of the Prince had been moderate and blameless. *My letter must be in the archives;* it is the only one in which I ever introduced a Latin quotation. To give additional force to my ideas, and greater weight to my assertion, I borrowed these words from Tacitus — *Nec beneficio, nec injuriâ cognitus;* which perfectly explained the situation in which I stood with reference to the august personage, whom the cause of truth alone led me to defend."

But this letter, which could only have been written on the 15th of March, must have reached Paris on the 18th at latest; and it was not until that very day that the Prince quitted the citadel of Strasburg.

Let M. de Talleyrand inform us what efforts he employed

week, when I was appointed intendant of the city ; a post to which great emoluments are attached.

On my return to France, which my health obliged me to revisit, on leave of absence, the Emperor created me a baron, with authority to institute a majorate for my family.

in the interval, between the 18th and 20th, to substantiate
the clear evidence of an honest man, which must have dispelled, or at least have diminished, the alarms which had
been excited in the mind of the First Consul.

The evidence of M. de Massias is positive. Had it been
viewed solely with the object of elucidating the truth, it
could not in any way have squared with the portrait of the
individual who was supposed to be at the head of the conspiracy. Three previous days ought to have sufficed for M.
de Talleyrand to endeavour to undeceive the First Consul,
and to prevent the great catastrophe. How did he employ
this valuable time ? What said he ? What did he to corro-
borate the letter of M. de Massias, and to get it introduced
as a defensive document on the trial ? The sentence shows
that the documents for and against the prisoner amounted
to *one* only ; and it may be easily guessed that this one
was not the letter of M. de Massias.

Let M. de Talleyrand answer this.

This letter, * and other documents relative to the fatal
event, have disappeared from the archives of the department
of foreign affairs, at the head of which M. de Talleyrand has
successively been during the Republic, the Directory, the
Consulate, the Empire, and the Kingdom.

Let us proceed.

On the morning of the 29th Ventose (20th of March), the
day on which the sentence was pronounced, I saw M. de
Talleyrand at Malmaison. By a singular coincidence, it was
shortly after this that orders were given for the removal of
the Prince to Vincennes. In the afternoon he called on the
governor of Paris. His duty might have required his at-

---

* It is possible that this letter is the same to which the Emperor Napoleon
alluded, in replying to Mr. O'Meara, when he complained that it had not been
delivered to him until after the death of the Prince   From the declarations
of persons attached to the Emperor's cabinet, it appears that they had no knowledge of any letter of the Duke d'Enghien's.

tendance on the First Consul : but he, a minister, and the reporter of the privy-council which had determined the arrest of the Duke d'Enghien, what business could he have with the general who was appointed to nominate the Prince's judges, and to direct them to bring him before their tribunal ? If the letter of the First Consul, of which I was the bearer to the governor of Paris, said all, as it may be supposed it did, what was the object of M. de Talleyrand's extraordinary visit? Did he go to add his own comments to the letter, or to transmit the last instructions, the last commands of the First Consul? ... It must be observed, that the decree of the government of the same day, which directed that the Duke d'Enghien should be brought before a court-martial, certainly authorized the governor of Paris to nominate the court ; but that it should be *immediately* summoned by order of the governor, who selected its members, is not in the decree.

M. de Talleyrand, like Count Hullin, may justly exclaim, " How unfortunate I am !" He did every thing to bring about the catastrophe, and nothing to prevent it. After the event, he was so unlucky as to be the individual on whom devolved the task of announcing and justifying the death of the Duke d'Enghien to the foreign powers. If he acted against his inclination, it may truly be said that he has drained the cup of bitterness to the very dregs. But what is to be thought of the fate of the victim?

Will it now be said that I have done wrong in endeavouring to exculpate the Emperor at the expense of M. de Talleyrand, that is to say, candidly unfolding facts of which I entertain a thorough conviction? I am aware that the Emperor Napoleon, in his testament, seems to take upon himself the whole responsibility of the catastrophe; but I know him well enough to estimate differently from many other persons the value of his own declarations. Even in his last moments, the Emperor Napoleon was less concerned by the approach of death, than he was anxious to preserve unbroken, in public opinion, the illusion attached to his power; and I am certain that, even on the brink of the grave, he would have felt highly displeased at an attempt to prove that any event of his reign took place without his authority. " The Duke d'Enghien died because I willed it." Such is the language of the Emperor to posterity; which is as much as to say—" I being sovereign, nobody dared to conceive the thought of disposing of the life or liberty of any one whatever. I might have been misled, but no one dared for a moment to interfere with my power."

Penetrated with these ideas, to which all the facts I have recorded, as well as the words of the Emperor himself, add considerable weight, I propose this objection to those who persist in maintaining that the Emperor ordered the execution of the Duke d'Enghien, as the sultan sends the bow-string to a vizier.

The Emperor regretted the death of the Duke d'Enghien; but the deed was done, and he could not throw the blame of it on any one. His inflexible character, the strong feeling of his dignity and his duty as a sovereign, would not permit him to evade the responsibility of anything that had been done, still less to screen himself by throwing blame on another.

If matters had been managed at Vincennes by the president of the court-martial in such a way that M. Real had found the Prince still living; if the examination had proved that he was not the mysterious person who had been seen with George, and who was sought for, I ask all who knew the First Consul, whether it is their belief that he would have suffered the Duke d'Enghien to be sacrificed. I also ask what would have become of M. de Talleyrand, if, after his terrible proposition of removing the Prince and putting him out of the way, he had seen the chief of the state relinquish the prey, which he had been induced to seize as the means of protecting his life against the plots of his irreconcilable enemies.

Another trait yet remains to be recorded, and with it I shall wind up the observations which this statement of facts has suggested. In the evening of the Duke d'Enghien's execution, M. de Talleyrand gave a masked ball, to which all the diplomatic body were invited. Nothing could exceed the dulness of this ball, which was an outrage upon public feeling. Some individuals had spirit enough to refuse the invitations; among these were, Princess Dolgoroucky and M. de Moustier, now one of his Majesty's ambassadors, who informed me of this fact.

Such was the part which M. de Talleyrand performed in the catastrophe of the Duke d'Enghien. Let him now say whether the exchange of a few polite phrases with Baron Dalberg, and the silence he has maintained, suffice to remove the serious accusations which public opinion has affixed upon him for the share he took in that fatal event.

§ II.

The Conduct of General Hullin.

It certainly is not the least painful part of my task, easy though it be, to cast back upon General Hullin the charge which, for the sole purpose of gratifying a third person, he has dared to direct against me. His old age, his grey hairs, the melancholy loss of sight with which he is afflicted, the uniform he wears, and my constant repugnance to compromise by disclosures, are considerations sufficient to account for the reserve which I formerly observed respecting General Hullin. I was not then aware that, taking advantage of the kind of proscription which compelled me to remain at a distance from my country, he had, in 1815, presented a memo-

rial to the government, in which, for the purpose of obtaining
leave to reside in France, he thought it advisable to fix upon
me the consequences of the judgment pronounced against the
Duke d'Enghien. The hypocrite took good care never to
say a word to me about this memorial, in 1823, when I published my pamphlet.

This disingenuous conduct, and Count Hullin's perseverance in his former assertions, would authorize my making
severe reprisals on him in the name of truth. My own honour
renders this a duty.

According to his statement, he received, at seven o'clock
in the evening of the 20th of March, a verbal order from the
governor of Paris to repair to Vincennes, and preside over a
court-martial, the object of which was not made known to him :
he even would have it believed, that he was not informed of
its object until he received at Vincennes the government
decree, and the order of the commander-in-chief, General
Murat, containing the names of the members of the court,
and an injunction to proceed forthwith, and on the spot.

General Hullin, as well as the captain-reporter, and even
the secretary, are alleged to have had no experience in
trials by courts-martial, which explains the irregularities in
the judgment.

The court would have acceded to the Prince's request of
an interview with the First Consul, but a general (meaning me)
represented that the application was unseasonably made ;
and this induced General Hullin to give up the point. Besides, there was nothing in the law to authorize such a
course.

The documents produced on the trial consisted of intercepted letters, and other papers calculated to produce an
impression on the mind of the court.

Bound by his oath, he says, he could not declare the court
incompetent. He appointed no one to assist the prisoner in
his defence, because the Prince neither objected to the com-

petency of the tribunal, nor asked for a defender, and none of the members of the court reminded him of such a duty.

He admits that several draughts were made of the sentence; and among them that which directs that it shall be executed forthwith, and which has been published by the lawyer who made known the existence of the documents connected with the trial; but after that minute was signed, it seems it was found to be irregular. A new one was of course drawn up, which constituted the real judgment of the court. The other minute ought to have been destroyed immediately, but it must have been forgotten. The general attests that all this is the truth!

. At all events, as neither the first nor the second minute was regular, the captain-reporter and the officer who permitted the execution could not, without prevarication, admit the authority of the judgment, and cause it to be executed.

The order for the execution could only be given by the general-in-chief, governor of Paris: he cannot tell whether the person who so cruelly precipitated that fatal execution acted by order. As to himself, the judgment was no sooner pronounced, than he proposed to write to the First Consul to inform him of the Prince's request of an interview, and also to pray him to remit a punishment which the court, in the rigorous fulfilment of its duty, was bound to impose. But at that very instant a man (he again means me) prevented him, by taking up the pen, and saying—" That is my business;" which made him believe that the said person was himself going to write to the First Consul.

Finally, in confidence of that being done, he was waiting until the moment at which he was to withdraw, when he heard a terrible explosion . .

Such is in substance the romance to which it has been thought fit to affix the name of General Hullin.

In the first place, I cannot pass over the improbability of General Hullin having received, from the governor of Paris,

merely a verbal notice of his appointment as president of the
court, when the appointment of the other members was communicated to them in writing.   General Hullin also ought to
have received an official letter ; but as the governor might
wish to give him particular instructions, it is likely that he
would send for him.   General Murat too well understood the
importance attached to a trial which was to decide the fate of
such a person as the Duke d'Enghien, to permit it to be supposed that the appointment of General Hullin to be president of the court was a matter of accident, or that he would
be allowed to proceed to Vincennes without being informed
of the object of his mission.   On the contrary, the fact of
his appointment of itself attests, that he had been informed
without reserve of what was a mystery to all Paris.   When
it was determined to send the Prince before a court-martial,
can it be believed that means were not taken to ascertain the
sentiments of him who was to be the president, especially
when there was no witness against the prisoner, and nothing
to produce in support of the charge but the *single document*
—the decree of the 29th of Ventose ? . . .   But a fact which
was not publicly known until after my first publication, and
of which I was myself ignorant, contradicts General Hullin
on this point.   The Duke d'Enghien's carriage arrived about
midnight at the barrier of Bondi.   It was detained there
until four o'clock ; and it was not until that hour that an
order was given for it to proceed by the outer boulevards.
At this period, the barriers of the capital were very strictly
guarded.   Now, who but the governor of Paris could give
this order ; and through whom, if not through the commandant of the place, could it be transmitted ?—Let General Hullin answer.

On leaving General Murat's house, he could not be ignorant of the arrest, the arrival, and the approaching trial, of the
Duke d'Enghien, as he was not ignorant of the order which
the governor of Paris gave through him for the troops of the

garrison, including the gendarmerie d'élite, to march to Vincennes. I was the only colonel of these troops who was not a member of the court-martial ; and I was appointed to command them, because that command fell to me of right. This is the whole secret of the order which brought me to Vincennes. I was not then a man of sufficient importance to be intrusted with secrets.

But this command left me quite unconnected with the preliminary proceedings, the instruction of the process, the interrogatory, and the trial and condemnation of the prisoner. General Hullin alone was recognised as the chief authority. In his character of president, he was my superior : for where an authorized assembly deliberates, and a body of troops is appointed to protect the deliberation, the armed force is essentially passive. Unhappy the country where it is otherwise !

Such being our respective positions, General Hullin was every thing—I nothing. Even the commandant of Vincennes, M. Harel, was under his orders ; and we shall soon see that this was well understood by General Hullin. It was for him to command : we were bound to execute his orders, under the pain of being punished for mutiny, if we disobeyed our superior officer. Let us then follow him in the discharge of his duties.

However, I shall not scrutinize his actions on this occasion, except in so far as they are connected with my case. An eloquent lawyer has sufficiently exposed them. I therefore leave General Hullin in presence of the accuser, who has summoned him before the tribunal of the present age and of posterity. It is not my object to aggravate the moral suffering of one whom intrigue has made my enemy. I only wish to repel the calumnious imputations directed against myself.

In the first place I have to remark, that the officer who was appointed captain-reporter proceeded to the examination of the Prince, and that he commenced the interrogatory at twelve o'clock at night, on the 29th of Ventose (March 20). This is proved by the minutes.* The whole proceeding, and the manner in which the minutes are drawn up, in no respect indicate, on the part of this officer, that inexperience attributed to him by General Hullin. I must also observe, that though this general had served with distinction, he was not originally bred in camps; and that the commandant of such a place as Paris cannot be presumed to be so little acquainted with the military laws respecting courts-martial as he would have us to believe. His colleagues, too, were colonels; men not destitute of information, and who could not all be ignorant of the rules in such cases. One of them had practised as a lawyer at Besançon, before he embraced the career of arms.

After the interrogatory, the Prince was conducted to the room in which the court was held; but it was then two o'clock in the morning. That this time must have elapsed is plain; for the interrogatory, which was not begun until twelve o'clock, fills six pages of print. This circumstance ought to be borne in mind; it will serve to refute one of the numerous and important false allegations of General Hullin.

For my part, being occupied in stationing the troops as they successively arrived at Vincennes from different barracks in Paris, which made it late in the night before they could be completely collected, I only went into the court-room, which I found filled with superior or subaltern officers of the troops, at the moment when the Prince was defending himself with warmth against the imputation of being the head of a conspiracy to take the life of the First Consul. During the short time while the court sat after my arrival, I can with truth affirm, that no mention was made either of the application of the Prince for an interview with the First Consul, or of the

---

* Document, No. 3, of the *Recueil*, published by M. Dupin.

proposal of a member of the court to accede to his request; and consequently that no words spoken by me could impede the intentions of the court on this point. It is very true that the captain-reporter, an officer of high honour and integrity, did, on proceeding to the interrogatory, advise the Prince to solicit an interview with the First Consul; but I was not present at the reading of the interrogatory, nor when new questions were put to the Prince by the president after the opening of the court.

I ask Count Hullin, who only accuses me to relieve himself from the reproach of having neglected to fulfil a sacred duty, where is to be found any mention made of the alleged proposal by a member of the court, and of my interruption, or, if he will, my pretended observation on the unseasonableness of the request? Where is the record of the deliberation which must have followed? Why not also say that there is on the protocol of the court, a resolution to accede, after discussion, to the Prince's wish?

- I will go farther, I will for a moment suppose that I could have uttered so strange an observation.—Had I any authority—had I more power than General Hullin, my superior as to military rank and as president of the court? Did I, for example, present instructions, or an order from the First Consul, thus to control a tribunal, which ought to be impassive as the law?

Such was not the language of General Hullin while he was in exile at Brussels. Let him tax his memory a little; he may recollect what he then said to those who made observations on this subject. He stated that "he acted on the most strict instructions. The case of the Duke d'Enghien asking an interview with the First Consul was foreseen, and he was prohibited from transmitting that request to the government."

Here we have the real truth; and among the motives for making General Hullin repair to the governor of Paris, this prohibition must have been one of the most important. It was a capital offence in the instigators of the Duke d'Enghien's destruction thus to preclude him from all communication with the First Consul.

It has been publicly reported, that General Murat deposited with a notary of Paris documents, which attest that the instructions which he gave to General Hullin and the whole of his conduct in this affair were the result of perfidious insinuations. I know not whether such a deposit really exists. Those who believe it does, must be surprised that such important documents were not published in 1823, a period when every one was eager to contribute to the explanation of this page of our history. Can these documents be withheld because they disprove the fable of my adversary? Should they now be brought to light, and the contrary appear on the face of them, there will be reason to doubt their authenticity.

According to the statement of the lawyer to whom I have already alluded, the Duke d'Enghien was condemned in violation of every regular form and principle. All the papers in the case, both for the accusation and the defence, consisted of one document only; namely, the decree of the Consuls, dated the 29th Ventose. In the minute of the judgment drawn up at Vincennes, the doors of the court being shut, this is distinctly recorded. It is therein stated—

" Read the documents both for the charge and the defence in number ONE."

This completely refutes the false version of General Hullin:—" that there were several documents under one endorsed cover, some intercepted letters, a correspondence of M. Shee's, then prefect of the Lower Rhine, and in particular a long report by the counsellor of state, Real."

Had then Count Hullin in holding this language completely forgotten that he had himself acknowledged having received only two documents for the trial of the prisoner; namely, the decree of the Consuls, and the list of the judges, which the governor of Paris sent to him at Vincennes at ten o'clock in the evening?

It may, then, be conjectured, for whose interest General Hullin's story on this point was invented. It was thought necessary to create some uncertainty respecting the conduct of the Duke d'Enghien, by a vague reference to intercepted letters, and a report of the counsellor of state, Real, who never made any report on the subject. It was doubtless hoped, that by this means the compliance of him who condemned the Prince would be rendered less odious. It was expected, perhaps, on announcing in this vague manner documents which never were before the court, that if it were one day asked why the correspondence of M. de Massias had not been produced for the defence, it might be alleged that that correspondence formed part of the papers under the endorsed cover.

Let us now follow the other irregularities in the proceedings, which it is necessary to point out in order to refute. General Hullin. No person was appointed to defend the Prince; he was abandoned to himself, to his inexperience, to his imprudent vivacity, while a sentence of death was hanging over his head. But was General Hullin then so little acquainted with the holding of courts-martial, and the so clear custom of giving a defender to the person accused, that he had need to wait until the Prince asked for one himself; and that in his situation he knew too little of the law to suggest the incompetence of the court-martial? This forgetfulness on the part of General Hullin, and the rigour and illegality of the sentence, are not in accordance with his pretended wish to favour the Prince's application for an interview with the First Consul. Those who have suddenly resolved to listen to the counsel of humanity, do not usually manifest their determination in so cold a manner. No; the court-martial which, without hesitation, condemned the Duke d'Enghien, did not mean, or did not dare, to save him; but had it wished to save him, it could have done so. Never was a judge, well-disposed towards a prisoner, in a situation more favourable to his safety. There existed neither documents, proofs, nor witnesses against the Prince, and he persisted in strenuously denying the accusations against him. His relations with England in the rank in which he was born, and his correspondence with his grandfather, could not be taken for the acknowledgment of a conspiracy. Besides, what judge does not know that the confession of a person accused is not sufficient for his condemnation, when no *corpus delicti* is proved; and when there are no testimonies of witnesses to assure the court that the prisoner, in the despair of his situation, is not so far misled as to charge himself with a crime which he never committed? But if the court-martial had not the courage to acquit an innocent person, or at least one accused but not convicted of a crime, after fulfilling what was regarded as an imperious duty, nothing prevented that tribunal, I will not say from soliciting a pardon—for that perhaps there was not spirit enough—but from transmitting to the First Consul the just prayer of the Prince.

But since the president of the court-martial was so very favourably disposed to the Duke d'Enghien—how happened it that he did not adopt all the necessary means to prevent his error from becoming irreparable, instead of ordering—

" That the judgment should be forthwith executed by the care of the captain-reporter, in presence of detachments from the different corps of the garrison, after notice given to the prisoner ?"

Count Hullin felt by anticipation the reflections which might be made on this act; and he endeavoured to meet them by affirming that the judgment as here quoted is not the original sentence pronounced by the court-martial : that it was that which had appeared in the Moniteur of the

22nd of March, 1804, because different copies had been made of the minute.

Absurd as is this fable, it is proper here to explain the grounds on which it ought to be rejected by demonstrating its falsehood.

It was twelve o'clock when the captain-reporter commenced the interrogatory of the Duke d'Enghien, and he could not close it before two o'clock in the morning. This is, besides, clearly shown by the minute. The reading of the single document presented, the new interrogatories put by the president to the Prince, and the discussions which were long and animated, protracted the proceedings of the court until four o'clock. At that hour the president ordered the court to be cleared, and the judges proceeded to deliberate with closed doors. The time occupied by this deliberation could not be less than half an hour, after which it was necessary to draw up a minute of the judgment. Now the drawing up of this minute, which is contained in two pages of manuscript, could not take less time than another half hour; that is to say, the whole would be completed by five o'clock in the morning. But, if all the proceedings which have just been enumerated could have been completed in the three hours which elapsed from the opening of the court to the signing of the judgment, it is physically impossible that the copy of the judgment which was published in the Moniteur, and which makes seven pages of print in octavo, could also be drawn up at Vincennes. A mere copyist could not transcribe this judgment in less than three hours; and much more time must be allowed, when it is recollected that the composition of the text, the numerous questions proposed, the no less numerous grounds of decision detailed, and the minute references to laws, required that a rough draft should be made before it was written out clean, as it afterwards appeared on the file. If, then, we add the period indispensably necessary for the drawing up and the transcribing, to the hour when the court proceeded to deliberate with closed doors, we shall bring down the time to ten in the morning; and it is notorious that the Prince was executed at six o'clock!

The first judgment exhibits blanks, in which were afterwards to be inserted the dates and the articles of the laws held to be applicable to the case. The reason of this may be readily conceived : it was drawn up at Vincennes, and it was not likely that the bulletin of the laws should be found in that prison. But let this first judgment be compared with that published in the Moniteur. In the seven printed pages which it occupies, we find a minute citation of a great number of laws and articles of laws ; various documents stated to have been read at the trial are quoted ; and the description of the Prince is completely detailed, even to the statement of his height of one metre and seven hundred and five millemetres. Could a minute like this, which required a practised pen, have been drawn up at Vincennes, in the dead of the night, amidst the confusion and emotion of all the members of the court, perhaps even of General Hullin, in spite of his secret instructions? But if the library to which it was necessary to refer was transported to Vincennes, why are not the laws, decrees, &c., quoted in the second judgment, mentioned in the first? The rough draught of a document contains all that is found in the fair copy.

Another circumstance will suffice to prove the impudent imposture of General Hullin's. The judgment inserted in the Moniteur states, that, after the close of the proceedings on the charge and defence, " the reporter, the clerk, and the citizens who were admitted to hear the trial, retired at the request of the president."

It is indeed an indispensable rule that the captain-reporter should not be present at the deliberations of a court-martial, after the close of the proceedings on the charge and defence, because the prisoner, of whom he is the accuser, is not himself present.

However, the minute of the second judgment, which is on the file in the archives of courts-martial, is entirely in the hand-writing of the captain-reporter. Where then could he write it—since, according to General Hullin's story, it must have been drawn up while the doors of the court were closed, and the judgment declares that the reporter had then withdrawn—if he did not write it at Paris, after the instigators of this fatal event, alarmed by the rumour of the First Consul being displeased at their proceedings, and at the irregularity of what had been drawn up at Vincennes, became desirous of making it appear less serious with respect to themselves?

Answer this, General Hullin!

The truth, as every thing demonstrates it to be, is, that the judgment on the file directing that it shall be *executed forthwith*, is that which was drawn up in the closed court, and that which was delivered by General Hullin to the captain-reporter, in order that he might take measures for its execution. It is signed by all the members of the court, and also by the captain-reporter, whose signature was necessary to give it executory force. Can it be supposed that such a document, bearing the signatures of all the members of the tribunal, is nothing but a rough draught? Ridiculous fable l

But what can never be supposed is, that if, instead of this minute, General Hullin had delivered to the captain-reporter the minute inserted in the Moniteur, that estimable officer must have, in contempt of the tenour of the judgment, and contrary even to the constant usage of courts-martial held under special commission (which this was not), caused the Prince to be executed almost before the eyes of the judges, who had not sentenced him to such instantaneous execution. This allegation refutes itself by its absurd atrocity. The great falsehood of the accusation against the captain-reporter might be conjectured from the conduct of that officer; for he was extremely attentive to the Prince, and gave proofs of the interest he felt for him. It was he, as 1 have already stated, who suggested to the Prince the idea of expressing, at the bottom of his interrogatory, a desire to see the First Consul, and who dictated the words written by the Prince's own hand in that document.

Could General Hullin mean that the sentence which he had pronounced should only be executed on the authority of the governor of Paris, when, after delivering the fatal decree to the captain-reporter, he gave orders to the commandant of Vincennes, Harel, the only officer present acquainted with the subterraneous passages of the prison, to conduct the prisoner into the castle-ditch, where his execution would occasion no danger to the passers-by? This fact is attested by the deposition of the Sieur Anfort, made in 1806, and published, in 1822, by a man who appears to have been solely actuated by the desire of discovering truth. The following is an extract from this deposition :—

" The examination being ended, the Duke d'Enghien was summoned to an adjoining apartment. These gentlemen announced that they were going to put the question to the vote ; and after an interval, the commandant, Harel, was again called. The condemnation of the prisoner was announced to him ; and he was directed to bring him down at the proper time to the castle-ditch. Another interval elapsed ; after which, the definitive order was given to the commandant by the president of the council. In a low and faltering voice, Harel requested the prisoner to follow him ; and with a torch in his hand, he advanced beneath the narrow winding stair-case." *

Amidst all these overwhelming facts, what becomes of the story of the letter which General Hullin thought himself

---

* Extract from a work entitled, *Notice Historique sur S. A. R. Monseigneur le Duc d'Enghien, par un bourgeois de Paris.*—Paris, 1822.

bound to write to the First Consul, as soon as the sentence was pronounced, conjuring him to remit a punishment which the strict duty of the court obliged it to impose?

What, too, becomes of the assertion, that " at this moment a man, who had been constantly in the council-chamber, said to him, taking up the pen—" That is my business!"

What! General Hullin was so impatient for the execution of the sentence, that he ordered Harel to conduct the Prince to the castle-ditch, instead of consigning this melancholy task to the captain-reporter; and yet he conceived it to be his duty to write to solicit the prisoner's pardon!

In a court-martial, the captain-reporter represents the public prosecutor in other criminal courts. Now, as the privilege of appeal was neither proposed nor permitted to the Duke d'Enghien, since his sentence was immediately executed, he was delivered up by General Hullin in the same situation in which a prisoner stands, when, after having exhansted every resource, he is consigned to the proper officer for execution. Immediate death is the prompt and inevitable consequence of this last measure.

I have little more to say on the subject of this calumny. It has already been proved by the documents of the trial (and it is besides an invariable custom in similar cases), that the chamber in which the court-martial sat at Vincennes was cleared after the proceedings on the charge and defence, and was immediately transformed into a council-chamber, where the members deliberated with *closed doors;* and it has not been insinuated, hitherto at least, that I remained there during the deliberation. By what right could I have done so? On what ground could the members, who had to deliberate among themselves, have permitted me to remain with them? It must be borne in mind, that, with the exception of General Hullin, none of the colonels who formed part of the court-martial had been informed of their nomination in any other way than by a letter addressed to them individually by the governor of Paris. Consequently, none of them could have been practised upon. The instigators of the catastrophe depended on the private instructions given to General Hullin, and on the willingness with which he had doubtless promised to perform the task prescribed to him.

By what right, too, could I have taken the pen from the hand of the president, when he was going to write respecting the result of the deliberations of the court? And is it possible that General Hullin felt so little self-respect, as to yield to the threat of a person whose power was inferior to his own, and to renounce the consoling privilege of demanding the pardon of an unfortunate prisoner whose condemnation was a subject of regret? Would he have obeyed an order, of which his situation and his functions did not permit him to admit the existence in my hands, and would he not in consequence immediately have asserted his own authority? But have I not already sufficiently proved the absurdity of supposing that Count Hullin wished to intercede for the Prince, while he coolly surrendered him up to certain death? How could his intercession have met with any obstacle; or how could I, having no authority to suspend the execution ordered by him, have taken upon me to solicit pardon in his stead?

In this new point of view, therefore, let justice be rendered to the misrepresentations of General Hullin.

I shall now leave him with those feelings which he says he experienced on hearing the fatal explosion. Then, no doubt, commenced the remorse which he says preyed upon him for more than twenty years, in consequence of his having yielded to the instigations of those who had predetermined the death of the unfortunate Prince.

§ III.

My Conduct in the command of the Troops.

At this time, though scarcely twenty-eight years of age, I was a general officer and aide-de-camp. This rank, which procured me the honour of executing perilous missions on the field of battle, could in no way serve to initiate me into the secrets of the state. I was not in a situation to correspond with foreign powers; I was not employed to watch the emigrants, and to communicate for that purpose with ministers and ambassadors; I had no rank in the civil government; no authority to make reports to the council of state, or to obtrude my opinion on any subject which that body might have under consideration; still less had I the power of instituting or of procuring the adoption of any measure whatsoever.

Besides, what personal reason had I to take any interest in what was going on? Had I any anxieties respecting the future which it was necessary to calm, or securities to ask on account of the past? I knew the revolution only by the wars which it had occasioned, the battles which it had caused to be fought, and the glory which our arms had thereby acquired. Fortune and my sword had given me all I wished for. I was happy in my lot—my ambition was satisfied; and assuredly nothing then gave me reason to presume that I ever should be selected for the high offices to which I was afterwards appointed. I had nothing to care for but to discharge with honour and zeal the duties of my station; and it is well known that the First Consul left to such as me no idle time, and still less that which would have been necessary to enable us to meddle with things altogether foreign to our military functions.

While on duty at Malmaison, just after my return from a long mission, I was ordered to carry a sealed letter to General Murat, then governor of Paris. It will easily be conceived that the contents of this letter were not disclosed to me. The First Consul was not in the habit of entering into such explanations with the bearers of his messages as that communication would suppose; but what would it signify if I did know the contents? Whatever might be the business in hand, I had only to obey my superiors in rank, and was not in a situation to be called on to deliberate. Accordingly, on the 20th of March, at five o'clock in the evening, I departed from Malmaison with the letter for General Murat.

Nothing can be plainer than what my situation in those circumstances was; and the line of my duty was so clear, that I had not occasion to reflect for a moment on what my conduct should be.

What would any other person have done in my situation?

I was colonel of the corps of select gendarmerie, which was not then included in the guard, but formed part of the garrison of Paris; and it was solely in that character that I was ordered by General Murat to repair to Vincennes, and to take the command of the troops there assembled. Was I not bound to obey?

Having arrived at the appointed place, whither I was sent to guard a court-martial, convoked by the competent authority, could I refuse to fulfil my mission?

Being responsible, to a certain extent, for the conduct of the troops intrusted to my direction, was it not my duty to station them, and to overlook them during the continuance of the business which was the cause of their being assembled?

Did it belong to me, whose first duty was obedience, to scrutinize the object for which the court-martial was convoked, or the legality of the acts in virtue of which it was to proceed?

To military men, in particular, I address with confidence these questions, as well as those which I have yet to submit. '

Military discipline, the responsibility which attached to me on this important occasion, when the arrest of General Moreau had already caused some ferment among the troops, rendered the most active vigilance necessary on my part.

The barracks of Paris are situated in quarters remote from each other; consequently, some of the corps ordered out had to march across the whole town, as they departed from opposite points very distant from the Barrière du Trône. On this account some corps, which had not received their marching orders till late in the evening, did not arrive at Vincennes until nearly three in the morning.

Therefore, it was not until after all the troops were assembled, and after I had stationed them on the ésplanade in front of the Castle of Vincennes, that I could gratify my curiosity to see the Prince; and to learn the circumstances, 'of which I till then knew nothing, which had caused him to be brought to trial.

I have stated that the night, which I passed among the troops, being very cold, I was induced, on entering the court; to draw near to the fire, before which the president's chair was placed. It was in this way that I came to be, for a few moments only, seated behind General Hullin, while the trial was going on; and it was there that I heard what I have related of the brief part of the proceedings which I witnessed. A quarter of an hour had scarcely elapsed when the Prince was ordered to withdraw, and the court was cleared for the close sitting. Having no authority nor office which entitled me to remain, or to take any part in the private discussions of the court, I immediately joined my troops; and, with them, awaited the result of the deliberation.

I have already proved the twofold falsehood of General Hullin's story relative to the influence which he alleges I exercised over the court during its sitting, and over himself to prevent his forwarding the request of the Prince for an interview with the First Consul. I shall here add two observations not less decisive than those already made.

The court deliberated with closed doors; and, consequently, I was excluded. In order, therefore, to give me an opportunity to say to the president, with the view of preventing him from writing to the First Consul—"That is my business," either the judgment must have been read publicly, and I must have heard it after the doors of the court were re-opened; or the court must, before deliberating, have recognised me to be invested with a superior authority; and in virtue of previous and formal instructions have called me in, after the signing of the judgment, to submit it to my veto. It is only under the one or the other of these suppositions, that it could be possible for me to be in a situation to say to the president— "That is my business."

Now the genuine judgment pronounced at Vincennes, that which was executed, does not record the re-opening of the court, which, in fact, did not take place. General Hullin did not then think it necessary to resort to this fiction. On the contrary, the judgment is declared in the minute to be *done*, *closed*, and *determined*, without adjourning, *to be executed forthwith*, on the mere reading of the sentence by the captain-reporter, in presence of the different detachments of the troops of the garrison.

It was, then, impossible for me to know the tenour of the sentence by its being read in open court, since there was no such reading; and, consequently, it was also impossible that I could reply to General Hullin, taking the pen out of his hand—"That is my business."

As to the instructions which must have been given to the court to refer to me the sentence, after having delivered it to be executed, even though immediate execution had not been ordered (for all this is necessary to give any probability to the general's version), I ask, through what channel were these

instructions received ; in what document do they appear ; and
by whom were they given ? No mention is made of them in
the only document of the process ; namely, the decree of the
29th of Ventose : the order of the governor of Paris, appoint-
ing the members of the court, takes no notice of such instructions ; and finally, there is no allusion to any thing of the kind
in the two minutes of the judgment.

The court then, or, if it be wished that I should speak with
more precision, the president, did not submit to me the sentence which was pronounced ; and therefore I cannot admit,
and still less subscribe to the fact, that the arbitrary will of an
inferior controlled the legal will of his superior. But to go
farther ; let it be for a moment admitted that General Hullin's tardy version might be true : take it for granted that,
subordinate as I was, I not only disobeyed my superior,
which would have been a breach of discipline, but that I
forcibly mastered his hand, which would have been almost
rebellion, how does General Hullin justify himself for not
immediately ordering me under arrest, or at least preferring a
complaint against me? Did he do any thing of the kind?
Moreover, to whom did he ever impart his resentment on this
subject? Assuredly neither to the Emperor nor to me. It
was then only after the restoration that General Hullin recollected this important fact. His memory must have returned to him along with the very just regrets which his
uneasy forebodings respecting the future had awakened.

He says he believed that I had orders ; but he ought to
have asked me to exhibit them, and certainly he would not
now forget to mention his having seen them. He, my adversaries, or the Emperor's enemies, would not be silent on
this point. But this question is one of those which common
sense suffices to answer. What instructions could I have received in the situation in which I stood?

Finally, as a last objection, some persons have blamed me
for endeavouring to justify the First Consul at the expense

of the minister for foreign affairs. I may, with much better reason, reproach my adversaries with having constantly sought to justify themselves at the expense of the Emperor. Besides, to this imputation, and to every other of the same nature, I have but one word to say in reply ; which is, that I never considered myself released by the fall of Napoleon and his death from the gratitude due by me to him. I have made this sentiment the basis of my conduct, and in doing so I conceive I have only fulfilled a duty.

In recapitulation, and to avoid reverting to the same points again, the whole of this part of the subject may be reduced to a few simple questions, to which the public may now reply :—

By whom was the arrest of the Prince suggested ?

By whom was he tried ?

By whom was he condemned ?

By whom was the sentence signed ?

The documents which follow, and more especially the correspondence of the Duke Dalberg, will assist the reader in solving these questions.

DOCUMENTS

AND CORRESPONDENCE

OF

THE DUKE DALBERG.

DOCUMENTS AND CORRESPONDENCE

OF

THE DUKE DALBERG.

§ I.

Letter from the First Consul to the Minister for the War Department.[*]

Paris, the 19th Ventose, year XII. (10th March, 1804.)

You will be pleased, citizen-general, to direct General Ordener, whom I, for this purpose, place at your disposal, to proceed this night by express to Strasburg. He will travel under a borrowed name. He will see the general of the division.

The object of his mission is to proceed to Ettenheim, to surround the town, and carry off the Duke d'Enghien, Dumouriez, an English colonel, and any other person who may be in their suite.

The general of the division, the quarter-master of the gendarmerie who has been reconnoitring at Ettenheim, and also the police-commissary, will give him every necessary information.

You will order General Ordener to make 300 men of the

---

[*] This order was issued on the day the privy-council was held.

26th dragoons proceed from Schlestadt to Rheinau, where they will arrive at eight in the evening.

The commandant of the division will send fifteen pontoniers to Rheinau, who will also arrive at eight in the evening, and who, that they may do so, will proceed by post, or on the horses of the light artillery. Independently of the usual ferry, four or five large boats must be provided, so that 300 horses may pass over at once.

The troops will take with them bread for four days, and will be provided with cartridges. The general of division will unite to them a captain or other officer, and a lieutenant of gendarmerie, and three or four brigades (thirties) of gendarmerie.

As soon as General Ordener shall pass the Rhine, he will proceed straight-forward to Ettenheim, and march direct to the houses of the Duke and Dumouriez. This expedition being terminated, he will return to Strasburg.

In passing through Luneville, General Ordener will direct the officer of carbineers who commanded the depôt at Ettenheim to proceed by post to Strasburg, and there await his orders.

General Ordener, having arrived at Strasburg, must secretly dispatch two agents, either civil or military, and arrange with them that they shall come and meet him.

You will order that, on the same day and at the same hour, 200 of the 26th dragoons, under the command of General Caulaincourt (to whom you will give directions accordingly), shall proceed to Offenburg, to surround the town, and arrest the Baroness de Reich, if she has not already been taken at Strasburg, and other agents of the English government, of whom the prefect and citizen Mehée, now at Strasburg, will give him information.

From Offenburg, General Caulaincourt will send patroles on Ettenheim, until he learns that General Ordener has succeeded. They must mutually aid each other.

At the same time, the general of division will forward **300** cavalry to Kehl, with four pieces of light artillery ; and will send a post of light cavalry to Wilstadt, the intermediate point between the two roads.

The two generals will take care that the best discipline shall prevail, and that the troops shall exact nothing from the inhabitants: you will accordingly furnish them with **12,000** francs.

If it should happen that they cannot fulfil their mission, and that they should hope to succeed by staying three or four days, and by sending out patroles, they are authorized to do so.

They will inform the baillis of the two towns, that if they continue to afford refuge to the enemies of France, they will bring themselves into great difficulty.

You will order the commandant of Neuf-Brissac to send **100** men on the right bank of the Rhine, with two pieces of cannon.

The posts of Kehl, as well as those of the right bank, shall be evacuated as soon as the two detachments shall have returned.

General Caulaincourt will have with him thirty gendarmes : he, together with General Ordener and the general of division, will hold a council, and will make whatever changes they may think necessary for the present arrangements.

If it should happen that neither Dumouriez nor the Duke d'Enghien are at Ettenheim, an extraordinary courier must be dispatched with intelligence of the state of things.

You will order the arrest of the postmaster of Kehl, and other individuals capable of furnishing information.

(Signed) BONAPARTE.

§ II.

*Instructions to General Ordener from the Minister of the War Department.**

Paris, 20th Ventose, year XII. (March, 1804.)

In consequence of the arrangements of the government, by which General Ordener is placed at the disposal of the minister of war, he is directed to leave Paris by post immediately on the receipt of the present order, and to proceed to Strasburg with the utmost expedition, without stopping a moment. He will travel under a borrowed name. On his arrival at Strasburg, he will see the general of the division. *The object of the mission is to proceed to Ettenheim, to surround the town, and to arrest the Duke d'Enghien, Dumouriez,* an English colonel, and any other individual who may be with them. The general commanding the 5th division, the quarter-master who has been reconnoitring Ettenheim, and also the commissary of police, will furnish him with every necessary information.

General Ordener will give orders for sending from Scbles-tadt 300 hundred of the 26th dragoons, who will proceed to Rheinau, where they will arrive at eight in the evening. The commander of the 5th division will send fifteen pontoniers to Rheinau, who will likewise arrive there at eight in the evening, and who, for that purpose, will set out on light artillery horses. Independently of the ferry, he must secure four or five other large boats, so that 300 horses may be conveyed

---

* The preceding order of the First Consul to the minister of the war department is dated March 10th, eleven o'clock in the evening. The minister would transmit it to General Ordener at the earliest at two or three o'clock on the morning of the 11th. It is probable that the general did not depart until the evening of the same day.

across at once. The troops will take with them a supply of
bread for four days, and will provide themselves with a sufficient quantity of cartridges. To the above-mentioned force
the general of division will add a captain, a lieutenant of
gendarmerie, and thirty gendarmes. As soon as General Ordener shall have crossed the Rhine, *he will proceed straight to
Ettenheim, and on his arrival there, he will go to the residence of the Duke d'Enghien and to that of Dumouriez.*
This expedition being terminated, he will return to Strasburg.
On his way through Luneville, General Ordener will direct
the officer of carbineers who commanded the depôt at Ettenheim to proceed by post to Strasburg, there to await further
orders. On reaching Strasburg, General Ordener will secretly dispatch two agents, either civil or military, and will
arrange so that they shall come and meet him. General
Ordener is informed that General Caulaincourt is to depart
with him for the purpose of aiding him in this mission.
General Ordener will take care to maintain the strictest discipline, and to prevent the troops from exacting any thing
from the inhabitants. If it should happen that General
Ordener cannot fulfil his mission, but should hope to succeed
by staying three or four days, and sending out patroles, he is
authorized to do so. He will inform the bailli of the town,
that if he continue to afford refuge to the enemies of France,
he will bring himself into difficulty. He will direct the commandant of Neuf-Brissac to send 100 men on the right bank
of the Rhine, with two pieces of cannon. The posts of Kehl,
as well as those of the right bank, will be evacuated as soon as
the two detachments shall return.

General Ordener, General Caulaincourt, and the general
commanding the 5th division, will hold a council, and make
such changes as they may deem necessary for the present arrangements. Should it happen that neither Dumouriez nor
the Duke d'Enghien is at Ettenheim, General Ordener will
dispatch an extraordinary courier to inform me of the state of

things, and he will await further orders. General Ordener will direct the commander of the 5th division to order the arrest of the postmaster of Kehl, and any other individuals who may be able to furnish information.

. I transmit to General Ordener the sum of **12,000** francs for his use, and that of General Caulaincourt. You will request the general commanding the 5th military division, while you and General Caulaincourt are engaged on your expedition, to dispatch **300** cavalry to Kehl, with four pieces of light artillery. He will also send a post of light cavalry to Wilstadt, the intermediate point between the two routes.

(Signed)   ALEX. BERTHIER.

§ III.

Liberty.—Equality.

Extract from the Registers of the Deliberations of the Consuls of the Republic.

Paris, 29th Ventose, year XII. of the Republic, one and indivisible.

The government of the Republic decrees as follows :

ARTICLE I. The heretofore Duke d'Enghien, accused of having borne arms against the Republic, and of having been and still being paid by England for taking part in the plots contrived by that power against the internal and external safety of the Republic, is to be brought before a court-martial, composed of seven members appointed by the governor of Paris, which court will assemble at Vincennes.

ART. II. The grand-judge, the minister of the war department, and· the governor of Paris, are. charged with the execution of the present decree.

(Signed)   BONAPARTE, First Consul.

A true Copy, by order of the First Consul,

(Signed)   HUGUES MARET.

(Signed)   MURAT, general-in-chief and governor of Paris.

§ IV.

Nomination of the Members of the Court-martial.

To the Government of Paris, 29th Ventose, year XII. of the Republic.

The general-in-chief, governor of Paris, in fulfilment of the decree of the government, dated this day, ordering that the heretofore Duke d'Enghien shall be brought before a court-martial, composed of seven members appointed by the governor of Paris, has nominated and nominates for forming this court the seven officers whose names are subjoined.

General Hullin, commander of the foot-grenadiers of the consular guard, president.

Colonel Guitton, commander of the 1st regiment of cuirassiers.

Colonel Bazancourt, commander of the 4th regiment of light infantry.

Colonel Ravier, commander of the 18th regiment of infantry of the line.

Colonel Barrois, commander of the 96th of the line.

Colonel Rabbe, commander of the 2nd regiment of the Paris municipal guards.

Citizen Dautancourt, major of the select gendarmerie, who will fill the office of captain-reporter.

The court is to assemble immediately at the Castle of Vincennes, to try the accused (without adjourning) on the charges specified in the decree of the government, of which a copy will be delivered to the president.

J. MURAT.

§ V.

Interrogatory.

Year XII. of the French Republic, this day, 29th Ventose, at twelve o'clock in the evening, I, captain-major of the select gendarmerie, in obedience to the order of the general commanding the corps, waited upon the general-in-chief, Murat, governor of Paris, who immediately directed me to proceed to the Castle of Vincennes, there to take and receive further orders from General Hullin, commander of the grenadiers of the consular guard.

On my arrival at the Castle of Vincennes, General Hullin communicated to me, 1st, a copy of the government-decree of the 29th Ventose, present month, ordering that the heretofore Duke d'Enghien should be brought before a court-martial, composed of seven members appointed by the governor-general of Paris; 2nd, the order of the general-in-chief, governor of Paris, of this day, nominating the members of the court-martial, in execution of the aforesaid decree. These members are, Citizens Hullin, general of the grenadiers of the guard; Guitton, colonel of the 1st cuirassiers; Bazancourt, commander of the 4th regiment of light infantry; Ravier, commander of the 18th infantry of the line; Barrois, commander of the 96th of the line; and Rabbe, commander of the 2nd regiment of the guard of Paris.

The order, moreover, directs that the undersigned captain-major shall fill the office of captain-reporter of the court-

martial: the court is also ordered to assemble immediately at
the Castle of Vincennes, to try (without adjournment) the
accused on the charges specified in the government-decree
above-mentioned.

In fulfilment of these measures, and by virtue of the orders
of General Hullin, the president of the court, the undersigned captain proceeded to the chamber in which the Duke
d'Enghien was in bed, accompanied by the chef d'escadron,
Jacquin, of the select legion; two foot-gendarmes of the
same corps, named Lerva and Tharsis; and Citizen Noirot,
lieutenant of the same corps: the undersigned captain-
reporter immediately received the following replies to the
questions which he addressed to the Duke, being assisted by
Citizen Molin, captain of the 18th regiment, the secretary
chosen by the reporter.

— Asked his name, surname, age, and birth-place.

Answered—That his name is Louis-Antoine-Henri de Bourbon, Duke d'Enghien, and that he was born at Chantilly, on
the 2nd of August, 1772.

— Asked at what period he quitted France.

Answered—He cannot say precisely; but thinks it was on
the 16th of July, 1789. That he departed with the Prince
de Condé, his grandfather, his father, the Count d'Artois,
and the children of the Count d'Artois.

— Asked where he has resided since he quitted France.

Answered—On leaving France, I proceeded with my relations, whom I have always followed, to Mons and Brussels:
thence we removed to Turin, and we passed nearly sixteen
months with the King of Sardinia. I afterwards went, still
in company with my relations, to Worms and its neighbourhood, on the banks of the Rhine. The corps of Condé was
then formed, and I served throughout the whole war. I had
previously made the campaign of 1792 in Brabant, with the
corps of Bourbon in the army of Duke Albert.

— Asked where he has resided since. the peace concluded between the French Republic and the Emperor.

Answered—We closed the last campaign in the neighbourhood of Gratz. There the corps of Condé, which was in the pay of England, was disbanded; that is to say, at Wendisch-Facstrictz in Styria. That he afterwards remained for his pleasure in Gratz and its neighbourhood, about six or nine months, awaiting news from his grandfather, the Prince de Condé, who had gone to England, and who was to inform him what allowance that power would make him ; a point which was not yet determined. During this interval, he applied to Cardinal Rohan for permission to go to Ettenheim in Brisgau, formerly the bishopric of Strasburg, and that he had been there for two years and a half. After the death of the cardinal, he applied to the Elector of Baden, officially, for permission to remain in that country, as he did not wish to stay without his consent. That permission was granted.

— Asked whether he did not go to England, and whether that power does not still allow him a pension.

Answered—That he never went thither ; but that England allows him a pension, which is all he has to live on.

He requested to add, that, as the reasons which had induced him to remain at Ettenheim no longer existed, he proposed to fix his abode at Friburg in Brisgau, which is a much more agreeable town than Ettenheim, where he remained only because the Emperor granted him permission to hunt, a diversion of which he is very fond.

— Asked whether he corresponded with the French princes who had emigrated to London, and whether he had seen them lately.

Answered—That he had, as might naturally be supposed, corresponded with his grandfather since he had quitted Vienna, whither he had conducted him after the disbanding of the corps: that he likewise corresponded with his father, whom he had not seen, to the best of his recollection, since 1794 or 1795.

— Asked what rank he held in the army of Condé.

Answered—Commander of the advanced-guard before 1796. Before that campaign, he was a volunteer at the head-quarters of his grandfather; and since 1796, he has been a commander of advanced-guard. He observed, that after the army of Condé proceeded to Russia, it was combined in two corps, one of infantry and one of dragoons, of which he was made colonel by the Emperor, and in that rank he returned to the armies of the Rhine.

— Asked whether he knew General **Pichegru**, and whether he had had any connexion with him.

Answered—I never saw him to my knowledge; and I never had any connexion with him. I know he wished to see me. I congratulate myself on never having known him, if it be true that he intended to employ the odious measures of which he is accused.

— Asked whether he knew the Ex-general **Dumouriez**, and whether he had any connexion with him.

Answered—I never saw him.

— Asked whether, since the peace, he has not maintained correspondence with the interior of the Republic.

Answered—That he has written to some friends who served with him in the army, and who are still attached to him, upon business concerning himself and them. This is not the correspondence which he presumes is alluded to.

From the above the present minute was drawn up; and signed by the Duke d'Enghien, the Chef d'escadron Jacquin, Lieutenant Noirot, the two gendarmes, and the captain-reporter.

" Before I sign the present minute, I earnestly request to have a private audience with the First Consul. My name,

my rank, my manner of thinking, and the horror of my
situation, induce me to hope that he will not refuse my
request."

(Signed)   L. A. H. DE BOURBON.

Lower down:

Lieutenant NOIROT and JACQUIN.

A true Copy,
DAUTANCOURT,
(The Captain filling the office of Reporter.)
MOLIN, (Captain-secretary.)

§ VI.

Judgment on which the Duke d'Enghien was executed.

This day, the 30th Ventose, year XII. of the Republic.

The court-martial, constituted in pursuance of the decree
of the government, dated the 29th current, composed of the
Citizens Hullin, general, commanding the grenadiers of the
consular guard, president; Guitton, colonel of the 1st regiment of cuirassiers; Bazancourt, colonel of the 4th regiment
of light infantry; Ravier, colonel of the 18th regiment of the
line; Barrois, colonel of the 96th; Rabbe, colonel of the 2nd
regiment of the Paris guards; the Citizen Dautancourt,
filling the office of captain-reporter, assisted by the Citizen
Molin, captain of the 18th regiment of infantry of the line,
chosen to fill the office of secretary; all appointed by the
general-in-chief, governor of Paris;

Assembled in the Castle of Vincennes,

For the purpose of trying the heretofore Duke d'Enghien, on the charges preferred against him in the above-cited decree.

The president caused the prisoner to be brought in free and unfettered; and ordered the captain-reporter to exhibit the documents both for the prosecution and the defence in number ONE.

The decree before-mentioned being read to the prisoner, the president put to him the following questions :

— Your name, surname, age, and birth-place.

Answered—That his name is Louis-Antoine-Henri de Bourbon, Duke d'Enghien, born at Chantilly, on the 2nd of August, 1772.

— Asked whether he bore arms against France.

Answered—That he had served all the war; and that he persisted in the declaration which he had made to the captain-reporter, and which he had signed. He further added, that he was ready to take the field, and wished to serve in the new war of England against France.

— Asked whether he was still in the pay of England.

Answered—That he was; that he received 150 guineas per month from that power.

The court, after causing, through the medium of the president, the prisoner's declaration be read over to him, asked him whether he had any thing to add to his grounds of defence; to which he replied, that he had nothing more to say, and therein persisted.

The president directed the prisoner to be removed; the court proceeding to deliberate with closed doors. The president collected the votes, beginning with the youngest in rank. The president having delivered his own opinion last, the court, by a unanimity of voices, declared the prisoner guilty, and applied to him article —— of the law of the ——, to this effect ——, and in consequence condemned him to suffer the pain of death.

Orders, that the present judgment shall be executed FORTHWITH, by the care of the captain-reporter, after causing it to be read to the prisoner in the presence of the different detachments of the corps of the garrison.

Done, closed, and determined, without adjourning, at Vincennes, the day, month, and year as above, and signed by us,

(Signed)   P. HULLIN, BAZANCOURT, RABBE, BARROIS, DAUTANCOURT, Reporter, GUITTON, RAVIER.

Note. The signature of Molin, the secretary, is not on the minute.

§ VII.

Second Judgment drawn up on the Day after the Execution.

Special court-martial,

Constituted in the first military division, in virtue of the decree of the government, dated the 29th Ventose, year XII. of the Republic, one and indivisible.

JUDGMENT.

In the name of the French people,

This day, the 30th Ventose, year XII. of the Republic, the special court-martial, formed in the first military division, in pursuance of the decree of the government, dated the 29th Ventose, year XII. and composed, according to the law of the 19th Fructidor, year V. of seven members; namely, the citizens—

· Hullin, general of brigade, commanding the foot-grenadiers of the guards, president ;

Guitton, colonel, commanding the 1st regiment of cuirassiers ;

Bazancourt, commanding the 4th regiment of light infantry;

Ravier, colonel of the 18th regiment of infantry of the line;

Barrois, colonel, commanding the 96th regiment of the line;

Rabbe, colonel, commanding the 2nd regiment of the municipal guard of Paris ;

Dautancourt, captain-major of the select gendarmerie, performing the duty of captain-reporter ;

Molin, captain of the 18th regiment of infantry of the line, secretary : all nominated by the general-in-chief, Murat, governor of Paris, and commanding the first military division.

The which president, members, reporter, and secretary, are not related or allied to each other, or with the prisoner, within the degree prohibited by the law.

The court, convoked by order of the general-in-chief, governor of Paris, assembled, at the Castle of Vincennes, in the apartment of the commandant of the fortress, to try the person named Louis-Antoine-Henri de Bourbon, Duke d'Enghien, born at Chantilly, on the 2nd of August, 1772; height, 1 metre 705 millimetres—hair and eyebrows, bright chesnut—countenance, oval, long, well-formed—eyes, grey, inclining to brown—nose, aquiline—chin, somewhat pointed, well-formed : accused,

1st. Of having borne arms against the French republic.

2nd. Of having offered his services to the English government, the enemy of the French people.

3rd. Of having received and accredited near him agents of the said English government; of having procured for them the means of obtaining secret communications from France, and of having conspired with them against the internal and external security of the state.

4th. Of having put himself at the head of a number of French emigrants, and others paid by England, and collected on the frontiers of France, in the territories of Friburg and Baden.

5th. Of having carried on correspondence with Strasburg, for the purpose of instigating the adjoining departments to revolt, and thus effecting a diversion in favour of England.

6th. Of being one of the promoters and accomplices of the conspiracy formed by the English against the life of the First Consul; and intending, in case of success in that conspiracy, to enter France.

The court being opened, the president ordered the reporter to read all the documents both for the prosecution and the defence.

The reading being finished, the president ordered the guard to bring in the prisoner, who was accordingly introduced, free and unfettered, before the court.

— Asked his name, surname, age, birth-place, and domicile.

Answered—That his name is Louis-Antoine-Henri de Bourbon, Duke d'Enghien, aged thirty-two, born at Chantilly near Paris, having left France since the 16th of July, 1789.

The prisoner, having been interrogated by the president on all the points of the charge against him; the reporter having been heard in support of his report and his conclusions, and the prisoner on his grounds of defence; after the latter had declared that he had nothing farther to add in his justification, the president asked the members whether they had any observations to make; on their replying in the negative, and before proceeding to collect the votes, he ordered the prisoner to be removed.

The prisoner was re-conducted to prison by his escort; and the reporter, the secretary, as well as the citizens who were present at the trial, withdrew on intimation from the president.

The court proceeded to deliberate with closed doors, and the president put the following questions :—

Louis-Antoine-Henri de Bourbon, Duke d'Enghien, accused,

1st. Of having borne arms against the French republic—is he guilty ?

2nd. Of having offered his services to the English government, the enemy of the French people—is he guilty ?

3rd. Of having received and accredited near him agents of the said English government ; of having procured for them the means of obtaining secret communications from France, and of having conspired with them against the internal and external security of the state—is he guilty ?

4th. Of having put himself at the head of a number of French emigrants and others paid by England, and collected on the frontiers of France, in the territories of Friburg and Baden—is he guilty ?

5th. Of having carried on correspondence with Strasburg, for the purpose of instigating the adjoining departments to revolt, and thus effect a diversion in favour of England—is he guilty ?

6th. Of being one of the promoters and accomplices of the conspiracy formed by the English against the life of the First Consul, and intending in case of success in that conspiracy to enter France—is he guilty ?

The votes being taken separately on each of the above questions, beginning with the junior officer in rank, the president giving his vote last,

The court declared the said Louis-Antoine-Henri de Bourbon, Duke d'Enghien,

1st. Unanimously, guilty of having borne arms against the French republic.

2nd. Unanimously, of having offered his services to the English government, the enemy of the French people.

3rd. Unánimously, guilty of having received and accredited near him agents of the said English government; of having procured for them the means of obtaining secret communications from France, and of having conspired with them against the internal and external security of the state.

4th. Unanimously, guilty of having put himself at the head of a number of emigrants and others paid by England, and collected on the frontiers of France, in the territories of Friburg and Baden.

5th. Unanimously, guilty of having carried on correspondence with Strasburg, for the purpose of instigating the adjoining departments to revolt, and thus effect a diversion in favour of England.

6th. Unanimously, guilty of being one of the promoters and accomplices of the conspiracy formed by the English against the life of the First Consul, and intending in case of success in that conspiracy to enter France.

Whereupon the president put the question relative to the application of the punishment. The votes being again taken in the form above indicated, the special court-martial unanimously condemns to the pain of death the aforesaid Louis-Antoine-Henri de Bourbon, Duke d'Enghien, in reparation of the crimes of espionage, of correspondence with the enemies of the republic, and of attempts against the internal and external security of the state.

The said penalty is inflicted in conformity with articles 2, title 4, of the military code of offences and punishments, of the 21st Brumaire, year V.; 1st and 2nd section of title 1st of the ordinary penal-code of the 6th of October, 1791, which runs thus, viz. :—

ART. II. (Of the 21st Brumaire, year V.) " Every individual, whatever may be his condition, quality, or profession, convicted of espionage for the enemy, shall be punished with death."

ART. I. (Of the 6th of October, 1791.) " Every plot or enterprise against the republic shall be punished with death."

ART. II. (Ibid.) " Every conspiracy and plot tending to trouble the state by a civil war, and arming citizens against

each other, or against the exercise of the legitimate authority, shall be punished by death."

The court enjoins the captain-reporter to read immediately
the present judgment to the prisoner, in presence of the
guard assembled under arms.

Orders that there be sent, within the period prescribed by
law, by the care of the president and the reporter, copies of
the judgment to the minister for war, the grand-judge,
minister for justice, and the general-in-chief, governor of
Paris.

Done, closed and determined, without adjourning, the day,
month, and year aforesaid; and the members of the special
court-martial have, with the reporter and the secretary,
signed the minute of the judgment.

(Signed) GUITTON, BAZANCOURT, RAVIER, BAR-
ROIS, RABBE, DAUTANCOURT, Captain-
reporter, MOLIN, Captain-secretary, and
HULLIN, President.

A true Copy,

P. HULLIN, President of the Special Court-
martial.

P. DAUTANCOURT, Captain-reporter.

MOLIN, Captain-secretary.

§ VIII.

Letter from M. de Talleyrand, Minister of State for Foreign Affairs, to the Baron d'Edelsheim, Minister of State at Carlsruhe.

Paris, the 20th Ventose, year XII. (11th of March, 1804.)

M. LE BARON,—I transmitted to you a note* requiring the arrest of the committee of French emigrants at Offenburg, when the First Consul had, by the successive arrest of brigands sent into France by the English government, as well as by the progress and result of the trials here, learned the part taken by the English agents at Offenburg in the terrible plots formed against his person, and against the security of France. In like manner, he has learned that the Duke d'Enghien and General Dumouriez have been at Ettenheim; and as it is impossible that they could be in that town without the permission of his Electoral Highness, the First Consul cannot without profound regret perceive that a prince whom he took a pleasure in making experience, in the most signal manner, the effects of his friendship with France, should give an asylum to its cruelest enemies, and permit such notorious conspiracies to be tranquilly formed.

On this very extraordinary occasion, the First Consul conceives it to be his duty to order two small detachments to march to Offenburg and Ettenheim to seize the instigators of a crime, which, from its nature, places out of the law of nations all who manifestly take part therein. General Cau-

---

* It thus appears that attention was called to these emigrants before the privy-council held on the 10th. Why then did not M. de Talleyrand send notice to the Duke d'Enghien even before that council was held.

laincourt is intrusted with the First Consul's orders in this respect. You need not doubt that in executing them he will observe all the attention which his Highness may desire. He will have the honour of delivering to your Excellency the letter which I have been ordered to write to you.

Receive, M. le Baron, the assurance of my high esteem.

(Signed)   Ch. M. Talleyrand.

Next day, the 12th of March (corresponding with the 21st of Ventose), General Caulaincourt received the letter above referred to from the war minister.

The Duke d'Enghien was arrested on the night between the 14th and 15th of March (the 23rd and 24th Ventose).

The Elector published the following decree, dated Carls-ruhe, March 16th, 1804. *

" Immediately after the re-establishment of peace between the German empire and the French republic, his Serene and Electoral Highness issued, on the 14th of May, 1798, in his ancient states, precise and strict orders to permit no transported French emigrants to continue to reside within his territories.

" The war which afterwards broke out having given to these persons different motives for entering his states, his Serene and Electoral Highness seized the first favourable moment, the 20th of June, 1799, to order their removal.

" Peace being again concluded, and several individuals attached to the army of Condé having taken upon themselves to repair to this neighbourhood, his Serene and Electoral Highness thought fit to issue the following orders, which

---

* This decree, dated the 16th, is the consequence of M. de Talleyrand's letter, dated the 11th. It must therefore have been delivered, at least, on the 15th.

Probably M. de Massias wrote on the same day; and if so, his letter must have arrived at Paris before the Duke d'Enghien, who did not leave Strasburg until the 18th in the evening.

are the last, the most recent, and those which are still observed.

" There shall not be granted to any individual returning from the army of Condé, nor in general to any French emigrant, unless he have obtained permission before the peace, any other residence than that permitted to travellers. His Serene and Electoral Highness, by his express resolution, allows no exception from this ordinance, save individually persons who may prove their having obtained, or having reason soon to expect, their erasure from the list of emigrants, and who may on that account have a sufficient reason for preferring a residence in the neighbourhood of France to any other, without being regarded as suspected by the French government. The residence of these persons having hitherto been attended by no disagreeable consequence or disadvantage to the French government, and the chargé d'affaires of France residing here never having proposed more rigour, his Serene and Electoral Highness judged proper, in the month of December, 1802, on his entering into possession of his new states, to grant to the French emigrants, as well as to all other foreigners therein with respect to residence, the same indulgence which they enjoyed in some districts under the preceding government, without, however, assuring to them any new protection; but always with the firm determination of withdrawing this indulgence from them, whenever his Serene and Electoral Highness should ascertain that the residence, on the frontiers of the Rhine, of any individual, having become an object of suspicion with the French government, threatened to disturb the repose of the empire.

" That government having required the arrest of certain emigrants implicated in the plot formed against the constitution, and a military patrol having come to arrest the persons included in this class, the moment is arrived in which his Serene and Electoral Highness is obliged to regard the residence of emigrants in his states as prejudicial to the repose of the empire, and suspicious to the French government. Consequently, he considers it indispensable to renew in full rigour the prohibition against French emigrants, both the old and the new, sojourning in his states, and to revoke all permissions, limited or unlimited, given by the preceding or the present government. He, besides, orders that all those who cannot immediately prove their erasure or their submission to the French government, shall immediately remove ; and that if they do not voluntarily depart within three days, they shall be conveyed beyond the frontiers. With respect to those who, in this manner, believe they may be entitled to obtain permission for a residence unattended with any prejudice, it is ordered that a list of them be addressed to his Serene and Electoral Highness, while they await the decision for permitting or refusing the continuance of their residence.

" All the officers of the great bailiwicks, the magistrates of districts, and officers of police, are personally responsible for the punctual execution of this ordinance, and are declared liable for any damage which may result from delay."

§ IX.

Letter from M. de Dalberg, Minister Plenipotentiary from Baden to Paris, to Baron Edelsheim, Minister for Foreign Affairs.

Paris, March 20th, 1804.

MONSIEUR LE BARON,

The arrests which have just taken place in Baden must have been a source of great embarrassment to the court. There was no possibi-

, I beg the reader will compare the language of the preamble of this letter with the letter of the 11th from M. de Talleyrand to the prime

lity of making you acquainted with what was going on; all having been done with the utmost secrecy and precipitation.

The measures having compromised the emigrants at Ettenheim and Offenburg, the First Consul ordered M. de Caulaincourt to set out immediately, and to take with him the order for the arrest, which was executed accordingly. M. de Caulaincourt had only time to see his mother. He set out on Sunday, the 11th. On the evening of Monday, the 12th, I learned that he had gone to Strasburg, and the arrest of Dumouriez was talked of. The Duke d'Enghien was not yet publicly mentioned. I calculated that as M. de Caulaincourt must have arrived on Tuesday, the 13th, my letter to your Excellency would be too late to convey to you any information, as it could not reach you until the 16th or 17th. I therefore resolved to wait until I procured further intelligence. A courier could not have outstripped the First Consul's aide-de-camp.

At length, on Tuesday, the 15th, I learned positively the order of which M. de Caulaincourt was the bearer. The affair was mentioned for the *first time* by Madame Bonaparte in the morning to a lady with whom I was acquainted, and who communicated it to me. She added,

minister of Baden. There is in both such a coincidence, that this is nearly a repetition of the other; and yet M. de Dalberg maintains that, at that period, he kept himself at a great distance from the French ministry.

This is the letter of a man, who finding himself obliged to communicate the business to his court, took his time for so doing, in order that he might save his own responsibility, and avoid compromising the secure execution of the measure.

He was informed of the departure of M. de Caulaincourt on the 12th (he probably knew it earlier, but no matter); and he calculated that on the 12th it would be too late to dispatch a courier, who, however, would have had the advantage of the chance of M. de Caulaincourt's delay. And to make amends for this negligence, he writes on the 20th, when all was over.

By writing on the 11th or 12th, and dispatching a courier straight to Ettenheim, every chance would have been in his favour. The court of Baden could have viewed such a step only as a proof of zeal for its service. There could have been no risk in writing on the 11th or 12th; while on the 20th it was perfectly useless.

And besides: after M. de Dalberg found himself (at

that Madame Bonaparte was very much concerned about it, and that it was likely to increase the difficulties of the government.

As my letter could not then be of any use, I resolved to wait until we could procure certain intelligence. The particulars of the expedition were only known yesterday evening; and as the violation of the foreign territory is a circumstance which cannot be concealed, it has occasioned a great sensation here.

The Swedish and Austrian ministers and M. Oubril are the only persons who have expressed their opinions in a decided way.

When I joined the diplomatic circle on Monday, I was questioned respecting the particulars of the affair. I replied, that I knew nothing of it.

As the government here has not succeeded in seizing all suspected persons, domiciliary visits are spoken of;

least) mystified, and that he was authorized to make a remonstrance, in which he would have been supported by all the diplomatic body, he waited for further information. What reason had he to wait? especially, as he himself says that he chose the Prussian minister for making the remonstrance.

It appears to me that a minister who was free from self-reproach, would have urged inquiry instead of suspending it. There is something obscure in this conduct, particularly when it is remarked that if M. de Dalberg had declared himself as he ought to have done, he would have placed France under the necessity of either not following up the arrest of the Duke d'Enghien, or of demanding the recall of M. de Dalberg for having presumed to declare himself against the arrest. But what ensued?—nothing; except, indeed, that M. de Dalberg suddenly became an object of favour with the imperial government of France. Now let the reader judge.

Why, it may be asked of M. Dalberg, did you not tell these gentlemen that M. de Talleyrand had employed you to lull your court into security, while he was preparing the violation of your sovereign's territory? On the Monday then your eyes must have been opened. What excuse

and if they take place, the houses of the ambassadors will certainly be searched. For five or six days past it has been reported that there is a suspicion of some one being concealed in the house of M. de Cobentzel. The barriers are still guarded, and nobody can quit Paris without a passport.

M. de Beust has just informed me that he yesterday saw M. de Talleyrand, who told him that all the French ministers in Germany had received orders to demand the removal of the emigrants from the states of the princes, and he (M. Beust) was accordingly requested to write to his court. M. de Saint Genest will not of course be excepted, if M. Massias has received a similar order.

will you make for your negligence ?

DALBERG.

§ X.

Letter from the Same to the Same.

Paris, March 21st, 1804.

It is alleged that the Duke d'Enghien arrived yesterday at five o'clock, escorted by fifty gendarmes. Every body is inquiring—What is intended to be done with him ?

The government suspected

This is a pitiful assertion on the part of a man who, on the 19th (as he himself says in his letter of the 20th), knew of the arrests at Ettenheim.

How ! The Duke d'Enghien was shot at six in the

for a moment that the Duke de Berri and M. de Montpensier were here. Consequently, for the last fortnight all Paris has been imprisoned. A person about the First Consul informed me, that documents had been obtained which would sufficiently prove that the individuals arrested entertained the design of assassination; that the First Consul would pardon some, and execute others; that as to the princes they would be kept in prison, and that the powers will be held responsible for any new attempt.

Since the discovery of this conspiracy, the First Consul will not hear a word about peace, or any arrangement with England. He is resolved to wage deadly war against that power. I am convinced that a change in the English ministry, which is spoken of, will make no alteration in the political system of England.

morning, in the presence of 1800 troops, who passed under your windows to return to their quarters. Your porter, no doubt, knew the event. And on the same day, at four in the afternoon, (the hour of the departure of the post at that period), you write to your court that people are asking what is intended to be done with the Duke d'Enghien!

This was insinuated for the purpose of lulling your vigilance, and affording the intriguers time to consummate their crime.

You were the only person who was entitled to raise just complaints, and consequently it was above all important to mislead you.

DALBERG.

§ XI.

Letter from the Same to the Same.

Paris, March 22nd, 1804.

The Moniteur of this day, of which I have the honour to enclose a copy, publishes the sentence of death pronounced

How! You learned this from the Moniteur? The sources whence you derived your information about the

by a special court-martial on the unfortunate Duke d'Enghien, who was brought to Paris on Tuesday

The sentence was, *as it was understood yesterday*, executed at the Castle of Vincennes, at two o'clock on the morning of Wednesday.

The atrocious execution of the unfortunate Duke d'Enghien has produced a sensation which it would be difficult to describe. All Paris is horror-struck, as all France will be when the intelligence spreads. Europe must shudder at the event. We are approaching the most terrible crisis. Bonaparte's ambition knows no bounds. He respects nothing; and will sacrifice every thing to his passions.

The character of his Serene and Electoral Highness demands that the courts of Europe should know that he had no participation in the arrest of the unfortunate Prince; and I think he cannot refuse to inform the Emperor of Russia of the circumstances of this event. The channel of communication, by which he would be least compromised, is that of the Margravine.

The death of the Duke d'Enghien was determined for three reasons : 1st, the danger of keeping him in France; 2nd, the necessity of producing a feeling of awe; and 3rd, the fear of interference on the part of the courts. MM.

ambition and violence of the First Consul gave you no hint of this matter, and you knew nothing of it until the appearance of the Moniteur of the 22nd of March.

Sum total. On this affair, upon which you now express yourself with so much vehemence, you wrote two letters.

The first on the 20th, when all was over at Ettenheim; and the second on the 21st, when all was over in Paris.

Besides, this *yesterday morning* was the 21st of March, the day on which you wrote, at four in the afternoon, to inform your court that people were inquiring what was intended to be done with the Duke d'Enghien. The time for dispatching a courier is generally between four and six in the afternoon, and you confess that you knew all in the morning.

How could the Elector be compromised, since he was ignorant of the event? Why resort to indirect means, instead of openly and vehemently declaring against this violation of his territory?

de Luchesini, de Cobentzel, and Oubril, deliberated together upon the affair, for the purpose of pointing out the offence which was thus again offered to all the sovereigns of Europe. I cannot express the sorrow I feel for what has occurred, or the apprehensions I entertain for the future. I regret to be at this moment in Paris.

There are few among us who do not share these sentiments.

A new military conscription is talked of, which implies the fear of, or the wish for, a continental war, which, indeed, I have always conceived to be inevitable.

DALBERG.

It was necessary then to make the diplomatic body act before the catastrophe, since you knew of the arrest on the 19th. Why did you not act in concert with them, considering the opinions you entertained respecting the personal character of the First Consul?

§ XII.

Letter from the Same to the Same.

Paris, March 27th, 1804.

I received yesterday evening the dispatch, No. 17, which your Excellency did me the honour to address to me, to inform me of all that relates to the arrest made in our territory. In an affair of such high importance, and which produces generally the most lively sensation, it was certainly necessary that I should know the truth; and I express to you my gratitude for having transmitted to me, without delay, what was calculated to throw light upon the business.

I think, however, it might have been wished that his Serene and Electoral Highness had authorized his ambassador to reply to unjust accusations, and that a courier had brought me the letter which your Excellency wrote to M. de Talleyrand, directing me to state verbally all that that letter contained.

The copies of the other informations which your Excellency has transmitted to me, suffice, in the meanwhile, to prescribe what I have to do, and to determine the opinion which it is necessary to maintain in this affair.

I have already had the honour to mention, that owing to the impossibility of informing you of this expedition, (an impossibility which is sufficiently evident from the two *letters of M. de Talleyrand, who himself appeared, until the last moment, to be ignorant of the resolution that was adopted,*) I waited until the matter should be cleared up, being unwilling, by false or precipitate information, to influence the resolutions which it might please his Serene Electoral Highness to adopt.

The historical narrative, drawn up with the view of recording the facts such as they were, perfectly fulfils its object, and sufficiently proves

These two letters must be curious. But how could you presume to say that he appeared ignorant of every thing until the last moment? You must have known this to be a falsehood, of which you had proof.

Here the mystery is explained. You were afraid of knowing too much, and consequently you allowed things to take their course. In this

that his Serene Electoral Highness was not informed of the object of the military expedition until thirty-six hours after it was undertaken.

If, on the one hand, we must render justice, and admit how necessary it was for France to know the plots that were hatching against her peace; on the other hand, the illegality of the means resorted to, and the violence of a military arrest, on a foreign territory, in defiance of all customs and laws, must also be acknowledged. It therefore behoves his Serene Electoral Highness to make known how little he was acquainted with the machinations of which France herself was ignorant, in spite of her police and its agents, and to declare that it was not with his consent that foreign troops marched on the territory of the empire.

It is then necessary to unfold the circumstances which attended the Duke d'Enghien's abode at Ettenheim, and the permission which was tacitly granted for his residing there, by the rights of hospitality and with the knowledge of France.

It is, nevertheless, infinitely proper, according to the determination of his Serene Electoral Highness, to communicate to the members of

way the Duke d'Enghien could not escape.

The decree of the court of Baden, dated the 16th, which speaks of the arrests of the preceding day, proves that the court received intimation earlier than you state.

All this is mere foolery. Every thing was arranged by the intriguers in Paris; and it never entered the head of any one to accuse the Elector of Baden. But it is not so with respect to the person whose business it was to apprize him of the affair.

The greater the mystery which prevailed in Paris (but the truth is there was none), the worse must have been your opinion of the private character of the First Consul; and the more you ought to have been on the alert, for you were the advance-sentinel, on whose vigilance every thing depended. A single step on your part would have prevented all.

the Electoral College all that relates to this affair. I am, however, of opinion, that this should not be done verbally, but by communicating to each the historical statement, with copies of the documents thereunto annexed.

In order to fulfil the intentions of the court, I cannot, in the very difficult and dangerous situation in which I am placed, do otherwise than simply explain to the ministers of the courts with which we are most intimately connected, the circumstances such as they occurred.

I have done this with regard to the Russian, Swedish, Prussian, and Austrian embassies; and they are of opinion that, as this affair took place at Carlsruhe without my knowledge, I ought not to adopt any measure, at least, until I receive positive instructions.

I find none in your Excellency's dispatch, and I have therefore determined to say nothing, unless I am provoked to speak. It may be readily supposed that no measure will be adopted with reference to me; and that consequently I shall not, in all probability, have any opportunity of speaking of the business, or of supporting the statements contained in your Excellency's letter.

The French public are very hasty in forming their judgments and opinions; and thus it happens that many persons come to question me for the purpose of correcting statements which are advanced according as people are animated by conflicting sentiments.

The public papers are endeavouring to prove that the arrest took place with the consent of the Elector. On this point I merely state that I am authorized to contradict that assertion, and to declare that his Serene Electoral Highness had no knowledge of the event until thirty-six hours after the arrest.

Accept, &c.

DALBERG.

§ XIII.

Letter from the Same to the Same.

Paris, April 11th, 1804.

The death of Pichegru has occasioned a profound sensation here. It was known that he gave no information, that he constantly declared he would speak before the court, and that it was vain to hope that he would accuse or denounce any one whatever.

George evinced equal courage and firmness. It was consequently deemed necessary to get rid of one or the other; and it appears that

This is a misrepresentation, which only proves the extent

Pichegru was fixed upon as the victim.

The history of the Roman emperors and the Lower Empire affords a picture of this country and of the present reign.

DALBERG.

of your malignity. And yet, shortly after this, you marched with arms and baggage into the camp of this chief of the Lower Empire, who loaded you with wealth and honours, and whom you yourself acknowledge having betrayed.

Judge yourself, and respect the memory of him who might have saved France, but for the manœuvres which you attribute to fate, and in which you took part.

Enjoy your fortune in repose, if your conscience will allow you to do so; but do not slander him who stood with respect to you only in the light of a benefactor.

§ XIV.

To M. le Baron de Berstedt, Minister for Foreign Affairs at Carlsruhe.

Herrensheim, Nov. 12, 1823.

I have just become acquainted with the scandalous libel and odious inculpations which M. de Rovigo has published in his pamphlet, respecting the assassination of the Duke d'Enghien.

It is twenty years since that great crime was committed; I was then at Paris, in the character of envoy from his Serene Highness the Elector of Baden. Your Excellency must be sensible that I

I will not answer M. de Dalberg by returning insult for insult. That would prove nothing but weakness and cowardice.

People should prove by good arguments that they are in the right. The date of the event signifies little. There is no prescription for crimes, and besides this one belongs to history. But I am writing

cannot but revolt at finding myself even obscurely marked out in such a libel.

In my correspondence with the court, and with Baron d'Edelsheim, will be found evidence of the conduct prescribed to me on that melancholy occasion, and how far I was from making reports which might have compromised the security of the country, and the persons residing there. My dispatches still prove how little I was inclined to consent that this atrocity should not *strike* public opinion in the way it ought to do. I had no relations with the French minister, except those which the duties of my office prescribed.

I fixed myself in France when the total destruction of our political forms in Germany, and our relations, which I defended to the last moment, was unfortunately completed, when the daughter of the Emperor of Austria had arrived in France, and when a French law prohibited persons born in the united departments from remaining in foreign service. I was born at Mentz, and my property was situated within the united departments. It had previously been laid under sequestration during seven years, and had been subjected to the operation of part of the laws against emigrants.

on materials and facts, and not upon insults.

Vain pretexts these. The real cause will be seen in the course of these Memoirs, and will appear, too, from your own statement.

There were in the electorates of Treves and Cologne, and in Belgium, many persons in the same situation as you. But, on submitting to the law of necessity, we did not see any one of them become, in the twinkling of an eye, a counsellor of state, a senator, a duke, with a dotation of four millions, nor their wives admitted to intimate intercourse with the consort of the sovereign.

For a long time there had been no sequestration on your property; and, besides, a proof that that was not a reason with you is, that, since 1812, that property is again situated in Germany, and protected by the restoration of the forms which you say you defended to the last moment.

The daughter of the Emperor of Germany is no longer in Paris to induce your residence in France, and yet you not only do not return to Germany, but you render yourself distinguished among those who work the destruction of the old Germanic forms, and that you might labour with more security, you have sheltered yourself under an act of naturalization of the King of France. Before that act you had again become a German on the same principle that you formerly made yourself a Frenchman. Why did you not remain a German, unless it be that the opinion of your countrymen warned you of the reception you had reason to expect?

I have preserved the minutes of my official correspondence; but I wish to print, if it should become necessary, only what relates to the fact, and to submit to your Excellency the minutes which ought to be published. I address myself then to you, M. le Baron, with confidence ; and I beg of you to examine the numbered series of my letters in 1804. Would not the dignity of the court of Baden, perhaps, require that it should be expressed by a simple ar-

Your propensity to intrigue kept you in France ; and in the course of these Memoirs you will see what you have done there. In vain you now plead the cause of the Greeks; you can deceive no one.

This is a singular overture from a man of talent and finesse. Had the court of

ticle in a journal without any signature, that the perfidious insinuations of M. de Rovigo against a minister of Baden, who was continued in his post after the atrocity in question, are regarded as calumnious and unfounded? I may also hope, from the justice and benevolence of his Royal Highness the Grand-duke, that he will be pleased to make the contradiction officially known at Paris.

You, M. le Baron, are too much a man of the world, as well as a man of business, not to feel that I am justified in making use of the proofs and documents which are at my disposal for the purpose of disproving such calumnies, and that I have a just right to clear up my conduct at that fatal period.

You will, then, I am sure, do justice to my claim. I await your Excellency's reply with that confidence which your old friendship for me inspires; and I beg of you to accept the assurance of my high consideration, and of my devoted sentiments.

DALBERG.

Baden acceded to your demand, it would have been from interest felt for you, doubtless, as much and even more than from regard to its own dignity, which I did not offend, because a diplomatic person represents two very distinct individuals, whose characters are never confounded.

Now it is the private individual whom this concerns; but, after all, how would the declaration which you have solicited affect me?

Would it change any thing in the facts?

If your court should take them on itself, that might be of some importance to you; but how would that affect the truth of the arguments which I have addressed to you?

Is it in despair of your cause that you resort to this course? You have no right to complain of my attack; you even yourself proclaim your treason against him who was your benefactor and the benefactor of all your family. You insult his ashes, after having acquired honours, fortune, and consideration, under the shade of his glory. You have made yourself the pilot of foreign intrigues to destroy a trophy which protected you.

I, on the contrary, defend the memory of him whom you insult when he is no more. I obey the commands of gratitude; and in doing so, I certainly expect no justice on

the part of those who endeavour to bend public opinion
to the yoke of their personal
hatred.   But it is not for
them that I write ; others
will read this work with more
equity.   The day of justice
may be late, but it will arrive.

§ XV.

To M. le Prince Talleyrand.

Herrensheim, near Worms, November 13th, 1823.

MY PRINCE,

M. de Rovigo, no doubt,
expects great favour for having ushered into the world
such an infamous libel. I have
received it here, at a hundred
leagues distance from Paris.
He points me out in a note ;
it contains as many falsehoods
as phrases. I possess the minutes of my official correspondence with the court of Baden,
which will suffice to confound
such absurd and perfidious insinuations, made to please I
know not whom.   I expect
from you, my Prince, the declaration that, at the epoch of
this drama, I kept myself distant, as it was my duty to do,
from the French ministry.
My more intimate intercourse
with you, and of which I
am proud, began in Poland,
where, in common with the
Baron de Vincent, we made
efforts to prevent the war of
1807 from laying waste a
great part of the world.

Though I have already ex-
plained M. de Dalberg's part
in the transaction, I think
myself bound to make some
reply to the attacks upon me
in his correspondence.

I had no plan of ambition
or interest in endeavouring
to bring to light an historical
fact, which intriguers had enveloped in darkness.

For a long time private
information had strengthened
my suspicions against M. de
Dalberg, and his official correspondence has confirmed
them. I must, therefore, congratulate myself for having
caused the publication.

My readers will judge whether the remarks which I
make on his correspondence
are just, and they alone are
competent to decide.

As to the opinion here manifested by M. de Dalberg
respecting me, I cannot reasonably expect that he should

treat me with more deference than he has done his benefactors.

Were you not a German minister? Why did you contribute to prevent Germany from having one chance more?

You were then already as officious as official, and only two years had elapsed since the death of the Duke d'Enghien.

The resistance which the powers of Europe opposed to Bonaparte, when he wished to ascend the throne of France, revived the hopes of the emigrants.

The trial of Pichegru, of MM. de Polignac and de Rivière, was in progress at Paris. I arrived there as envoy from the Elector of Baden. I was ordered to ascertain whether any complaints existed against the emigrants who inhabited the electorate, and whether their residence was considered improper. You replied to me, that you did not think that the government of Baden need be more severe than the French government; that you knew of no complaint on the subject of the emigrants, and that they ought to be allowed to remain undisturbed. I transmitted this answer to the Elector.

The arrest took place in consequence of false reports of Bonaparte's secret police. Here M. de Rovigo states the truth. I was assured that the agents of that police then committed the mistake of pointing out M. de Thumery, who was in the Duke d'Enghien's suite, as General Dumouriez arrived from England at Ettenheim.

This false information must have added to the First Con-

When you saw the territory of Baden violated, you could no longer doubt that you had been deceived. You ought then to have spoken out openly; but, far from that, your prince afterwards married a princess of the family of Napoleon, and you became the friend of his policy.

sul's alarm.   He was afraid
that an immediate movement
would take place on the frontier.

I know that the King of
Sweden, who was then at
Carlsruhe, and the Elector
warned the Prince that he
might incur danger, and advised him to remove.   He
delayed, and became the unfortunate victim of his security.

This is the only hint which
the Duke d'Enghien received;
and not that sent by a pretended courier from M. de
Talleyrand, which was not
heard of till after the restoration.

If, as I have already said,
the Duke d'Enghien had received notice from Paris, he
would neither have delayed
nor hesitated to go away.

After this event, and when
Russia declared herself at
Ratisbon on this violation of
a foreign territory, it was
wished that the Elector should
enter into official explanations;
and the court of Berlin wishing that war might be avoided,
made the affair a subject of
negotiation at Paris.   You
must recollect, my Prince, the
opposition I made to M. de
Luchesini, in order that the
Elector might yield nothing
calculated to compromise his
moral dignity, and the high
opinion which prevailed of his
integrity and virtues.   My
correspondence includes these
details.   In the times in which
we live, when pains are taken
to arouse all the passions anew,
we are bound, my Prince,
when calumniated, to clear up
the part we have taken in
public affairs.

It is well known that under
your administration you always moderated the violent

passions of Bonaparte. You wished that the long misfortunes of Europe should be finished with him, and by him. But such was not the will of fate. Your name is attached to a great event, and I shall always congratulate myself on the small share which I also had in it. The fatal catastrophe to which public attention is now again called, was sufficiently known at the time to be rightly attributed to whom it belonged. Bonaparte alone, being ill-informed by the vilest part of the police, and listening only to his fury, proceeded to this excess without consulting. He caused the Prince to be carried off with the intention of putting him to death. It is deplorable to be obliged again to discuss facts by which poor human nature is so much dishonoured.

If you do me the honour to reply to this communication, send your letter, my Prince, to my hotel, whence it will be transmitted to me, and accept the respectful and devoted homage which I offer you.

DALBERG.

There is no doubt of this; but, with such sentiments, how happened it that, less than a year before, you put your name at the bottom of a decree of the section of the council of state, to which you then belonged, which condemned the respectable M. Frochot (prefect of the Seine) for not opposing, with sufficient rigour, the enterprise of Mallet, on the 23rd of October, 1812?

It seems to me that this sentence, signed by you, is become your own. It is only necessary to await the day of justice. It was not, as you pretend, the agents of the police who deceived the Emperor, for he did not interfere in the affair.

No, Sir, the Emperor did not cause the Prince to be carried off with the intention of putting him to death. If, however, that were your opinion, you would be a thousand times more guilty for not having informed your court when there was still time so to do, as may be seen by your correspondence.

But, whether you be guilty, or whether you have only been deceived, what is the world not authorized to think, on seeing you, in less than two years afterwards, concerned in the secrets of the policy of him whom you now so ungratefully insult?

§ XVI.

Copy of M. le Baron de Berstedt's Letter.

Carlsruhe, November 16th, 1823.

M. LE DUC,

Immediately on the receipt of the letter, dated the 12th, which your Excellency did me the honour to address to me, I proceeded in conformity with your desire to look over the series of your official correspondence in 1804 with the Baron d'Edelsheim. I found therein only what I expected to find relative to the indignation which you felt at the horrible assassination of the Duke d'Enghien. All your letters at that period express this sentiment with energy; and if you think proper, M. le Duc, to make use of any of the minutes which you have preserved, I think that the deciphering of your dispatch, No. 25, dated the 22nd of March, 1804, will be more than sufficient to confound your calumniators.

Perhaps you may add to it an extract from that of the 27th of March, No. 27, to prove that at the fatal epoch you could not flatter yourself with enjoying the confidence of the minister for foreign

It is remarkable that M. de Dalberg has not published this number. It is a pity it is withheld; and it is much to be wished that the old minister of Baden would give it to the public, otherwise there is no

affairs at Paris, if you really should think it worth while to vindicate yourself from the ridiculous reproach of your having been intimate with him.

I shall send by post to-morrow to the Bailli de Ferrette copies of the most interesting parts of your correspondence at that period, to be used wherever they may be of any service to you, as authentic documents preserved among the papers of the legation.

I hope that this measure will meet your views; and I shall be happy if it contribute to tranquillize you respecting the effects of a calumny which you, certainly, had no reason to expect.

Glad to find an opportunity for renewing to your Excellency the assurance of my high consideration, I beg of you never to doubt the sincerity of my perfect attachment.

(Signed) BERSTEDT.

explaining this reserve except by the supposition that the dispatch expresses opinions respecting M. de Talleyrand which the writer has powerful reasons for not now holding.

At this period, 1804, M. de Berstedt was a young man, little conversant in affairs, and besides, placed at too remote a point of view to judge rightly of the effect of the picture the scene of which has been retraced.

Besides, this letter proves nothing except that the letters published by M. de Dalberg may be regarded as authentic.

§ XVII.

Letter from M. de Talleyrand to M. de Dalberg.

Paris, November 20th, 1823.

I have received, my dear Duke, your letter of the 13th of November. It is excellent. I have read it to several

Here is a quick decision of

persons of different opinions. They are all agreed respecting it. It is considered unanswerable. I was tempted to print it; but farther reflection has induced me to think that it would, perhaps, be better to follow another course. Too much importance should not be given to the Duke of Rovigo's attack. The public has done justice, and complete justice on it. You will perceive that every body is indignant at the baseness of the Duke of Rovigo's calumnies. The judgment of the public is pronounced, and no more need be said on the affair.

For my part, I have nothing to publish, and I shall publish nothing. I have written a letter to the King. It is all that has been done, and all that will be done by me in this infamous affair. Adieu! I hope to see you in a few days. A thousand good wishes.

the question. It is said that, when Satan grew old, he turned monk - to absolve his colleagues; it remains to be known whether the absolution was efficacious.

The public, say you? What public? You doubtless mean that of certain saloons; for the real public—that which is out of the reach of intrigue and influence, and whose judgment is, therefore, without appeal—thinks that there is baseness in making a traffic of the independence of one's country, but never in unmasking a traitor or tearing off the veil of hypocrisy.

I believe it. What could you say that would not accuse you more than your silence? After having excited all the great disorders in the state, and caused the waste of the public wealth, you have been compelled to blame your own work in order to preserve some credit with your old friends; but even that credit will pass away, and there will remain to you only the pretension of fixing ridicule, and bringing vice into vogue.

N.B. I must here ask the reader whether this letter does not give reason to suspect that that of the Duke de Dalberg was concerted between the two correspondents. I was tempted to print it, says M. de Talleyrand, and immediately M. de Dalberg prints it. This manœuvre, of making another act, and advance every thing under his name, without his appearing, in order that his own manœuvres may be preserved independent; the confidence with which he appears to rely on having succeeded in suppressing all the documents in this affair, a security which may, however, be disturbed, are all traits belonging to the well-known character of M. de Talleyrand, and perfectly accordant with his preceding transactions. To strike in the dark, and keep himself aloof ; to put others forward, and preserve the means of easily gathering the fruit of their intrigues, or of disavowing them, according to circumstances, is what many persons have denominated talent, without reflecting that history will, probably, one day give it a very different name.

END OF VOL. I.

LONDON:

PRINTED BY A. J. VALPY, RED LION COURT, FLEET STREET.

Lightning Source UK Ltd.
Milton Keynes UK
UKOW06f2327250416

272971UK00017B/560/P